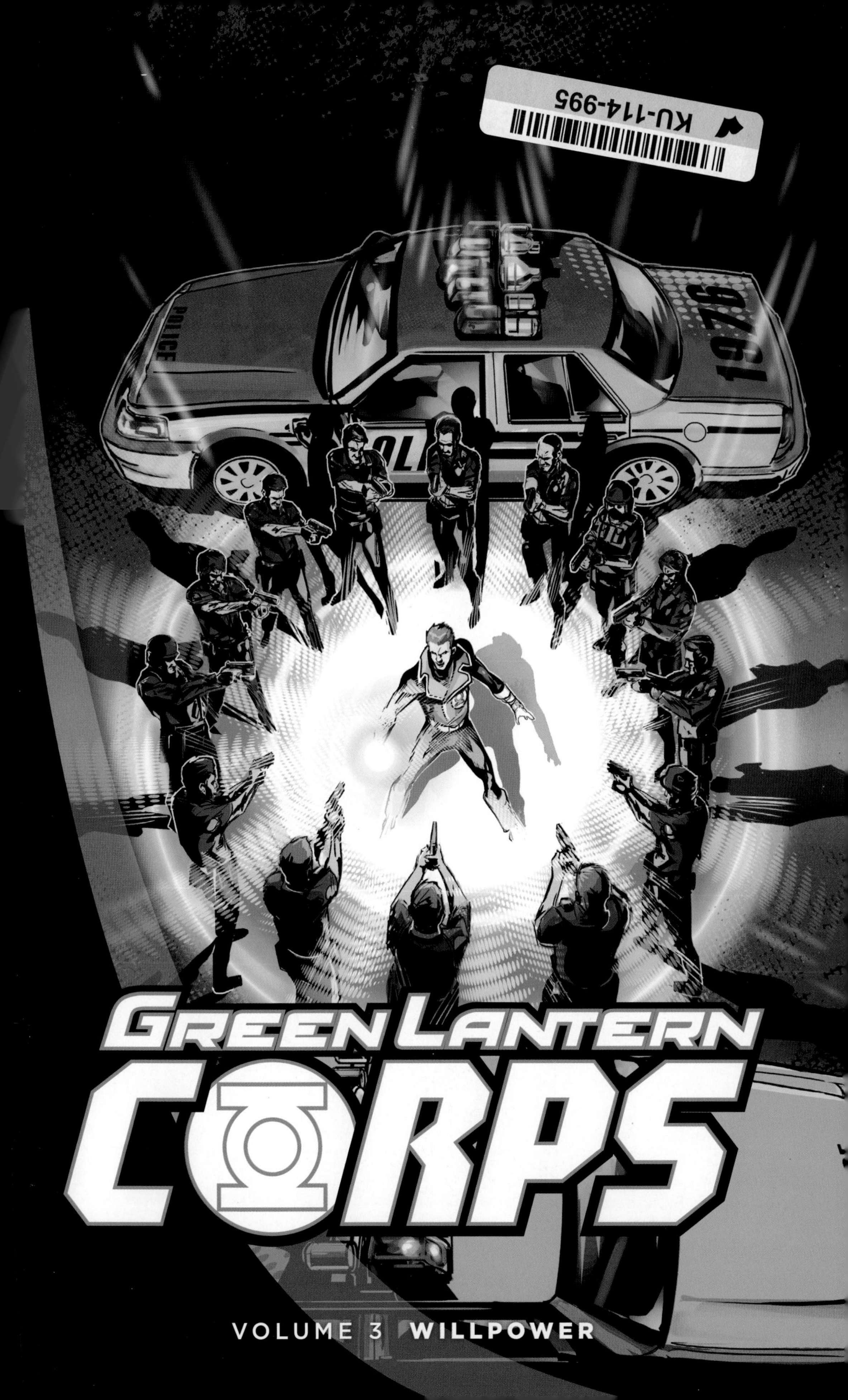
POLICE

Green Lantern Corps

VOLUME 3 WILLPOWER

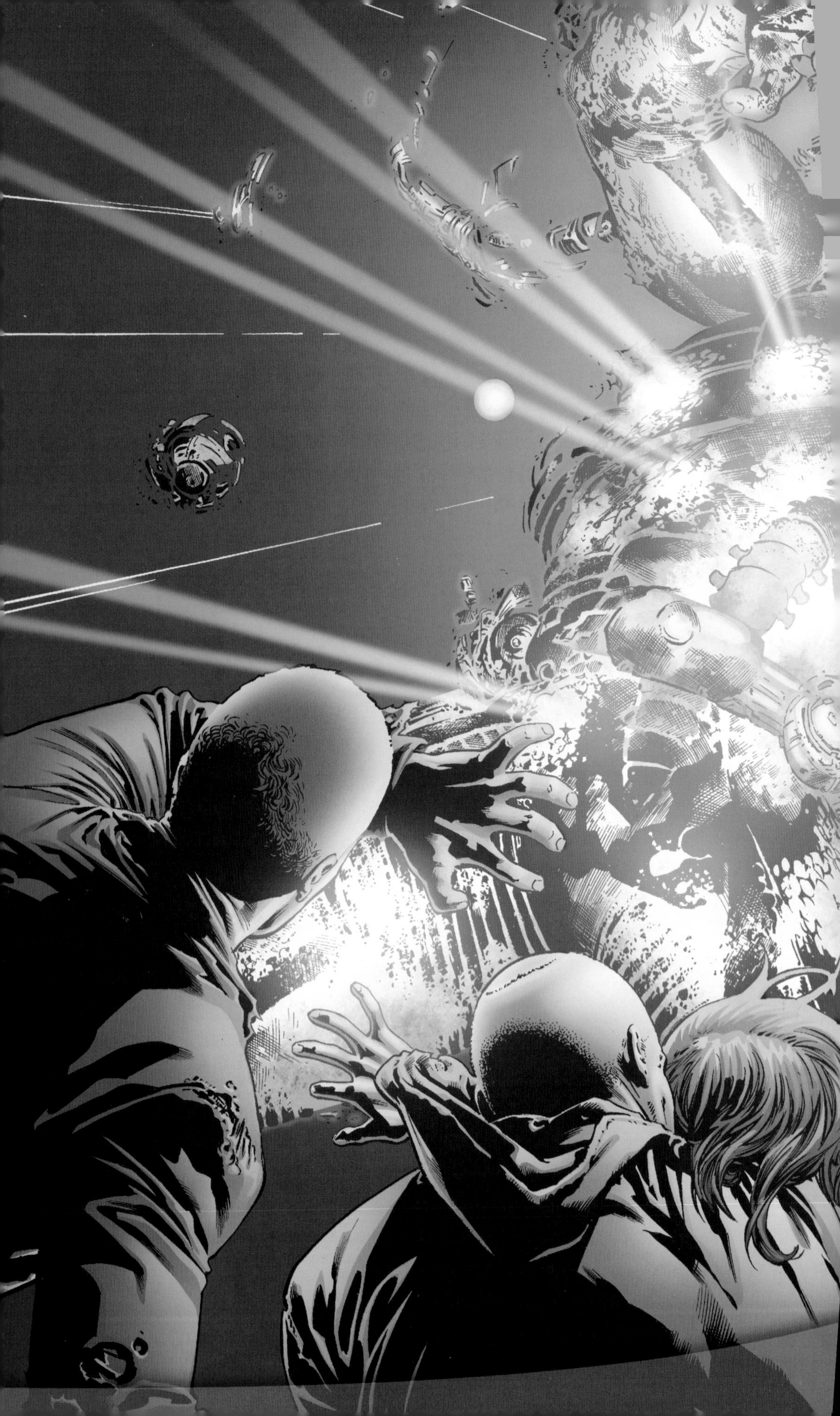

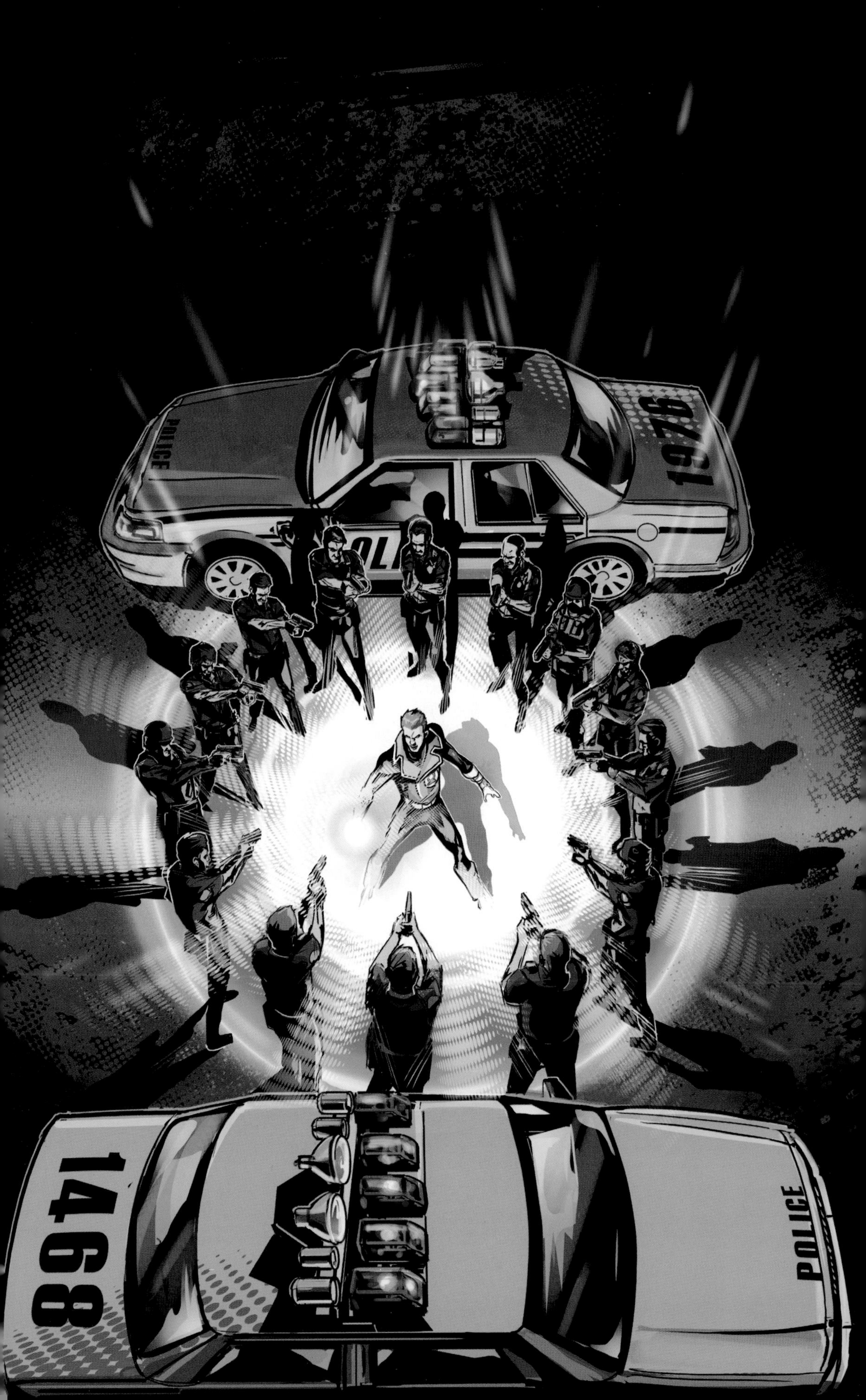
POLICE
1276
1468
POLICE

FALLING STAR

PETER J. TOMASI writer **FERNANDO PASARIN** penciller **SCOTT HANNA** inker cover art by **TREVOR MCCARTHY**

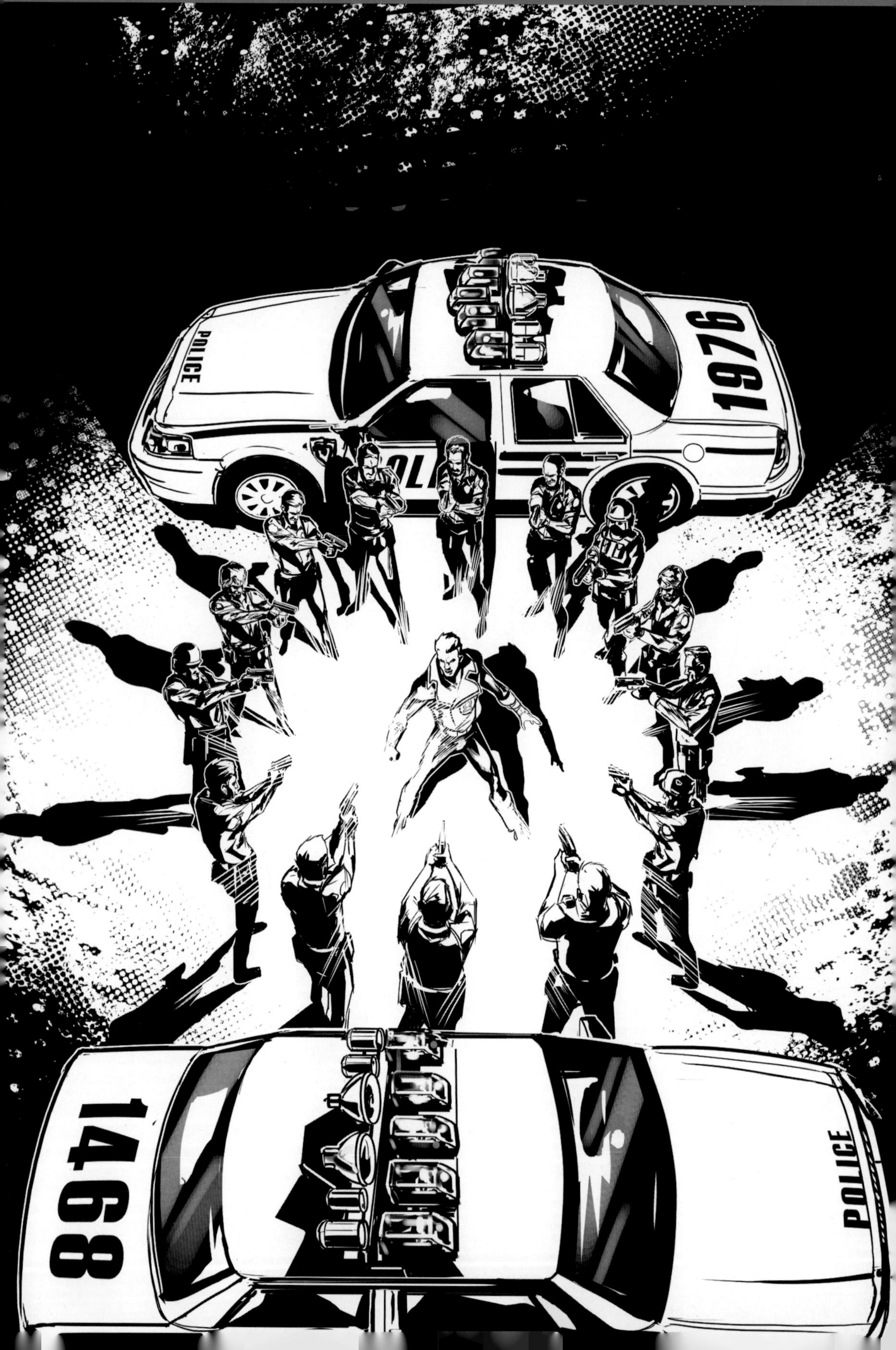

POLICE
1976
POLICE
1468

BALTIMORE, MARYLAND.

EVERYTHING WAS *PERFECT!*

KRSHKRSHKRSHKRSH

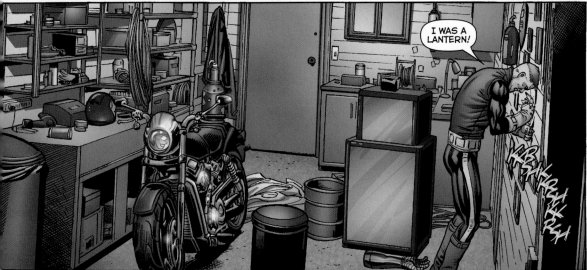

I WAS A LANTERN!

KRSHKRSHKRSH

A SENTINEL!

KRSH KRSH

RESPECTED!

MY DAMN *NAME* BURNED INTO THE BOOK OF OA!

SKRAK

...WHAT HAPPENED...?

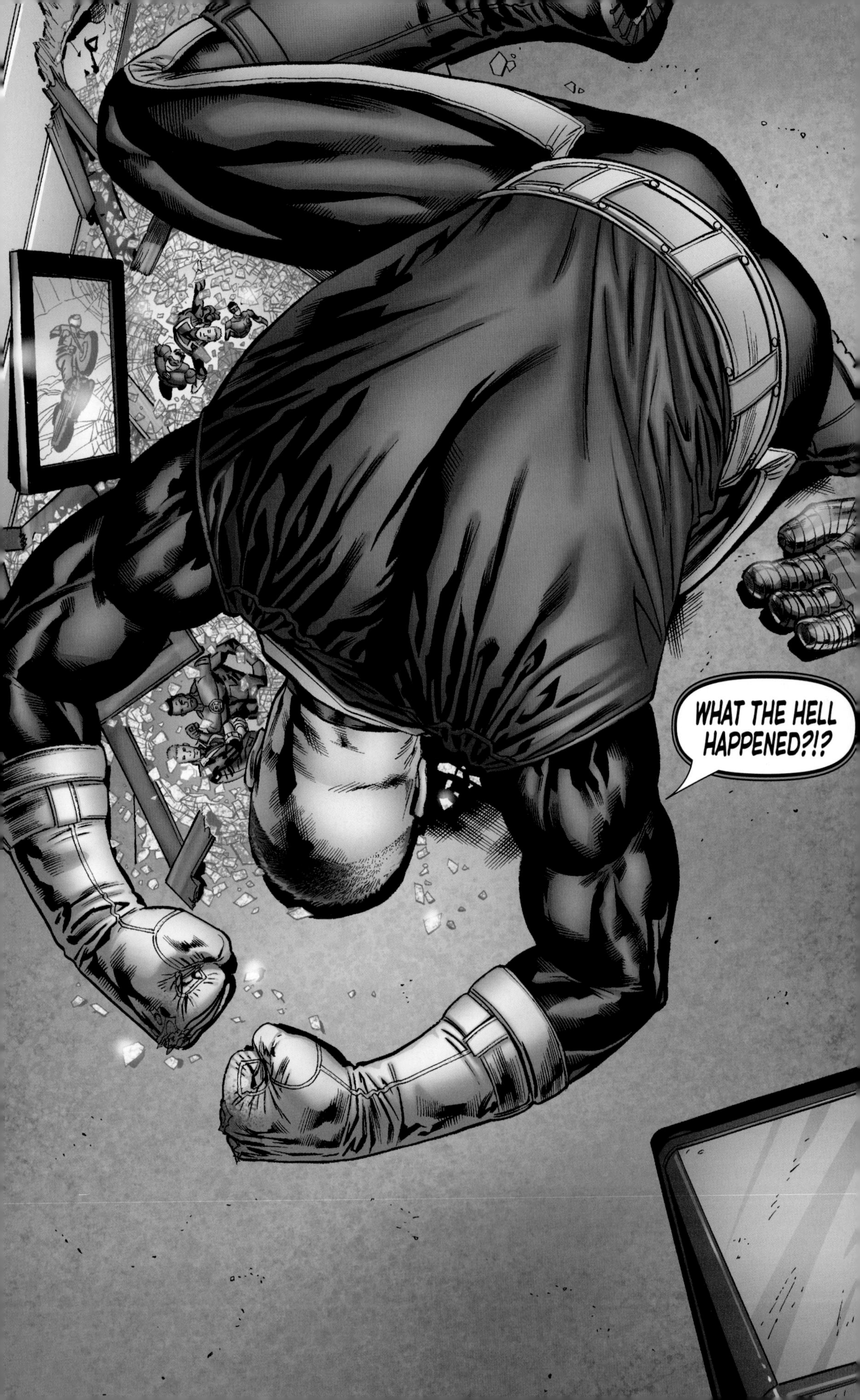
WHAT THE HELL HAPPENED?!?

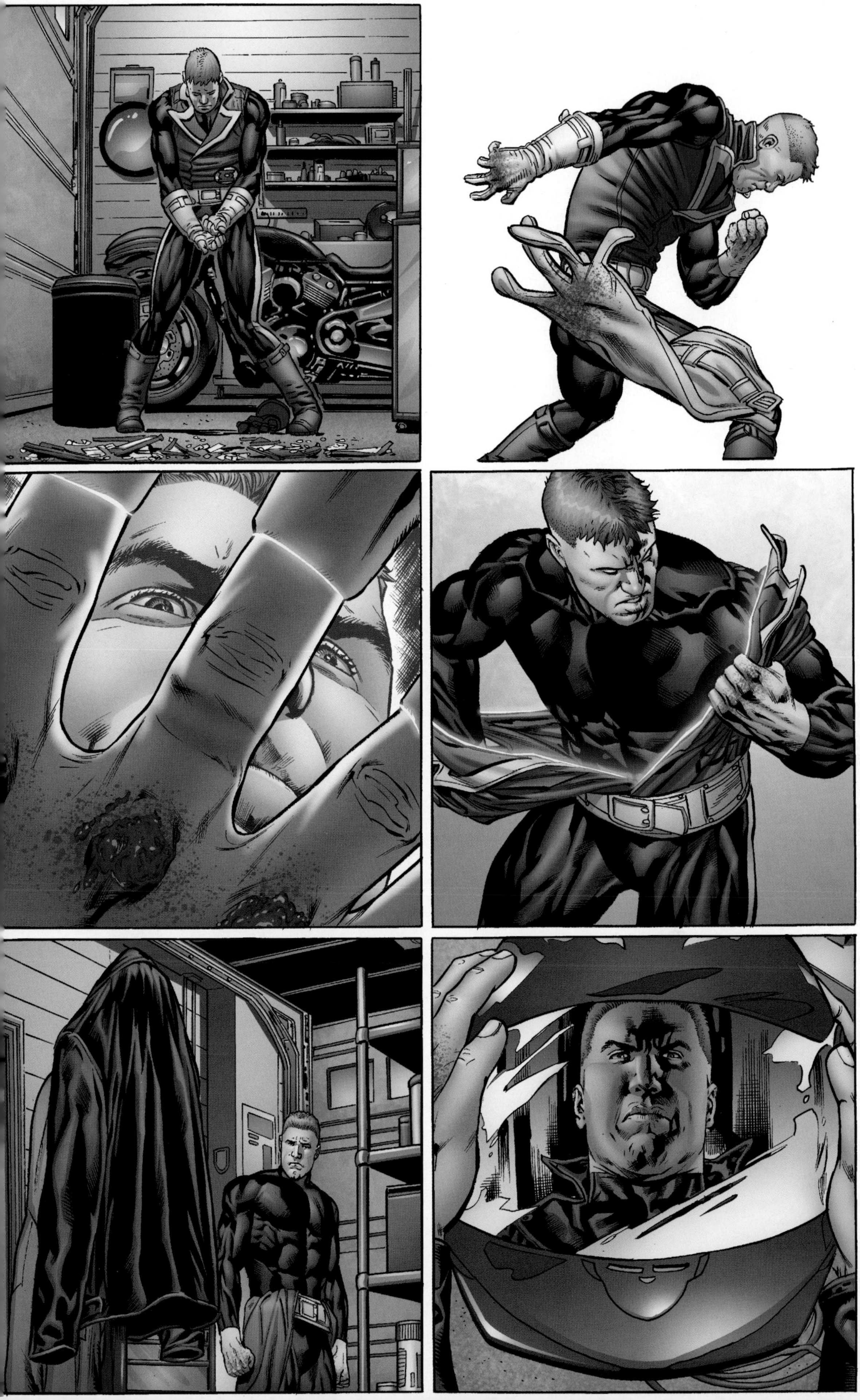

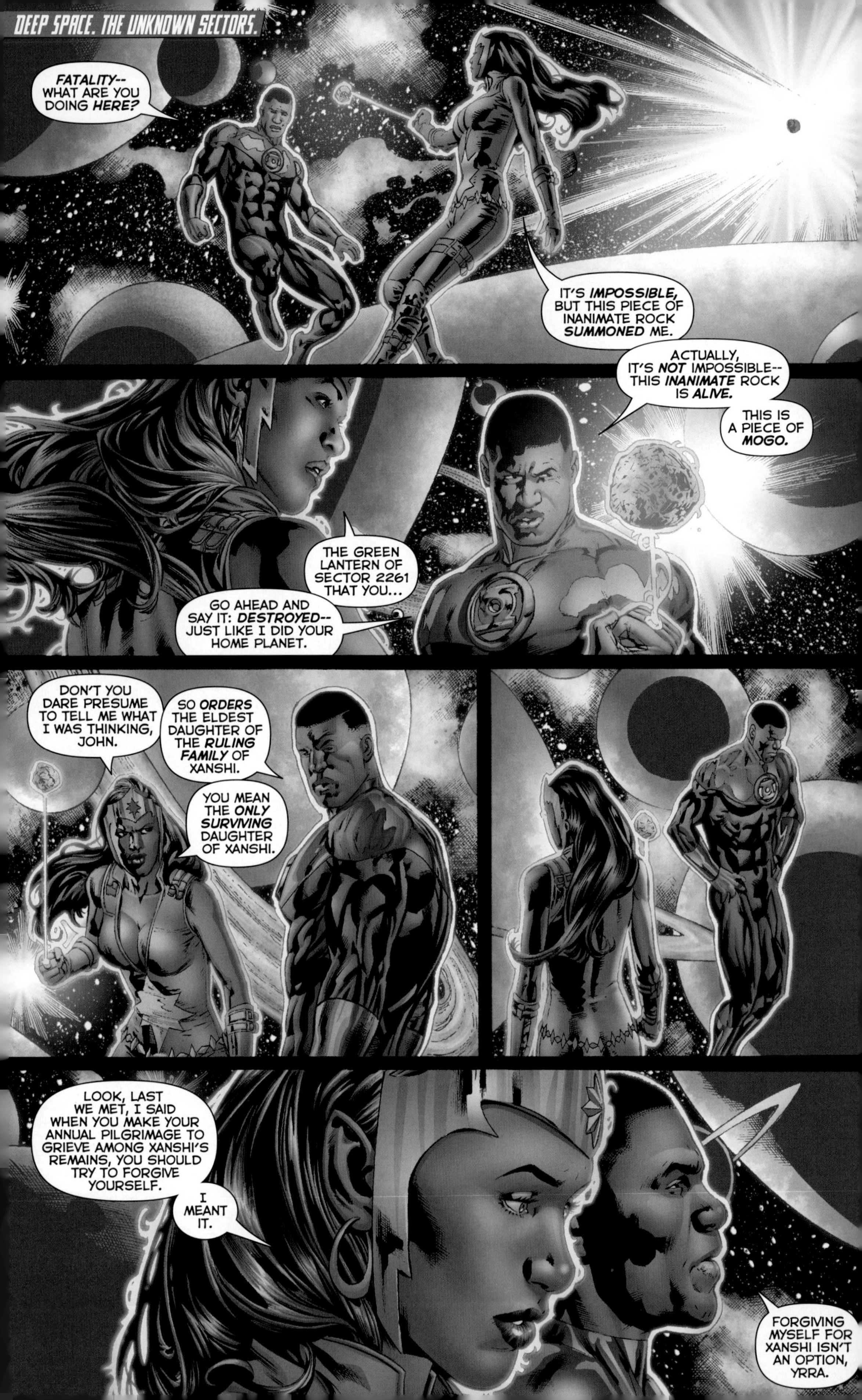
DEEP SPACE. THE UNKNOWN SECTORS.
FATALITY-- WHAT ARE YOU DOING HERE?
IT'S IMPOSSIBLE, BUT THIS PIECE OF INANIMATE ROCK SUMMONED ME.
ACTUALLY, IT'S NOT IMPOSSIBLE-- THIS INANIMATE ROCK IS ALIVE.
THIS IS A PIECE OF MOGO.
THE GREEN LANTERN OF SECTOR 2261 THAT YOU...
GO AHEAD AND SAY IT: DESTROYED-- JUST LIKE I DID YOUR HOME PLANET.
DON'T YOU DARE PRESUME TO TELL ME WHAT I WAS THINKING, JOHN.
SO ORDERS THE ELDEST DAUGHTER OF THE RULING FAMILY OF XANSHI.
YOU MEAN THE ONLY SURVIVING DAUGHTER OF XANSHI.
LOOK, LAST WE MET, I SAID WHEN YOU MAKE YOUR ANNUAL PILGRIMAGE TO GRIEVE AMONG XANSHI'S REMAINS, YOU SHOULD TRY TO FORGIVE YOURSELF.
I MEANT IT.
FORGIVING MYSELF FOR XANSHI ISN'T AN OPTION, YRRA.

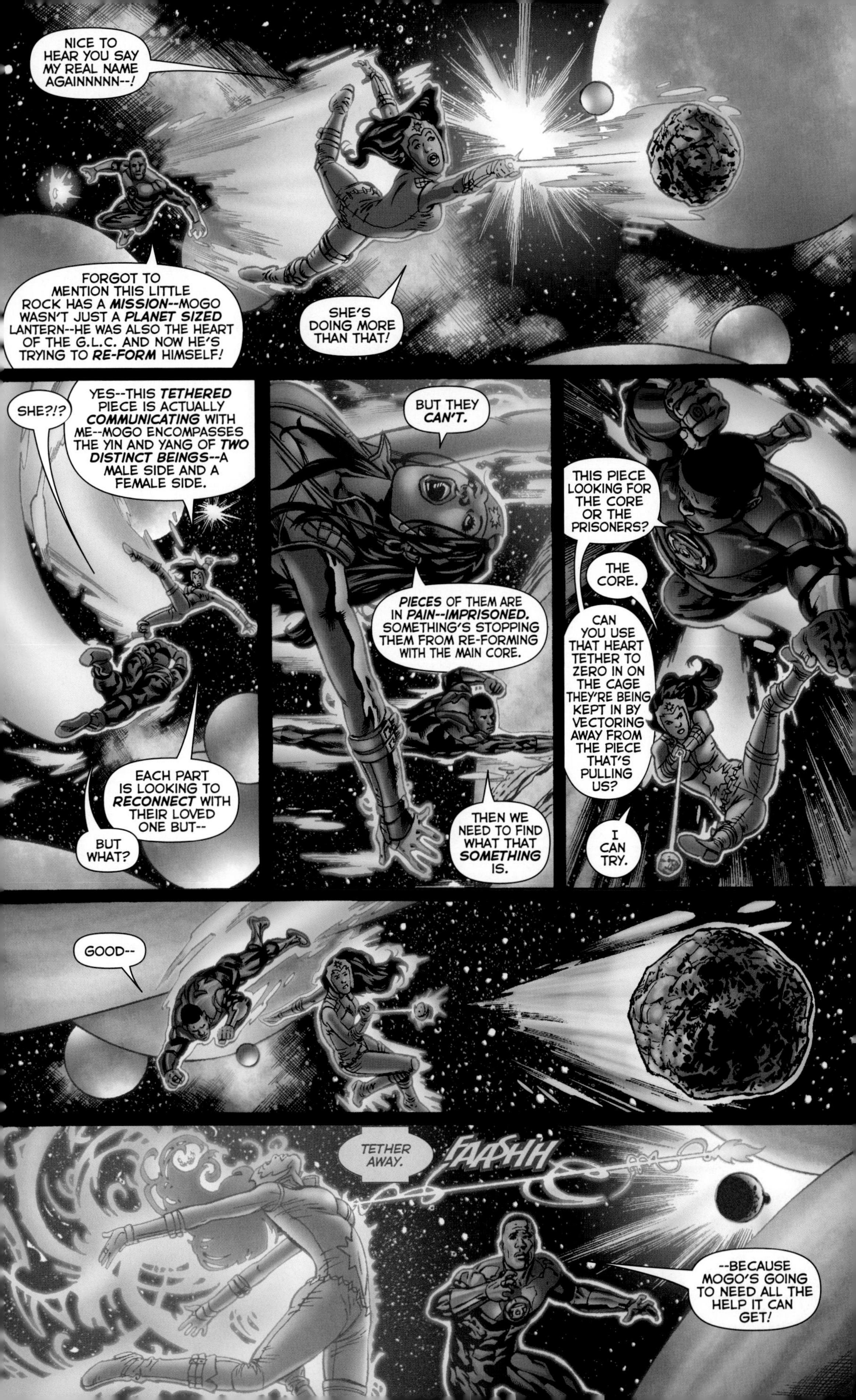

NICE TO HEAR YOU SAY MY REAL NAME AGAINNNNN--!
FORGOT TO MENTION THIS LITTLE ROCK HAS A *MISSION*--MOGO WASN'T JUST A *PLANET SIZED* LANTERN--HE WAS ALSO THE HEART OF THE G.L.C. AND NOW HE'S TRYING TO *RE-FORM* HIMSELF!
SHE'S DOING MORE THAN THAT!
SHE?!?
YES--THIS *TETHERED* PIECE IS ACTUALLY *COMMUNICATING* WITH ME--MOGO ENCOMPASSES THE YIN AND YANG OF *TWO DISTINCT BEINGS*--A MALE SIDE AND A FEMALE SIDE.
EACH PART IS LOOKING TO *RECONNECT* WITH THEIR LOVED ONE BUT--
BUT WHAT?
BUT THEY *CAN'T.*
PIECES OF THEM ARE IN *PAIN--IMPRISONED.* SOMETHING'S STOPPING THEM FROM RE-FORMING WITH THE MAIN CORE.
THEN WE NEED TO FIND WHAT THAT *SOMETHING* IS.
THIS PIECE LOOKING FOR THE CORE OR THE PRISONERS?
THE CORE.
CAN YOU USE THAT HEART TETHER TO ZERO IN ON THE CAGE THEY'RE BEING KEPT IN BY VECTORING AWAY FROM THE PIECE THAT'S PULLING US?
I CAN TRY.
GOOD--
TETHER AWAY.
FAASHH
--BECAUSE MOGO'S GOING TO NEED ALL THE HELP IT CAN GET!

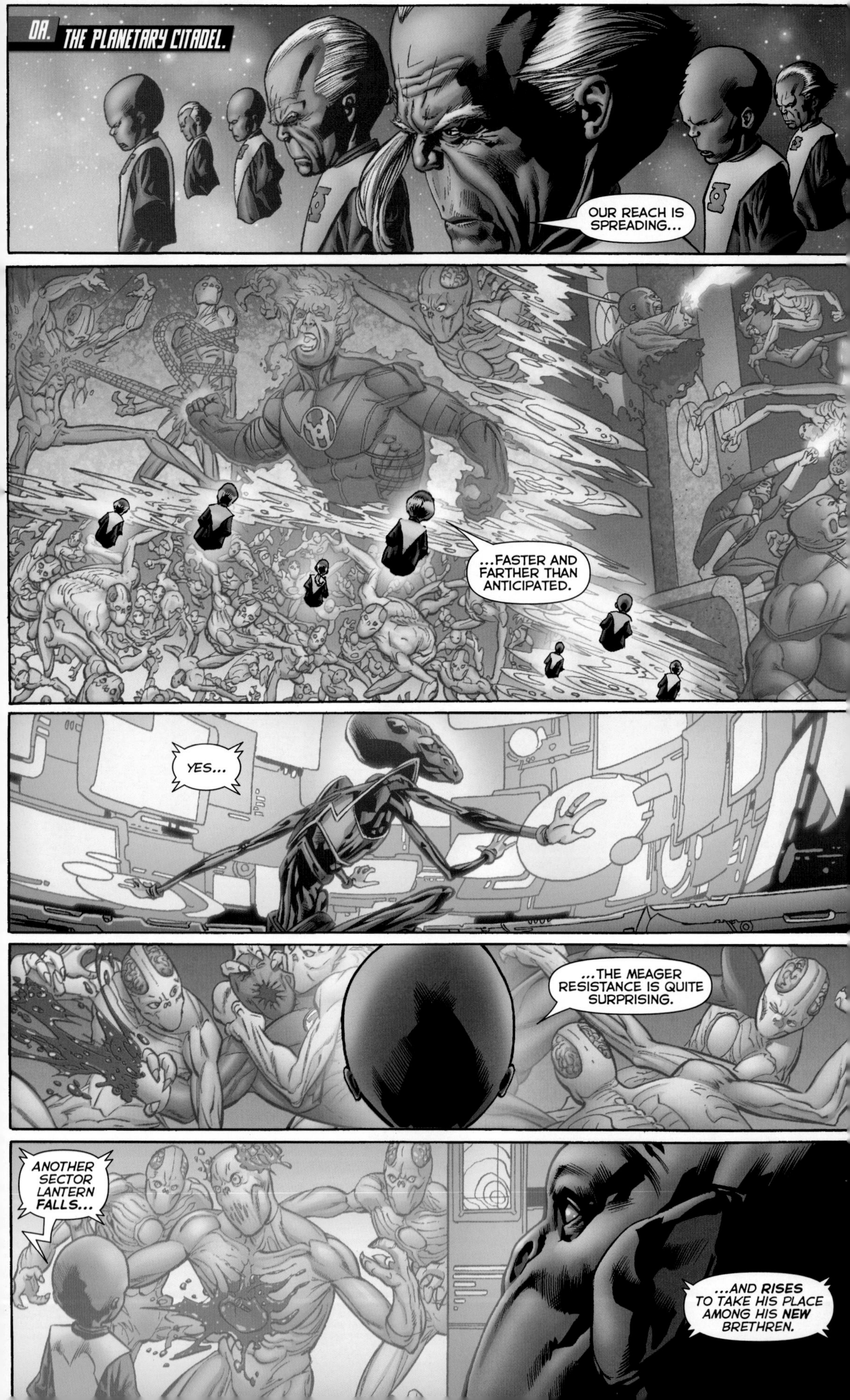
OA. THE PLANETARY CITADEL.
OUR REACH IS SPREADING...
...FASTER AND FARTHER THAN ANTICIPATED.
YES...
...THE MEAGER RESISTANCE IS QUITE SURPRISING.
ANOTHER SECTOR LANTERN FALLS...
...AND RISES TO TAKE HIS PLACE AMONG HIS NEW BRETHREN.

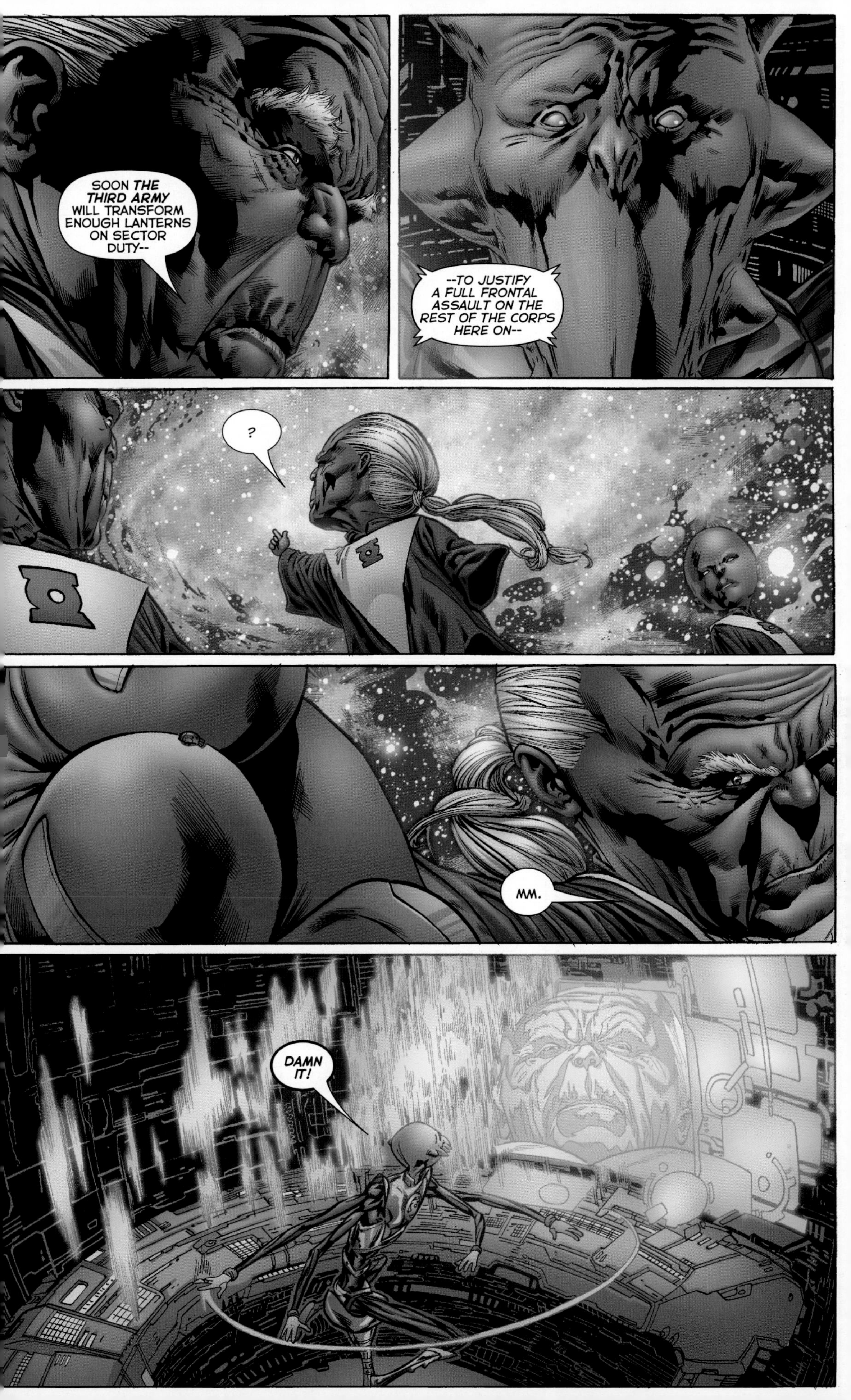
SOON THE THIRD ARMY WILL TRANSFORM ENOUGH LANTERNS ON SECTOR DUTY--
--TO JUSTIFY A FULL FRONTAL ASSAULT ON THE REST OF THE CORPS HERE ON--
?
MM.
DAMN IT!

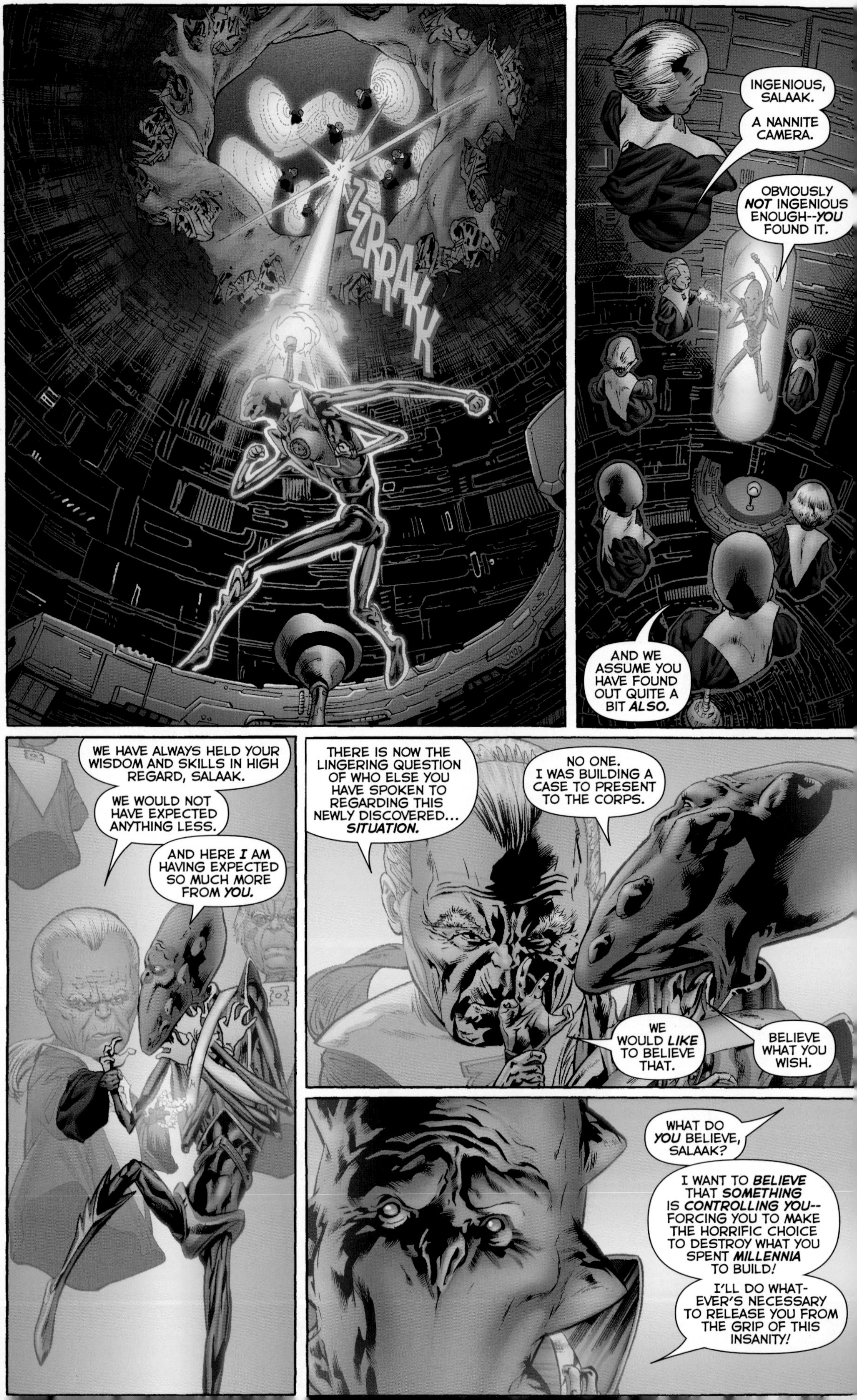
ZZRRAKK
INGENIOUS, SALAAK.
A NANNITE CAMERA.
OBVIOUSLY NOT INGENIOUS ENOUGH--YOU FOUND IT.
AND WE ASSUME YOU HAVE FOUND OUT QUITE A BIT ALSO.
WE HAVE ALWAYS HELD YOUR WISDOM AND SKILLS IN HIGH REGARD, SALAAK.
WE WOULD NOT HAVE EXPECTED ANYTHING LESS.
AND HERE I AM HAVING EXPECTED SO MUCH MORE FROM YOU.
THERE IS NOW THE LINGERING QUESTION OF WHO ELSE YOU HAVE SPOKEN TO REGARDING THIS NEWLY DISCOVERED... SITUATION.
NO ONE. I WAS BUILDING A CASE TO PRESENT TO THE CORPS.
WE WOULD LIKE TO BELIEVE THAT.
BELIEVE WHAT YOU WISH.
WHAT DO YOU BELIEVE, SALAAK?
I WANT TO BELIEVE THAT SOMETHING IS CONTROLLING YOU--FORCING YOU TO MAKE THE HORRIFIC CHOICE TO DESTROY WHAT YOU SPENT MILLENNIA TO BUILD!
I'LL DO WHAT-EVER'S NECESSARY TO RELEASE YOU FROM THE GRIP OF THIS INSANITY!

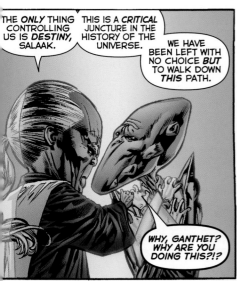

THE **ONLY** THING CONTROLLING US IS **DESTINY**, SALAAK.

THIS IS A **CRITICAL** JUNCTURE IN THE HISTORY OF THE UNIVERSE.

WE HAVE BEEN LEFT WITH NO CHOICE **BUT** TO WALK DOWN **THIS** PATH.

WHY, GANTHET? WHY ARE YOU DOING THIS?!?

FREE WILL IS THE ENEMY.

NO, YOU'RE WRONG--HOW CAN YOU BE SO BLIND AFTER ALL THIS TIME?!?

FREE WILL IS **LIFE**--WITHOUT IT THE UNIVERSE IS **HOLLOW!**

WITH IT, THE UNIVERSE IS **DEAD.**

THE ABILITY TO ACT AND MAKE CHOICES AS FREE AND AUTONOMOUS BEINGS HAS ONLY CREATED HAVOC AND UNREST.

FREE WILL IS A CANCER THAT NEEDS TO BE CUT OUT IF THE UNIVERSE IS TO SURVIVE AND ASCEND.

SHAME ON ME FOR PUTTING MY TRUST IN YOU ALL THESE YEARS AND TAKING YOUR SIDE AGAINST THE FREE THINKERS OF THE CORPS.

WITH YOUR INHERENT SENSE OF ORDER AND ADHERENCE TO REGULATIONS WE THOUGHT **YOU,** OF ALL LANTERNS, WOULD EMBRACE THE GLORIOUS NEW EPOCH WE ARE SHAPING.

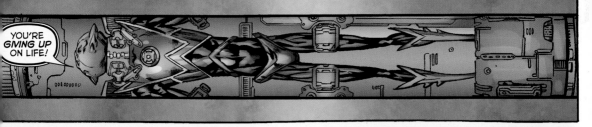

YOU'RE **GIVING UP** ON LIFE!

NO, SALAAK...

...WE ARE **SAVING** IT.

C'MON--THAT WAS PLAIN AS DAY PASSING INTERFERENCE!

GOT THAT RIGHT!

BETTER OFF GOING BACK TO REPLACEMENT REFS WITH ALL THESE BLOWN CALLS.

BRRING BRRING

AREN'T YOU GOING TO ANSWER IT?

ANYBODY I'D WANNA TALK TO IS WATCHING THE GAME AND NOT LOOKING TO YAP WITH ME.

ANYBODY EVER SAY YOU SHOULD STOP BEING SO ANTI-SOCIAL?

ANYBODY WHO'D SAY THAT ISN'T SOMEONE I WANNA SOCIALIZE WITH.

BRRING BRRING

EBENEZER GARDNER'S RESIDENCE, WHO MAY I ASK IS--

HEY, GUY! HOW'S MY FAVORITE SPACE COP BROTHER-- SAVING PLANETS AND ALIENS?

YEAH, YOU KNOW, ALL THAT STUFF.

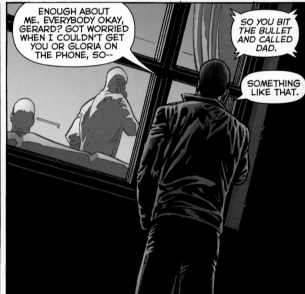

ENOUGH ABOUT ME. EVERYBODY OKAY, GERARD? GOT WORRIED WHEN I COULDN'T GET YOU OR GLORIA ON THE PHONE, SO--

SO YOU BIT THE BULLET AND CALLED DAD.

SOMETHING LIKE THAT.

WELL, IT'S NOT EVERY DAY THE GARDNER FAMILY GETS GREEN ENERGY SPHERES POPPED AROUND THEM AND ZIPPED INTO SPACE TO MEET THE *JUSTICE LEAGUE*--WHAT THE HELL WAS *THAT* ABOUT?

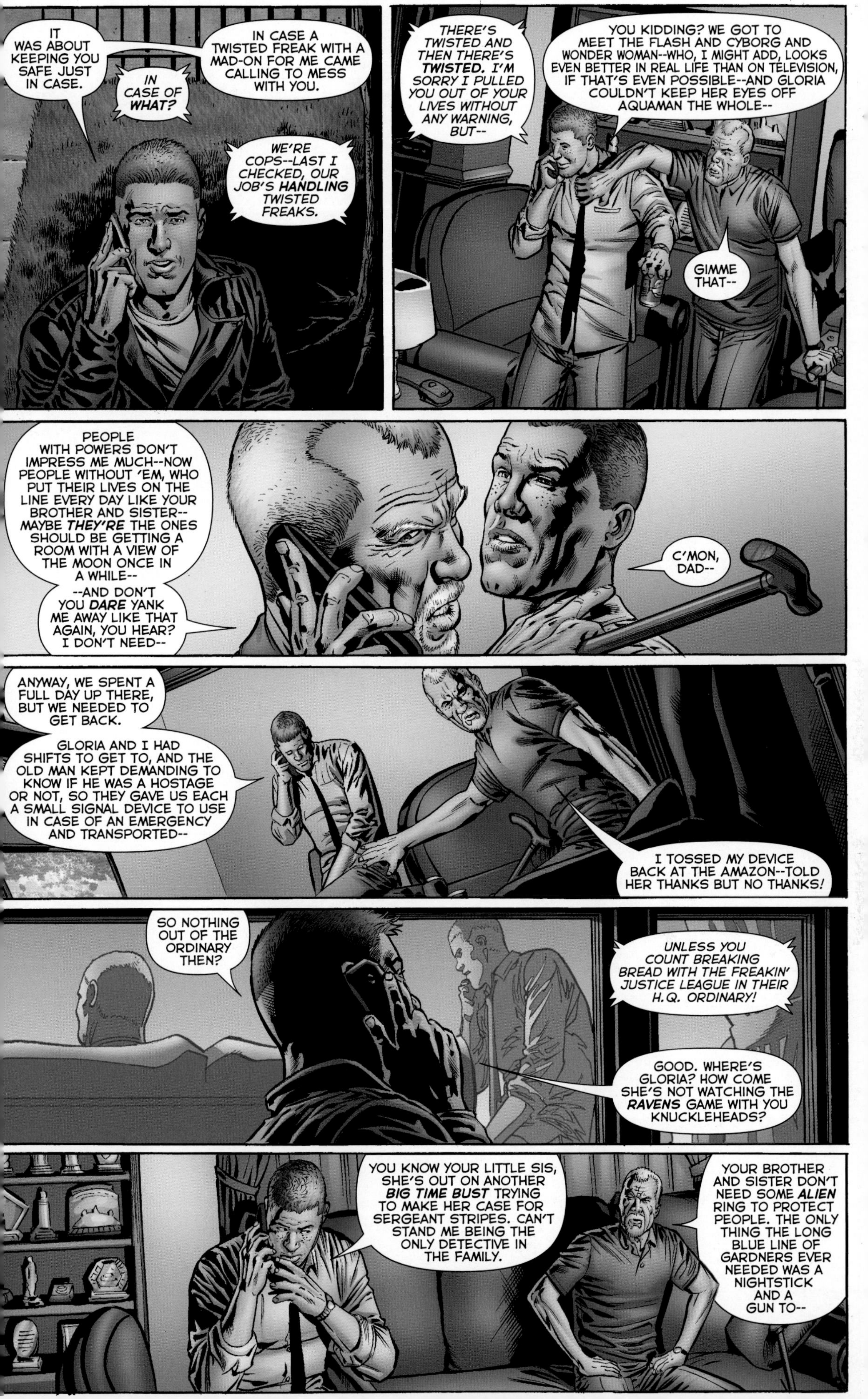

IT WAS ABOUT KEEPING YOU SAFE JUST IN CASE.
IN CASE OF *WHAT?*
IN CASE A TWISTED FREAK WITH A MAD-ON FOR ME CAME CALLING TO MESS WITH YOU.
WE'RE COPS--LAST I CHECKED, OUR JOB'S ***HANDLING*** *TWISTED FREAKS.*
THERE'S TWISTED AND THEN THERE'S ***TWISTED.*** *I'M SORRY I PULLED YOU OUT OF YOUR LIVES WITHOUT ANY WARNING, BUT--*
YOU KIDDING? WE GOT TO MEET THE FLASH AND CYBORG AND WONDER WOMAN--WHO, I MIGHT ADD, LOOKS EVEN BETTER IN REAL LIFE THAN ON TELEVISION, IF THAT'S EVEN POSSIBLE--AND GLORIA COULDN'T KEEP HER EYES OFF AQUAMAN THE WHOLE--
GIMME THAT--
PEOPLE WITH POWERS DON'T IMPRESS ME MUCH--NOW PEOPLE WITHOUT 'EM, WHO PUT THEIR LIVES ON THE LINE EVERY DAY LIKE YOUR BROTHER AND SISTER--MAYBE *THEY'RE* THE ONES SHOULD BE GETTING A ROOM WITH A VIEW OF THE MOON ONCE IN A WHILE--
--AND DON'T YOU *DARE* YANK ME AWAY LIKE THAT AGAIN, YOU HEAR? I DON'T NEED--
C'MON, DAD--
ANYWAY, WE SPENT A FULL DAY UP THERE, BUT WE NEEDED TO GET BACK.
GLORIA AND I HAD SHIFTS TO GET TO, AND THE OLD MAN KEPT DEMANDING TO KNOW IF HE WAS A HOSTAGE OR NOT, SO THEY GAVE US EACH A SMALL SIGNAL DEVICE TO USE IN CASE OF AN EMERGENCY AND TRANSPORTED--
I TOSSED MY DEVICE BACK AT THE AMAZON--TOLD HER THANKS BUT NO THANKS!
SO NOTHING OUT OF THE ORDINARY THEN?
UNLESS YOU COUNT BREAKING BREAD WITH THE FREAKIN' JUSTICE LEAGUE IN THEIR H.Q. ORDINARY!
GOOD. WHERE'S GLORIA? HOW COME SHE'S NOT WATCHING THE ***RAVENS*** GAME WITH YOU KNUCKLEHEADS?
YOU KNOW YOUR LITTLE SIS, SHE'S OUT ON ANOTHER ***BIG TIME BUST*** TRYING TO MAKE HER CASE FOR SERGEANT STRIPES. CAN'T STAND ME BEING THE ONLY DETECTIVE IN THE FAMILY.
YOUR BROTHER AND SISTER DON'T NEED SOME ***ALIEN*** RING TO PROTECT PEOPLE. THE ONLY THING THE LONG BLUE LINE OF GARDNERS EVER NEEDED WAS A NIGHTSTICK AND A GUN TO--

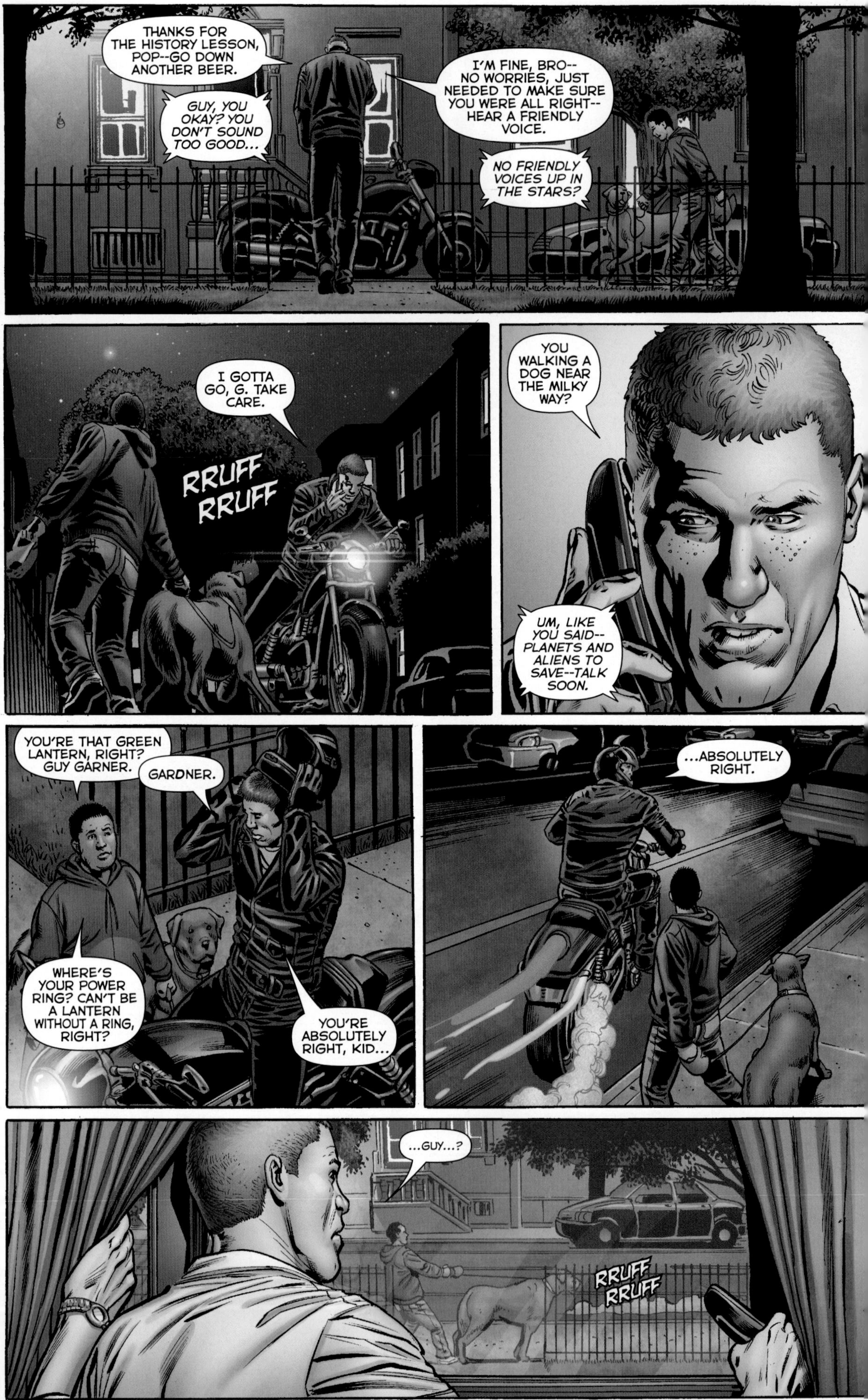
THANKS FOR THE HISTORY LESSON, POP--GO DOWN ANOTHER BEER.
GUY, YOU OKAY? YOU DON'T SOUND TOO GOOD...
I'M FINE, BRO-- NO WORRIES, JUST NEEDED TO MAKE SURE YOU WERE ALL RIGHT-- HEAR A FRIENDLY VOICE.
NO FRIENDLY VOICES UP IN THE STARS?
I GOTTA GO, G. TAKE CARE.
RRUFF RRUFF
YOU WALKING A DOG NEAR THE MILKY WAY?
UM, LIKE YOU SAID-- PLANETS AND ALIENS TO SAVE--TALK SOON.
YOU'RE THAT GREEN LANTERN, RIGHT? GUY GARNER.
GARDNER.
WHERE'S YOUR POWER RING? CAN'T BE A LANTERN WITHOUT A RING, RIGHT?
YOU'RE ABSOLUTELY RIGHT, KID...
...ABSOLUTELY RIGHT.
...GUY...?
RRUFF RRUFF

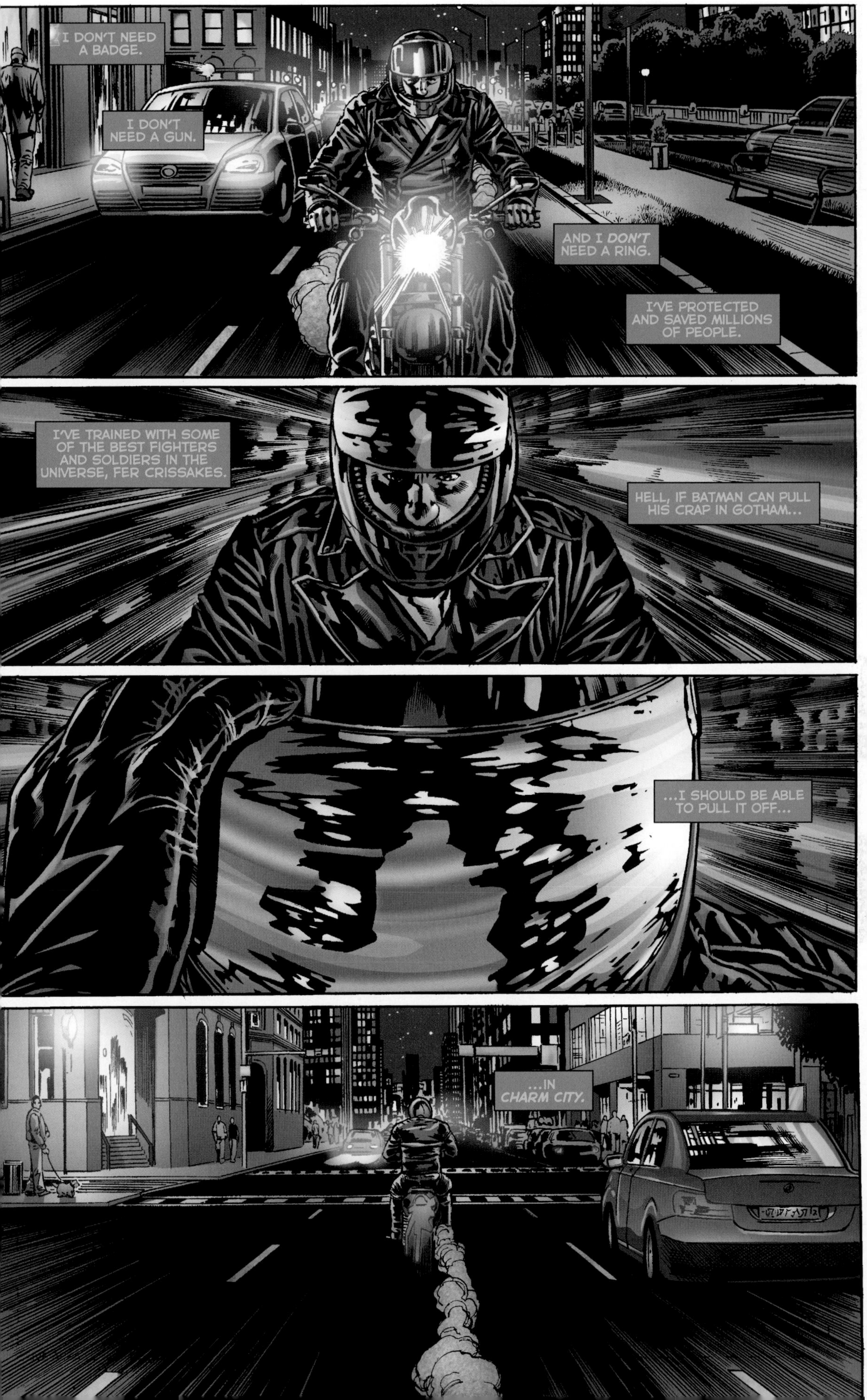
I DON'T NEED A BADGE.
I DON'T NEED A GUN.
AND I *DON'T* NEED A RING.
I'VE PROTECTED AND SAVED MILLIONS OF PEOPLE.
I'VE TRAINED WITH SOME OF THE BEST FIGHTERS AND SOLDIERS IN THE UNIVERSE, FER CRISSAKES.
HELL, IF BATMAN CAN PULL HIS CRAP IN GOTHAM...
...I SHOULD BE ABLE TO PULL IT OFF...
...IN *CHARM CITY.*

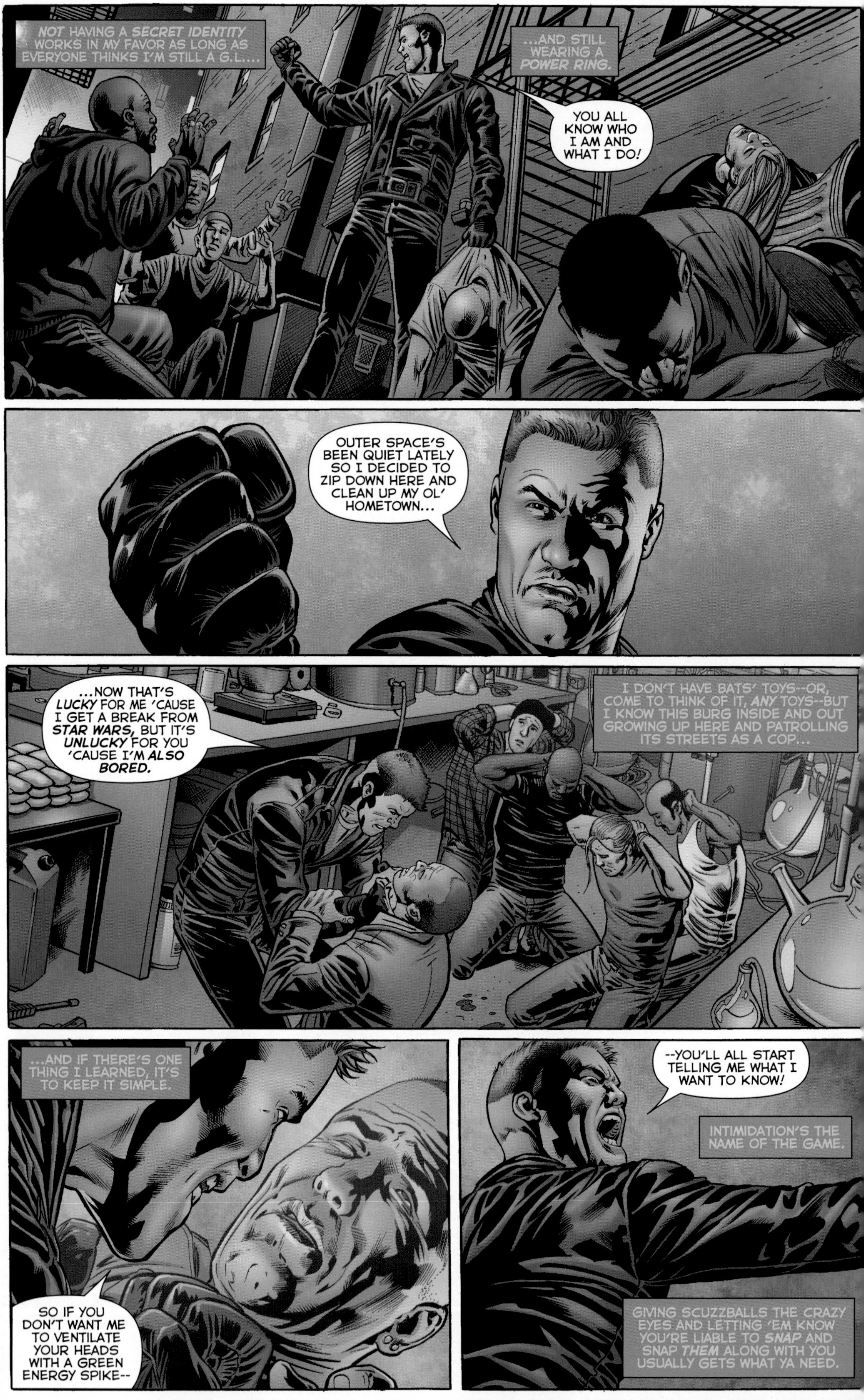
NOT HAVING A SECRET IDENTITY WORKS IN MY FAVOR AS LONG AS EVERYONE THINKS I'M STILL A G.L....
...AND STILL WEARING A POWER RING.
YOU ALL KNOW WHO I AM AND WHAT I DO!
OUTER SPACE'S BEEN QUIET LATELY SO I DECIDED TO ZIP DOWN HERE AND CLEAN UP MY OL' HOMETOWN...
...NOW THAT'S LUCKY FOR ME 'CAUSE I GET A BREAK FROM STAR WARS, BUT IT'S UNLUCKY FOR YOU 'CAUSE I'M ALSO BORED.
I DON'T HAVE BATS' TOYS--OR, COME TO THINK OF IT, ANY TOYS--BUT I KNOW THIS BURG INSIDE AND OUT GROWING UP HERE AND PATROLLING ITS STREETS AS A COP...
...AND IF THERE'S ONE THING I LEARNED, IT'S TO KEEP IT SIMPLE.
SO IF YOU DON'T WANT ME TO VENTILATE YOUR HEADS WITH A GREEN ENERGY SPIKE--
--YOU'LL ALL START TELLING ME WHAT I WANT TO KNOW!
INTIMIDATION'S THE NAME OF THE GAME.
GIVING SCUZZBALLS THE CRAZY EYES AND LETTING 'EM KNOW YOU'RE LIABLE TO SNAP AND SNAP THEM ALONG WITH YOU USUALLY GETS WHAT YA NEED.

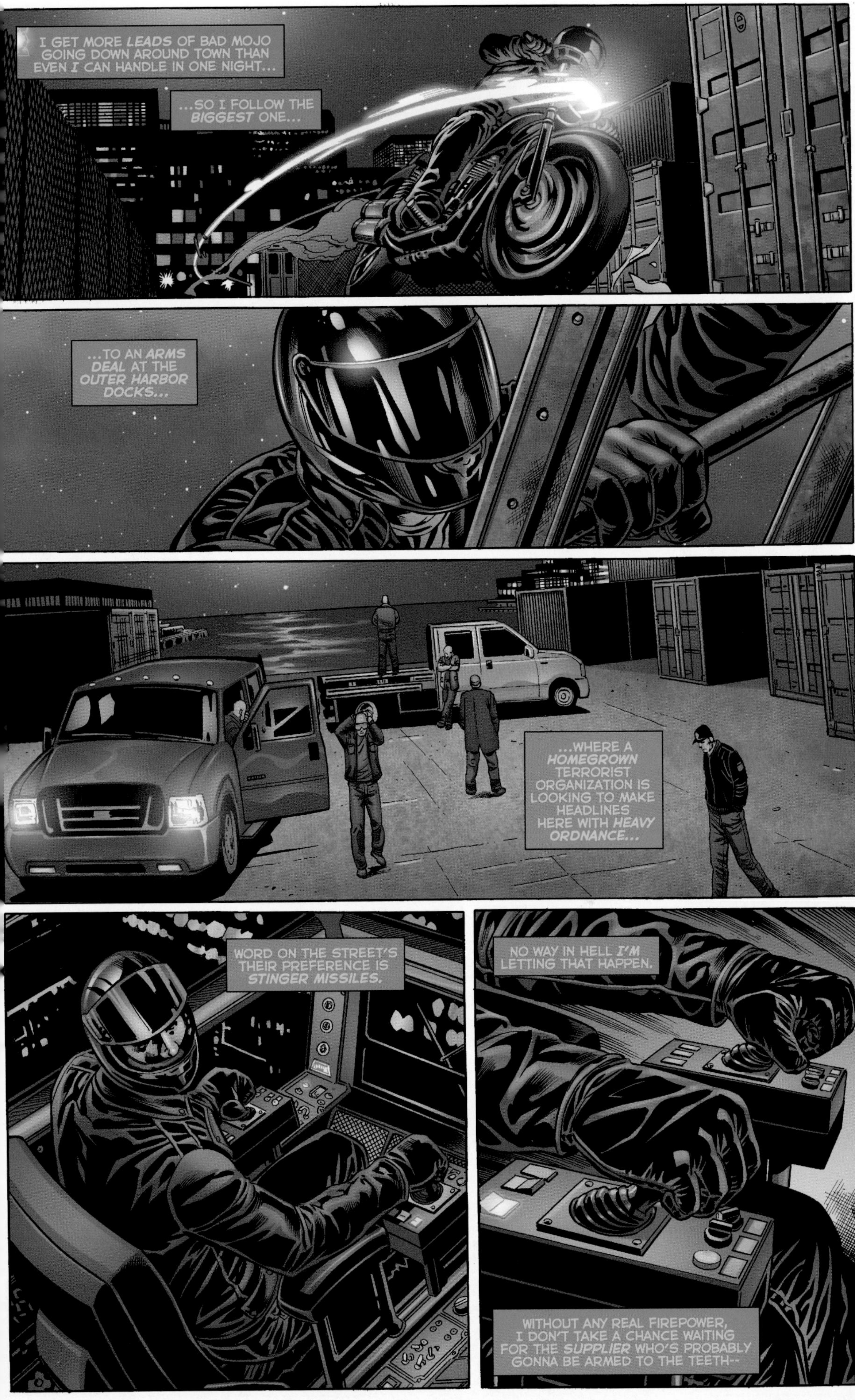
I GET MORE LEADS OF BAD MOJO GOING DOWN AROUND TOWN THAN EVEN I CAN HANDLE IN ONE NIGHT...
...SO I FOLLOW THE BIGGEST ONE...
...TO AN ARMS DEAL AT THE OUTER HARBOR DOCKS...
...WHERE A HOMEGROWN TERRORIST ORGANIZATION IS LOOKING TO MAKE HEADLINES HERE WITH HEAVY ORDNANCE...
WORD ON THE STREET'S THEIR PREFERENCE IS STINGER MISSILES.
NO WAY IN HELL I'M LETTING THAT HAPPEN.
WITHOUT ANY REAL FIREPOWER, I DON'T TAKE A CHANCE WAITING FOR THE SUPPLIER WHO'S PROBABLY GONNA BE ARMED TO THE TEETH--

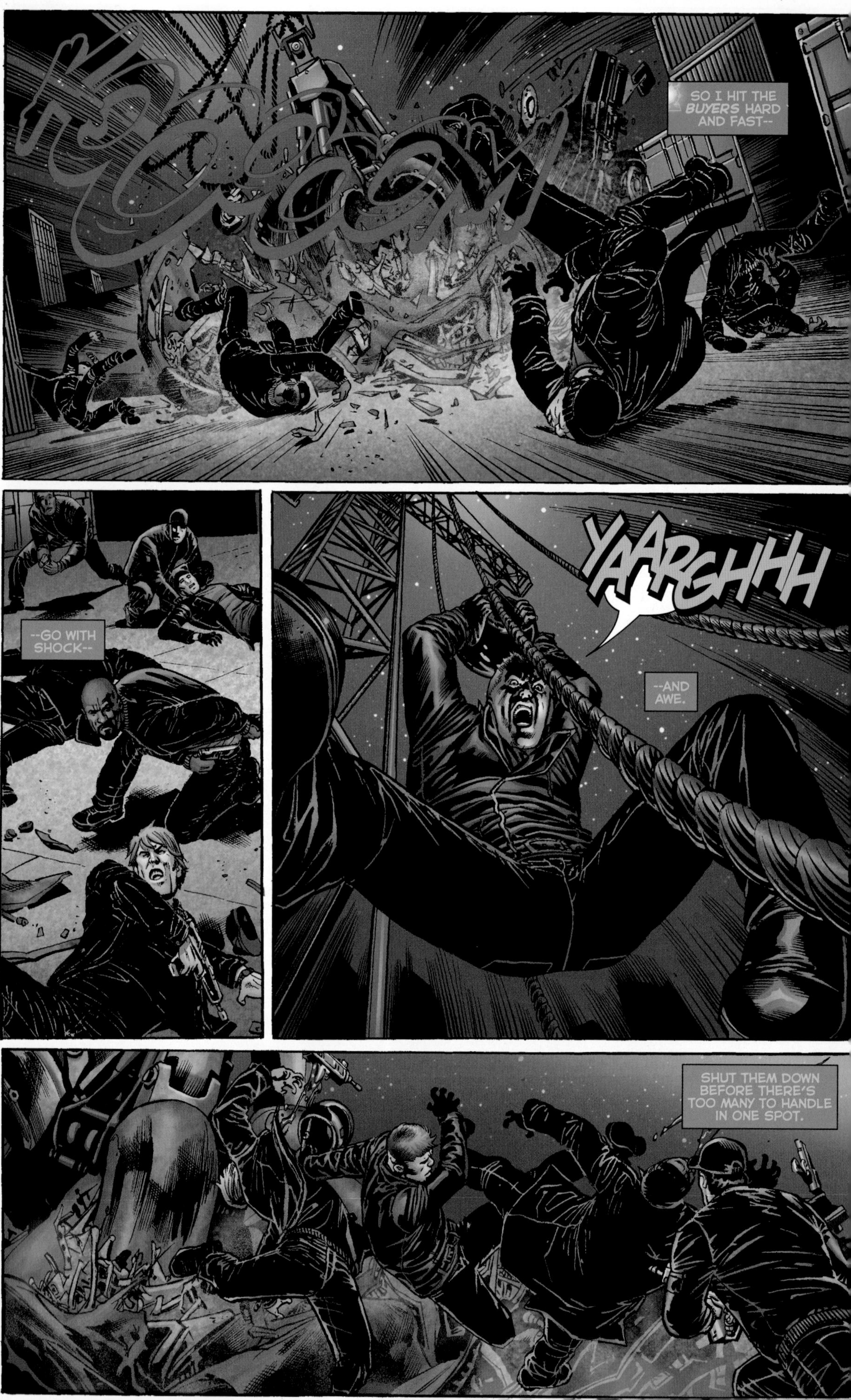
KRA-BOOOOM
SO I HIT THE BUYERS HARD AND FAST--
--GO WITH SHOCK--
YAARGHHH
--AND AWE.
SHUT THEM DOWN BEFORE THERE'S TOO MANY TO HANDLE IN ONE SPOT.

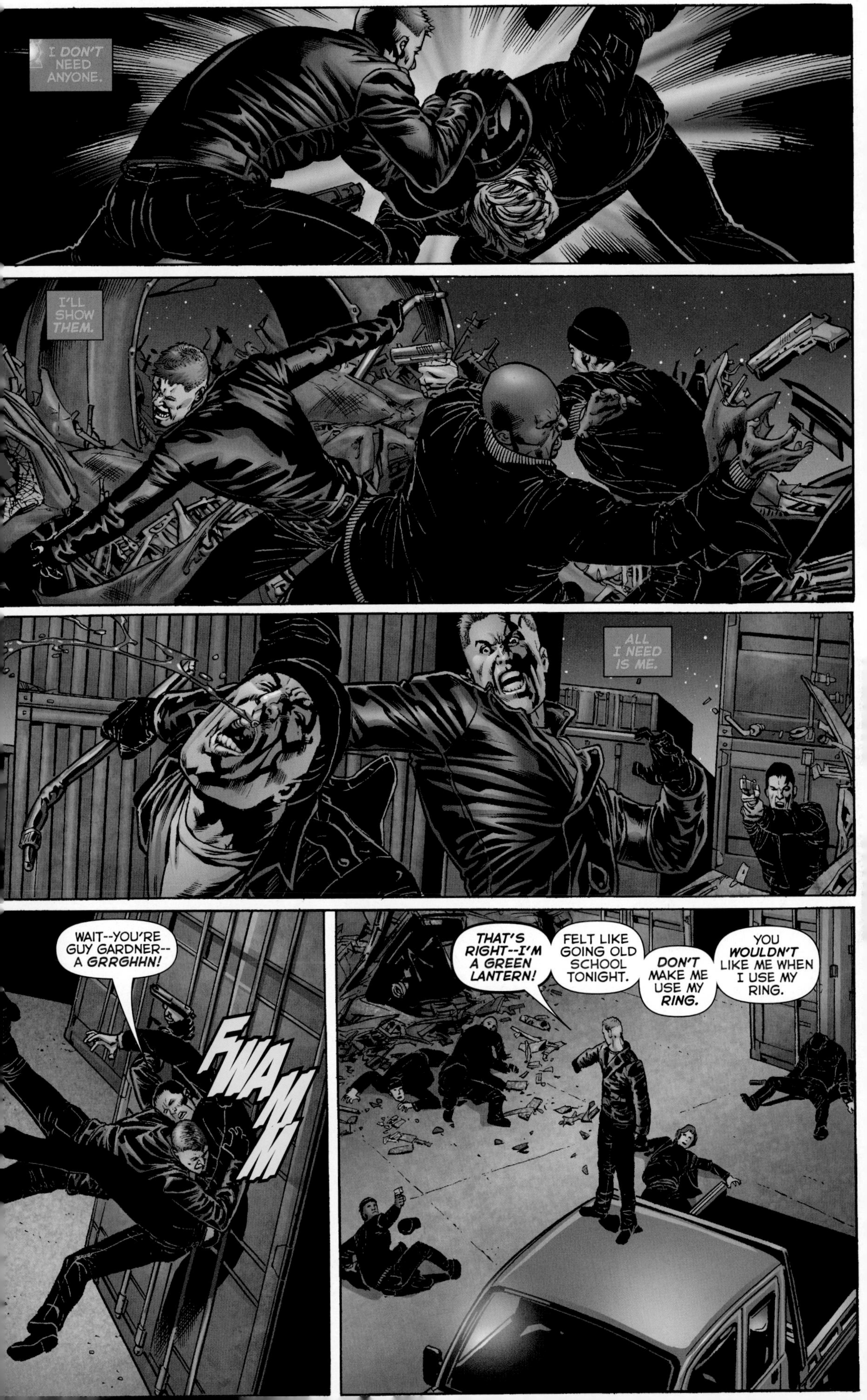
I DON'T NEED ANYONE.
I'LL SHOW THEM.
ALL I NEED IS ME.
WAIT--YOU'RE GUY GARDNER--A GRRGHHN!
FWAMM
THAT'S RIGHT--I'M A GREEN LANTERN!
FELT LIKE GOING OLD SCHOOL TONIGHT.
DON'T MAKE ME USE MY RING.
YOU WOULDN'T LIKE ME WHEN I USE MY RING.

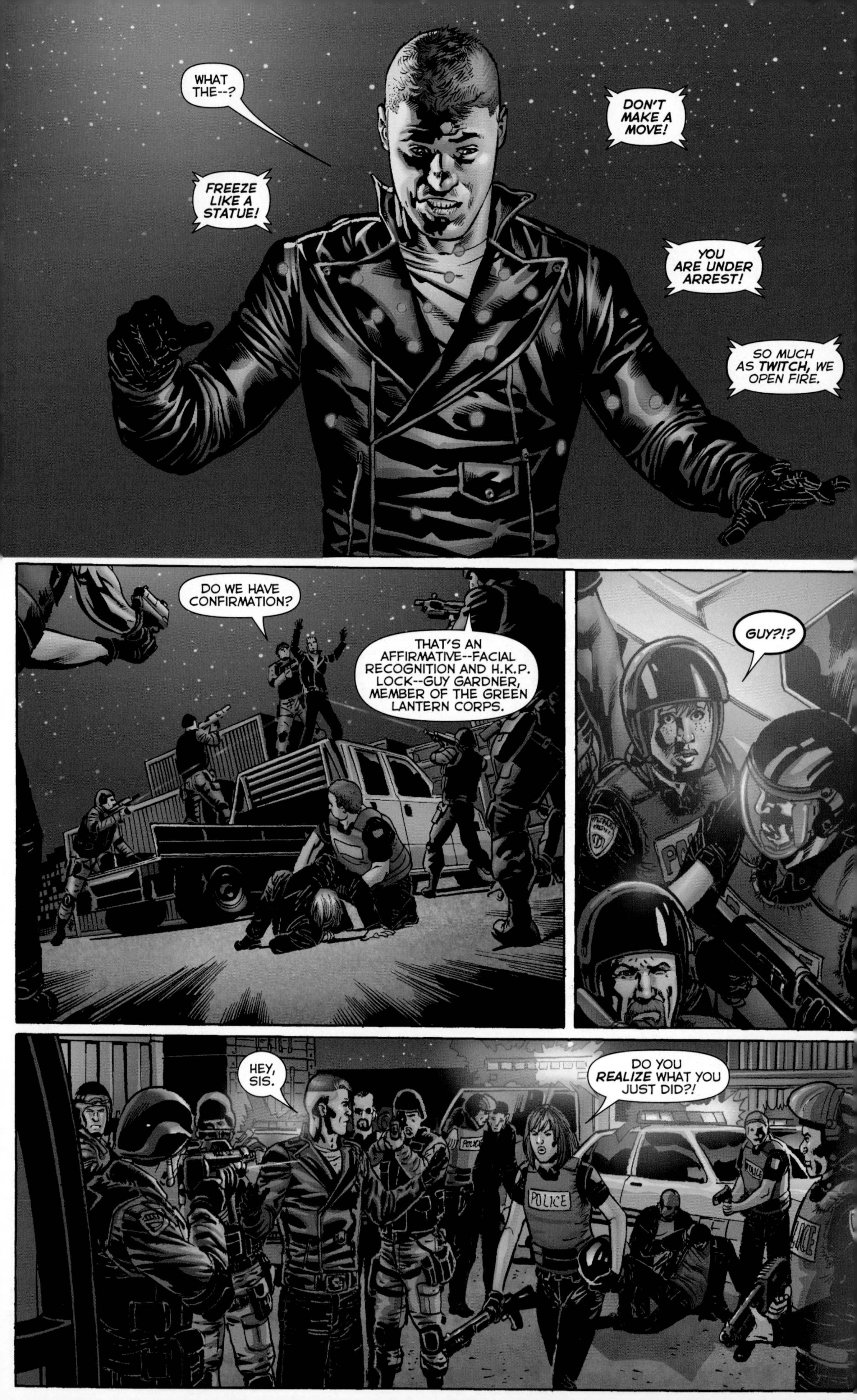

WHAT THE--?
DON'T MAKE A MOVE!
FREEZE LIKE A STATUE!
YOU ARE UNDER ARREST!
SO MUCH AS TWITCH, WE OPEN FIRE.
DO WE HAVE CONFIRMATION?
THAT'S AN AFFIRMATIVE--FACIAL RECOGNITION AND H.K.P. LOCK--GUY GARDNER, MEMBER OF THE GREEN LANTERN CORPS.
GUY?!?
HEY, SIS.
DO YOU REALIZE WHAT YOU JUST DID?!
POLICE

I'M KINDA THINKING I STEPPED INTO THE *MIDDLE* OF SOMETHING HERE, GLORIA.

YOU *STEPPED* INTO SOMETHING ALL RIGHT! THOSE ARE *FEDERAL UNDERCOVER AGENTS* YOU'VE BEEN *SMASHING* AROUND, *BIG BROTHER*, AND--

PLEASE, ALLOW ME...

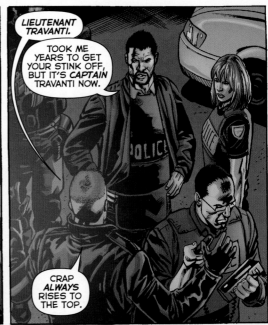

LIEUTENANT TRAVANTI.

TOOK ME YEARS TO GET YOUR STINK OFF, BUT IT'S *CAPTAIN* TRAVANTI NOW.

CRAP *ALWAYS* RISES TO THE TOP.

YES IT DOES, WHICH EXPLAINS HOW SOMEONE LIKE YOU GOT TO BE SOME FAMOUS *SPACE* COP AFTER *FAILING* SO SPECTACULARLY AS A *BALTIMORE* COP.

THOSE AGENTS GOING TO THE EMERGENCY ROOM WERE UNDER DEEP COVER FOR TWO YEARS AND WERE ABOUT TO LEAD US TO AN ARMS DEALER WHO'S MADE IT HIS PERSONAL MISSION TO SUPPLY HIS WARES TO AS MANY ZEALOTS AND NUT JOBS WITH CASH AS HE CAN.

YOU JUST FLUSHED THEIR WORK *AND* OURS DOWN THE TOILET WITH YOUR ONE-MAN-ARMY NONSENSE.

NO ENERGY SIGNATURE. HE'S CLEAN. NO RING.

NO RING? YOU COULD'VE GOTTEN KILLED PULLING THIS *INDIANA JONES* CRAP--WHY AREN'T--

LONG STORY.

GET THE CUFFS ON HIM, OFFICER GARDNER, THEN PROCESS YOUR BROTHER'S ASS DOWNTOWN, LANTERN OR NO LANTERN.

KLAK

DÉJÀ VU ALL OVER AGAIN, JOHN.

WHAT?

NOTHING.

GO AHEAD, SIS. DO WHAT YA NEED TO DO.

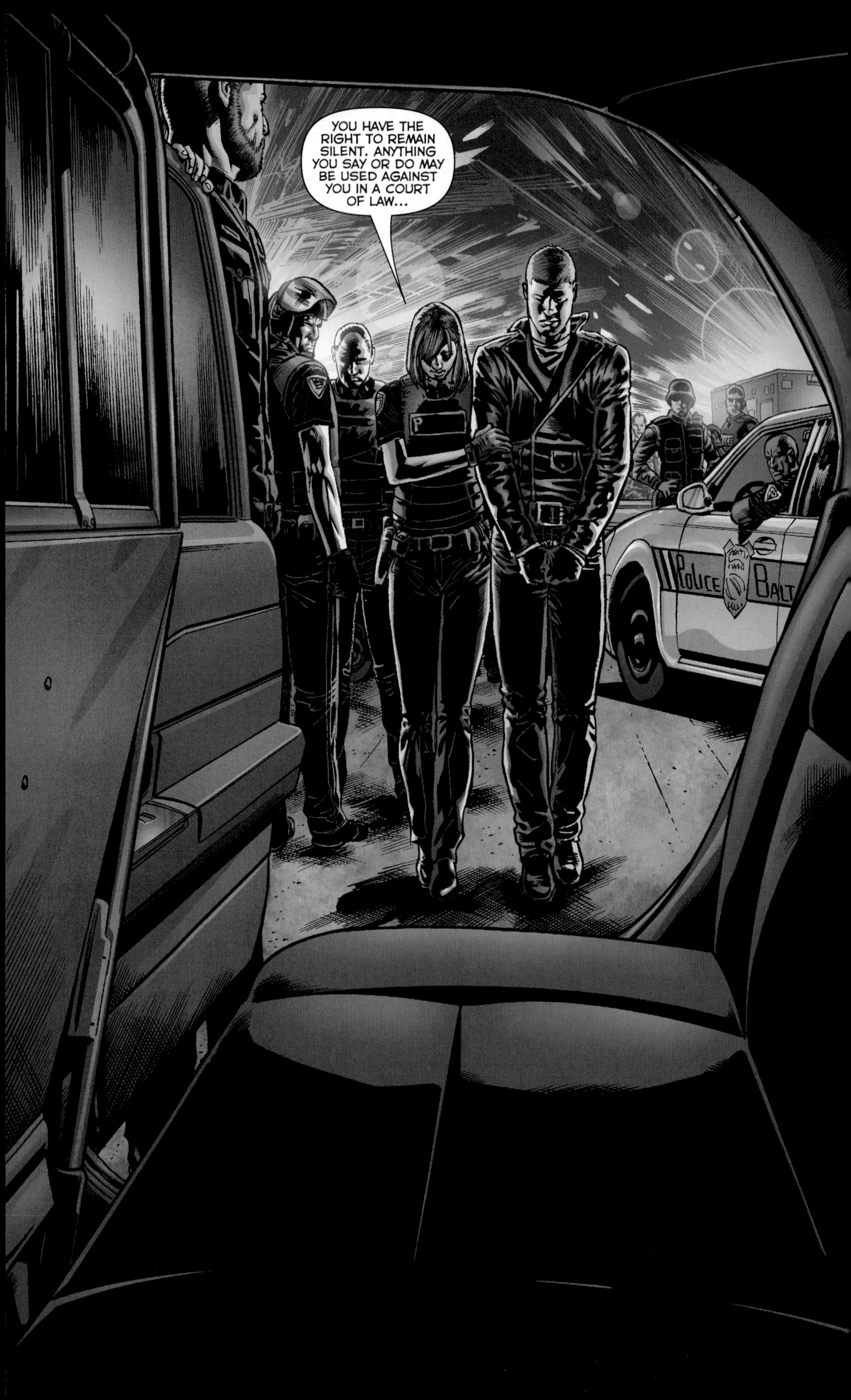
YOU HAVE THE RIGHT TO REMAIN SILENT. ANYTHING YOU SAY OR DO MAY BE USED AGAINST YOU IN A COURT OF LAW...
POLICE
BALT

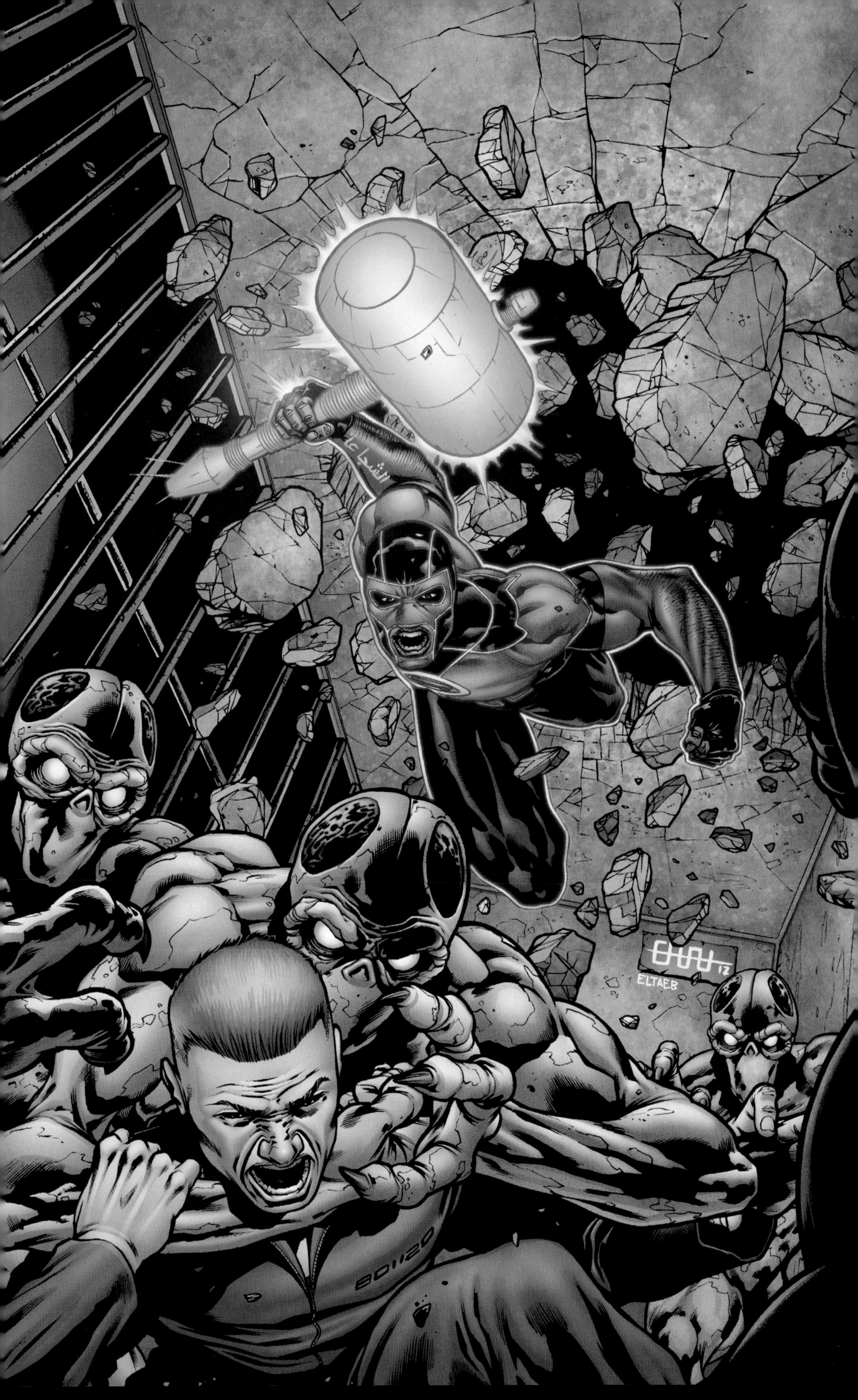

ELTAEB
12

BAD GUYS

PETER J. TOMASI writer **FERNANDO PASARIN** penciller **SCOTT HANNA** inker cover art by **CAFU** & **GABE ELTAEB**

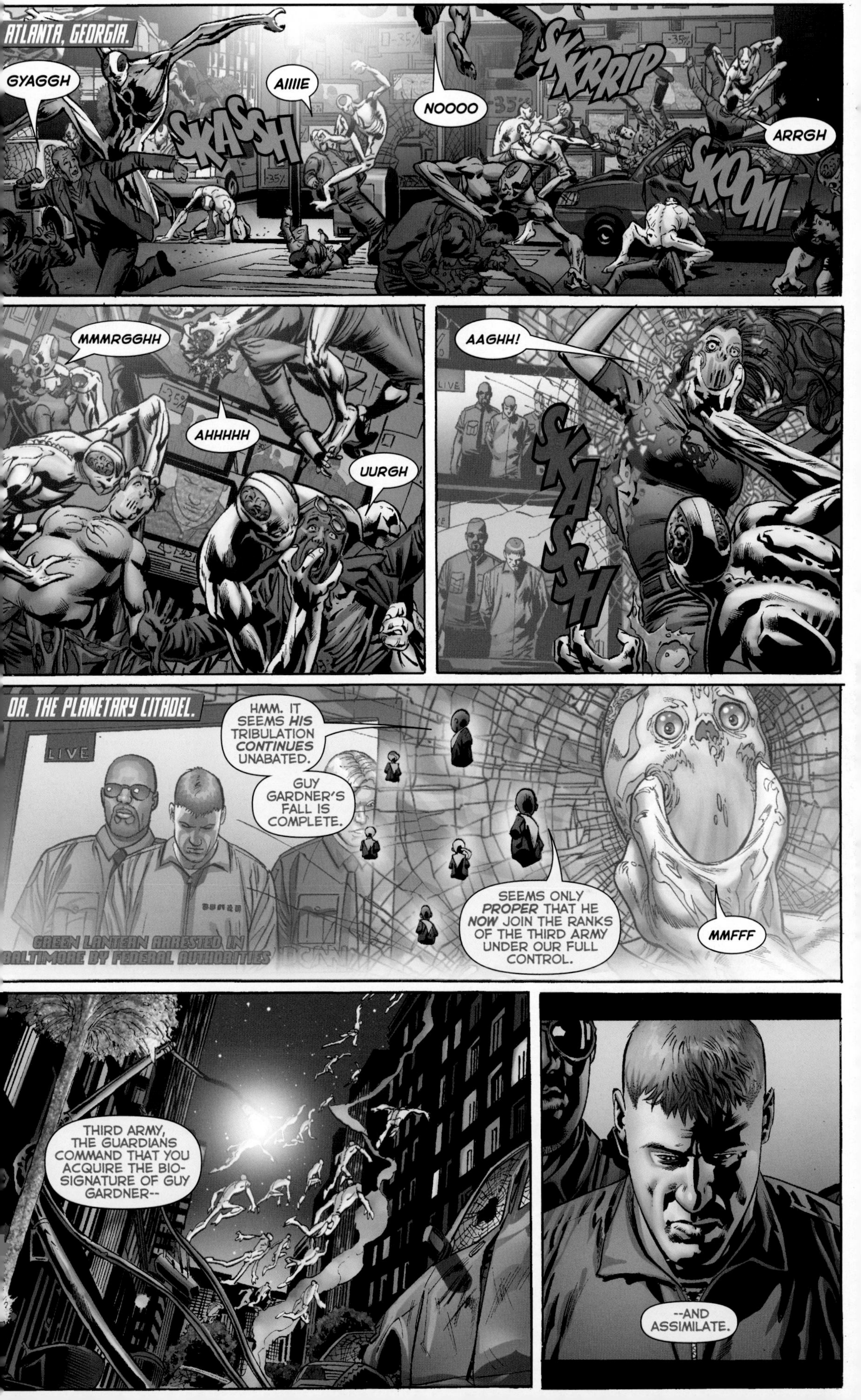
ATLANTA, GEORGIA.
GYAGGH
SKASSH
AIIIIE
NOOOO
SKKRRIP
ARRGH
SKOOM
MMMRGGHH
AHHHHH
UURGH
AAGHH!
SKASSH
OA. THE PLANETARY CITADEL.
HMM. IT SEEMS HIS TRIBULATION CONTINUES UNABATED.
GUY GARDNER'S FALL IS COMPLETE.
SEEMS ONLY PROPER THAT HE NOW JOIN THE RANKS OF THE THIRD ARMY UNDER OUR FULL CONTROL.
MMFFF
LIVE
GREEN LANTERN ARRESTED IN BALTIMORE BY FEDERAL AUTHORITIES
THIRD ARMY, THE GUARDIANS COMMAND THAT YOU ACQUIRE THE BIO-SIGNATURE OF GUY GARDNER--
--AND ASSIMILATE.

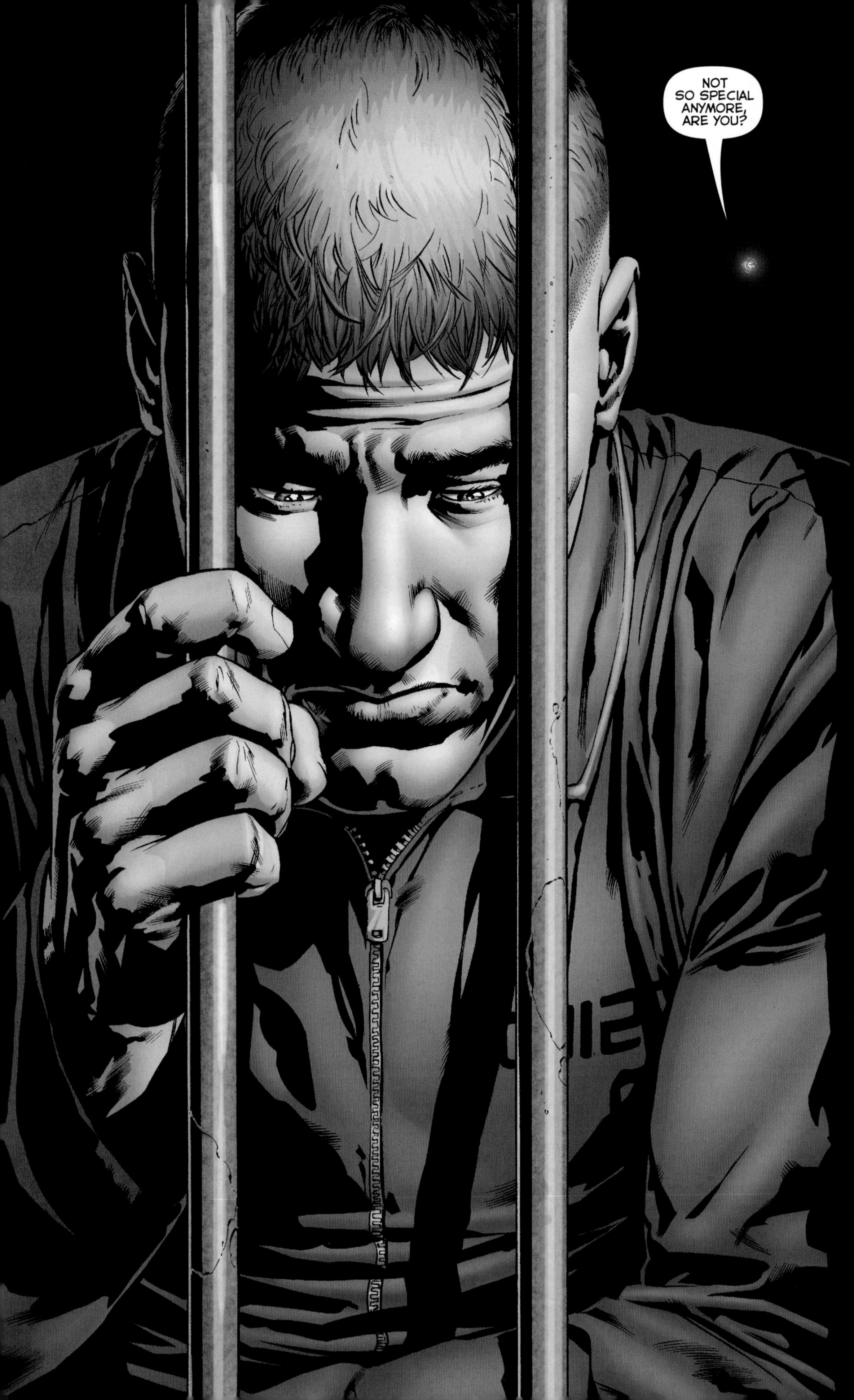
NOT SO SPECIAL ANYMORE, ARE YOU?

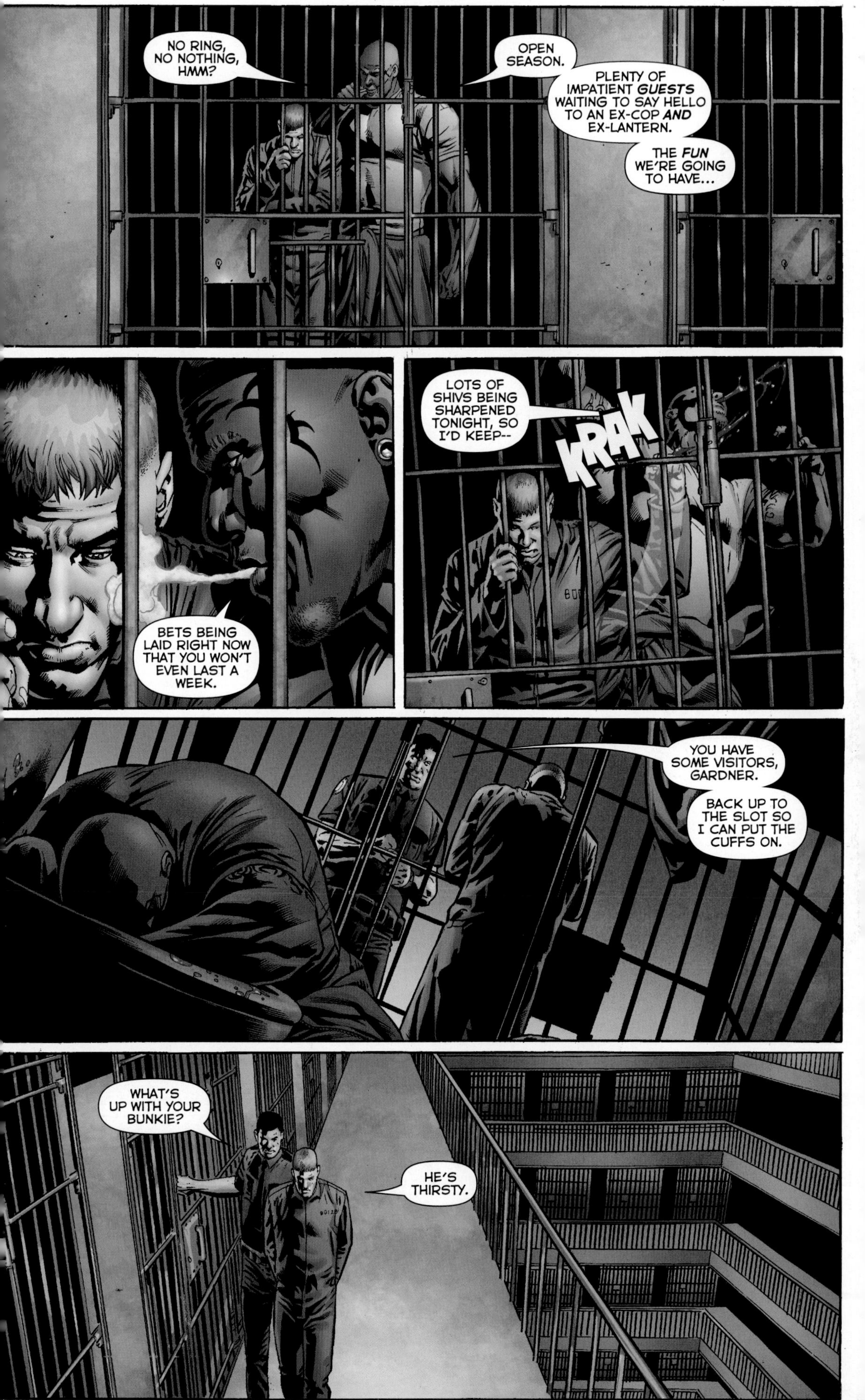
NO RING, NO NOTHING, HMM?
OPEN SEASON.
PLENTY OF IMPATIENT GUESTS WAITING TO SAY HELLO TO AN EX-COP AND EX-LANTERN.
THE FUN WE'RE GOING TO HAVE...
BETS BEING LAID RIGHT NOW THAT YOU WON'T EVEN LAST A WEEK.
LOTS OF SHIVS BEING SHARPENED TONIGHT, SO I'D KEEP--
KRAK
YOU HAVE SOME VISITORS, GARDNER.
BACK UP TO THE SLOT SO I CAN PUT THE CUFFS ON.
WHAT'S UP WITH YOUR BUNKIE?
HE'S THIRSTY.

PULLED SOME SPECIAL FAVORS TO COME TUCK ME IN AFTER REGULAR ZOO HOURS, HUH?

WE'RE HERE TO HELP, GUY.

TO TRY AND FIGURE OUT A WAY--

--TO RESCUE POOR OL' ME FROM MYSELF AGAIN, GLORIA.

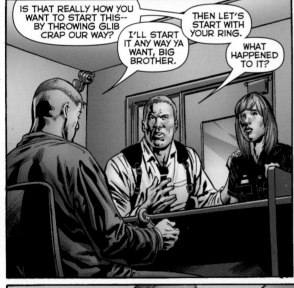

IS THAT REALLY HOW YOU WANT TO START THIS-- BY THROWING GLIB CRAP OUR WAY?

I'LL START IT ANY WAY YA WANT, BIG BROTHER.

THEN LET'S START WITH YOUR RING.

WHAT HAPPENED TO IT?

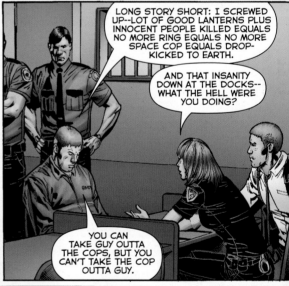

LONG STORY SHORT: I SCREWED UP--LOT OF GOOD LANTERNS PLUS INNOCENT PEOPLE KILLED EQUALS NO MORE RING EQUALS NO MORE SPACE COP EQUALS DROP-KICKED TO EARTH.

AND THAT INSANITY DOWN AT THE DOCKS-- WHAT THE HELL WERE YOU DOING?

YOU CAN TAKE GUY OUTTA THE COPS, BUT YOU CAN'T TAKE THE COP OUTTA GUY.

YOU'RE HOLDING BACK, AS USUAL. WHY ARE YOU BOXING YOURSELF INTO A CORNER?

BEING THE *GREAT DETECTIVE* YOU ARE, I'M SURE YOU'LL FIGURE IT OUT, GERARD.

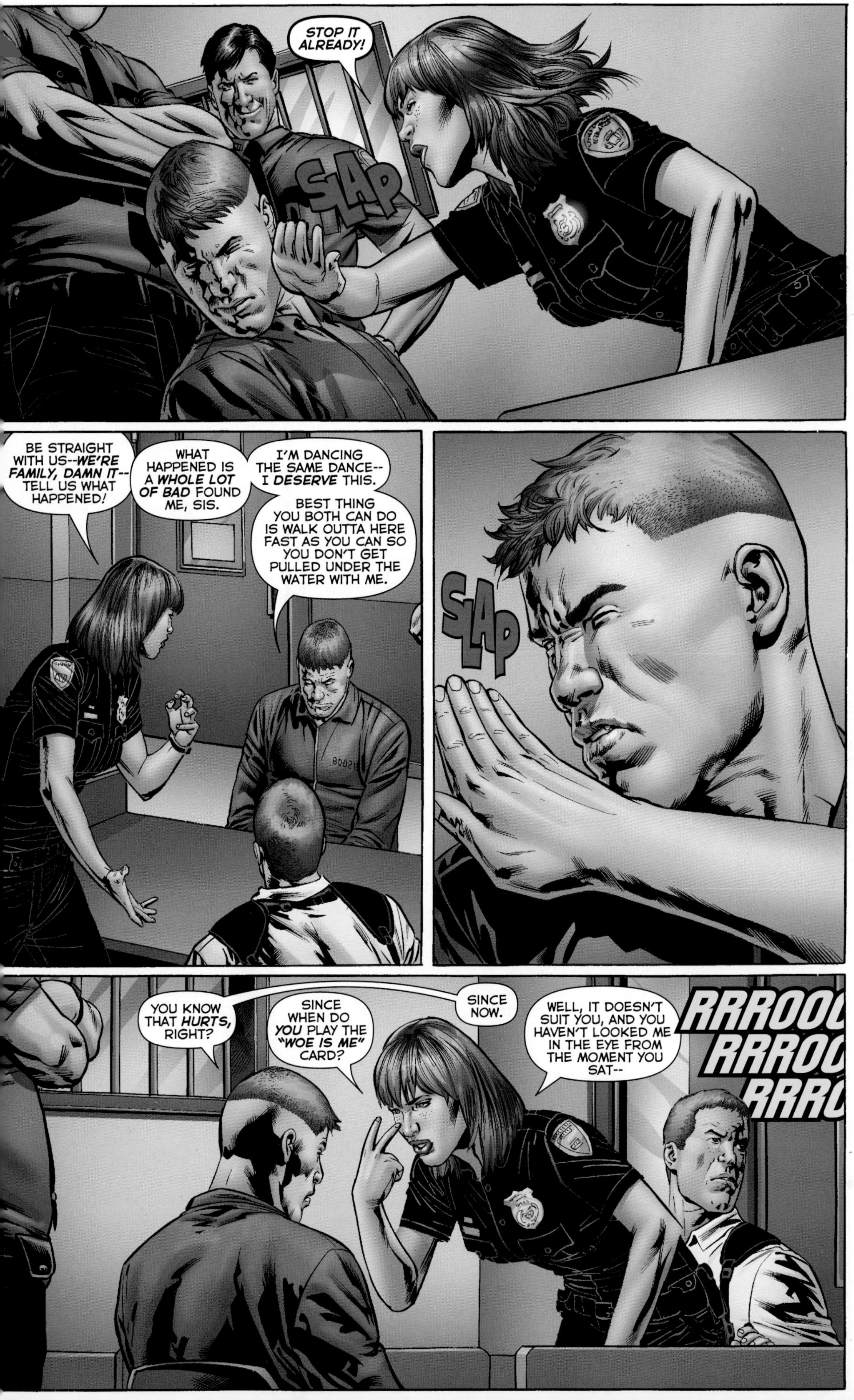
STOP IT ALREADY!
SLAP
BE STRAIGHT WITH US--WE'RE FAMILY, DAMN IT--TELL US WHAT HAPPENED!
WHAT HAPPENED IS A WHOLE LOT OF BAD FOUND ME, SIS.
I'M DANCING THE SAME DANCE--I DESERVE THIS.
BEST THING YOU BOTH CAN DO IS WALK OUTTA HERE FAST AS YOU CAN SO YOU DON'T GET PULLED UNDER THE WATER WITH ME.
SLAP
YOU KNOW THAT HURTS, RIGHT?
SINCE WHEN DO YOU PLAY THE "WOE IS ME" CARD?
SINCE NOW.
WELL, IT DOESN'T SUIT YOU, AND YOU HAVEN'T LOOKED ME IN THE EYE FROM THE MOMENT YOU SAT--
RRROOO
RRROO
RRRO

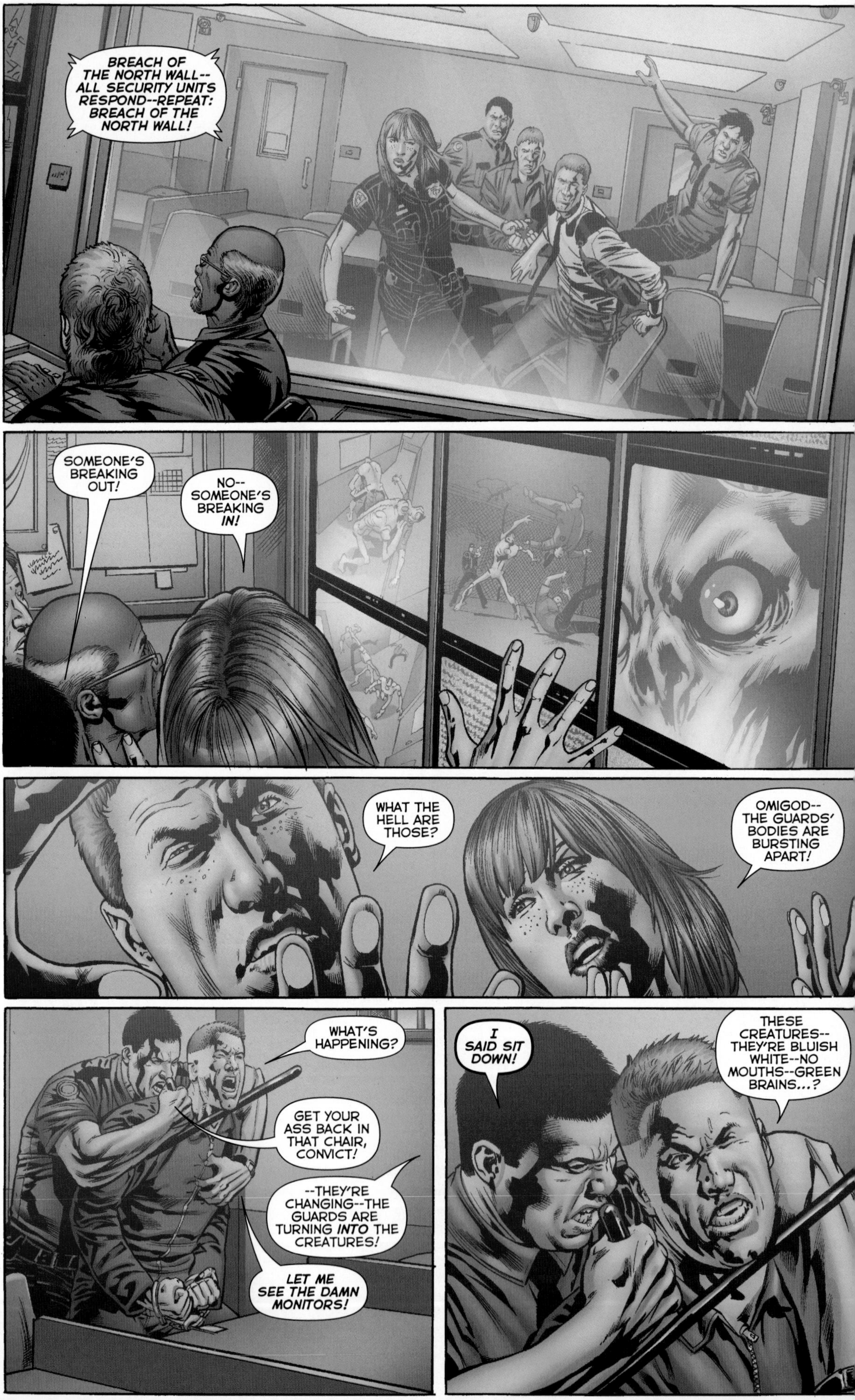
BREACH OF THE NORTH WALL-- ALL SECURITY UNITS RESPOND--REPEAT: BREACH OF THE NORTH WALL!
SOMEONE'S BREAKING OUT!
NO-- SOMEONE'S BREAKING IN!
WHAT THE HELL ARE THOSE?
OMIGOD-- THE GUARDS' BODIES ARE BURSTING APART!
WHAT'S HAPPENING?
GET YOUR ASS BACK IN THAT CHAIR, CONVICT!
--THEY'RE CHANGING--THE GUARDS ARE TURNING INTO THE CREATURES!
LET ME SEE THE DAMN MONITORS!
I SAID SIT DOWN!
THESE CREATURES-- THEY'RE BLUISH WHITE--NO MOUTHS--GREEN BRAINS...?

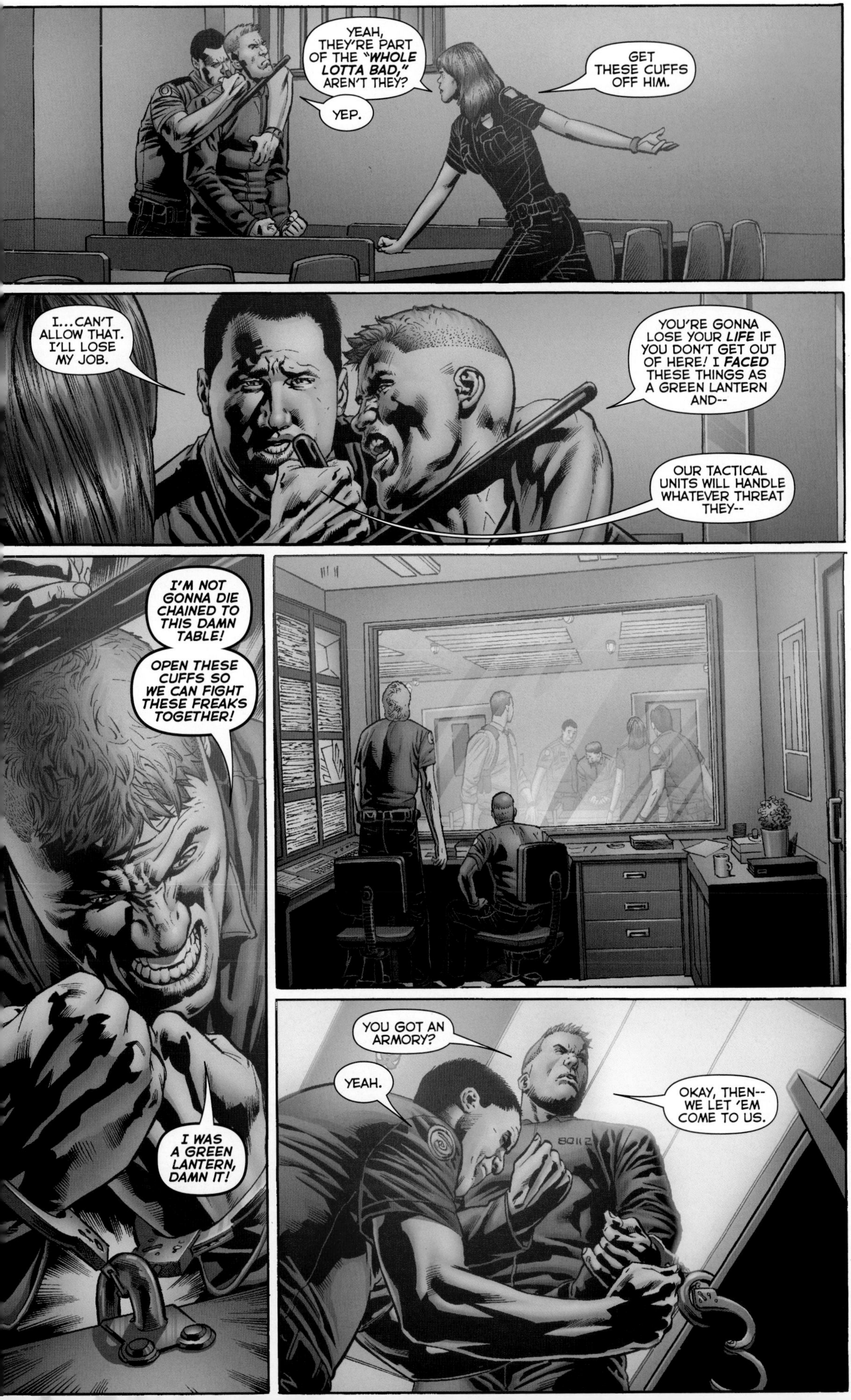
YEAH, THEY'RE PART OF THE "WHOLE LOTTA BAD," AREN'T THEY?
YEP.
GET THESE CUFFS OFF HIM.
I...CAN'T ALLOW THAT. I'LL LOSE MY JOB.
YOU'RE GONNA LOSE YOUR LIFE IF YOU DON'T GET OUT OF HERE! I FACED THESE THINGS AS A GREEN LANTERN AND--
OUR TACTICAL UNITS WILL HANDLE WHATEVER THREAT THEY--
I'M NOT GONNA DIE CHAINED TO THIS DAMN TABLE!
OPEN THESE CUFFS SO WE CAN FIGHT THESE FREAKS TOGETHER!
I WAS A GREEN LANTERN, DAMN IT!
YOU GOT AN ARMORY?
YEAH.
OKAY, THEN-- WE LET 'EM COME TO US.

THIS IS OUR END POINT, JOHN.

I CAN FEEL THE PIECES SCREAMING TO BE REUNITED WITH MOGO'S CORE.

SHIP TO PLANET TRANSMISSION INTERCEPTED.

LET'S HEAR IT.

--STOP STALLING--THE DEADLINE HAS PASSED--

--CONSIDER YOURSELVES FORTUNATE WE'RE ONLY TARGETING A BODY OF WATER AT THIS MOMENT--

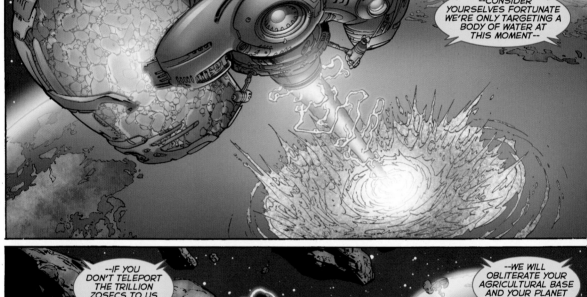

--IF YOU DON'T TELEPORT THE TRILLION ZOSECS TO US IMMEDIATELY--

--WE WILL OBLITERATE YOUR AGRICULTURAL BASE AND YOUR PLANET WILL STARVE!

YOU HAVE FOUR MINUTES LEFT.

TERRORISTS.

RING, ARE FRAGMENTS OF MOGO INSIDE THAT SHIP?

AFFIRMATIVE.

LANTERN MOGO'S TERRA FIRMA IS BEING UTILIZED TO GENERATE THE DESTRUCTIVE ENERGY BEAM FROM THE UNKNOWN SHIP.

OKAY, I'VE HEARD ENOUGH--

--LET'S GO TO WORK, YRRA!
ZZZRAAAAAAKKKKK
UGNN
THIS IS GREEN LANTERN STEWART. CEASE AND DESIST ALL HOSTILITIES OR FACE THE CONSEQUENCES!
THE ONLY THING *CEASING*-- NOT COUNTING THE FOOLS ON THE PLANET BELOW--WILL BE *YOU* IF YOU DON'T GET OUT OF OUR WAY, LANTERN!
WRONG ANSWER!
FOR LOVE!

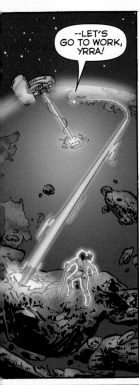

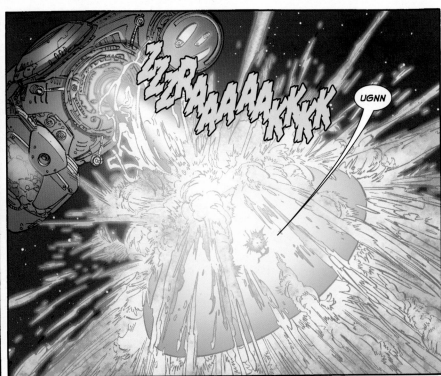

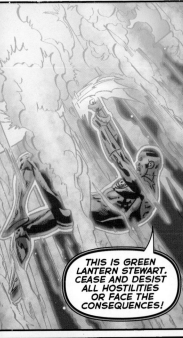

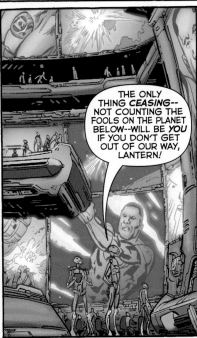

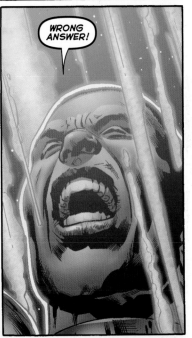

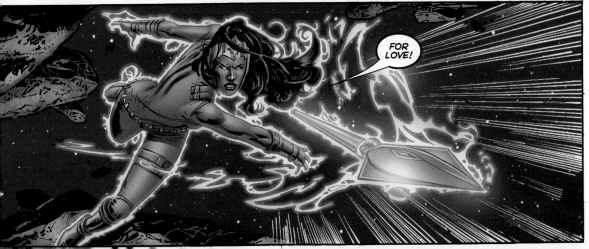

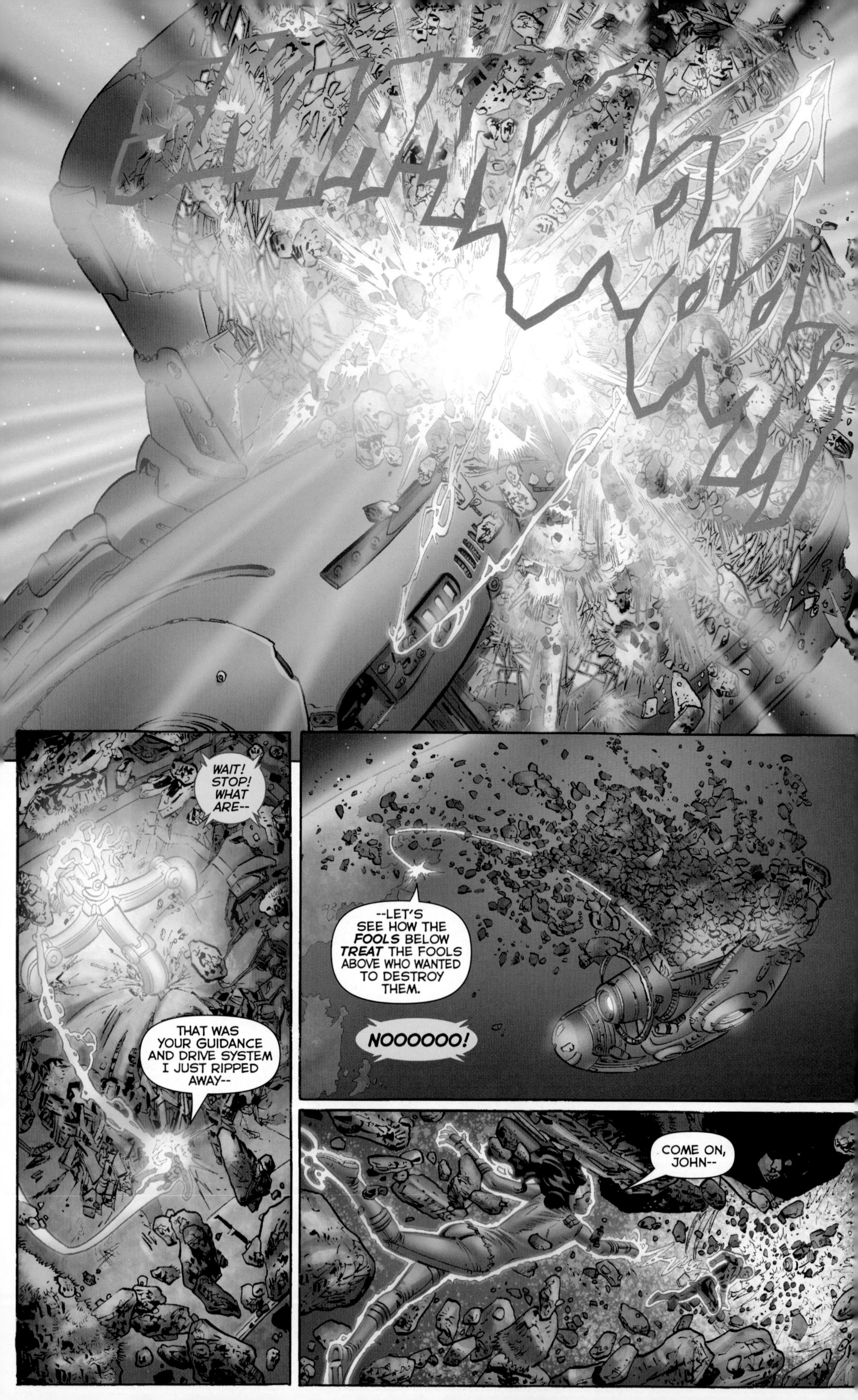
WAIT! STOP! WHAT ARE--
THAT WAS YOUR GUIDANCE AND DRIVE SYSTEM I JUST RIPPED AWAY--
--LET'S SEE HOW THE *FOOLS* BELOW *TREAT* THE FOOLS ABOVE WHO WANTED TO DESTROY THEM.
NOOOOOO!
COME ON, JOHN--

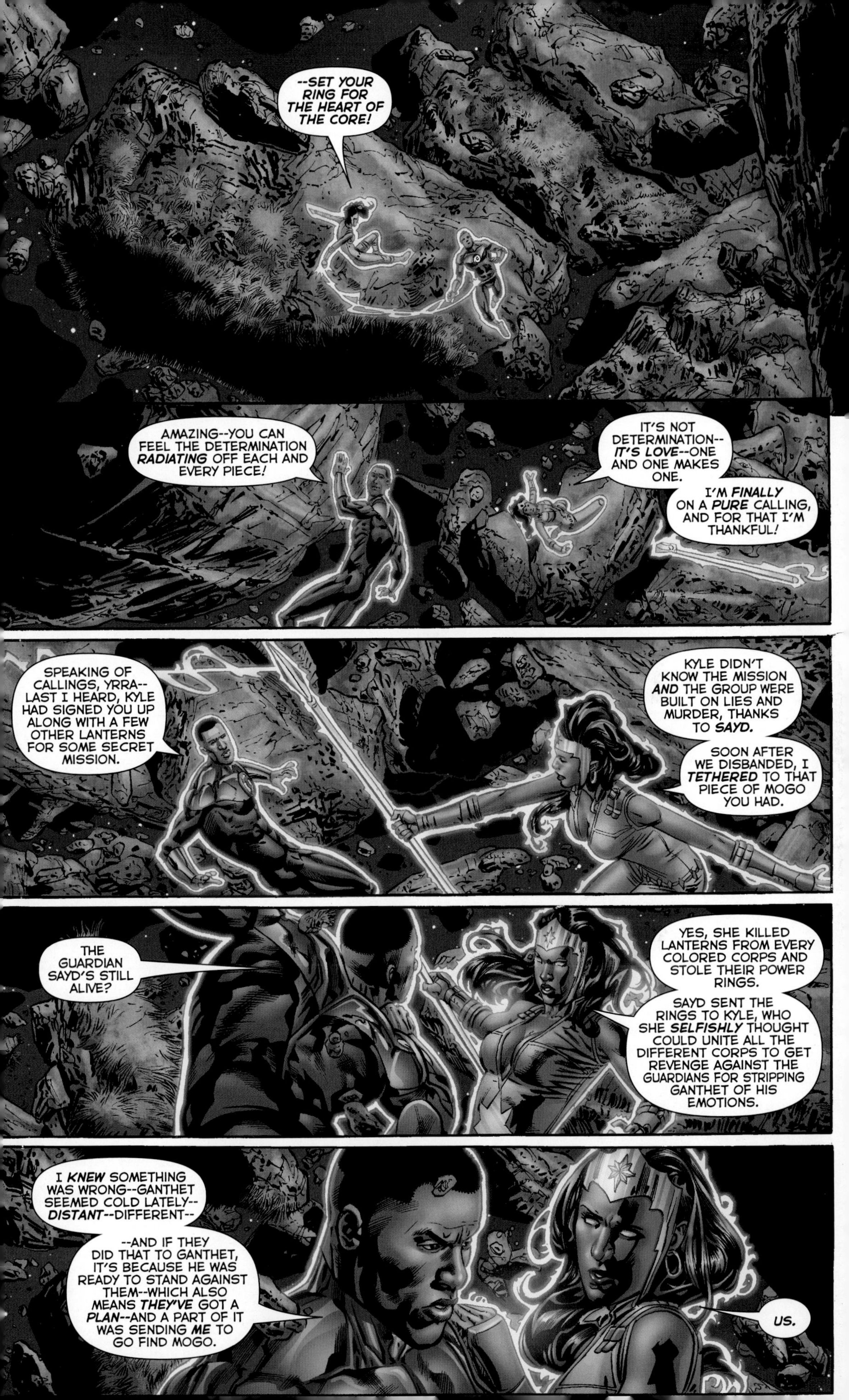
--SET YOUR RING FOR THE HEART OF THE CORE!
AMAZING--YOU CAN FEEL THE DETERMINATION RADIATING OFF EACH AND EVERY PIECE!
IT'S NOT DETERMINATION-- IT'S LOVE--ONE AND ONE MAKES ONE.
I'M FINALLY ON A PURE CALLING, AND FOR THAT I'M THANKFUL!
SPEAKING OF CALLINGS, YRRA-- LAST I HEARD, KYLE HAD SIGNED YOU UP ALONG WITH A FEW OTHER LANTERNS FOR SOME SECRET MISSION.
KYLE DIDN'T KNOW THE MISSION AND THE GROUP WERE BUILT ON LIES AND MURDER, THANKS TO SAYD.
SOON AFTER WE DISBANDED, I TETHERED TO THAT PIECE OF MOGO YOU HAD.
THE GUARDIAN SAYD'S STILL ALIVE?
YES, SHE KILLED LANTERNS FROM EVERY COLORED CORPS AND STOLE THEIR POWER RINGS.
SAYD SENT THE RINGS TO KYLE, WHO SHE SELFISHLY THOUGHT COULD UNITE ALL THE DIFFERENT CORPS TO GET REVENGE AGAINST THE GUARDIANS FOR STRIPPING GANTHET OF HIS EMOTIONS.
I KNEW SOMETHING WAS WRONG--GANTHET SEEMED COLD LATELY-- DISTANT--DIFFERENT--
--AND IF THEY DID THAT TO GANTHET, IT'S BECAUSE HE WAS READY TO STAND AGAINST THEM--WHICH ALSO MEANS THEY'VE GOT A PLAN--AND A PART OF IT WAS SENDING ME TO GO FIND MOGO.
US.

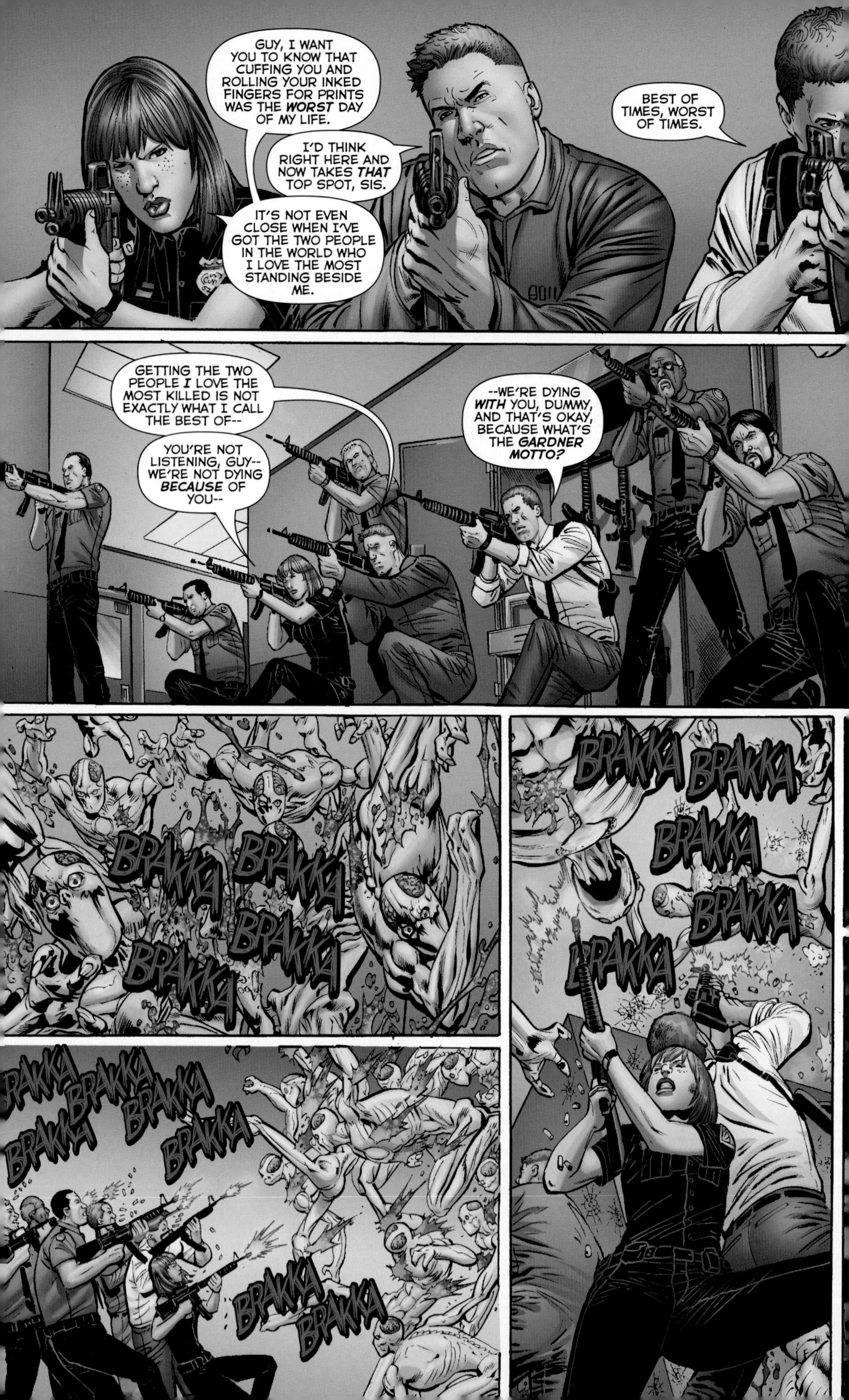
GUY, I WANT YOU TO KNOW THAT CUFFING YOU AND ROLLING YOUR INKED FINGERS FOR PRINTS WAS THE *WORST* DAY OF MY LIFE.
I'D THINK RIGHT HERE AND NOW TAKES *THAT* TOP SPOT, SIS.
IT'S NOT EVEN CLOSE WHEN I'VE GOT THE TWO PEOPLE IN THE WORLD WHO I LOVE THE MOST STANDING BESIDE ME.
BEST OF TIMES, WORST OF TIMES.
GETTING THE TWO PEOPLE *I* LOVE THE MOST KILLED IS NOT EXACTLY WHAT I CALL THE BEST OF--
YOU'RE NOT LISTENING, GUY-- WE'RE NOT DYING *BECAUSE* OF YOU--
--WE'RE DYING *WITH* YOU, DUMMY, AND THAT'S OKAY, BECAUSE WHAT'S THE *GARDNER MOTTO?*
BRAKKA BRAKKA
BRAKKA
BRAKKA
BRAKKA BRAKKA
BRAKKA
BRAKKA
BRAKKA
BRAKKA BRAKKA BRAKKA BRAKKA BRAKKA BRAKKA
BRAKKA BRAKKA

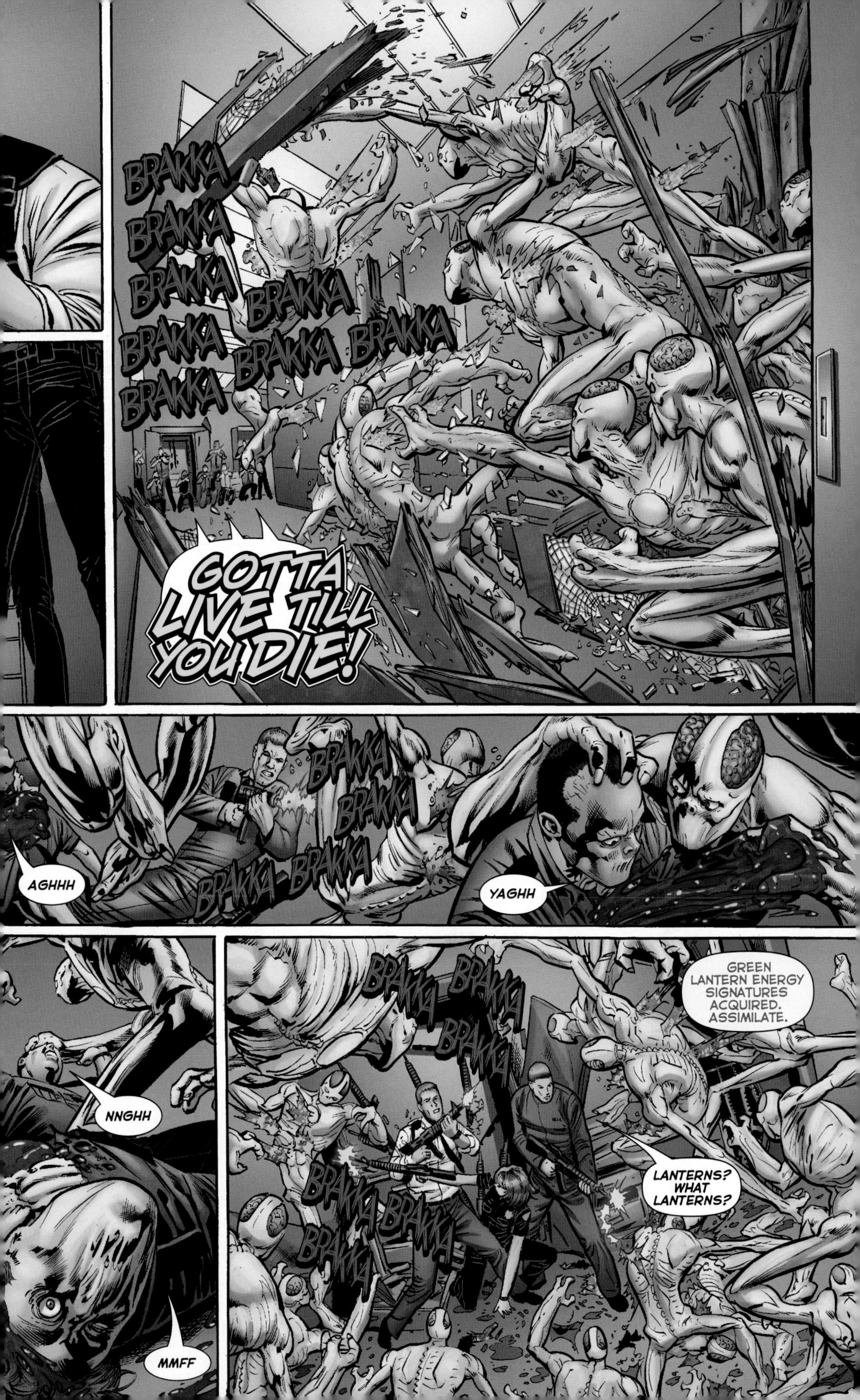
BRAKKA
BRAKKA
BRAKKA
BRAKKA
BRAKKA
BRAKKA
BRAKKA
BRAKKA
GOTTA LIVE TILL YOU DIE!
AGHHH
BRAKKA
BRAKKA
BRAKKA
BRAKKA
YAGHH
NNGHH
MMFF
BRAKKA
BRAKKA
BRAKKA
GREEN LANTERN ENERGY SIGNATURES ACQUIRED. ASSIMILATE.
LANTERNS? WHAT LANTERNS?
BRAKKA
BRAKKA
BRAKKA

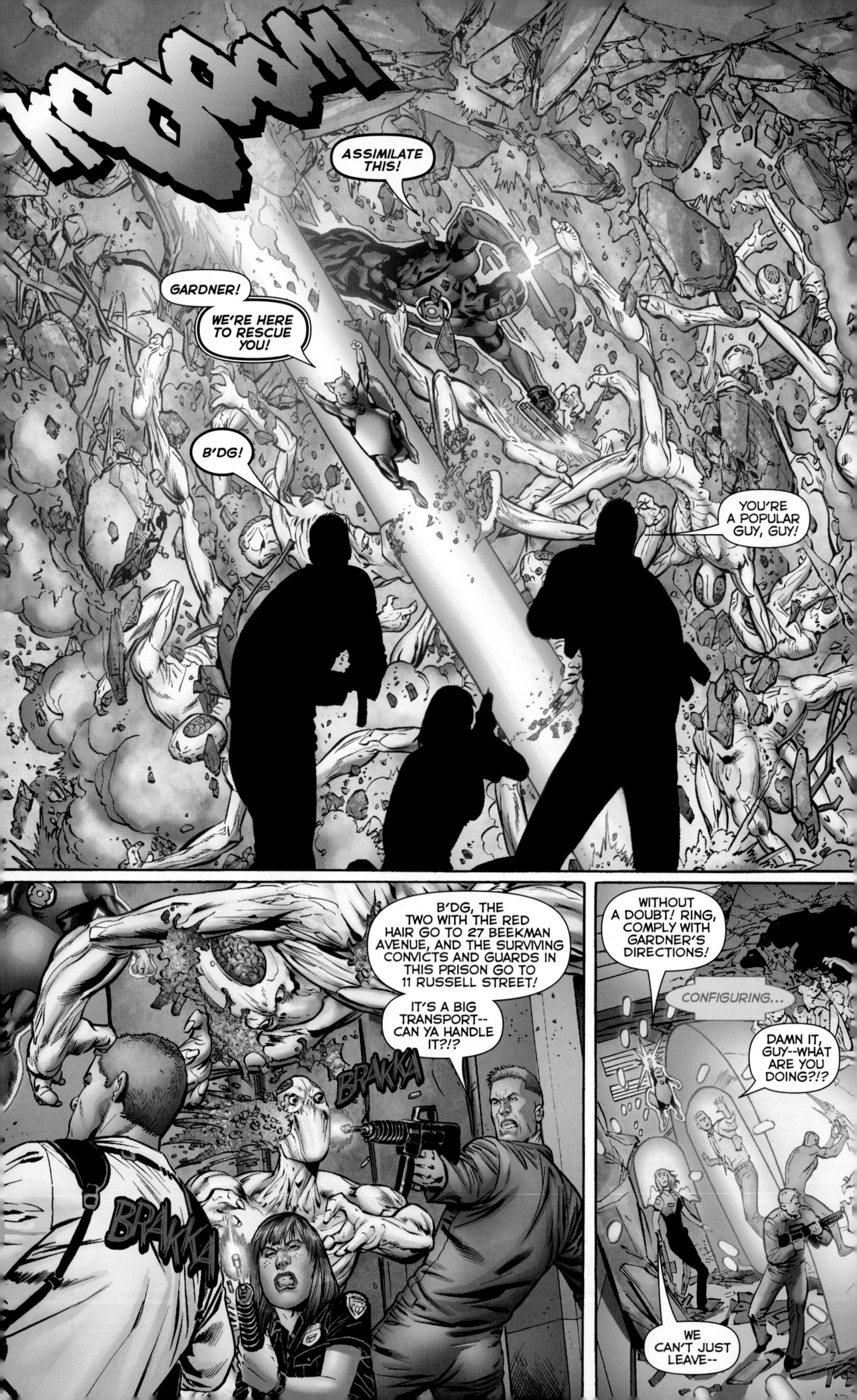
KA-BOOM
ASSIMILATE THIS!
GARDNER!
WE'RE HERE TO RESCUE YOU!
B'DG!
YOU'RE A POPULAR GUY, GUY!
B'DG, THE TWO WITH THE RED HAIR GO TO 27 BEEKMAN AVENUE, AND THE SURVIVING CONVICTS AND GUARDS IN THIS PRISON GO TO 11 RUSSELL STREET!
IT'S A BIG TRANSPORT-- CAN YA HANDLE IT?!?
BRAKKA
BRAKKA
WITHOUT A DOUBT! RING, COMPLY WITH GARDNER'S DIRECTIONS!
CONFIGURING...
DAMN IT, GUY--WHAT ARE YOU DOING?!?
WE CAN'T JUST LEAVE--

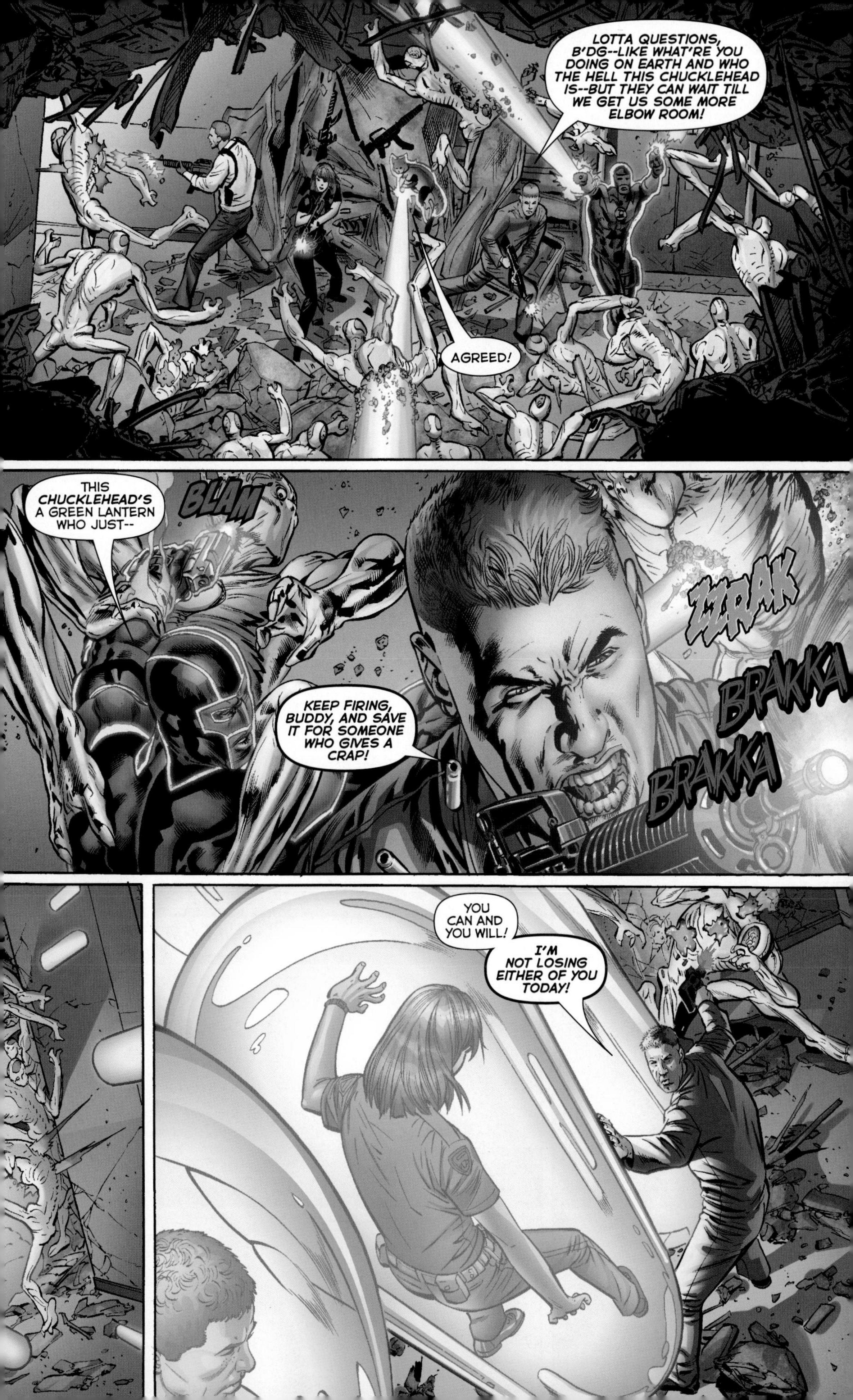
LOTTA QUESTIONS, B'DG--LIKE WHAT'RE YOU DOING ON EARTH AND WHO THE HELL THIS CHUCKLEHEAD IS--BUT THEY CAN WAIT TILL WE GET US SOME MORE ELBOW ROOM!
AGREED!
THIS CHUCKLEHEAD'S A GREEN LANTERN WHO JUST--
BLAM
KEEP FIRING, BUDDY, AND SAVE IT FOR SOMEONE WHO GIVES A CRAP!
ZZRAK
BRAKKA
BRAKKA
YOU CAN AND YOU WILL!
I'M NOT LOSING EITHER OF YOU TODAY!

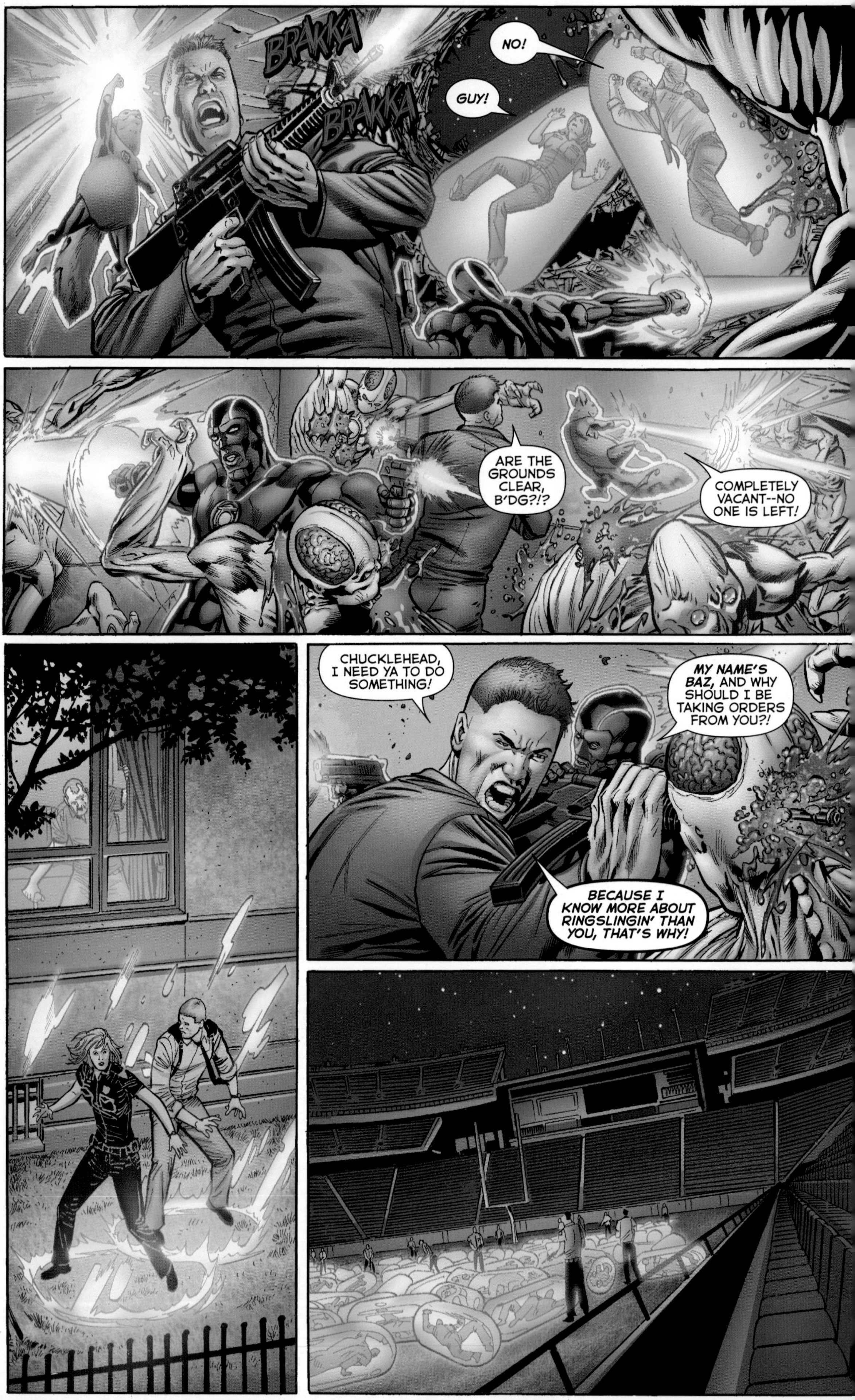
BRAKKA
BRAKKA
NO!
GUY!
ARE THE GROUNDS CLEAR, B'DG?!?
COMPLETELY VACANT--NO ONE IS LEFT!
CHUCKLEHEAD, I NEED YA TO DO SOMETHING!
MY NAME'S BAZ, AND WHY SHOULD I BE TAKING ORDERS FROM YOU?!
BECAUSE I KNOW MORE ABOUT RINGSLINGIN' THAN YOU, THAT'S WHY!

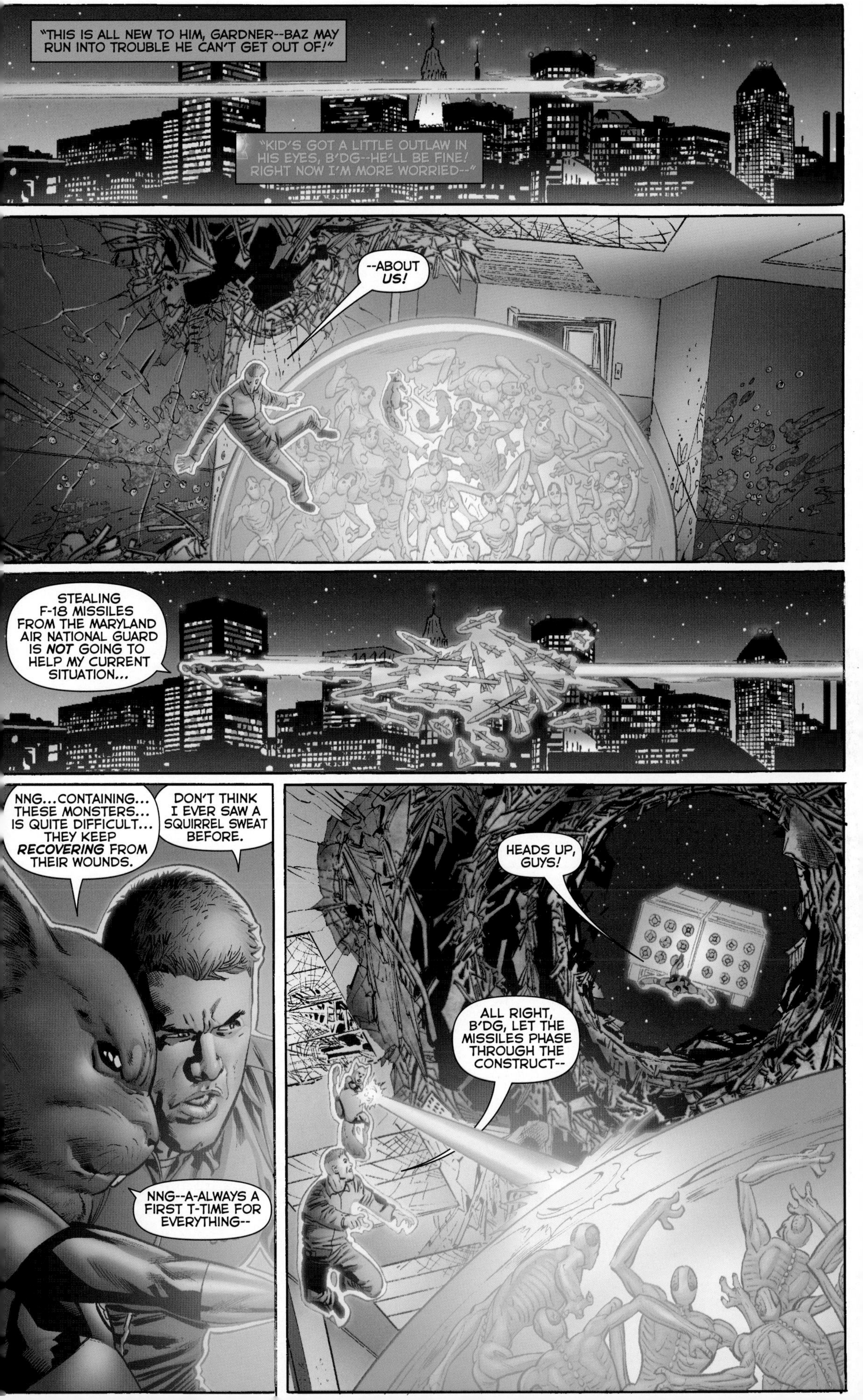
"THIS IS ALL NEW TO HIM, GARDNER--BAZ MAY RUN INTO TROUBLE HE CAN'T GET OUT OF!"
"KID'S GOT A LITTLE OUTLAW IN HIS EYES, B'DG--HE'LL BE FINE! RIGHT NOW I'M MORE WORRIED--"
--ABOUT *US!*
STEALING F-18 MISSILES FROM THE MARYLAND AIR NATIONAL GUARD IS *NOT* GOING TO HELP MY CURRENT SITUATION...
NNG...CONTAINING... THESE MONSTERS... IS QUITE DIFFICULT... THEY KEEP *RECOVERING* FROM THEIR WOUNDS.
DON'T THINK I EVER SAW A SQUIRREL SWEAT BEFORE.
NNG--A-ALWAYS A FIRST T-TIME FOR EVERYTHING--
HEADS UP, GUYS!
ALL RIGHT, B'DG, LET THE MISSILES PHASE THROUGH THE CONSTRUCT--

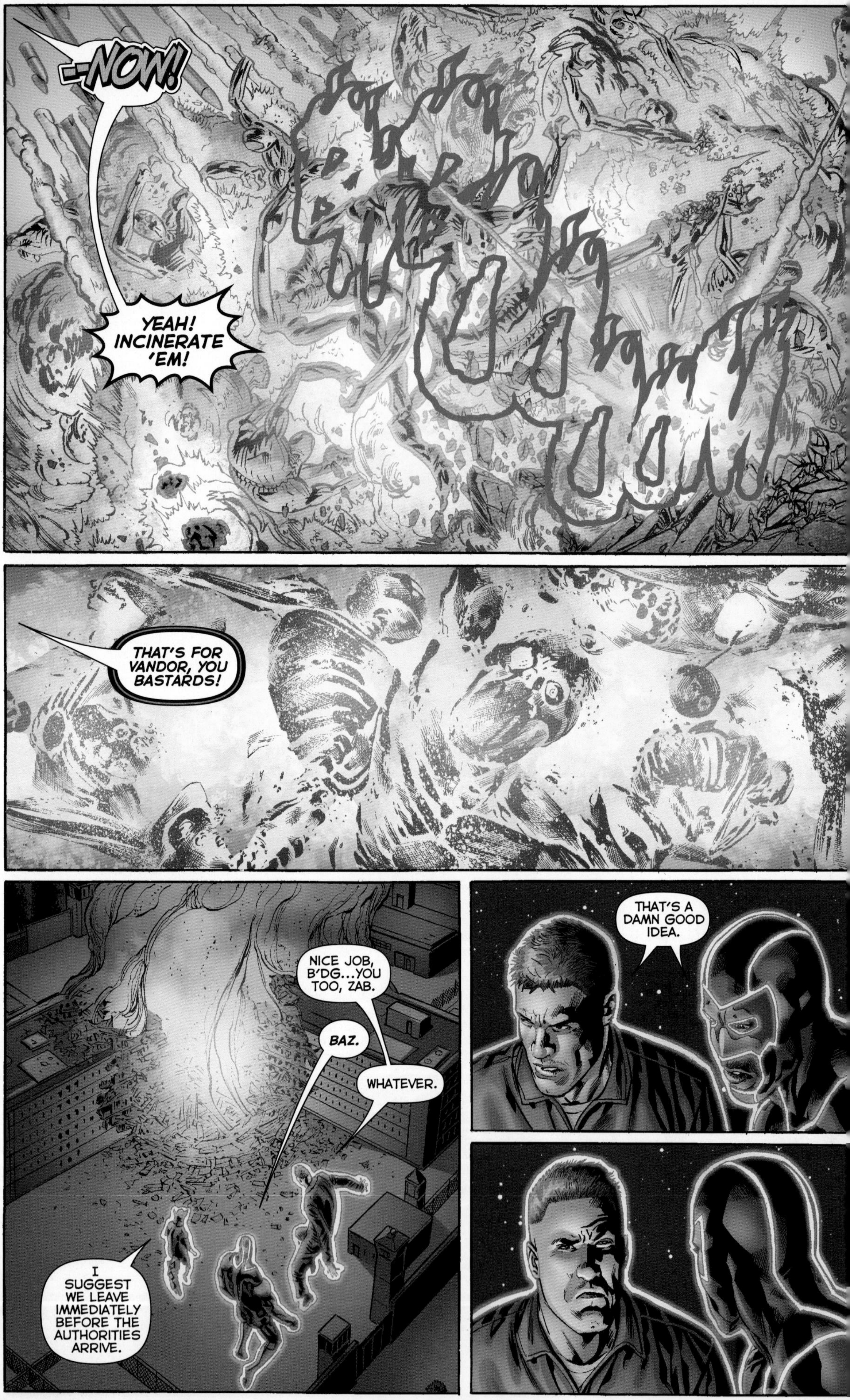
--NOW!
YEAH! INCINERATE 'EM!
THAT'S FOR VANDOR, YOU BASTARDS!
NICE JOB, B'DG...YOU TOO, ZAB.
BAZ.
WHATEVER.
I SUGGEST WE LEAVE IMMEDIATELY BEFORE THE AUTHORITIES ARRIVE.
THAT'S A DAMN GOOD IDEA.

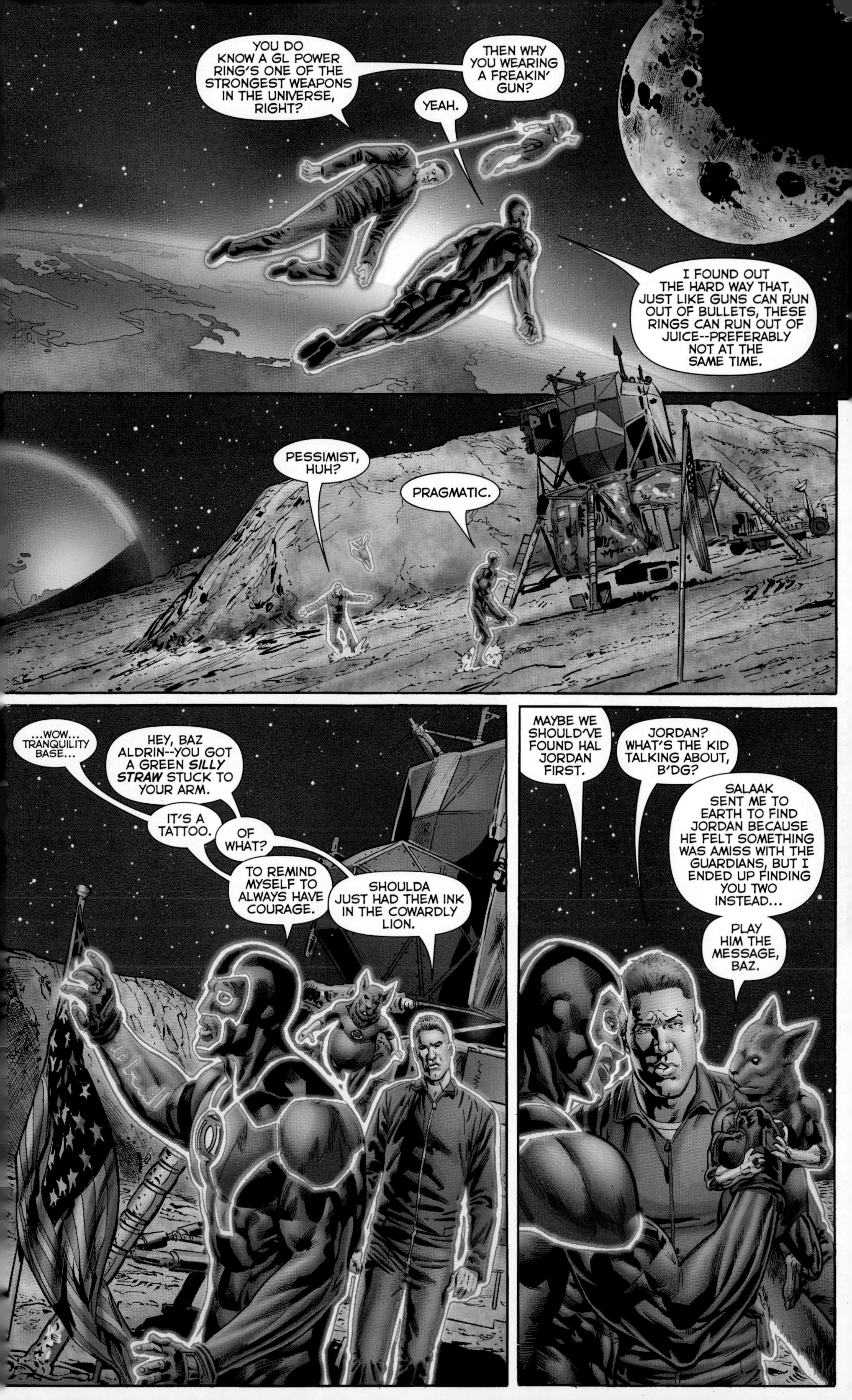
YOU DO KNOW A GL POWER RING'S ONE OF THE STRONGEST WEAPONS IN THE UNIVERSE, RIGHT?
YEAH.
THEN WHY YOU WEARING A FREAKIN' GUN?
I FOUND OUT THE HARD WAY THAT, JUST LIKE GUNS CAN RUN OUT OF BULLETS, THESE RINGS CAN RUN OUT OF JUICE--PREFERABLY NOT AT THE SAME TIME.
PESSIMIST, HUH?
PRAGMATIC.
...WOW... TRANQUILITY BASE...
HEY, BAZ ALDRIN--YOU GOT A GREEN SILLY STRAW STUCK TO YOUR ARM.
IT'S A TATTOO.
OF WHAT?
TO REMIND MYSELF TO ALWAYS HAVE COURAGE.
SHOULDA JUST HAD THEM INK IN THE COWARDLY LION.
MAYBE WE SHOULD'VE FOUND HAL JORDAN FIRST.
JORDAN? WHAT'S THE KID TALKING ABOUT, B'DG?
SALAAK SENT ME TO EARTH TO FIND JORDAN BECAUSE HE FELT SOMETHING WAS AMISS WITH THE GUARDIANS, BUT I ENDED UP FINDING YOU TWO INSTEAD...
PLAY HIM THE MESSAGE, BAZ.

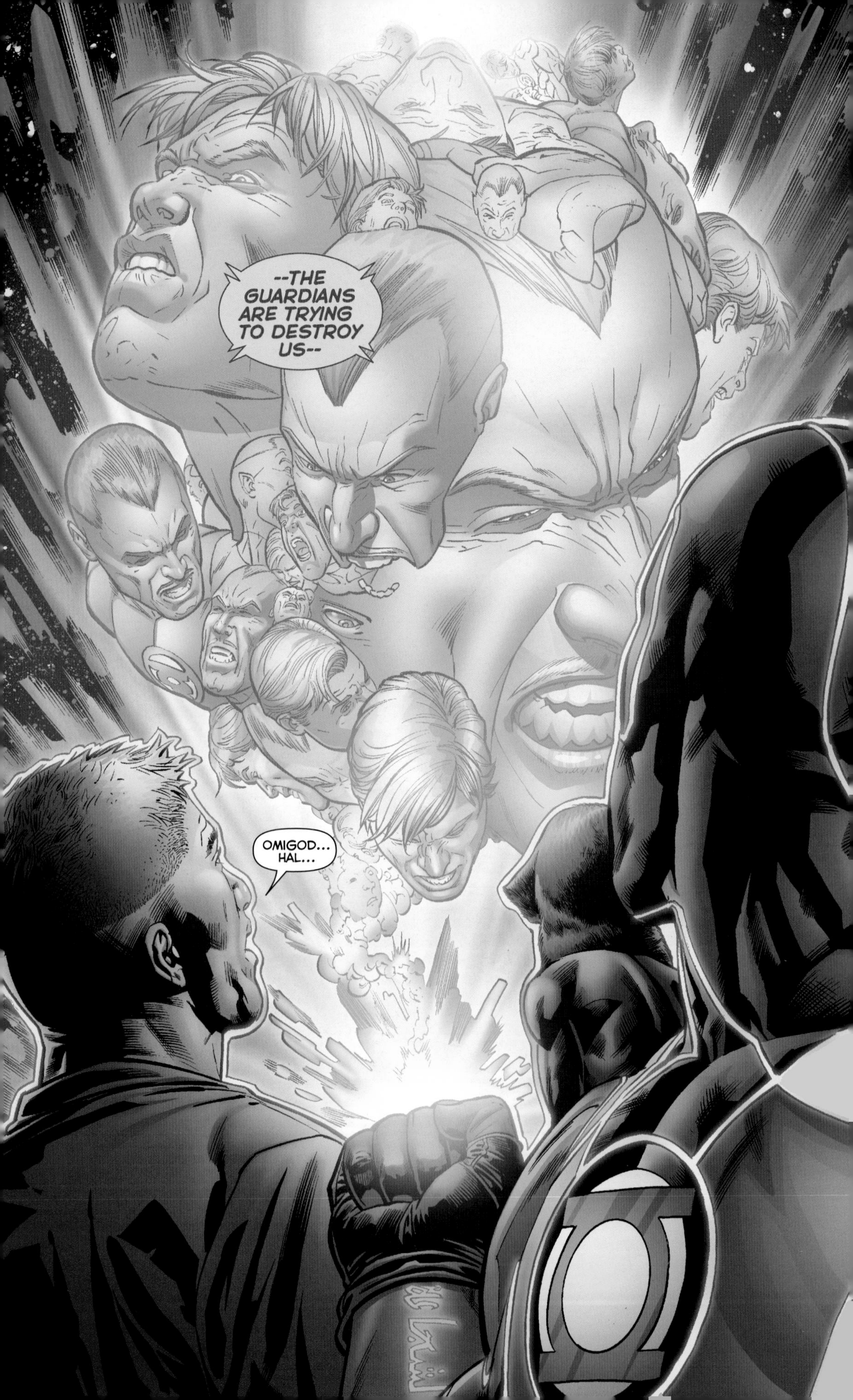
--THE GUARDIANS ARE TRYING TO DESTROY US--
OMIGOD... HAL...

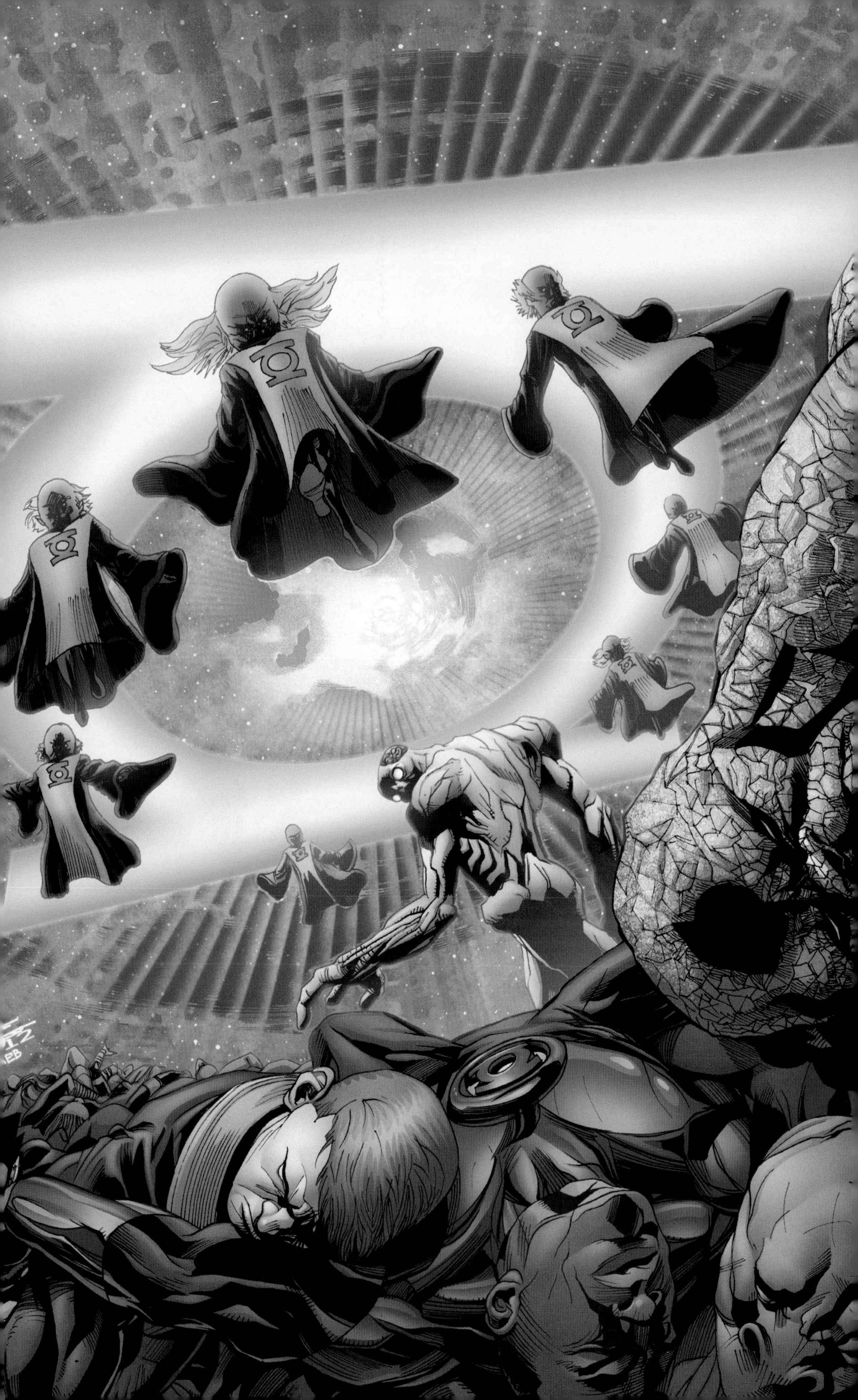

RISE OF THE FIRST LANTERN

PETER J. TOMASI writer **CHRISCROSS** penciller **SCOTT HANNA & MARIO ALQUIZA** inkers cover art by **CHRISCROSS & GAEB ELTAEB**

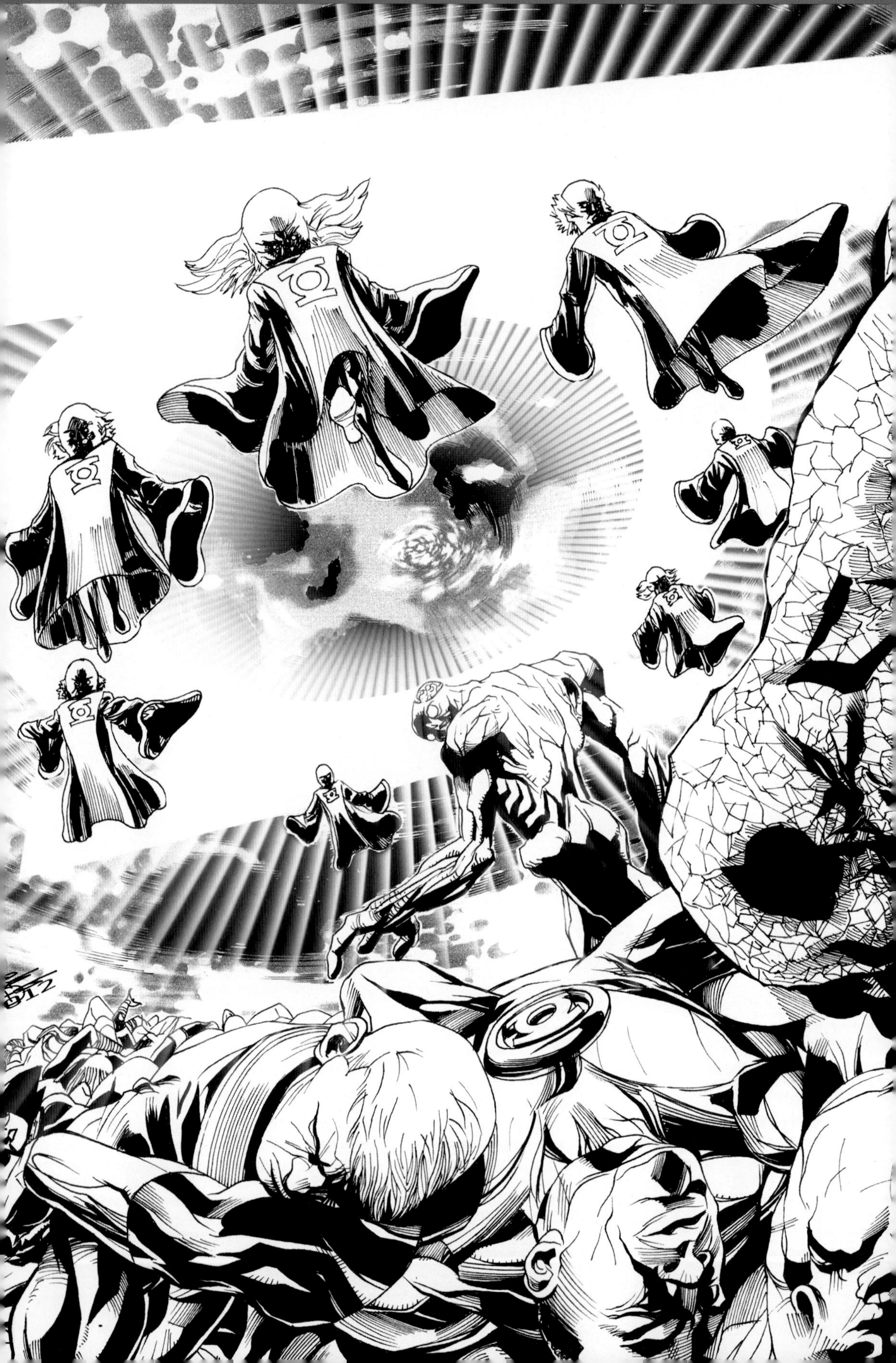

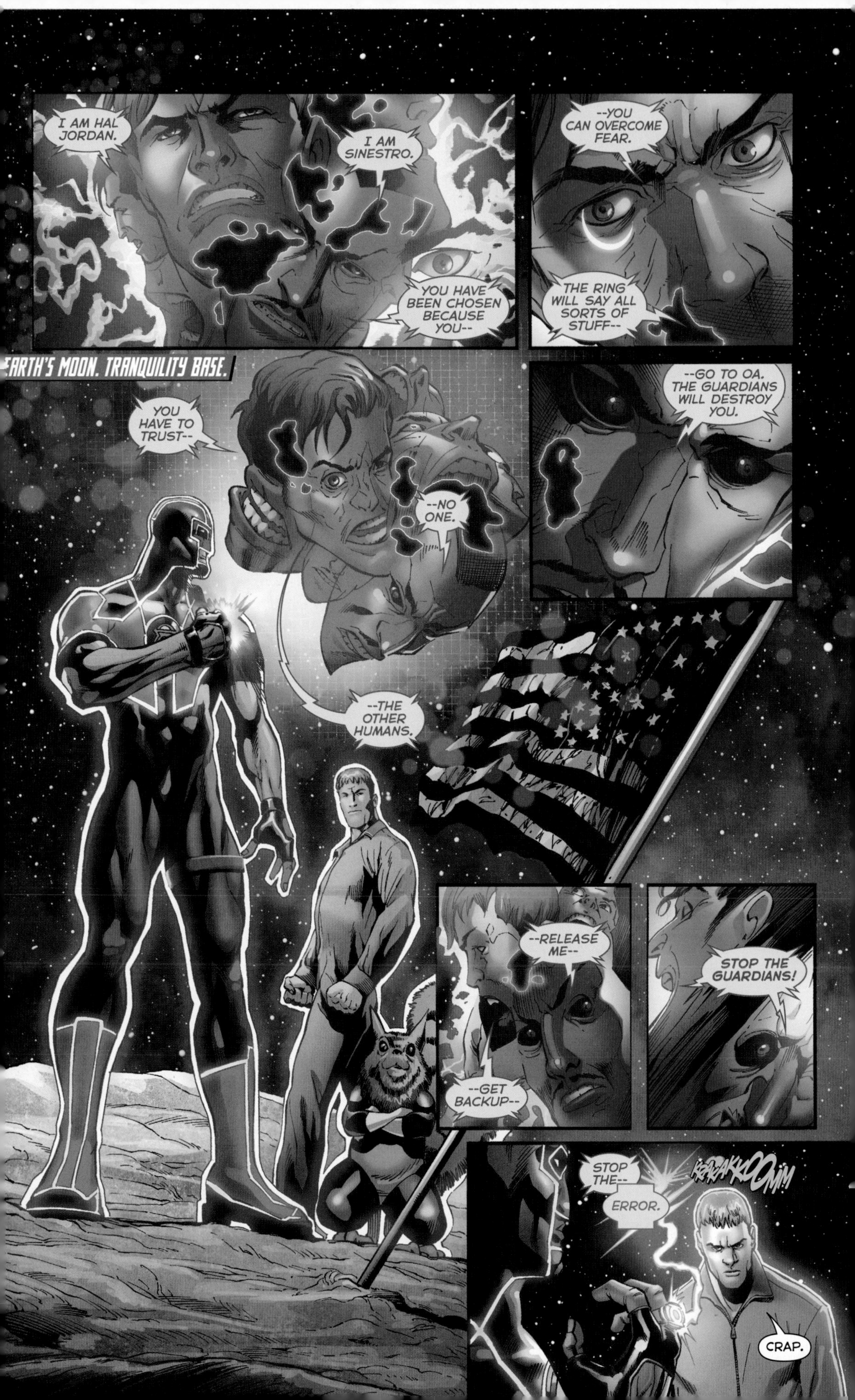
I AM HAL JORDAN.
I AM SINESTRO.
YOU HAVE BEEN CHOSEN BECAUSE YOU--
--YOU CAN OVERCOME FEAR.
THE RING WILL SAY ALL SORTS OF STUFF--
EARTH'S MOON. TRANQUILITY BASE.
YOU HAVE TO TRUST--
--NO ONE.
--THE OTHER HUMANS.
--GO TO OA. THE GUARDIANS WILL DESTROY YOU.
--RELEASE ME--
--GET BACKUP--
STOP THE GUARDIANS!
STOP THE--
ERROR.
KRAKAKKOOMM
CRAP.

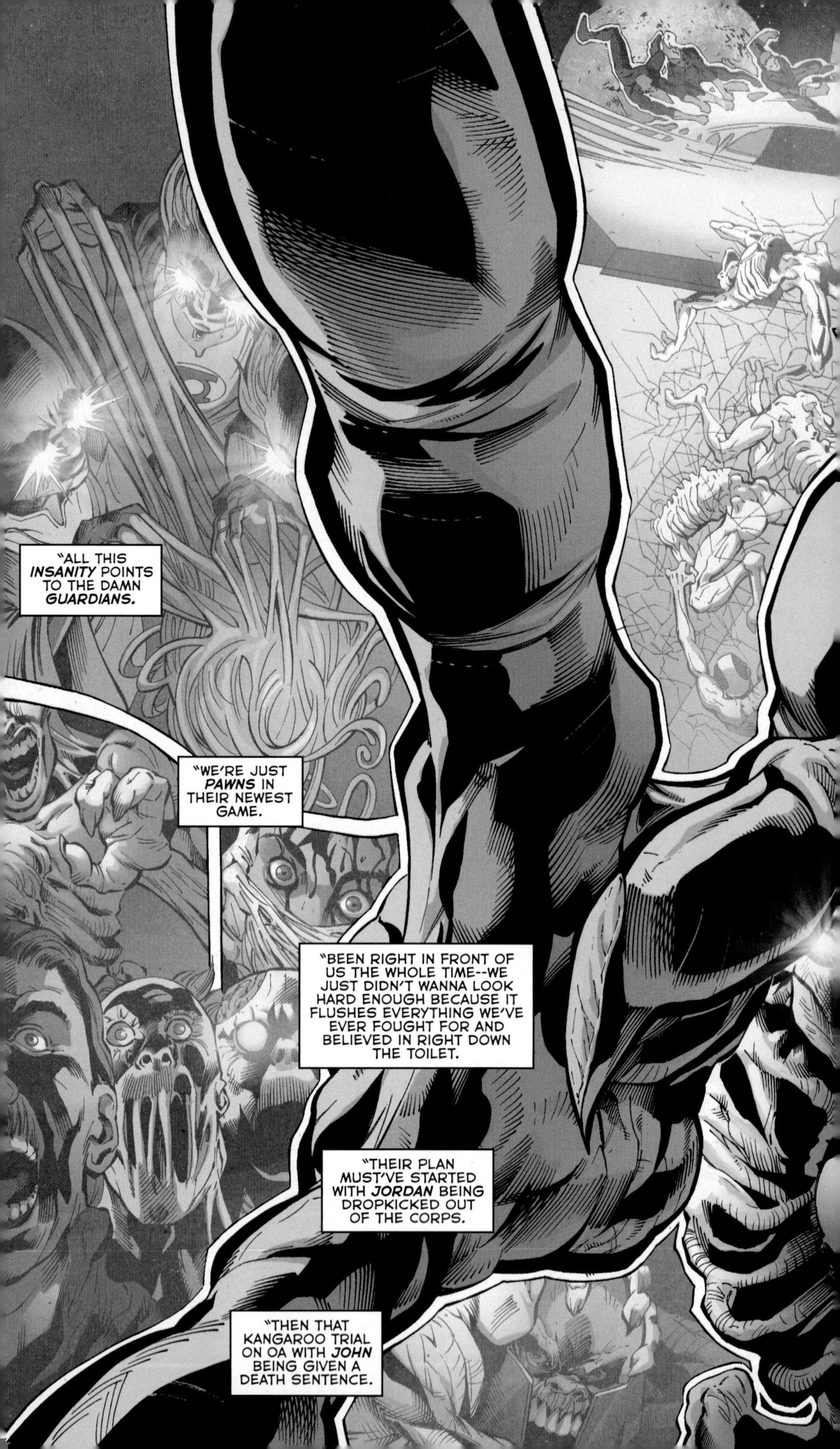
"ALL THIS *INSANITY* POINTS TO THE DAMN *GUARDIANS.*
"WE'RE JUST *PAWNS* IN THEIR NEWEST GAME.
"BEEN RIGHT IN FRONT OF US THE WHOLE TIME--WE JUST DIDN'T WANNA LOOK HARD ENOUGH BECAUSE IT FLUSHES EVERYTHING WE'VE EVER FOUGHT FOR AND BELIEVED IN RIGHT DOWN THE TOILET.
"THEIR PLAN MUST'VE STARTED WITH *JORDAN* BEING DROPKICKED OUT OF THE CORPS.
"THEN THAT KANGAROO TRIAL ON OA WITH *JOHN* BEING GIVEN A DEATH SENTENCE.

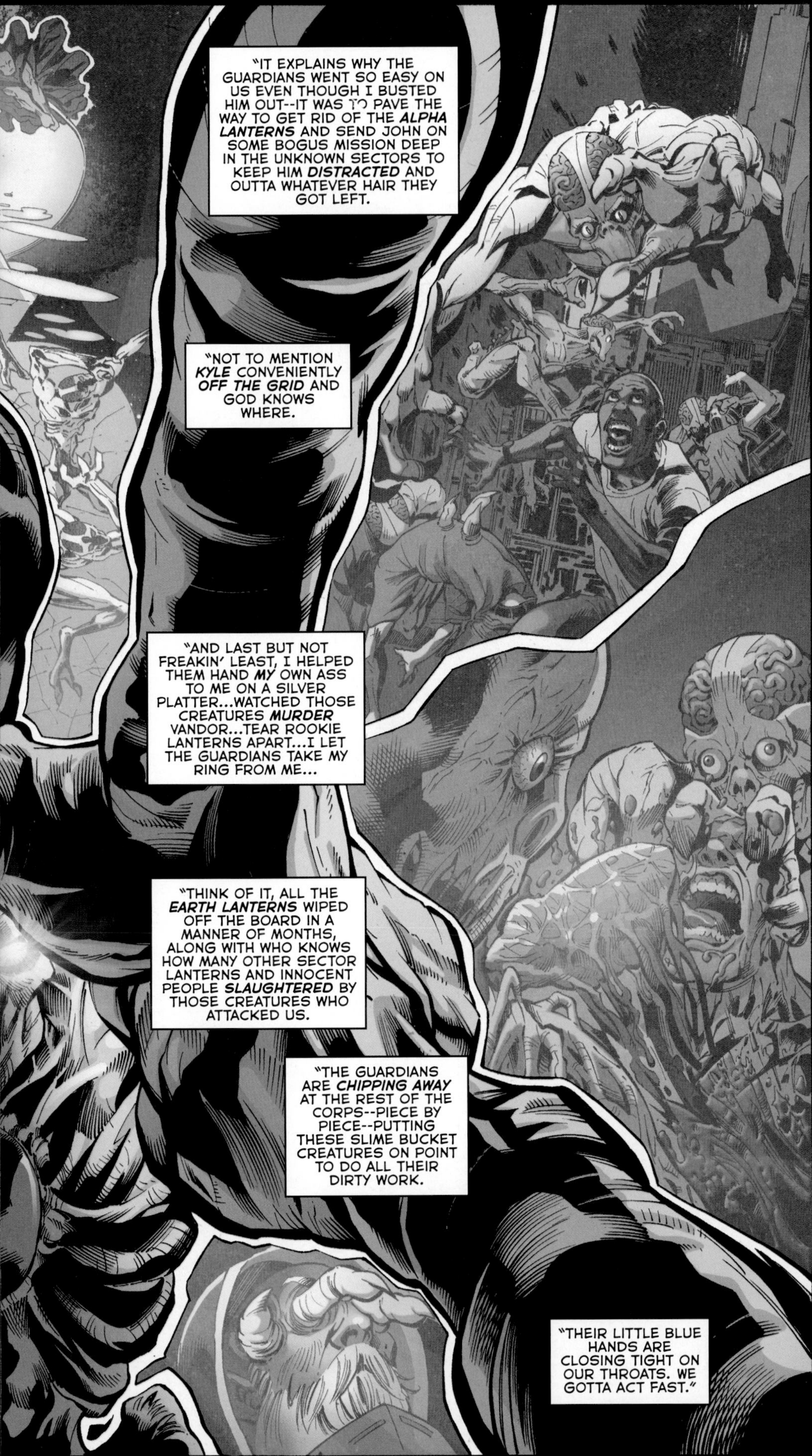
"IT EXPLAINS WHY THE GUARDIANS WENT SO EASY ON US EVEN THOUGH I BUSTED HIM OUT--IT WAS TO PAVE THE WAY TO GET RID OF THE *ALPHA LANTERNS* AND SEND JOHN ON SOME BOGUS MISSION DEEP IN THE UNKNOWN SECTORS TO KEEP HIM *DISTRACTED* AND OUTTA WHATEVER HAIR THEY GOT LEFT.
"NOT TO MENTION *KYLE* CONVENIENTLY *OFF THE GRID* AND GOD KNOWS WHERE.
"AND LAST BUT NOT FREAKIN' LEAST, I HELPED THEM HAND *MY* OWN ASS TO ME ON A SILVER PLATTER...WATCHED THOSE CREATURES *MURDER* VANDOR...TEAR ROOKIE LANTERNS APART...I LET THE GUARDIANS TAKE MY RING FROM ME...
"THINK OF IT, ALL THE *EARTH LANTERNS* WIPED OFF THE BOARD IN A MANNER OF MONTHS, ALONG WITH WHO KNOWS HOW MANY OTHER SECTOR LANTERNS AND INNOCENT PEOPLE *SLAUGHTERED* BY THOSE CREATURES WHO ATTACKED US.
"THE GUARDIANS ARE *CHIPPING AWAY* AT THE REST OF THE CORPS--PIECE BY PIECE--PUTTING THESE SLIME BUCKET CREATURES ON POINT TO DO ALL THEIR DIRTY WORK.
"THEIR LITTLE BLUE HANDS ARE CLOSING TIGHT ON OUR THROATS. WE GOTTA ACT FAST."

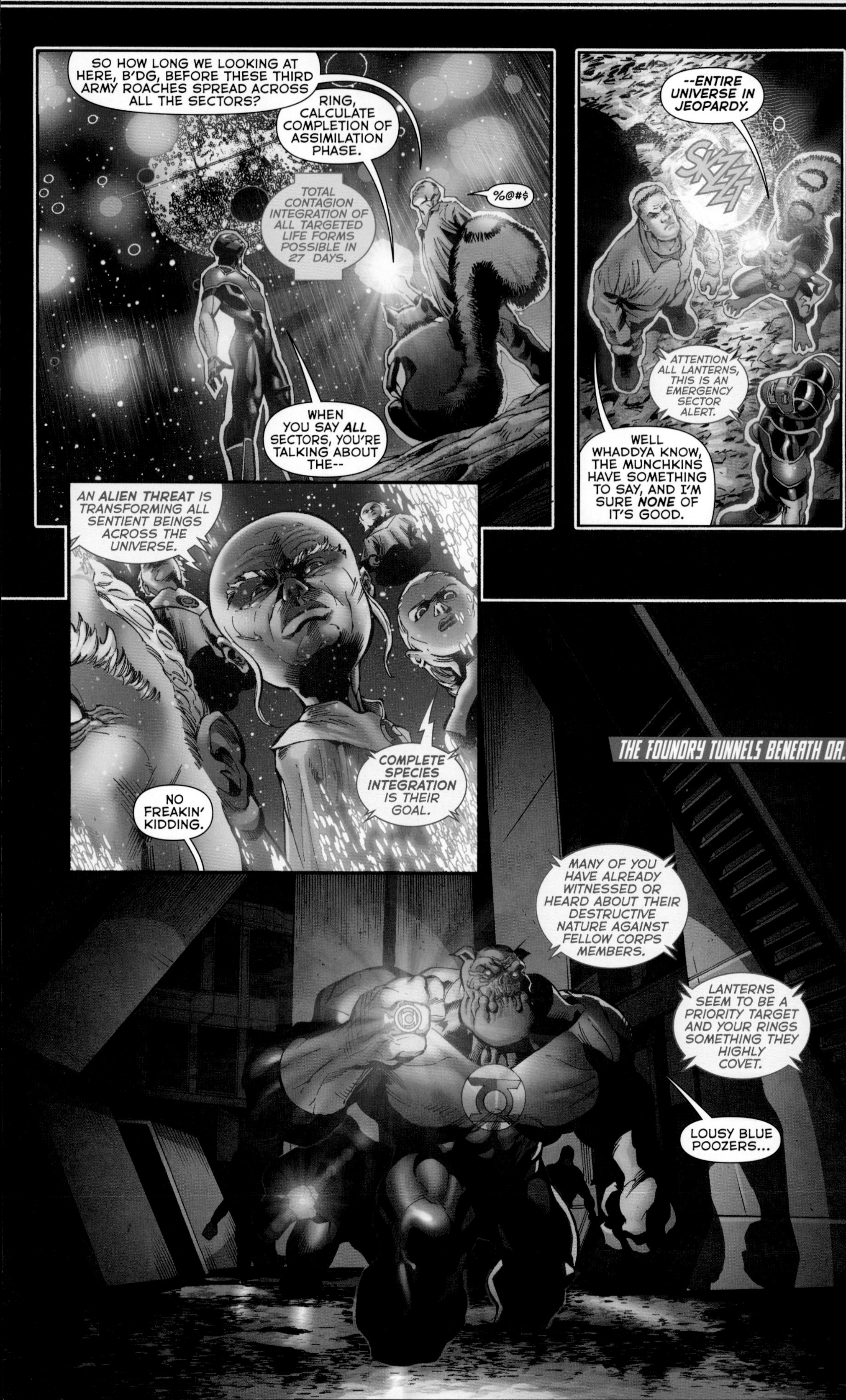
SO HOW LONG WE LOOKING AT HERE, B'DG, BEFORE THESE THIRD ARMY ROACHES SPREAD ACROSS ALL THE SECTORS?
RING, CALCULATE COMPLETION OF ASSIMILATION PHASE.
%@#$
TOTAL CONTAGION INTEGRATION OF ALL TARGETED LIFE FORMS POSSIBLE IN 27 DAYS.
WHEN YOU SAY ALL SECTORS, YOU'RE TALKING ABOUT THE--
--ENTIRE UNIVERSE IN JEOPARDY.
SKZZZT
ATTENTION ALL LANTERNS, THIS IS AN EMERGENCY SECTOR ALERT.
WELL WHADDYA KNOW, THE MUNCHKINS HAVE SOMETHING TO SAY, AND I'M SURE NONE OF IT'S GOOD.
AN ALIEN THREAT IS TRANSFORMING ALL SENTIENT BEINGS ACROSS THE UNIVERSE.
COMPLETE SPECIES INTEGRATION IS THEIR GOAL.
NO FREAKIN' KIDDING.
THE FOUNDRY TUNNELS BENEATH OA.
MANY OF YOU HAVE ALREADY WITNESSED OR HEARD ABOUT THEIR DESTRUCTIVE NATURE AGAINST FELLOW CORPS MEMBERS.
LANTERNS SEEM TO BE A PRIORITY TARGET AND YOUR RINGS SOMETHING THEY HIGHLY COVET.
LOUSY BLUE POOZERS...

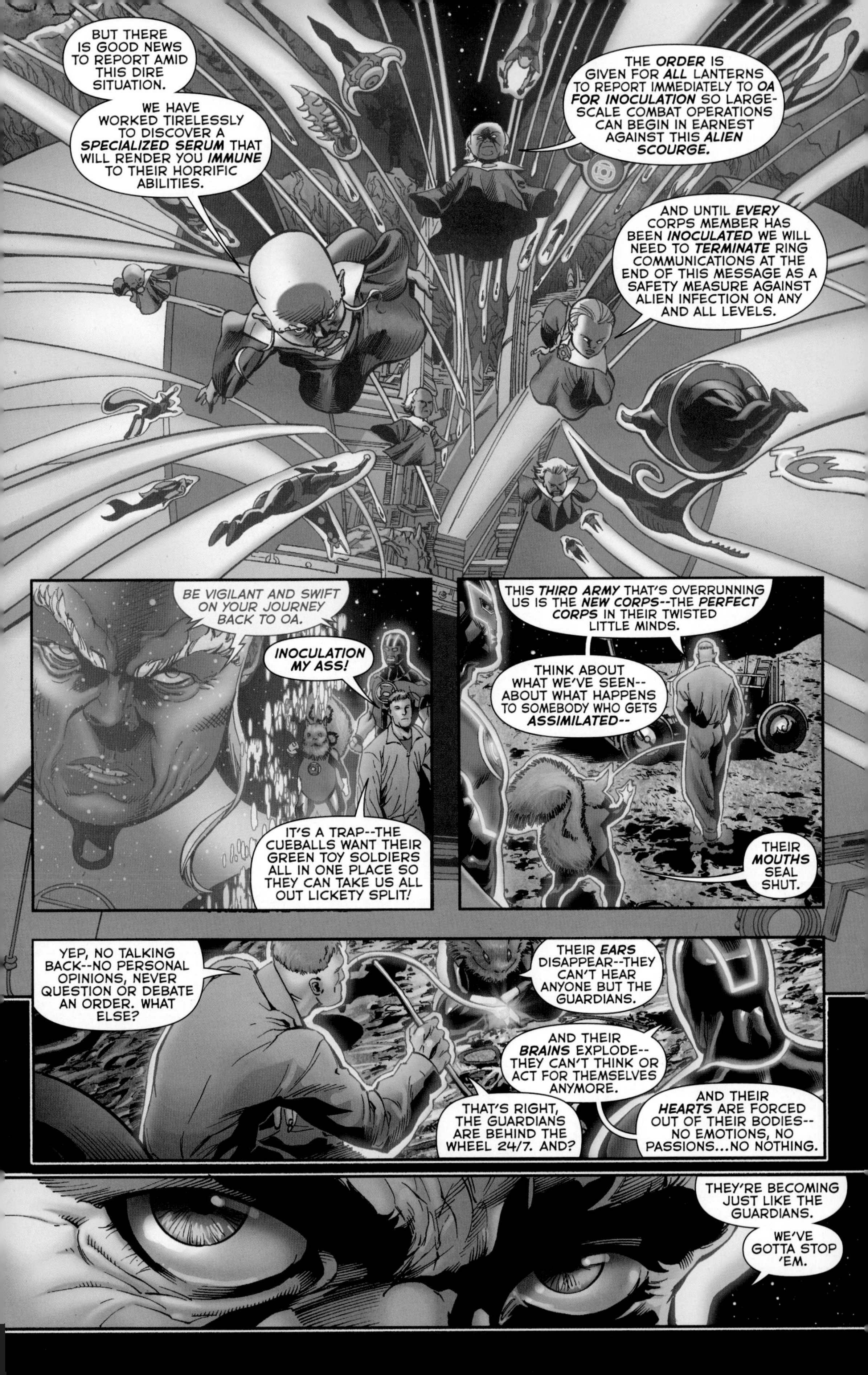

BUT THERE IS GOOD NEWS TO REPORT AMID THIS DIRE SITUATION.
WE HAVE WORKED TIRELESSLY TO DISCOVER A SPECIALIZED SERUM THAT WILL RENDER YOU IMMUNE TO THEIR HORRIFIC ABILITIES.
THE ORDER IS GIVEN FOR ALL LANTERNS TO REPORT IMMEDIATELY TO OA FOR INOCULATION SO LARGE-SCALE COMBAT OPERATIONS CAN BEGIN IN EARNEST AGAINST THIS ALIEN SCOURGE.
AND UNTIL EVERY CORPS MEMBER HAS BEEN INOCULATED WE WILL NEED TO TERMINATE RING COMMUNICATIONS AT THE END OF THIS MESSAGE AS A SAFETY MEASURE AGAINST ALIEN INFECTION ON ANY AND ALL LEVELS.
BE VIGILANT AND SWIFT ON YOUR JOURNEY BACK TO OA.
INOCULATION MY ASS!
IT'S A TRAP--THE CUEBALLS WANT THEIR GREEN TOY SOLDIERS ALL IN ONE PLACE SO THEY CAN TAKE US ALL OUT LICKETY SPLIT!
THIS THIRD ARMY THAT'S OVERRUNNING US IS THE NEW CORPS--THE PERFECT CORPS IN THEIR TWISTED LITTLE MINDS.
THINK ABOUT WHAT WE'VE SEEN--ABOUT WHAT HAPPENS TO SOMEBODY WHO GETS ASSIMILATED--
THEIR MOUTHS SEAL SHUT.
YEP, NO TALKING BACK--NO PERSONAL OPINIONS, NEVER QUESTION OR DEBATE AN ORDER. WHAT ELSE?
THEIR EARS DISAPPEAR--THEY CAN'T HEAR ANYONE BUT THE GUARDIANS.
THAT'S RIGHT, THE GUARDIANS ARE BEHIND THE WHEEL 24/7. AND?
AND THEIR BRAINS EXPLODE--THEY CAN'T THINK OR ACT FOR THEMSELVES ANYMORE.
AND THEIR HEARTS ARE FORCED OUT OF THEIR BODIES--NO EMOTIONS, NO PASSIONS...NO NOTHING.
THEY'RE BECOMING JUST LIKE THE GUARDIANS.
WE'VE GOTTA STOP 'EM.

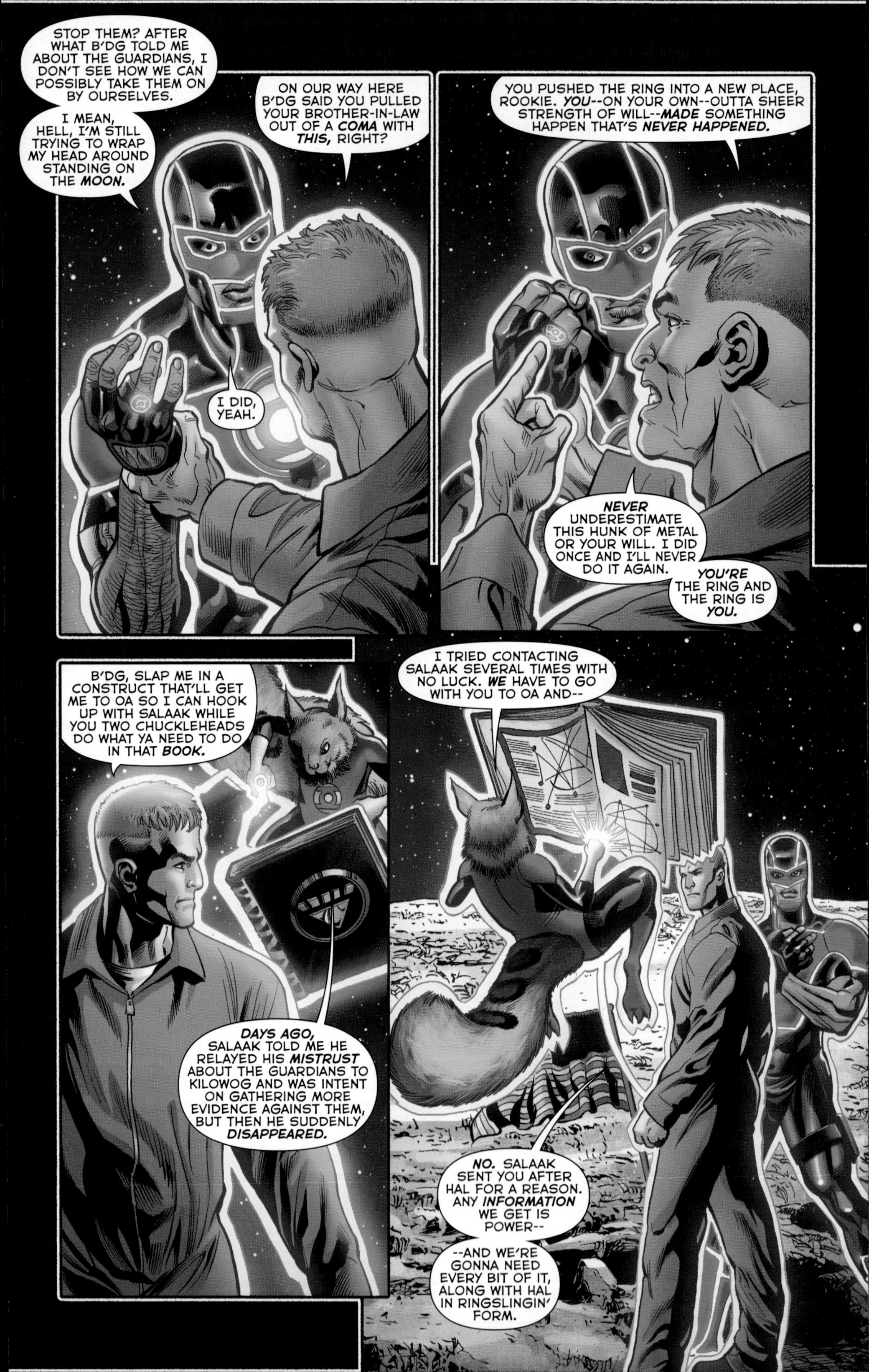

STOP THEM? AFTER WHAT B'DG TOLD ME ABOUT THE GUARDIANS, I DON'T SEE HOW WE CAN POSSIBLY TAKE THEM ON BY OURSELVES.
I MEAN, HELL, I'M STILL TRYING TO WRAP MY HEAD AROUND STANDING ON THE *MOON.*
ON OUR WAY HERE B'DG SAID YOU PULLED YOUR BROTHER-IN-LAW OUT OF A *COMA* WITH *THIS,* RIGHT?
I DID, YEAH.
YOU PUSHED THE RING INTO A NEW PLACE, ROOKIE. *YOU*--ON YOUR OWN--OUTTA SHEER STRENGTH OF WILL--*MADE* SOMETHING HAPPEN THAT'S *NEVER HAPPENED.*
NEVER UNDERESTIMATE THIS HUNK OF METAL OR YOUR WILL. I DID ONCE AND I'LL NEVER DO IT AGAIN.
YOU'RE THE RING AND THE RING IS *YOU.*
B'DG, SLAP ME IN A CONSTRUCT THAT'LL GET ME TO OA SO I CAN HOOK UP WITH SALAAK WHILE YOU TWO CHUCKLEHEADS DO WHAT YA NEED TO DO IN THAT *BOOK.*
DAYS AGO, SALAAK TOLD ME HE RELAYED HIS *MISTRUST* ABOUT THE GUARDIANS TO KILOWOG AND WAS INTENT ON GATHERING MORE EVIDENCE AGAINST THEM, BUT THEN HE SUDDENLY *DISAPPEARED.*
I TRIED CONTACTING SALAAK SEVERAL TIMES WITH NO LUCK. *WE* HAVE TO GO WITH YOU TO OA AND--
NO. SALAAK SENT YOU AFTER HAL FOR A REASON. ANY *INFORMATION* WE GET IS POWER--
--AND WE'RE GONNA NEED EVERY BIT OF IT, ALONG WITH HAL IN RINGSLINGIN' FORM.

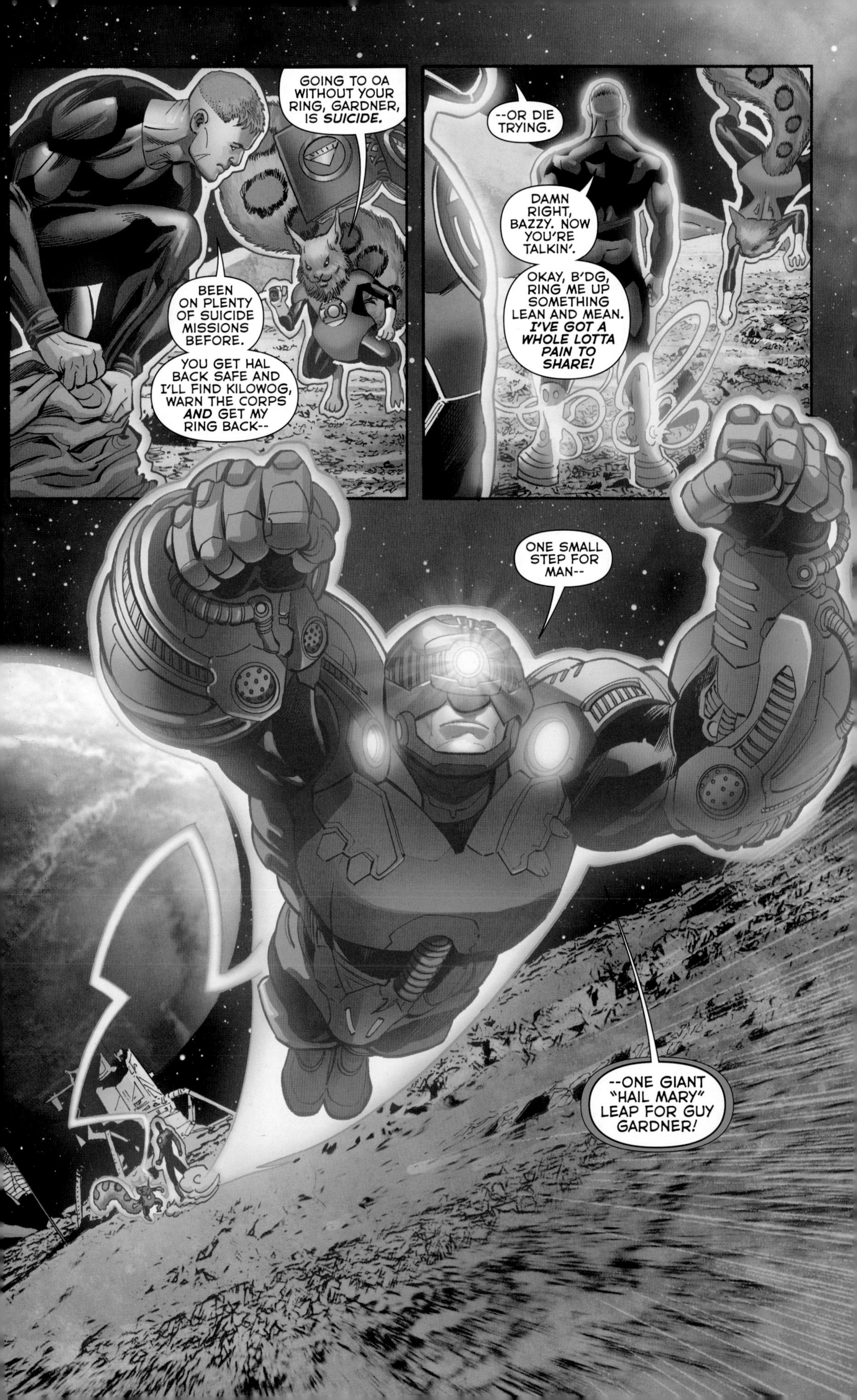
GOING TO OA WITHOUT YOUR RING, GARDNER, IS *SUICIDE.*
BEEN ON PLENTY OF SUICIDE MISSIONS BEFORE.
YOU GET HAL BACK SAFE AND I'LL FIND KILOWOG, WARN THE CORPS *AND* GET MY RING BACK--
--OR DIE TRYING.
DAMN RIGHT, BAZZY. NOW YOU'RE TALKIN'.
OKAY, B'DG, RING ME UP SOMETHING LEAN AND MEAN. ***I'VE GOT A WHOLE LOTTA PAIN TO SHARE!***
ONE SMALL STEP FOR MAN--
--ONE GIANT "HAIL MARY" LEAP FOR GUY GARDNER!

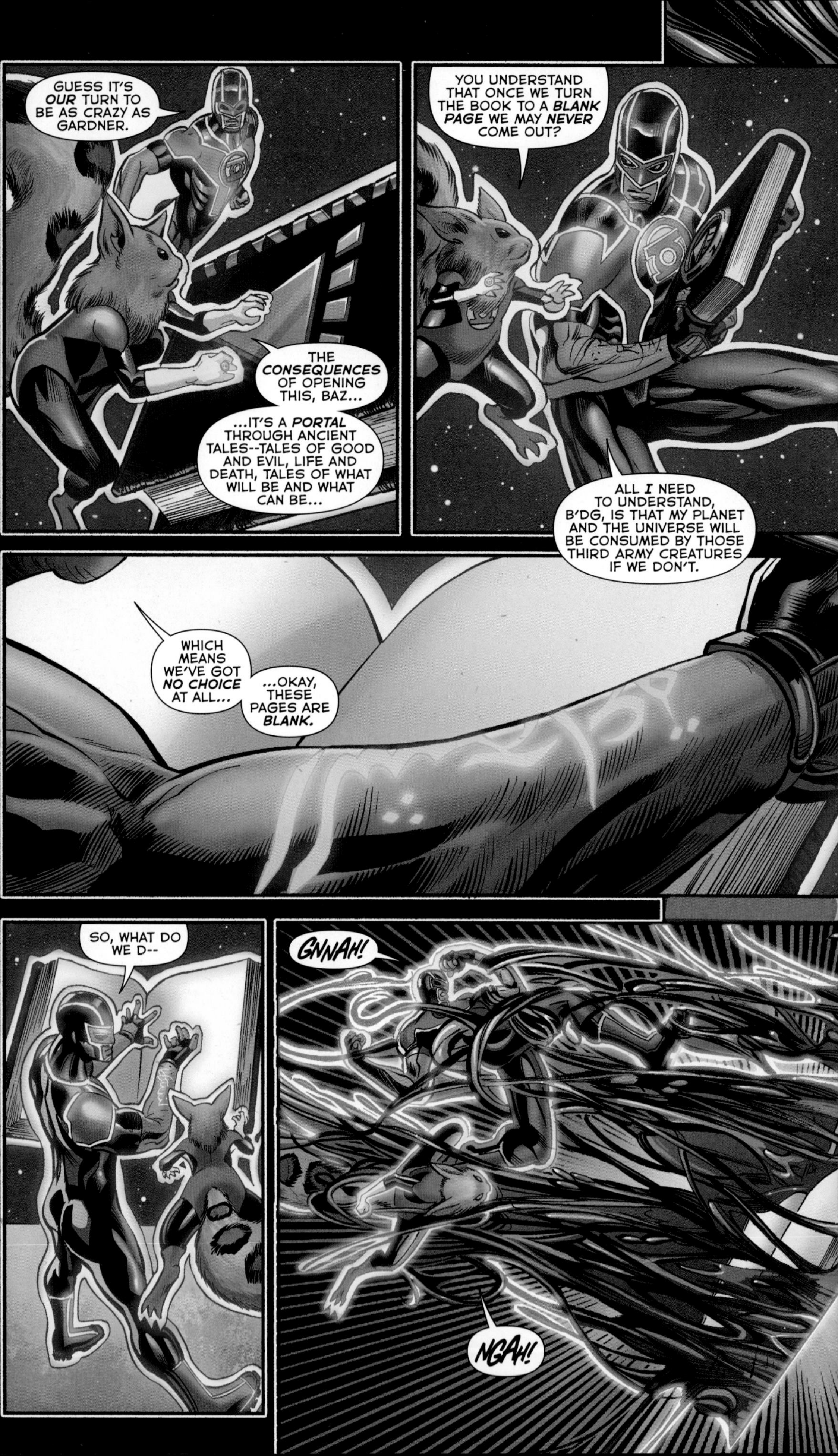
GUESS IT'S **OUR** TURN TO BE AS CRAZY AS GARDNER.
THE **CONSEQUENCES** OF OPENING THIS, BAZ...
...IT'S A **PORTAL** THROUGH ANCIENT TALES--TALES OF GOOD AND EVIL, LIFE AND DEATH, TALES OF WHAT WILL BE AND WHAT CAN BE...
YOU UNDERSTAND THAT ONCE WE TURN THE BOOK TO A **BLANK PAGE** WE MAY **NEVER** COME OUT?
ALL **I** NEED TO UNDERSTAND, B'DG, IS THAT MY PLANET AND THE UNIVERSE WILL BE CONSUMED BY THOSE THIRD ARMY CREATURES IF WE DON'T.
WHICH MEANS WE'VE GOT **NO CHOICE** AT ALL...
...OKAY, THESE PAGES ARE **BLANK.**
SO, WHAT DO WE D--
GNNAH!
NGAH!

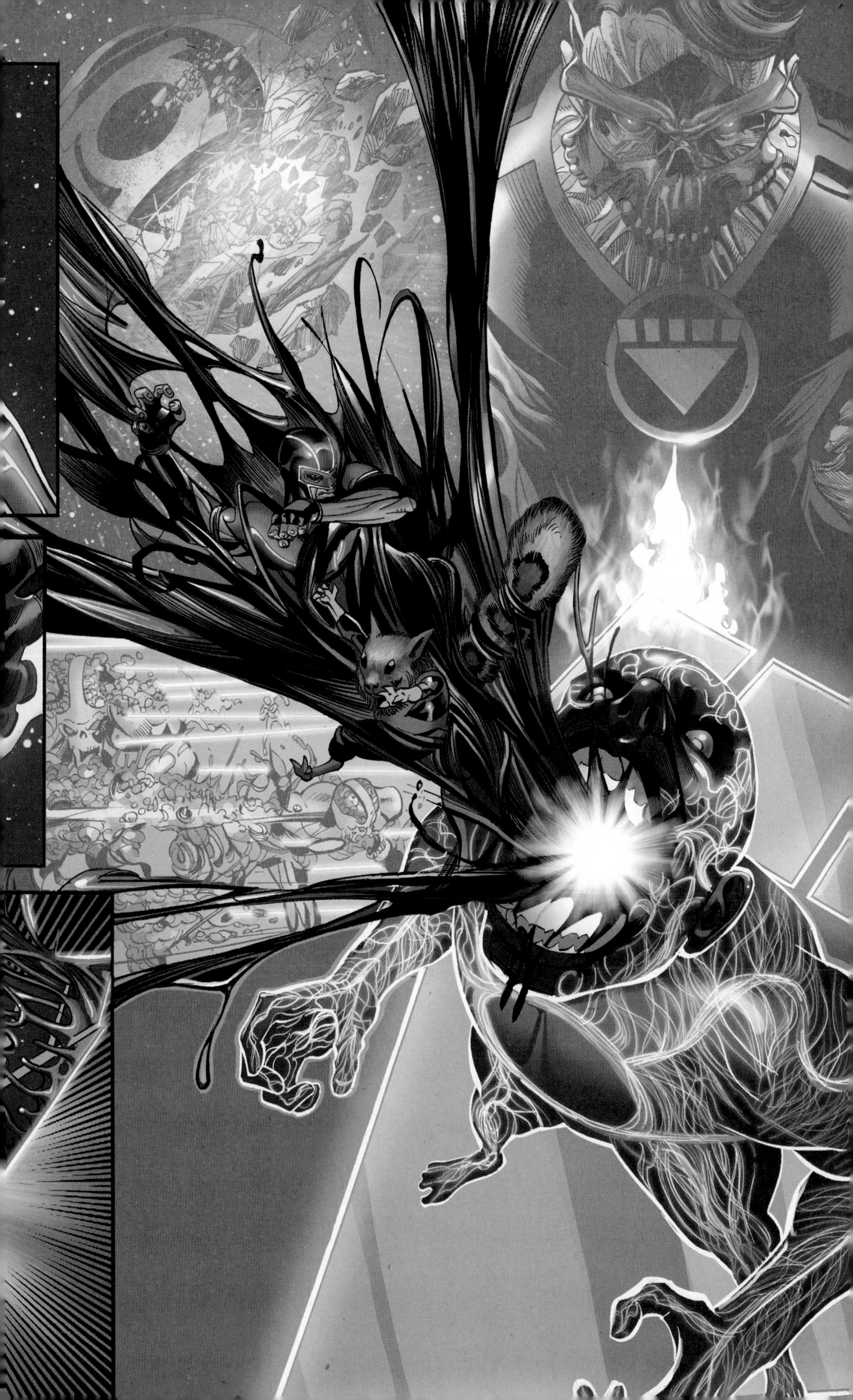

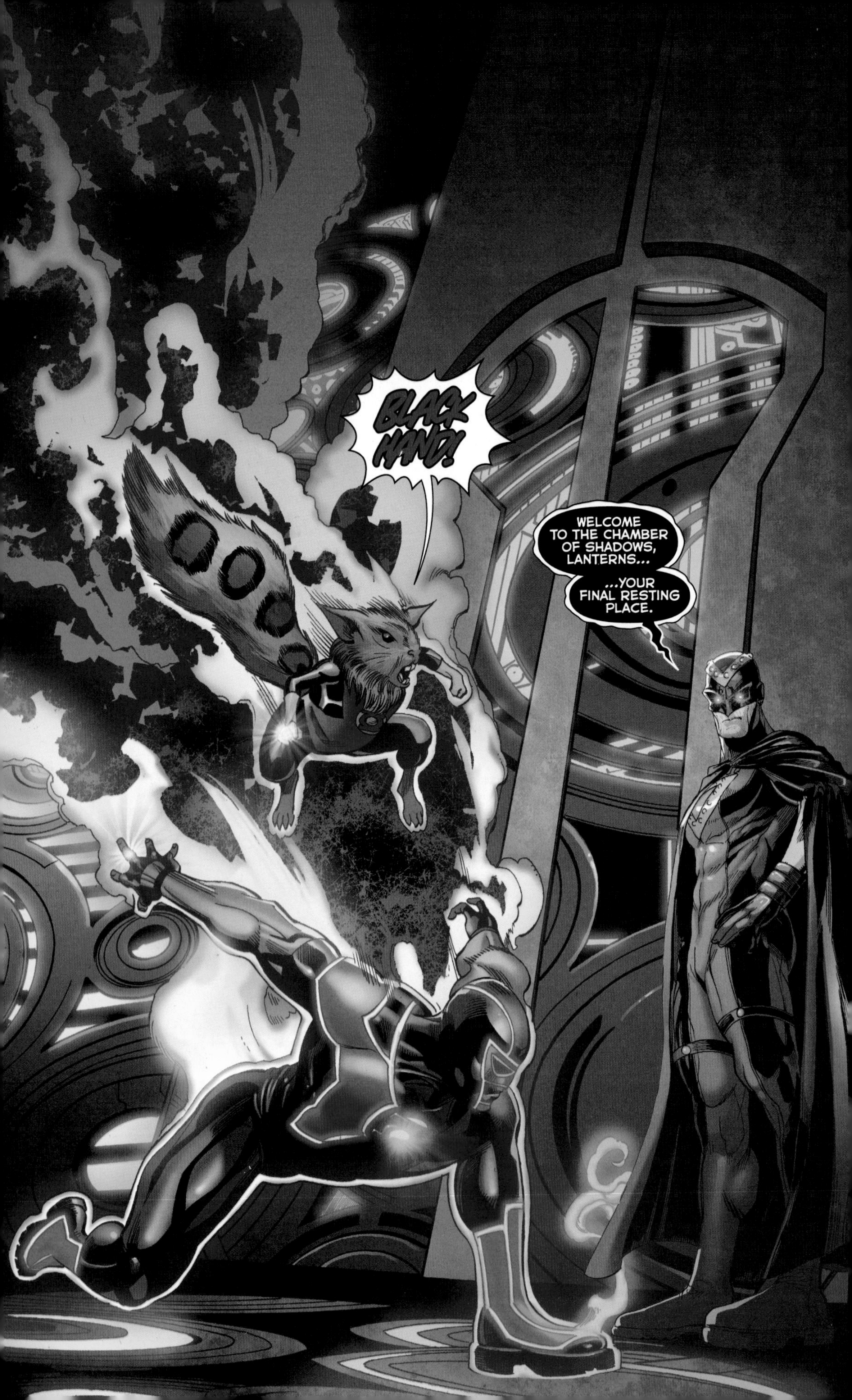
BLACK HAND!
WELCOME TO THE CHAMBER OF SHADOWS, LANTERNS...
...YOUR FINAL RESTING PLACE.

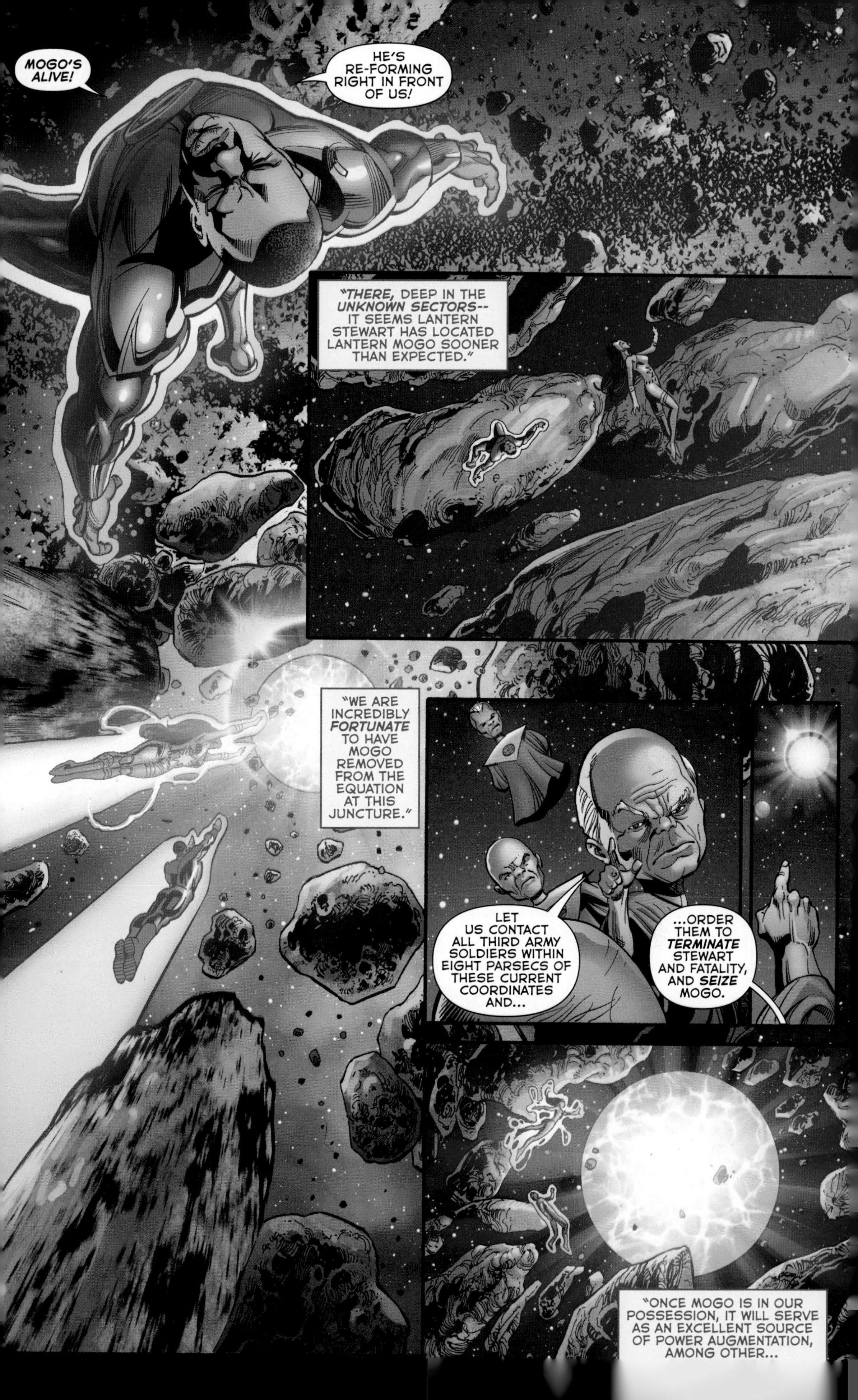
MOGO'S ALIVE!
HE'S RE-FORMING RIGHT IN FRONT OF US!
"THERE, DEEP IN THE UNKNOWN SECTORS-- IT SEEMS LANTERN STEWART HAS LOCATED LANTERN MOGO SOONER THAN EXPECTED."
"WE ARE INCREDIBLY FORTUNATE TO HAVE MOGO REMOVED FROM THE EQUATION AT THIS JUNCTURE."
LET US CONTACT ALL THIRD ARMY SOLDIERS WITHIN EIGHT PARSECS OF THESE CURRENT COORDINATES AND...
...ORDER THEM TO TERMINATE STEWART AND FATALITY, AND SEIZE MOGO.
"ONCE MOGO IS IN OUR POSSESSION, IT WILL SERVE AS AN EXCELLENT SOURCE OF POWER AUGMENTATION, AMONG OTHER...

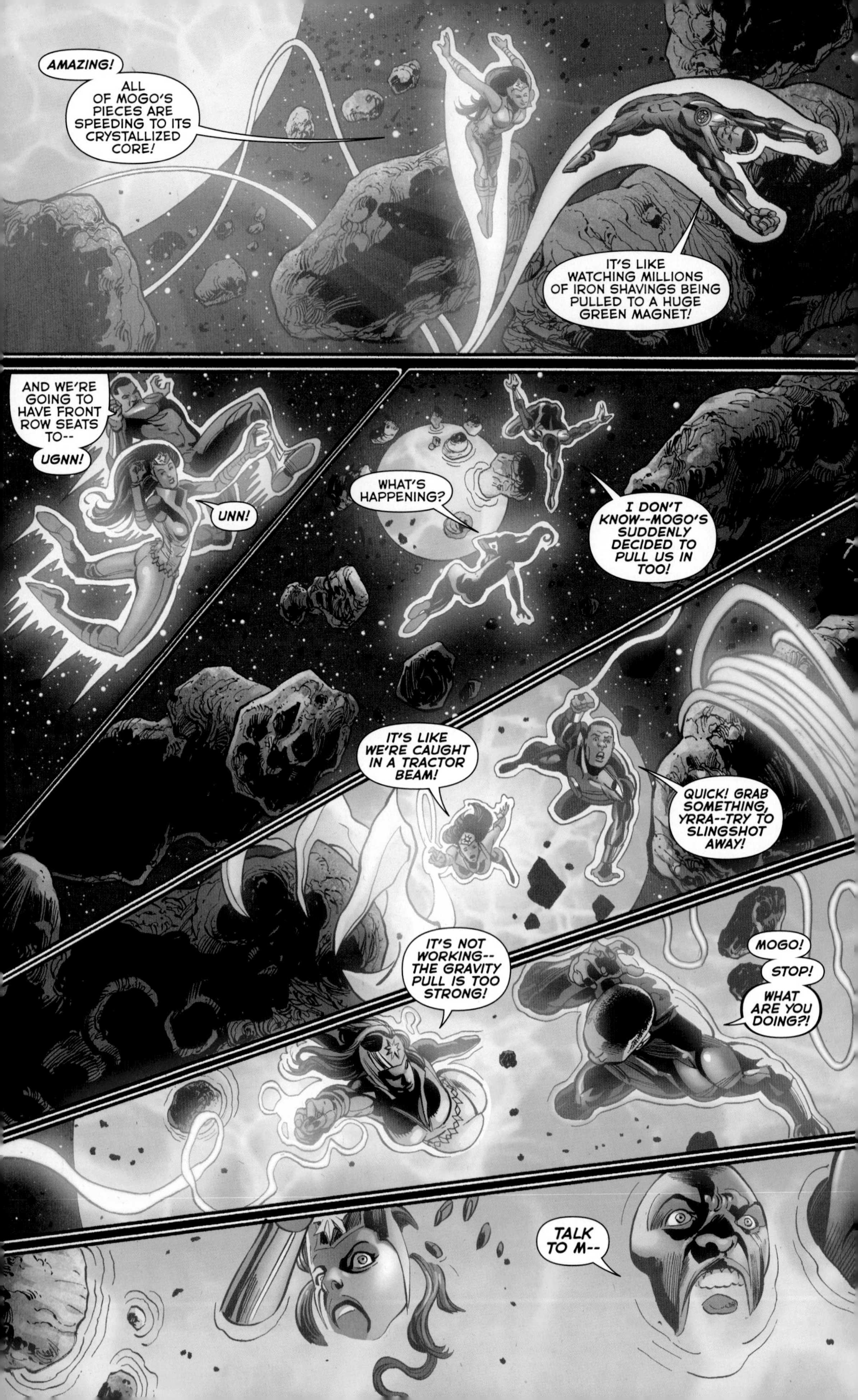
AMAZING!
ALL OF MOGO'S PIECES ARE SPEEDING TO ITS CRYSTALLIZED CORE!
IT'S LIKE WATCHING MILLIONS OF IRON SHAVINGS BEING PULLED TO A HUGE GREEN MAGNET!
AND WE'RE GOING TO HAVE FRONT ROW SEATS TO--
UGNN!
UNN!
WHAT'S HAPPENING?
I DON'T KNOW--MOGO'S SUDDENLY DECIDED TO PULL US IN TOO!
IT'S LIKE WE'RE CAUGHT IN A TRACTOR BEAM!
QUICK! GRAB SOMETHING, YRRA--TRY TO SLINGSHOT AWAY!
IT'S NOT WORKING-- THE GRAVITY PULL IS TOO STRONG!
MOGO!
STOP!
WHAT ARE YOU DOING?!
TALK TO M--

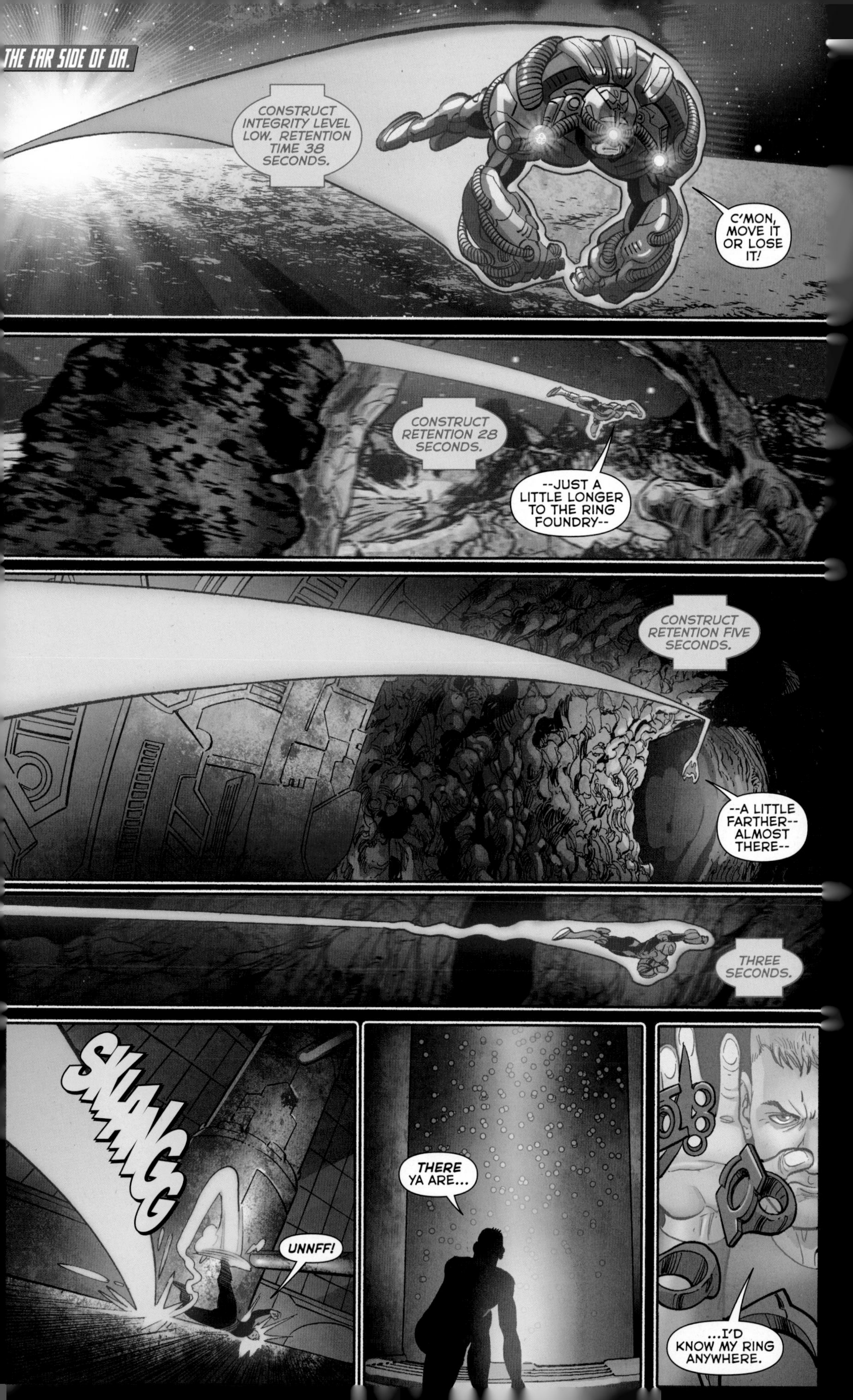
THE FAR SIDE OF OA.
CONSTRUCT INTEGRITY LEVEL LOW. RETENTION TIME 38 SECONDS.
C'MON, MOVE IT OR LOSE IT!
CONSTRUCT RETENTION 28 SECONDS.
--JUST A LITTLE LONGER TO THE RING FOUNDRY--
CONSTRUCT RETENTION FIVE SECONDS.
--A LITTLE FARTHER-- ALMOST THERE--
THREE SECONDS.
SKLANGG
UNNFF!
THERE YA ARE...
...I'D KNOW MY RING ANYWHERE.

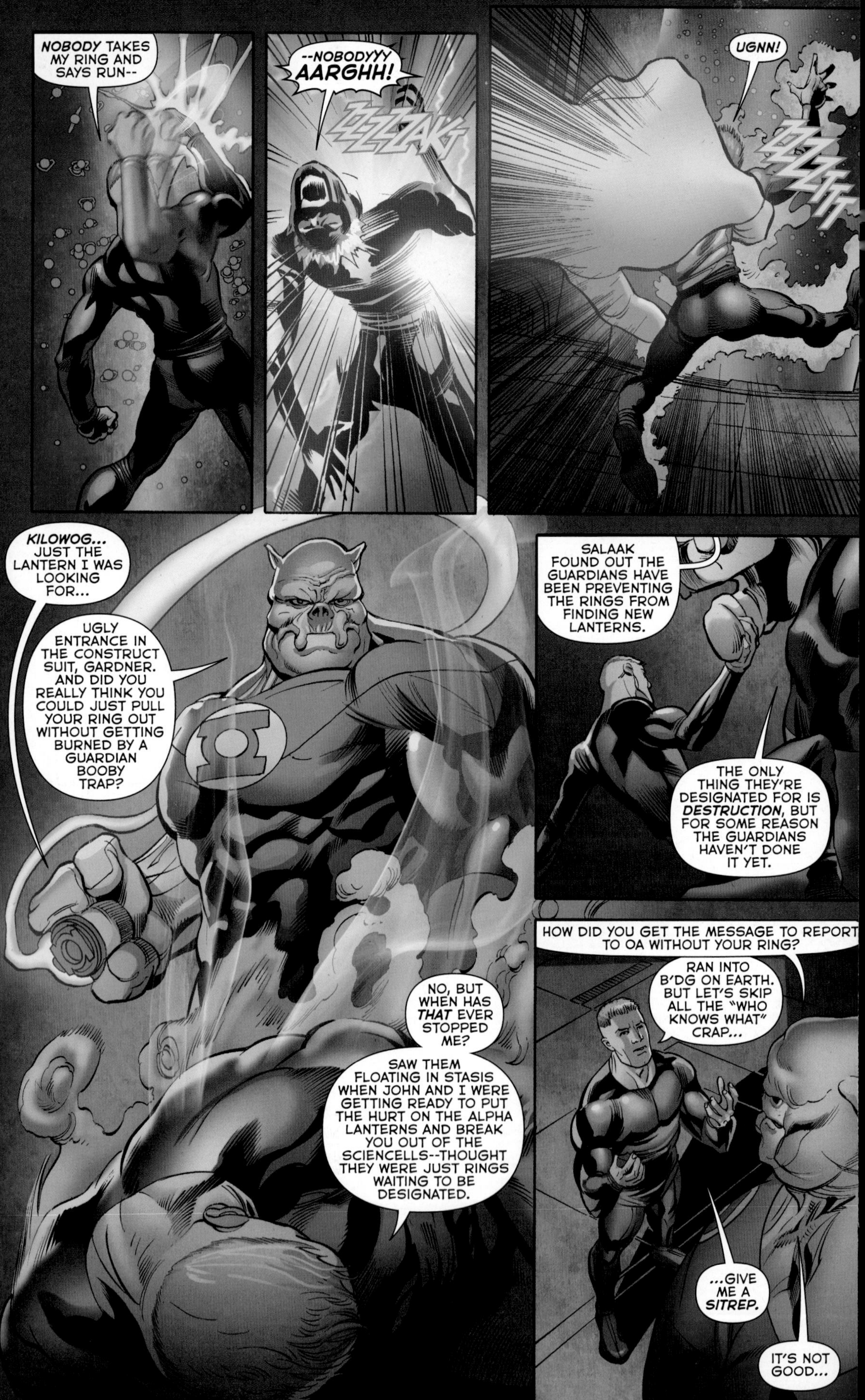

NOBODY TAKES MY RING AND SAYS RUN--
--NOBODYYY AARGHH!
ZZZZZAKT
UGNN!
ZZZZTTT
KILOWOG... JUST THE LANTERN I WAS LOOKING FOR...
UGLY ENTRANCE IN THE CONSTRUCT SUIT, GARDNER. AND DID YOU REALLY THINK YOU COULD JUST PULL YOUR RING OUT WITHOUT GETTING BURNED BY A GUARDIAN BOOBY TRAP?
NO, BUT WHEN HAS THAT EVER STOPPED ME?
SAW THEM FLOATING IN STASIS WHEN JOHN AND I WERE GETTING READY TO PUT THE HURT ON THE ALPHA LANTERNS AND BREAK YOU OUT OF THE SCIENCELLS--THOUGHT THEY WERE JUST RINGS WAITING TO BE DESIGNATED.
SALAAK FOUND OUT THE GUARDIANS HAVE BEEN PREVENTING THE RINGS FROM FINDING NEW LANTERNS.
THE ONLY THING THEY'RE DESIGNATED FOR IS DESTRUCTION, BUT FOR SOME REASON THE GUARDIANS HAVEN'T DONE IT YET.
HOW DID YOU GET THE MESSAGE TO REPORT TO OA WITHOUT YOUR RING?
RAN INTO B'DG ON EARTH. BUT LET'S SKIP ALL THE "WHO KNOWS WHAT" CRAP...
...GIVE ME A SITREP.
IT'S NOT GOOD...

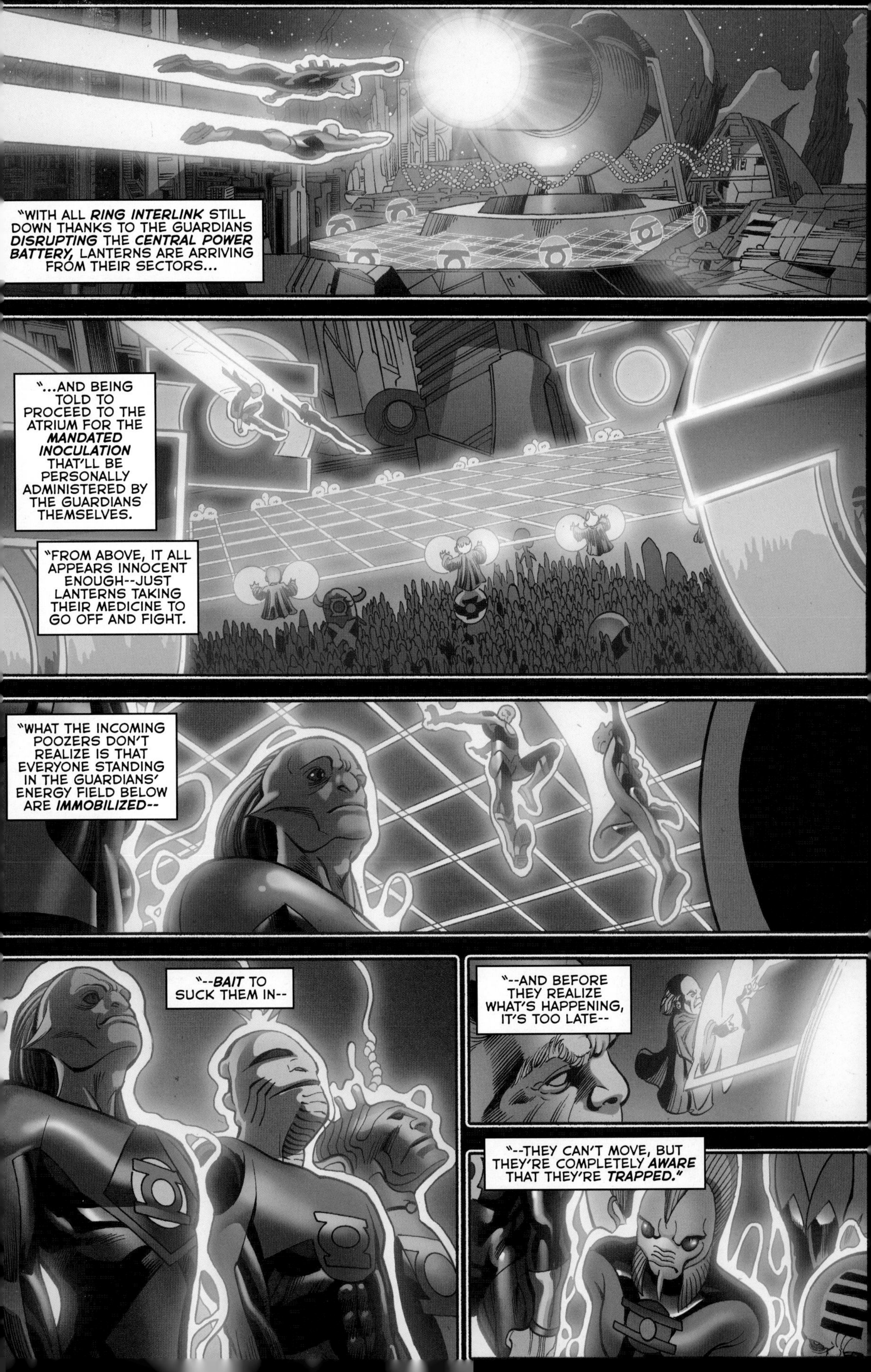
"WITH ALL *RING INTERLINK* STILL DOWN THANKS TO THE GUARDIANS *DISRUPTING* THE *CENTRAL POWER BATTERY,* LANTERNS ARE ARRIVING FROM THEIR SECTORS...
"...AND BEING TOLD TO PROCEED TO THE ATRIUM FOR THE *MANDATED INOCULATION* THAT'LL BE PERSONALLY ADMINISTERED BY THE GUARDIANS THEMSELVES.
"FROM ABOVE, IT ALL APPEARS INNOCENT ENOUGH--JUST LANTERNS TAKING THEIR MEDICINE TO GO OFF AND FIGHT.
"WHAT THE INCOMING POOZERS DON'T REALIZE IS THAT EVERYONE STANDING IN THE GUARDIANS' ENERGY FIELD BELOW ARE *IMMOBILIZED*--
"--*BAIT* TO SUCK THEM IN--
"--AND BEFORE THEY REALIZE WHAT'S HAPPENING, IT'S TOO LATE--
"--THEY CAN'T MOVE, BUT THEY'RE COMPLETELY *AWARE* THAT THEY'RE *TRAPPED.*"

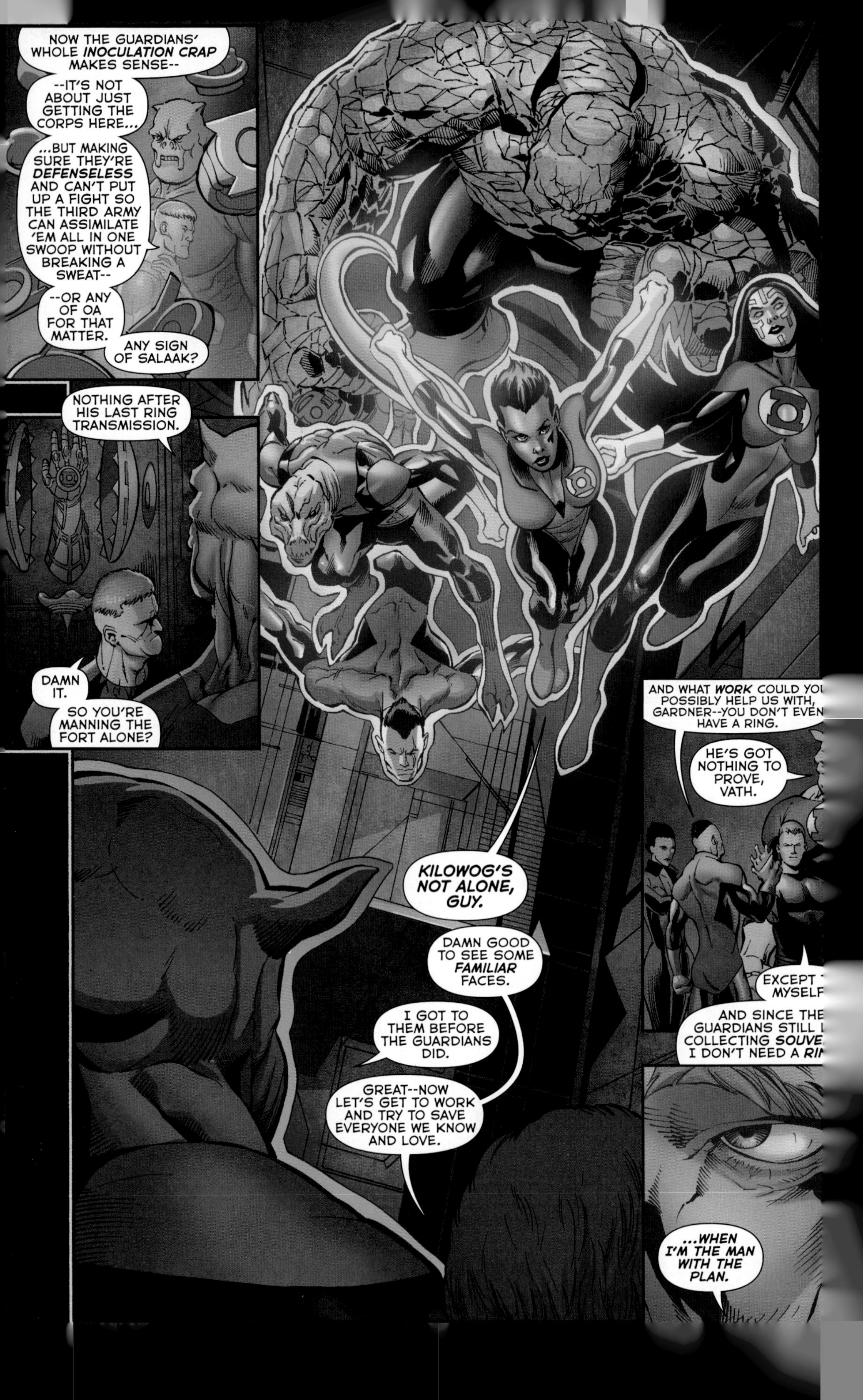
NOW THE GUARDIANS' WHOLE *INOCULATION CRAP* MAKES SENSE--
--IT'S NOT ABOUT JUST GETTING THE CORPS HERE...
...BUT MAKING SURE THEY'RE *DEFENSELESS* AND CAN'T PUT UP A FIGHT SO THE THIRD ARMY CAN ASSIMILATE 'EM ALL IN ONE SWOOP WITHOUT BREAKING A SWEAT--
--OR ANY OF OA FOR THAT MATTER.
ANY SIGN OF SALAAK?
NOTHING AFTER HIS LAST RING TRANSMISSION.
DAMN IT.
SO YOU'RE MANNING THE FORT ALONE?
KILOWOG'S NOT ALONE, GUY.
DAMN GOOD TO SEE SOME *FAMILIAR* FACES.
I GOT TO THEM BEFORE THE GUARDIANS DID.
GREAT--NOW LET'S GET TO WORK AND TRY TO SAVE EVERYONE WE KNOW AND LOVE.
AND WHAT *WORK* COULD YOU POSSIBLY HELP US WITH, GARDNER--YOU DON'T EVEN HAVE A RING.
HE'S GOT NOTHING TO PROVE, VATH.
EXCEPT MYSELF
AND SINCE THE GUARDIANS STILL COLLECTING *SOUVE* I DON'T NEED A *RI*
...WHEN I'M THE MAN WITH THE PLAN.

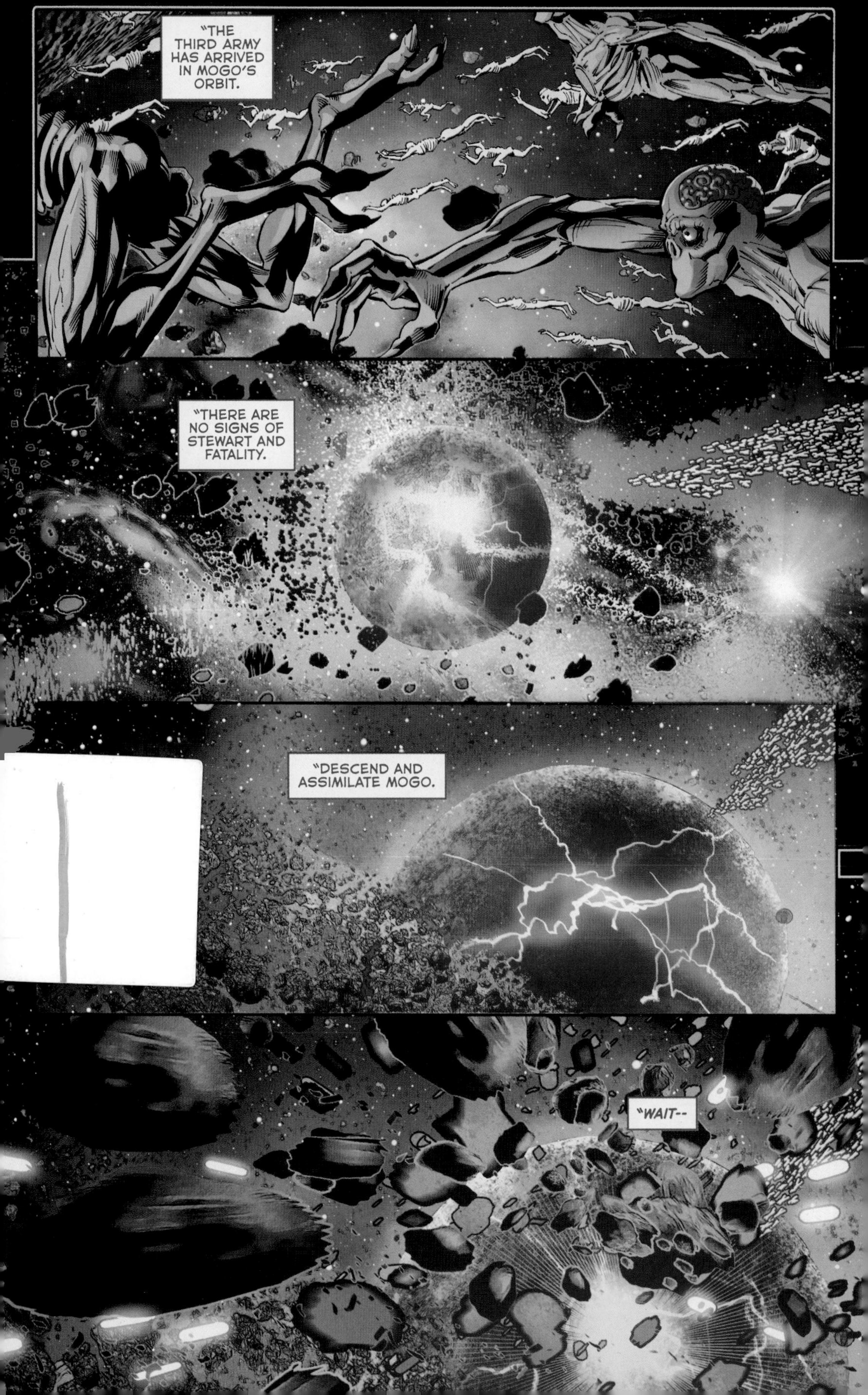
"THE THIRD ARMY HAS ARRIVED IN MOGO'S ORBIT.
"THERE ARE NO SIGNS OF STEWART AND FATALITY.
"DESCEND AND ASSIMILATE MOGO.
"WAIT--

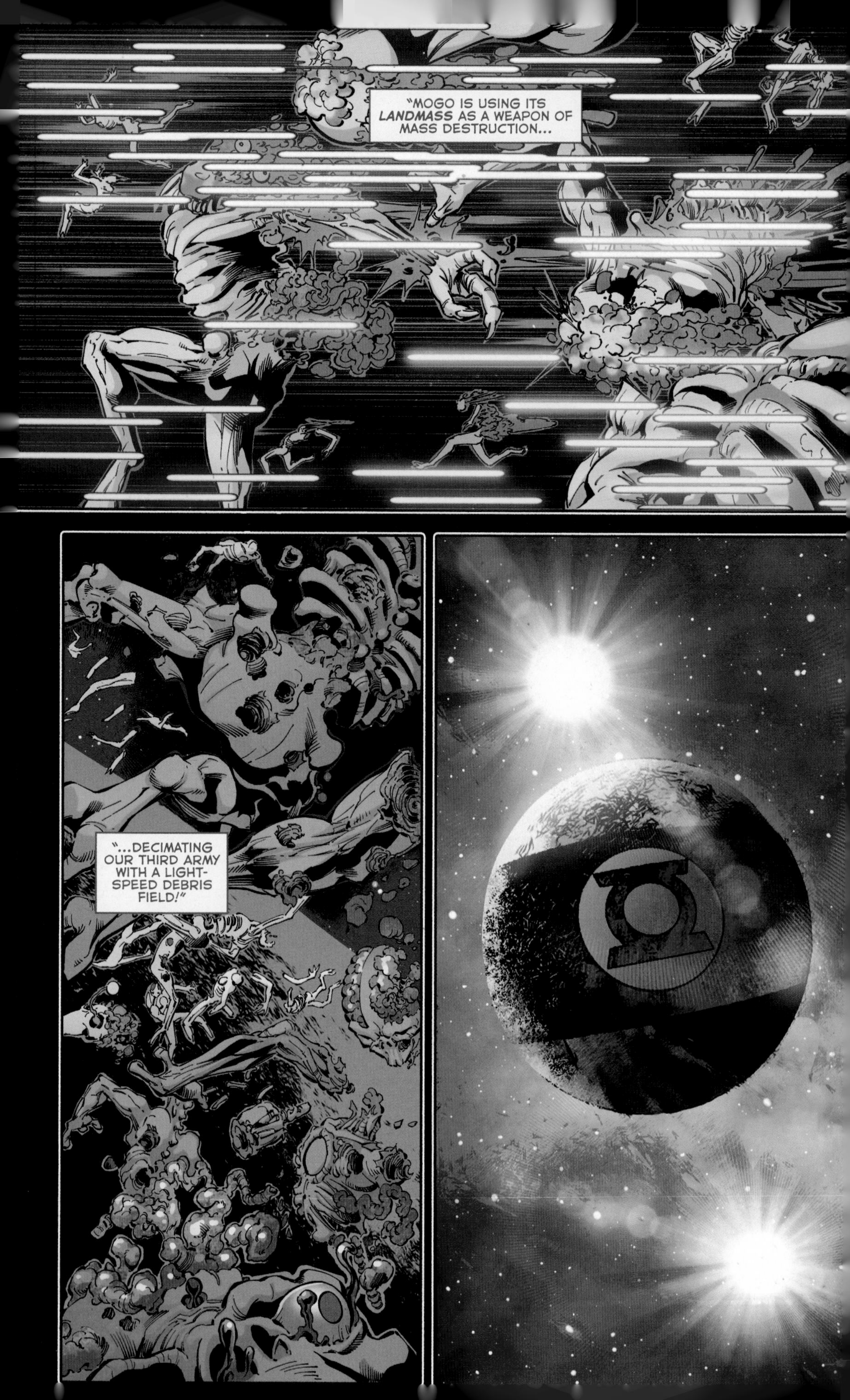
"MOGO IS USING ITS LANDMASS AS A WEAPON OF MASS DESTRUCTION...
"...DECIMATING OUR THIRD ARMY WITH A LIGHT-SPEED DEBRIS FIELD!"

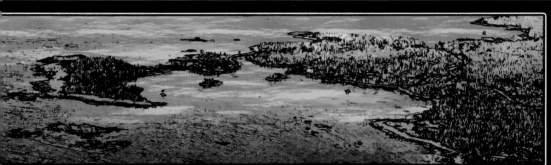

SPLARRSH

...RING... WHAT THE HELL JUST HAPPENED?

THIRD ARMY ATTACK HAS BEEN NEUTRALIZED.

...MOGO WASN'T TRYING TO KILL US... MOGO **SAVED** US.

AND YOU SAVED MOGO.

WE SAVED HIM.

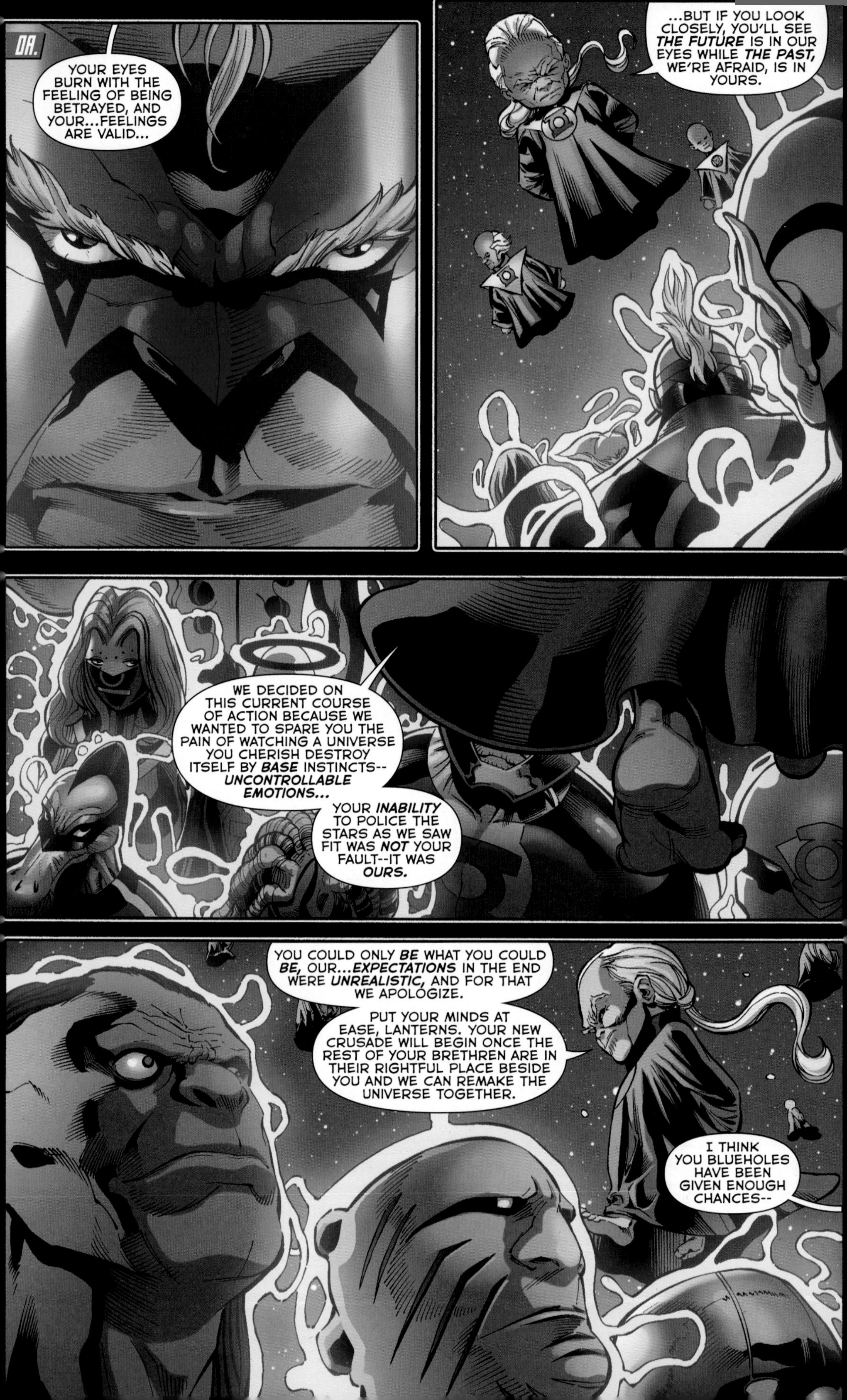
OA.
YOUR EYES BURN WITH THE FEELING OF BEING BETRAYED, AND YOUR...FEELINGS ARE VALID...
...BUT IF YOU LOOK CLOSELY, YOU'LL SEE THE FUTURE IS IN OUR EYES WHILE THE PAST, WE'RE AFRAID, IS IN YOURS.
WE DECIDED ON THIS CURRENT COURSE OF ACTION BECAUSE WE WANTED TO SPARE YOU THE PAIN OF WATCHING A UNIVERSE YOU CHERISH DESTROY ITSELF BY BASE INSTINCTS--UNCONTROLLABLE EMOTIONS...
YOUR INABILITY TO POLICE THE STARS AS WE SAW FIT WAS NOT YOUR FAULT--IT WAS OURS.
YOU COULD ONLY BE WHAT YOU COULD BE, OUR...EXPECTATIONS IN THE END WERE UNREALISTIC, AND FOR THAT WE APOLOGIZE.
PUT YOUR MINDS AT EASE, LANTERNS. YOUR NEW CRUSADE WILL BEGIN ONCE THE REST OF YOUR BRETHREN ARE IN THEIR RIGHTFUL PLACE BESIDE YOU AND WE CAN REMAKE THE UNIVERSE TOGETHER.
I THINK YOU BLUEHOLES HAVE BEEN GIVEN ENOUGH CHANCES--

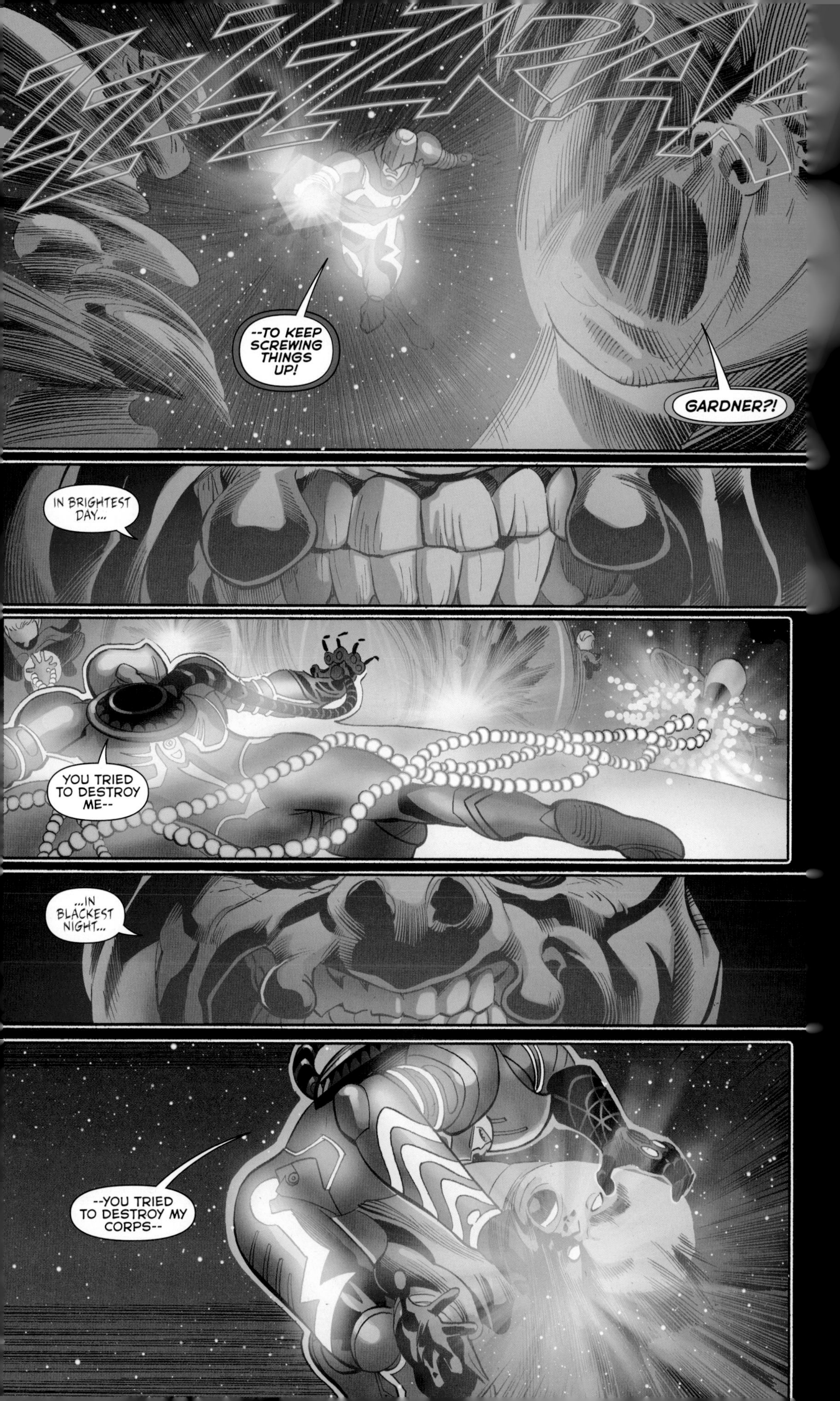
--TO KEEP SCREWING THINGS UP!
GARDNER?!
IN BRIGHTEST DAY...
YOU TRIED TO DESTROY ME--
...IN BLACKEST NIGHT...
--YOU TRIED TO DESTROY MY CORPS--

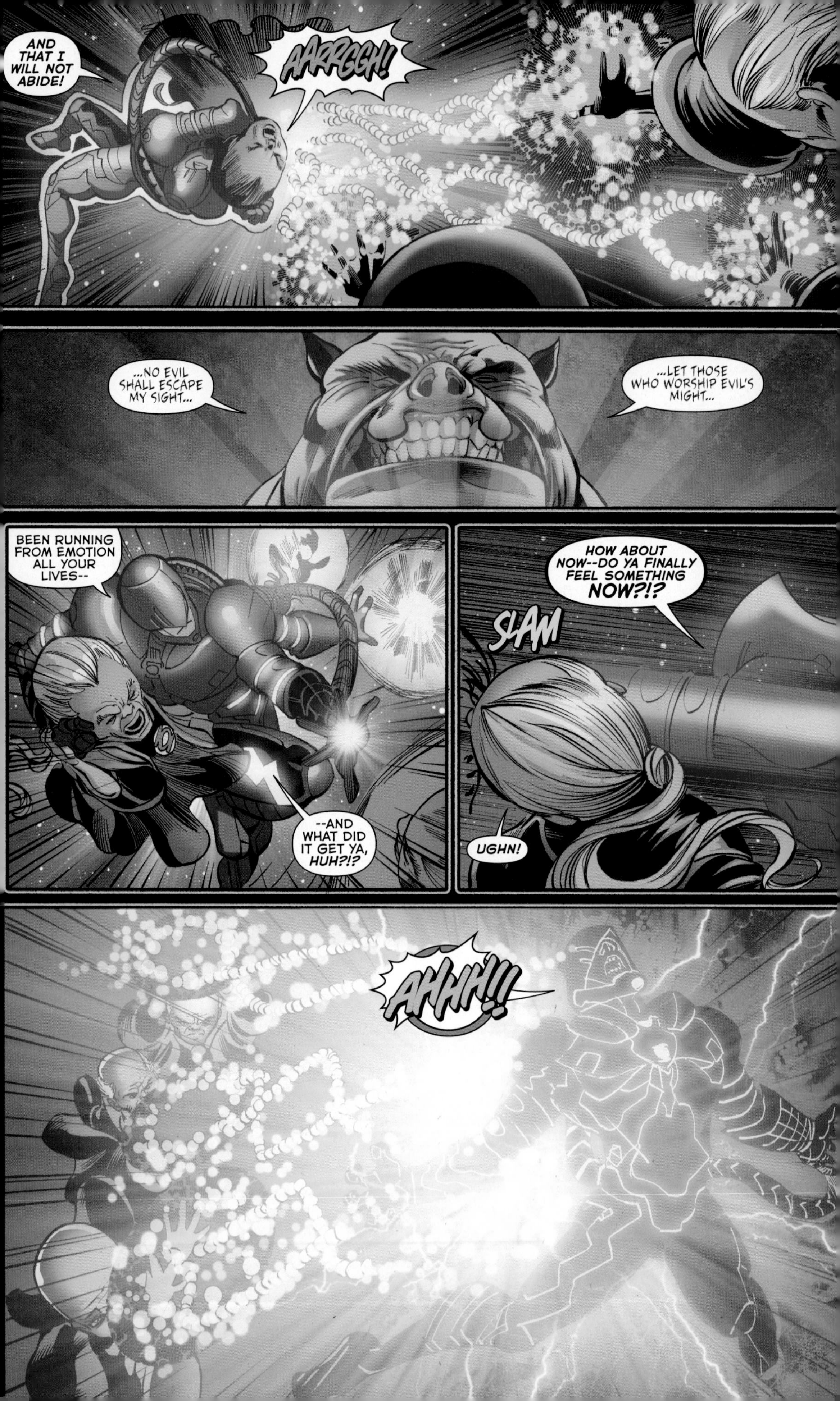
AND THAT I WILL NOT ABIDE!
AARRGGH!
...NO EVIL SHALL ESCAPE MY SIGHT...
...LET THOSE WHO WORSHIP EVIL'S MIGHT...
BEEN RUNNING FROM EMOTION ALL YOUR LIVES--
--AND WHAT DID IT GET YA, HUH?!?
HOW ABOUT NOW--DO YA FINALLY FEEL SOMETHING NOW?!?
SLAM
UGHN!
AHHH!!!

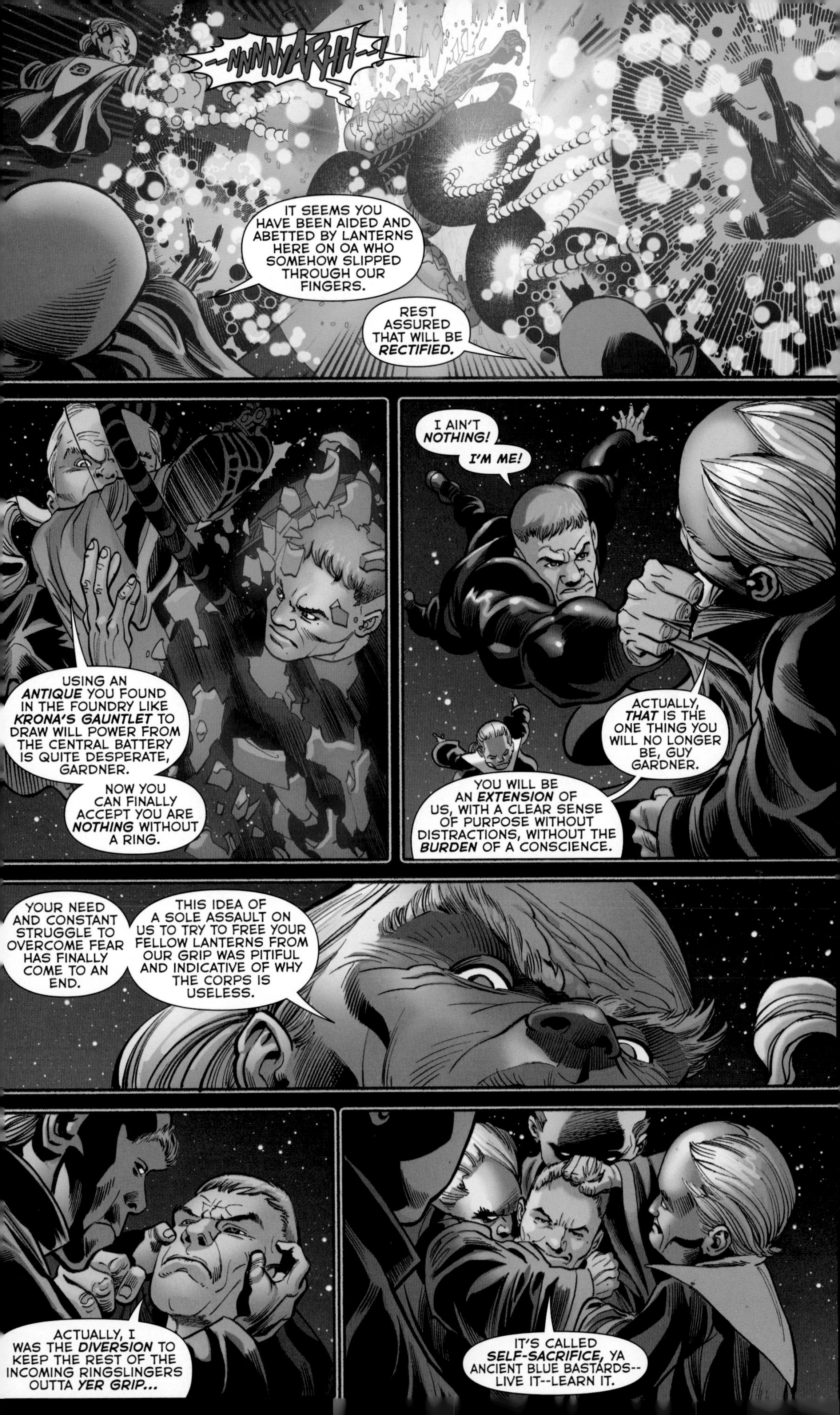
--NNNNYARHH--!
IT SEEMS YOU HAVE BEEN AIDED AND ABETTED BY LANTERNS HERE ON OA WHO SOMEHOW SLIPPED THROUGH OUR FINGERS.
REST ASSURED THAT WILL BE RECTIFIED.
USING AN ANTIQUE YOU FOUND IN THE FOUNDRY LIKE KRONA'S GAUNTLET TO DRAW WILL POWER FROM THE CENTRAL BATTERY IS QUITE DESPERATE, GARDNER.
NOW YOU CAN FINALLY ACCEPT YOU ARE NOTHING WITHOUT A RING.
I AIN'T NOTHING!
I'M ME!
ACTUALLY, THAT IS THE ONE THING YOU WILL NO LONGER BE, GUY GARDNER.
YOU WILL BE AN EXTENSION OF US, WITH A CLEAR SENSE OF PURPOSE WITHOUT DISTRACTIONS, WITHOUT THE BURDEN OF A CONSCIENCE.
YOUR NEED AND CONSTANT STRUGGLE TO OVERCOME FEAR HAS FINALLY COME TO AN END.
THIS IDEA OF A SOLE ASSAULT ON US TO TRY TO FREE YOUR FELLOW LANTERNS FROM OUR GRIP WAS PITIFUL AND INDICATIVE OF WHY THE CORPS IS USELESS.
ACTUALLY, I WAS THE DIVERSION TO KEEP THE REST OF THE INCOMING RINGSLINGERS OUTTA YER GRIP...
IT'S CALLED SELF-SACRIFICE, YA ANCIENT BLUE BASTARDS--LIVE IT--LEARN IT.

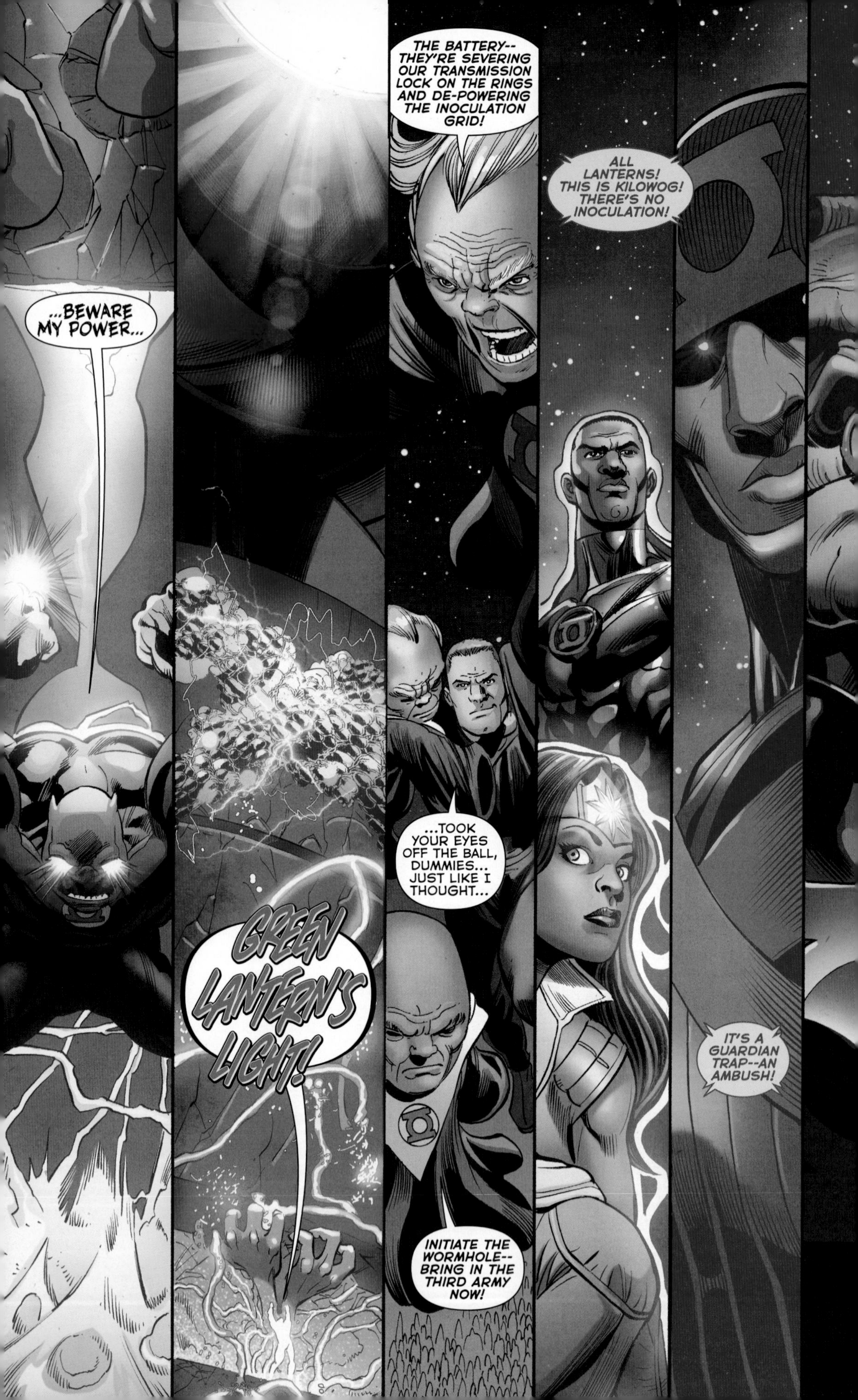
...BEWARE MY POWER...
GREEN LANTERN'S LIGHT!
THE BATTERY-- THEY'RE SEVERING OUR TRANSMISSION LOCK ON THE RINGS AND DE-POWERING THE INOCULATION GRID!
...TOOK YOUR EYES OFF THE BALL, DUMMIES... JUST LIKE I THOUGHT...
INITIATE THE WORMHOLE-- BRING IN THE THIRD ARMY NOW!
ALL LANTERNS! THIS IS KILOWOG! THERE'S NO INOCULATION!
IT'S A GUARDIAN TRAP--AN AMBUSH!

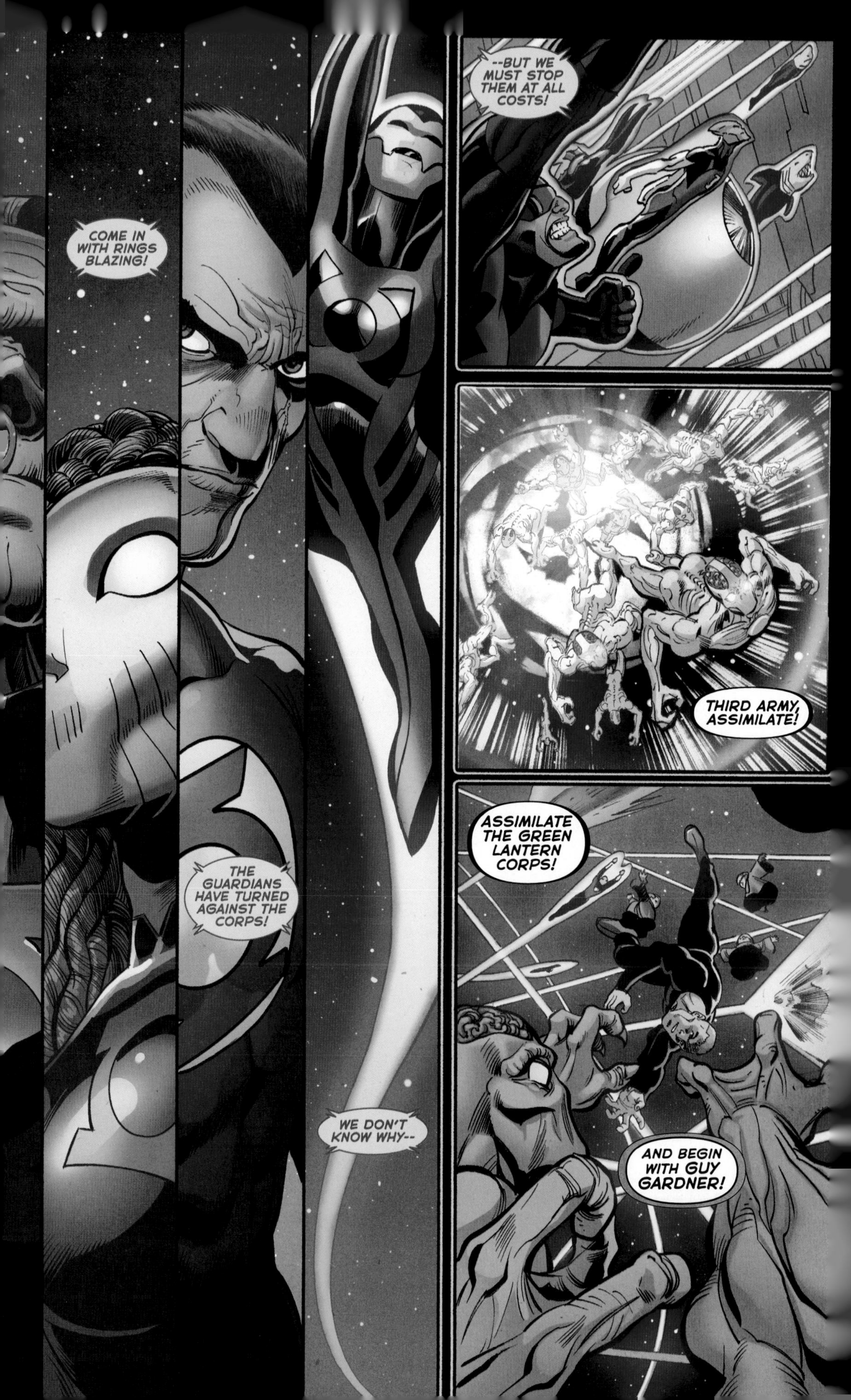
COME IN WITH RINGS BLAZING!
THE GUARDIANS HAVE TURNED AGAINST THE CORPS!
WE DON'T KNOW WHY--
--BUT WE MUST STOP THEM AT ALL COSTS!
THIRD ARMY, ASSIMILATE!
ASSIMILATE THE GREEN LANTERN CORPS!
AND BEGIN WITH GUY GARDNER!

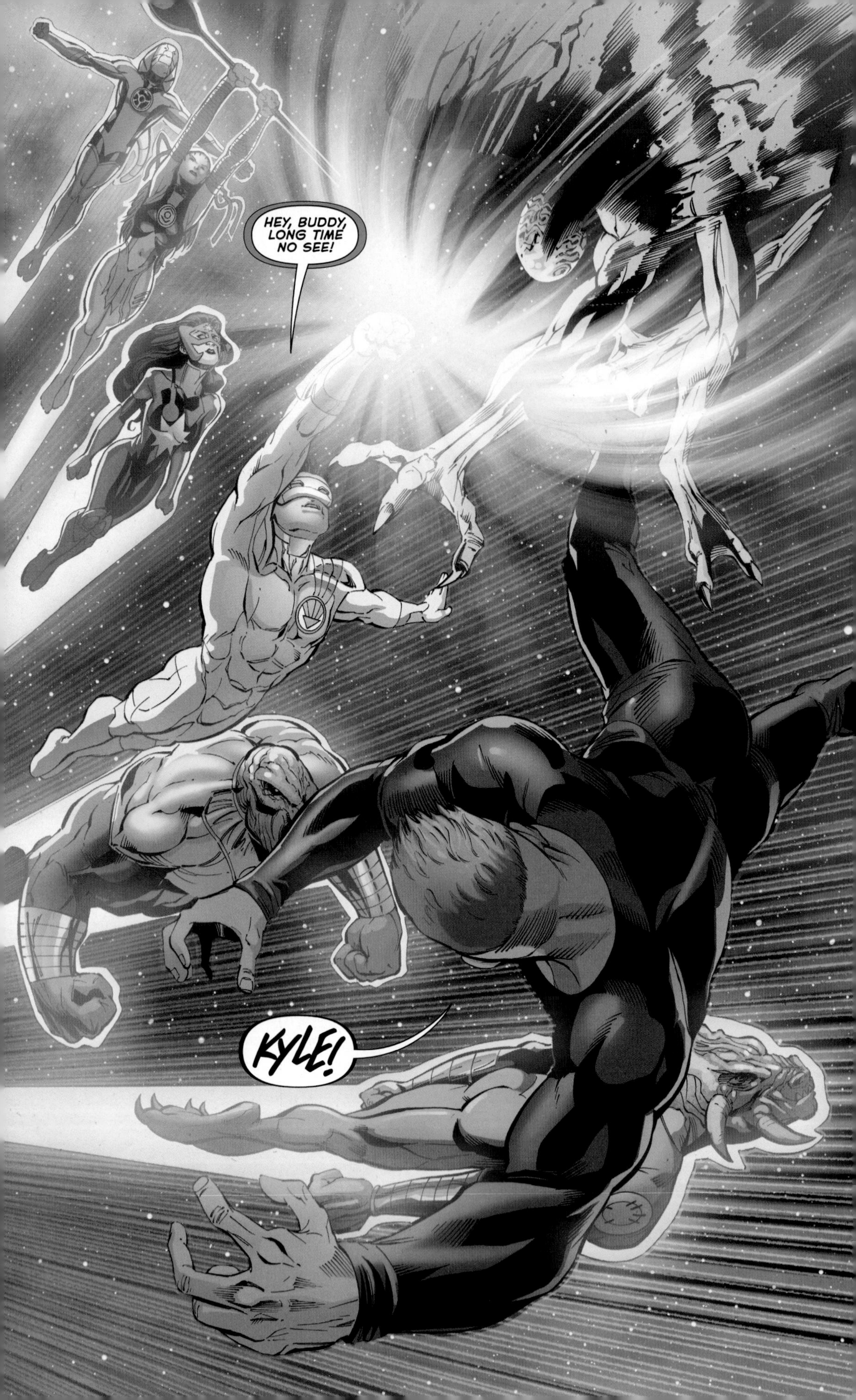
HEY, BUDDY, LONG TIME NO SEE!
KYLE!

FIRST AGAINST KRONA AND NOW HERE--ALWAYS SEEM TO BE CATCHING YOU BEFORE YOU GO SPLAT, GUY.

YOUR LIFE SIGNS ARE STRONG, YOU'LL BE OKAY.

YOU'RE JUST MY SHINING *WHITE* KNIGHT, KYLE, OL' BOY.

AND SPEAKING OF WHITE, WHAT THE HELL ARE YOU WEARING?

I'LL EXPLAIN LATER. WHERE'S YOUR RING?

"TRAPPED IN THE FOUNDRY."

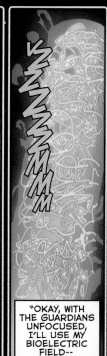

"OKAY, WITH THE GUARDIANS UNFOCUSED, I'LL USE MY BIOELECTRIC FIELD--

"--TO UNLEASH THE RINGS!"

ARE YOU SUICIDAL--TAKING ON GUARDIANS AND THESE CREATURES WITHOUT A RING?!

SEEMED LIKE A GOOD IDEA AT THE TIME!

I LIKE THE BLACK JUMPSUIT. ALL THAT'S MISSING IS A BLACK LANTERN SYMBOL.

C'MON, KYLE, YOU KNOW MY *FAVORITE* COLOR'S--

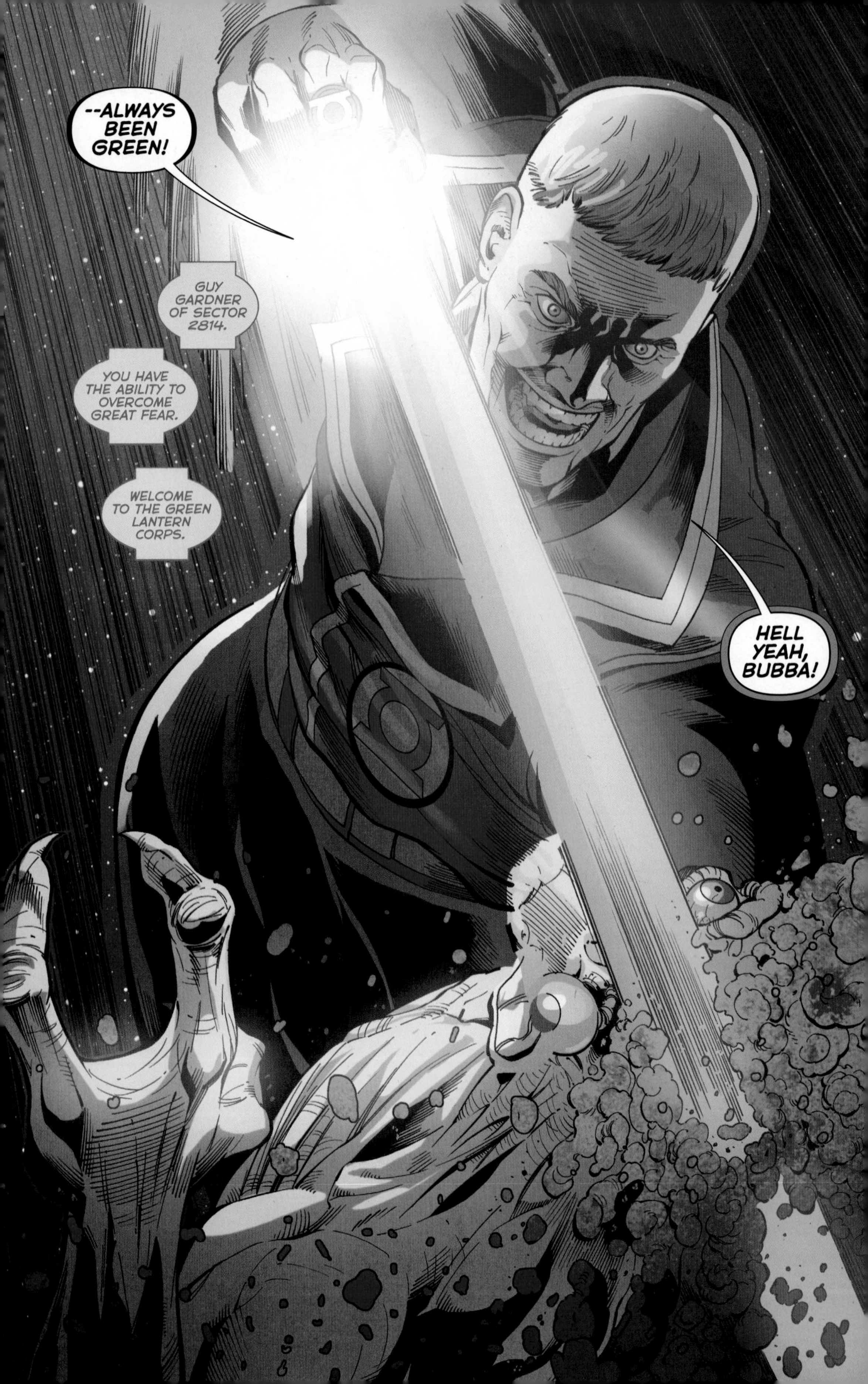
--ALWAYS BEEN GREEN!
GUY GARDNER OF SECTOR 2814.
YOU HAVE THE ABILITY TO OVERCOME GREAT FEAR.
WELCOME TO THE GREEN LANTERN CORPS.
HELL YEAH, BUBBA!

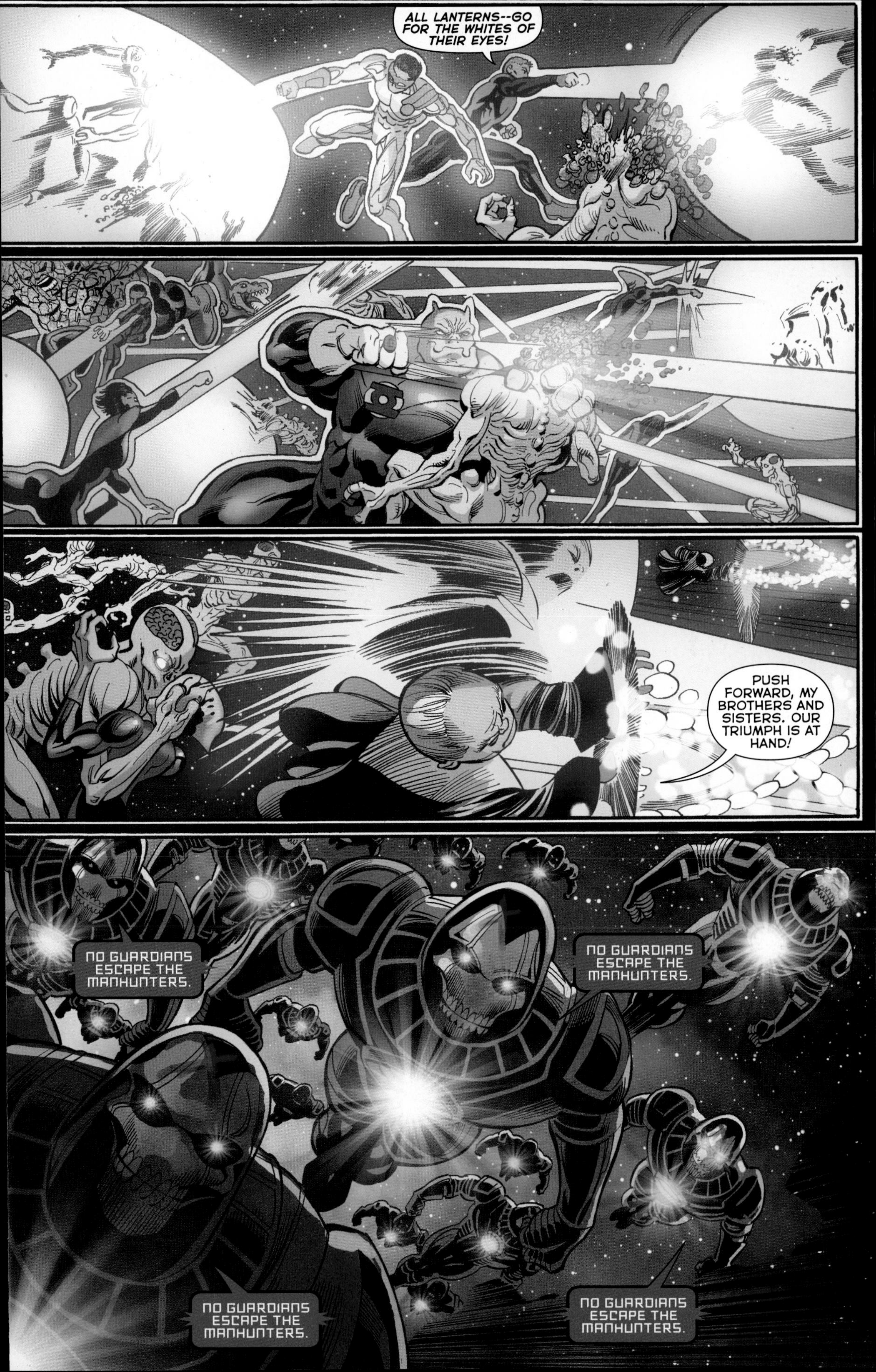
ALL LANTERNS--GO FOR THE WHITES OF THEIR EYES!
PUSH FORWARD, MY BROTHERS AND SISTERS. OUR TRIUMPH IS AT HAND!
NO GUARDIANS ESCAPE THE MANHUNTERS.
NO GUARDIANS ESCAPE THE MANHUNTERS.
NO GUARDIANS ESCAPE THE MANHUNTERS.
NO GUARDIANS ESCAPE THE MANHUNTERS.

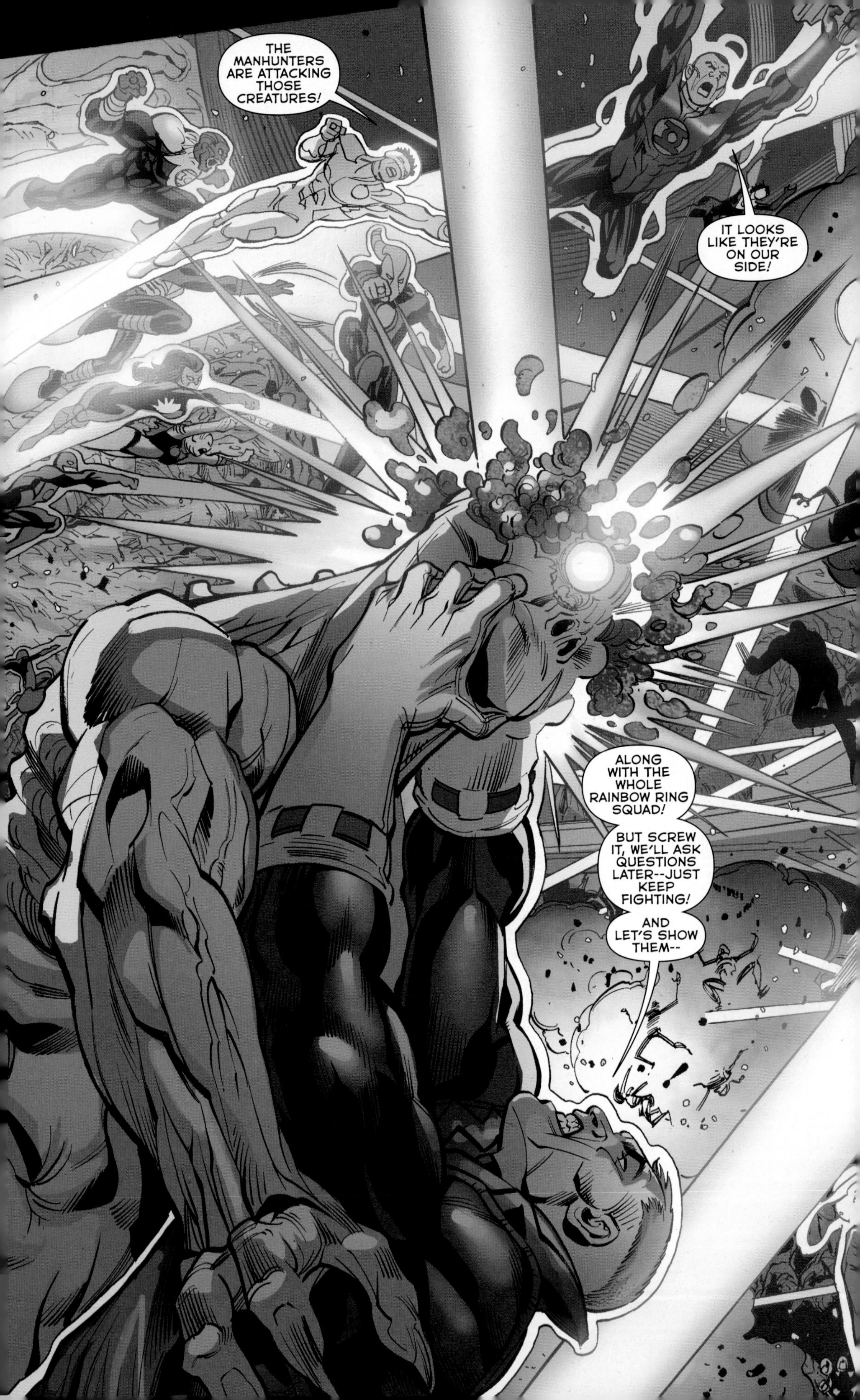
THE MANHUNTERS ARE ATTACKING THOSE CREATURES!
IT LOOKS LIKE THEY'RE ON OUR SIDE!
ALONG WITH THE WHOLE RAINBOW RING SQUAD!
BUT SCREW IT, WE'LL ASK QUESTIONS LATER--JUST KEEP FIGHTING!
AND LET'S SHOW THEM--

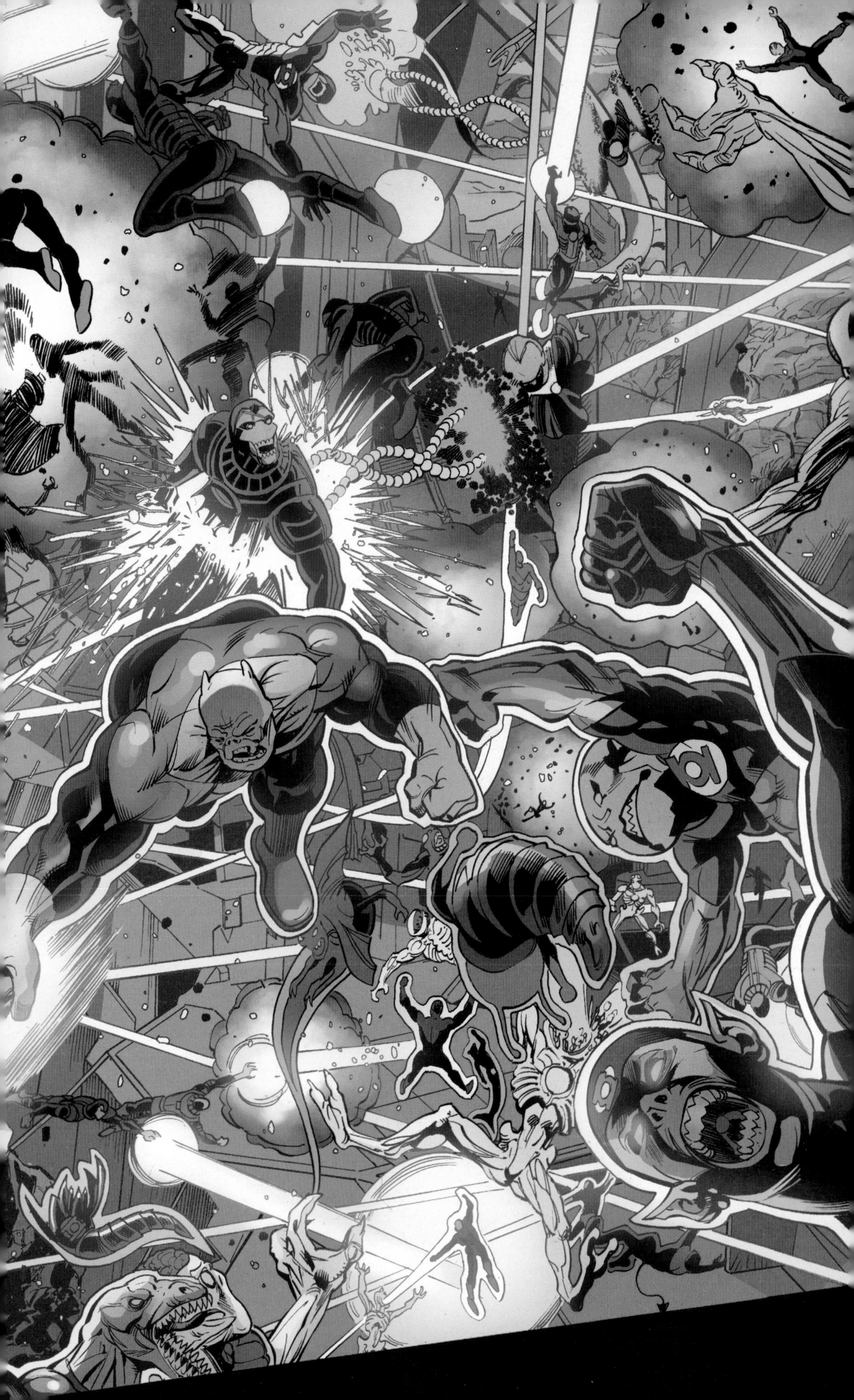

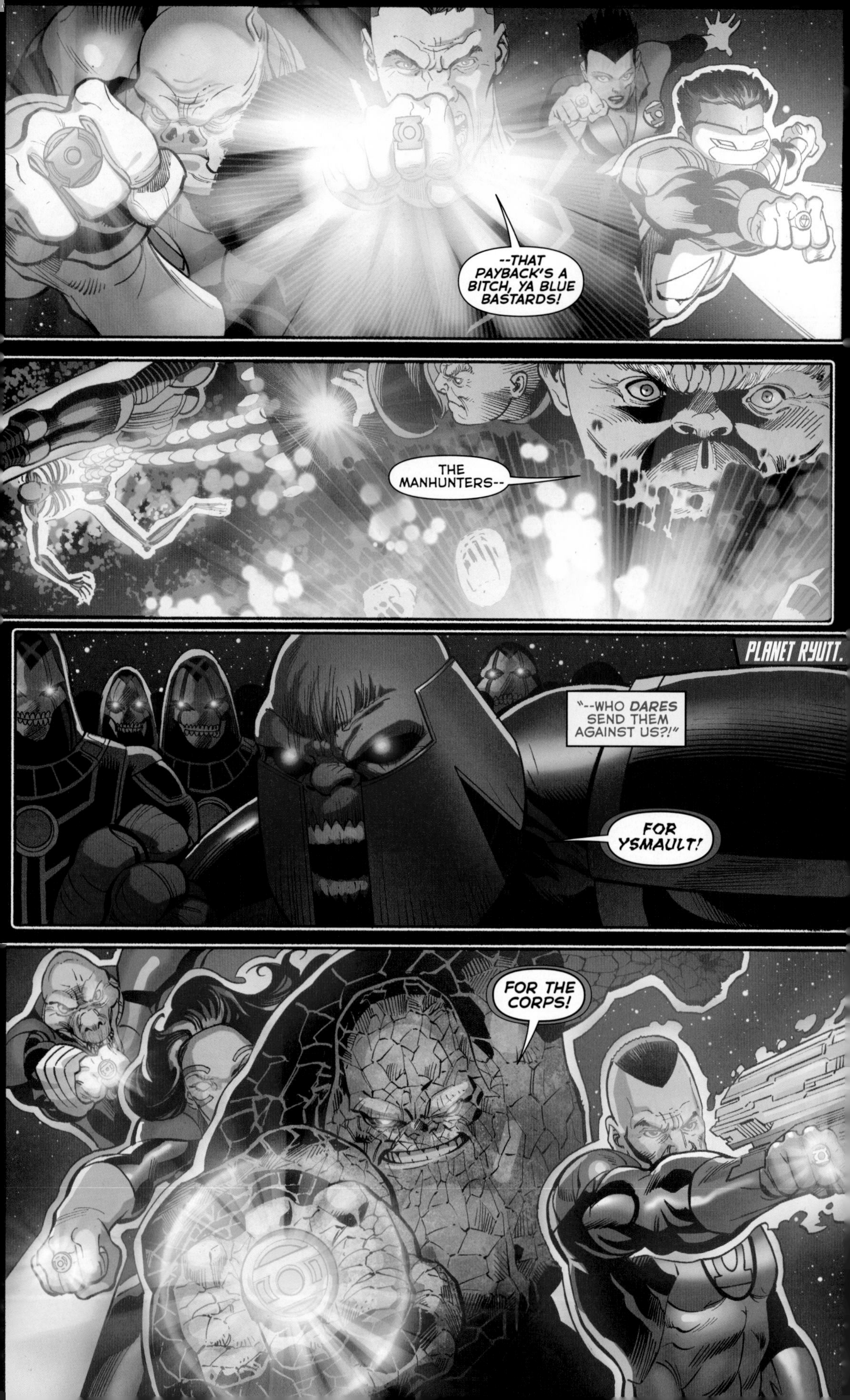
--THAT PAYBACK'S A BITCH, YA BLUE BASTARDS!
THE MANHUNTERS--
PLANET RYUTT.
"--WHO DARES SEND THEM AGAINST US?!"
FOR YSMAULT!
FOR THE CORPS!

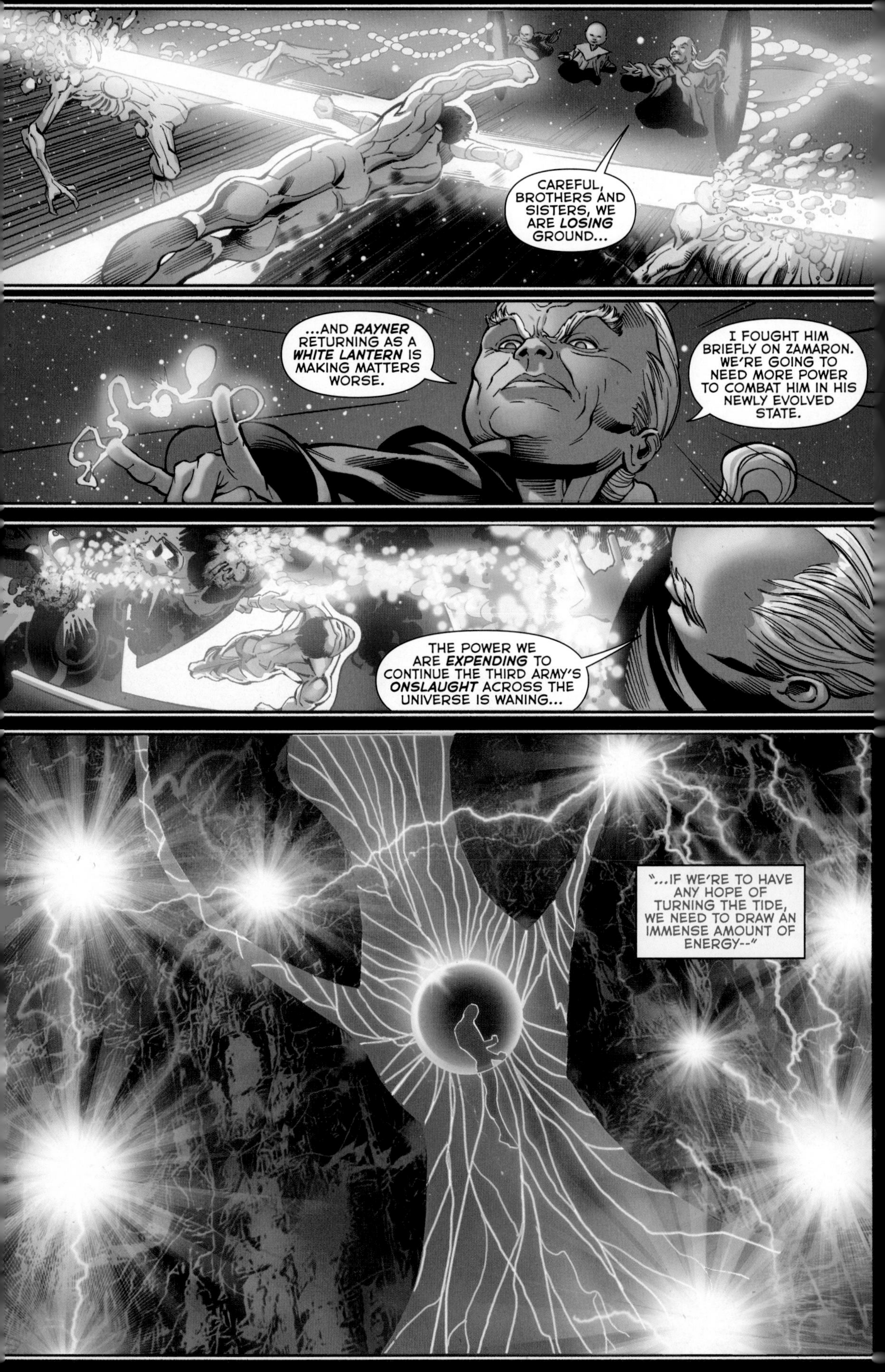
CAREFUL, BROTHERS AND SISTERS, WE ARE LOSING GROUND...
...AND RAYNER RETURNING AS A WHITE LANTERN IS MAKING MATTERS WORSE.
I FOUGHT HIM BRIEFLY ON ZAMARON. WE'RE GOING TO NEED MORE POWER TO COMBAT HIM IN HIS NEWLY EVOLVED STATE.
THE POWER WE ARE EXPENDING TO CONTINUE THE THIRD ARMY'S ONSLAUGHT ACROSS THE UNIVERSE IS WANING...
"...IF WE'RE TO HAVE ANY HOPE OF TURNING THE TIDE, WE NEED TO DRAW AN IMMENSE AMOUNT OF ENERGY--"

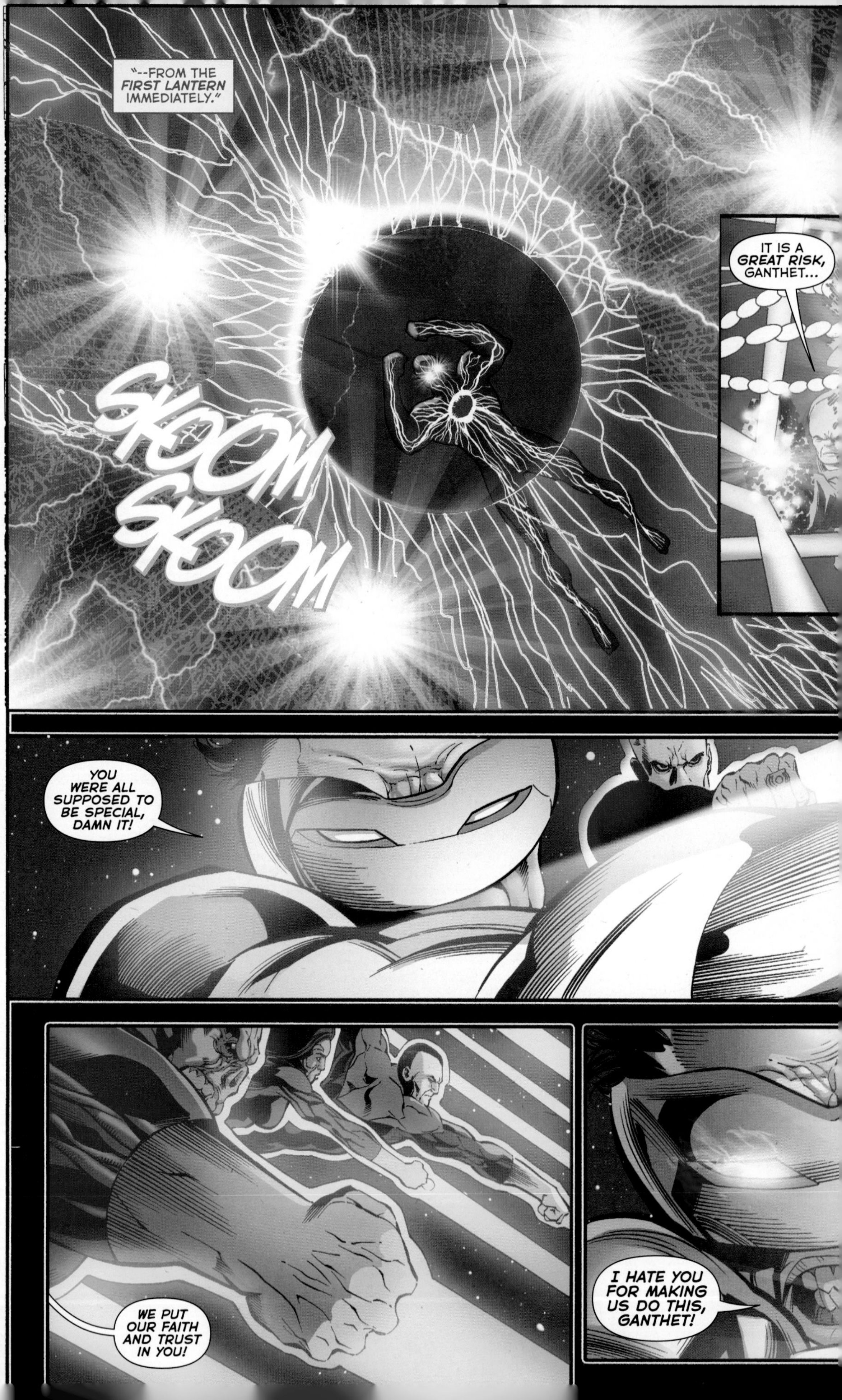
"--FROM THE FIRST LANTERN IMMEDIATELY."
SKOOM SKOOM
IT IS A GREAT RISK, GANTHET...
YOU WERE ALL SUPPOSED TO BE SPECIAL, DAMN IT!
WE PUT OUR FAITH AND TRUST IN YOU!
I HATE YOU FOR MAKING US DO THIS, GANTHET!

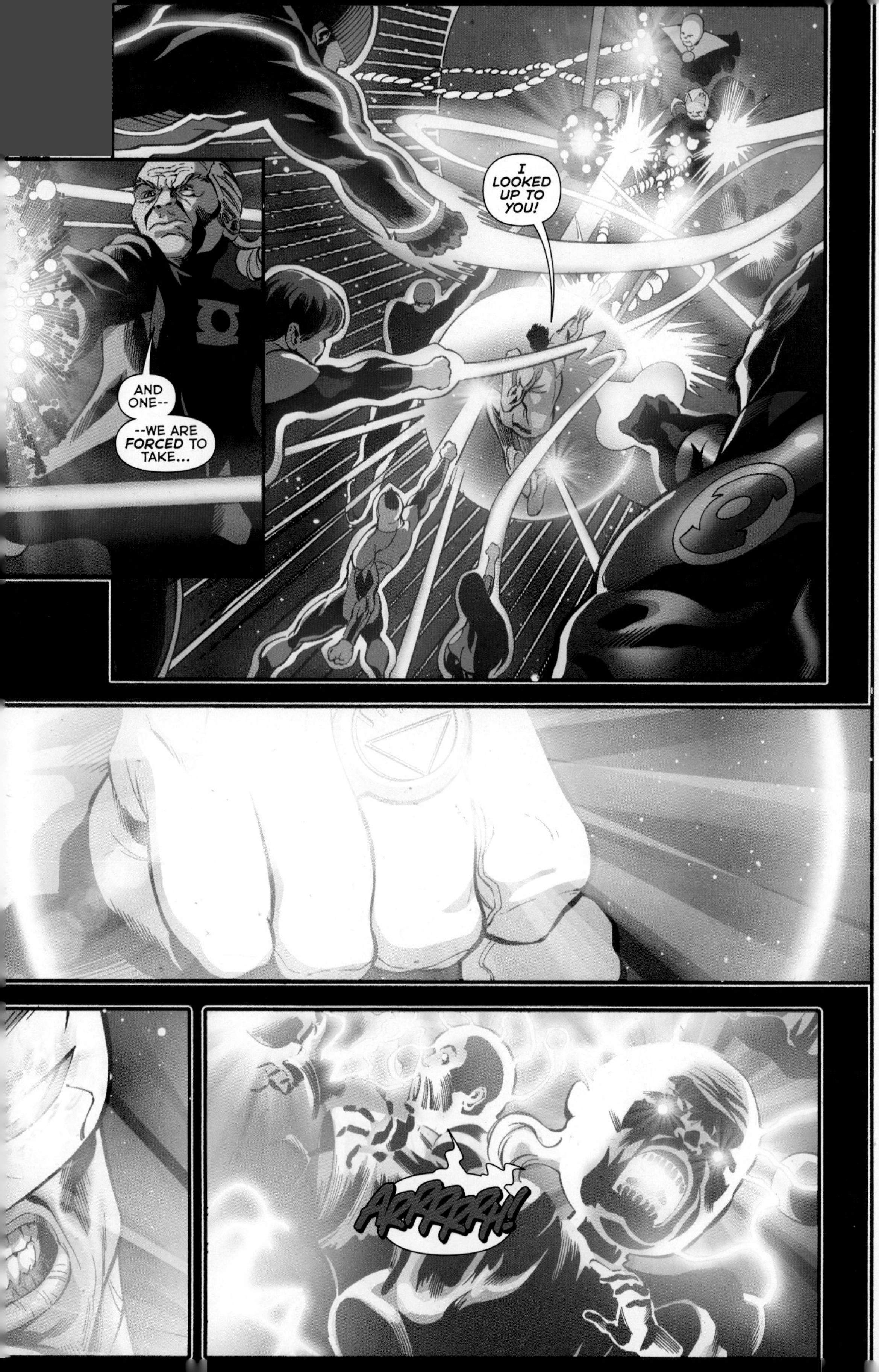
I LOOKED UP TO YOU!
AND ONE--
--WE ARE FORCED TO TAKE...
ARRRRRGH!

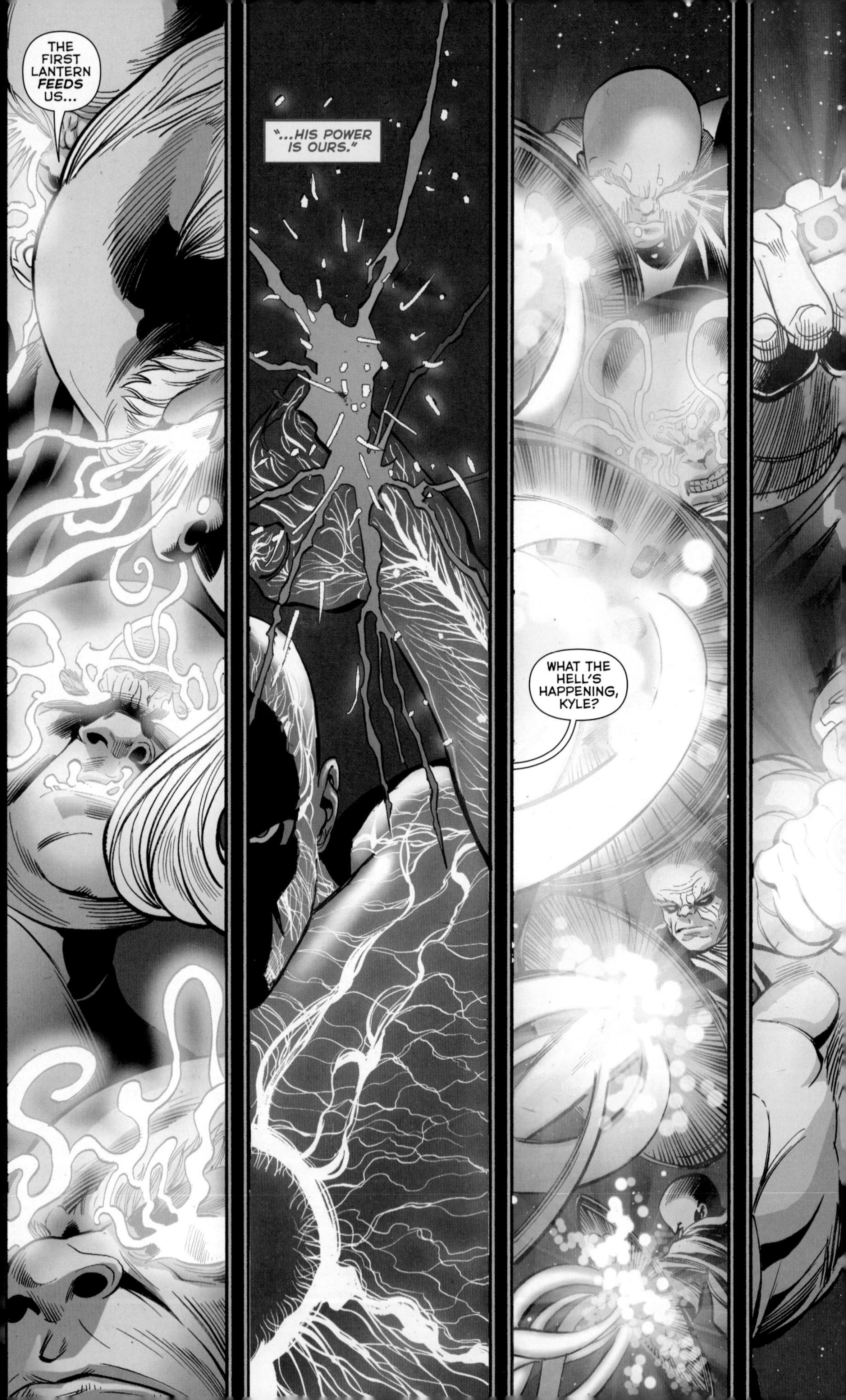
THE FIRST LANTERN FEEDS US...
"...HIS POWER IS OURS."
WHAT THE HELL'S HAPPENING, KYLE?

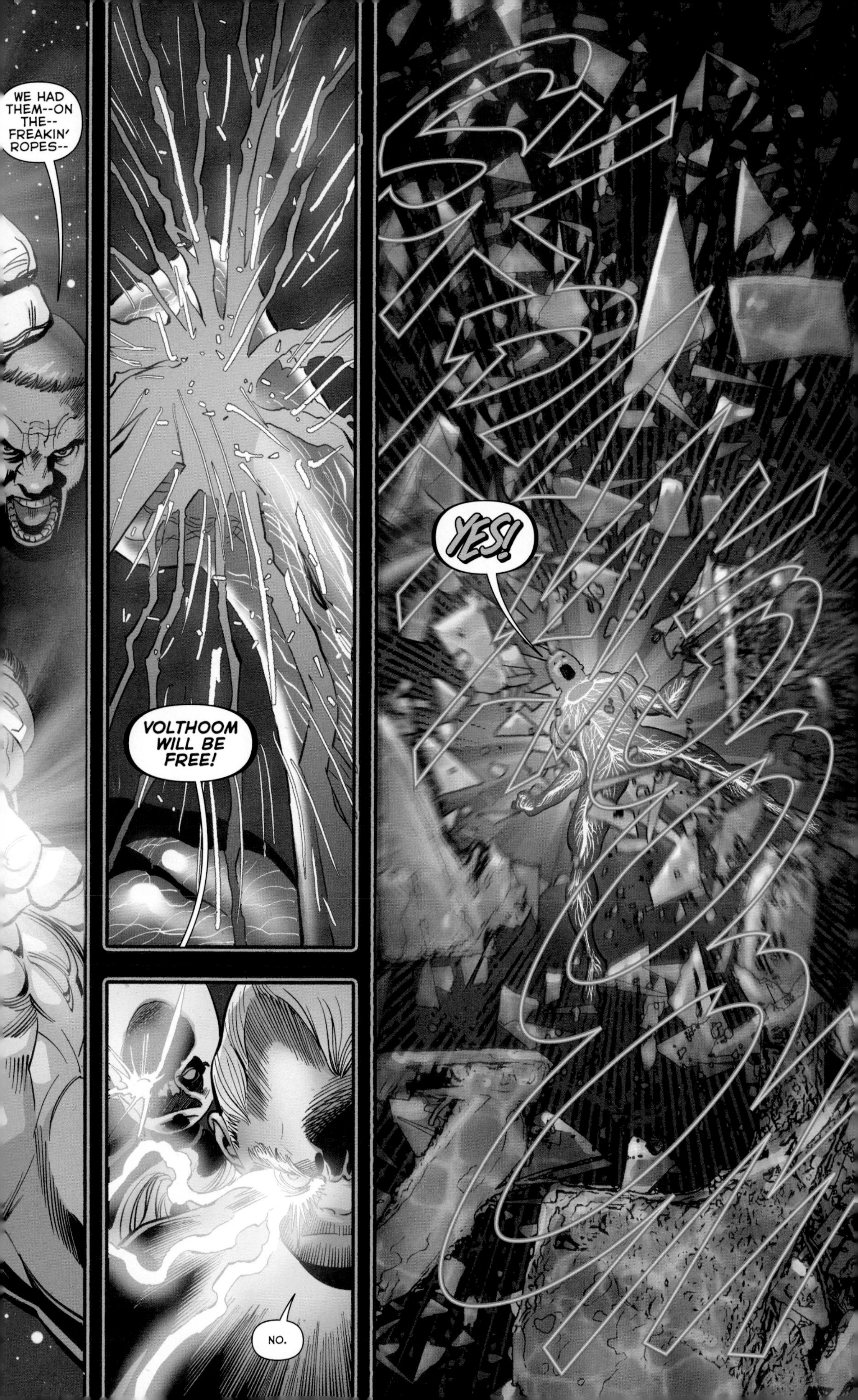
WE HAD THEM--ON THE--FREAKIN' ROPES--
VOLTHOOM WILL BE FREE!
NO.
YES!

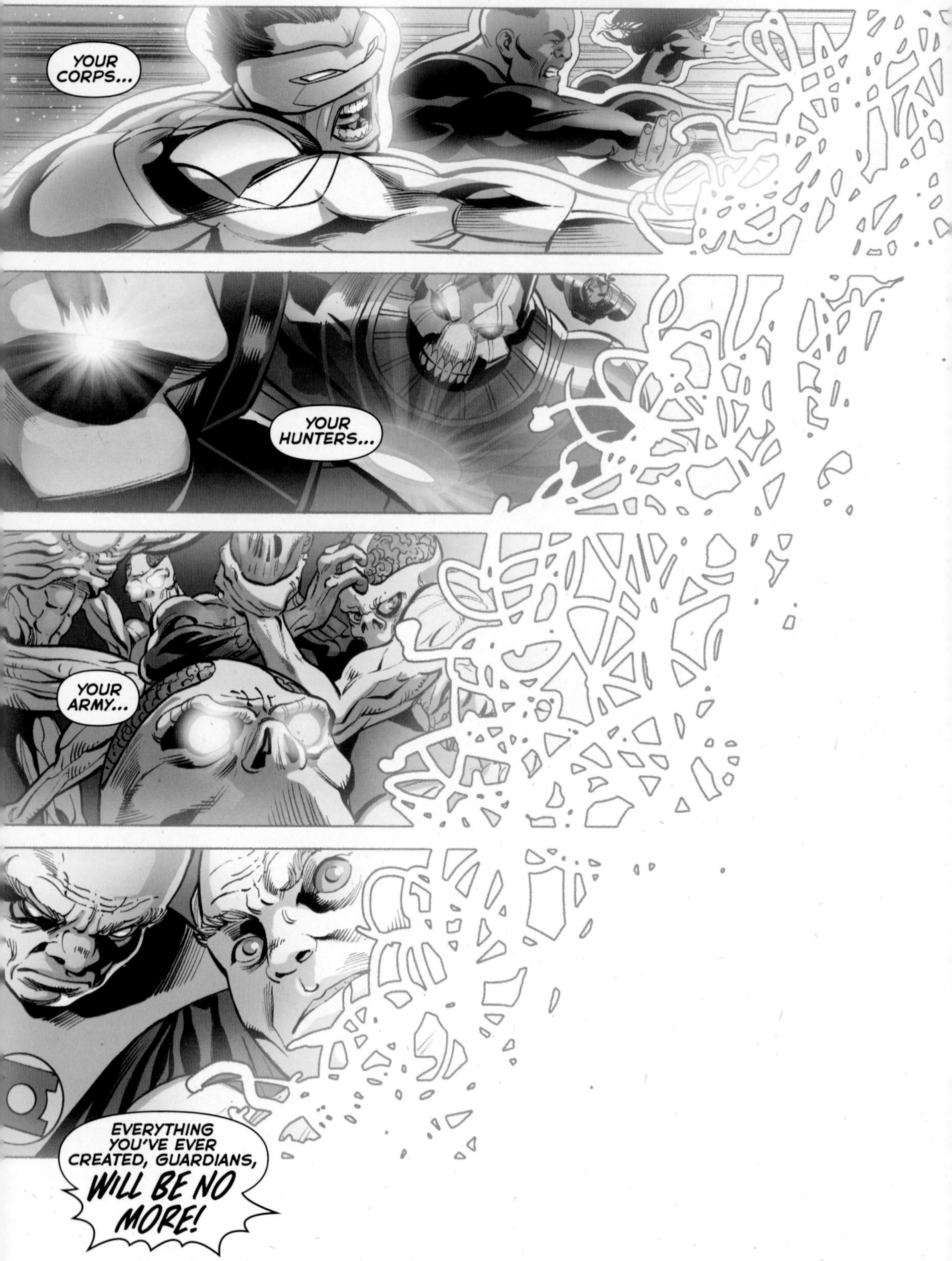
YOUR CORPS...
YOUR HUNTERS...
YOUR ARMY...
EVERYTHING YOU'VE EVER CREATED, GUARDIANS, WILL BE NO MORE!

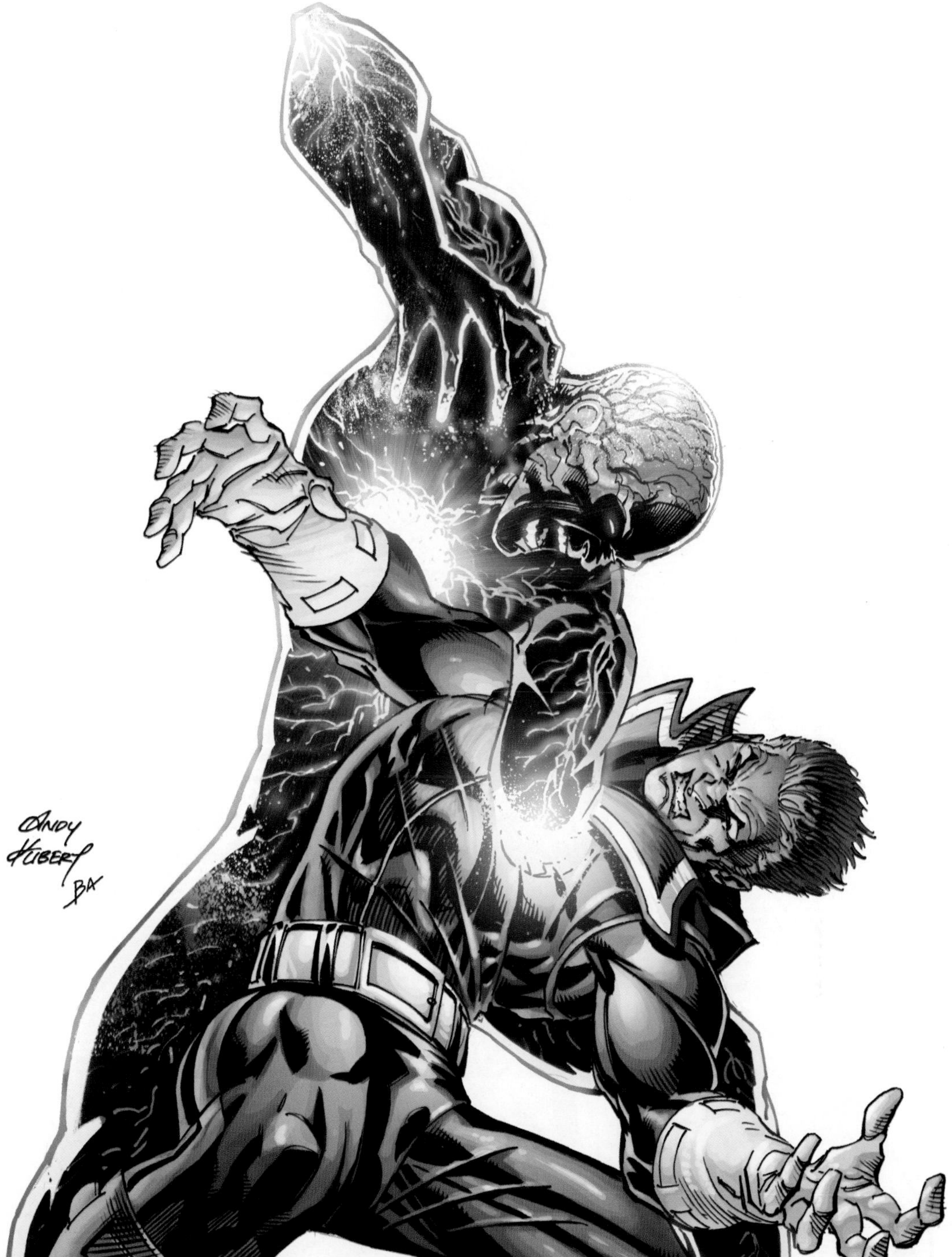
ANDY KUBERT BA

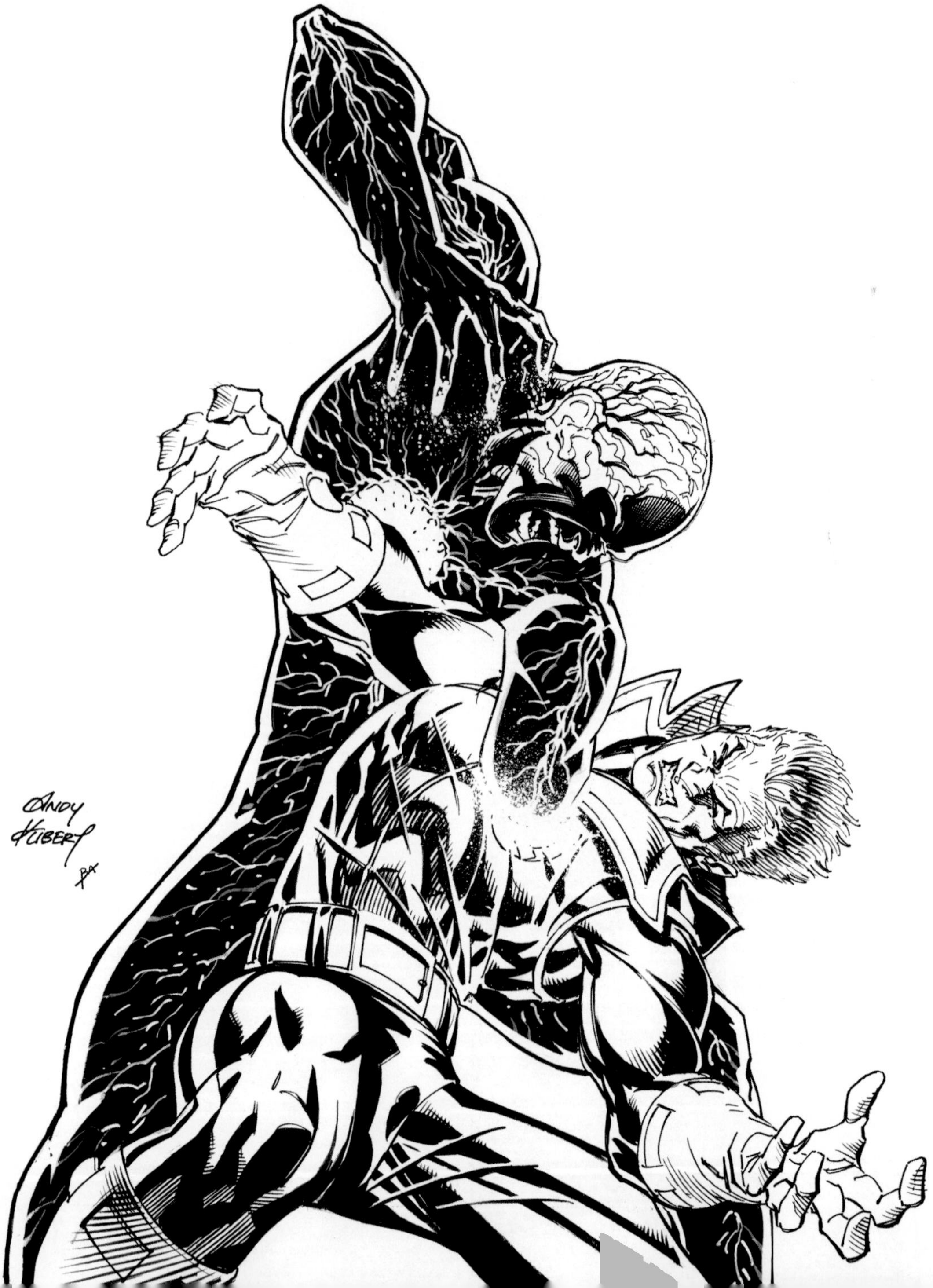

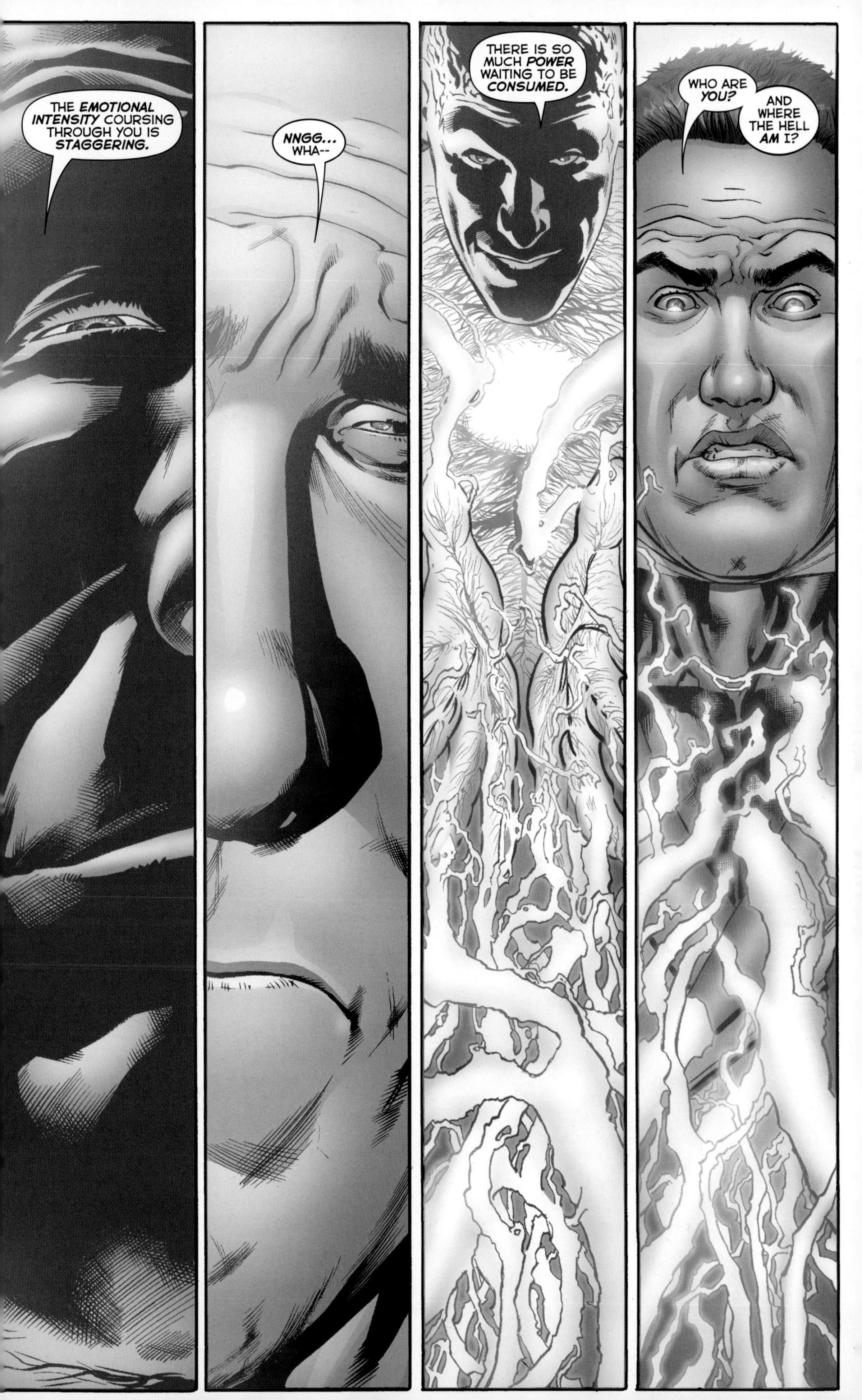
THE *EMOTIONAL INTENSITY* COURSING THROUGH YOU IS *STAGGERING.*
NNGG... WHA--
THERE IS SO MUCH *POWER* WAITING TO BE *CONSUMED.*
WHO ARE *YOU?*
AND WHERE THE HELL *AM* I?

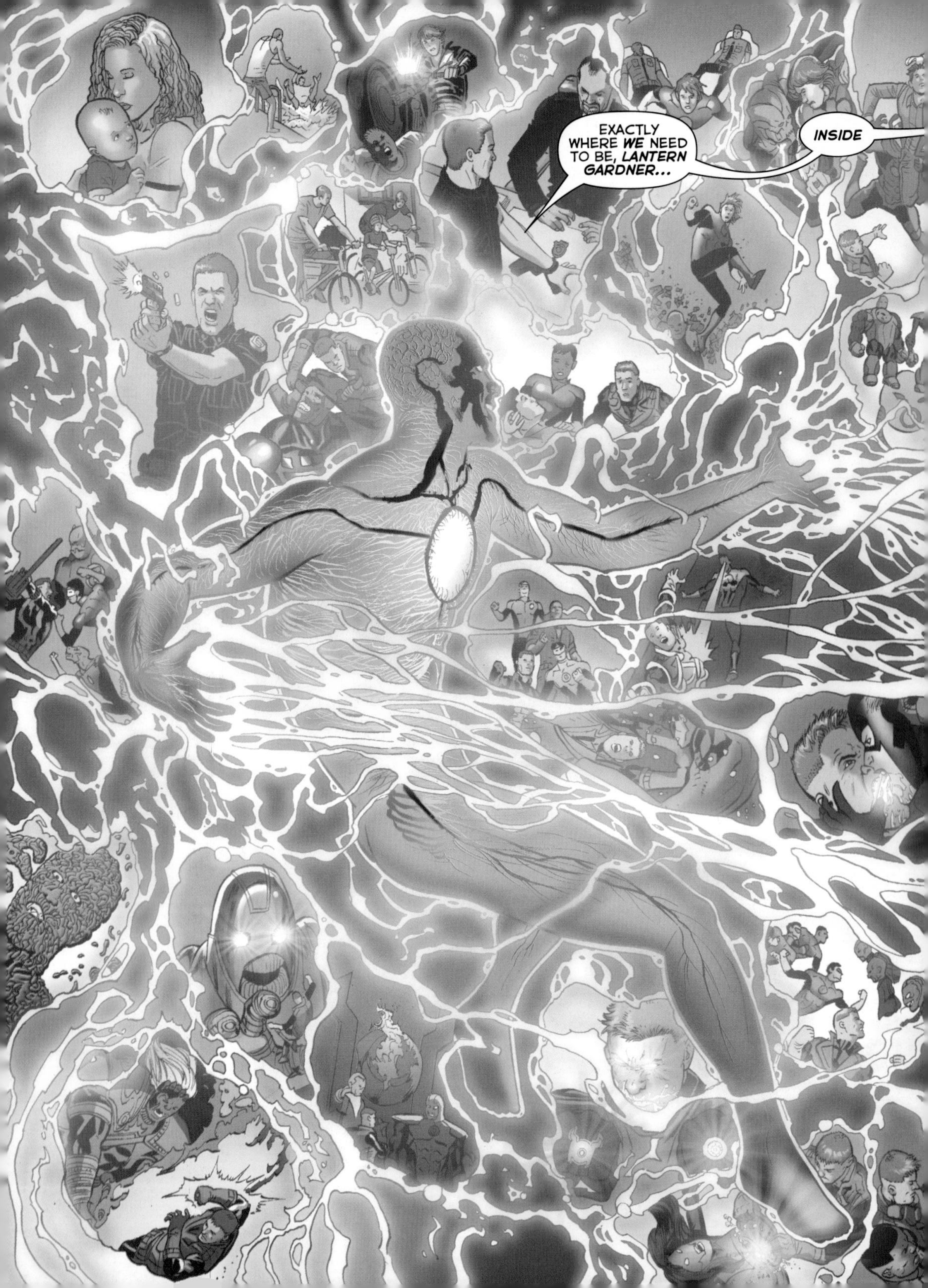
EXACTLY WHERE WE NEED TO BE, LANTERN GARDNER...
INSIDE

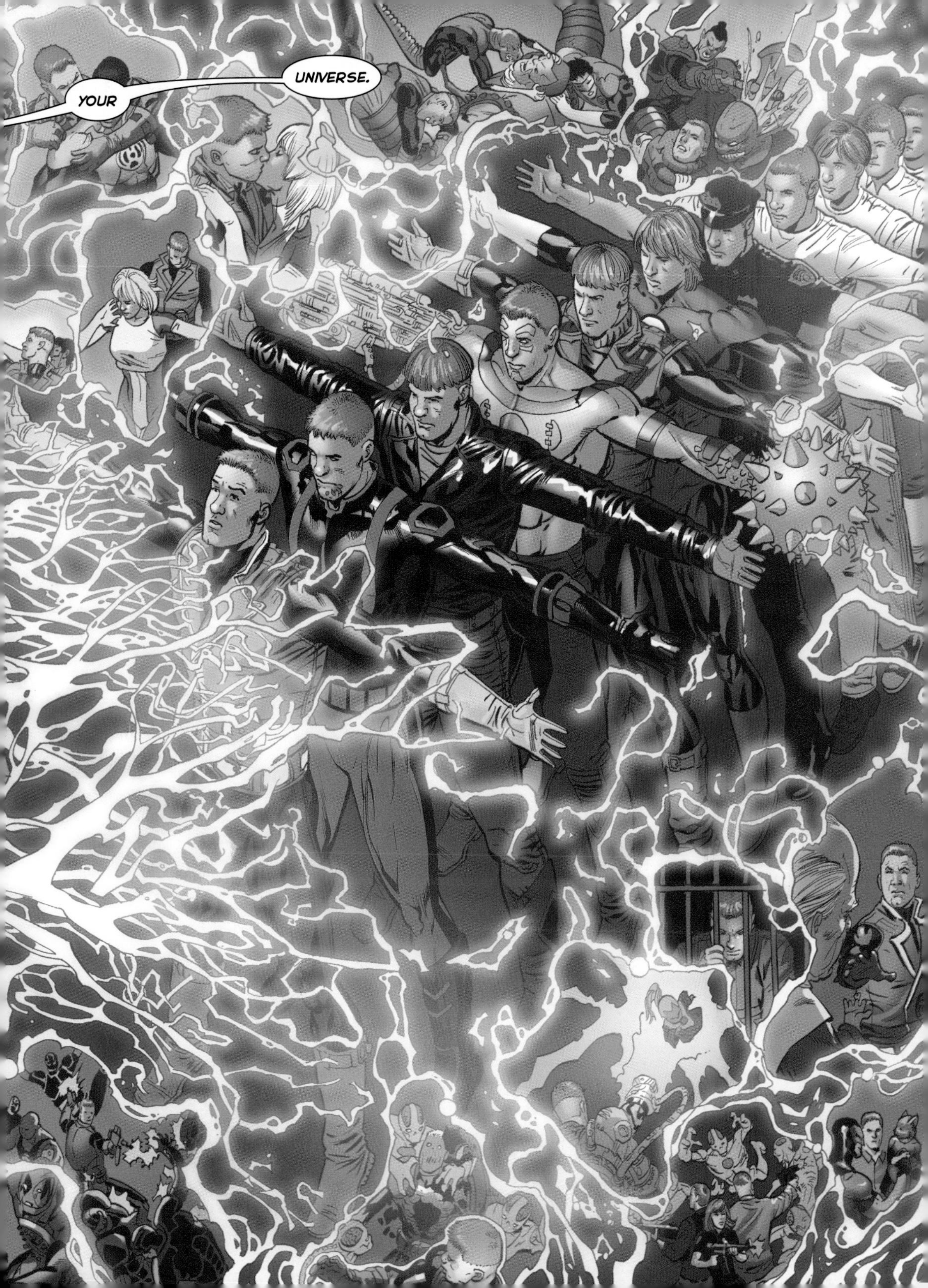

YOUR
UNIVERSE.

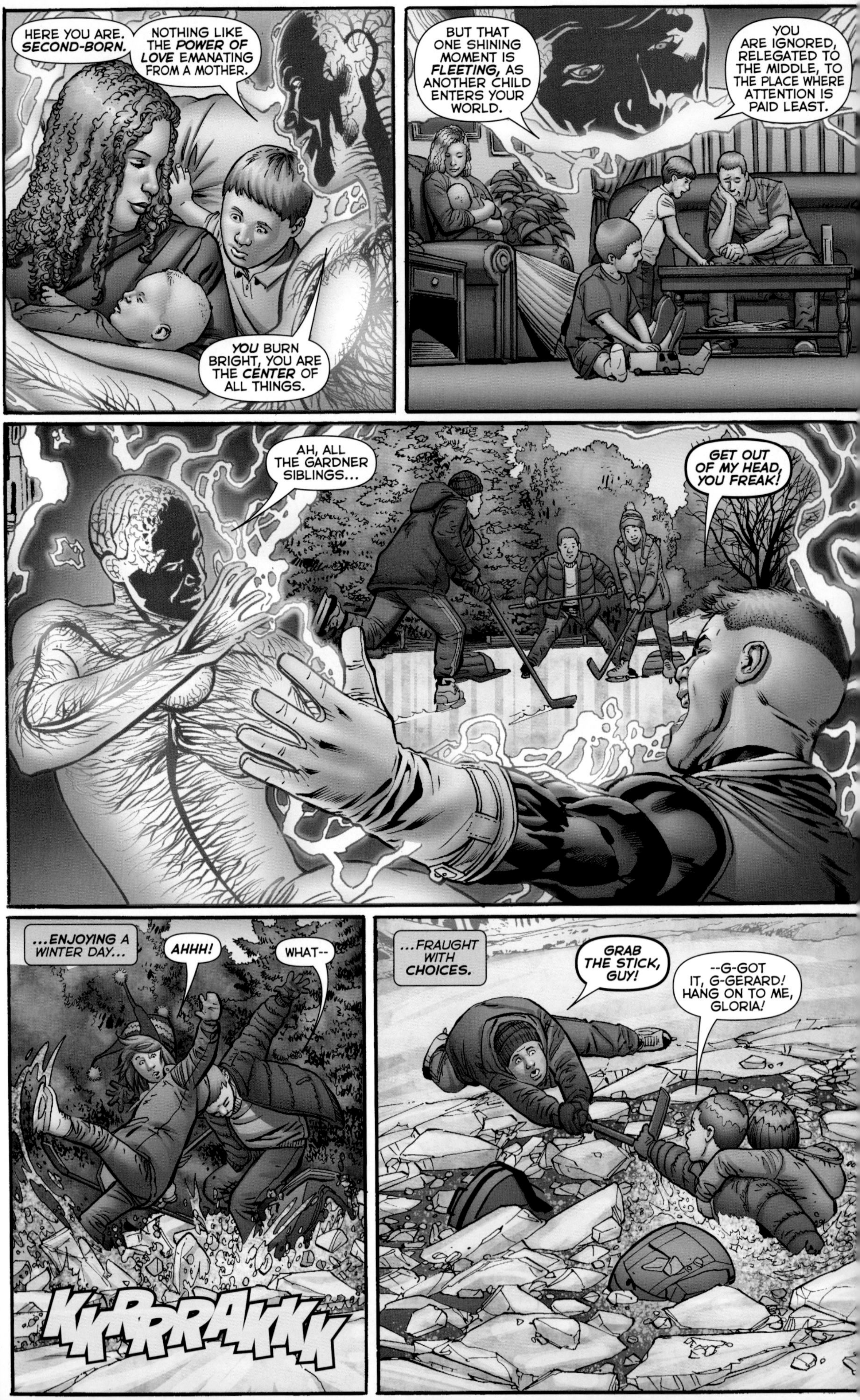
HERE YOU ARE. SECOND-BORN.
NOTHING LIKE THE POWER OF LOVE EMANATING FROM A MOTHER.
YOU BURN BRIGHT, YOU ARE THE CENTER OF ALL THINGS.
BUT THAT ONE SHINING MOMENT IS FLEETING, AS ANOTHER CHILD ENTERS YOUR WORLD.
YOU ARE IGNORED, RELEGATED TO THE MIDDLE, TO THE PLACE WHERE ATTENTION IS PAID LEAST.
AH, ALL THE GARDNER SIBLINGS...
GET OUT OF MY HEAD, YOU FREAK!
...ENJOYING A WINTER DAY...
AHHH!
WHAT--
KKRRRAKKKK
...FRAUGHT WITH CHOICES.
GRAB THE STICK, GUY!
--G-GOT IT, G-GERARD! HANG ON TO ME, GLORIA!

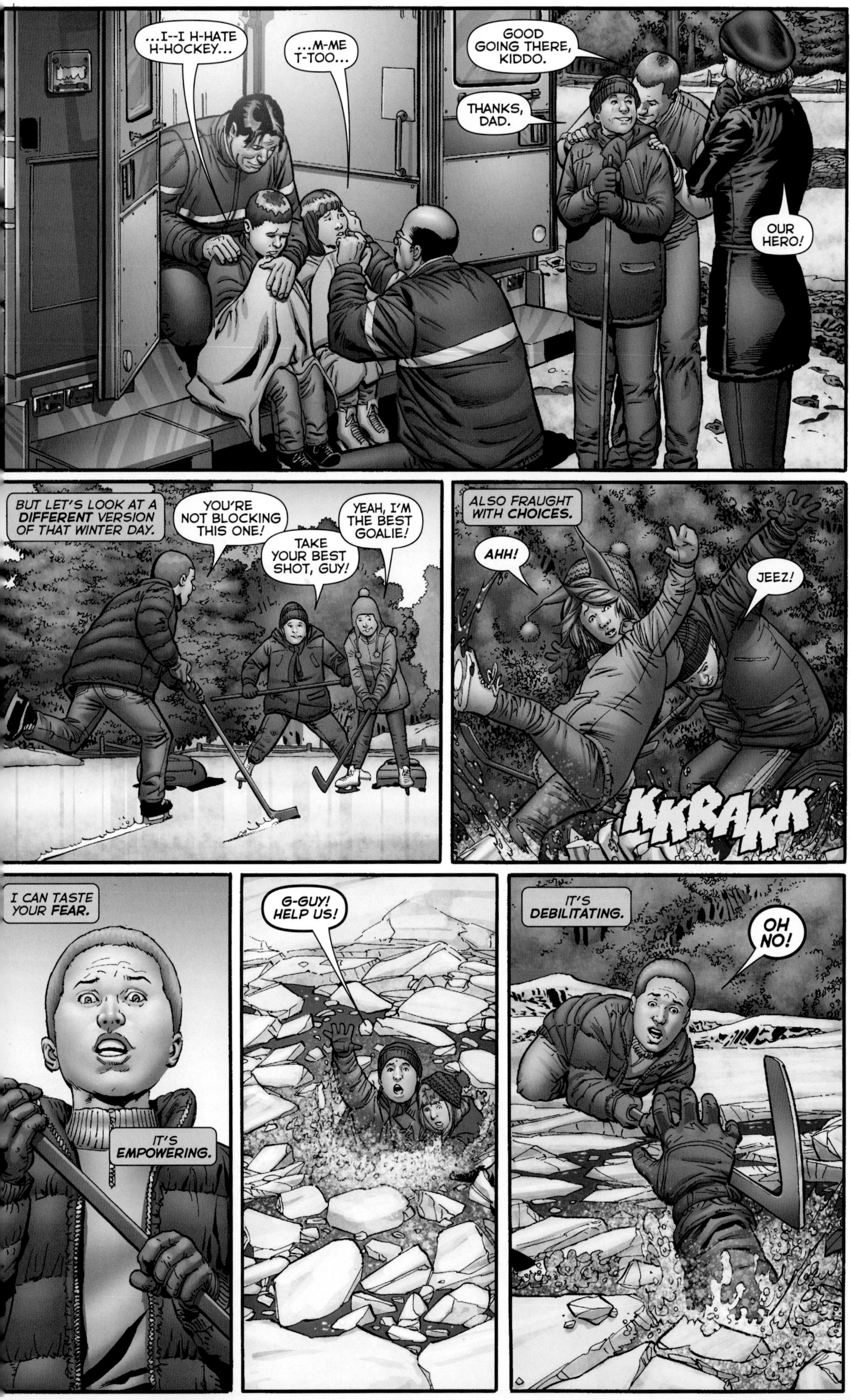
...I--I H-HATE H-HOCKEY...
...M-ME T-TOO...
GOOD GOING THERE, KIDDO.
THANKS, DAD.
OUR HERO!
BUT LET'S LOOK AT A DIFFERENT VERSION OF THAT WINTER DAY.
YOU'RE NOT BLOCKING THIS ONE!
TAKE YOUR BEST SHOT, GUY!
YEAH, I'M THE BEST GOALIE!
ALSO FRAUGHT WITH CHOICES.
AHH!
JEEZ!
KKRAKK
I CAN TASTE YOUR FEAR.
IT'S EMPOWERING.
G-GUY! HELP US!
IT'S DEBILITATING.
OH NO!

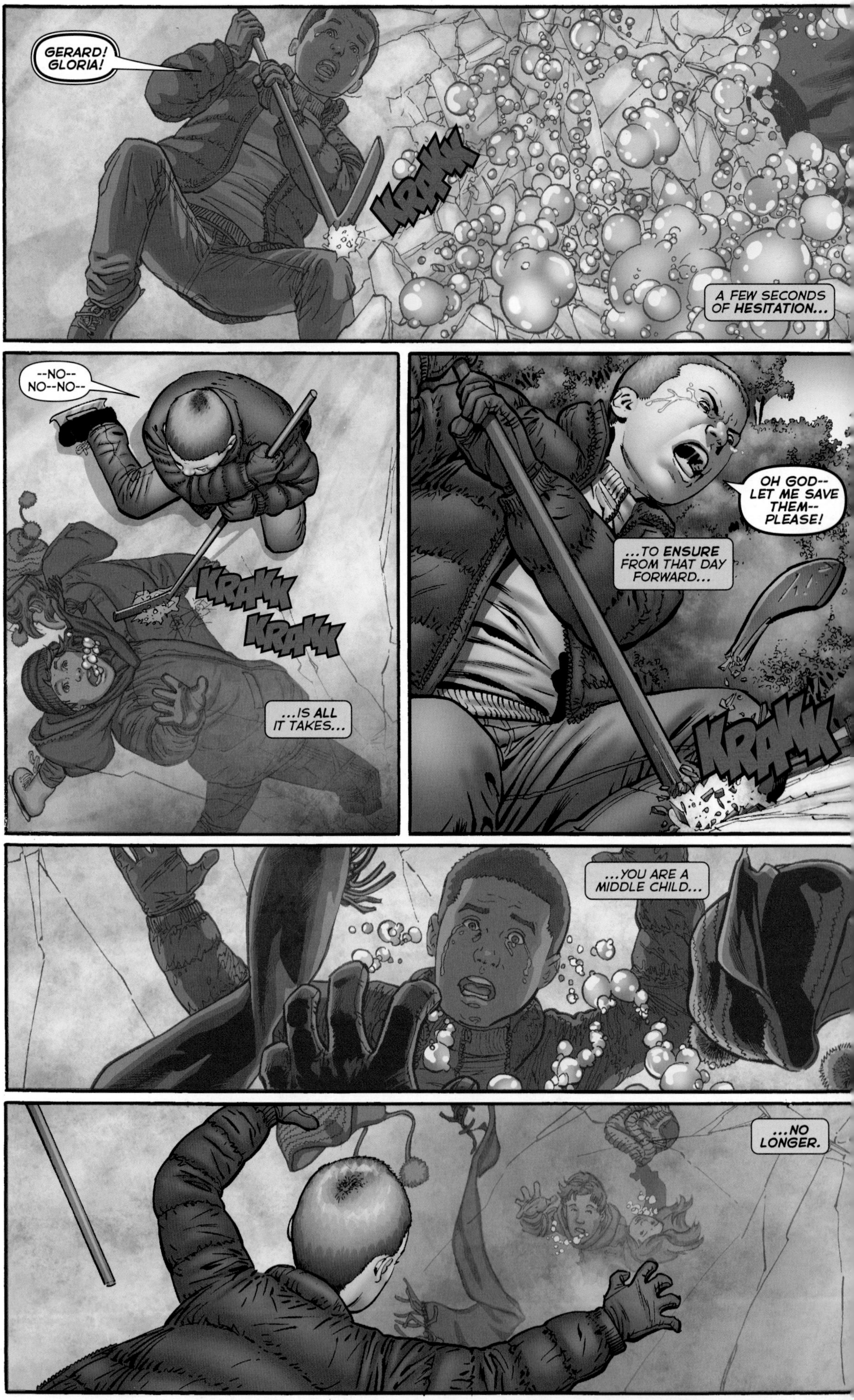
GERARD! GLORIA!
KRAKK
A FEW SECONDS OF HESITATION...
--NO-- NO--NO--
KRAKK
KRAKK
...IS ALL IT TAKES...
OH GOD-- LET ME SAVE THEM-- PLEASE!
...TO ENSURE FROM THAT DAY FORWARD...
KRAKK
...YOU ARE A MIDDLE CHILD...
...NO LONGER.

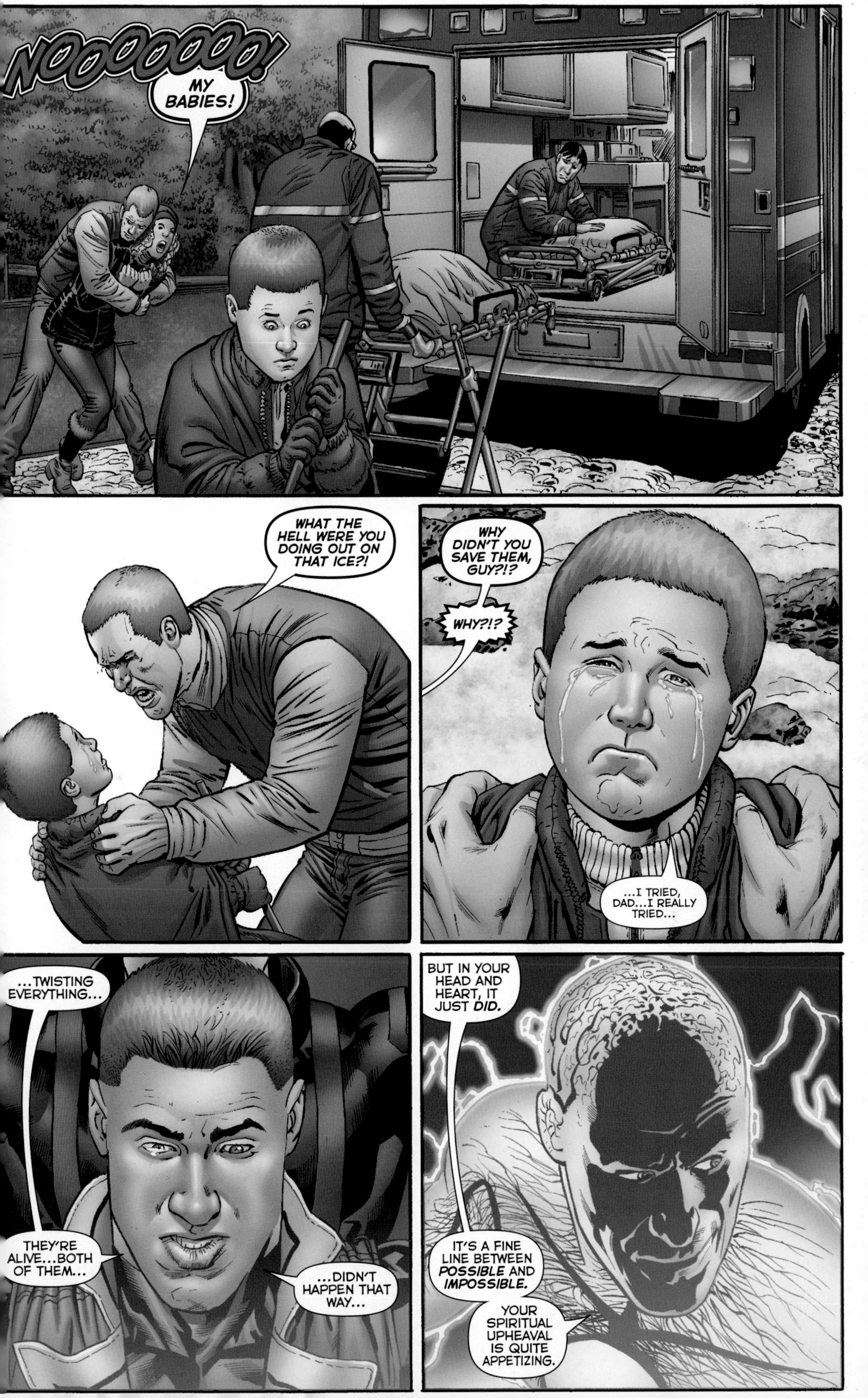
NOOOOOOO!
MY BABIES!
WHAT THE HELL WERE YOU DOING OUT ON THAT ICE?!
WHY DIDN'T YOU SAVE THEM, GUY?!?
WHY?!?
...I TRIED, DAD...I REALLY TRIED...
...TWISTING EVERYTHING...
THEY'RE ALIVE...BOTH OF THEM...
...DIDN'T HAPPEN THAT WAY...
BUT IN YOUR HEAD AND HEART, IT JUST DID.
IT'S A FINE LINE BETWEEN POSSIBLE AND IMPOSSIBLE.
YOUR SPIRITUAL UPHEAVAL IS QUITE APPETIZING.

HMM, LET'S SEE WHAT OTHER *MOMENTS* DEMAND OUR ATTENTION.

RRNN

WHEN I GET OUTTA THIS, I'LL--

--DO NOTHING.

THIS LOOKS FASCINATING.

YOUR THIRD YEAR AS A LAW ENFORCEMENT OFFICIAL.

YOU DO POSSESS A *KEEN* SENSE OF CIVIC DUTY, DON'T YOU?

STAY CLEAR!

OUT OF THE WAY, DAMN IT!

OFFICERS IN PURSUIT--KEY YOUR RADIO!

OFFICER GARDNER HERE!

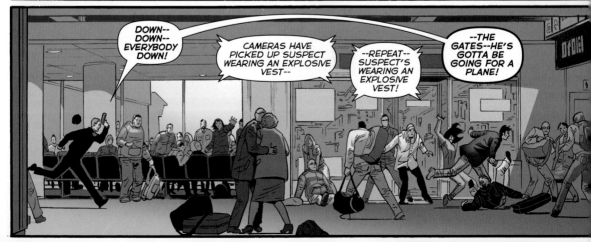

DOWN-- DOWN-- EVERYBODY DOWN!

CAMERAS HAVE PICKED UP SUSPECT WEARING AN EXPLOSIVE VEST--

--REPEAT-- SUSPECT'S WEARING AN EXPLOSIVE VEST!

--THE GATES--HE'S GOTTA BE GOING FOR A PLANE!

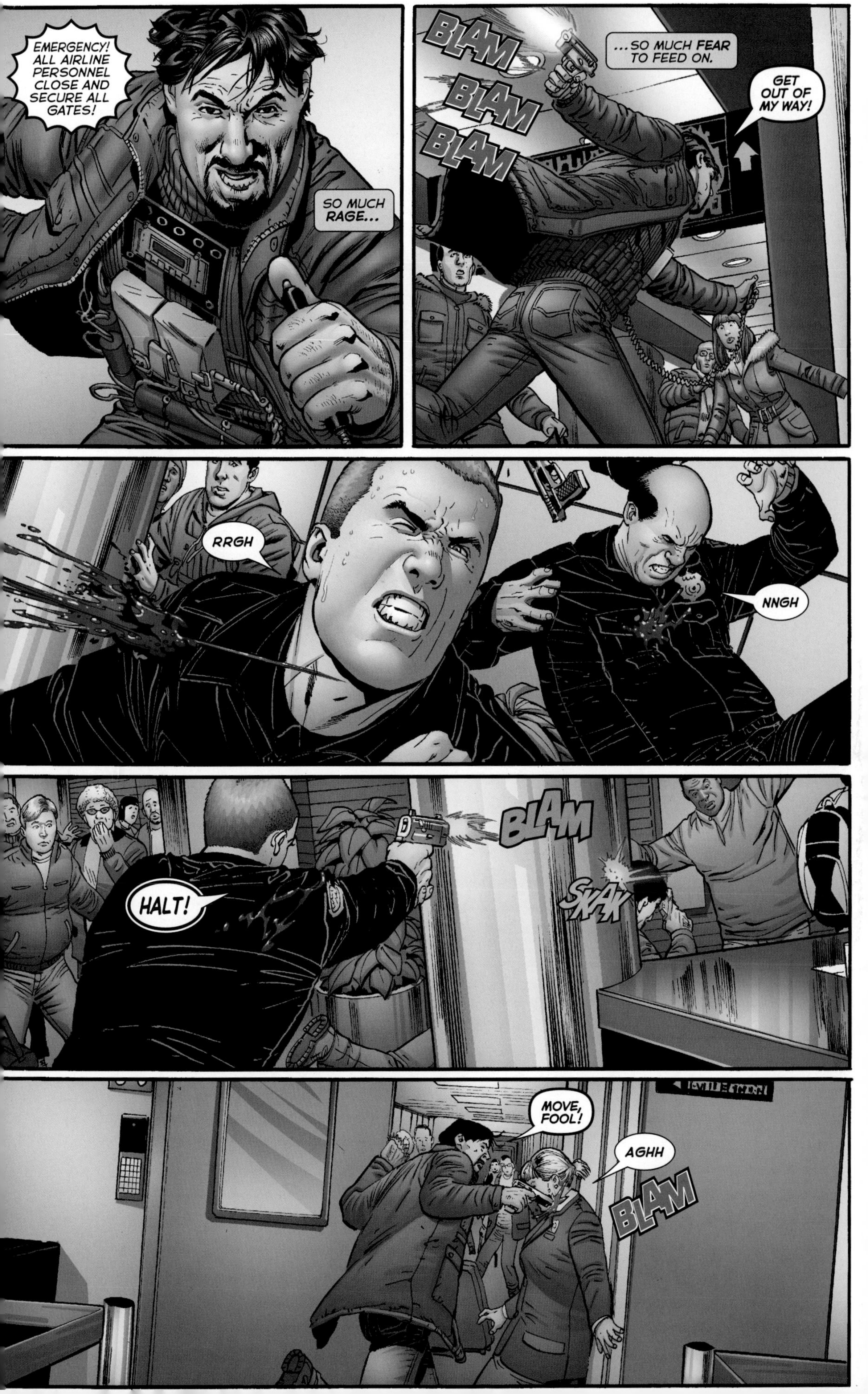
EMERGENCY! ALL AIRLINE PERSONNEL CLOSE AND SECURE ALL GATES!
SO MUCH RAGE...
BLAM
BLAM
BLAM
...SO MUCH FEAR TO FEED ON.
GET OUT OF MY WAY!
RRGH
NNGH
HALT!
BLAM
SKAK
MOVE, FOOL!
AGHH
BLAM

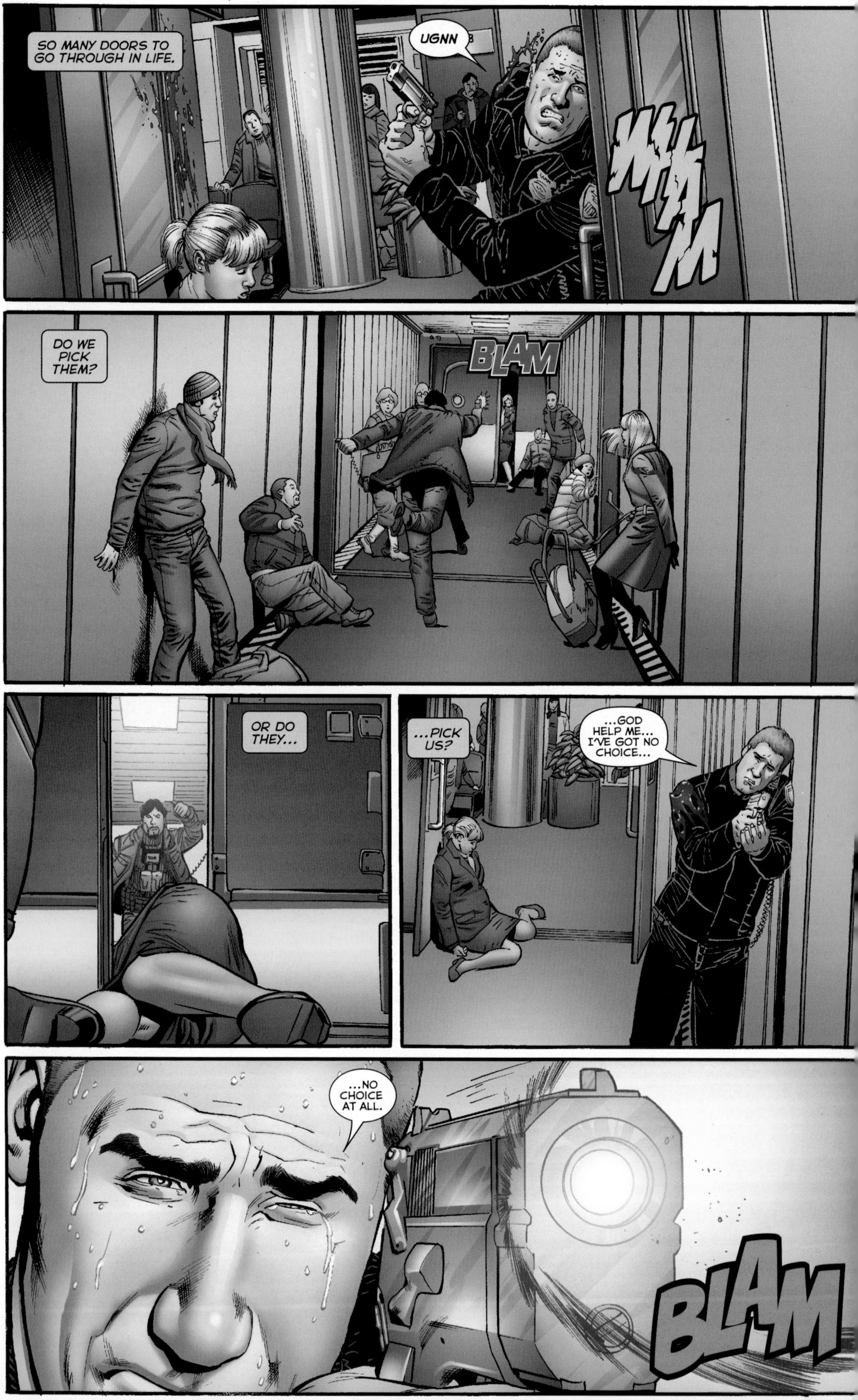
SO MANY DOORS TO GO THROUGH IN LIFE.
UGNN
WHAM
DO WE PICK THEM?
BLAM
OR DO THEY...
...PICK US?
...GOD HELP ME... I'VE GOT NO CHOICE...
...NO CHOICE AT ALL.
BLAM

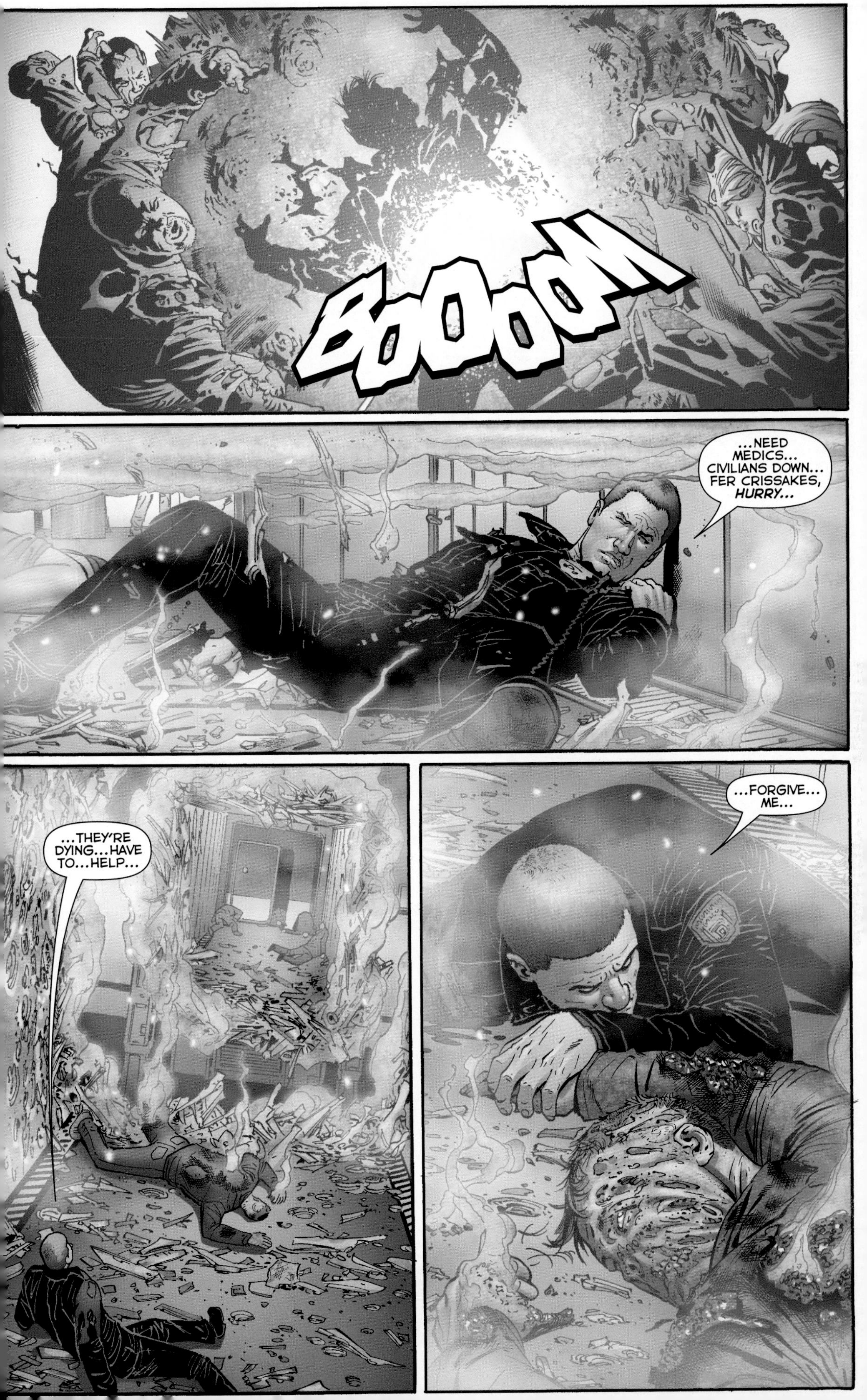
BOOOOOM
...NEED MEDICS... CIVILIANS DOWN... FER CRISSAKES, HURRY...
...THEY'RE DYING...HAVE TO...HELP...
...FORGIVE... ME...

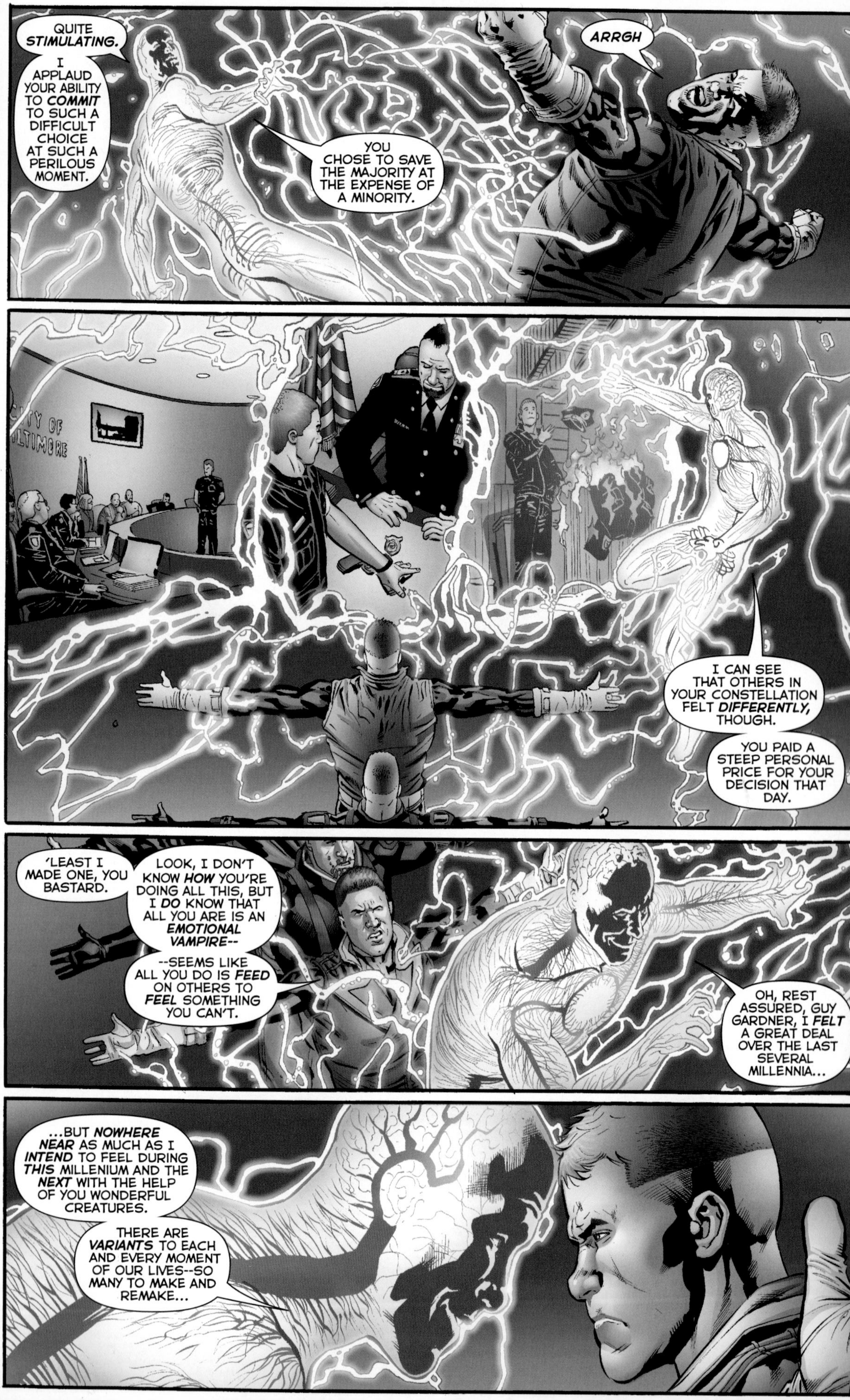
QUITE STIMULATING.
I APPLAUD YOUR ABILITY TO COMMIT TO SUCH A DIFFICULT CHOICE AT SUCH A PERILOUS MOMENT.
ARRGH
YOU CHOSE TO SAVE THE MAJORITY AT THE EXPENSE OF A MINORITY.
CITY OF BALTIMORE
I CAN SEE THAT OTHERS IN YOUR CONSTELLATION FELT DIFFERENTLY, THOUGH.
YOU PAID A STEEP PERSONAL PRICE FOR YOUR DECISION THAT DAY.
'LEAST I MADE ONE, YOU BASTARD.
LOOK, I DON'T KNOW HOW YOU'RE DOING ALL THIS, BUT I DO KNOW THAT ALL YOU ARE IS AN EMOTIONAL VAMPIRE--
--SEEMS LIKE ALL YOU DO IS FEED ON OTHERS TO FEEL SOMETHING YOU CAN'T.
OH, REST ASSURED, GUY GARDNER, I FELT A GREAT DEAL OVER THE LAST SEVERAL MILLENNIA...
...BUT NOWHERE NEAR AS MUCH AS I INTEND TO FEEL DURING THIS MILLENIUM AND THE NEXT WITH THE HELP OF YOU WONDERFUL CREATURES.
THERE ARE VARIANTS TO EACH AND EVERY MOMENT OF OUR LIVES--SO MANY TO MAKE AND REMAKE...

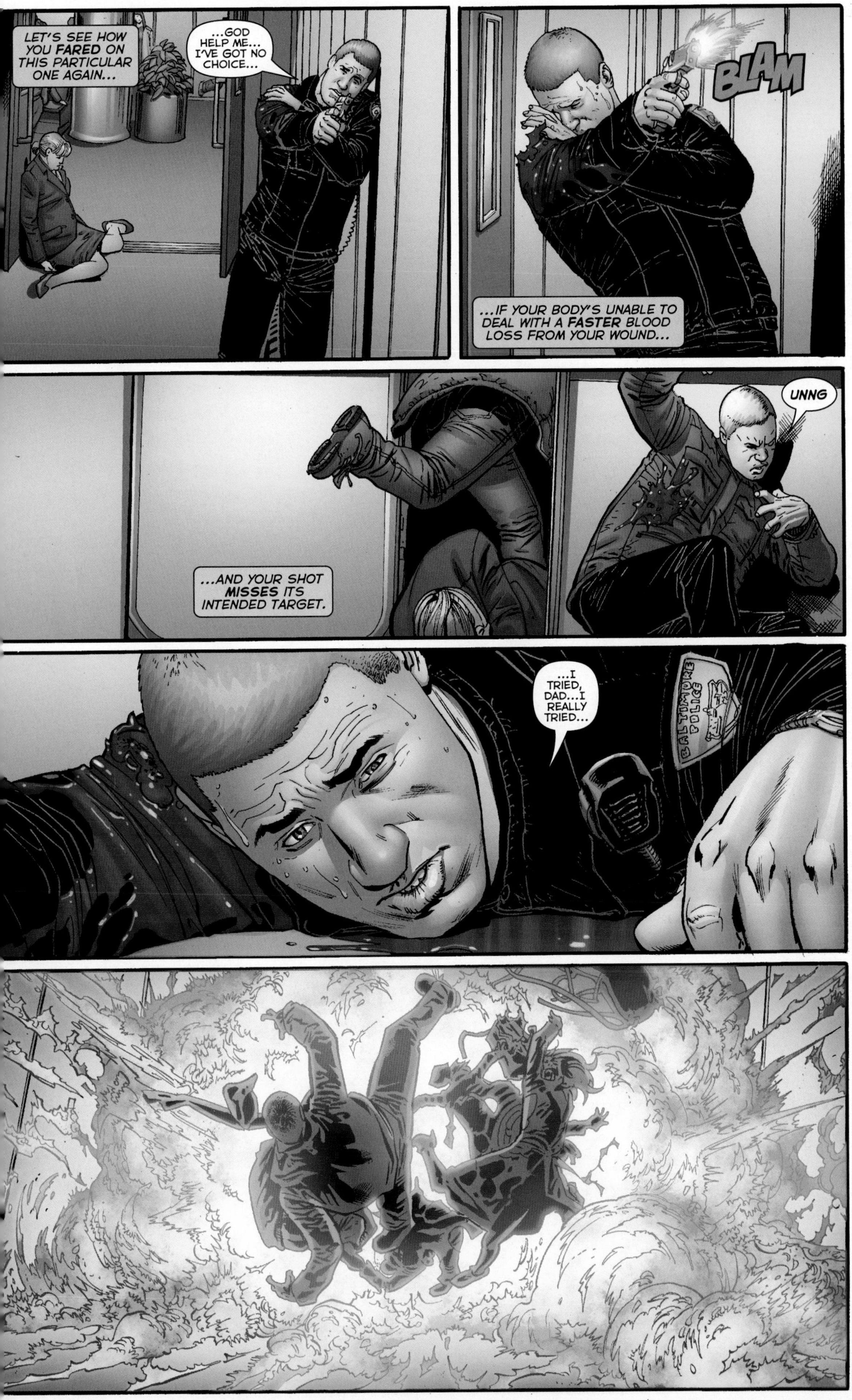
LET'S SEE HOW YOU FARED ON THIS PARTICULAR ONE AGAIN...
...GOD HELP ME... I'VE GOT NO CHOICE...
BLAM
...IF YOUR BODY'S UNABLE TO DEAL WITH A FASTER BLOOD LOSS FROM YOUR WOUND...
...AND YOUR SHOT MISSES ITS INTENDED TARGET.
UNNG
...I TRIED, DAD...I REALLY TRIED...
BALTIMORE POLICE

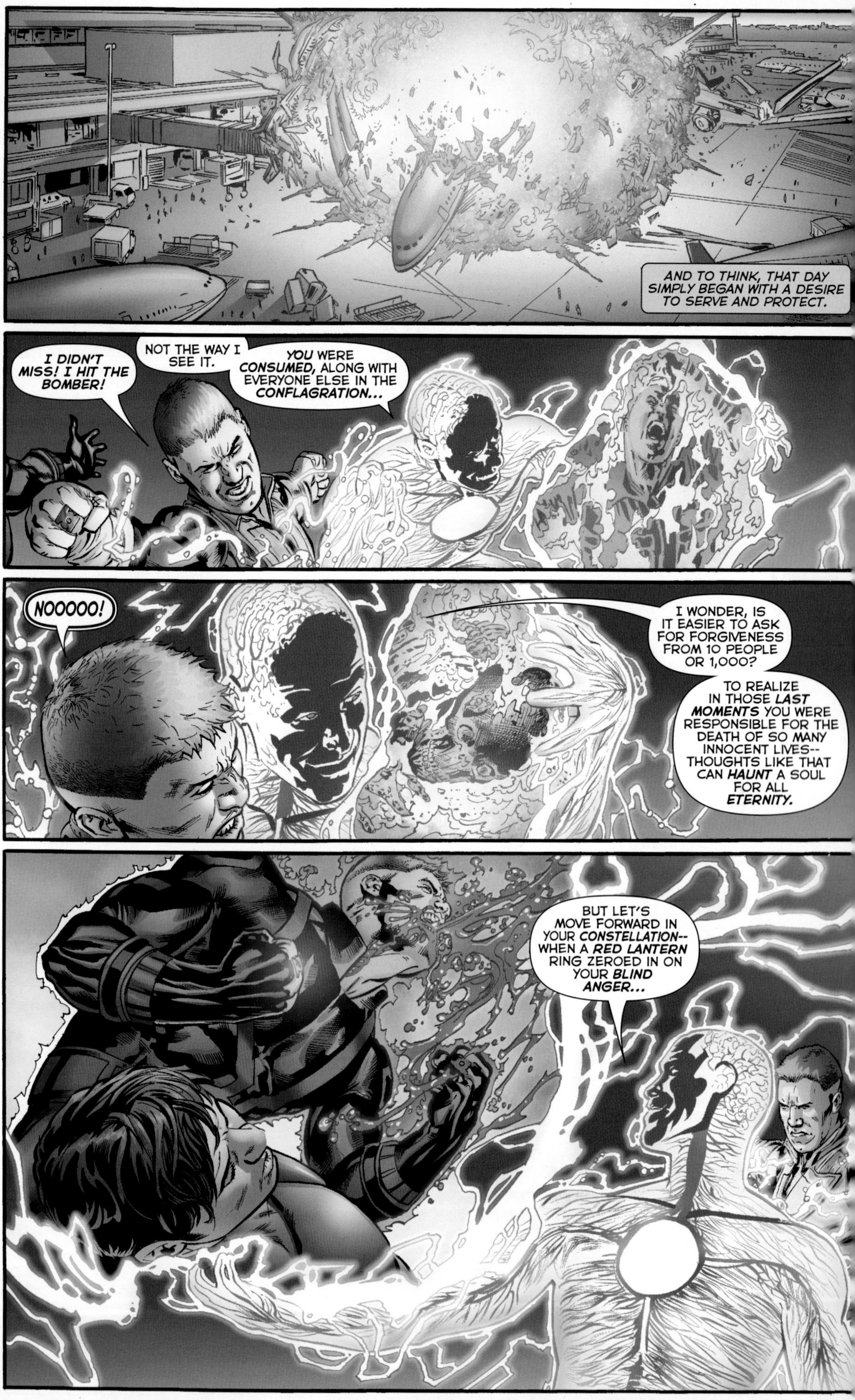
AND TO THINK, THAT DAY SIMPLY BEGAN WITH A DESIRE TO SERVE AND PROTECT.
I DIDN'T MISS! I HIT THE BOMBER!
NOT THE WAY I SEE IT.
YOU WERE CONSUMED, ALONG WITH EVERYONE ELSE IN THE CONFLAGRATION...
NOOOOO!
I WONDER, IS IT EASIER TO ASK FOR FORGIVENESS FROM 10 PEOPLE OR 1,000?
TO REALIZE IN THOSE LAST MOMENTS YOU WERE RESPONSIBLE FOR THE DEATH OF SO MANY INNOCENT LIVES-- THOUGHTS LIKE THAT CAN HAUNT A SOUL FOR ALL ETERNITY.
BUT LET'S MOVE FORWARD IN YOUR CONSTELLATION-- WHEN A RED LANTERN RING ZEROED IN ON YOUR BLIND ANGER...

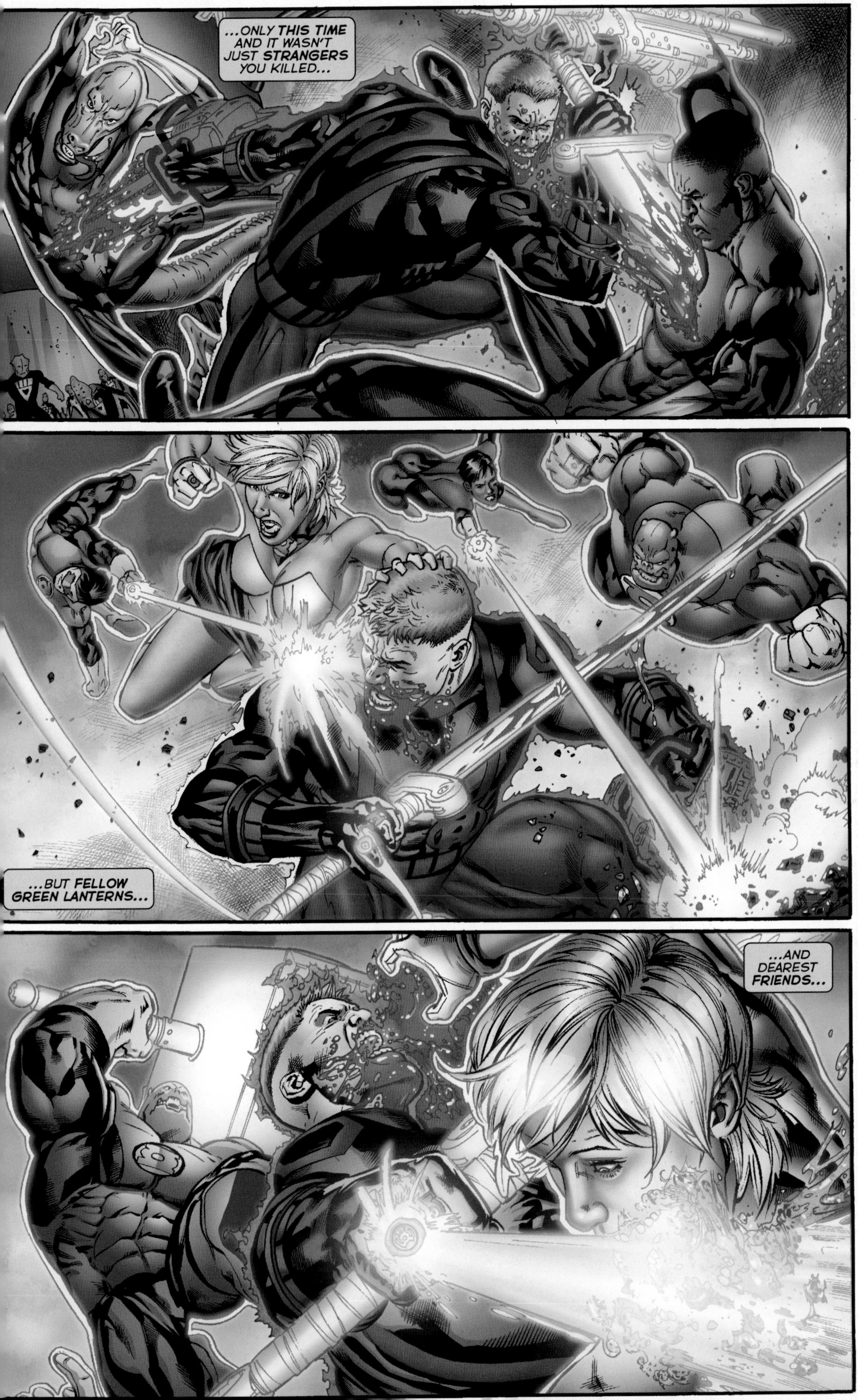
...ONLY THIS TIME AND IT WASN'T JUST STRANGERS YOU KILLED...
...BUT FELLOW GREEN LANTERNS...
...AND DEAREST FRIENDS...

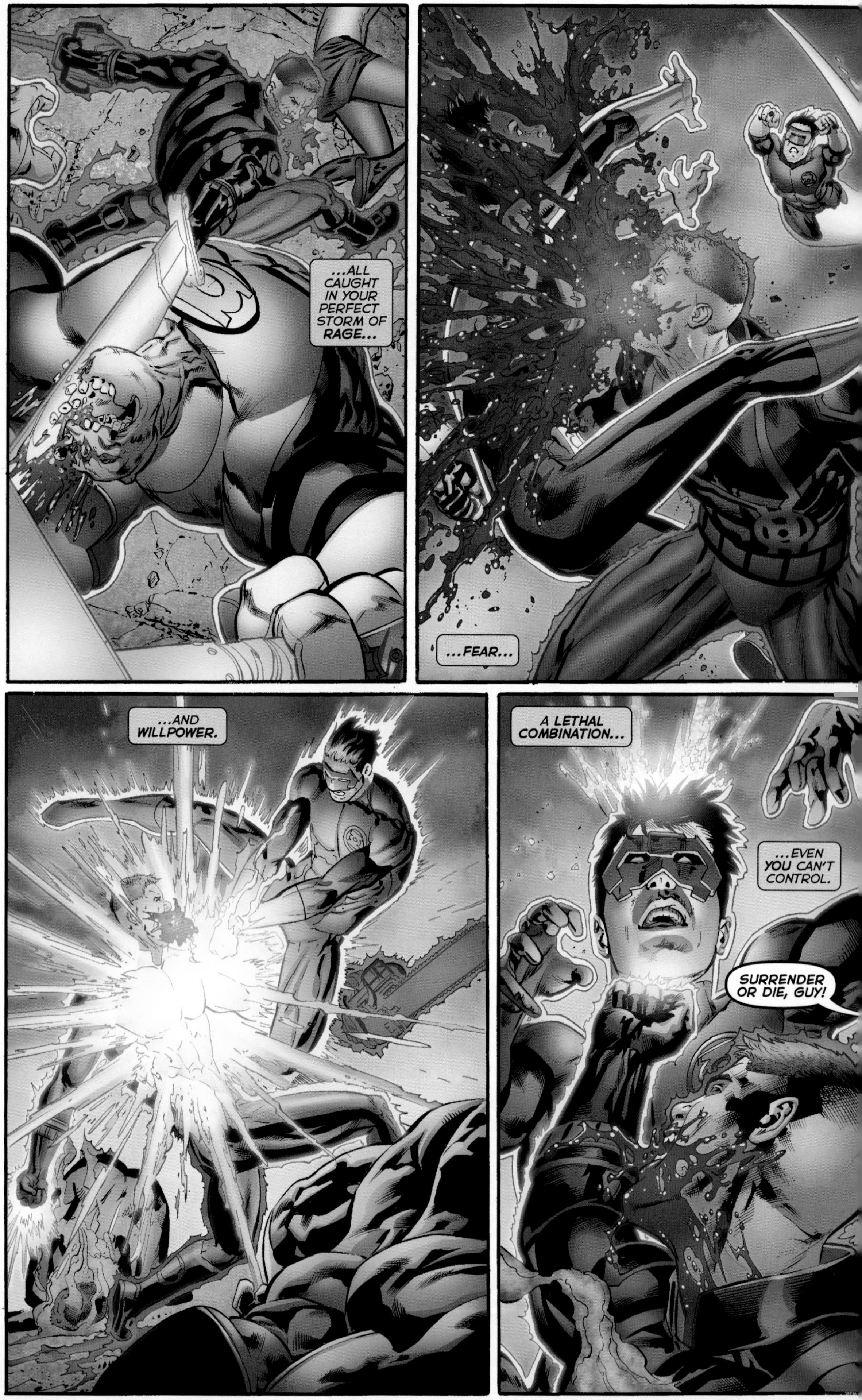
...ALL CAUGHT IN YOUR PERFECT STORM OF RAGE...
...FEAR...
...AND WILLPOWER.
A LETHAL COMBINATION...
...EVEN YOU CAN'T CONTROL.
SURRENDER OR DIE, GUY!

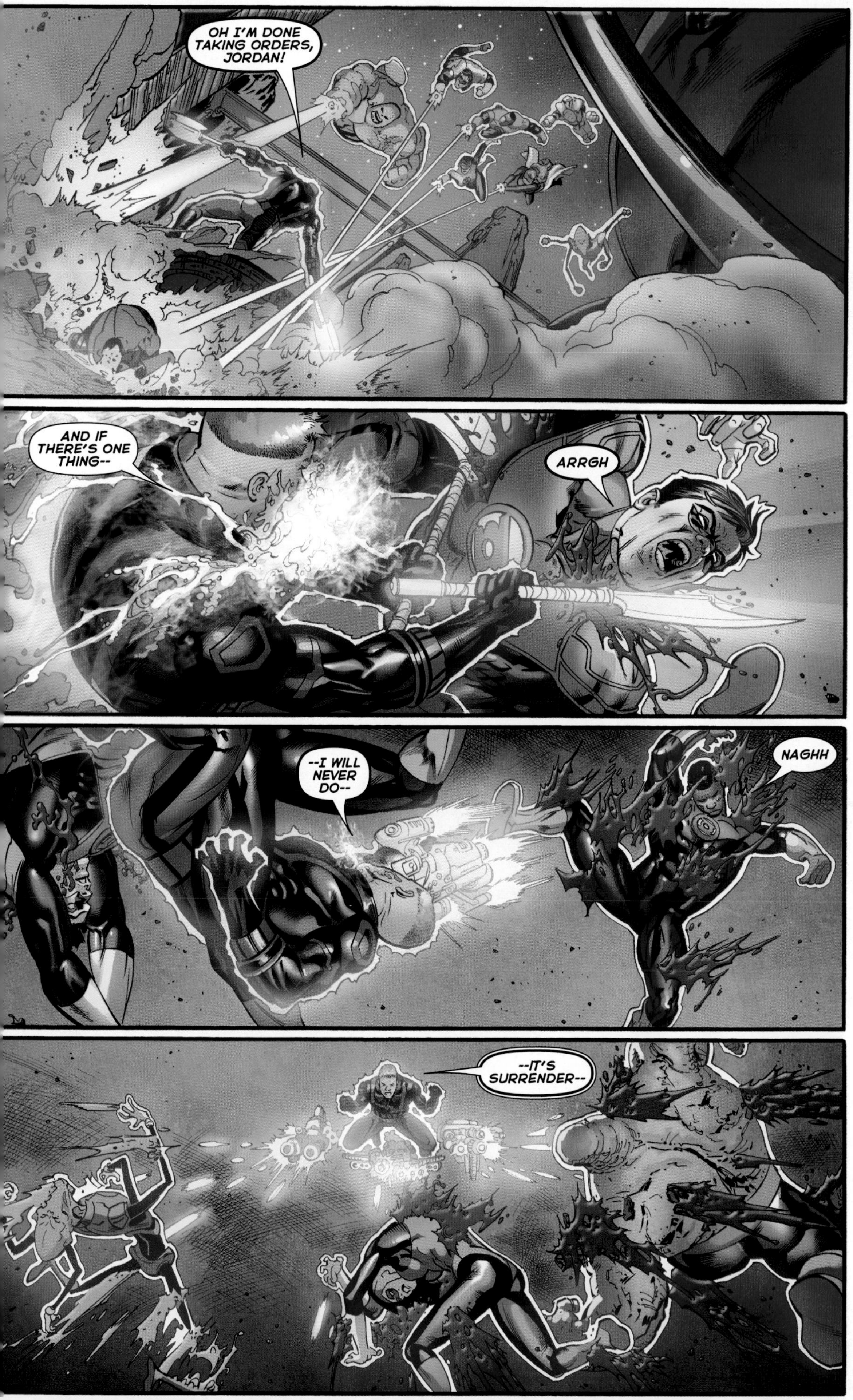
OH I'M DONE TAKING ORDERS, JORDAN!
AND IF THERE'S ONE THING--
ARRGH
--I WILL NEVER DO--
NAGHH
--IT'S SURRENDER--

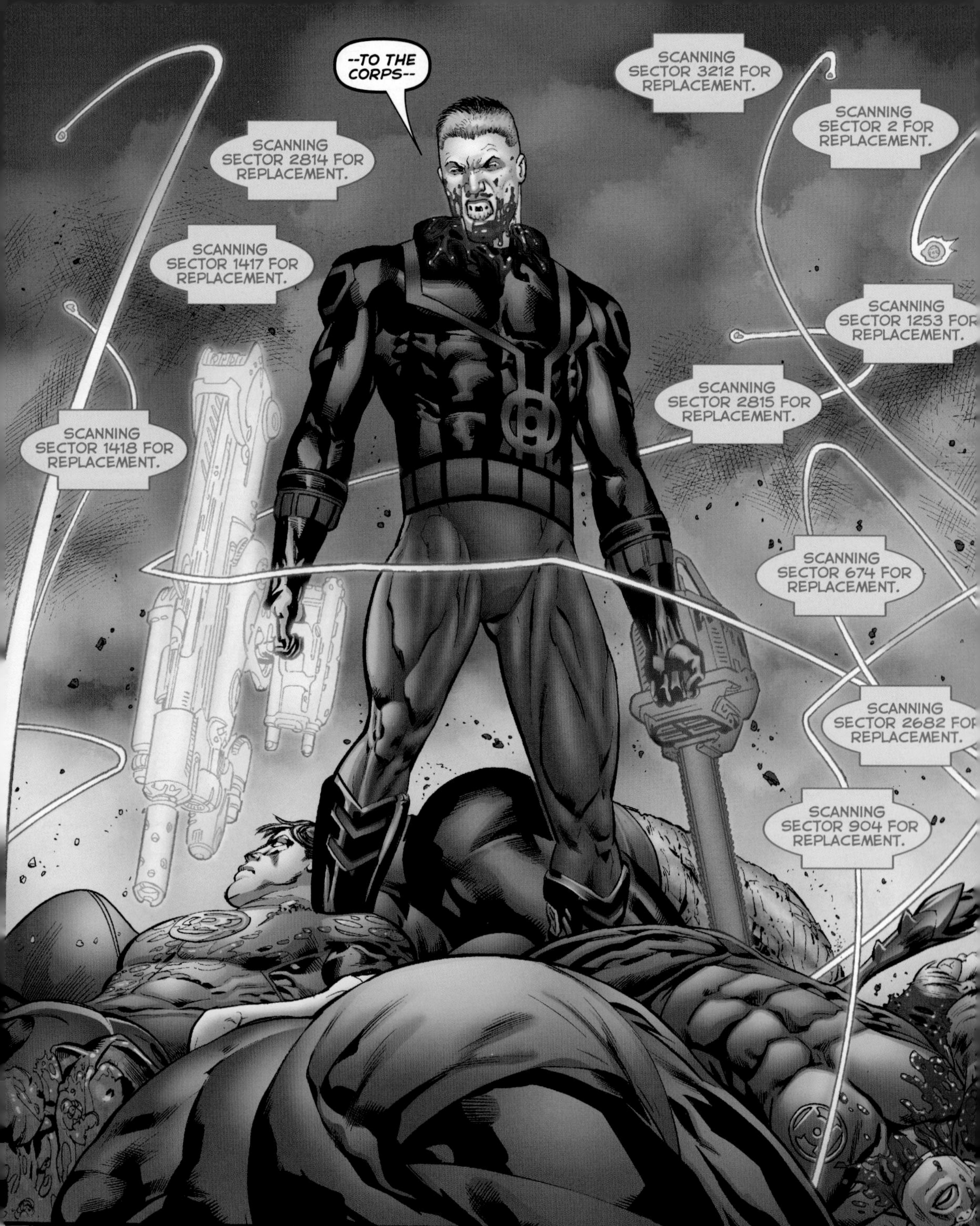
--TO THE CORPS--
SCANNING SECTOR 3212 FOR REPLACEMENT.
SCANNING SECTOR 2 FOR REPLACEMENT.
SCANNING SECTOR 2814 FOR REPLACEMENT.
SCANNING SECTOR 1417 FOR REPLACEMENT.
SCANNING SECTOR 1253 FOR REPLACEMENT.
SCANNING SECTOR 2815 FOR REPLACEMENT.
SCANNING SECTOR 1418 FOR REPLACEMENT.
SCANNING SECTOR 674 FOR REPLACEMENT.
SCANNING SECTOR 2682 FOR REPLACEMENT.
SCANNING SECTOR 904 FOR REPLACEMENT.

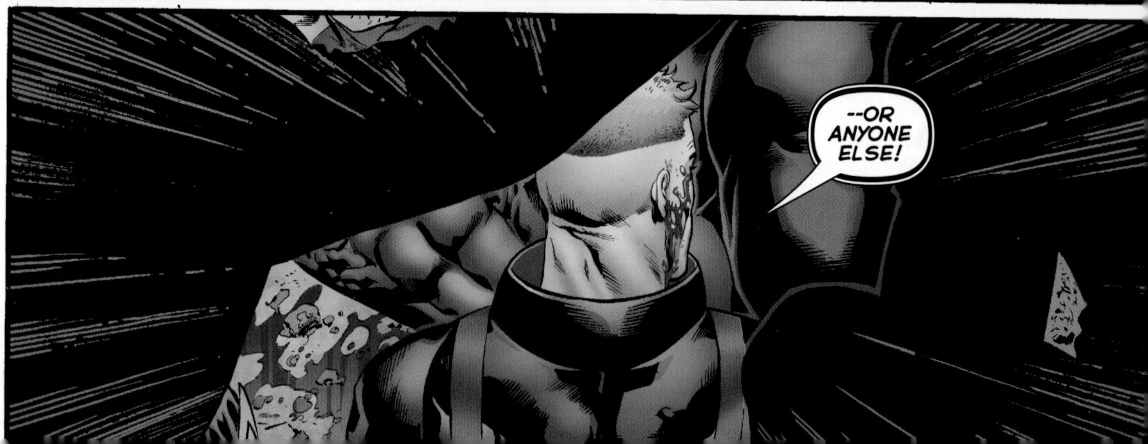
--OR ANYONE ELSE!

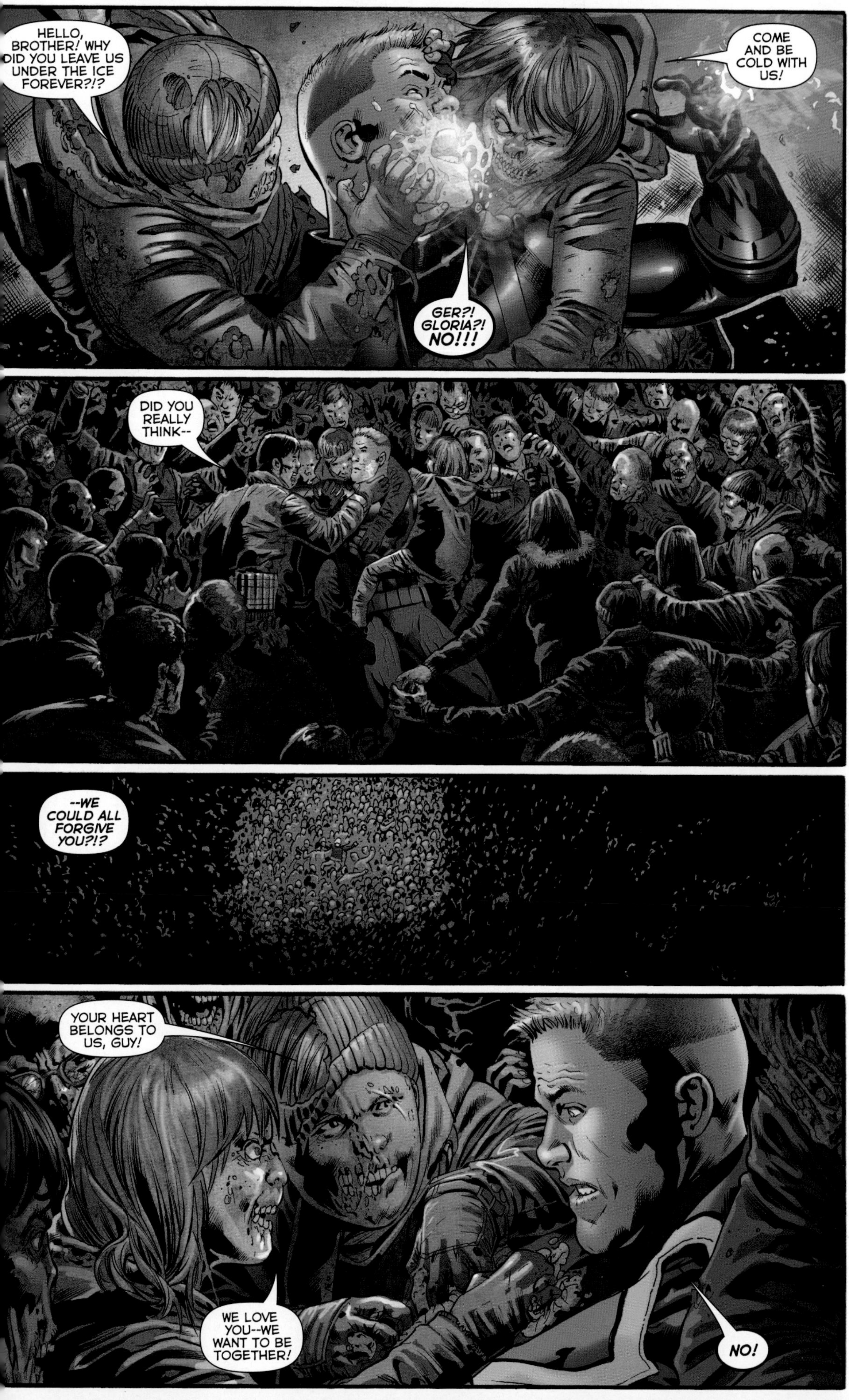
HELLO, BROTHER! WHY DID YOU LEAVE US UNDER THE ICE FOREVER?!?
COME AND BE COLD WITH US!
GER?! GLORIA?! NO!!!
DID YOU REALLY THINK--
--WE COULD ALL FORGIVE YOU?!?
YOUR HEART BELONGS TO US, GUY!
WE LOVE YOU--WE WANT TO BE TOGETHER!
NO!

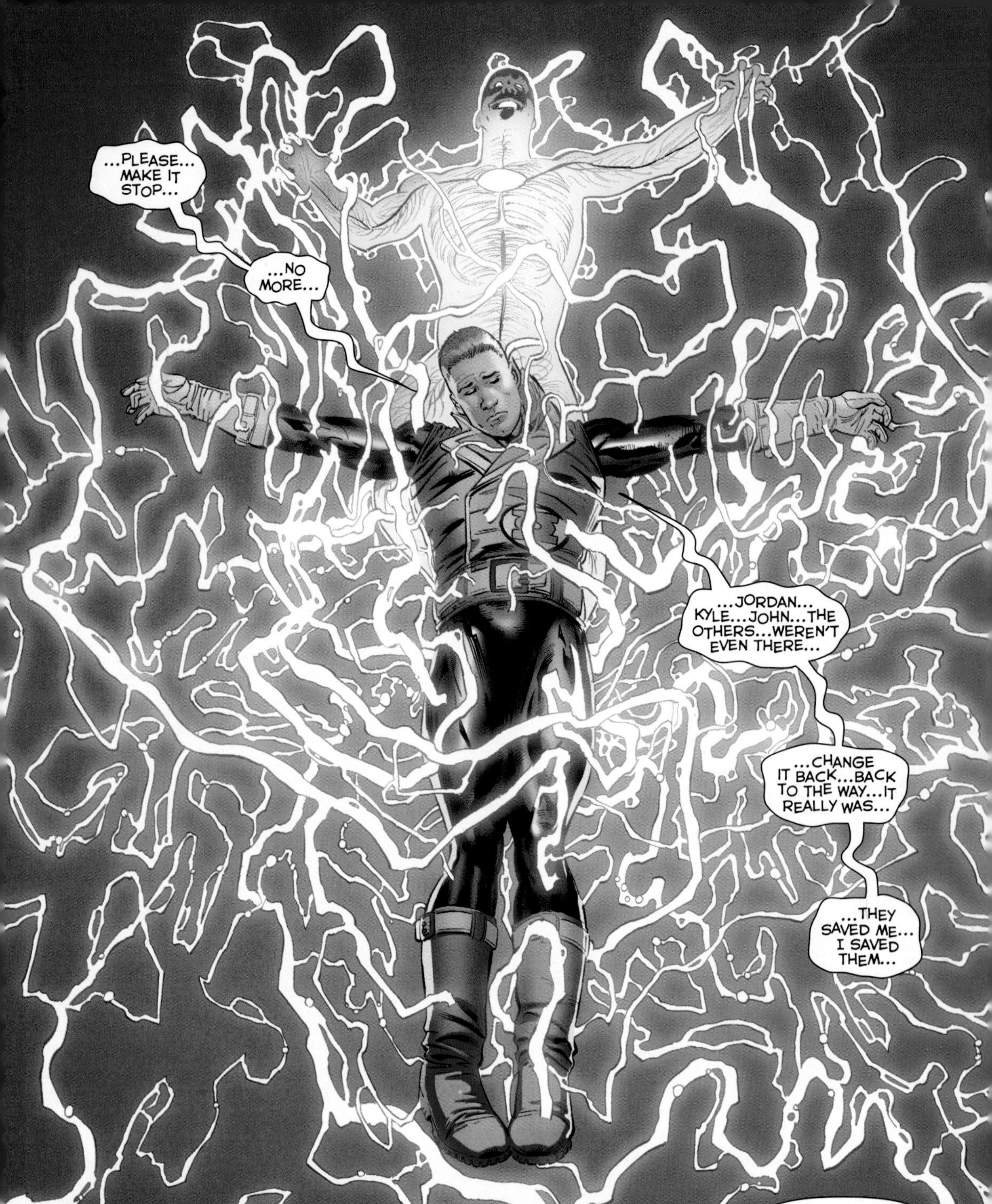
...PLEASE... MAKE IT STOP...
...NO MORE...
...JORDAN... KYLE...JOHN...THE OTHERS...WEREN'T EVEN THERE...
...CHANGE IT BACK...BACK TO THE WAY...IT REALLY WAS...
...THEY SAVED ME... I SAVED THEM...

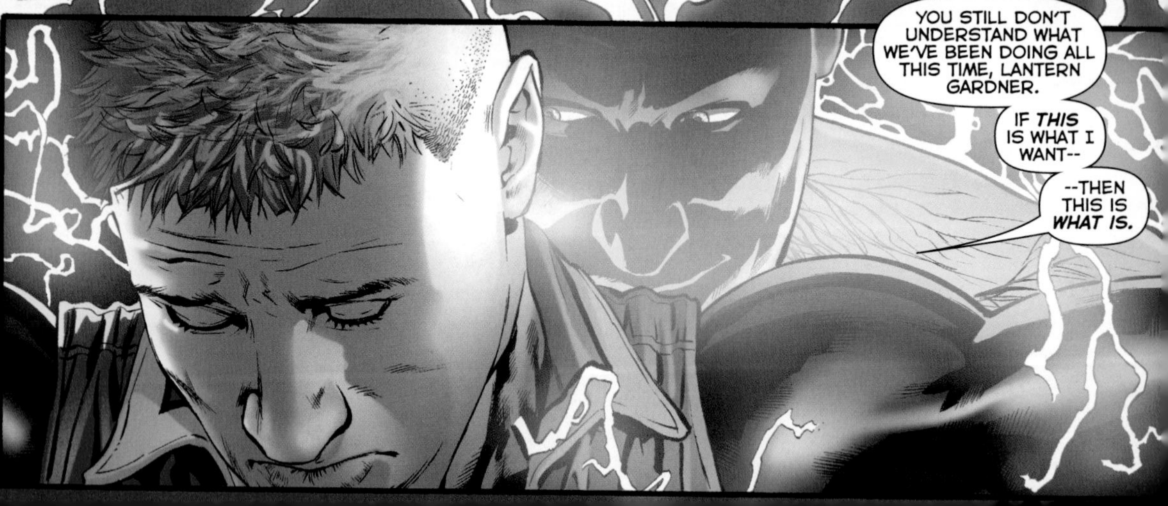
YOU STILL DON'T UNDERSTAND WHAT WE'VE BEEN DOING ALL THIS TIME, LANTERN GARDNER.
IF *THIS* IS WHAT I WANT--
--THEN THIS IS ***WHAT IS.***

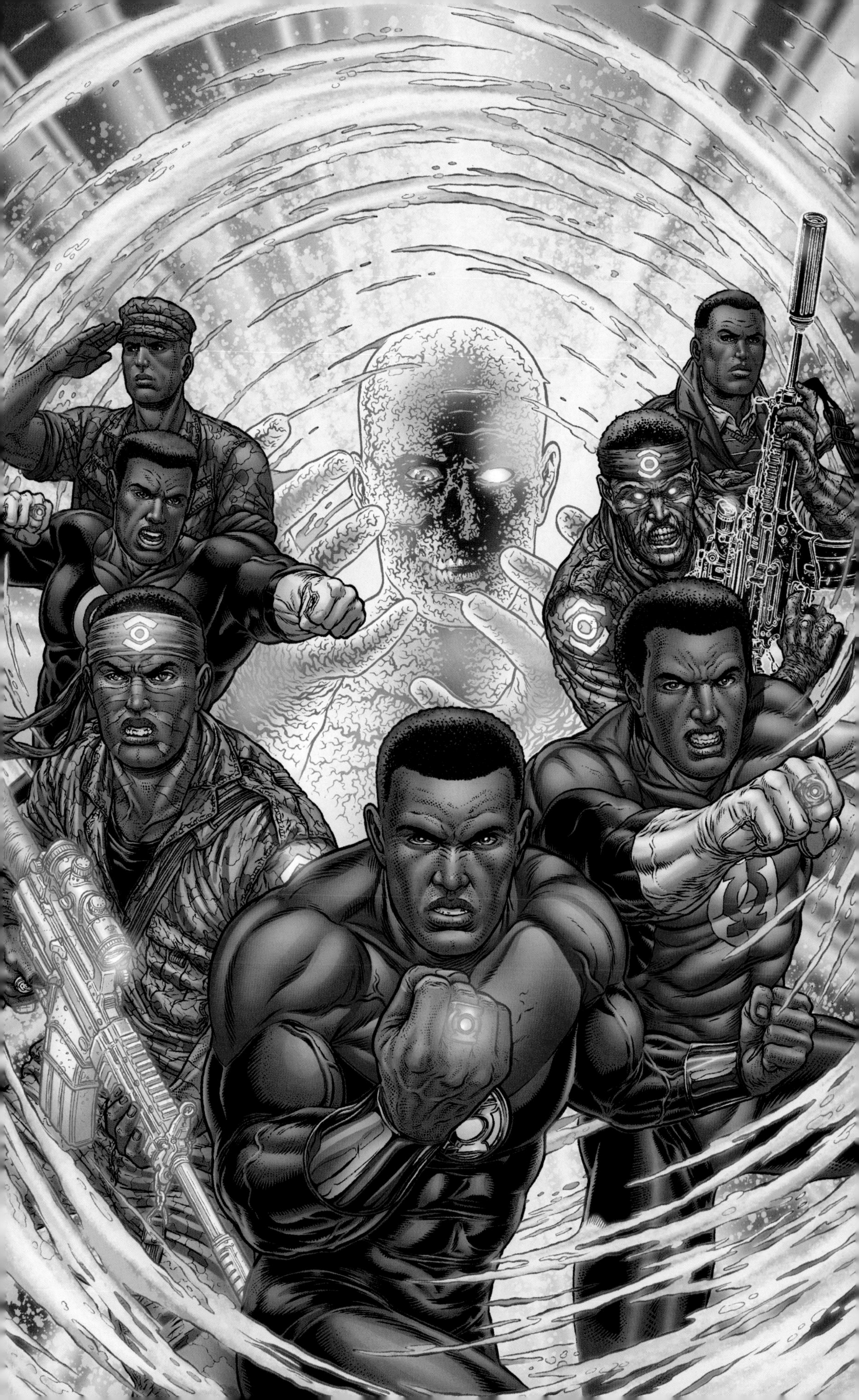

PIECES OF YOU

PETER J. TOMASI writer CHRISCROSS penciller SCOTT HANNA inker cover art by JUAN JOSÉ RYP & GABE ELTAEB

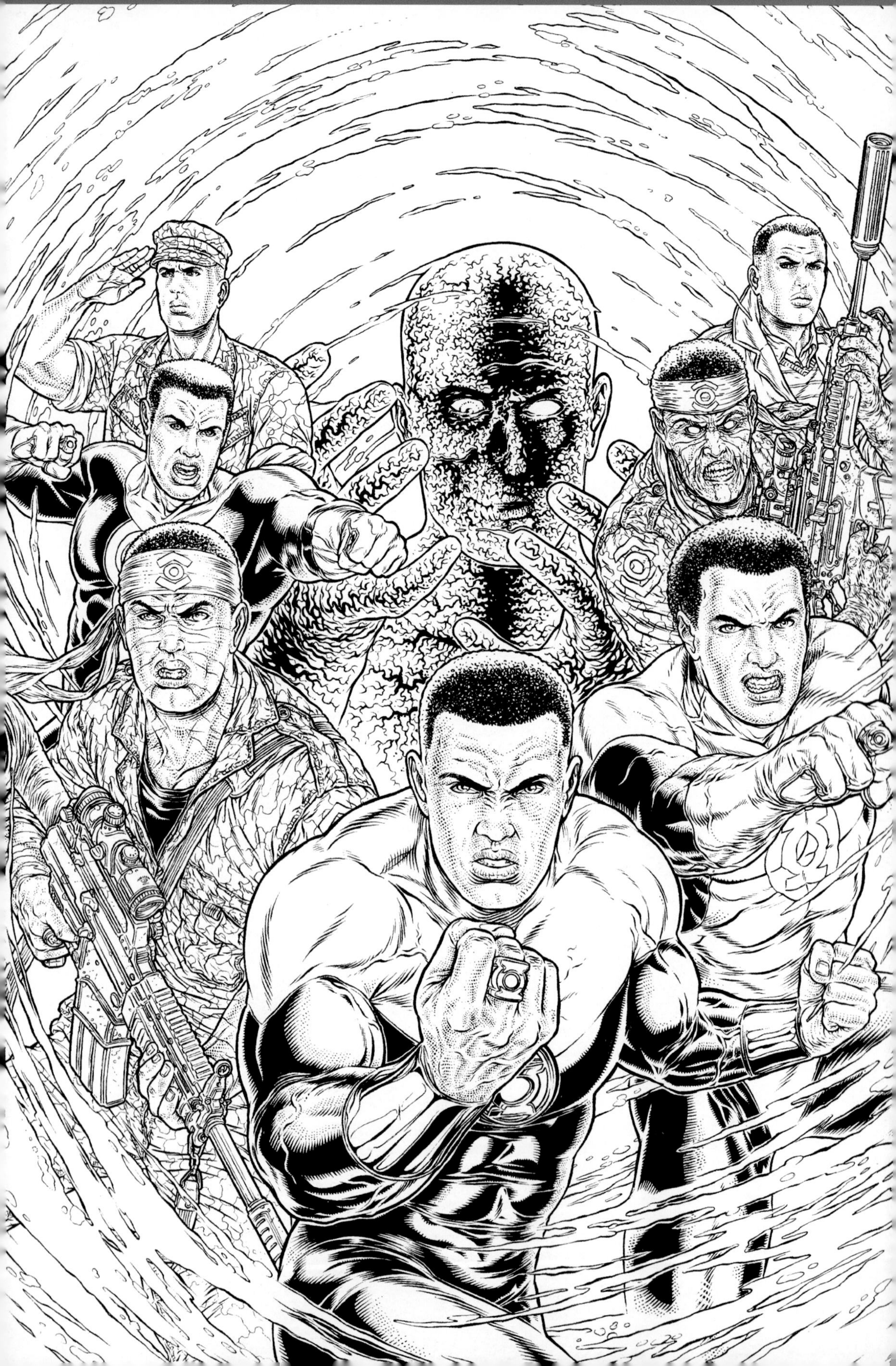

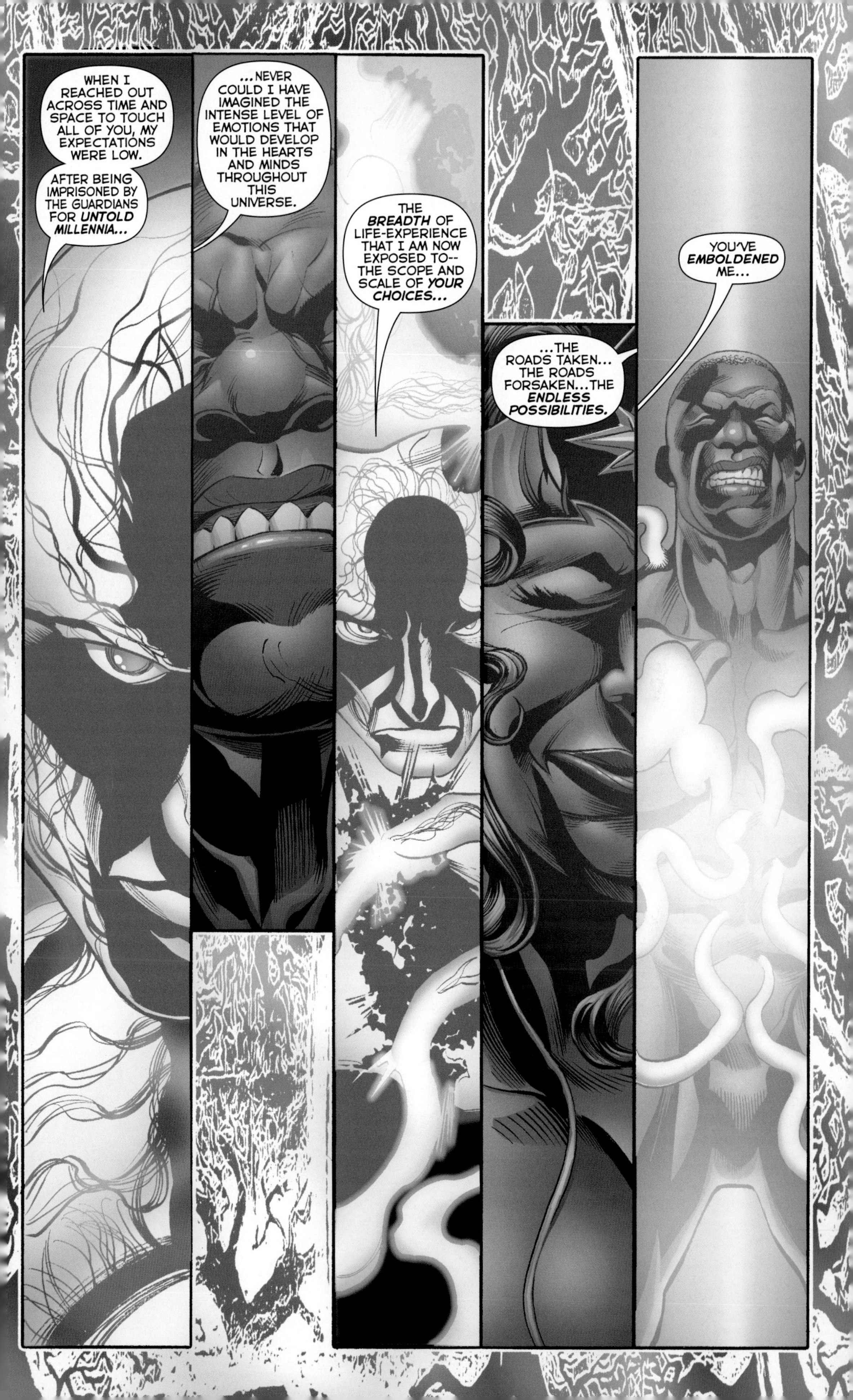

WHEN I REACHED OUT ACROSS TIME AND SPACE TO TOUCH ALL OF YOU, MY EXPECTATIONS WERE LOW.
AFTER BEING IMPRISONED BY THE GUARDIANS FOR *UNTOLD MILLENNIA...*
...NEVER COULD I HAVE IMAGINED THE INTENSE LEVEL OF EMOTIONS THAT WOULD DEVELOP IN THE HEARTS AND MINDS THROUGHOUT THIS UNIVERSE.
THE *BREADTH* OF LIFE-EXPERIENCE THAT I AM NOW EXPOSED TO-- THE SCOPE AND SCALE OF *YOUR CHOICES...*
...THE ROADS TAKEN... THE ROADS FORSAKEN...THE *ENDLESS POSSIBILITIES.*
YOU'VE *EMBOLDENED* ME...

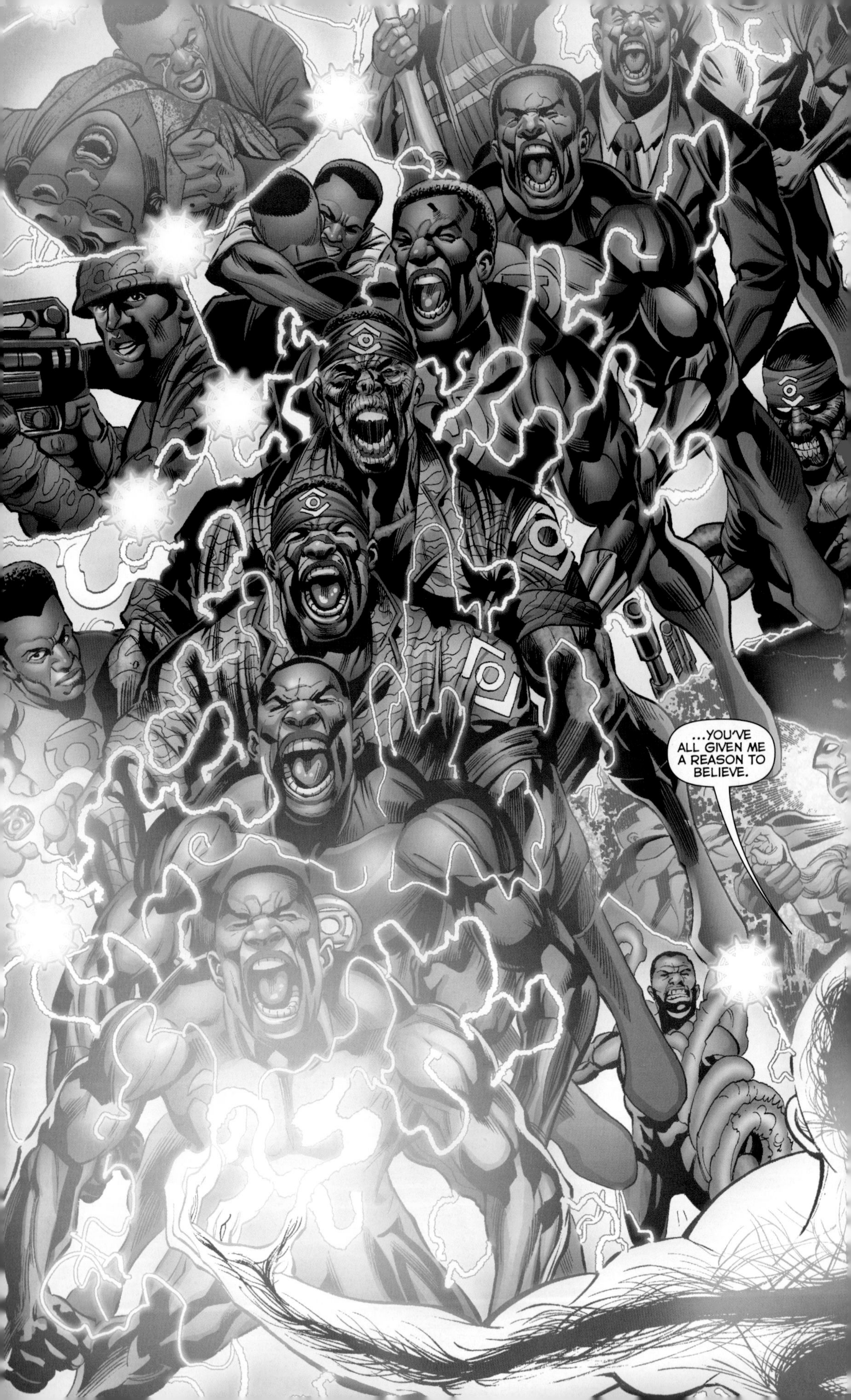
...YOU'VE ALL GIVEN ME A REASON TO BELIEVE.

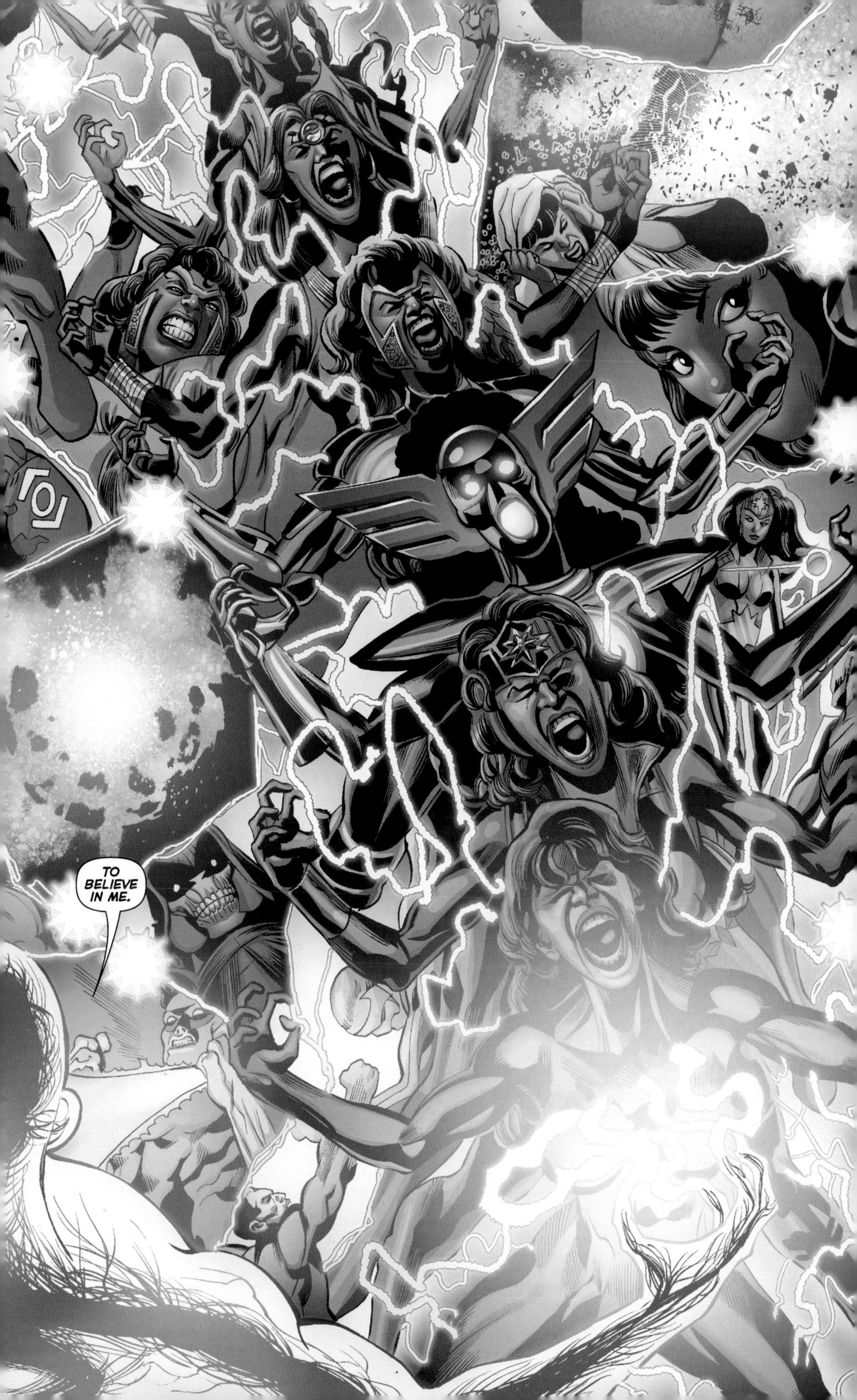
TO BELIEVE IN ME.

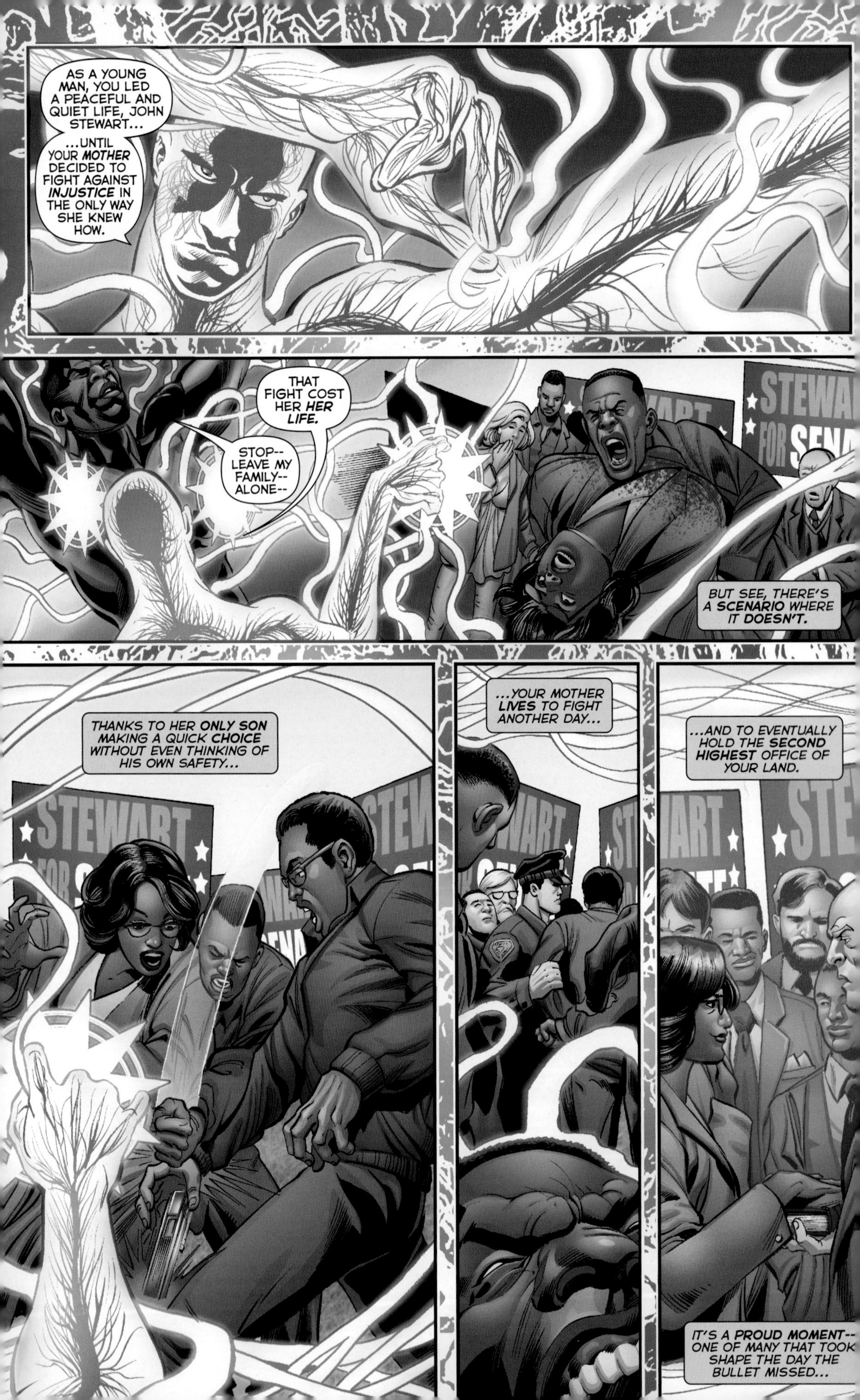
AS A YOUNG MAN, YOU LED A PEACEFUL AND QUIET LIFE, JOHN STEWART...
...UNTIL YOUR MOTHER DECIDED TO FIGHT AGAINST INJUSTICE IN THE ONLY WAY SHE KNEW HOW.
THAT FIGHT COST HER HER LIFE.
STOP-- LEAVE MY FAMILY-- ALONE--
STEWART FOR SENA
BUT SEE, THERE'S A SCENARIO WHERE IT DOESN'T.
THANKS TO HER ONLY SON MAKING A QUICK CHOICE WITHOUT EVEN THINKING OF HIS OWN SAFETY...
STEWART
...YOUR MOTHER LIVES TO FIGHT ANOTHER DAY...
...AND TO EVENTUALLY HOLD THE SECOND HIGHEST OFFICE OF YOUR LAND.
IT'S A PROUD MOMENT-- ONE OF MANY THAT TOOK SHAPE THE DAY THE BULLET MISSED...

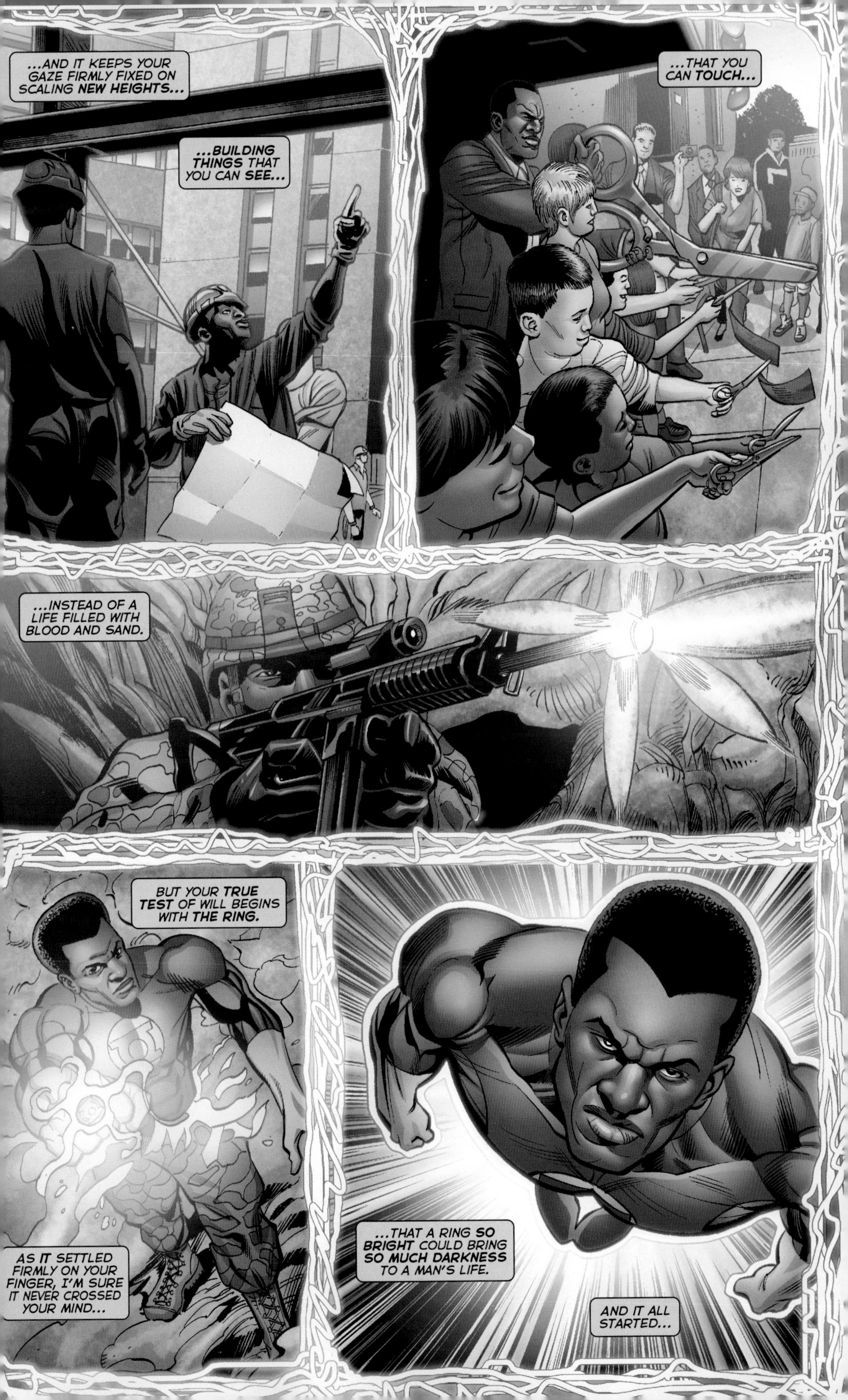
...AND IT KEEPS YOUR GAZE FIRMLY FIXED ON SCALING NEW HEIGHTS...
...BUILDING THINGS THAT YOU CAN SEE...
...THAT YOU CAN TOUCH...
...INSTEAD OF A LIFE FILLED WITH BLOOD AND SAND.
BUT YOUR TRUE TEST OF WILL BEGINS WITH THE RING.
AS IT SETTLED FIRMLY ON YOUR FINGER, I'M SURE IT NEVER CROSSED YOUR MIND...
...THAT A RING SO BRIGHT COULD BRING SO MUCH DARKNESS TO A MAN'S LIFE.
AND IT ALL STARTED...

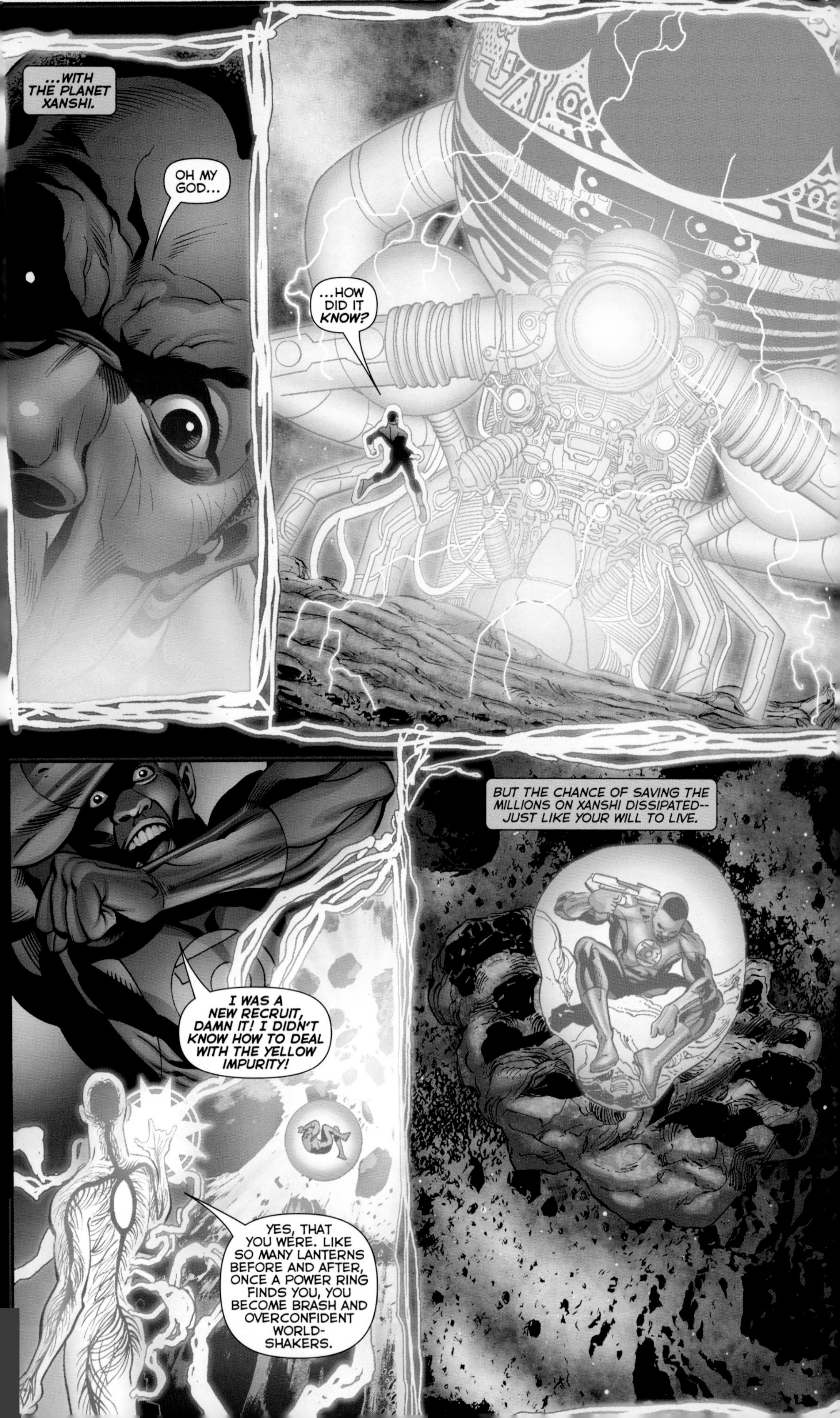
...WITH THE PLANET XANSHI.
OH MY GOD...
...HOW DID IT KNOW?
BUT THE CHANCE OF SAVING THE MILLIONS ON XANSHI DISSIPATED-- JUST LIKE YOUR WILL TO LIVE.
I WAS A NEW RECRUIT, DAMN IT! I DIDN'T KNOW HOW TO DEAL WITH THE YELLOW IMPURITY!
YES, THAT YOU WERE. LIKE SO MANY LANTERNS BEFORE AND AFTER, ONCE A POWER RING FINDS YOU, YOU BECOME BRASH AND OVERCONFIDENT WORLD-SHAKERS.

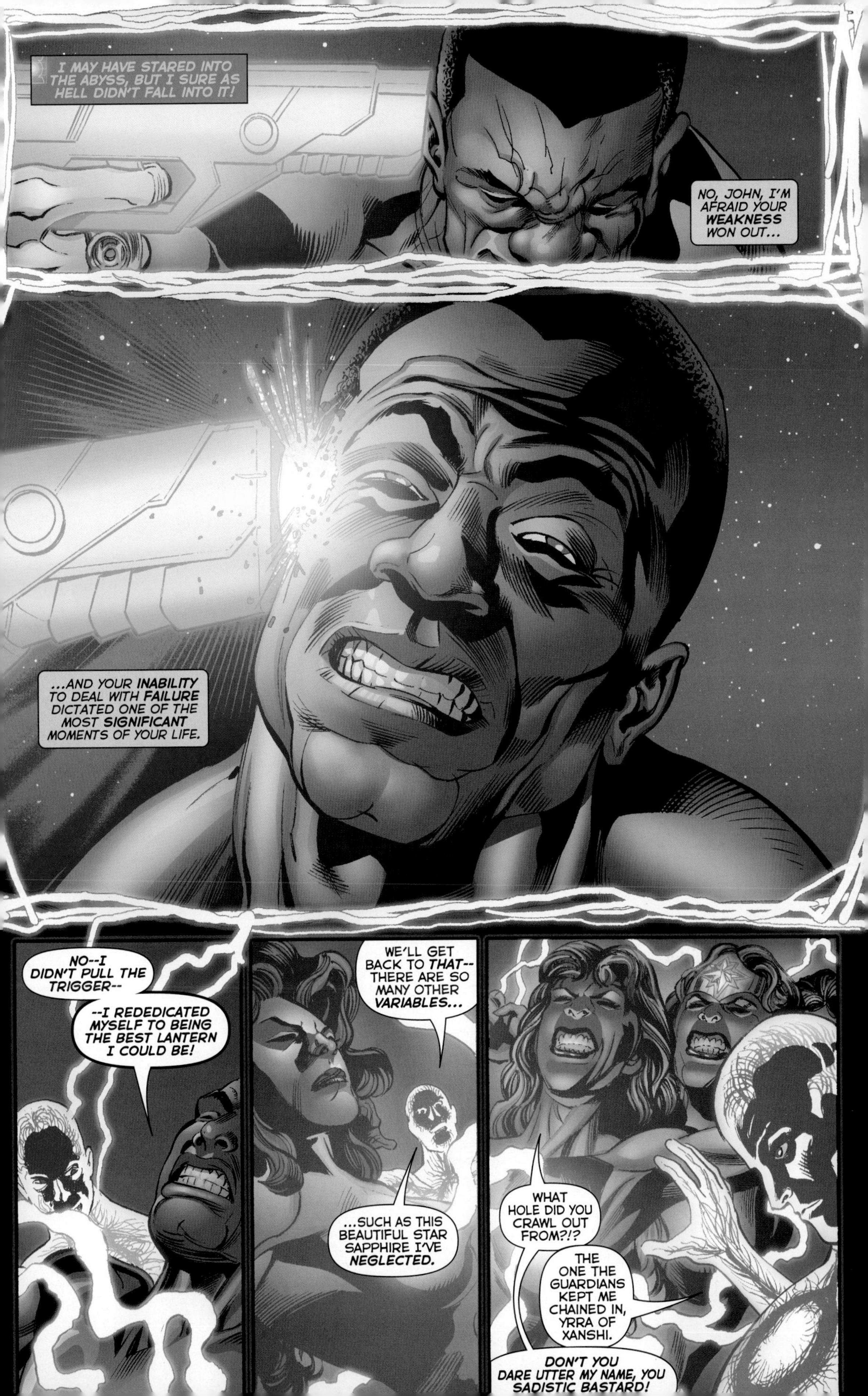
I MAY HAVE STARED INTO THE ABYSS, BUT I SURE AS HELL DIDN'T FALL INTO IT!
NO, JOHN, I'M AFRAID YOUR WEAKNESS WON OUT...
...AND YOUR INABILITY TO DEAL WITH FAILURE DICTATED ONE OF THE MOST SIGNIFICANT MOMENTS OF YOUR LIFE.
NO--I DIDN'T PULL THE TRIGGER--
--I REDEDICATED MYSELF TO BEING THE BEST LANTERN I COULD BE!
WE'LL GET BACK TO THAT--THERE ARE SO MANY OTHER VARIABLES...
...SUCH AS THIS BEAUTIFUL STAR SAPPHIRE I'VE NEGLECTED.
WHAT HOLE DID YOU CRAWL OUT FROM?!?
THE ONE THE GUARDIANS KEPT ME CHAINED IN, YRRA OF XANSHI.
DON'T YOU DARE UTTER MY NAME, YOU SADISTIC BASTARD!

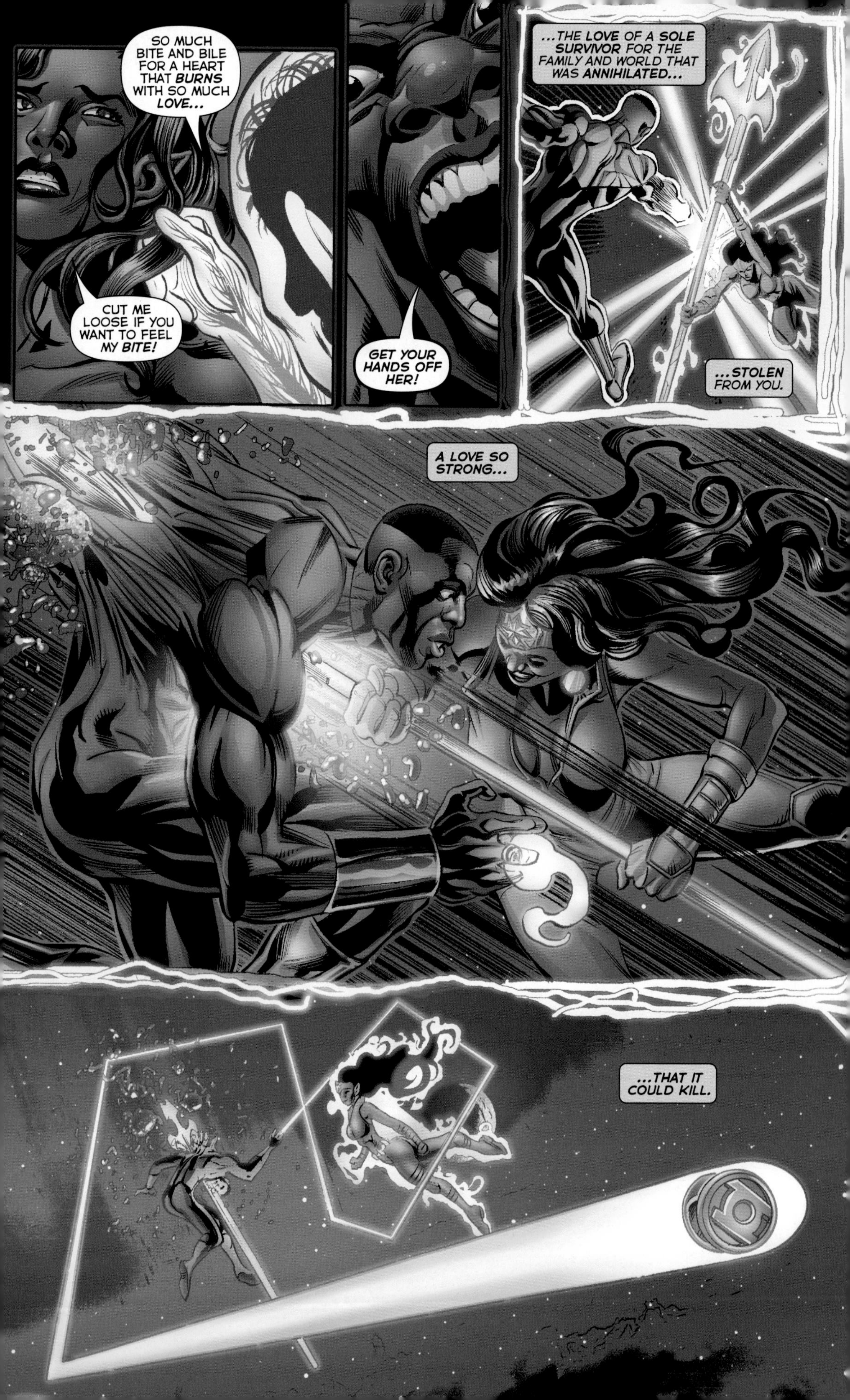
SO MUCH BITE AND BILE FOR A HEART THAT BURNS WITH SO MUCH LOVE...
CUT ME LOOSE IF YOU WANT TO FEEL MY BITE!
GET YOUR HANDS OFF HER!
...THE LOVE OF A SOLE SURVIVOR FOR THE FAMILY AND WORLD THAT WAS ANNIHILATED...
...STOLEN FROM YOU.
A LOVE SO STRONG...
...THAT IT COULD KILL.

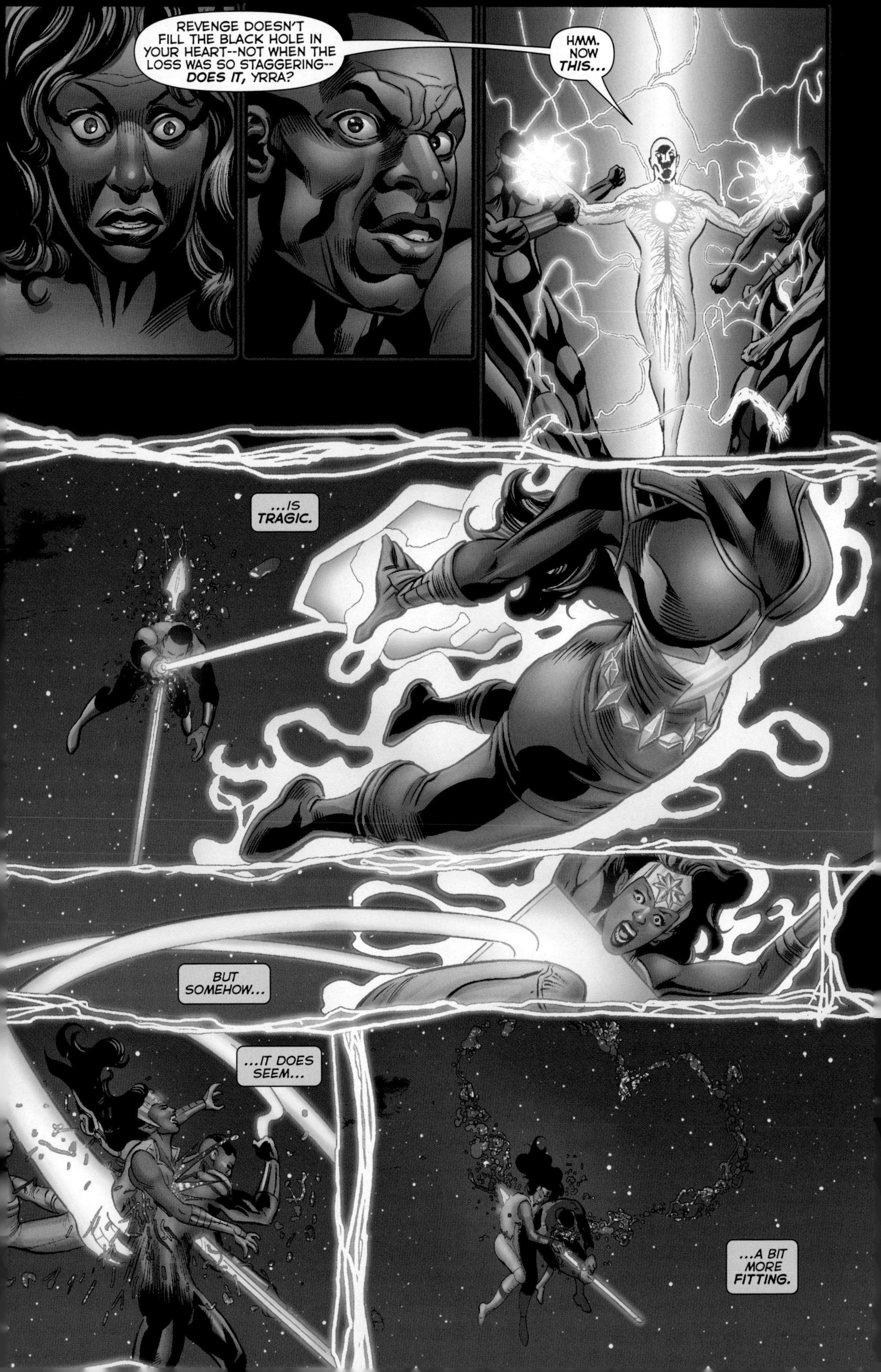
REVENGE DOESN'T FILL THE BLACK HOLE IN YOUR HEART--NOT WHEN THE LOSS WAS SO STAGGERING-- DOES IT, YRRA?
HMM. NOW THIS...
...IS TRAGIC.
BUT SOMEHOW...
...IT DOES SEEM...
...A BIT MORE FITTING.

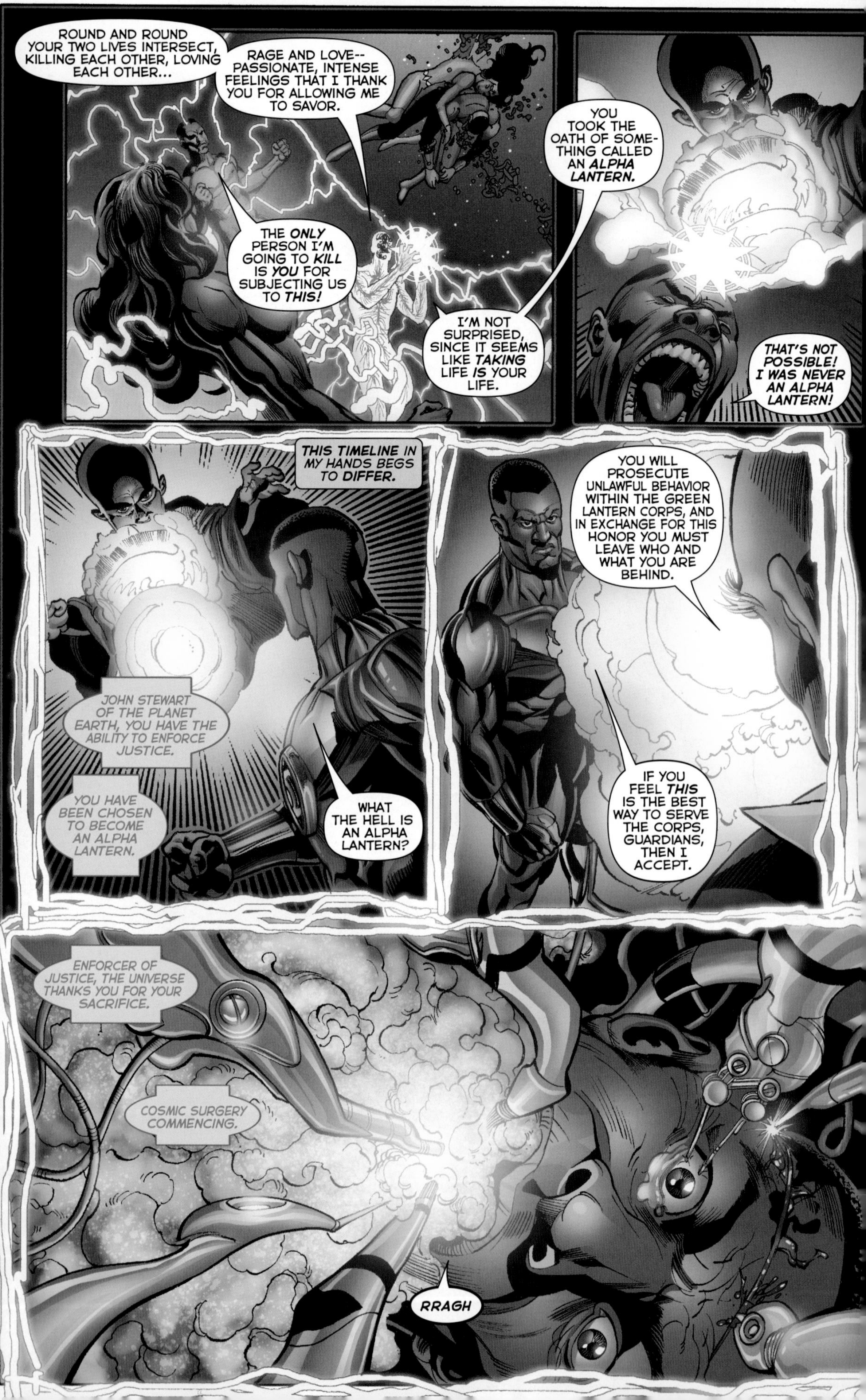
ROUND AND ROUND YOUR TWO LIVES INTERSECT, KILLING EACH OTHER, LOVING EACH OTHER...
RAGE AND LOVE-- PASSIONATE, INTENSE FEELINGS THAT I THANK YOU FOR ALLOWING ME TO SAVOR.
THE ONLY PERSON I'M GOING TO KILL IS YOU FOR SUBJECTING US TO THIS!
I'M NOT SURPRISED, SINCE IT SEEMS LIKE TAKING LIFE IS YOUR LIFE.
YOU TOOK THE OATH OF SOME-THING CALLED AN ALPHA LANTERN.
THAT'S NOT POSSIBLE! I WAS NEVER AN ALPHA LANTERN!
THIS TIMELINE IN MY HANDS BEGS TO DIFFER.
JOHN STEWART OF THE PLANET EARTH, YOU HAVE THE ABILITY TO ENFORCE JUSTICE.
YOU HAVE BEEN CHOSEN TO BECOME AN ALPHA LANTERN.
WHAT THE HELL IS AN ALPHA LANTERN?
YOU WILL PROSECUTE UNLAWFUL BEHAVIOR WITHIN THE GREEN LANTERN CORPS, AND IN EXCHANGE FOR THIS HONOR YOU MUST LEAVE WHO AND WHAT YOU ARE BEHIND.
IF YOU FEEL THIS IS THE BEST WAY TO SERVE THE CORPS, GUARDIANS, THEN I ACCEPT.
ENFORCER OF JUSTICE, THE UNIVERSE THANKS YOU FOR YOUR SACRIFICE.
COSMIC SURGERY COMMENCING.
RRAGH

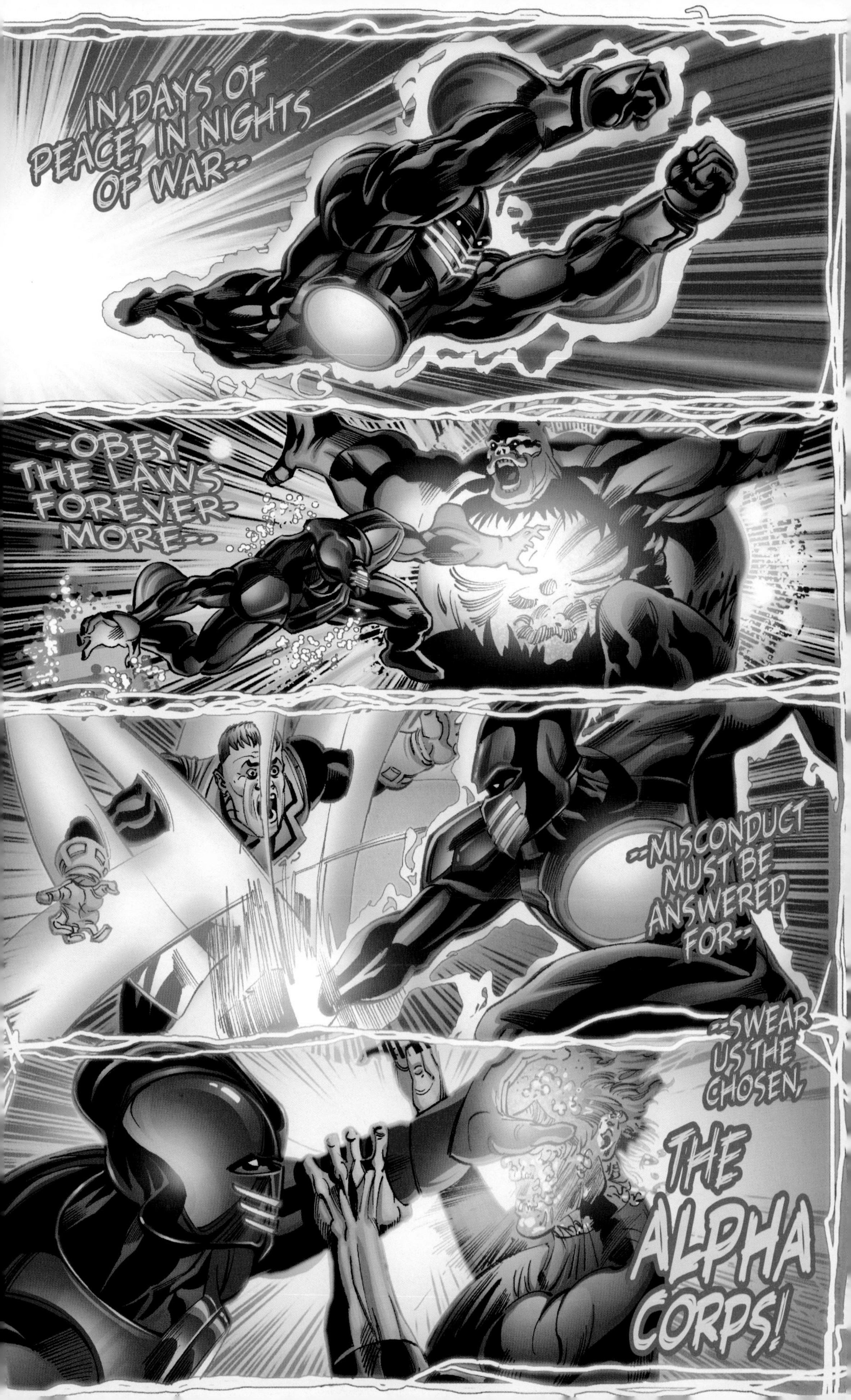
IN DAYS OF PEACE, IN NIGHTS OF WAR--
--OBEY THE LAWS FOREVERMORE--
--MISCONDUCT MUST BE ANSWERED FOR--
--SWEAR US THE CHOSEN,
THE ALPHA CORPS!

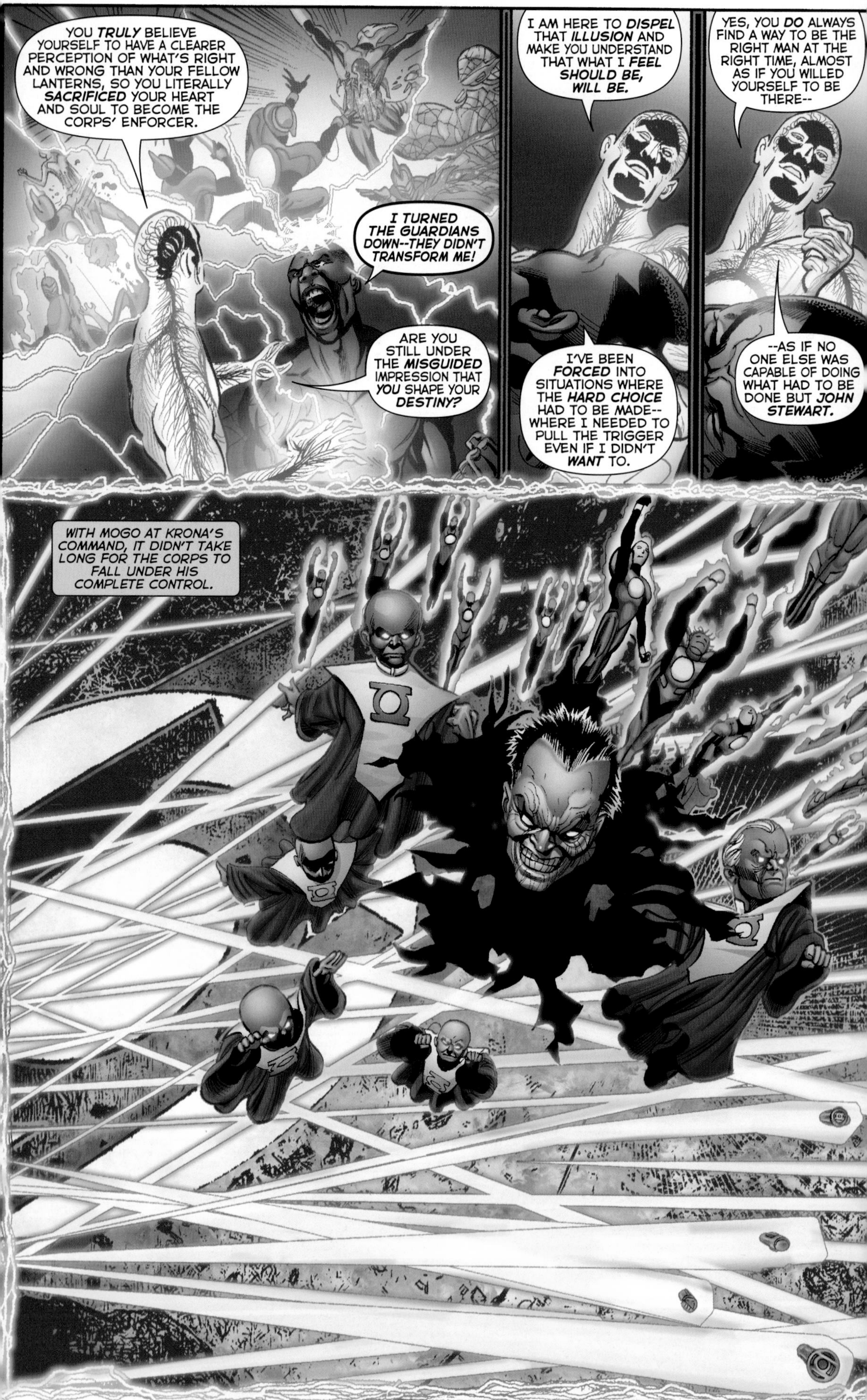
YOU TRULY BELIEVE YOURSELF TO HAVE A CLEARER PERCEPTION OF WHAT'S RIGHT AND WRONG THAN YOUR FELLOW LANTERNS, SO YOU LITERALLY SACRIFICED YOUR HEART AND SOUL TO BECOME THE CORPS' ENFORCER.
I TURNED THE GUARDIANS DOWN--THEY DIDN'T TRANSFORM ME!
ARE YOU STILL UNDER THE MISGUIDED IMPRESSION THAT YOU SHAPE YOUR DESTINY?
I AM HERE TO DISPEL THAT ILLUSION AND MAKE YOU UNDERSTAND THAT WHAT I FEEL SHOULD BE, WILL BE.
I'VE BEEN FORCED INTO SITUATIONS WHERE THE HARD CHOICE HAD TO BE MADE--WHERE I NEEDED TO PULL THE TRIGGER EVEN IF I DIDN'T WANT TO.
YES, YOU DO ALWAYS FIND A WAY TO BE THE RIGHT MAN AT THE RIGHT TIME, ALMOST AS IF YOU WILLED YOURSELF TO BE THERE--
--AS IF NO ONE ELSE WAS CAPABLE OF DOING WHAT HAD TO BE DONE BUT JOHN STEWART.
WITH MOGO AT KRONA'S COMMAND, IT DIDN'T TAKE LONG FOR THE CORPS TO FALL UNDER HIS COMPLETE CONTROL.

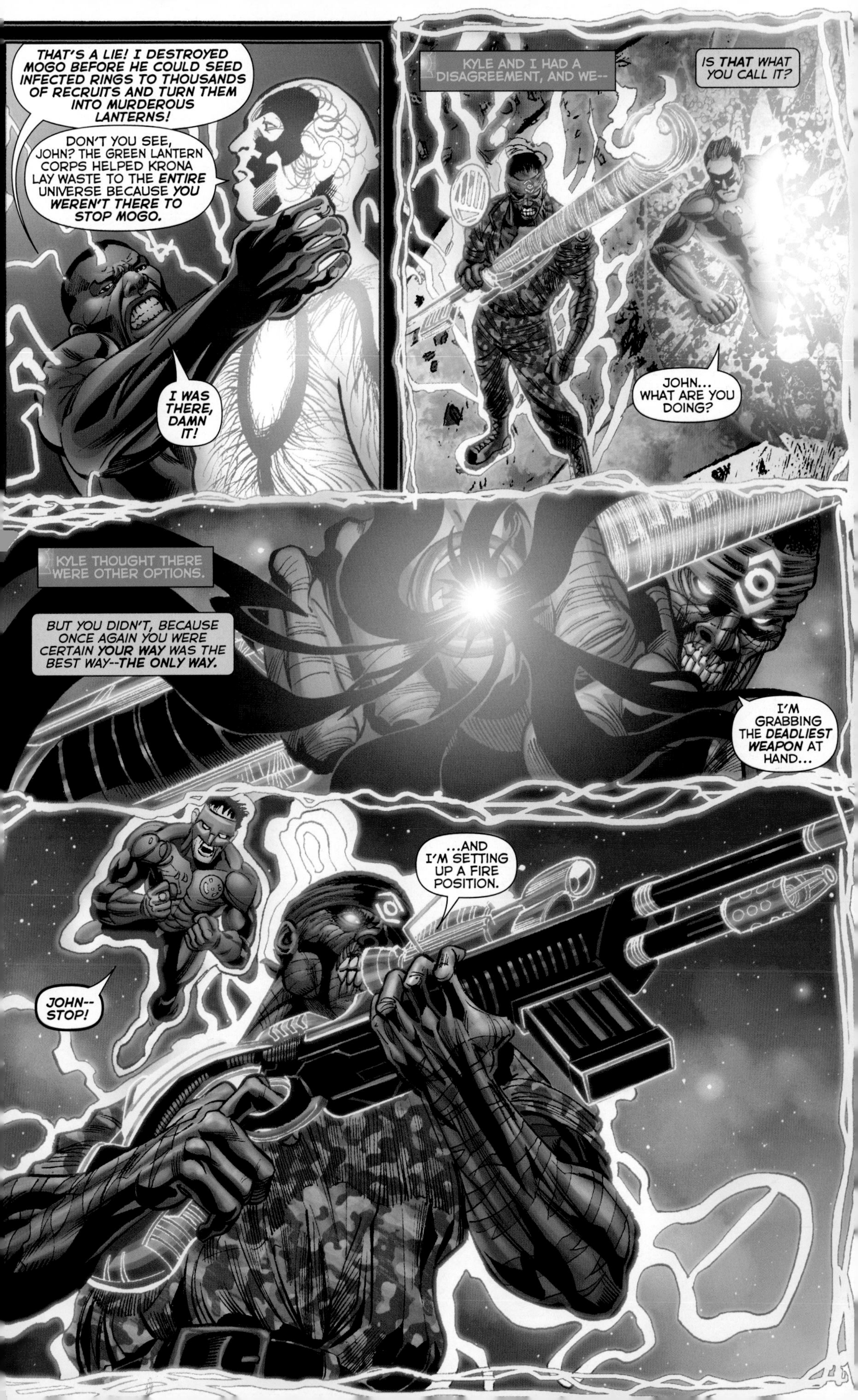
THAT'S A LIE! I DESTROYED MOGO BEFORE HE COULD SEED INFECTED RINGS TO THOUSANDS OF RECRUITS AND TURN THEM INTO MURDEROUS LANTERNS!
DON'T YOU SEE, JOHN? THE GREEN LANTERN CORPS HELPED KRONA LAY WASTE TO THE ENTIRE UNIVERSE BECAUSE YOU WEREN'T THERE TO STOP MOGO.
I WAS THERE, DAMN IT!
KYLE AND I HAD A DISAGREEMENT, AND WE--
IS THAT WHAT YOU CALL IT?
JOHN... WHAT ARE YOU DOING?
KYLE THOUGHT THERE WERE OTHER OPTIONS.
BUT YOU DIDN'T, BECAUSE ONCE AGAIN YOU WERE CERTAIN YOUR WAY WAS THE BEST WAY--THE ONLY WAY.
I'M GRABBING THE DEADLIEST WEAPON AT HAND...
...AND I'M SETTING UP A FIRE POSITION.
JOHN-- STOP!

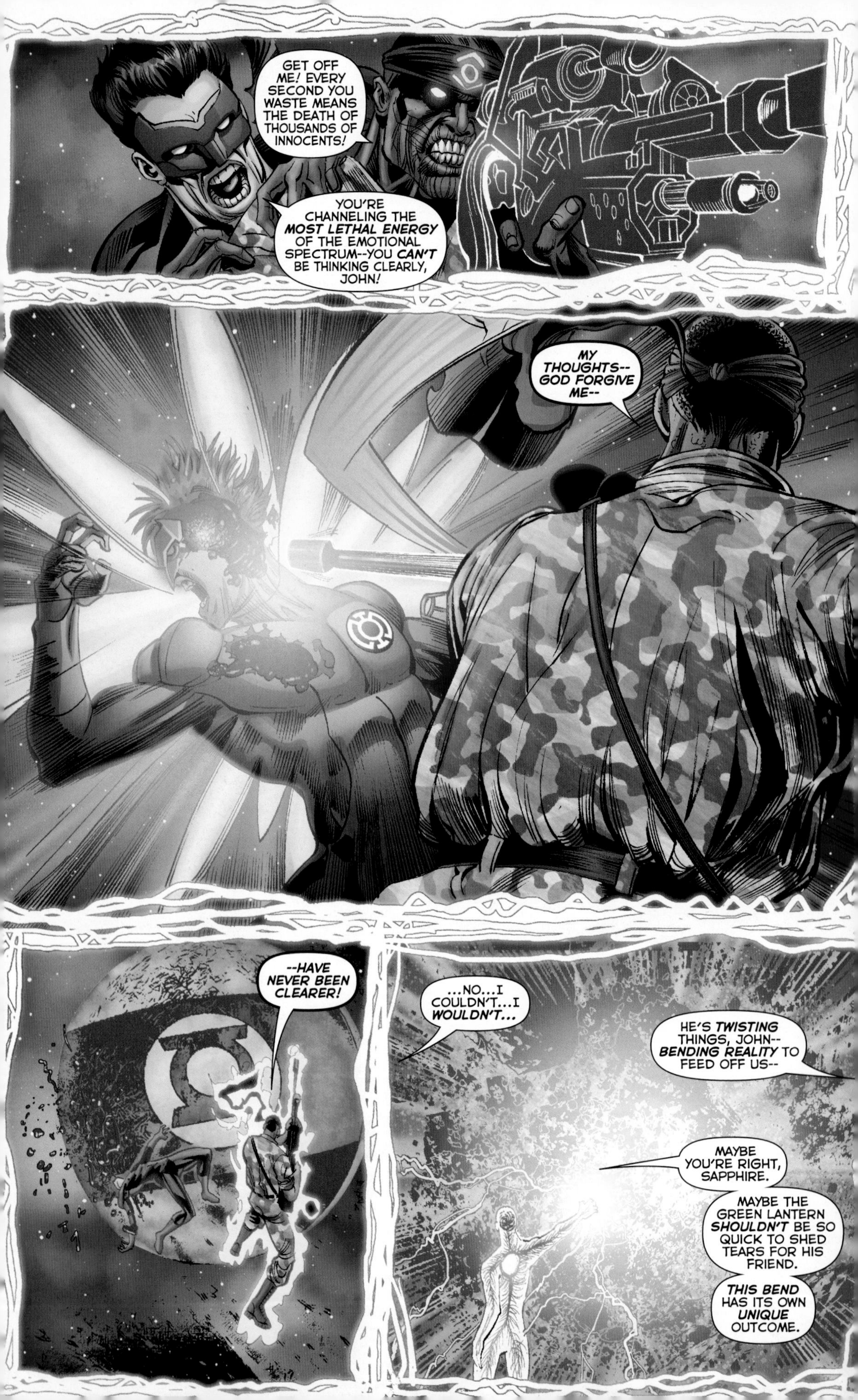
GET OFF ME! EVERY SECOND YOU WASTE MEANS THE DEATH OF THOUSANDS OF INNOCENTS!
YOU'RE CHANNELING THE MOST LETHAL ENERGY OF THE EMOTIONAL SPECTRUM--YOU CAN'T BE THINKING CLEARLY, JOHN!
MY THOUGHTS--GOD FORGIVE ME--
--HAVE NEVER BEEN CLEARER!
...NO...I COULDN'T...I WOULDN'T...
HE'S TWISTING THINGS, JOHN--BENDING REALITY TO FEED OFF US--
MAYBE YOU'RE RIGHT, SAPPHIRE.
MAYBE THE GREEN LANTERN SHOULDN'T BE SO QUICK TO SHED TEARS FOR HIS FRIEND.
THIS BEND HAS ITS OWN UNIQUE OUTCOME.

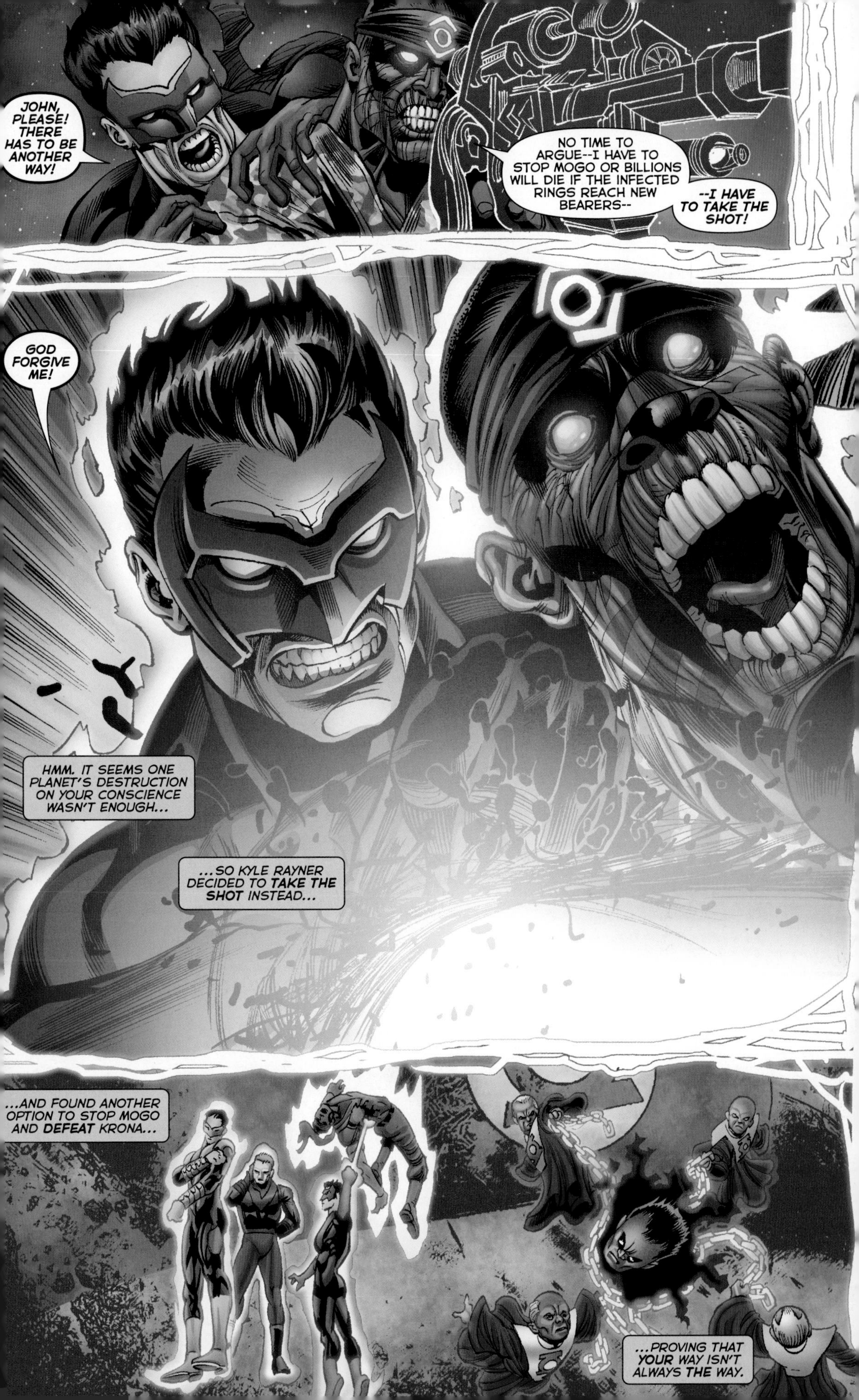
JOHN, PLEASE! THERE HAS TO BE ANOTHER WAY!
NO TIME TO ARGUE--I HAVE TO STOP MOGO OR BILLIONS WILL DIE IF THE INFECTED RINGS REACH NEW BEARERS--
--I HAVE TO TAKE THE SHOT!
GOD FORGIVE ME!
HMM. IT SEEMS ONE PLANET'S DESTRUCTION ON YOUR CONSCIENCE WASN'T ENOUGH...
...SO KYLE RAYNER DECIDED TO TAKE THE SHOT INSTEAD...
...AND FOUND ANOTHER OPTION TO STOP MOGO AND DEFEAT KRONA...
...PROVING THAT YOUR WAY ISN'T ALWAYS THE WAY.

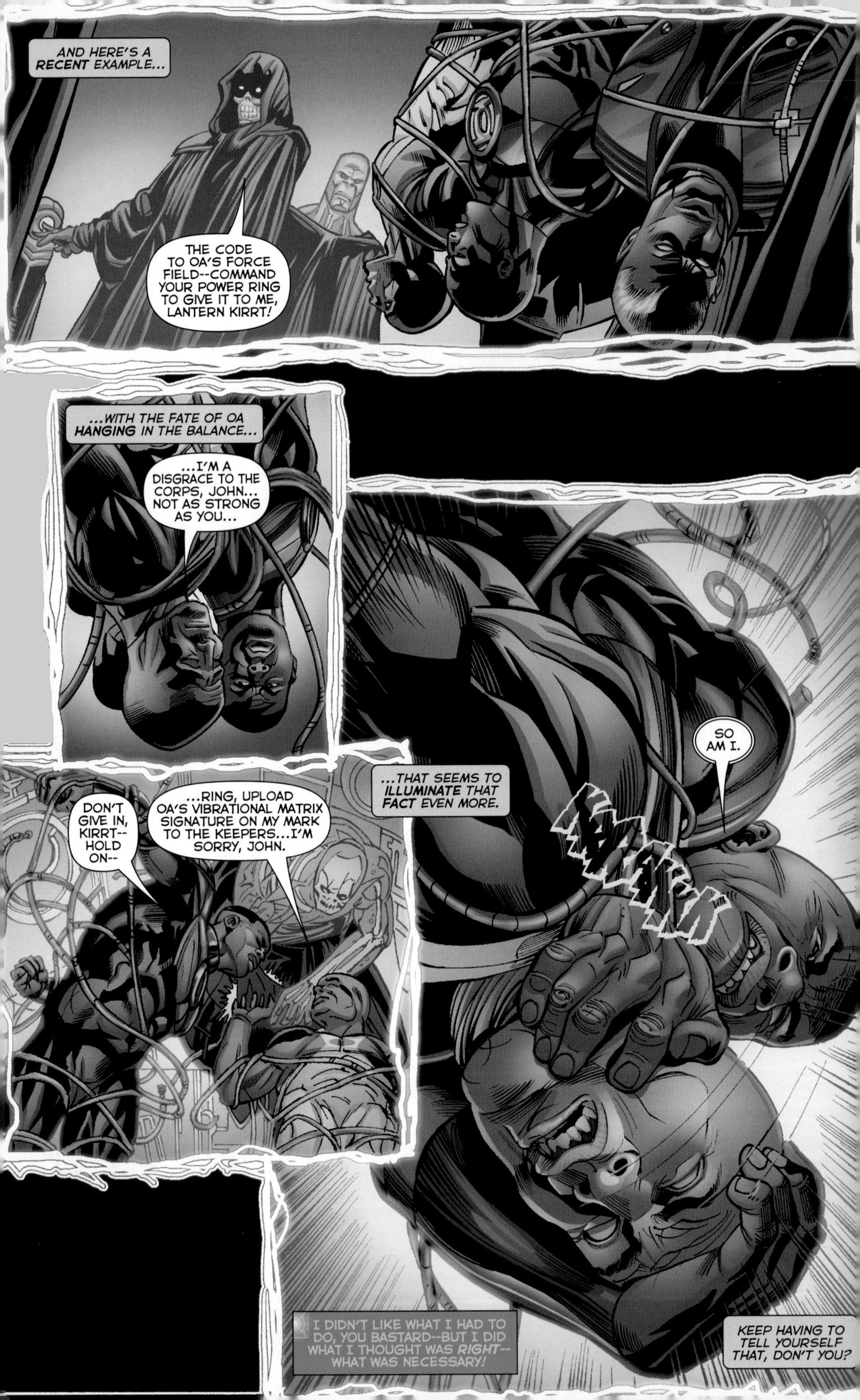
AND HERE'S A RECENT EXAMPLE...
THE CODE TO OA'S FORCE FIELD--COMMAND YOUR POWER RING TO GIVE IT TO ME, LANTERN KIRRT!
...WITH THE FATE OF OA HANGING IN THE BALANCE...
...I'M A DISGRACE TO THE CORPS, JOHN... NOT AS STRONG AS YOU...
DON'T GIVE IN, KIRRT--HOLD ON--
...RING, UPLOAD OA'S VIBRATIONAL MATRIX SIGNATURE ON MY MARK TO THE KEEPERS...I'M SORRY, JOHN.
...THAT SEEMS TO ILLUMINATE THAT FACT EVEN MORE.
SO AM I.
I DIDN'T LIKE WHAT I HAD TO DO, YOU BASTARD--BUT I DID WHAT I THOUGHT WAS RIGHT--WHAT WAS NECESSARY!
KEEP HAVING TO TELL YOURSELF THAT, DON'T YOU?

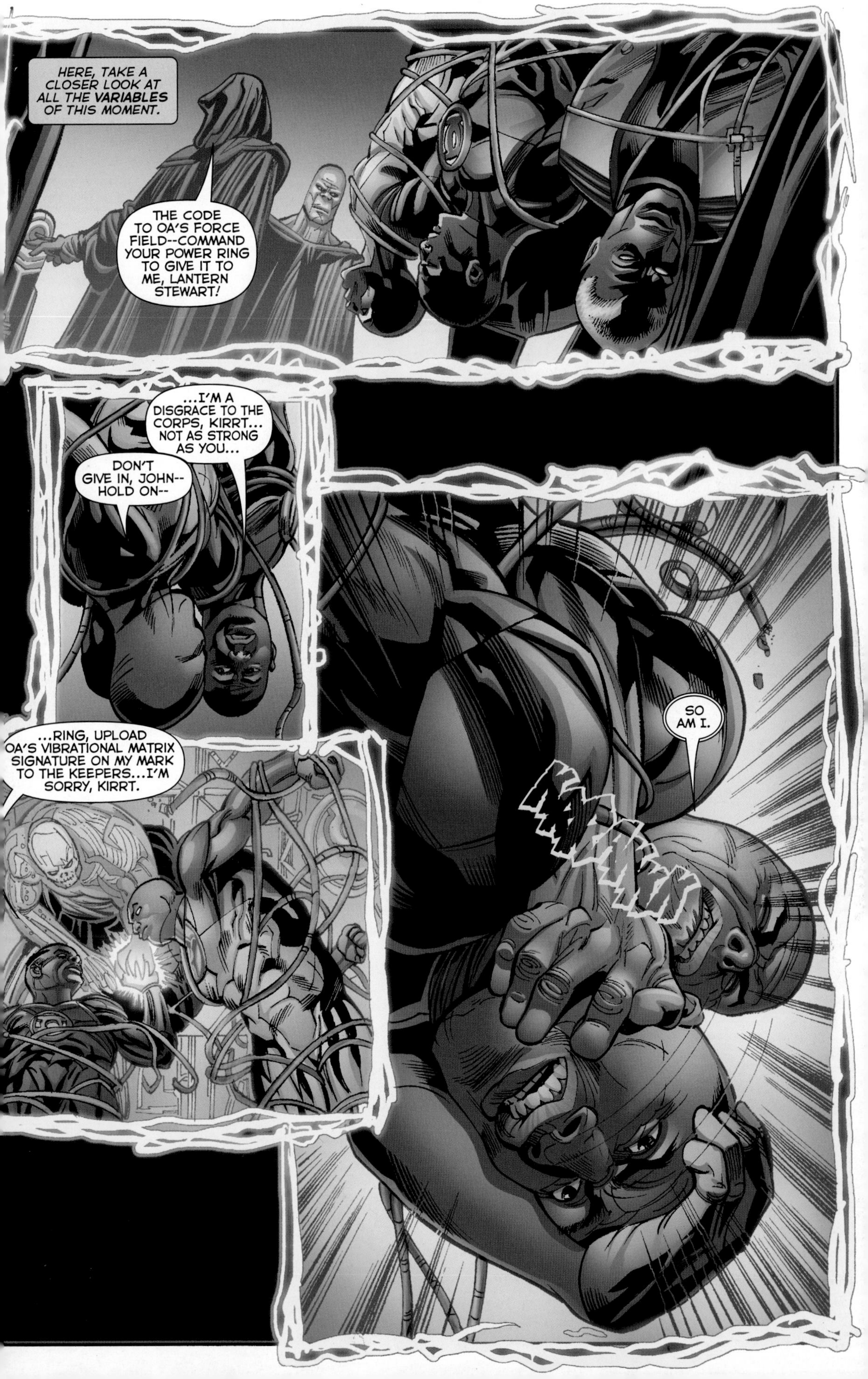
HERE, TAKE A CLOSER LOOK AT ALL THE VARIABLES OF THIS MOMENT.
THE CODE TO OA'S FORCE FIELD--COMMAND YOUR POWER RING TO GIVE IT TO ME, LANTERN STEWART!
...I'M A DISGRACE TO THE CORPS, KIRRT... NOT AS STRONG AS YOU...
DON'T GIVE IN, JOHN-- HOLD ON--
...RING, UPLOAD OA'S VIBRATIONAL MATRIX SIGNATURE ON MY MARK TO THE KEEPERS...I'M SORRY, KIRRT.
SO AM I.

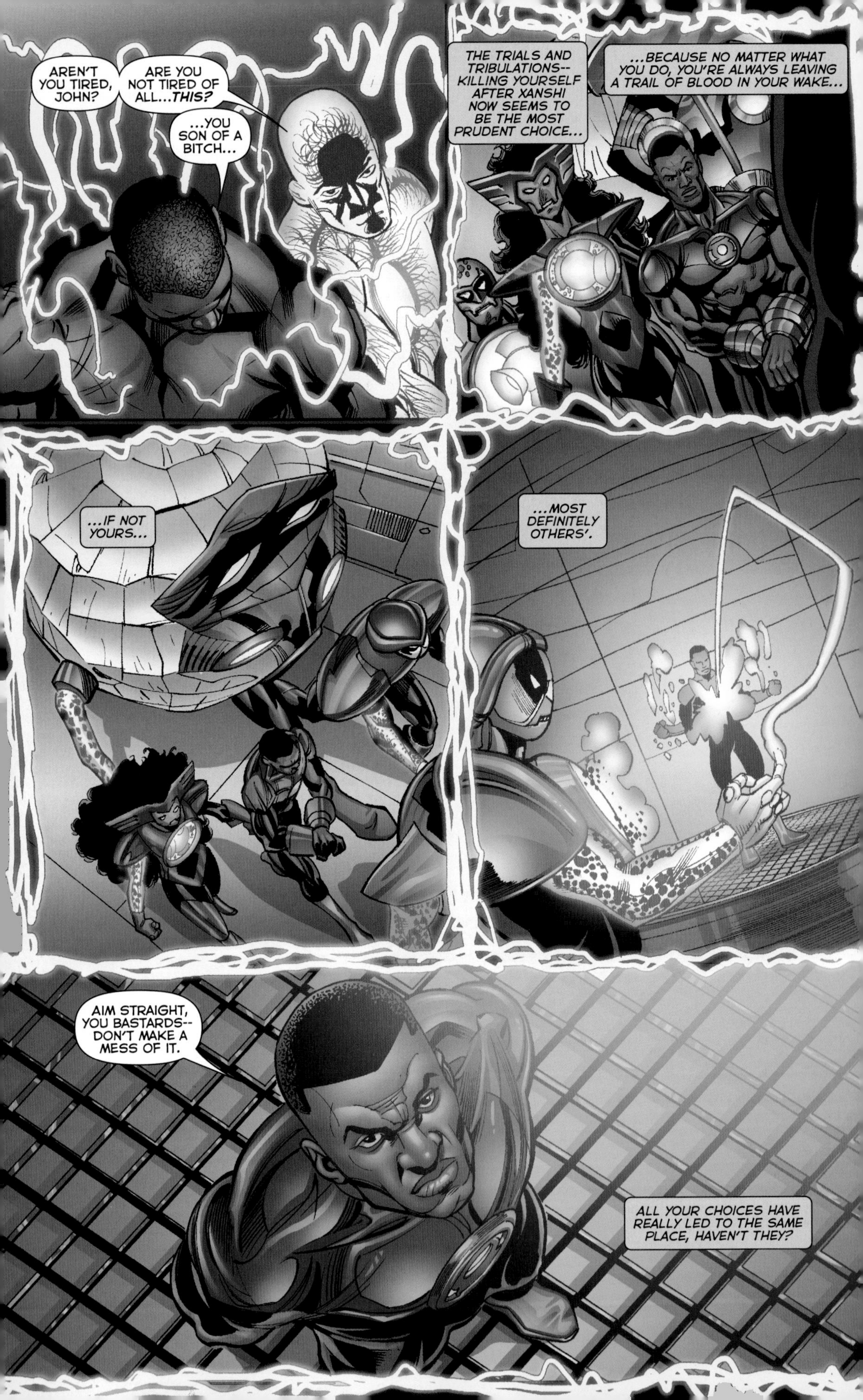
AREN'T YOU TIRED, JOHN?
ARE YOU NOT TIRED OF ALL...THIS?
...YOU SON OF A BITCH...
THE TRIALS AND TRIBULATIONS-- KILLING YOURSELF AFTER XANSHI NOW SEEMS TO BE THE MOST PRUDENT CHOICE...
...BECAUSE NO MATTER WHAT YOU DO, YOU'RE ALWAYS LEAVING A TRAIL OF BLOOD IN YOUR WAKE...
...IF NOT YOURS...
...MOST DEFINITELY OTHERS'.
AIM STRAIGHT, YOU BASTARDS-- DON'T MAKE A MESS OF IT.
ALL YOUR CHOICES HAVE REALLY LED TO THE SAME PLACE, HAVEN'T THEY?

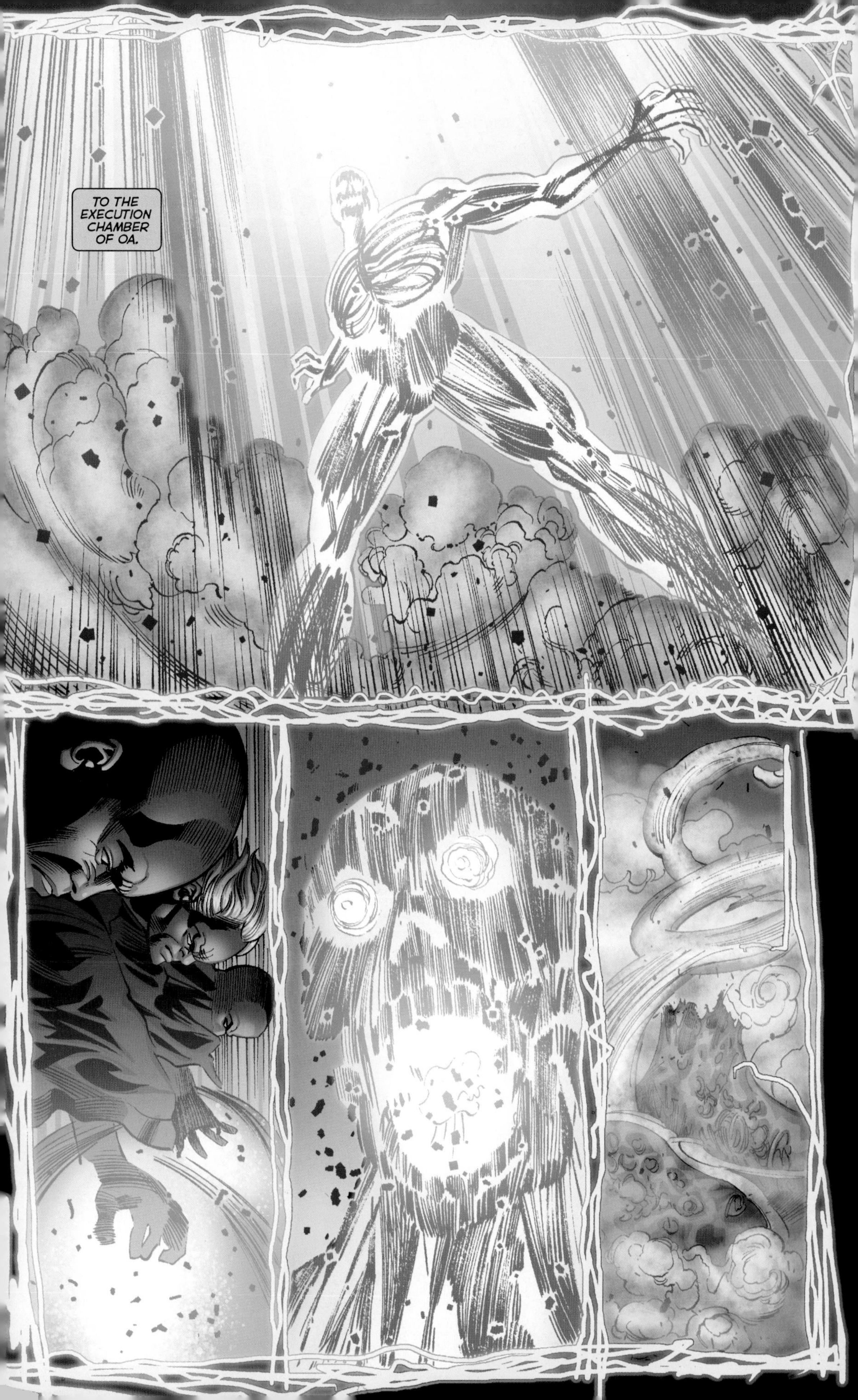
TO THE EXECUTION CHAMBER OF OA.

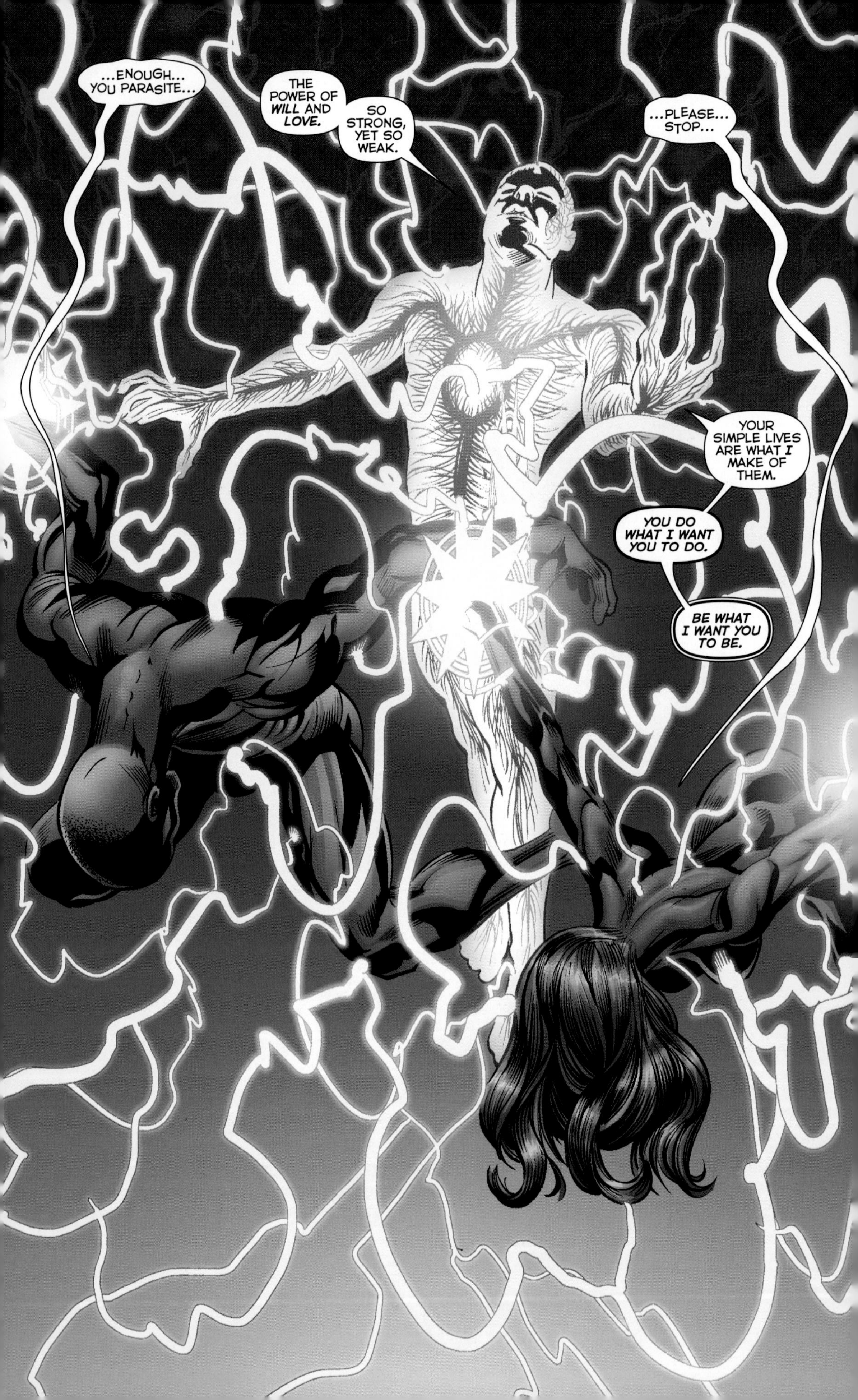
...ENOUGH... YOU PARASITE...
THE POWER OF *WILL* AND *LOVE.*
SO STRONG, YET SO WEAK.
...PLEASE... STOP...
YOUR SIMPLE LIVES ARE WHAT *I* MAKE OF THEM.
YOU DO WHAT I WANT YOU TO DO.
BE WHAT I WANT YOU TO BE.

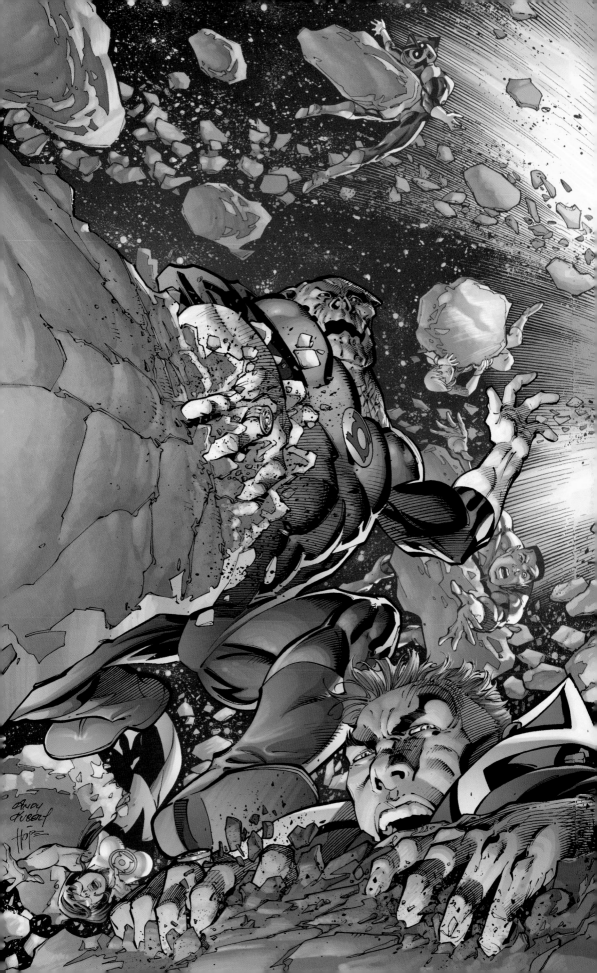

WILLING

PETER J. TOMASI writer **FERNANDO PASARIN** penciller **SCOTT HANNA** inker
cover art by **ANDY KUBERT, SANDRA HOPE & BRAD ANDERSON**

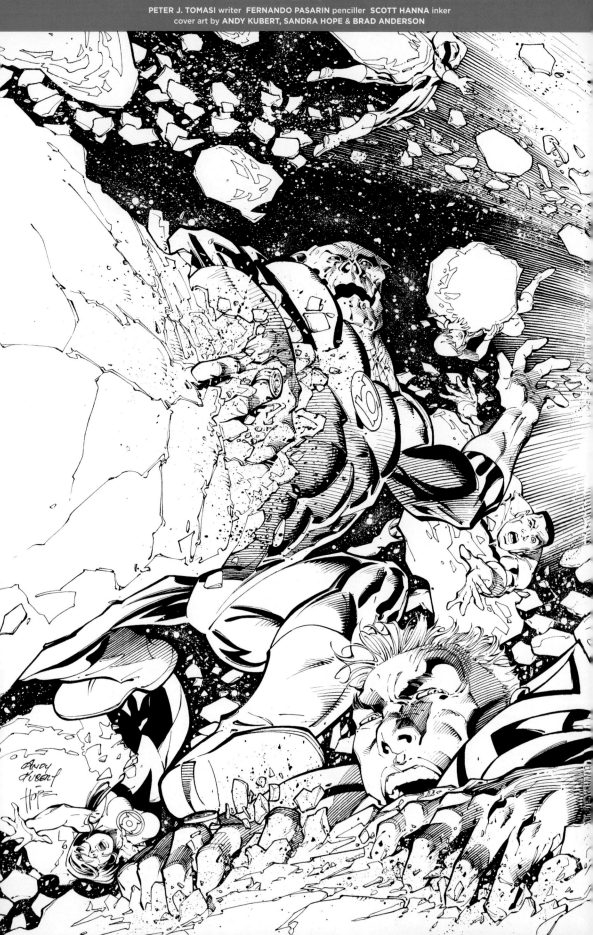

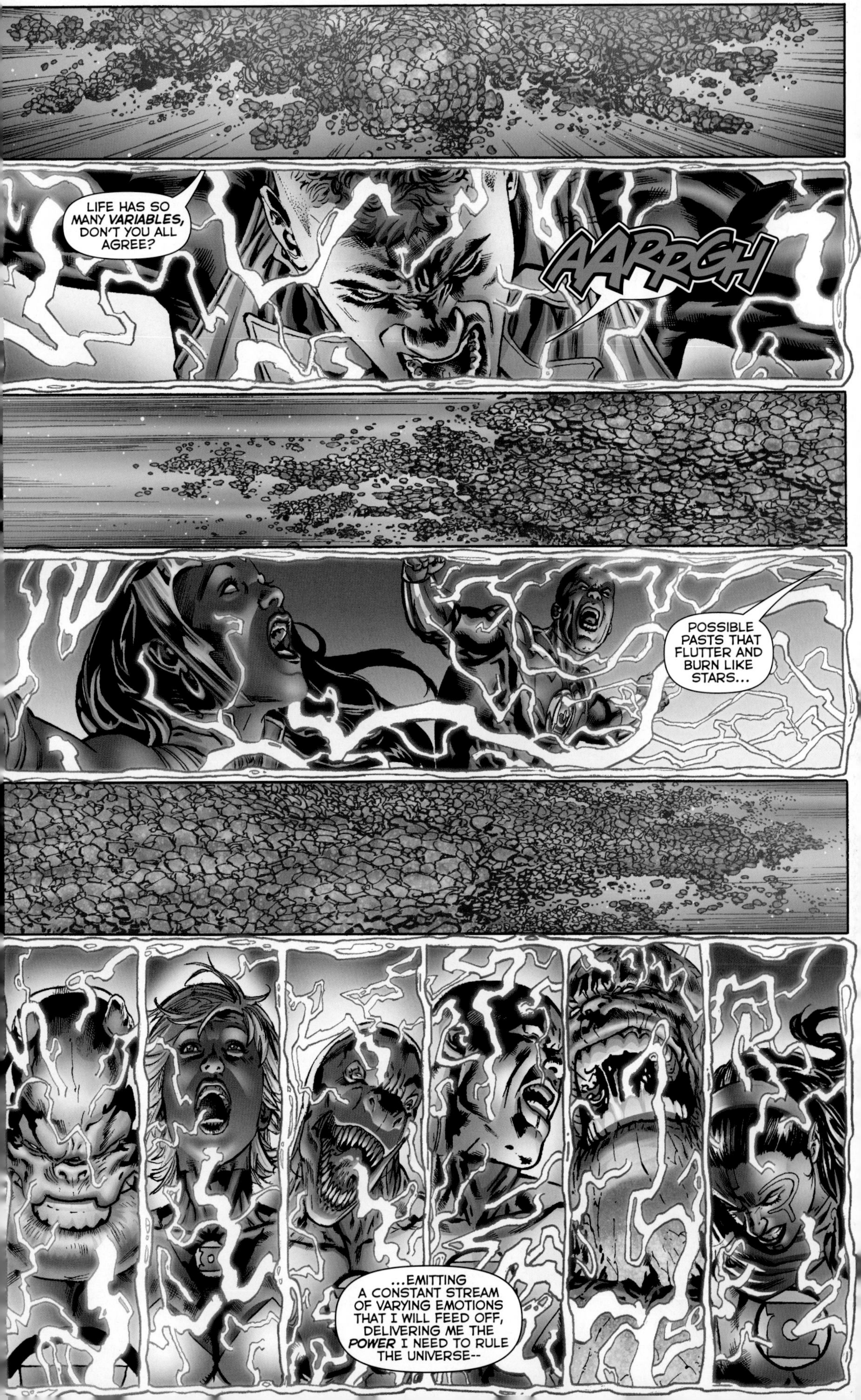
LIFE HAS SO MANY VARIABLES, DON'T YOU ALL AGREE?
AARRGH
POSSIBLE PASTS THAT FLUTTER AND BURN LIKE STARS...
...EMITTING A CONSTANT STREAM OF VARYING EMOTIONS THAT I WILL FEED OFF, DELIVERING ME THE POWER I NEED TO RULE THE UNIVERSE--

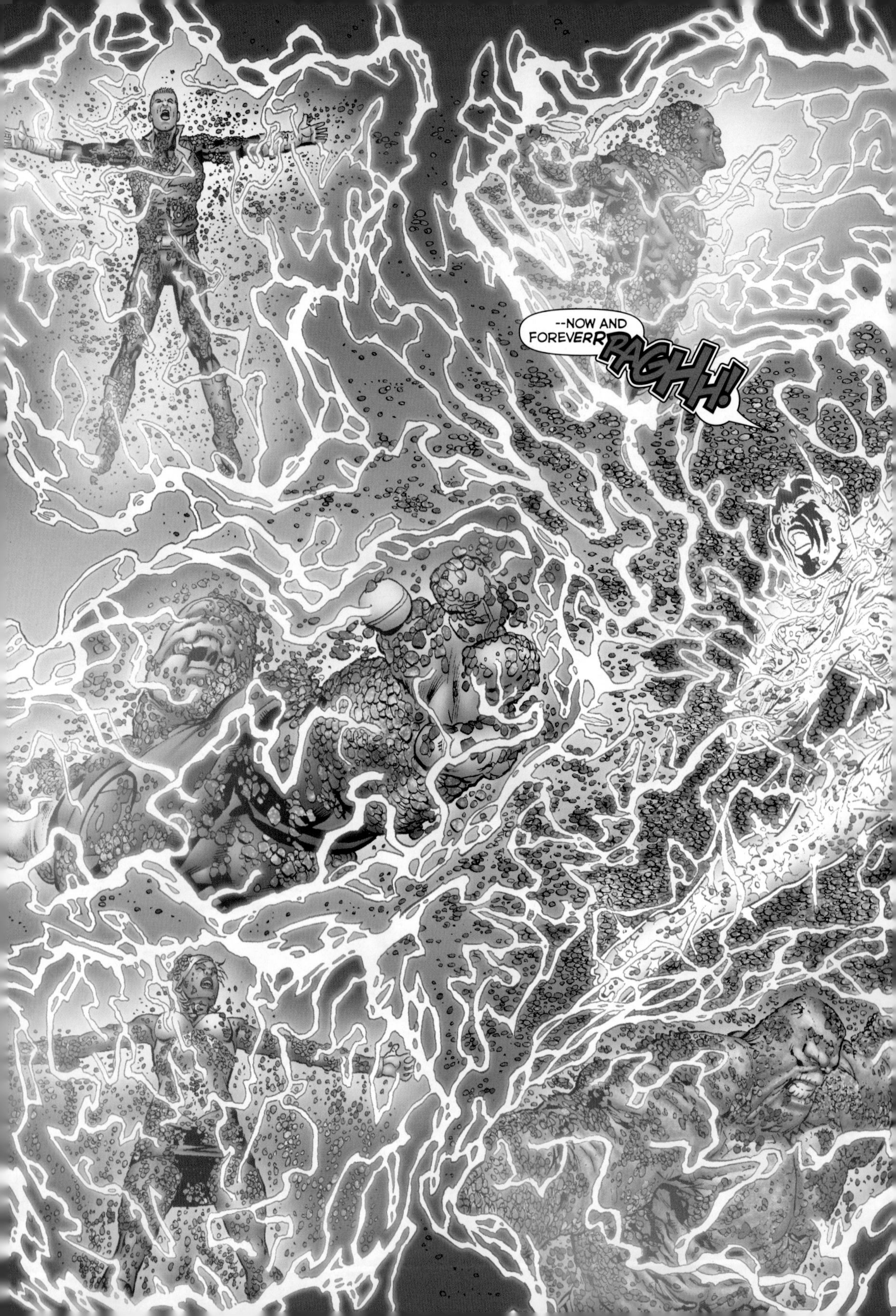
--NOW AND FOREVERR
RAGHH!

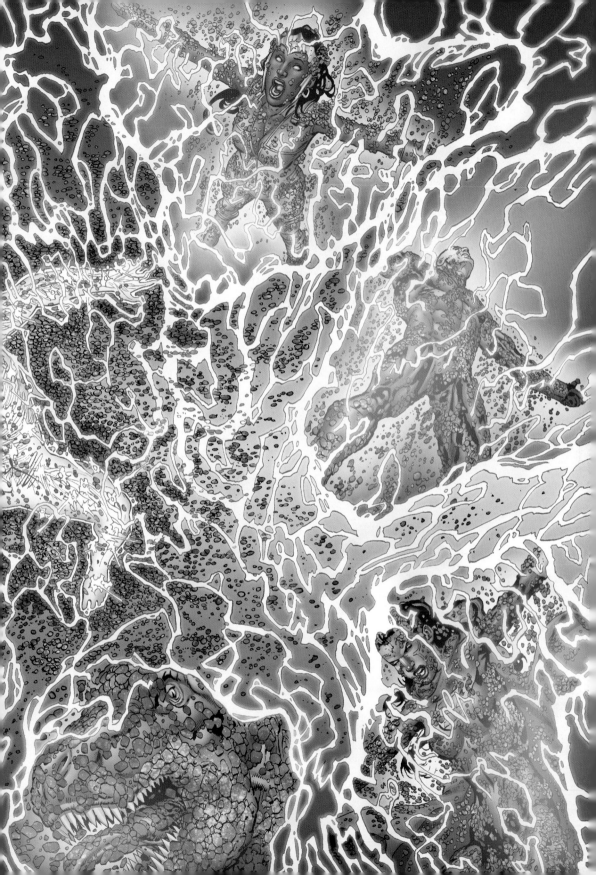

GAHH!
THESE ROCKS--
--CUTTING VOLTHOOM'S LINES--
--BASTARD'S FINALLY OUTTA MY HEAD--
UGNN!
WHO DARES?!?
JOHN!
YRAA, HANG ON!
WHATEVER'S HAPPENING--
"--IS HAPPENING ALL ACROSS OA--"

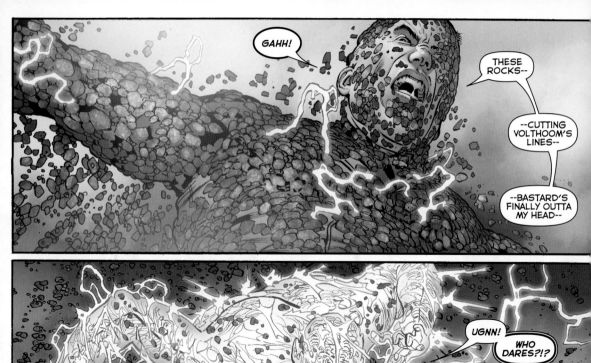

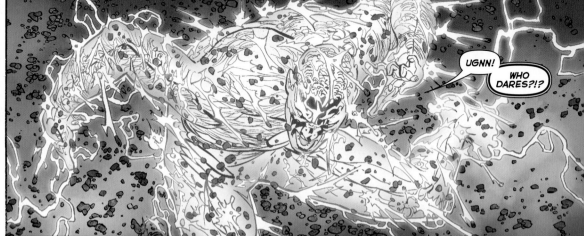

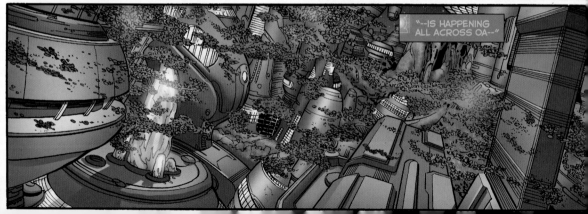

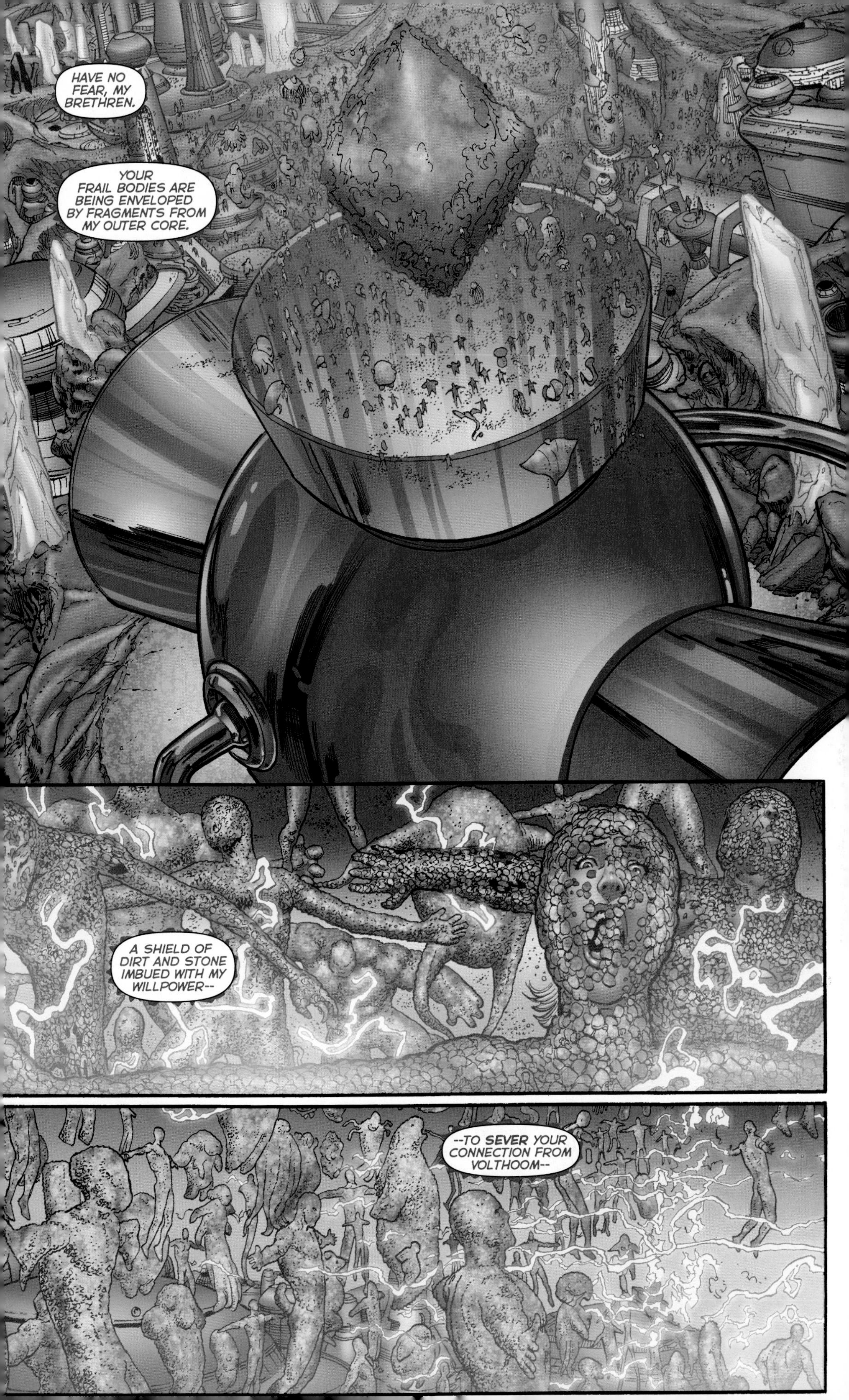
HAVE NO FEAR, MY BRETHREN.
YOUR FRAIL BODIES ARE BEING ENVELOPED BY FRAGMENTS FROM MY OUTER CORE.
A SHIELD OF DIRT AND STONE IMBUED WITH MY WILLPOWER--
--TO SEVER YOUR CONNECTION FROM VOLTHOOM--

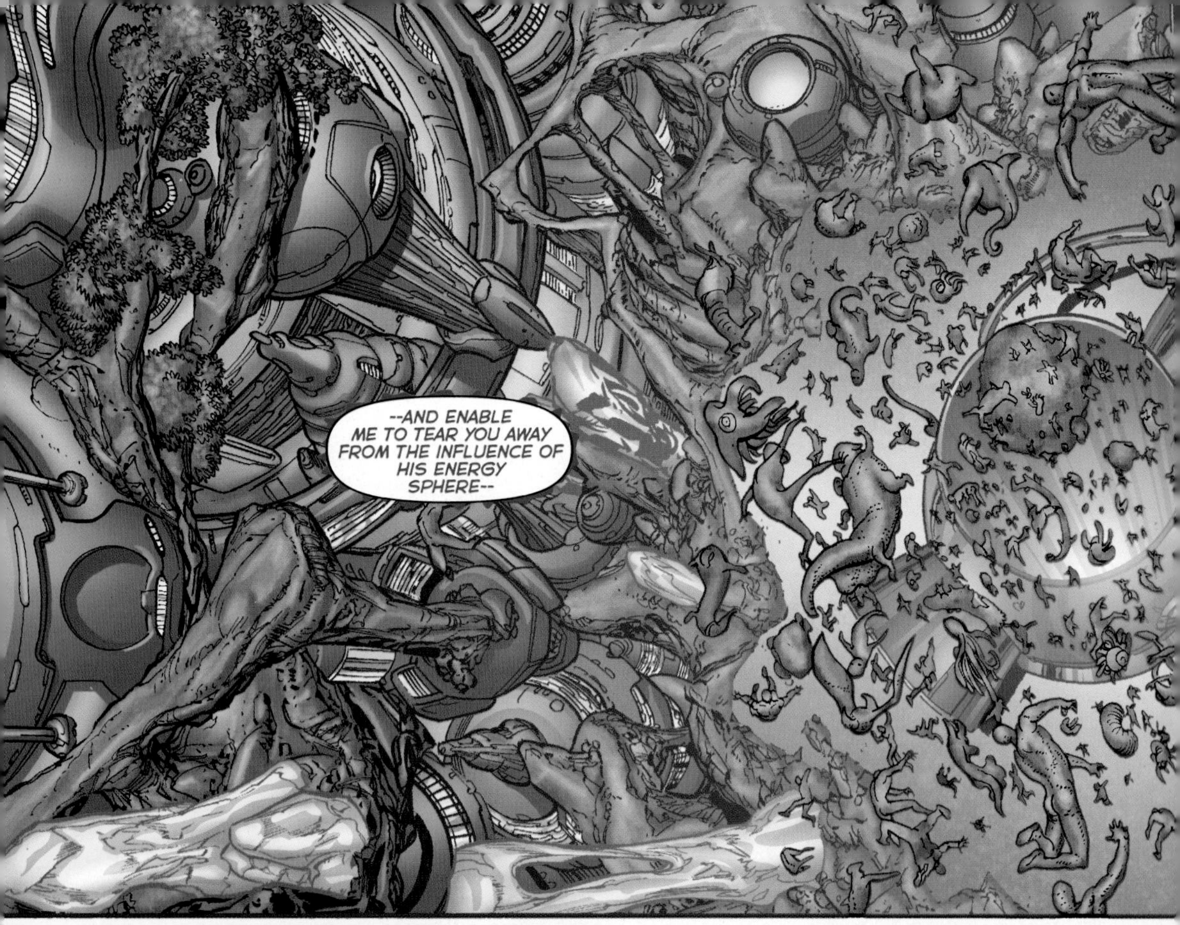
--AND ENABLE ME TO TEAR YOU AWAY FROM THE INFLUENCE OF HIS ENERGY SPHERE--

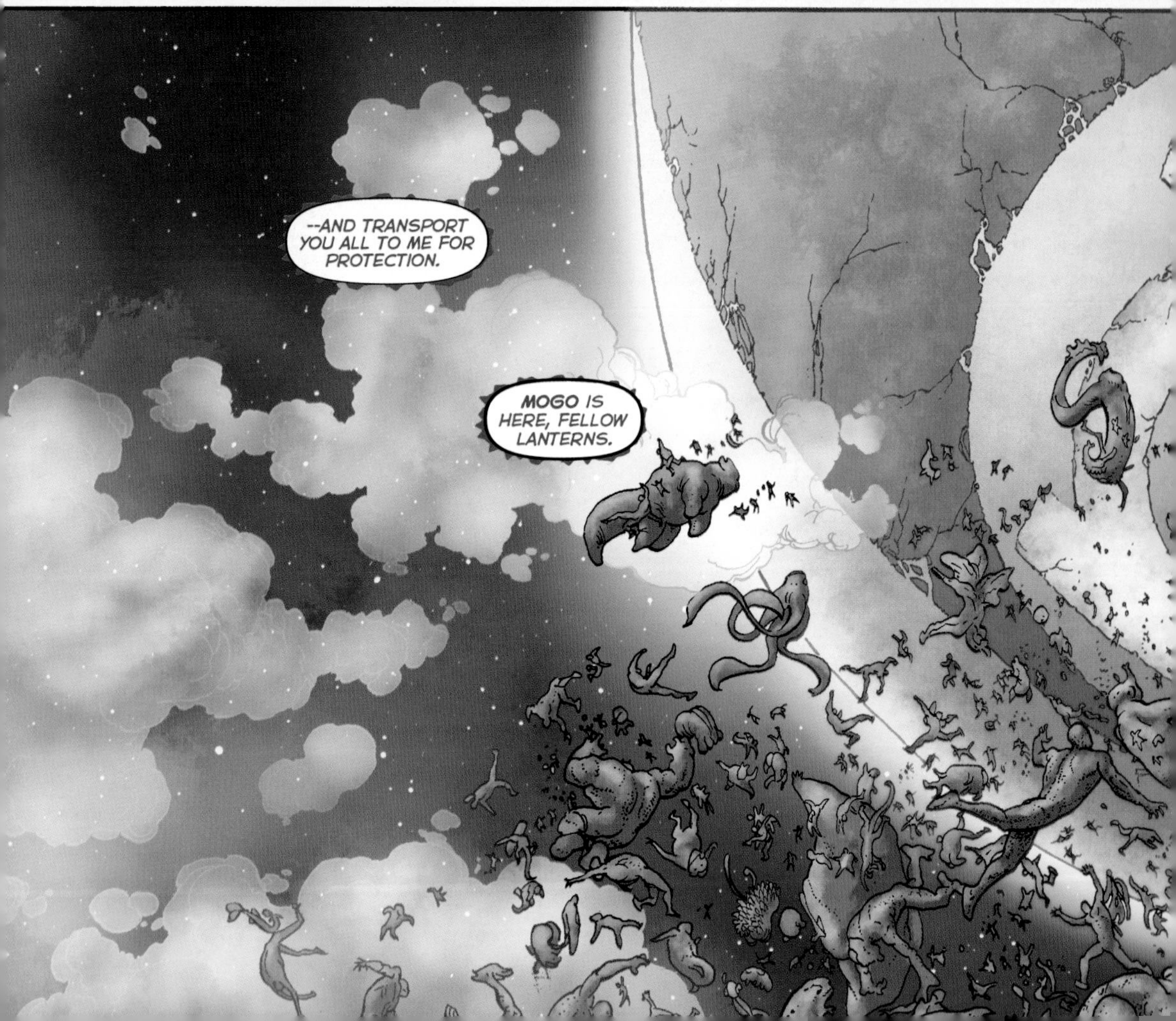
--AND TRANSPORT YOU ALL TO ME FOR PROTECTION.
MOGO IS HERE, FELLOW LANTERNS.

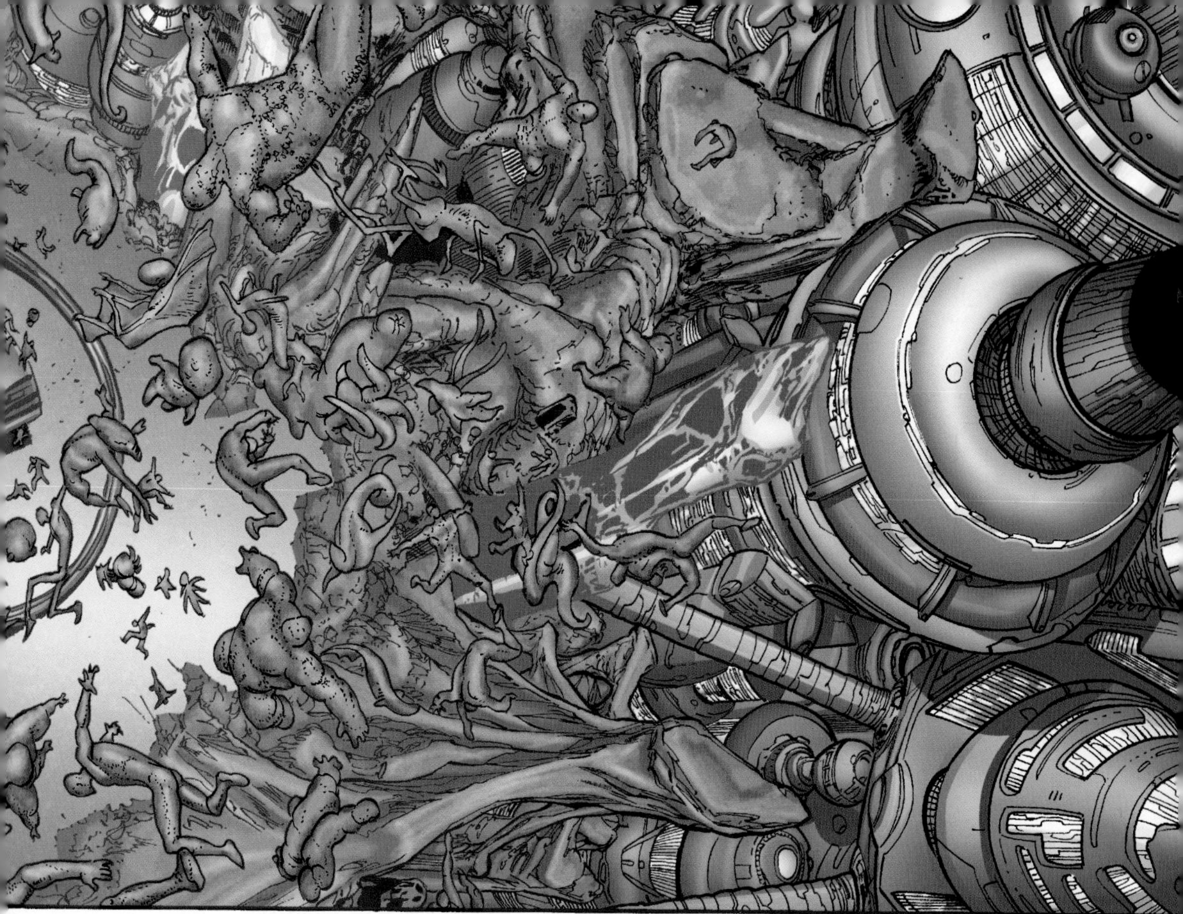
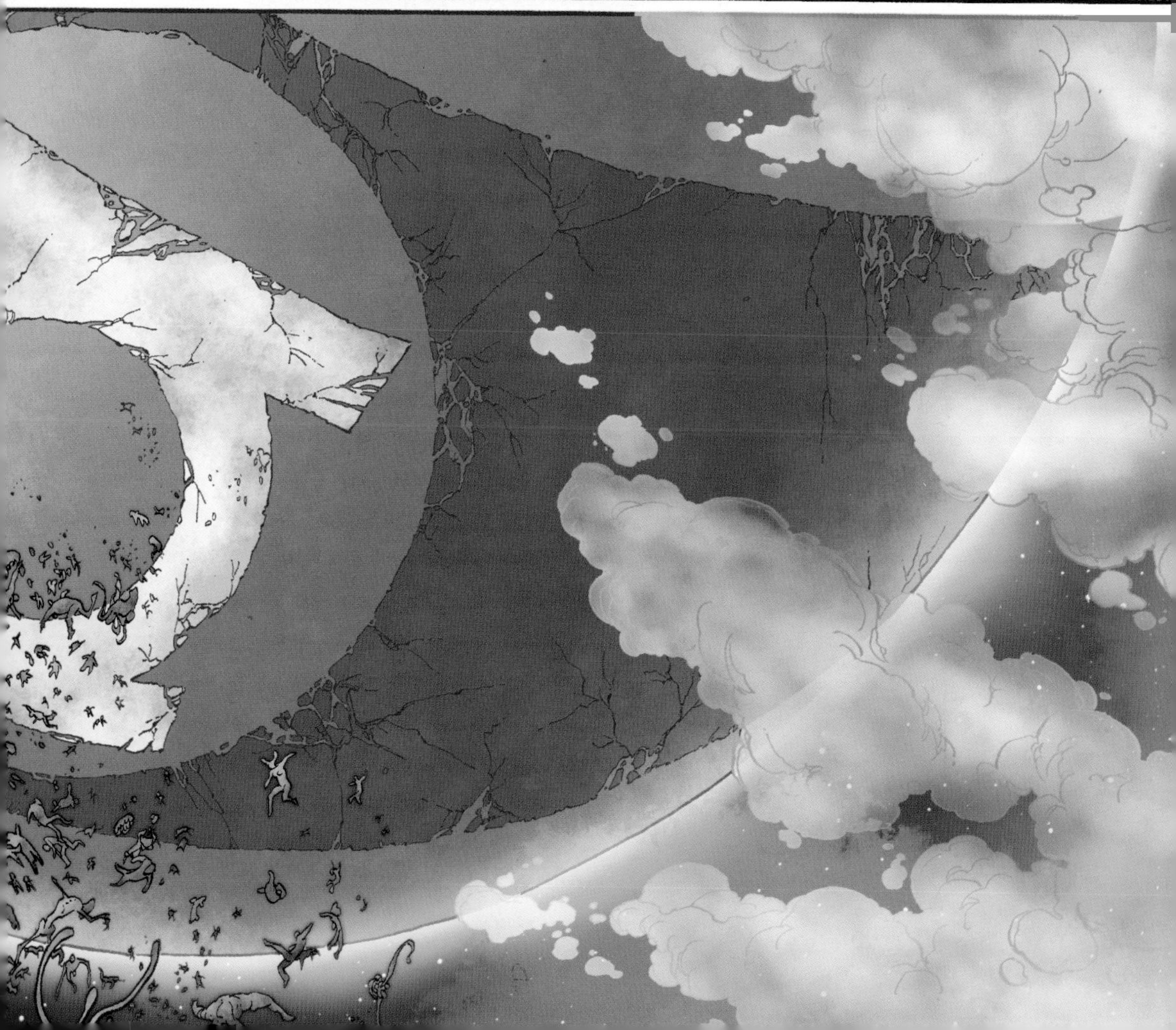

--NNGH--
--MOGO-- COMING IN-- TOO FAST--
TIME IS OF THE ESSENCE, LANTERN STEWART.
YOU WILL SUFFER NO PHYSICAL DAMAGE.
I WILL ABSORB YOUR IMPACTS.
AS I DRAW EACH AND EVERY ONE OF YOU--
--TO THE SAME POSITION ON MY SURFACE.

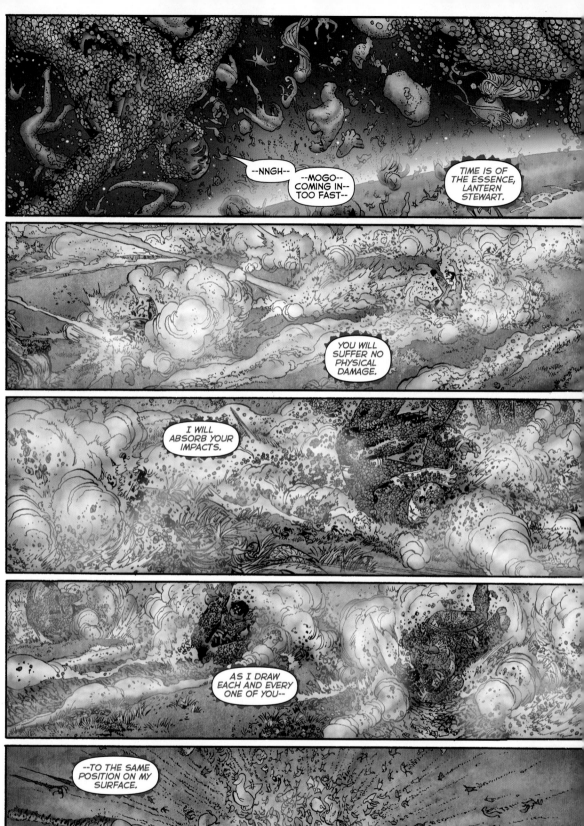

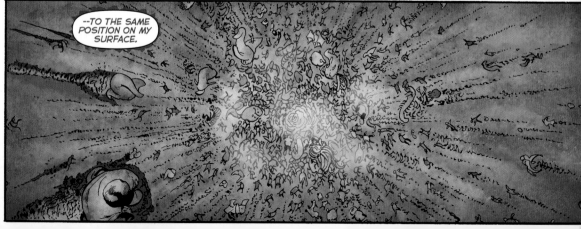

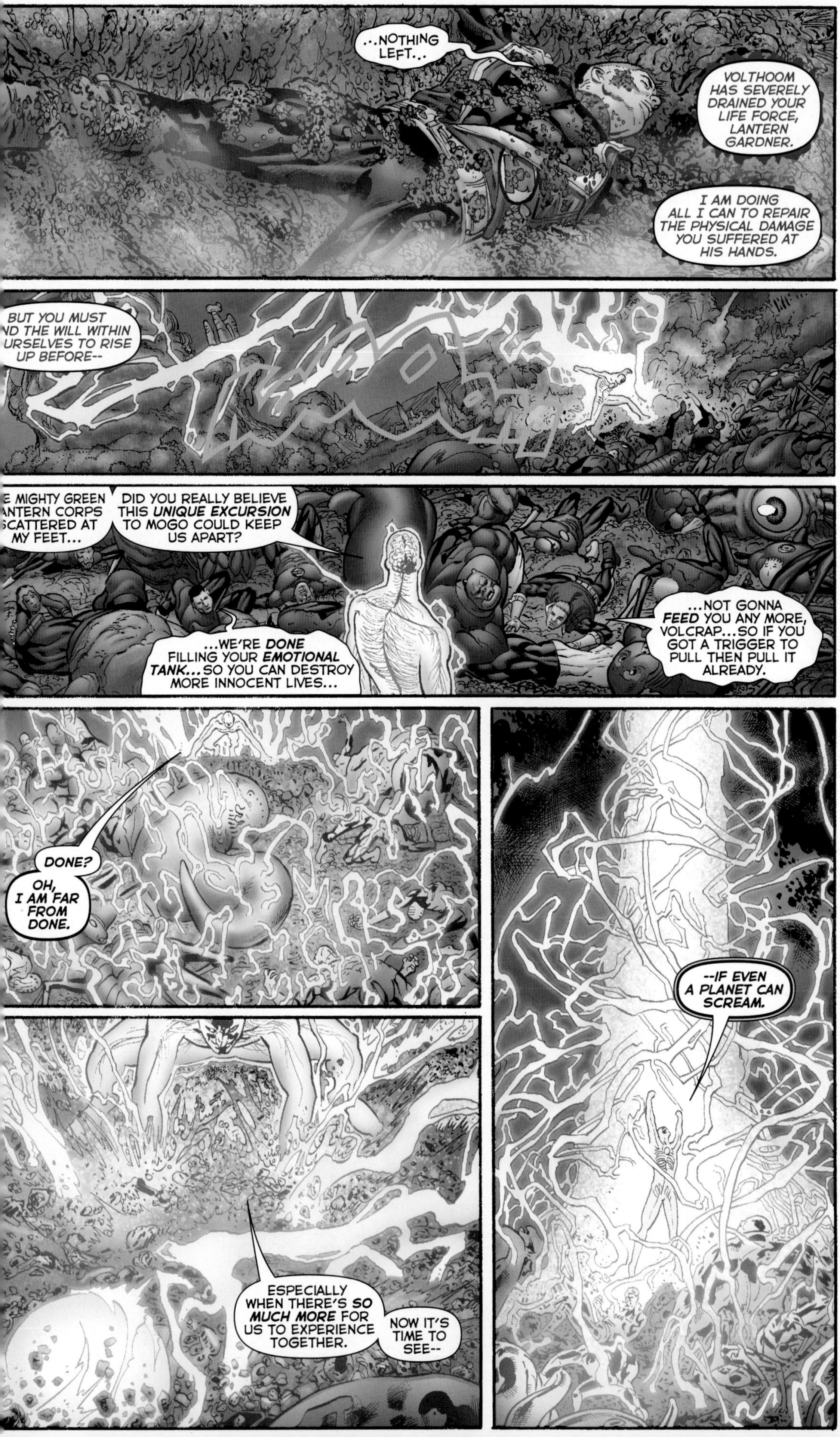
...NOTHING LEFT...
VOLTHOOM HAS SEVERELY DRAINED YOUR LIFE FORCE, LANTERN GARDNER.
I AM DOING ALL I CAN TO REPAIR THE PHYSICAL DAMAGE YOU SUFFERED AT HIS HANDS.
BUT YOU MUST ND THE WILL WITHIN URSELVES TO RISE UP BEFORE--
E MIGHTY GREEN ANTERN CORPS SCATTERED AT MY FEET...
DID YOU REALLY BELIEVE THIS UNIQUE EXCURSION TO MOGO COULD KEEP US APART?
...WE'RE DONE FILLING YOUR EMOTIONAL TANK...SO YOU CAN DESTROY MORE INNOCENT LIVES...
...NOT GONNA FEED YOU ANY MORE, VOLCRAP...SO IF YOU GOT A TRIGGER TO PULL THEN PULL IT ALREADY.
DONE?
OH, I AM FAR FROM DONE.
ESPECIALLY WHEN THERE'S SO MUCH MORE FOR US TO EXPERIENCE TOGETHER.
NOW IT'S TIME TO SEE--
--IF EVEN A PLANET CAN SCREAM.

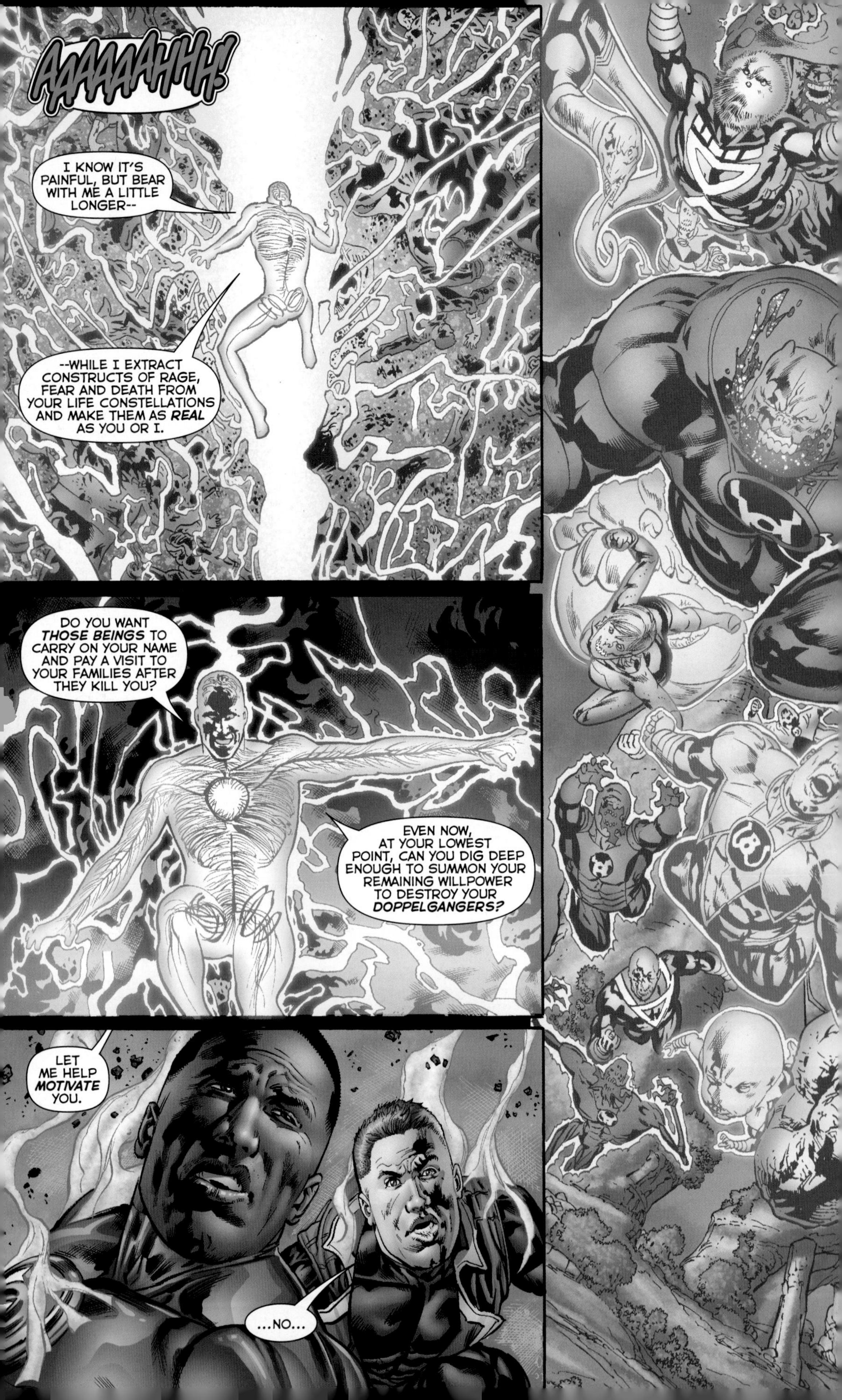
AAAAAAHHH!
I KNOW IT'S PAINFUL, BUT BEAR WITH ME A LITTLE LONGER--
--WHILE I EXTRACT CONSTRUCTS OF RAGE, FEAR AND DEATH FROM YOUR LIFE CONSTELLATIONS AND MAKE THEM AS *REAL* AS YOU OR I.
DO YOU WANT *THOSE BEINGS* TO CARRY ON YOUR NAME AND PAY A VISIT TO YOUR FAMILIES AFTER THEY KILL YOU?
EVEN NOW, AT YOUR LOWEST POINT, CAN YOU DIG DEEP ENOUGH TO SUMMON YOUR REMAINING WILLPOWER TO DESTROY YOUR *DOPPELGANGERS?*
LET ME HELP *MOTIVATE* YOU.
...NO...

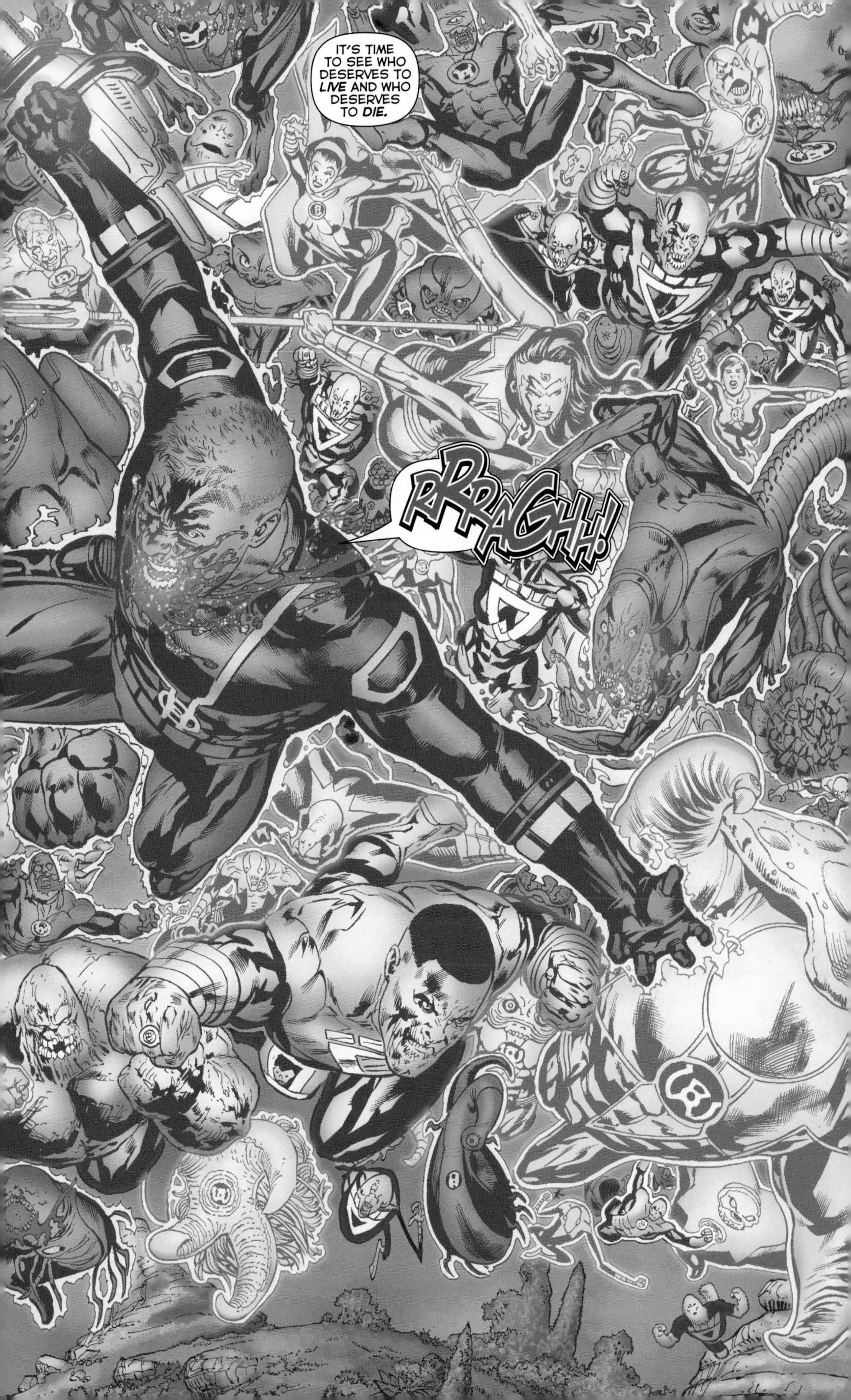
IT'S TIME TO SEE WHO DESERVES TO *LIVE* AND WHO DESERVES TO *DIE.*
RRRAGHH!

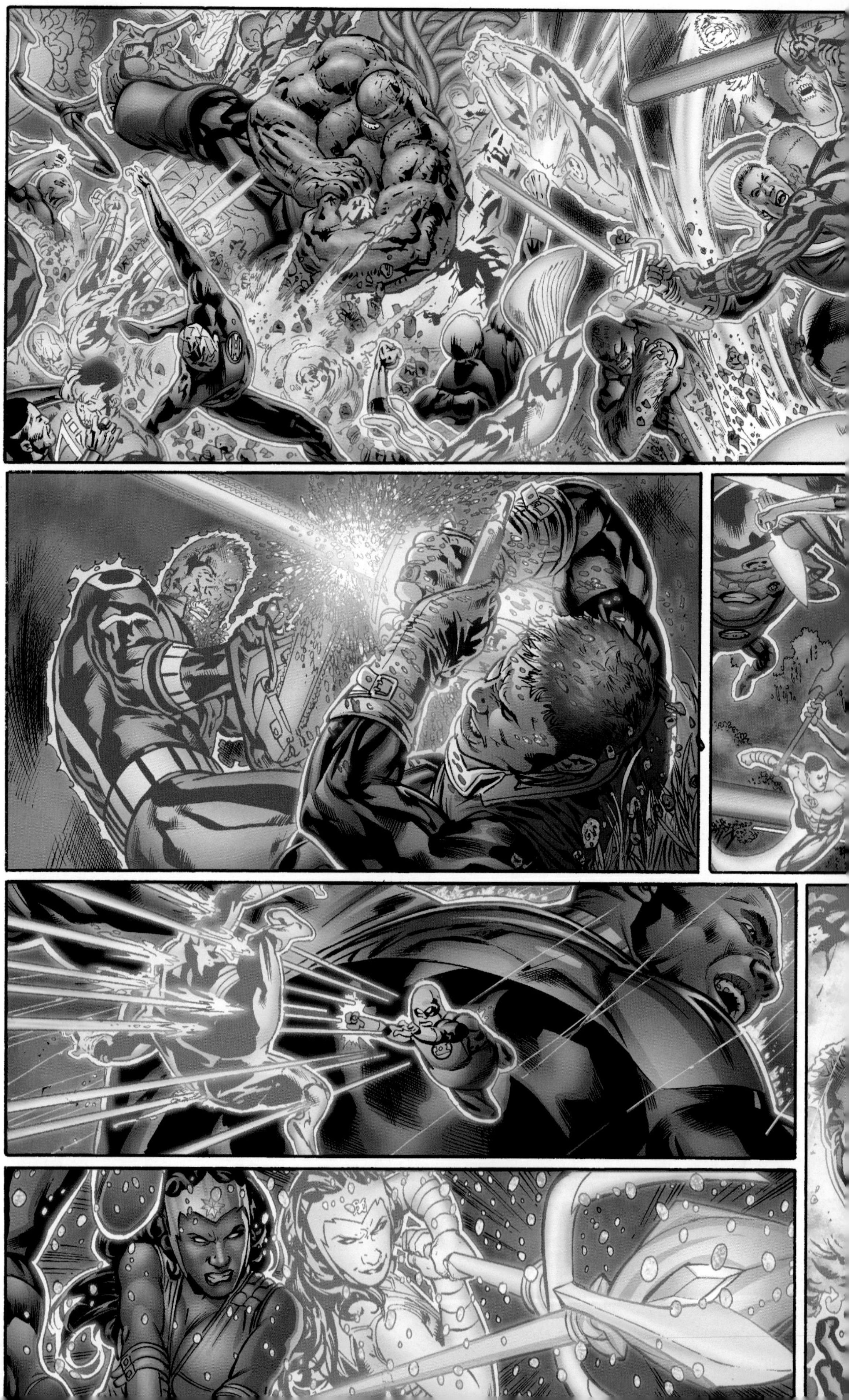

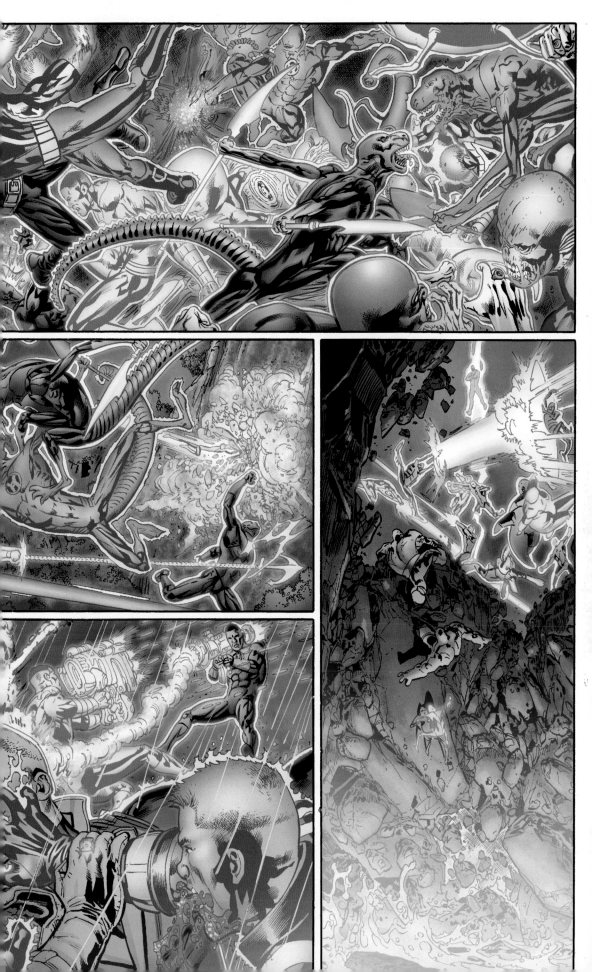

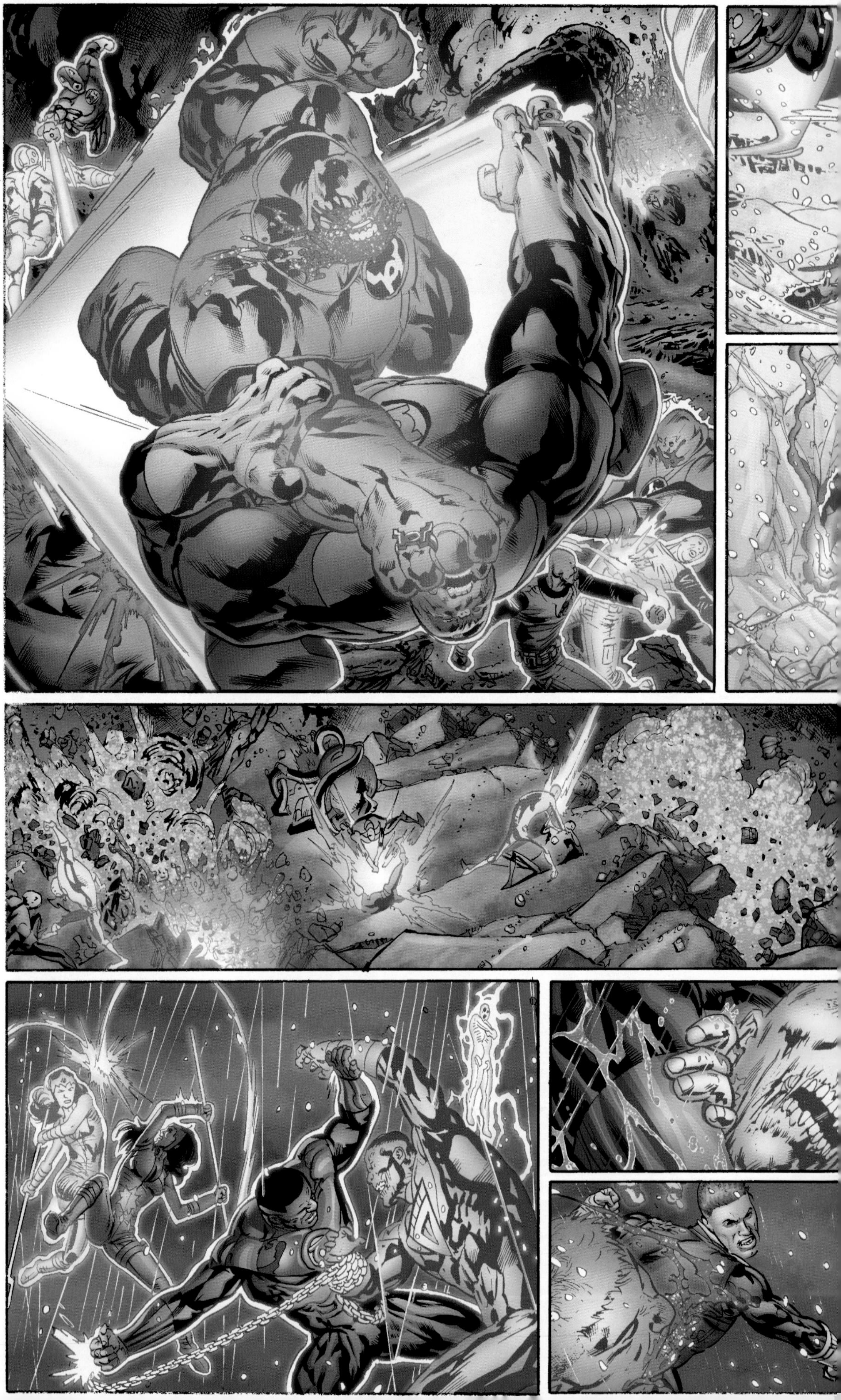

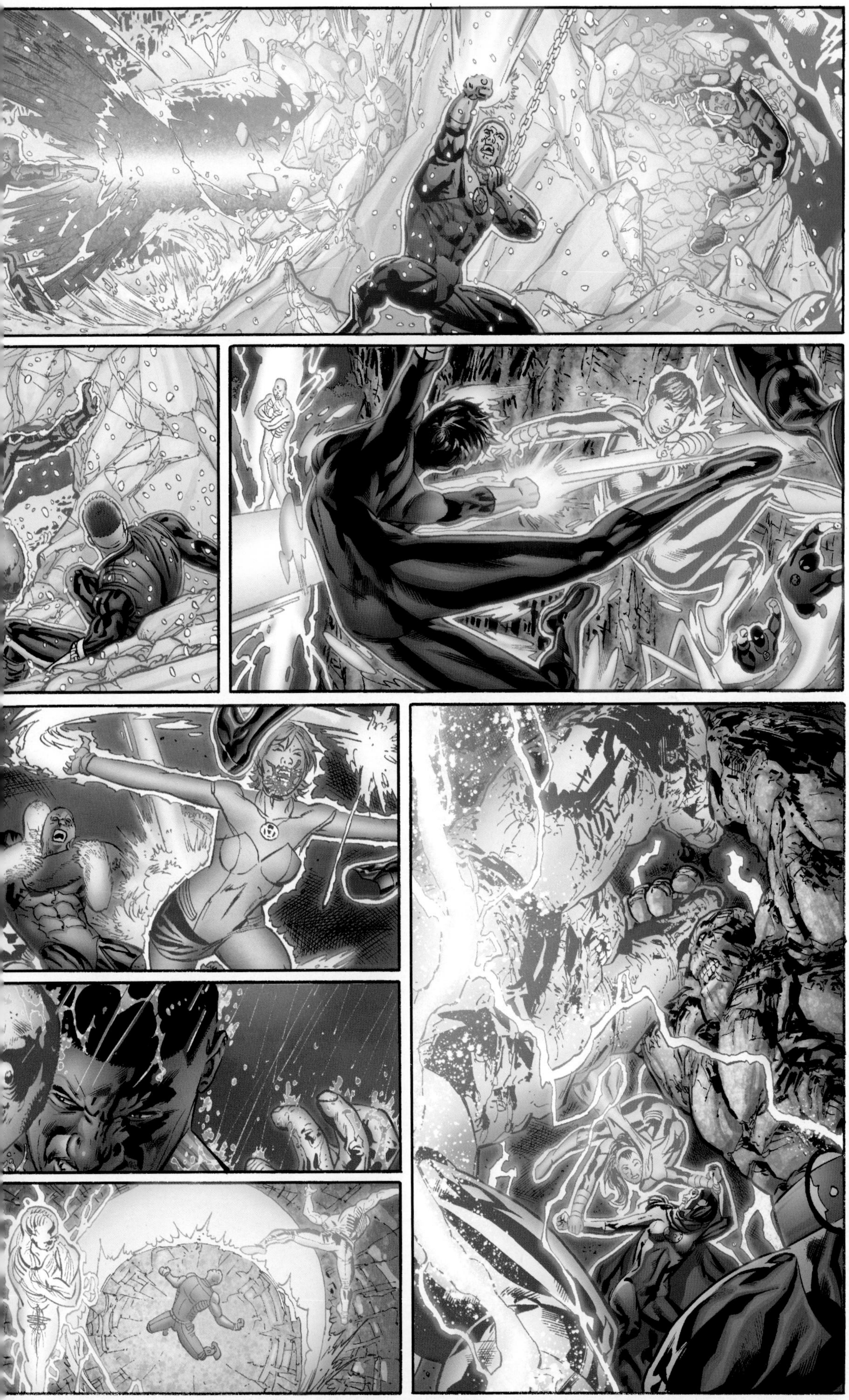

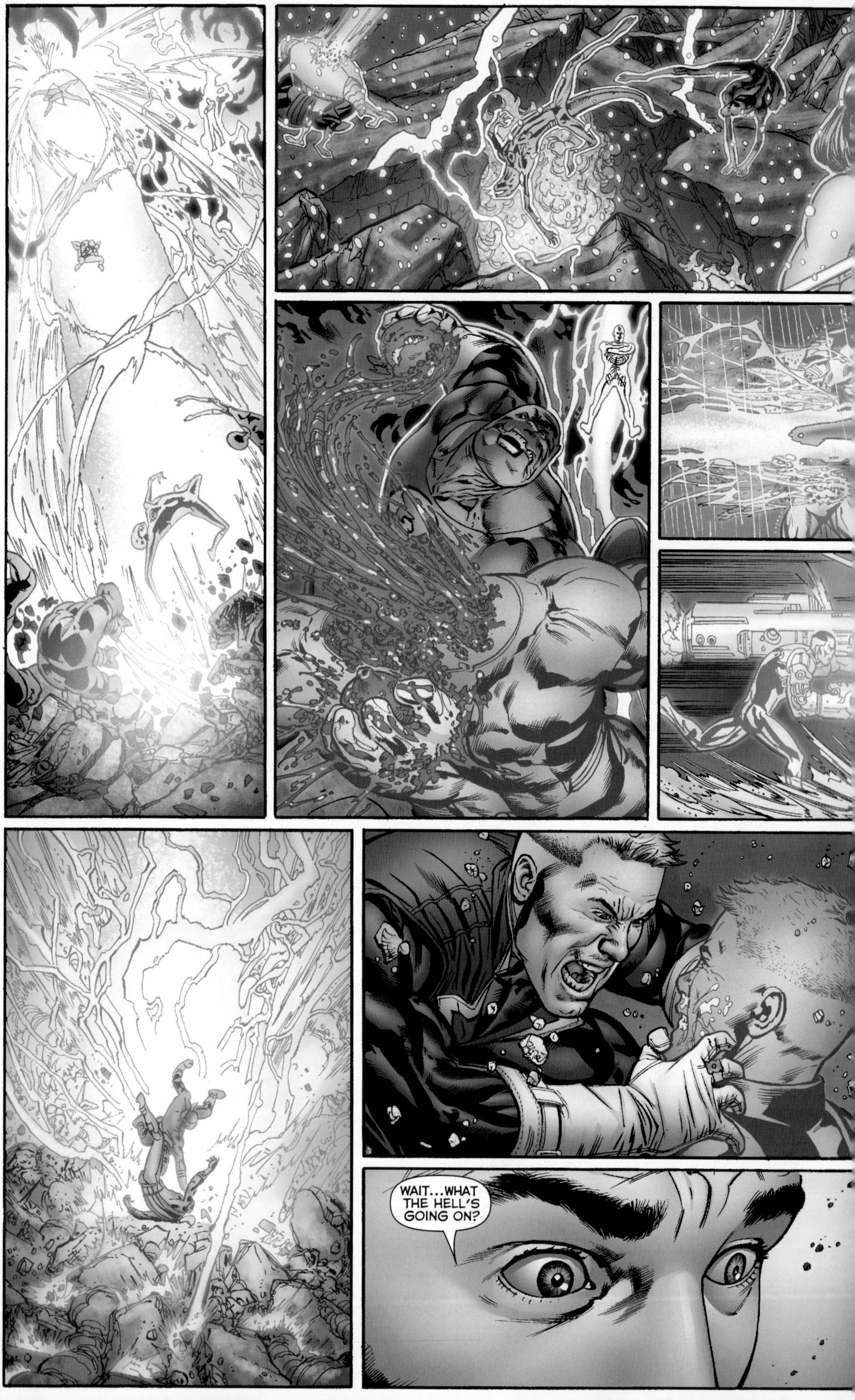
WAIT...WHAT THE HELL'S GOING ON?

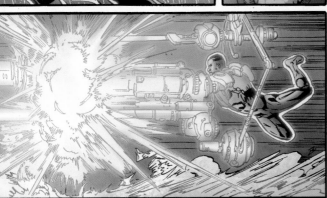

ALL THE DOPPELGANGERS HAVE STOPPED FIGHTING.

IT MUST BE ANOTHER PART OF THE FIRST LANTERN'S PLAN.

THEY'RE NOT MOVING--THEY'RE FROZEN IN THEIR TRACKS--

ACTUALLY, IT WAS ALL PART OF MY PLAN, LANTERN HANNU.

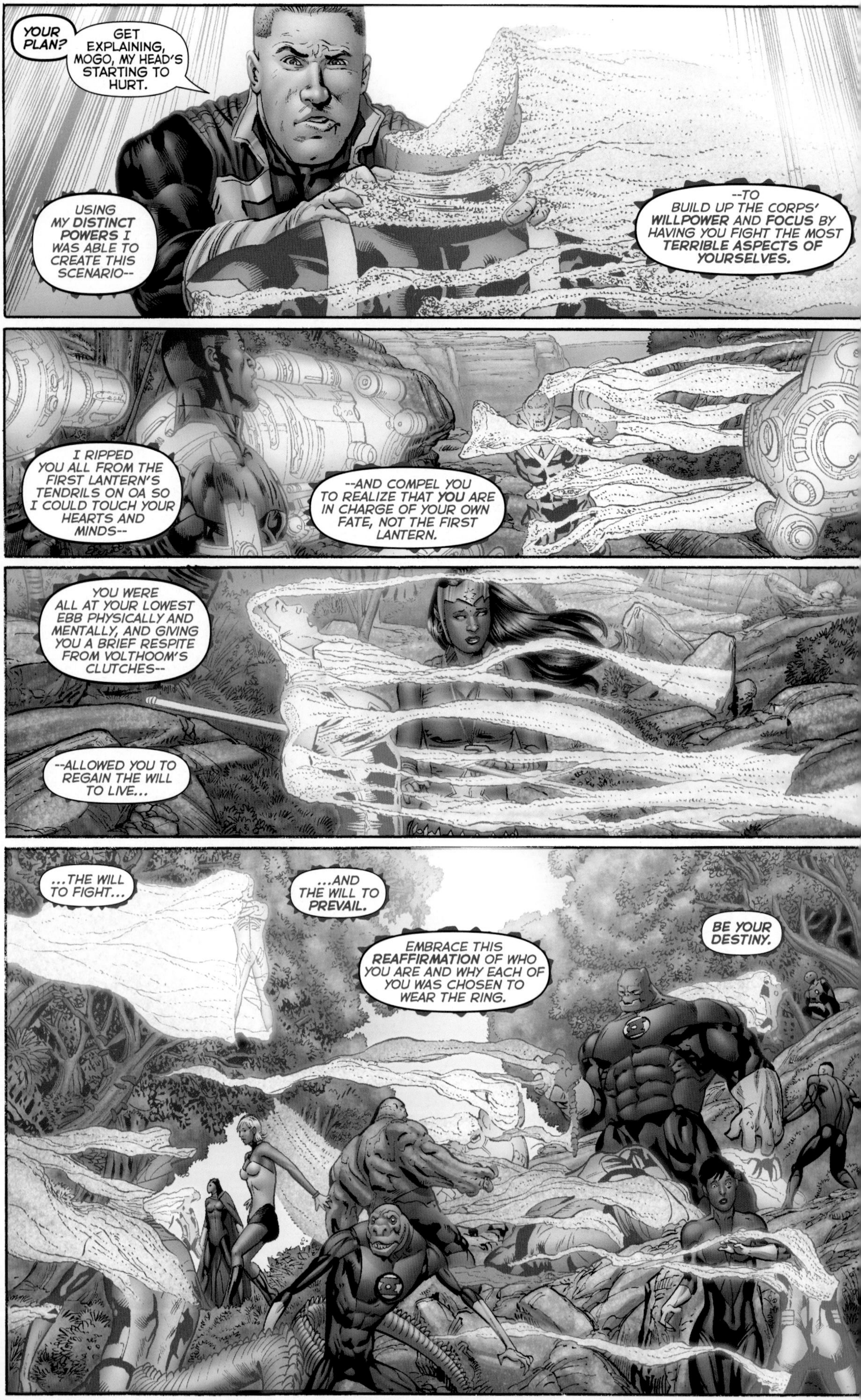
YOUR PLAN?
GET EXPLAINING, MOGO, MY HEAD'S STARTING TO HURT.
USING MY DISTINCT POWERS I WAS ABLE TO CREATE THIS SCENARIO--
--TO BUILD UP THE CORPS' WILLPOWER AND FOCUS BY HAVING YOU FIGHT THE MOST TERRIBLE ASPECTS OF YOURSELVES.
I RIPPED YOU ALL FROM THE FIRST LANTERN'S TENDRILS ON OA SO I COULD TOUCH YOUR HEARTS AND MINDS--
--AND COMPEL YOU TO REALIZE THAT YOU ARE IN CHARGE OF YOUR OWN FATE, NOT THE FIRST LANTERN.
YOU WERE ALL AT YOUR LOWEST EBB PHYSICALLY AND MENTALLY, AND GIVING YOU A BRIEF RESPITE FROM VOLTHOOM'S CLUTCHES--
--ALLOWED YOU TO REGAIN THE WILL TO LIVE...
...THE WILL TO FIGHT...
...AND THE WILL TO PREVAIL.
EMBRACE THIS REAFFIRMATION OF WHO YOU ARE AND WHY EACH OF YOU WAS CHOSEN TO WEAR THE RING.
BE YOUR DESTINY.

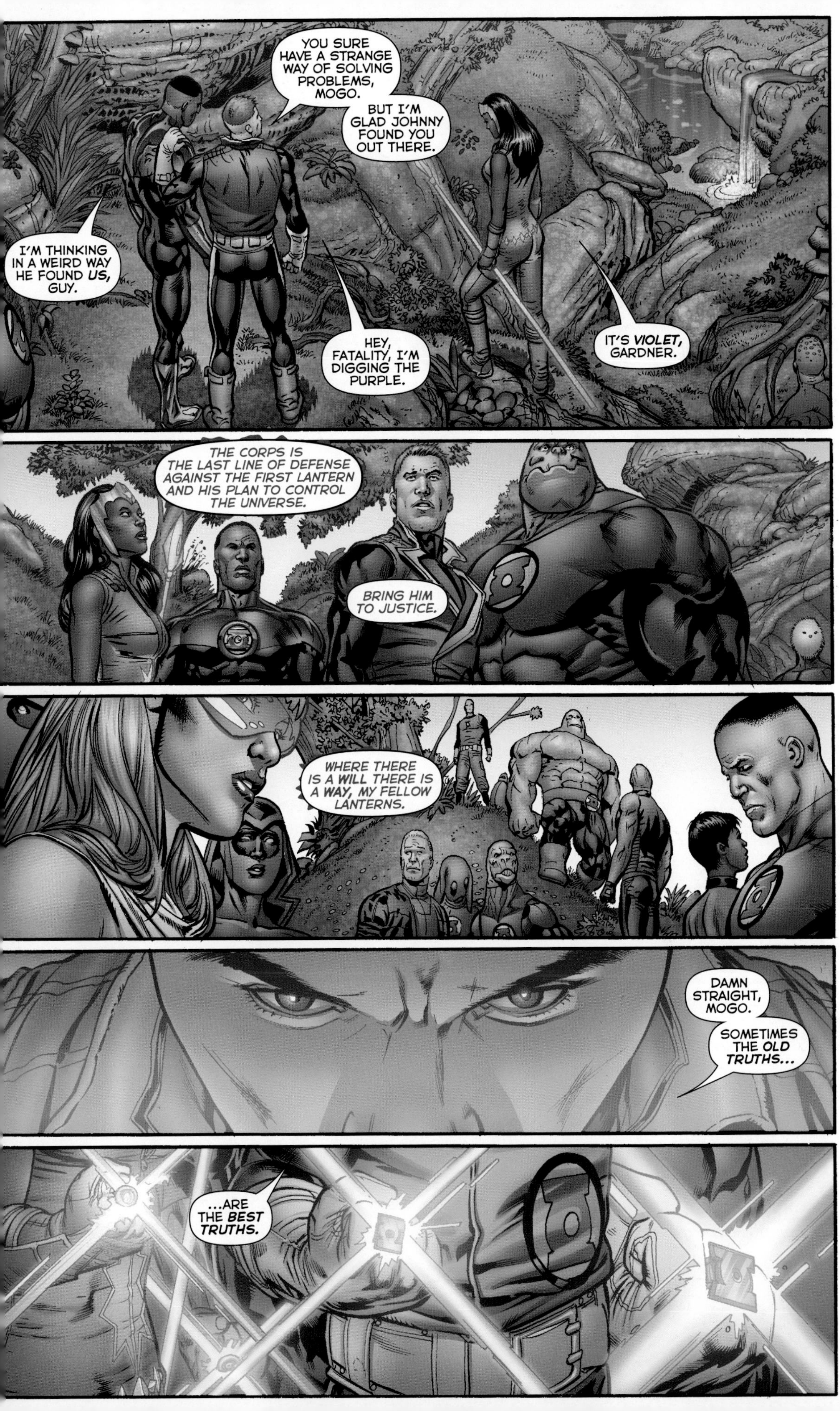
YOU SURE HAVE A STRANGE WAY OF SOLVING PROBLEMS, MOGO.
BUT I'M GLAD JOHNNY FOUND YOU OUT THERE.
I'M THINKING IN A WEIRD WAY HE FOUND US, GUY.
HEY, FATALITY, I'M DIGGING THE PURPLE.
IT'S VIOLET, GARDNER.
THE CORPS IS THE LAST LINE OF DEFENSE AGAINST THE FIRST LANTERN AND HIS PLAN TO CONTROL THE UNIVERSE.
BRING HIM TO JUSTICE.
WHERE THERE IS A WILL THERE IS A WAY, MY FELLOW LANTERNS.
DAMN STRAIGHT, MOGO.
SOMETIMES THE OLD TRUTHS...
...ARE THE BEST TRUTHS.

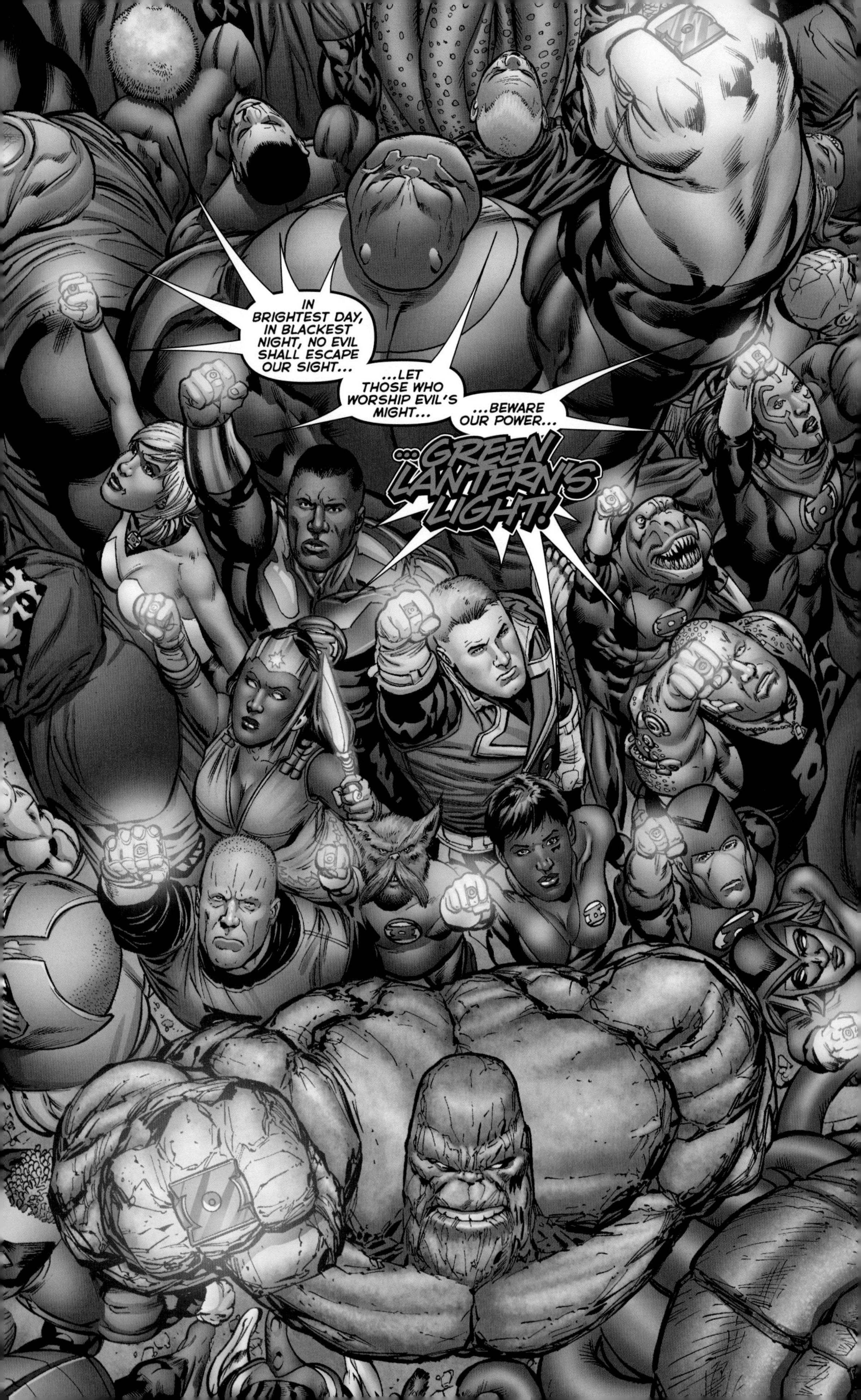
IN BRIGHTEST DAY, IN BLACKEST NIGHT, NO EVIL SHALL ESCAPE OUR SIGHT...
...LET THOSE WHO WORSHIP EVIL'S MIGHT...
...BEWARE OUR POWER...
...GREEN LANTERN'S LIGHT!

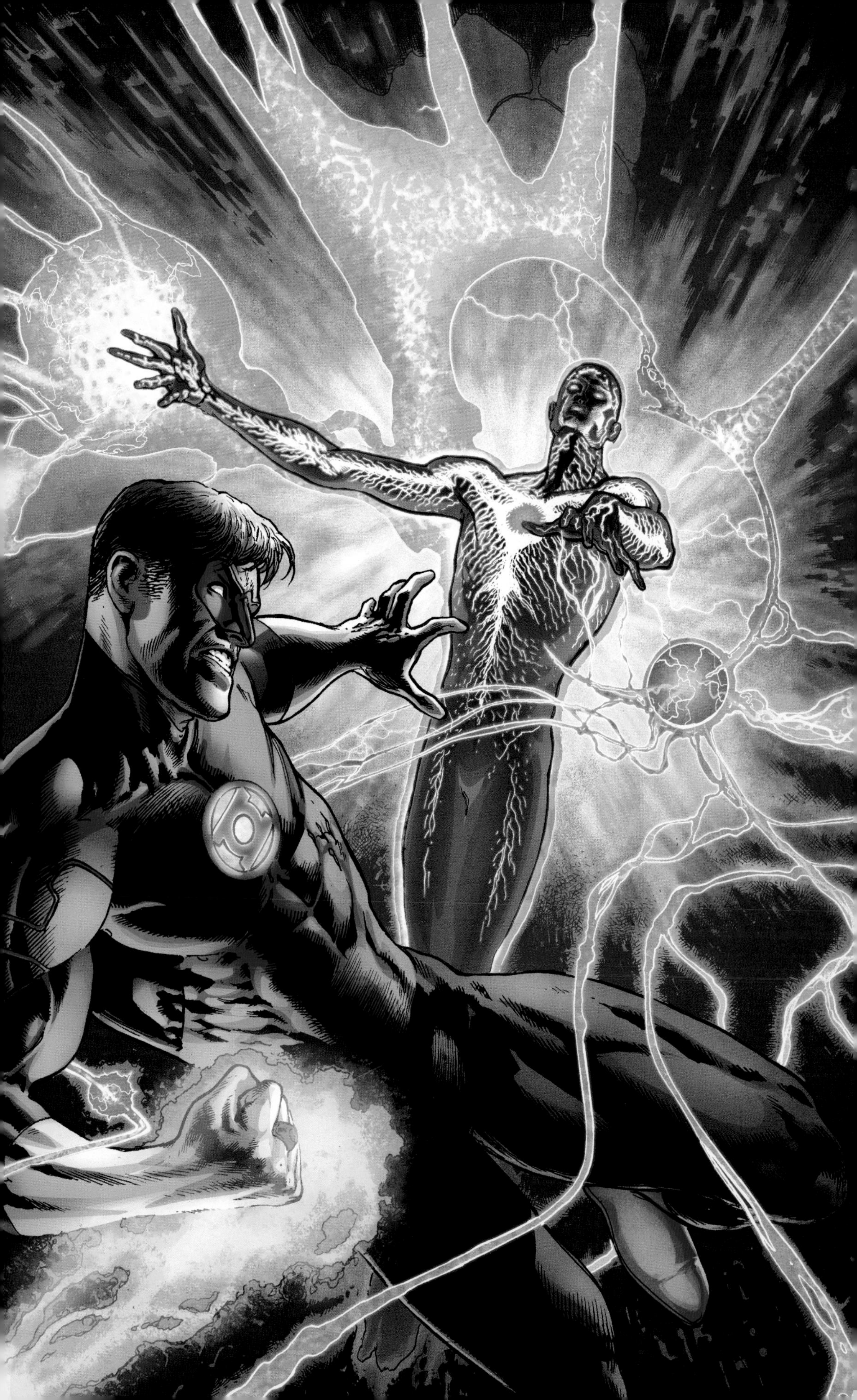

THE END

GEOFF JOHNS writer DOUG MAHNKE, PATRICK GLEASON, CULLY HAMNER, AARON KUDER, JERRY ORDWAY, ETHAN VAN SCIVER, IVAN REIS with OCLAIR ALBERT & JOE PRADO pencillers CHRISTIAN ALAMY, KEITH CHAMPAGNE, MARC DEERING, MARK IRWIN, WADE VON GRAWBADGER, TOM NGUYEN, & DOUG MAHNKE inkers cover art by DOUG MAHNKE with ALEX SINCLAIR

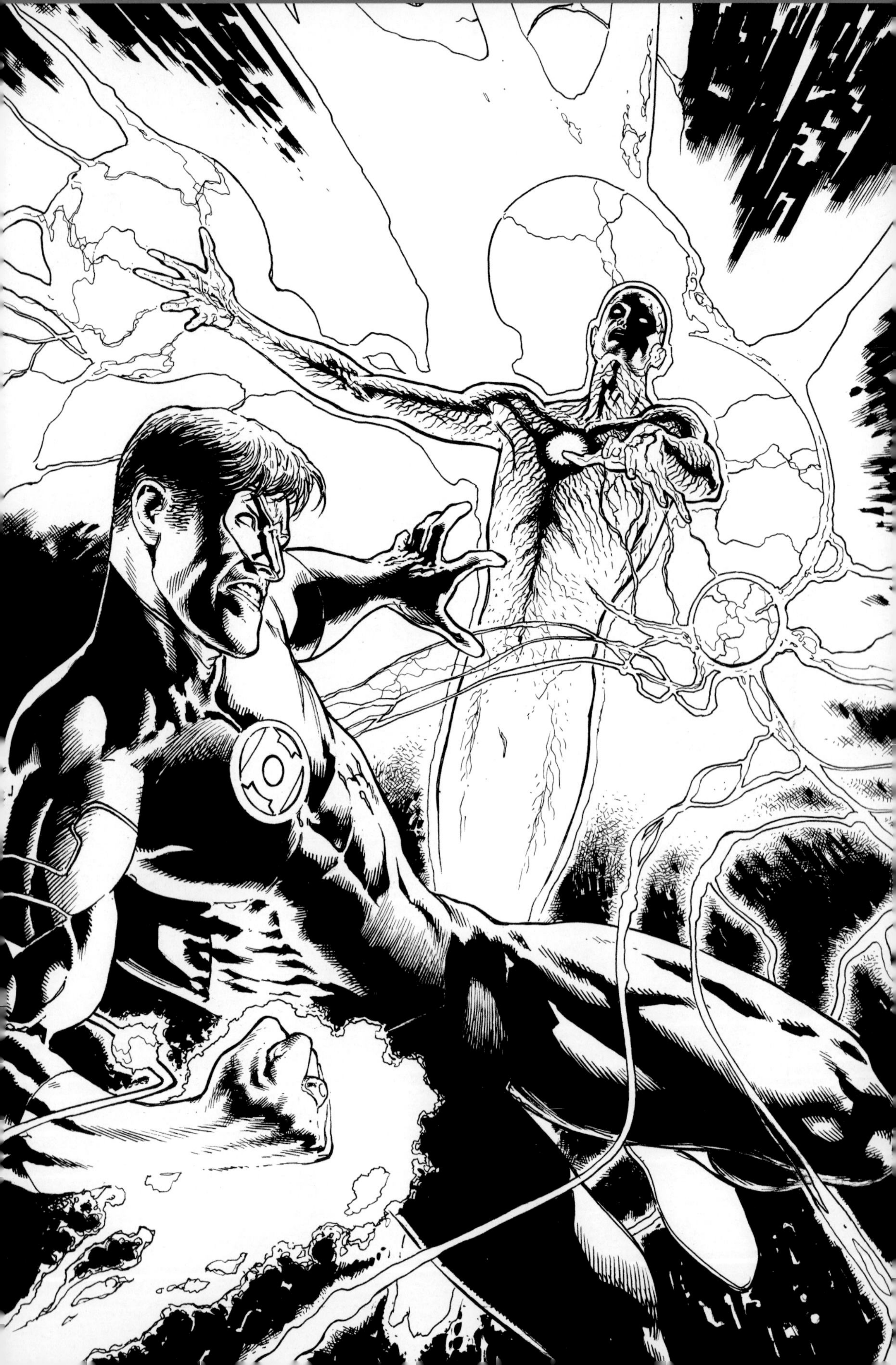

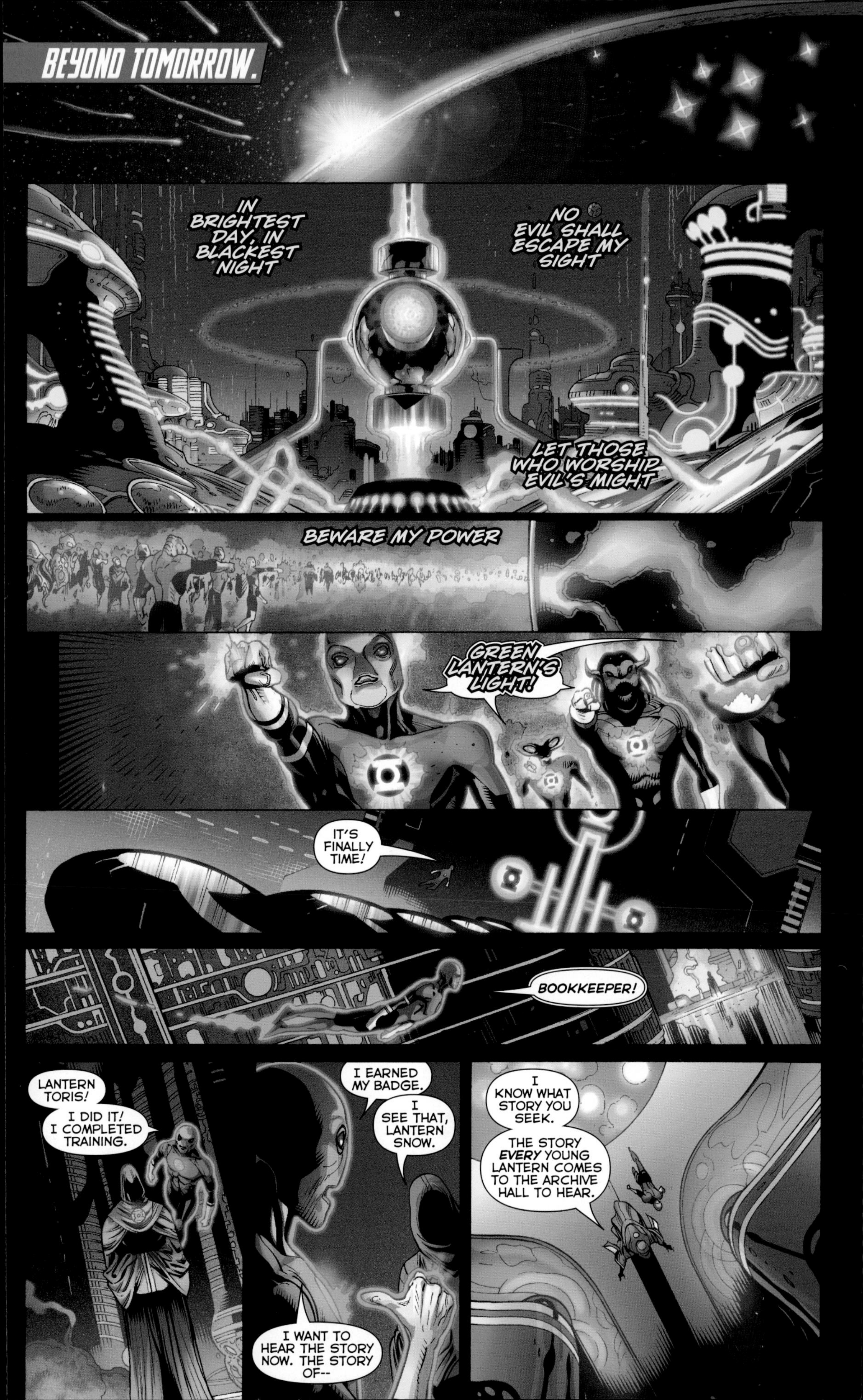
BEYOND TOMORROW.
IN BRIGHTEST DAY, IN BLACKEST NIGHT
NO EVIL SHALL ESCAPE MY SIGHT
LET THOSE WHO WORSHIP EVIL'S MIGHT
BEWARE MY POWER
GREEN LANTERN'S LIGHT!
IT'S FINALLY TIME!
BOOKKEEPER!
LANTERN TORIS!
I DID IT! I COMPLETED TRAINING.
I EARNED MY BADGE.
I SEE THAT, LANTERN SNOW.
I WANT TO HEAR THE STORY NOW. THE STORY OF--
I KNOW WHAT STORY YOU SEEK.
THE STORY EVERY YOUNG LANTERN COMES TO THE ARCHIVE HALL TO HEAR.

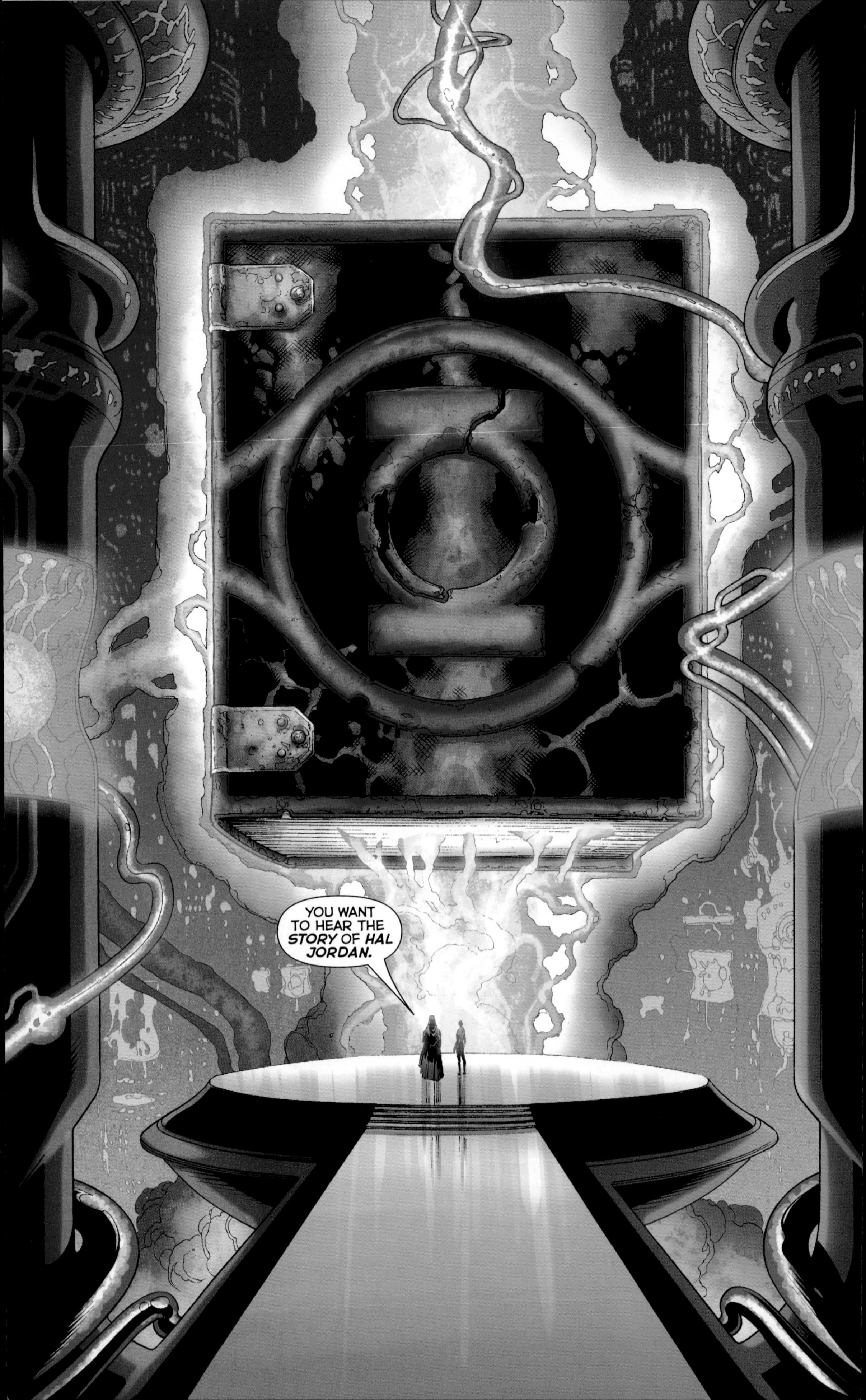
YOU WANT TO HEAR THE *STORY* OF *HAL JORDAN.*

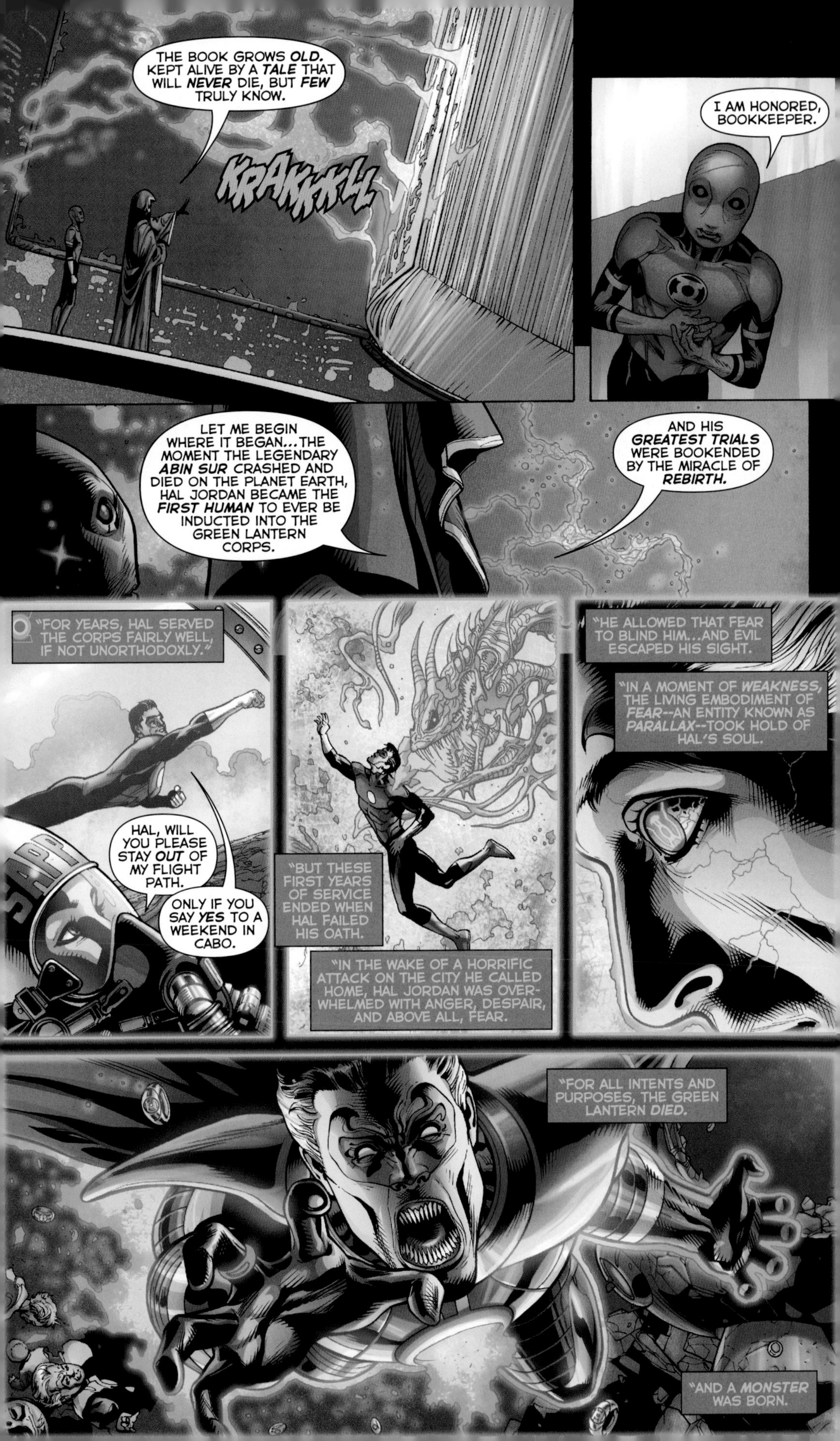
THE BOOK GROWS OLD. KEPT ALIVE BY A TALE THAT WILL NEVER DIE, BUT FEW TRULY KNOW.
KRAKKKLL
I AM HONORED, BOOKKEEPER.
LET ME BEGIN WHERE IT BEGAN...THE MOMENT THE LEGENDARY ABIN SUR CRASHED AND DIED ON THE PLANET EARTH, HAL JORDAN BECAME THE FIRST HUMAN TO EVER BE INDUCTED INTO THE GREEN LANTERN CORPS.
AND HIS GREATEST TRIALS WERE BOOKENDED BY THE MIRACLE OF REBIRTH.
"FOR YEARS, HAL SERVED THE CORPS FAIRLY WELL, IF NOT UNORTHODOXLY."
HAL, WILL YOU PLEASE STAY OUT OF MY FLIGHT PATH.
ONLY IF YOU SAY YES TO A WEEKEND IN CABO.
"BUT THESE FIRST YEARS OF SERVICE ENDED WHEN HAL FAILED HIS OATH.
"IN THE WAKE OF A HORRIFIC ATTACK ON THE CITY HE CALLED HOME, HAL JORDAN WAS OVERWHELMED WITH ANGER, DESPAIR, AND ABOVE ALL, FEAR.
"HE ALLOWED THAT FEAR TO BLIND HIM...AND EVIL ESCAPED HIS SIGHT.
"IN A MOMENT OF WEAKNESS, THE LIVING EMBODIMENT OF FEAR--AN ENTITY KNOWN AS PARALLAX--TOOK HOLD OF HAL'S SOUL.
"FOR ALL INTENTS AND PURPOSES, THE GREEN LANTERN DIED.
"AND A MONSTER WAS BORN.

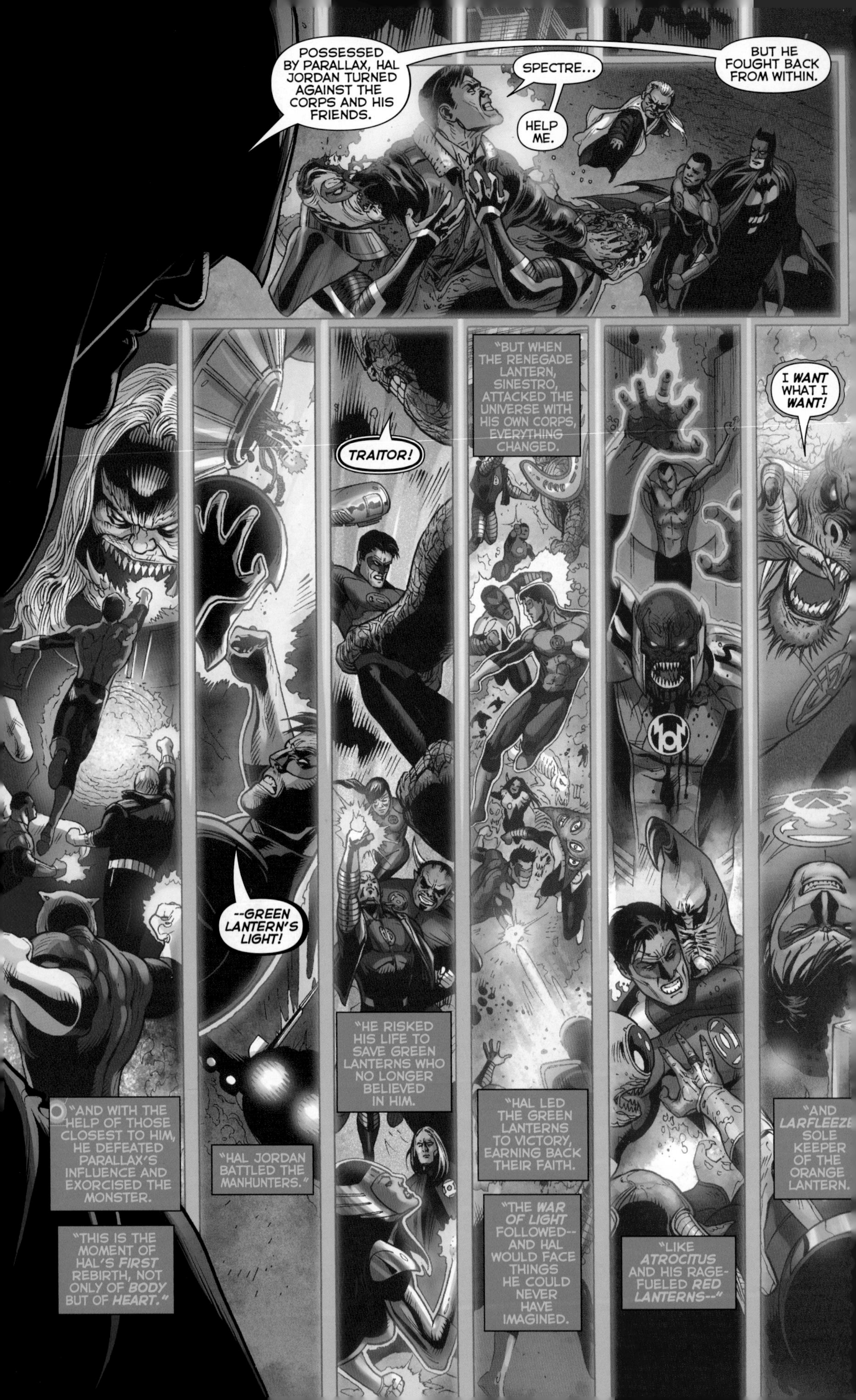

POSSESSED BY PARALLAX, HAL JORDAN TURNED AGAINST THE CORPS AND HIS FRIENDS.
SPECTRE...
HELP ME.
BUT HE FOUGHT BACK FROM WITHIN.
"AND WITH THE HELP OF THOSE CLOSEST TO HIM, HE DEFEATED PARALLAX'S INFLUENCE AND EXORCISED THE MONSTER.
"THIS IS THE MOMENT OF HAL'S FIRST REBIRTH, NOT ONLY OF BODY BUT OF HEART."
--GREEN LANTERN'S LIGHT!
"HAL JORDAN BATTLED THE MANHUNTERS."
TRAITOR!
"HE RISKED HIS LIFE TO SAVE GREEN LANTERNS WHO NO LONGER BELIEVED IN HIM.
"BUT WHEN THE RENEGADE LANTERN, SINESTRO, ATTACKED THE UNIVERSE WITH HIS OWN CORPS, EVERYTHING CHANGED.
"HAL LED THE GREEN LANTERNS TO VICTORY, EARNING BACK THEIR FAITH.
"THE WAR OF LIGHT FOLLOWED-- AND HAL WOULD FACE THINGS HE COULD NEVER HAVE IMAGINED.
"LIKE ATROCITUS AND HIS RAGE-FUELED RED LANTERNS--"
I WANT WHAT I WANT!
"AND LARFLEEZE SOLE KEEPER OF THE ORANGE LANTERN.

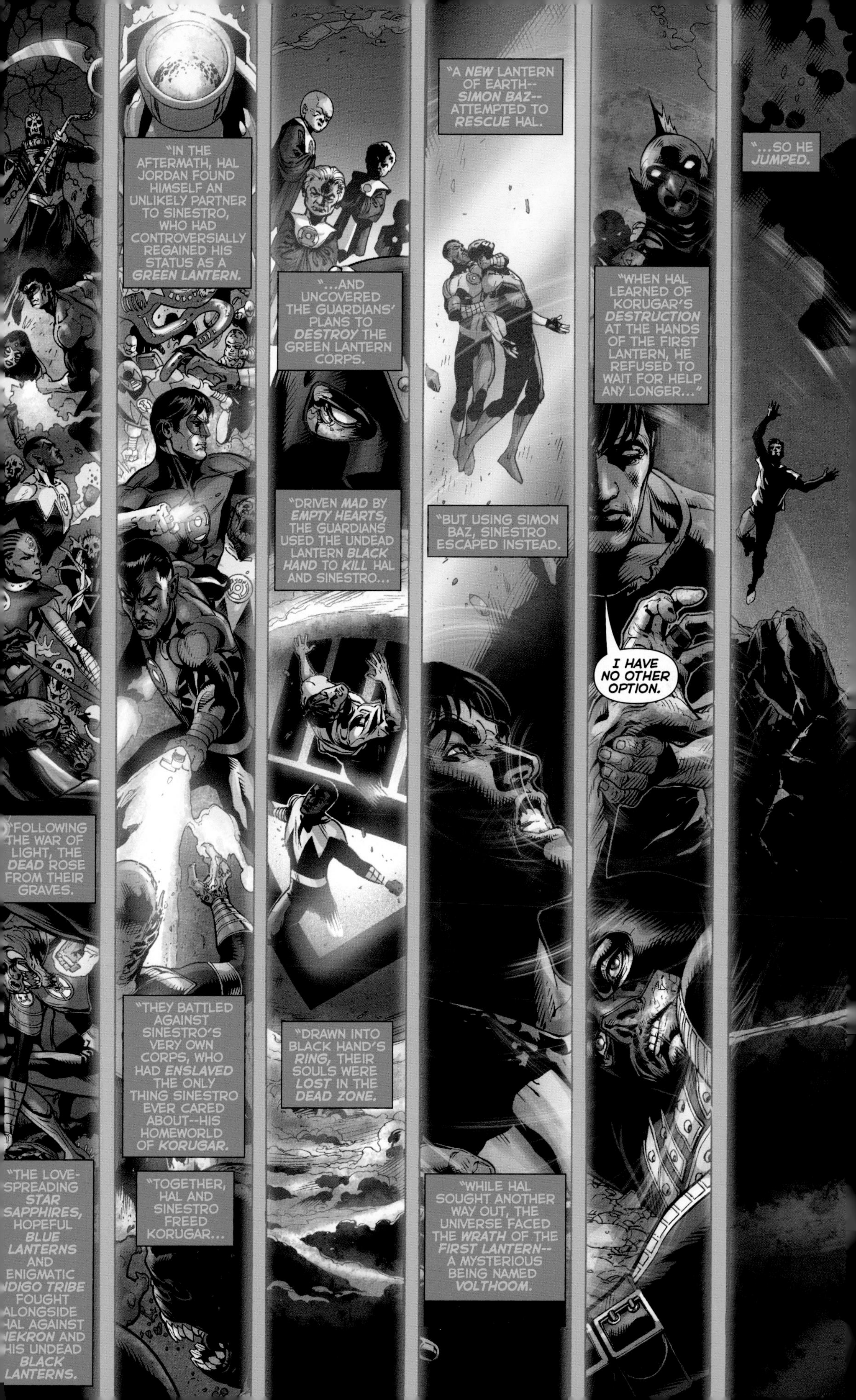
"FOLLOWING THE WAR OF LIGHT, THE DEAD ROSE FROM THEIR GRAVES.
"THE LOVE-SPREADING STAR SAPPHIRES, HOPEFUL BLUE LANTERNS AND ENIGMATIC NDIGO TRIBE FOUGHT ALONGSIDE HAL AGAINST NEKRON AND HIS UNDEAD BLACK LANTERNS.
"IN THE AFTERMATH, HAL JORDAN FOUND HIMSELF AN UNLIKELY PARTNER TO SINESTRO, WHO HAD CONTROVERSIALLY REGAINED HIS STATUS AS A GREEN LANTERN.
"THEY BATTLED AGAINST SINESTRO'S VERY OWN CORPS, WHO HAD ENSLAVED THE ONLY THING SINESTRO EVER CARED ABOUT--HIS HOMEWORLD OF KORUGAR.
"TOGETHER, HAL AND SINESTRO FREED KORUGAR...
"...AND UNCOVERED THE GUARDIANS' PLANS TO DESTROY THE GREEN LANTERN CORPS.
"DRIVEN MAD BY EMPTY HEARTS, THE GUARDIANS USED THE UNDEAD LANTERN BLACK HAND TO KILL HAL AND SINESTRO...
"DRAWN INTO BLACK HAND'S RING, THEIR SOULS WERE LOST IN THE DEAD ZONE.
"A NEW LANTERN OF EARTH--SIMON BAZ--ATTEMPTED TO RESCUE HAL.
"BUT USING SIMON BAZ, SINESTRO ESCAPED INSTEAD.
"WHILE HAL SOUGHT ANOTHER WAY OUT, THE UNIVERSE FACED THE WRATH OF THE FIRST LANTERN--A MYSTERIOUS BEING NAMED VOLTHOOM.
"WHEN HAL LEARNED OF KORUGAR'S DESTRUCTION AT THE HANDS OF THE FIRST LANTERN, HE REFUSED TO WAIT FOR HELP ANY LONGER..."
I HAVE NO OTHER OPTION.
"...SO HE JUMPED.

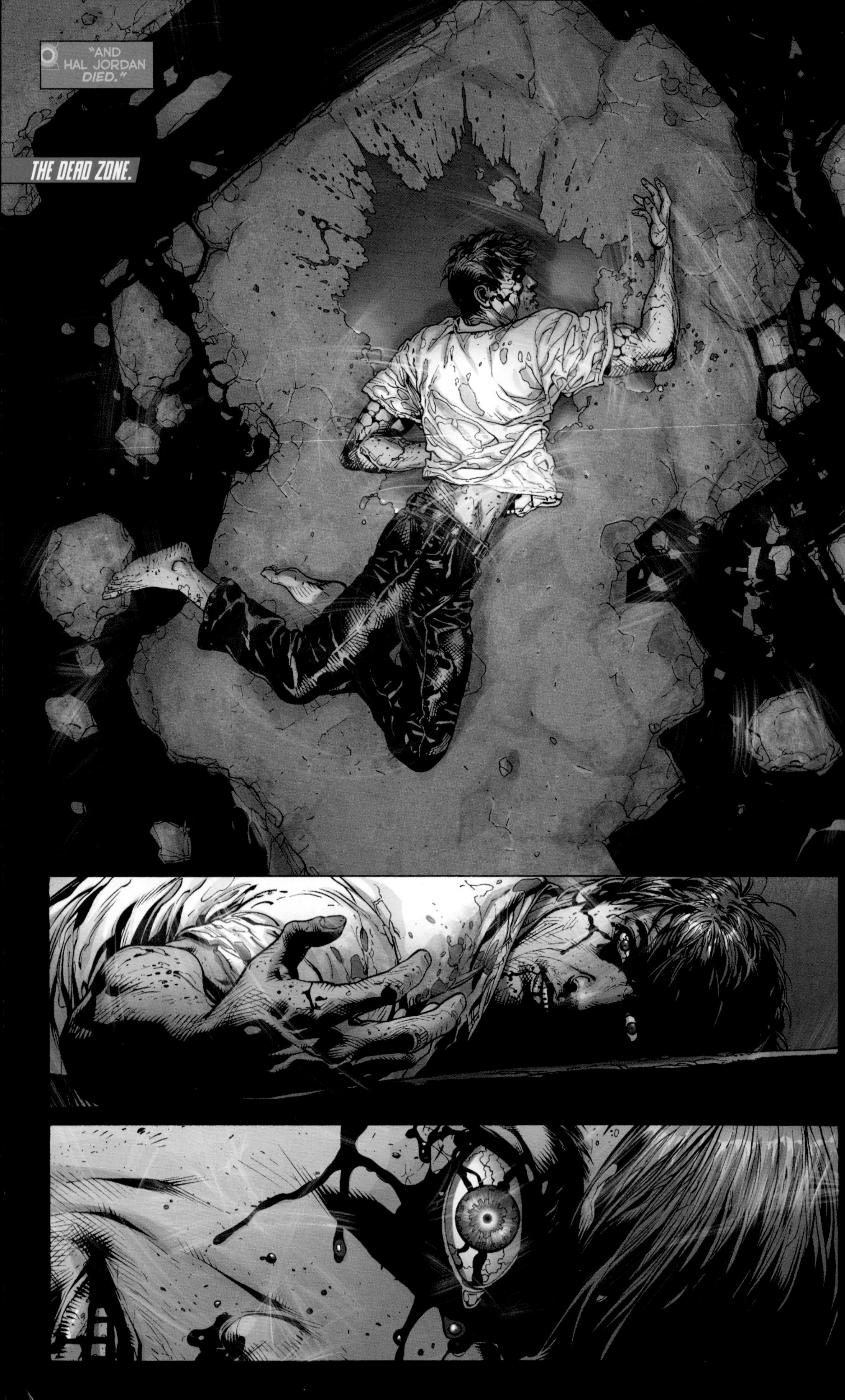
"AND HAL JORDAN DIED."
THE DEAD ZONE.

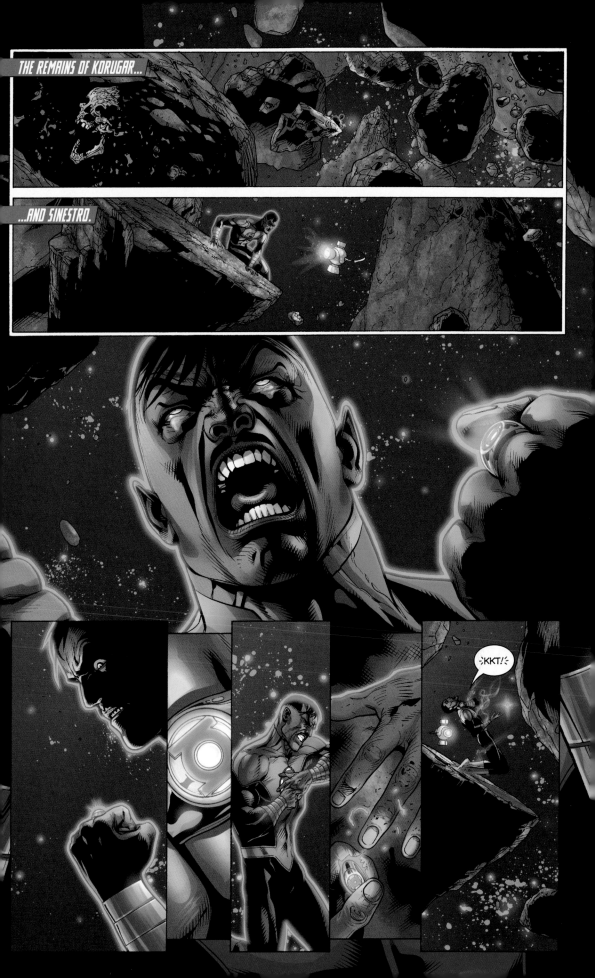

THE REMAINS OF KORUGAR...

...AND SINESTRO.

KKT!

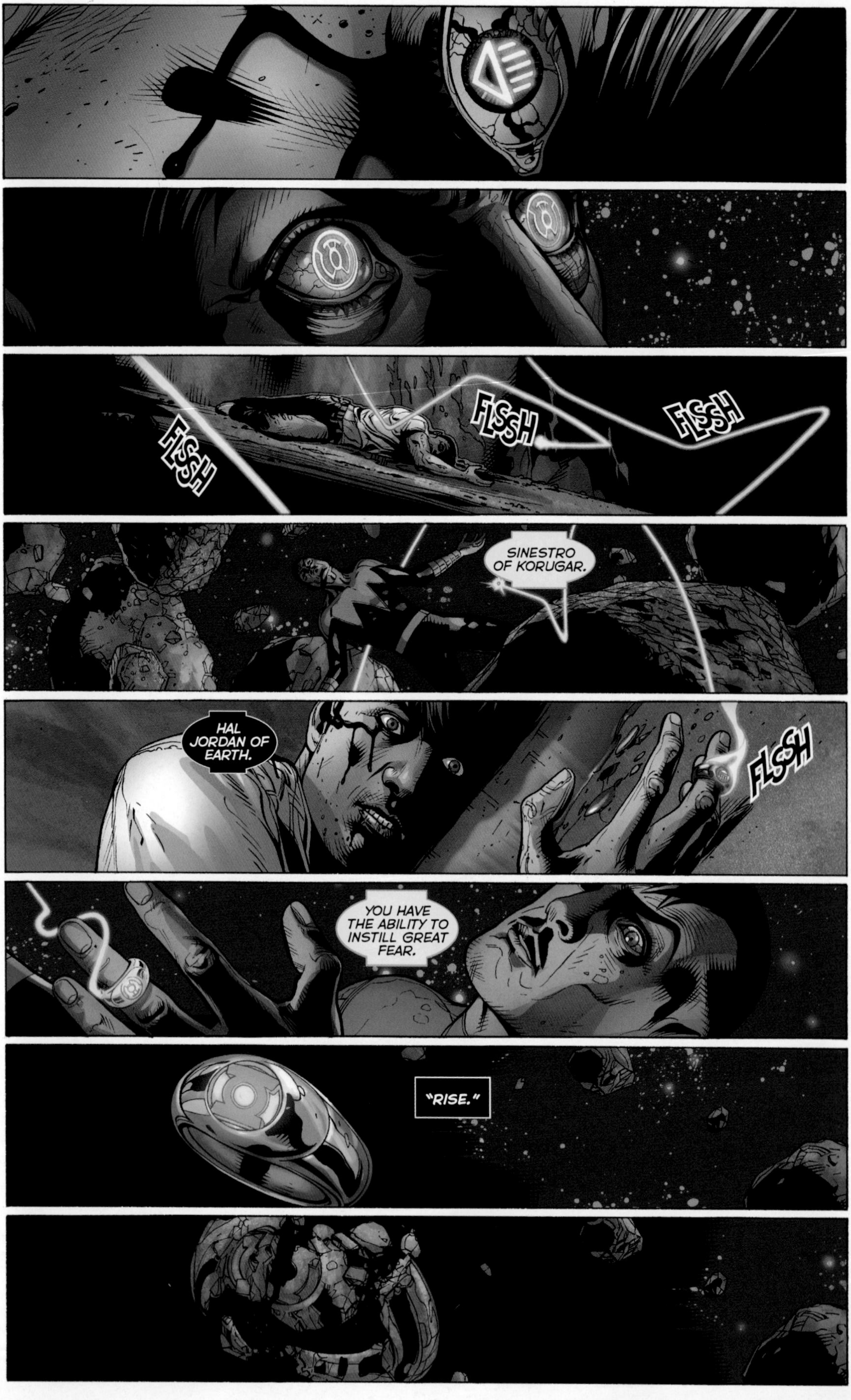
FLSSH
FLSSH
FLSSH
SINESTRO OF KORUGAR.
HAL JORDAN OF EARTH.
FLSSH
YOU HAVE THE ABILITY TO INSTILL GREAT FEAR.
"RISE."

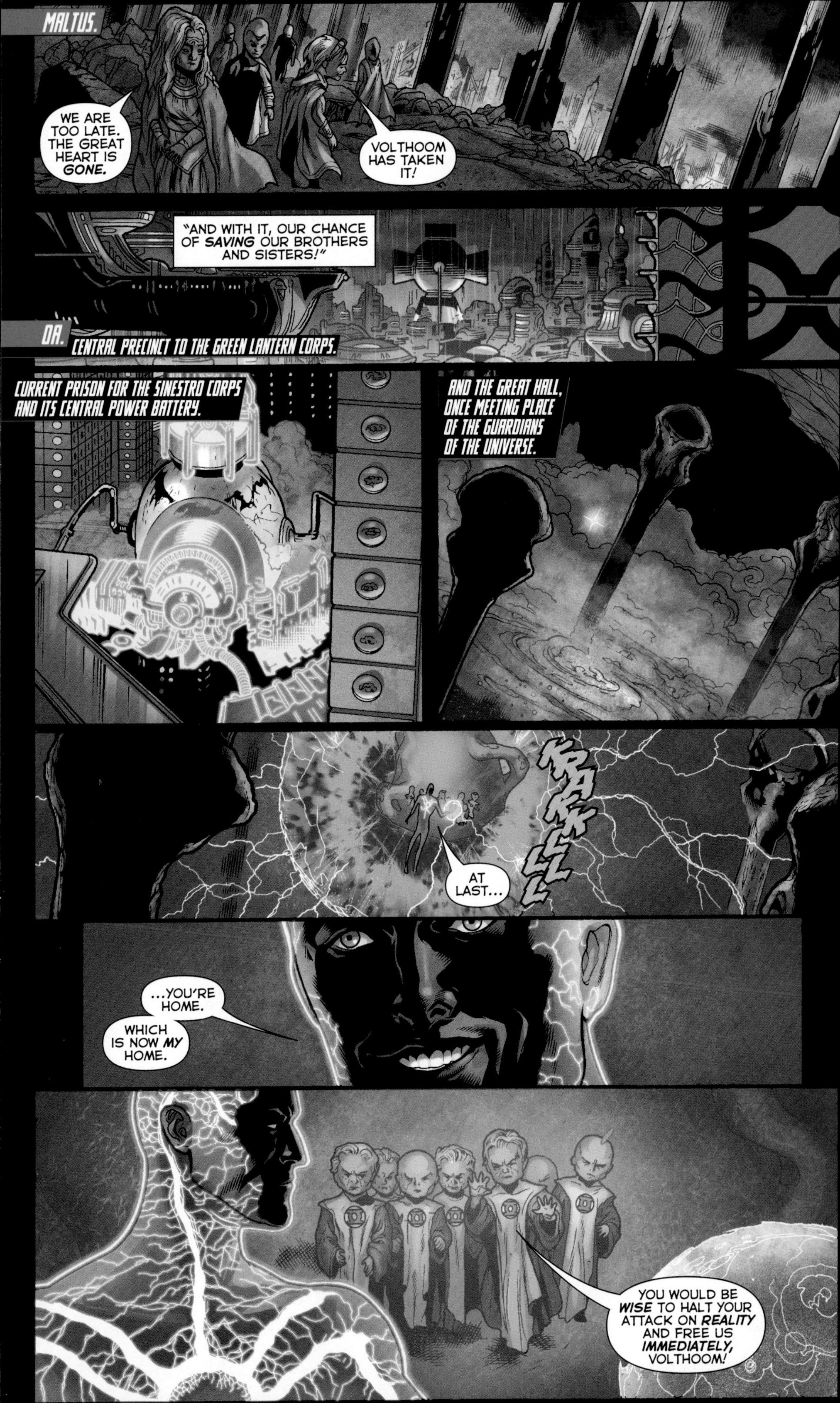
MALTUS.
WE ARE TOO LATE. THE GREAT HEART IS GONE.
VOLTHOOM HAS TAKEN IT!
"AND WITH IT, OUR CHANCE OF SAVING OUR BROTHERS AND SISTERS!"
OA.
CENTRAL PRECINCT TO THE GREEN LANTERN CORPS.
CURRENT PRISON FOR THE SINESTRO CORPS AND ITS CENTRAL POWER BATTERY.
AND THE GREAT HALL, ONCE MEETING PLACE OF THE GUARDIANS OF THE UNIVERSE.
KRAKKLLL
AT LAST...
...YOU'RE HOME.
WHICH IS NOW MY HOME.
YOU WOULD BE WISE TO HALT YOUR ATTACK ON REALITY AND FREE US IMMEDIATELY, VOLTHOOM!

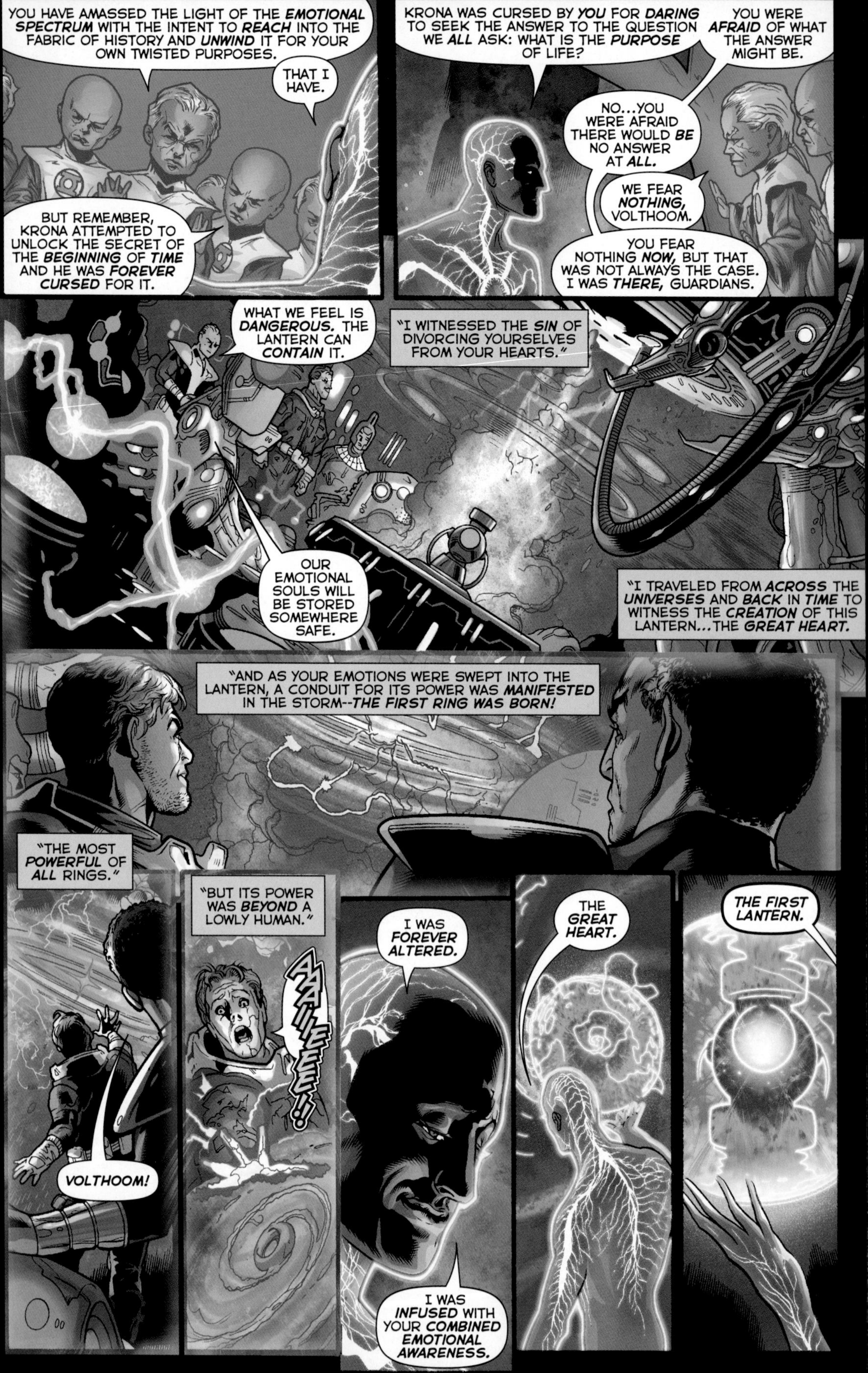
YOU HAVE AMASSED THE LIGHT OF THE EMOTIONAL SPECTRUM WITH THE INTENT TO REACH INTO THE FABRIC OF HISTORY AND UNWIND IT FOR YOUR OWN TWISTED PURPOSES.
THAT I HAVE.
BUT REMEMBER, KRONA ATTEMPTED TO UNLOCK THE SECRET OF THE BEGINNING OF TIME AND HE WAS FOREVER CURSED FOR IT.
KRONA WAS CURSED BY YOU FOR DARING TO SEEK THE ANSWER TO THE QUESTION WE ALL ASK: WHAT IS THE PURPOSE OF LIFE?
YOU WERE AFRAID OF WHAT THE ANSWER MIGHT BE.
NO...YOU WERE AFRAID THERE WOULD BE NO ANSWER AT ALL.
WE FEAR NOTHING, VOLTHOOM.
YOU FEAR NOTHING NOW, BUT THAT WAS NOT ALWAYS THE CASE. I WAS THERE, GUARDIANS.
WHAT WE FEEL IS DANGEROUS. THE LANTERN CAN CONTAIN IT.
"I WITNESSED THE SIN OF DIVORCING YOURSELVES FROM YOUR HEARTS."
OUR EMOTIONAL SOULS WILL BE STORED SOMEWHERE SAFE.
"I TRAVELED FROM ACROSS THE UNIVERSES AND BACK IN TIME TO WITNESS THE CREATION OF THIS LANTERN...THE GREAT HEART.
"AND AS YOUR EMOTIONS WERE SWEPT INTO THE LANTERN, A CONDUIT FOR ITS POWER WAS MANIFESTED IN THE STORM--THE FIRST RING WAS BORN!
"THE MOST POWERFUL OF ALL RINGS."
VOLTHOOM!
"BUT ITS POWER WAS BEYOND A LOWLY HUMAN."
AAAIIEEEE!!
I WAS FOREVER ALTERED.
I WAS INFUSED WITH YOUR COMBINED EMOTIONAL AWARENESS.
THE GREAT HEART.
THE FIRST LANTERN.

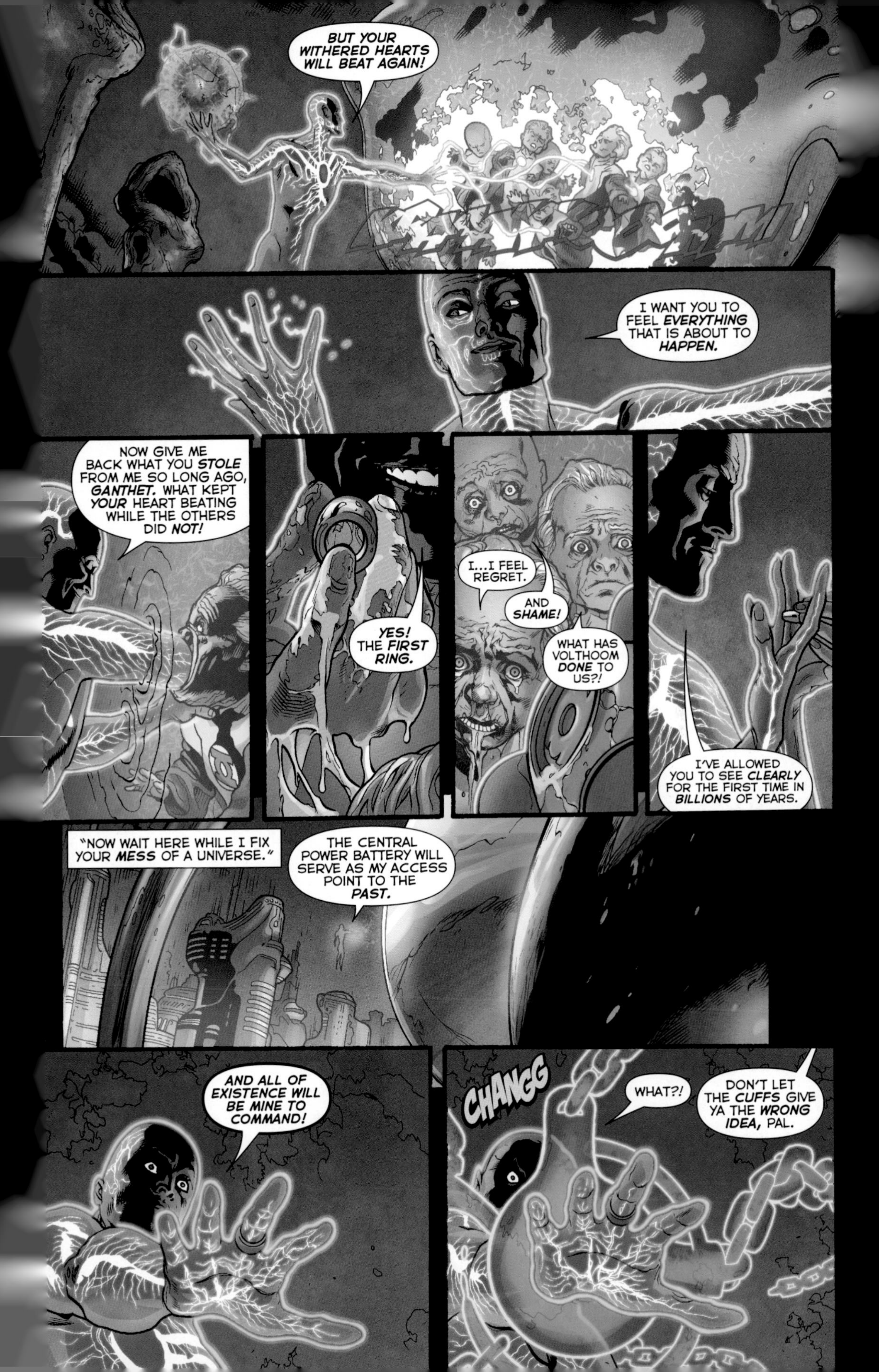

BUT YOUR WITHERED HEARTS WILL BEAT AGAIN!
I WANT YOU TO FEEL EVERYTHING THAT IS ABOUT TO HAPPEN.
NOW GIVE ME BACK WHAT YOU STOLE FROM ME SO LONG AGO, GANTHET. WHAT KEPT YOUR HEART BEATING WHILE THE OTHERS DID NOT!
YES! THE FIRST RING.
I...I FEEL REGRET.
AND SHAME!
WHAT HAS VOLTHOOM DONE TO US?!
I'VE ALLOWED YOU TO SEE CLEARLY FOR THE FIRST TIME IN BILLIONS OF YEARS.
"NOW WAIT HERE WHILE I FIX YOUR MESS OF A UNIVERSE."
THE CENTRAL POWER BATTERY WILL SERVE AS MY ACCESS POINT TO THE PAST.
AND ALL OF EXISTENCE WILL BE MINE TO COMMAND!
CHANGG
WHAT?!
DON'T LET THE CUFFS GIVE YA THE WRONG IDEA, PAL.

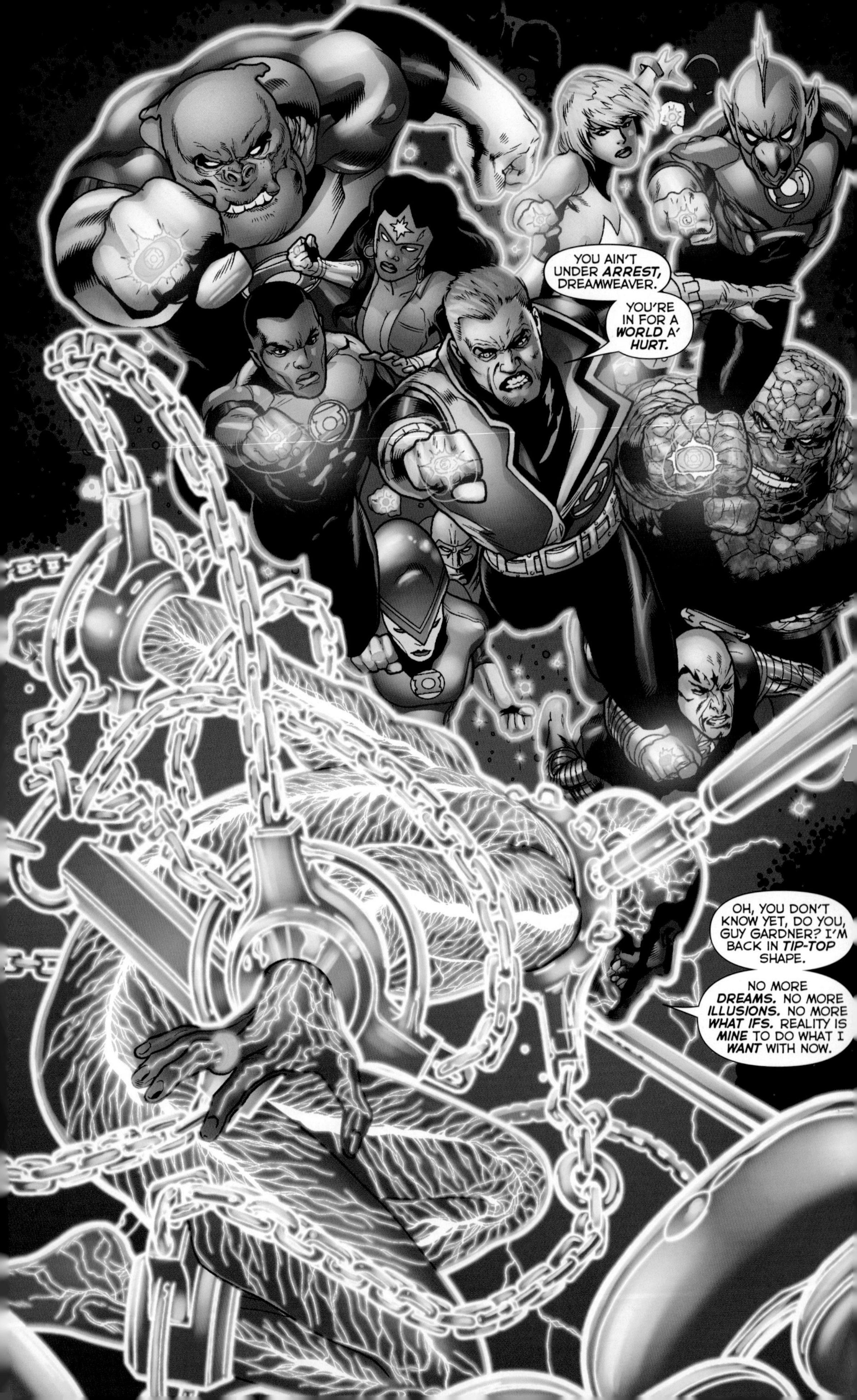
YOU AIN'T UNDER ARREST, DREAMWEAVER.
YOU'RE IN FOR A WORLD A' HURT.
OH, YOU DON'T KNOW YET, DO YOU, GUY GARDNER? I'M BACK IN TIP-TOP SHAPE.
NO MORE DREAMS. NO MORE ILLUSIONS. NO MORE WHAT IFS. REALITY IS MINE TO DO WHAT I WANT WITH NOW.

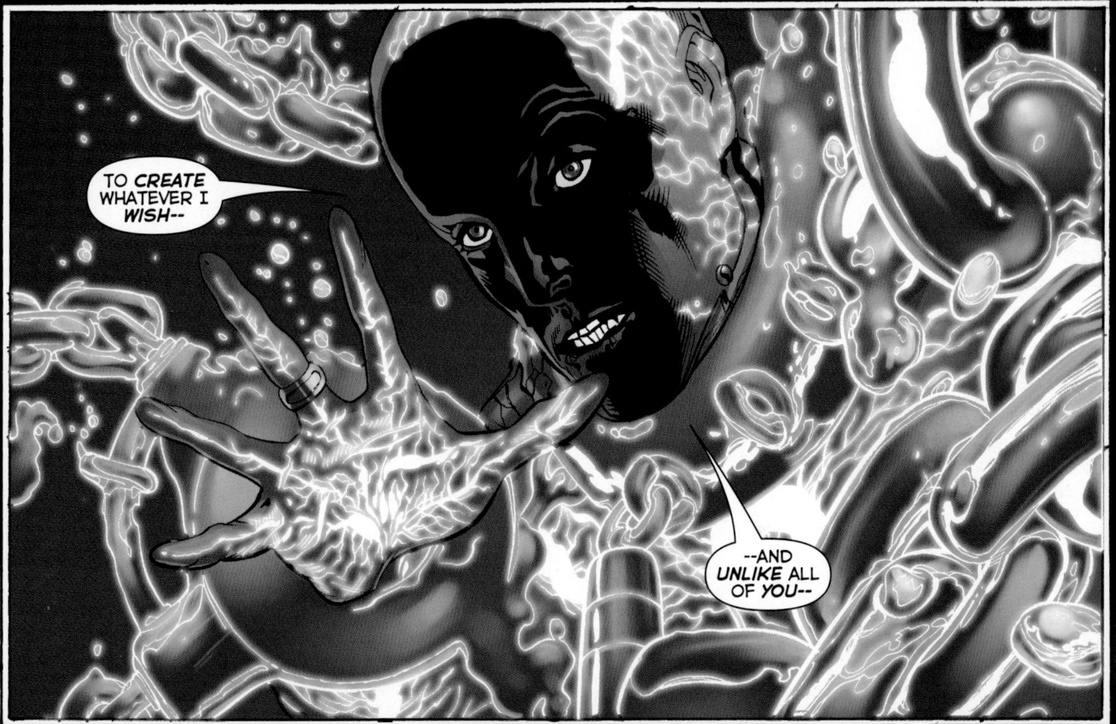
TO CREATE WHATEVER I WISH--
--AND UNLIKE ALL OF YOU--

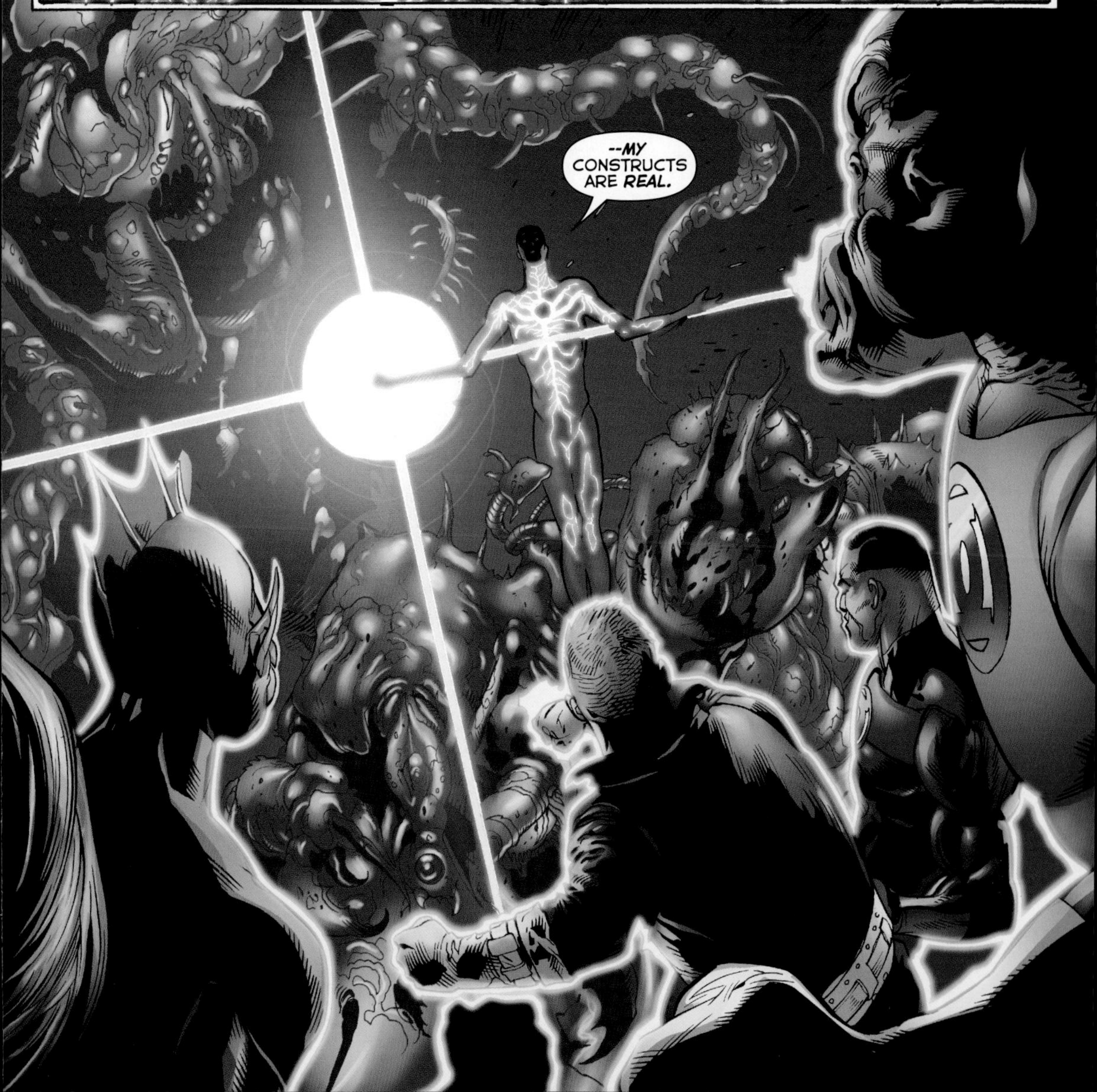
--MY CONSTRUCTS ARE REAL.

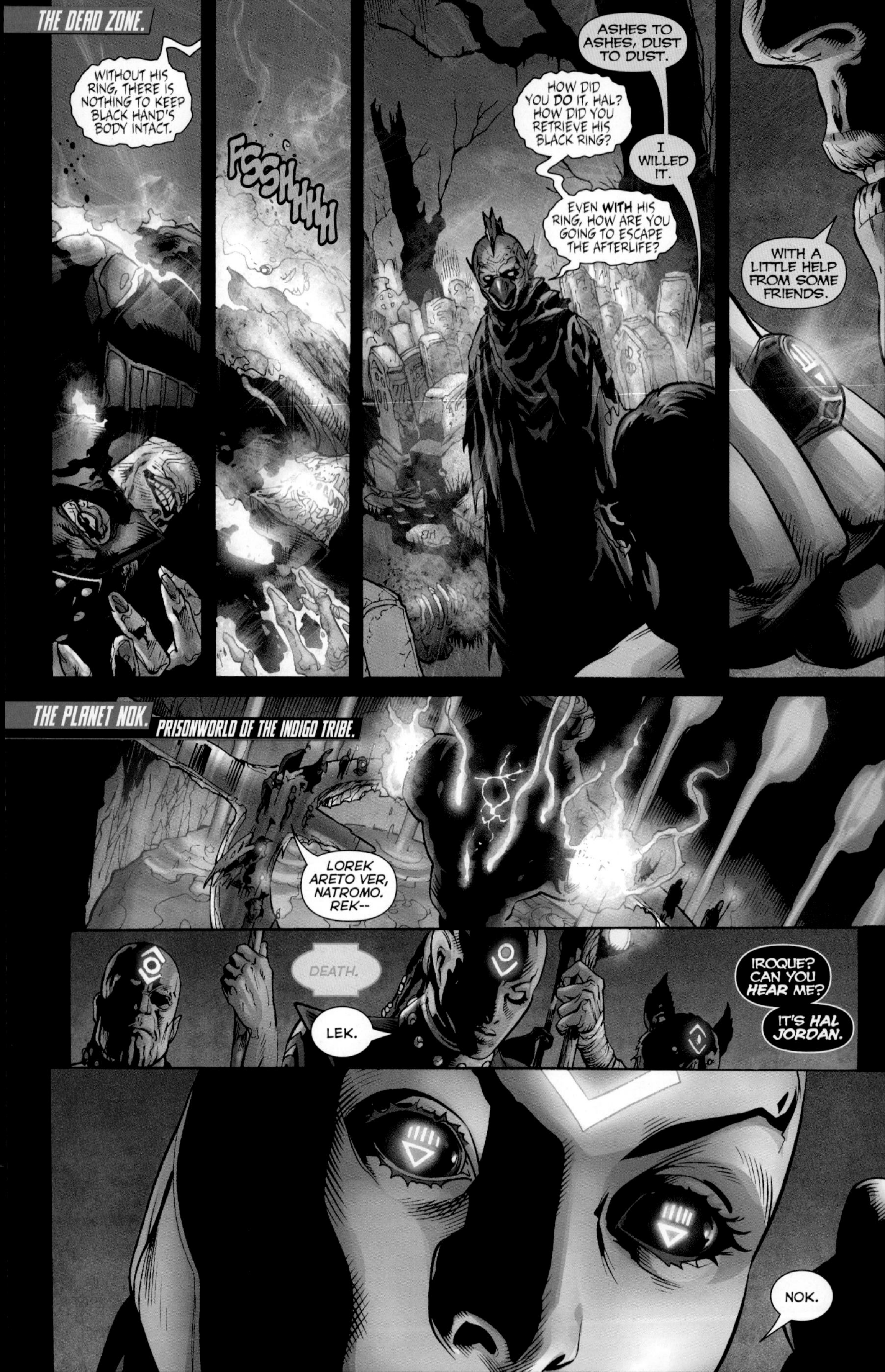
THE DEAD ZONE.
WITHOUT HIS RING, THERE IS NOTHING TO KEEP BLACK HAND'S BODY INTACT.
FSSHHHH
ASHES TO ASHES, DUST TO DUST.
HOW DID YOU DO IT, HAL? HOW DID YOU RETRIEVE HIS BLACK RING?
I WILLED IT.
EVEN WITH HIS RING, HOW ARE YOU GOING TO ESCAPE THE AFTERLIFE?
WITH A LITTLE HELP FROM SOME FRIENDS.
THE PLANET NOK.
PRISONWORLD OF THE INDIGO TRIBE.
LOREK ARETO VER, NATROMO. REK--
DEATH.
LEK.
IROQUE? CAN YOU HEAR ME?
IT'S HAL JORDAN.
NOK.

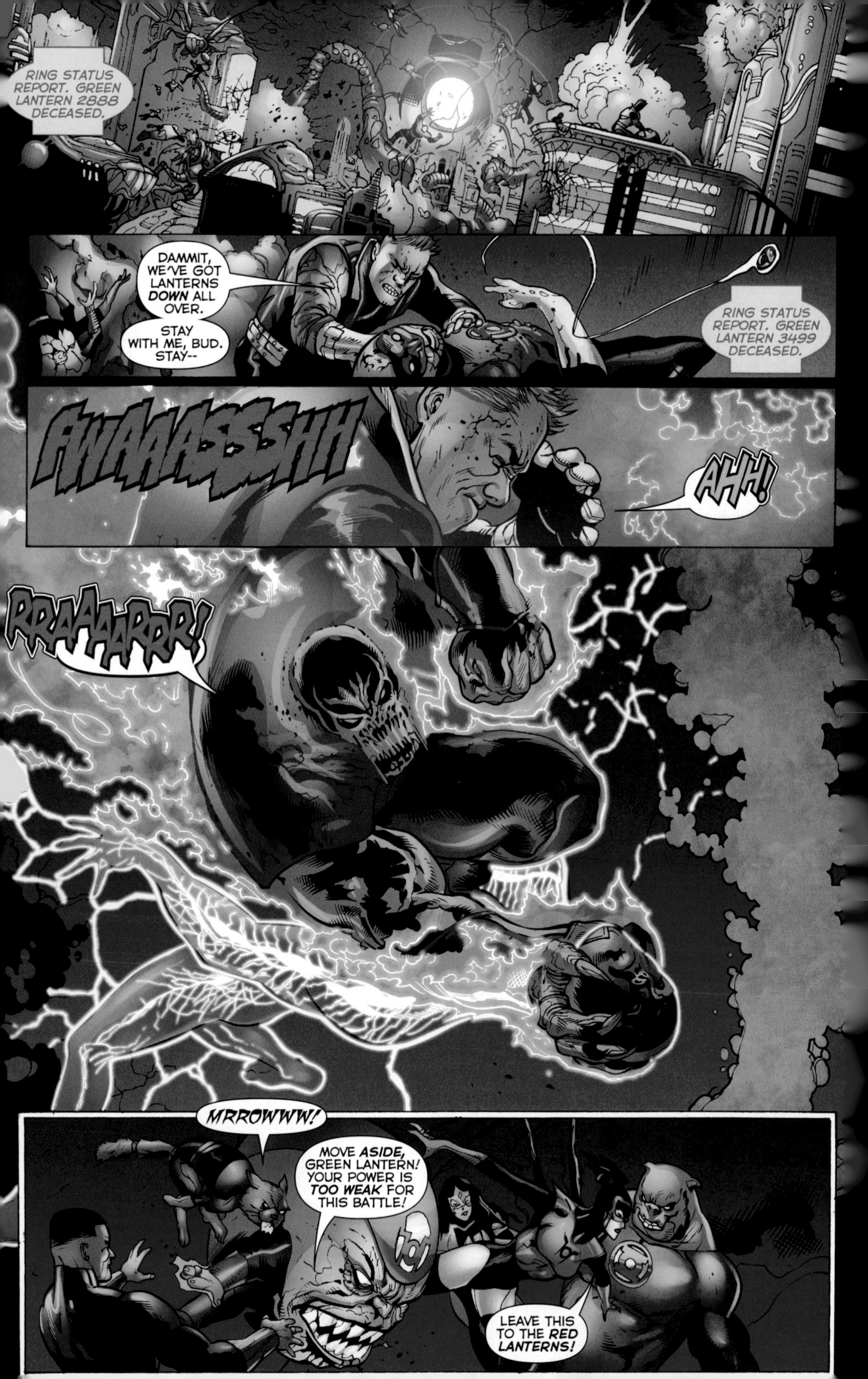
RING STATUS REPORT. GREEN LANTERN 2888 DECEASED.
DAMMIT, WE'VE GOT LANTERNS DOWN ALL OVER.
STAY WITH ME, BUD. STAY--
RING STATUS REPORT. GREEN LANTERN 3499 DECEASED.
FWAAAASSSHH
AHH!
RRAAAAARRR!
MRROWWW!
MOVE ASIDE, GREEN LANTERN! YOUR POWER IS TOO WEAK FOR THIS BATTLE!
LEAVE THIS TO THE RED LANTERNS!

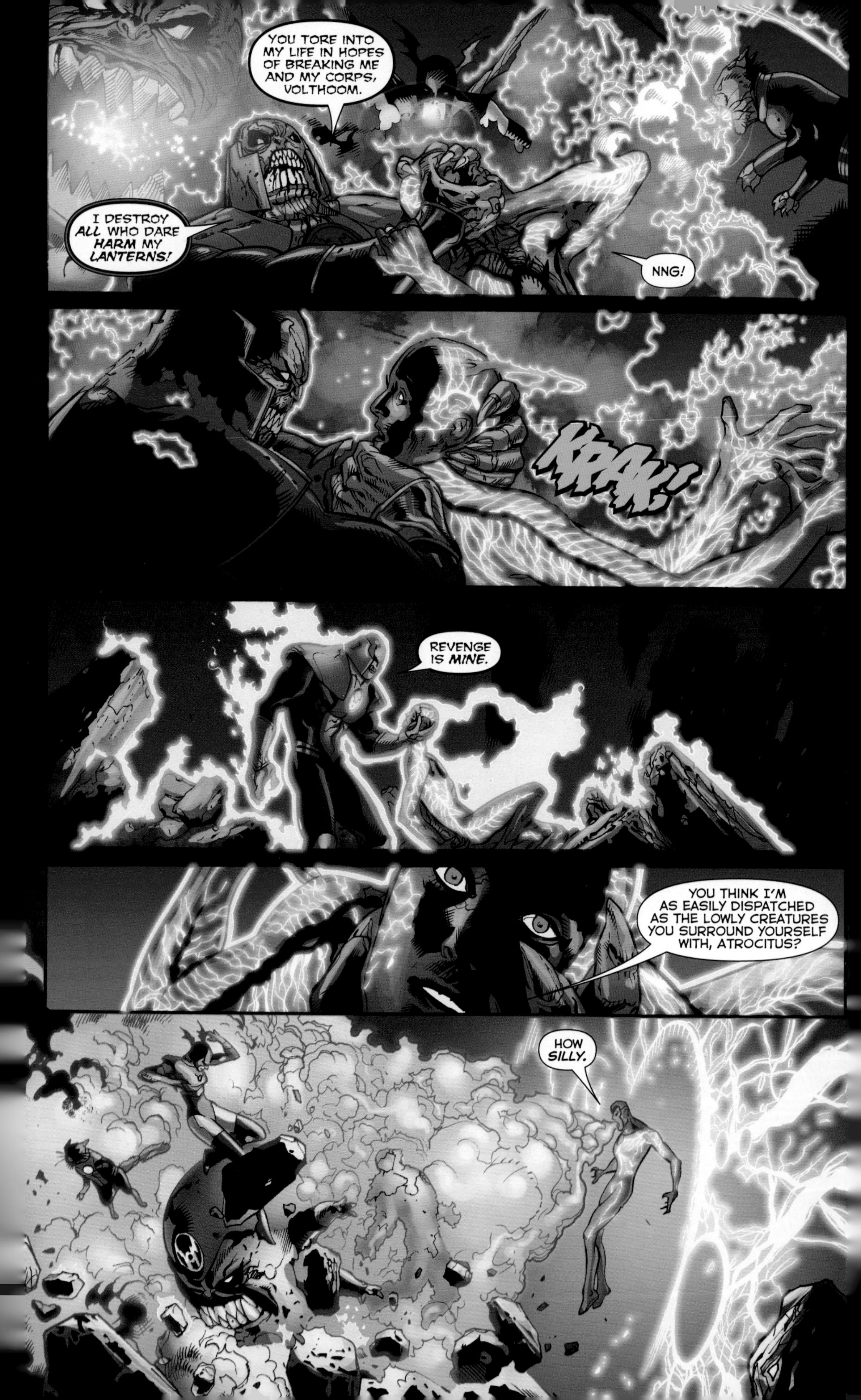
YOU TORE INTO MY LIFE IN HOPES OF BREAKING ME AND MY CORPS, VOLTHOOM.
I DESTROY ALL WHO DARE HARM MY LANTERNS!
NNG!
KRAK!
REVENGE IS MINE.
YOU THINK I'M AS EASILY DISPATCHED AS THE LOWLY CREATURES YOU SURROUND YOURSELF WITH, ATROCITUS?
HOW SILLY.

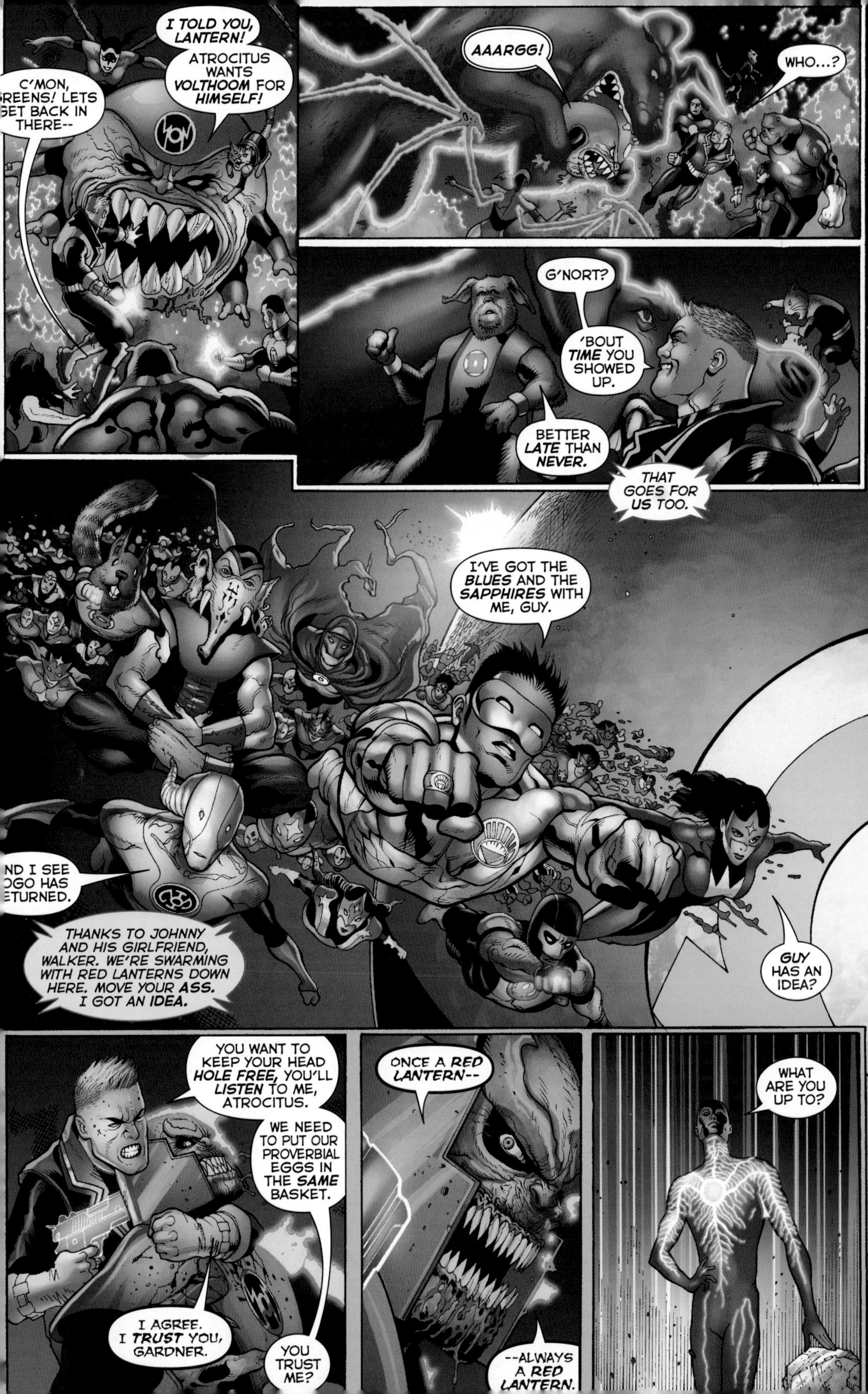
C'MON, GREENS! LETS GET BACK IN THERE--
I TOLD YOU, LANTERN!
ATROCITUS WANTS VOLTHOOM FOR HIMSELF!
AAARGG!
WHO...?
G'NORT?
'BOUT TIME YOU SHOWED UP.
BETTER LATE THAN NEVER.
THAT GOES FOR US TOO.
I'VE GOT THE BLUES AND THE SAPPHIRES WITH ME, GUY.
ND I SEE OGO HAS ETURNED.
THANKS TO JOHNNY AND HIS GIRLFRIEND, WALKER. WE'RE SWARMING WITH RED LANTERNS DOWN HERE. MOVE YOUR ASS. I GOT AN IDEA.
GUY HAS AN IDEA?
YOU WANT TO KEEP YOUR HEAD HOLE FREE, YOU'LL LISTEN TO ME, ATROCITUS.
WE NEED TO PUT OUR PROVERBIAL EGGS IN THE SAME BASKET.
I AGREE. I TRUST YOU, GARDNER.
YOU TRUST ME?
ONCE A RED LANTERN--
--ALWAYS A RED LANTERN.
WHAT ARE YOU UP TO?

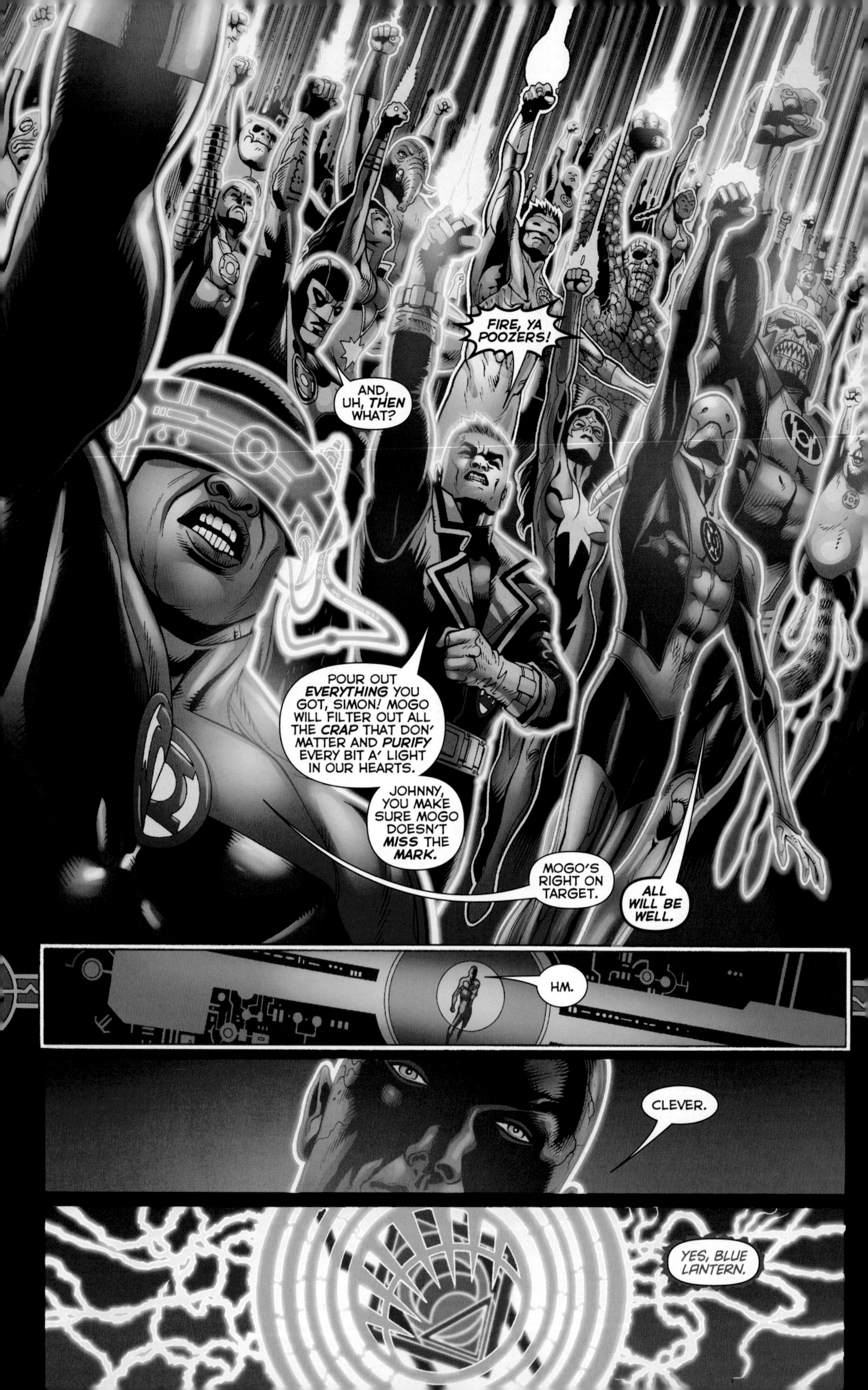

FIRE, YA POOZERS!
AND, UH, *THEN* WHAT?
POUR OUT *EVERYTHING* YOU GOT, SIMON! MOGO WILL FILTER OUT ALL THE *CRAP* THAT DON' MATTER AND *PURIFY* EVERY BIT A' LIGHT IN OUR HEARTS.
JOHNNY, YOU MAKE SURE MOGO DOESN'T *MISS* THE *MARK.*
MOGO'S RIGHT ON TARGET.
ALL WILL BE WELL.
HM.
CLEVER.
YES, BLUE LANTERN.

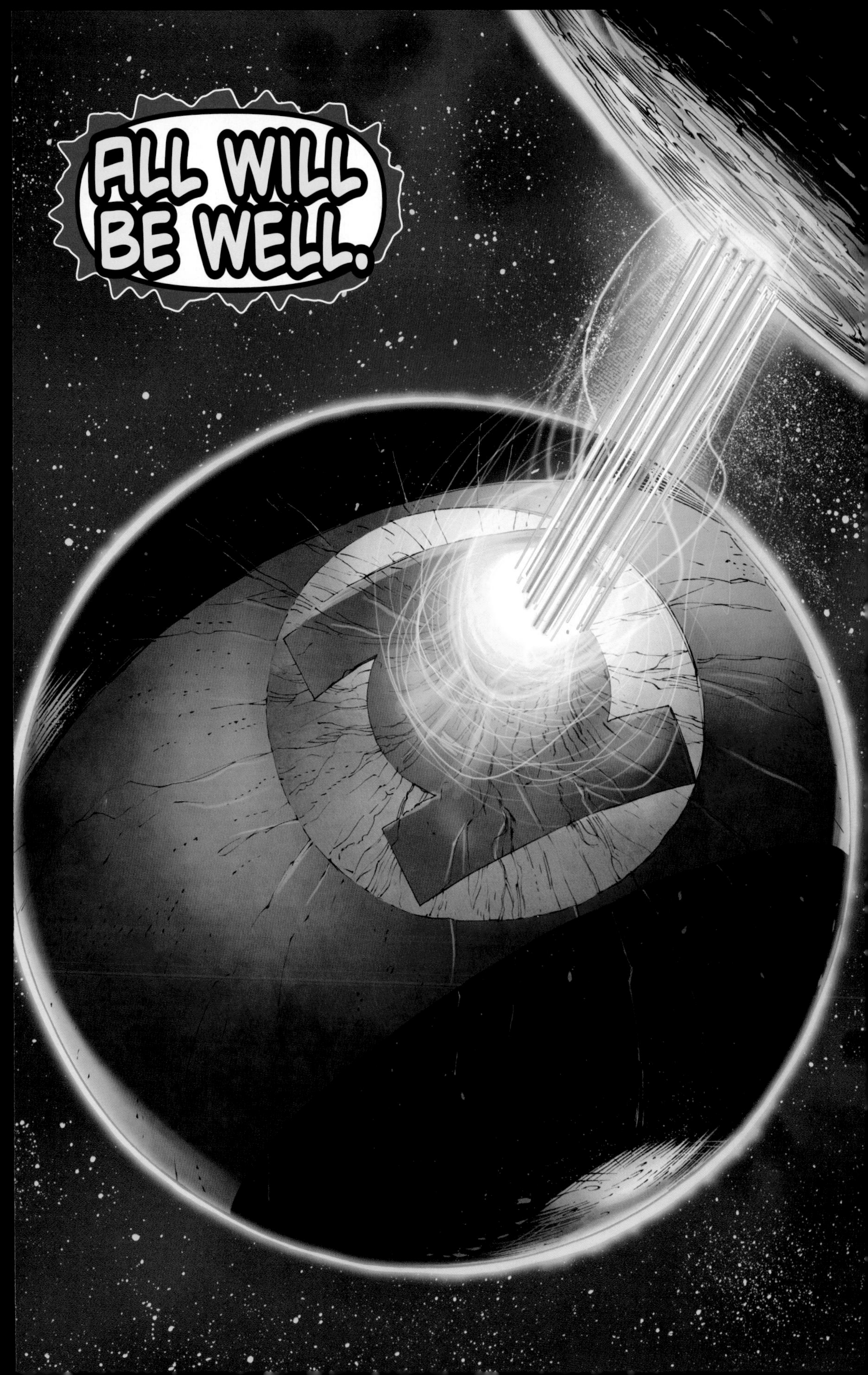
ALL WILL BE WELL.

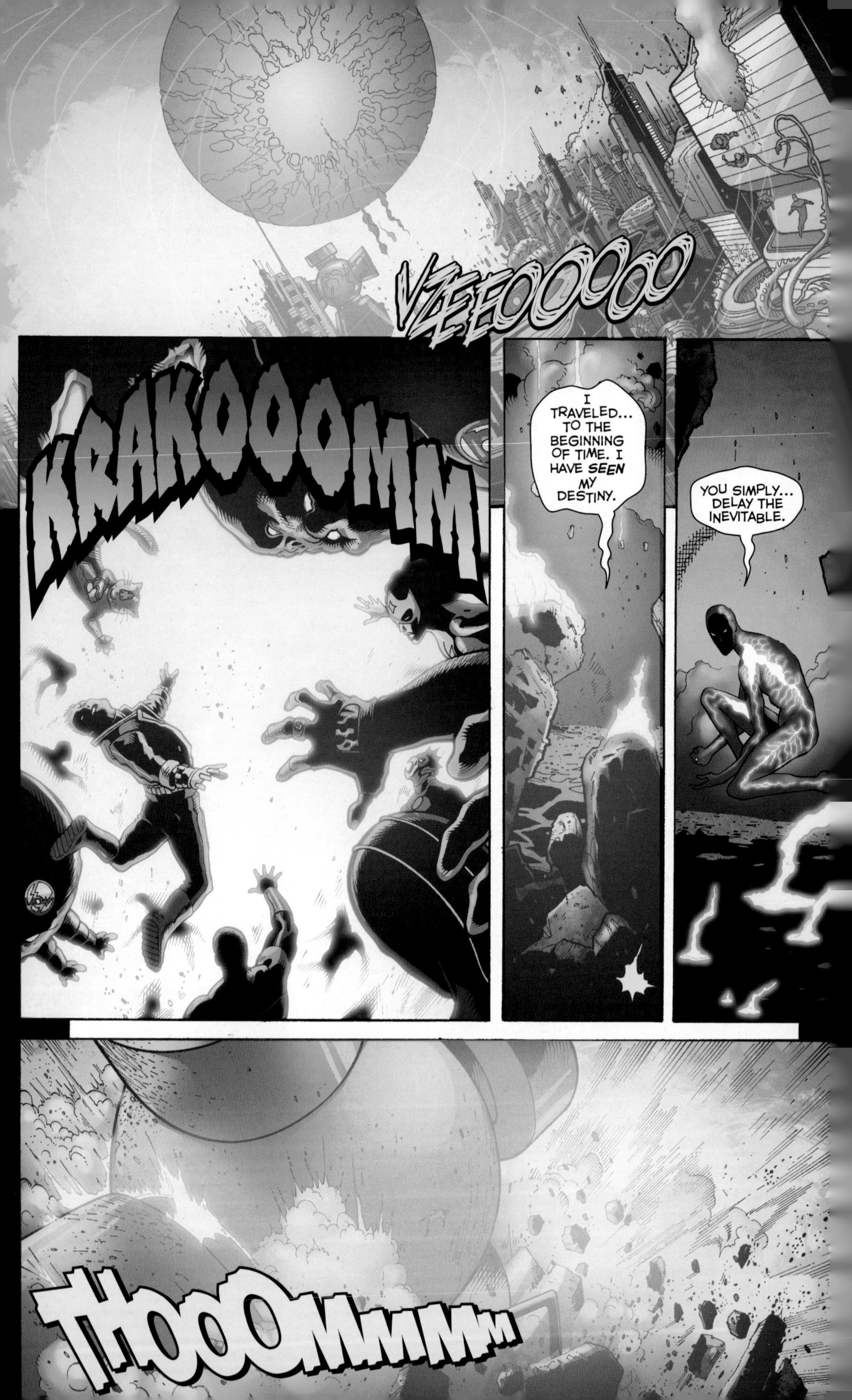
VZEEOOOOOO
KRAKOOOMM
I TRAVELED... TO THE BEGINNING OF TIME. I HAVE *SEEN* MY DESTINY.
YOU SIMPLY... DELAY THE INEVITABLE.
THOOOMMMMM

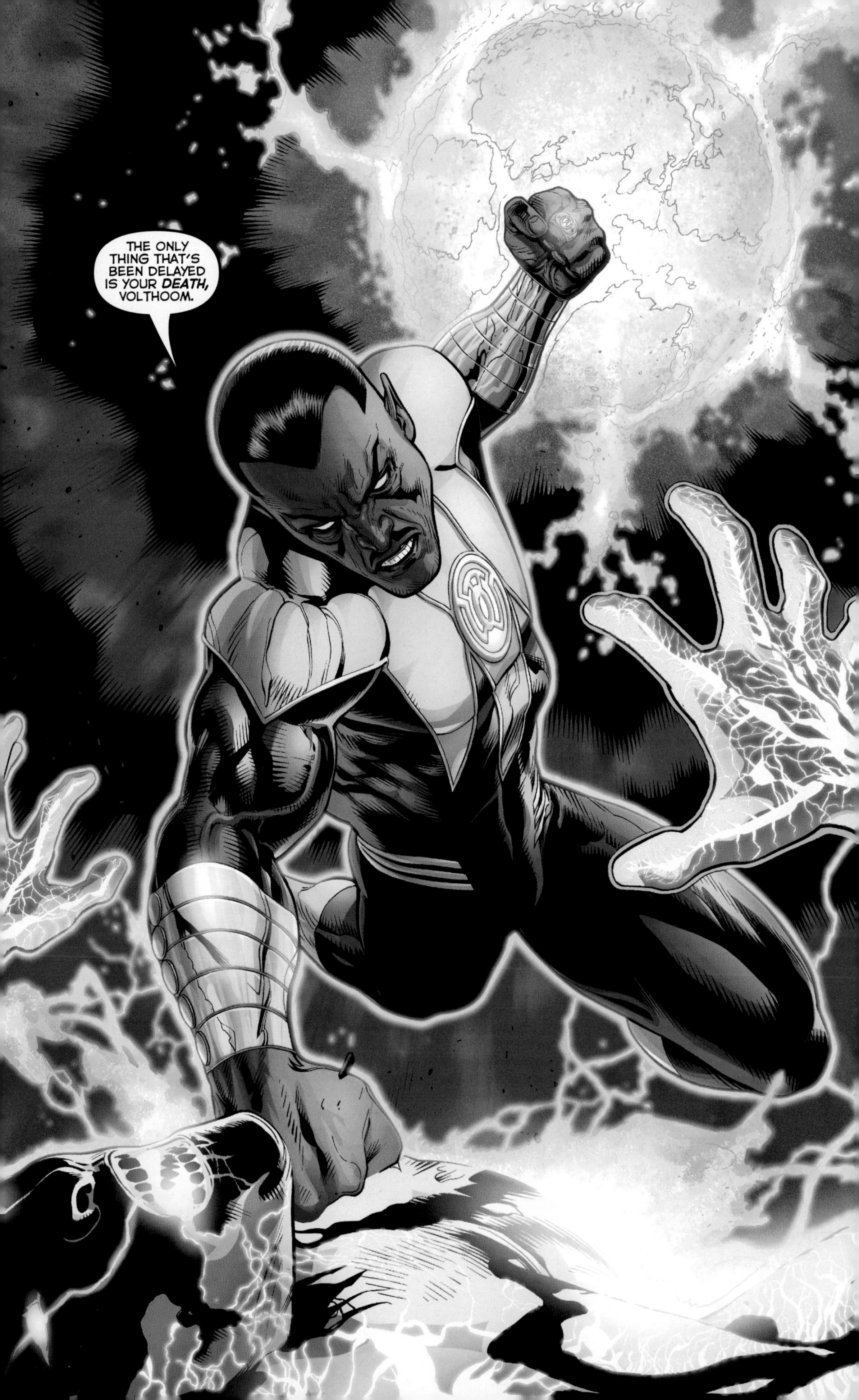
THE ONLY THING THAT'S BEEN DELAYED IS YOUR DEATH, VOLTHOOM.

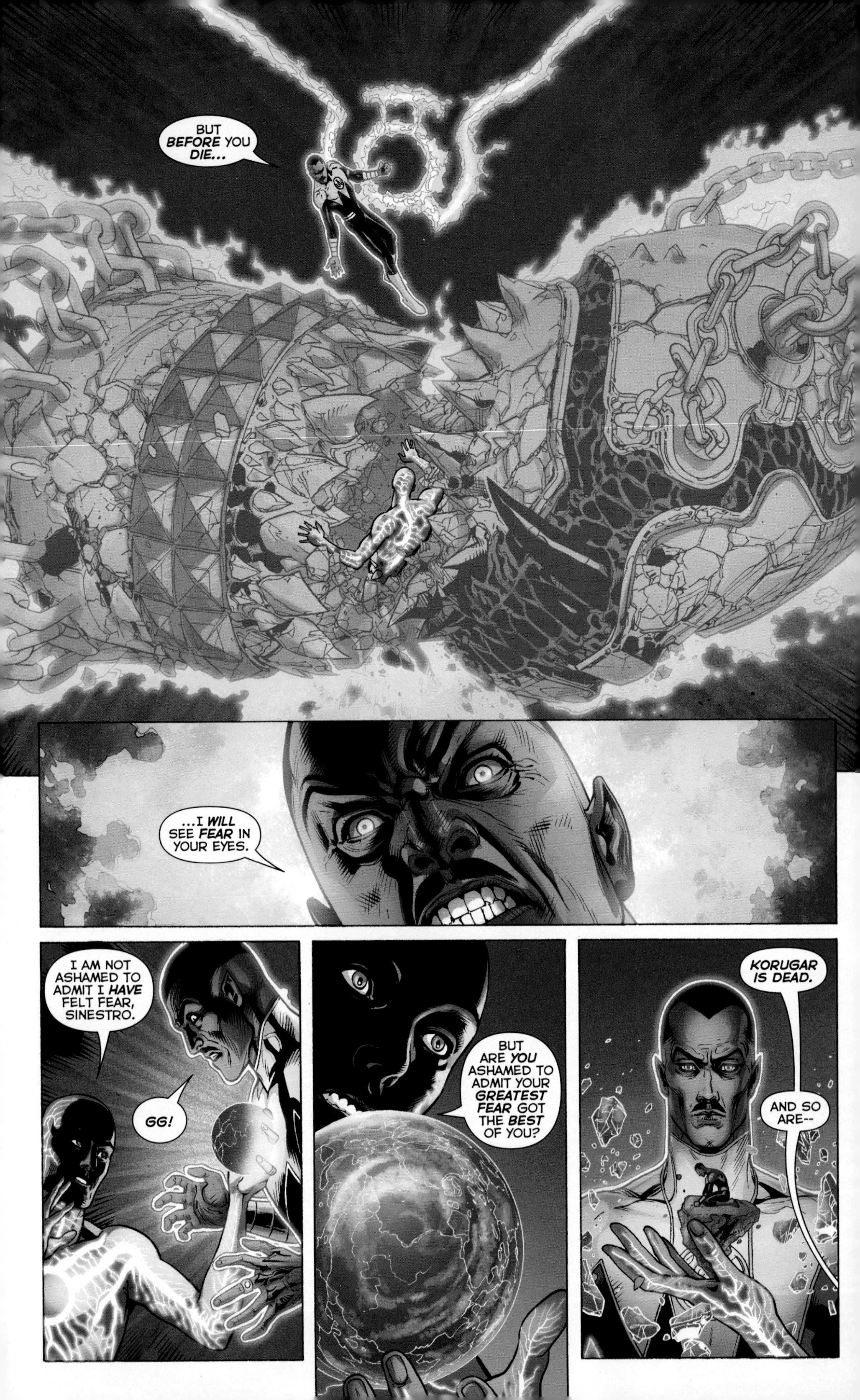
BUT BEFORE YOU DIE...
...I WILL SEE FEAR IN YOUR EYES.
I AM NOT ASHAMED TO ADMIT I HAVE FELT FEAR, SINESTRO.
GG!
BUT ARE YOU ASHAMED TO ADMIT YOUR GREATEST FEAR GOT THE BEST OF YOU?
KORUGAR IS DEAD.
AND SO ARE--

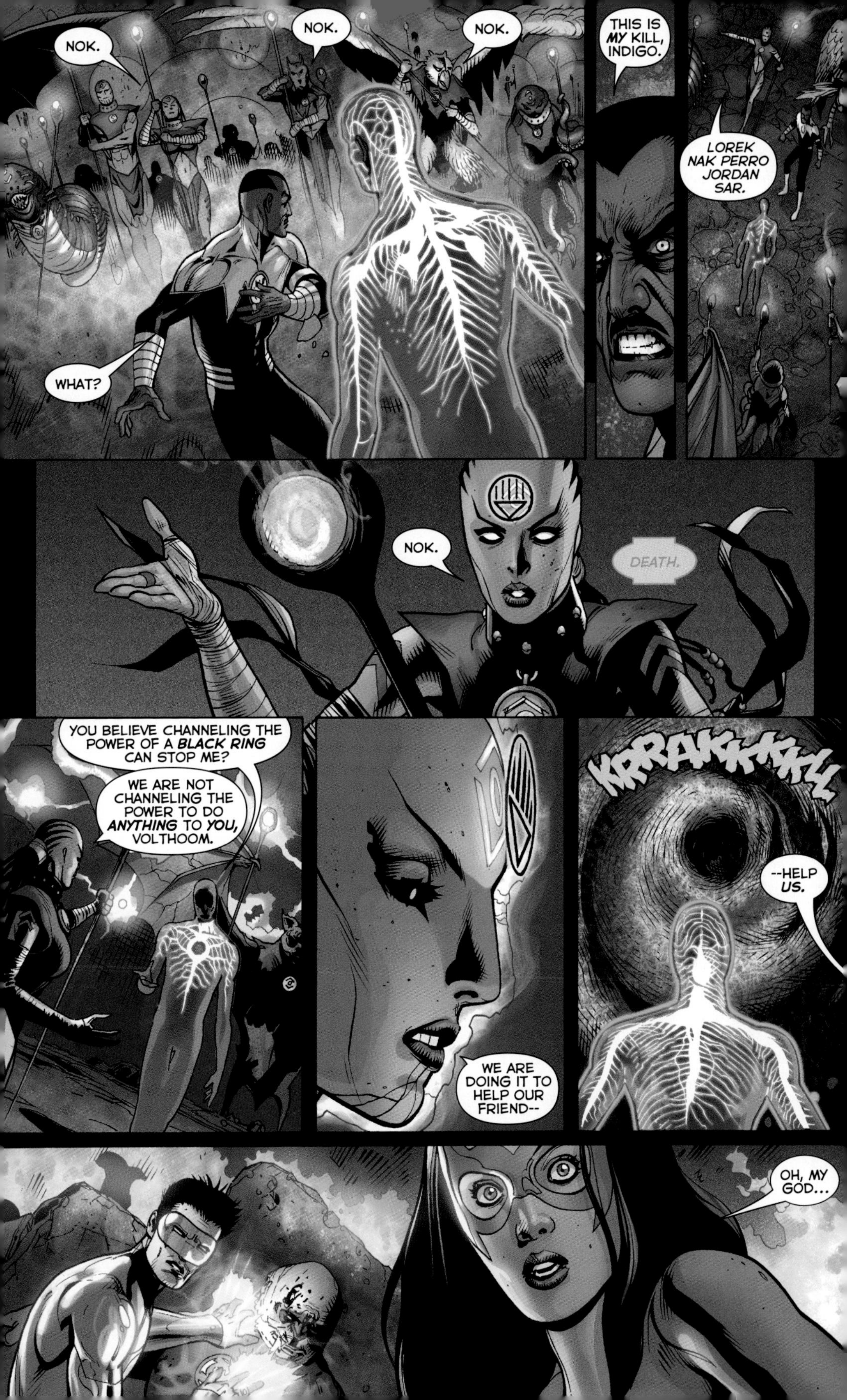
NOK.
NOK.
NOK.
WHAT?
THIS IS MY KILL, INDIGO.
LOREK NAK PERRO JORDAN SAR.
NOK.
DEATH.
YOU BELIEVE CHANNELING THE POWER OF A BLACK RING CAN STOP ME?
WE ARE NOT CHANNELING THE POWER TO DO ANYTHING TO YOU, VOLTHOOM.
WE ARE DOING IT TO HELP OUR FRIEND--
KRRAKKKKKL
--HELP US.
OH, MY GOD...

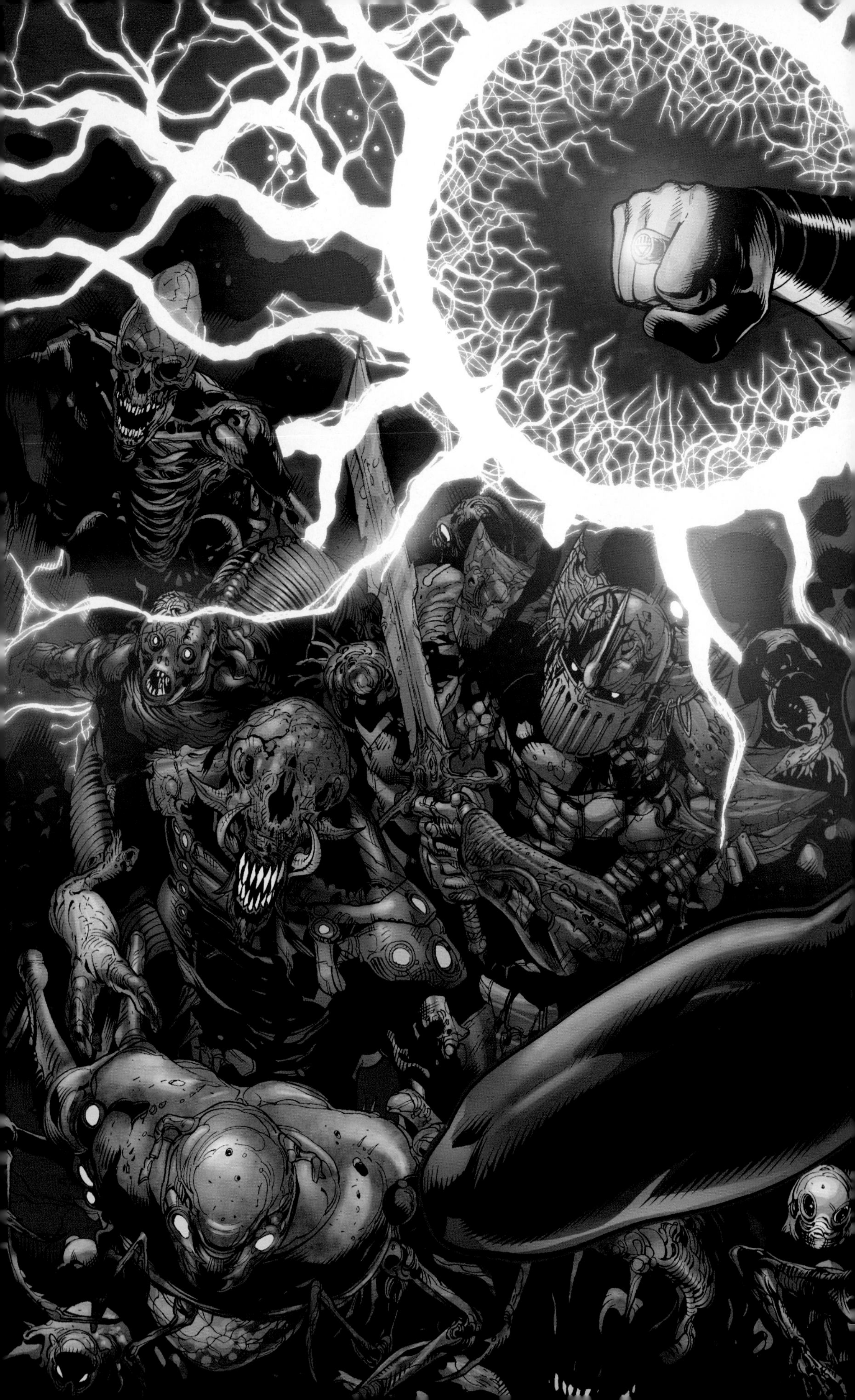

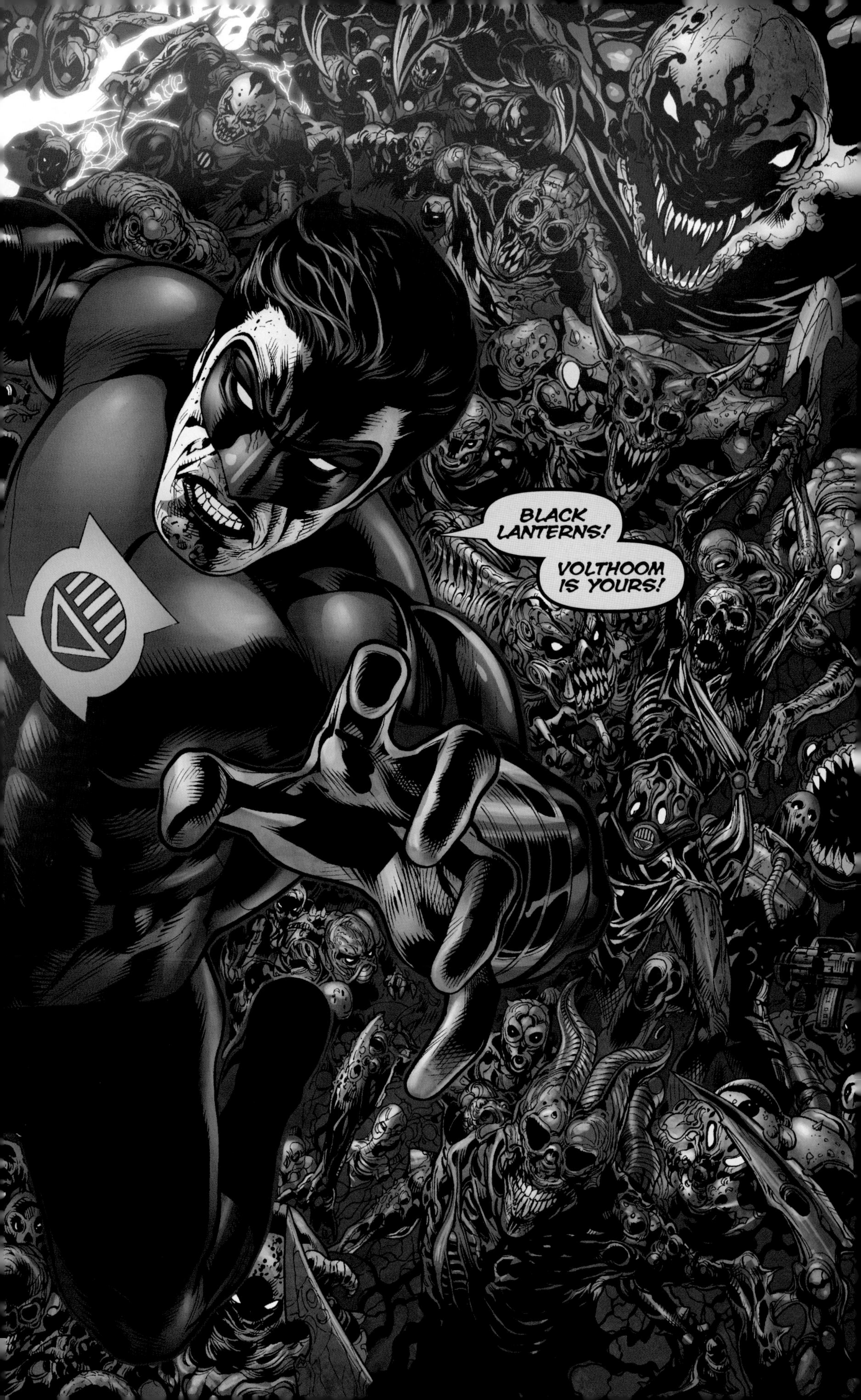
BLACK LANTERNS!
VOLTHOOM IS YOURS!

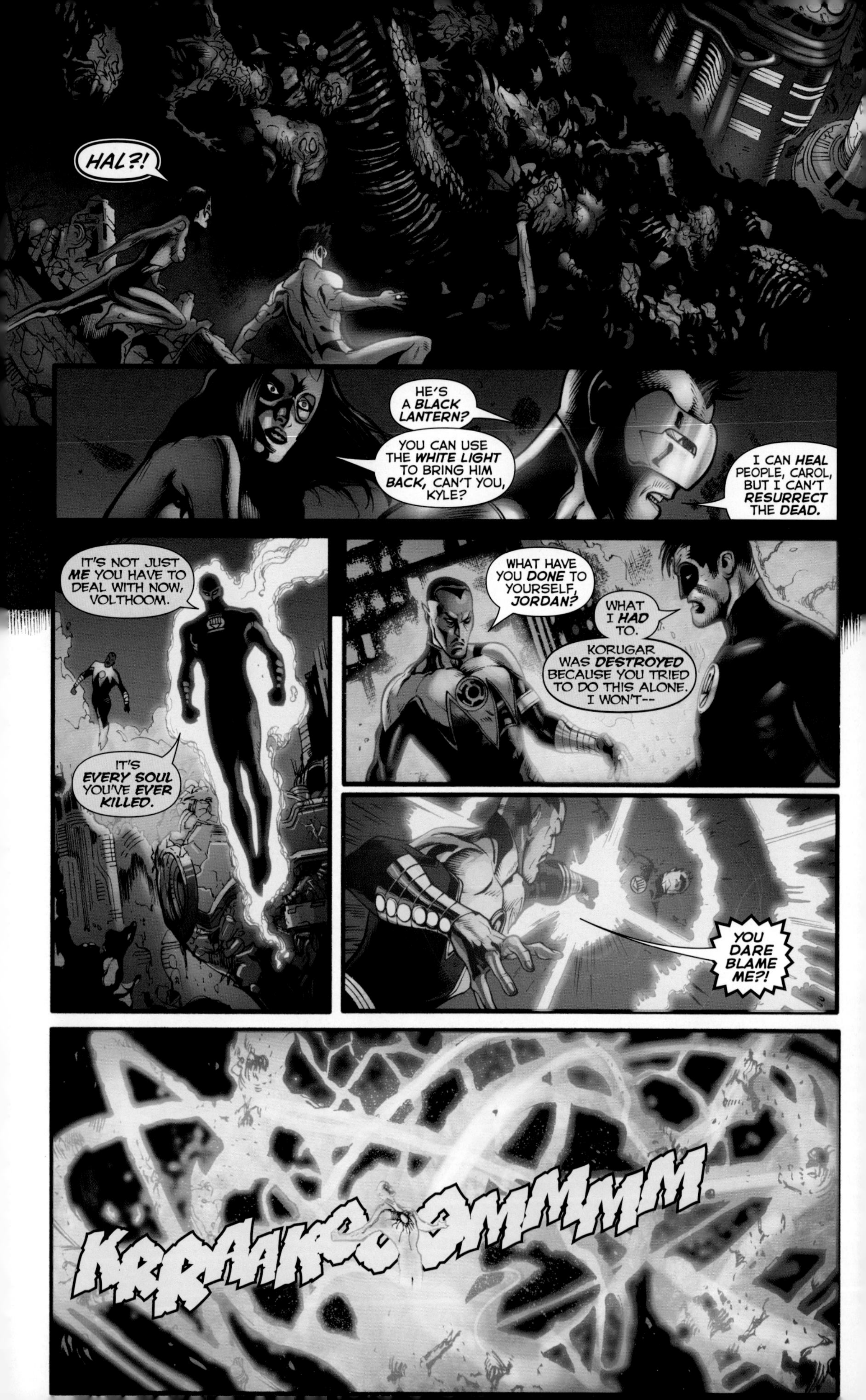

HAL?!
HE'S A BLACK LANTERN?
YOU CAN USE THE WHITE LIGHT TO BRING HIM BACK, CAN'T YOU, KYLE?
I CAN HEAL PEOPLE, CAROL, BUT I CAN'T RESURRECT THE DEAD.
IT'S NOT JUST ME YOU HAVE TO DEAL WITH NOW, VOLTHOOM.
IT'S EVERY SOUL YOU'VE EVER KILLED.
WHAT HAVE YOU DONE TO YOURSELF, JORDAN?
WHAT I HAD TO.
KORUGAR WAS DESTROYED BECAUSE YOU TRIED TO DO THIS ALONE. I WON'T--
YOU DARE BLAME ME?!
KRRAAKOOMMMMM

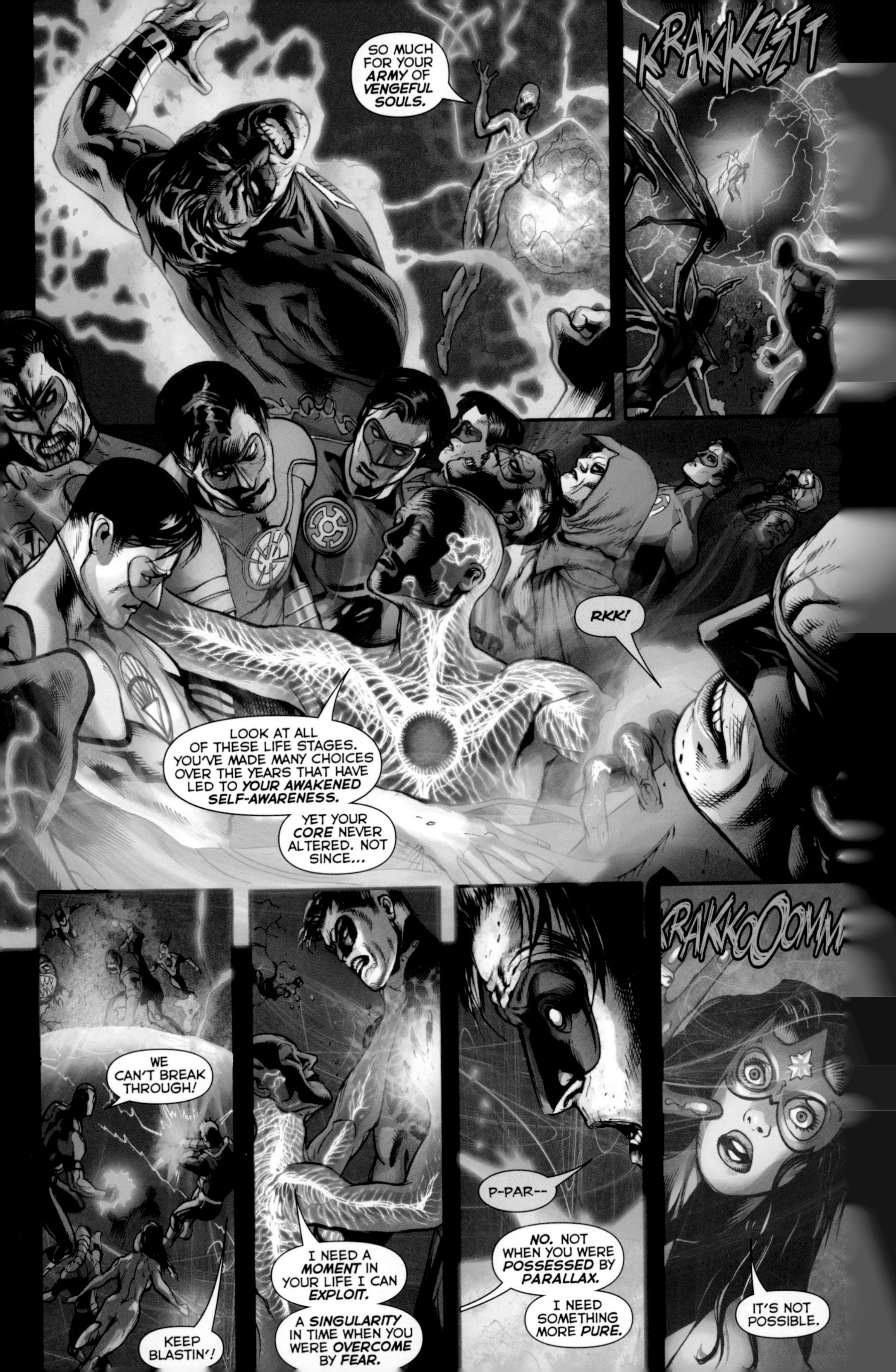
SO MUCH FOR YOUR ARMY OF VENGEFUL SOULS.
KRAKKZZTT
RKK!
LOOK AT ALL OF THESE LIFE STAGES. YOU'VE MADE MANY CHOICES OVER THE YEARS THAT HAVE LED TO YOUR AWAKENED SELF-AWARENESS.
YET YOUR CORE NEVER ALTERED. NOT SINCE...
WE CAN'T BREAK THROUGH!
KEEP BLASTIN'!
I NEED A MOMENT IN YOUR LIFE I CAN EXPLOIT.
A SINGULARITY IN TIME WHEN YOU WERE OVERCOME BY FEAR.
P-PAR--
NO. NOT WHEN YOU WERE POSSESSED BY PARALLAX.
I NEED SOMETHING MORE PURE.
KRAKKOOOMM
IT'S NOT POSSIBLE.

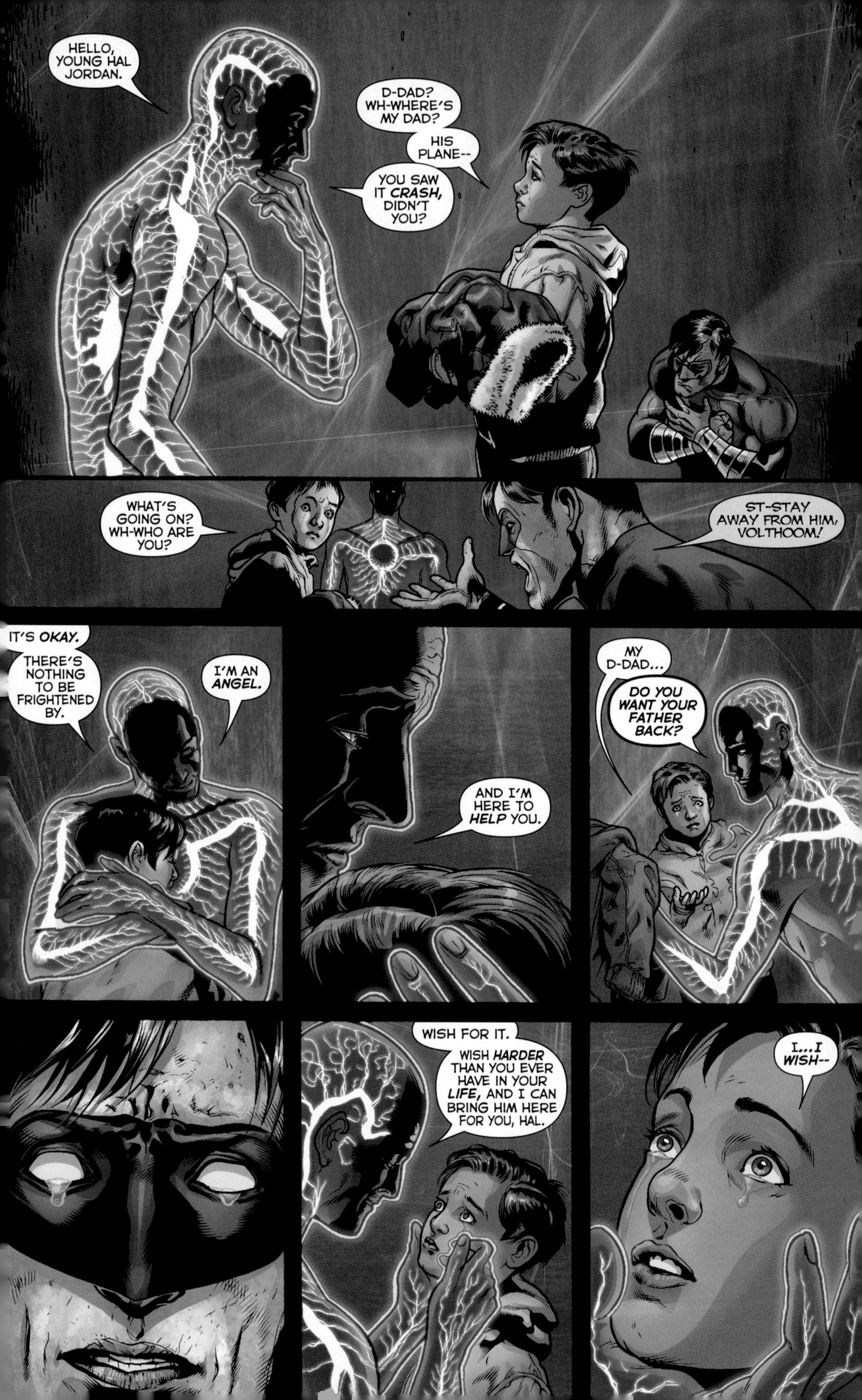
HELLO, YOUNG HAL JORDAN.
D-DAD? WH-WHERE'S MY DAD?
HIS PLANE--
YOU SAW IT CRASH, DIDN'T YOU?
WHAT'S GOING ON? WH-WHO ARE YOU?
ST-STAY AWAY FROM HIM, VOLTHOOM!
IT'S OKAY.
THERE'S NOTHING TO BE FRIGHTENED BY.
I'M AN ANGEL.
AND I'M HERE TO HELP YOU.
MY D-DAD...
DO YOU WANT YOUR FATHER BACK?
WISH FOR IT.
WISH HARDER THAN YOU EVER HAVE IN YOUR LIFE, AND I CAN BRING HIM HERE FOR YOU, HAL.
I...I WISH--

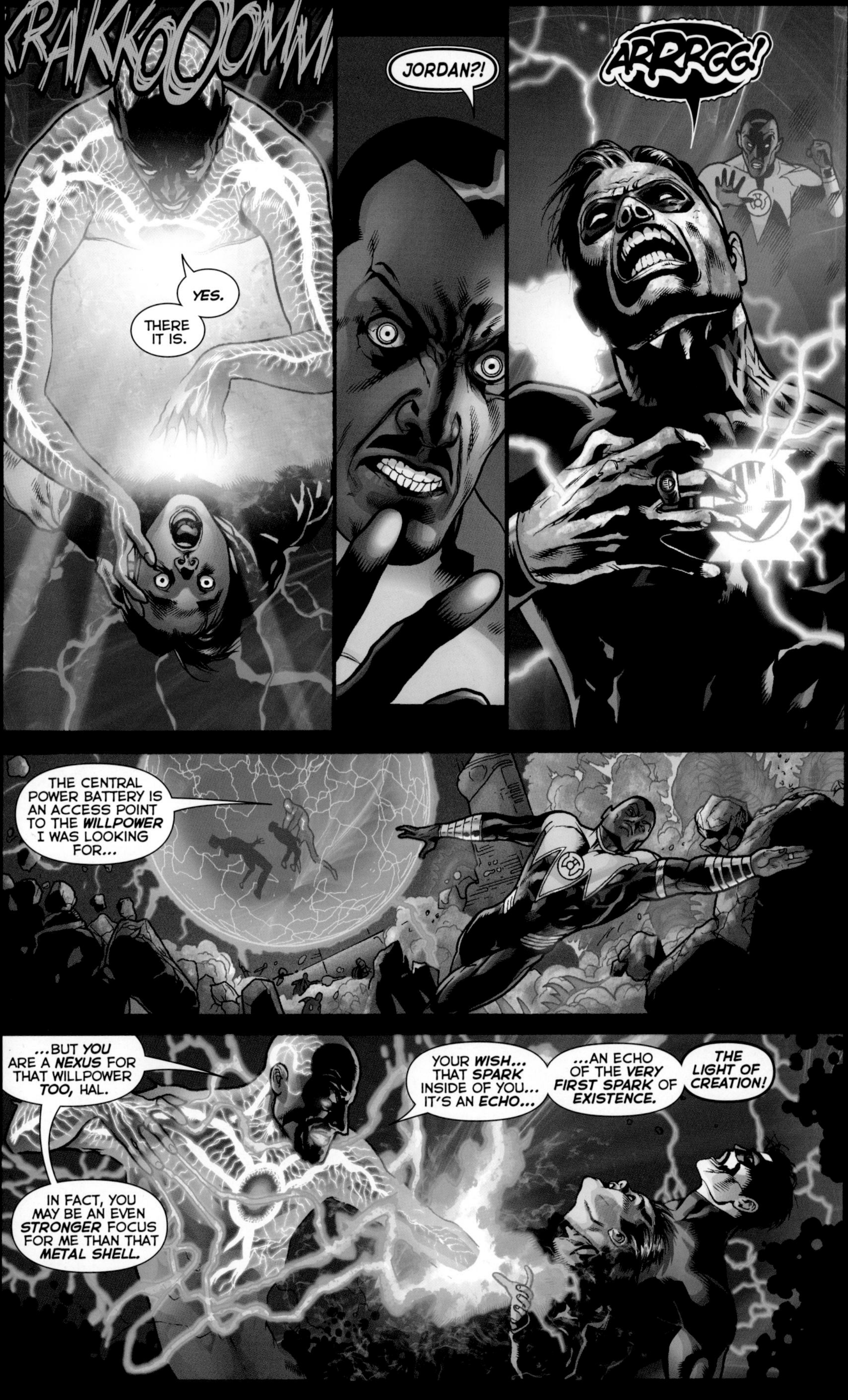
KRAKKOOOMM
YES.
THERE IT IS.
JORDAN?!
ARRRGG!
THE CENTRAL POWER BATTERY IS AN ACCESS POINT TO THE WILLPOWER I WAS LOOKING FOR...
...BUT YOU ARE A NEXUS FOR THAT WILLPOWER TOO, HAL.
IN FACT, YOU MAY BE AN EVEN STRONGER FOCUS FOR ME THAN THAT METAL SHELL.
YOUR WISH... THAT SPARK INSIDE OF YOU... IT'S AN ECHO...
...AN ECHO OF THE VERY FIRST SPARK OF EXISTENCE.
THE LIGHT OF CREATION!

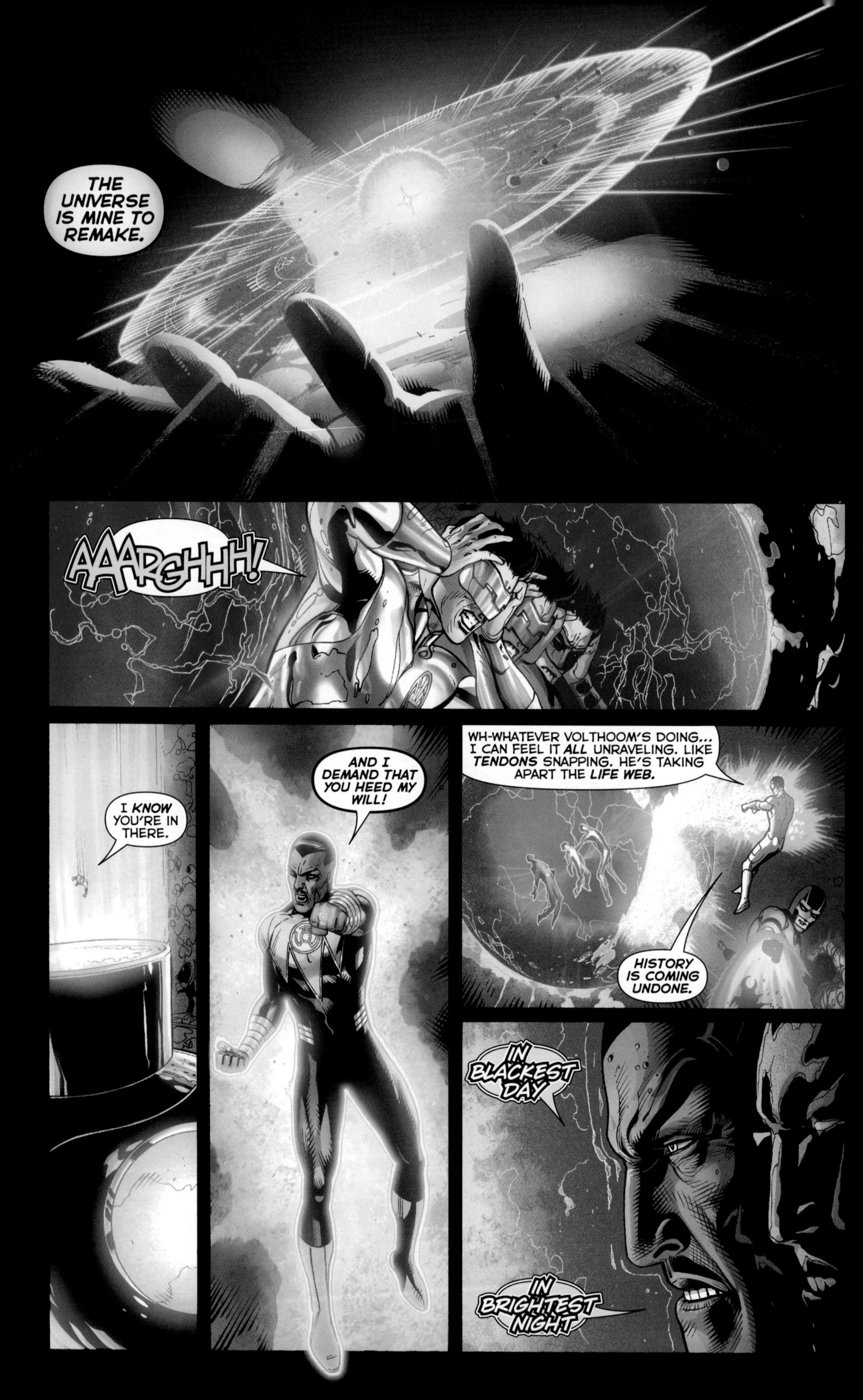
THE UNIVERSE IS MINE TO REMAKE.
AAARGHHH!
I KNOW YOU'RE IN THERE.
AND I DEMAND THAT YOU HEED MY WILL!
WH-WHATEVER VOLTHOOM'S DOING... I CAN FEEL IT ALL UNRAVELING. LIKE TENDONS SNAPPING. HE'S TAKING APART THE LIFE WEB.
HISTORY IS COMING UNDONE.
IN BLACKEST DAY
IN BRIGHTEST NIGHT

"BEWARE MY FEARS MADE INTO LIGHT"

VOLTHOOM'S MONSTERS ARE GOING AFTER SINESTRO!

SINESTRO IS *NOT* AN ALLY, SIMON. WHATEVER HE'S DOING--

WHATEVER HE'S DOING, IT'S TO *HELP* US. HE WANTS VOLTHOOM TAKEN OUT AS MUCH AS *WE* DO.

LET THOSE WHO TRY TO STOP WHAT'S RIGHT

BURN LIKE MY POWER

SINESTRO'S MIGHT!

AFSSSSSSSSS

WELL, CREATURE?

WHAT ARE YOU *WAITING* FOR?

Y-YOU MAY HAVE CONTROLLED YOUR *PAST* HOSTS, PARALLAX.

"BUT *NOT* ME."

KRRRGG!

BRAKKOOOMMMM

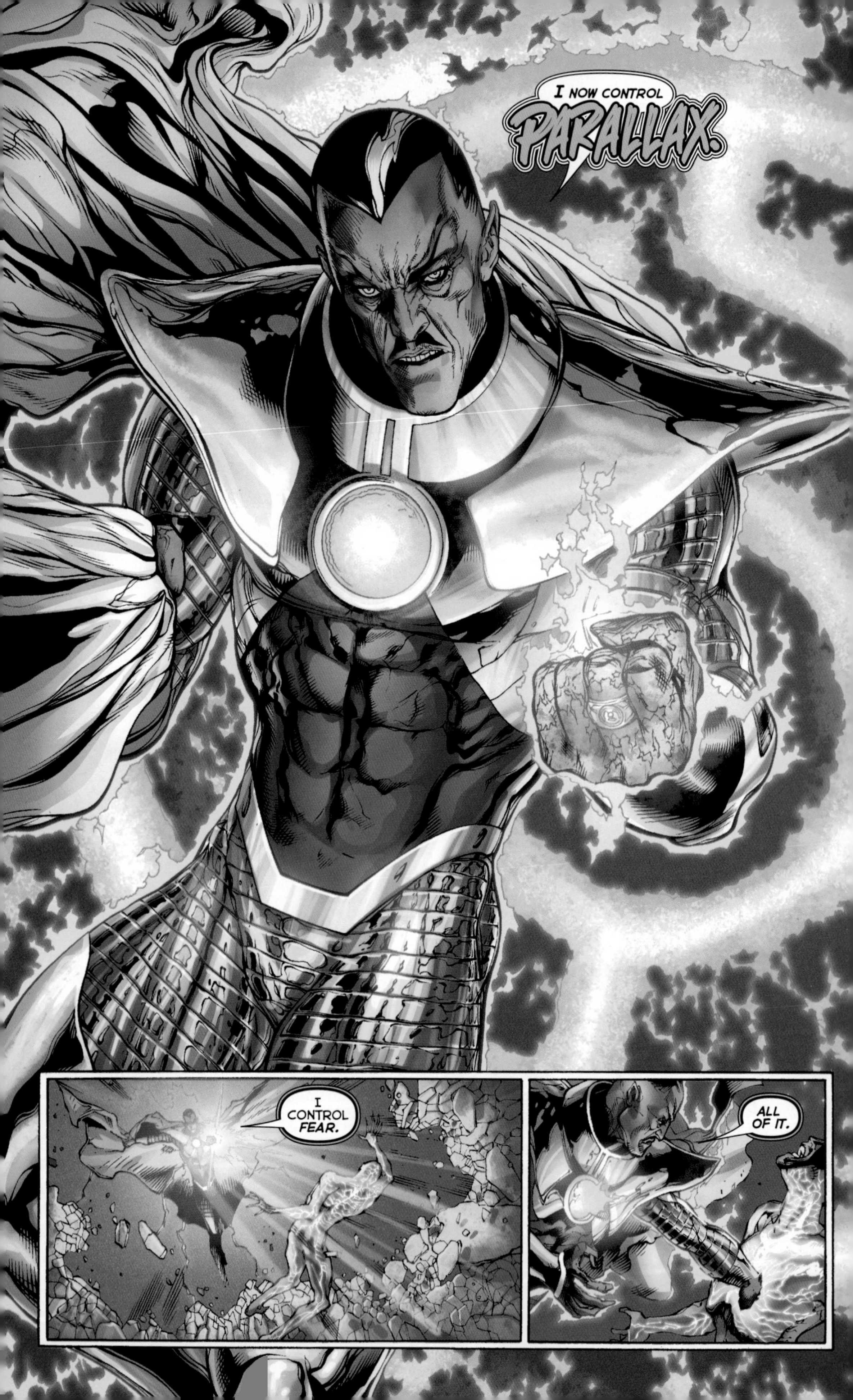
I NOW CONTROL
PARALLAX.
I CONTROL FEAR.
ALL OF IT.

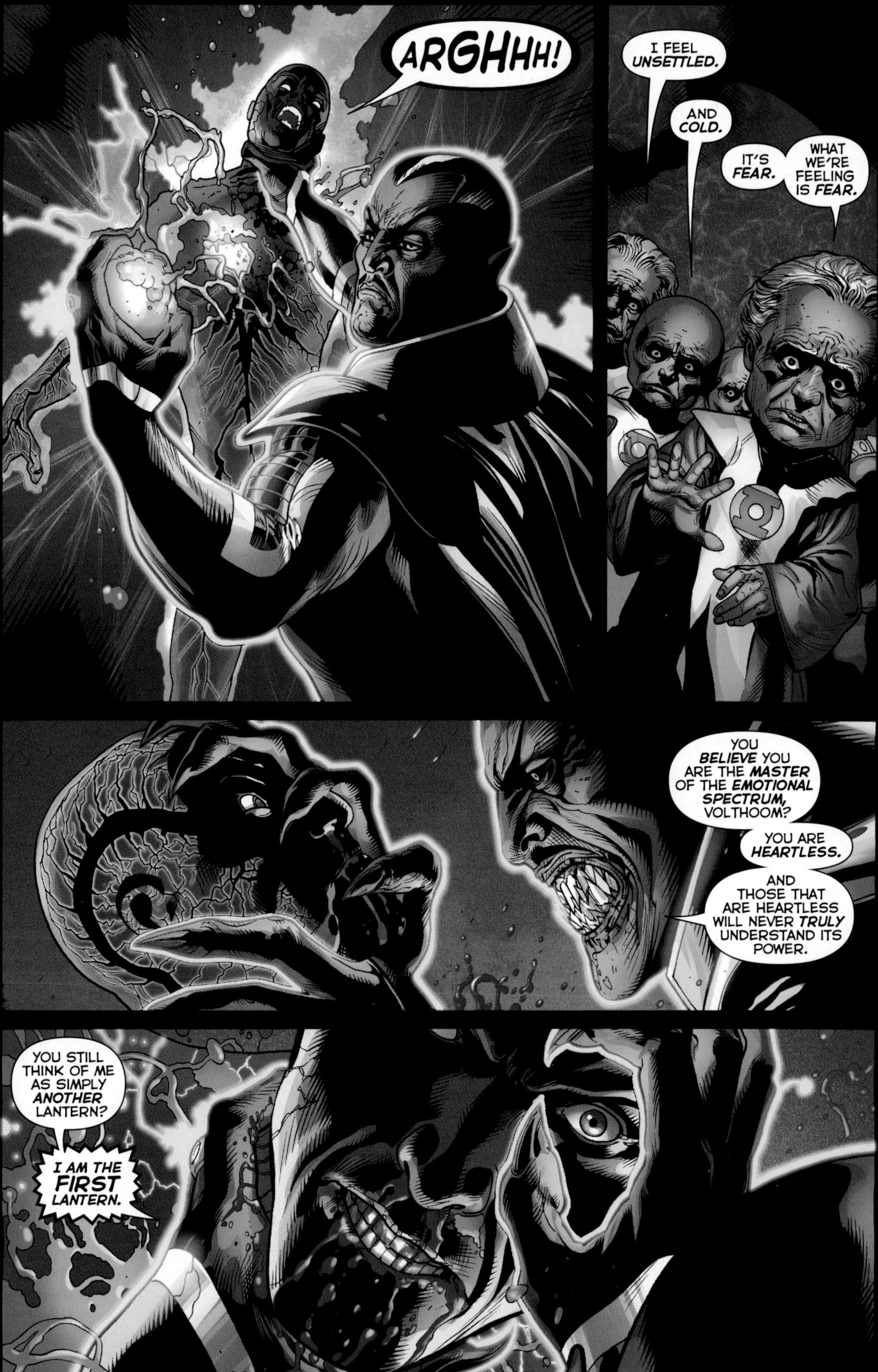
ARGHHH!
I FEEL UNSETTLED.
AND COLD.
IT'S FEAR.
WHAT WE'RE FEELING IS FEAR.
YOU BELIEVE YOU ARE THE MASTER OF THE EMOTIONAL SPECTRUM, VOLTHOOM?
YOU ARE HEARTLESS.
AND THOSE THAT ARE HEARTLESS WILL NEVER TRULY UNDERSTAND ITS POWER.
YOU STILL THINK OF ME AS SIMPLY ANOTHER LANTERN?
I AM THE FIRST LANTERN.

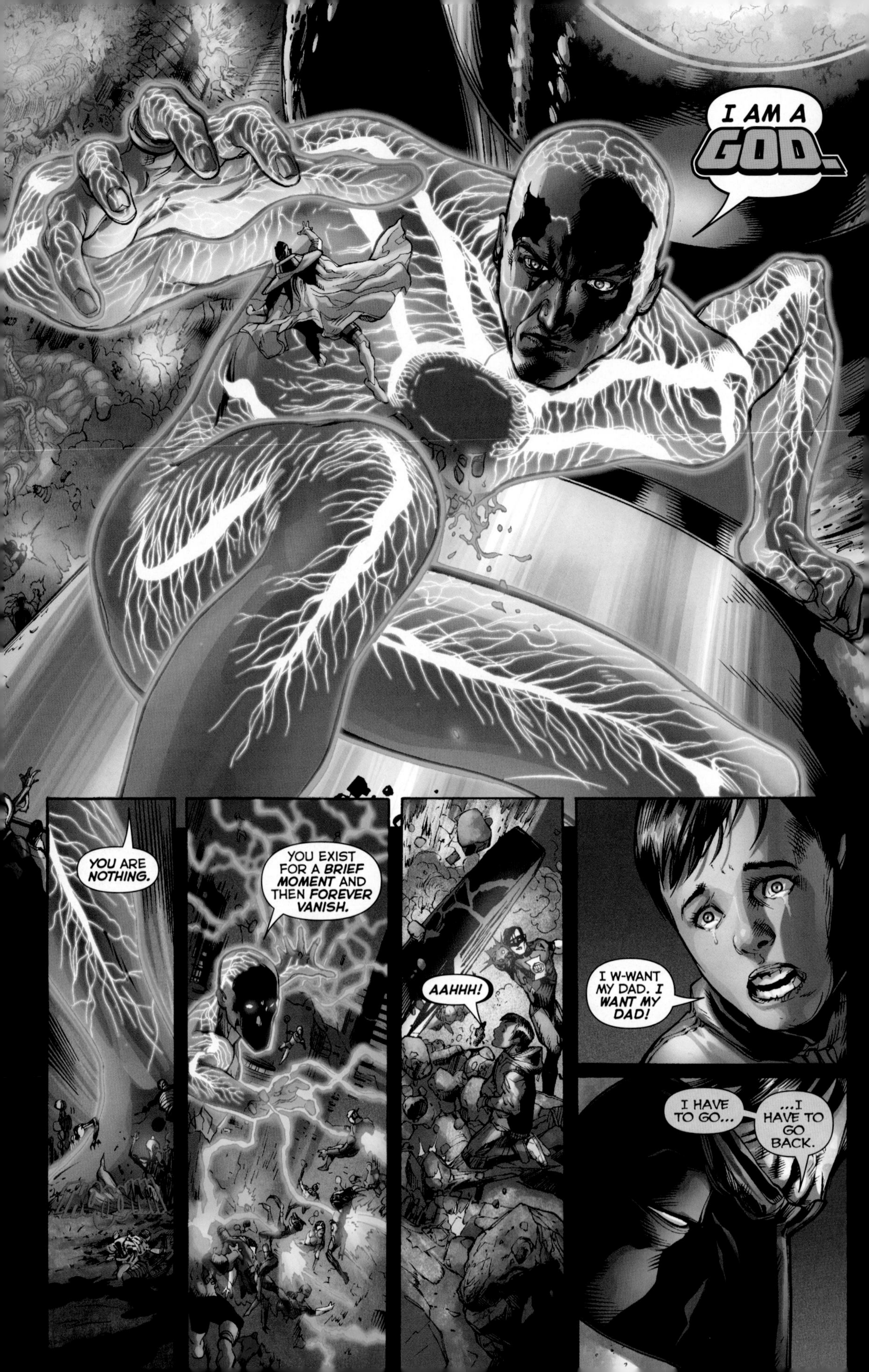
I AM A GOD.
YOU ARE NOTHING.
YOU EXIST FOR A BRIEF MOMENT AND THEN FOREVER VANISH.
AAHHH!
I W-WANT MY DAD. I WANT MY DAD!
I HAVE TO GO...
...I HAVE TO GO BACK.

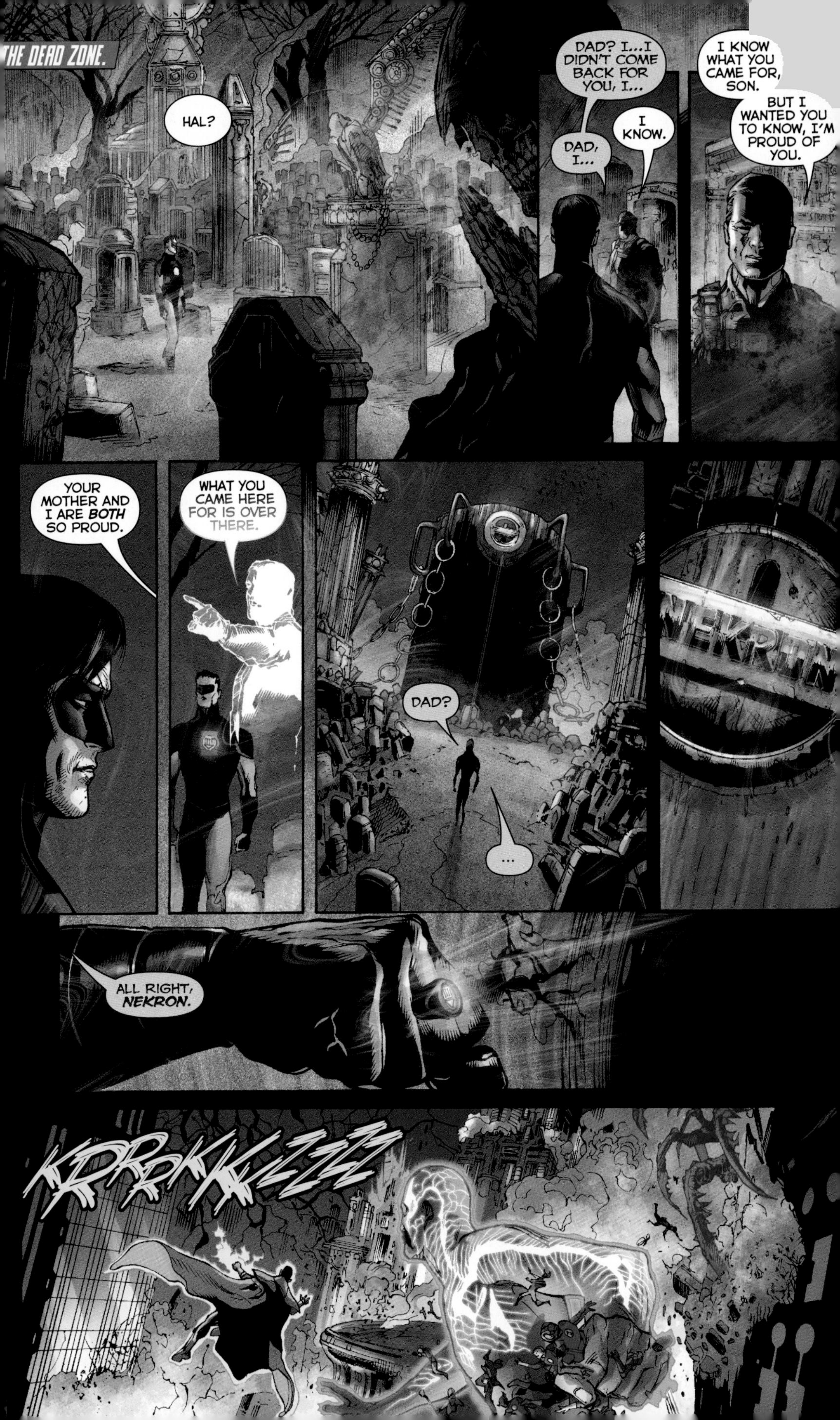
THE DEAD ZONE.
HAL?
DAD? I...I DIDN'T COME BACK FOR YOU, I...
DAD, I...
I KNOW.
I KNOW WHAT YOU CAME FOR, SON.
BUT I WANTED YOU TO KNOW, I'M PROUD OF YOU.
YOUR MOTHER AND I ARE BOTH SO PROUD.
WHAT YOU CAME HERE FOR IS OVER THERE.
DAD?
...
NEKRON
ALL RIGHT, NEKRON.
KRRRKKZZZZ

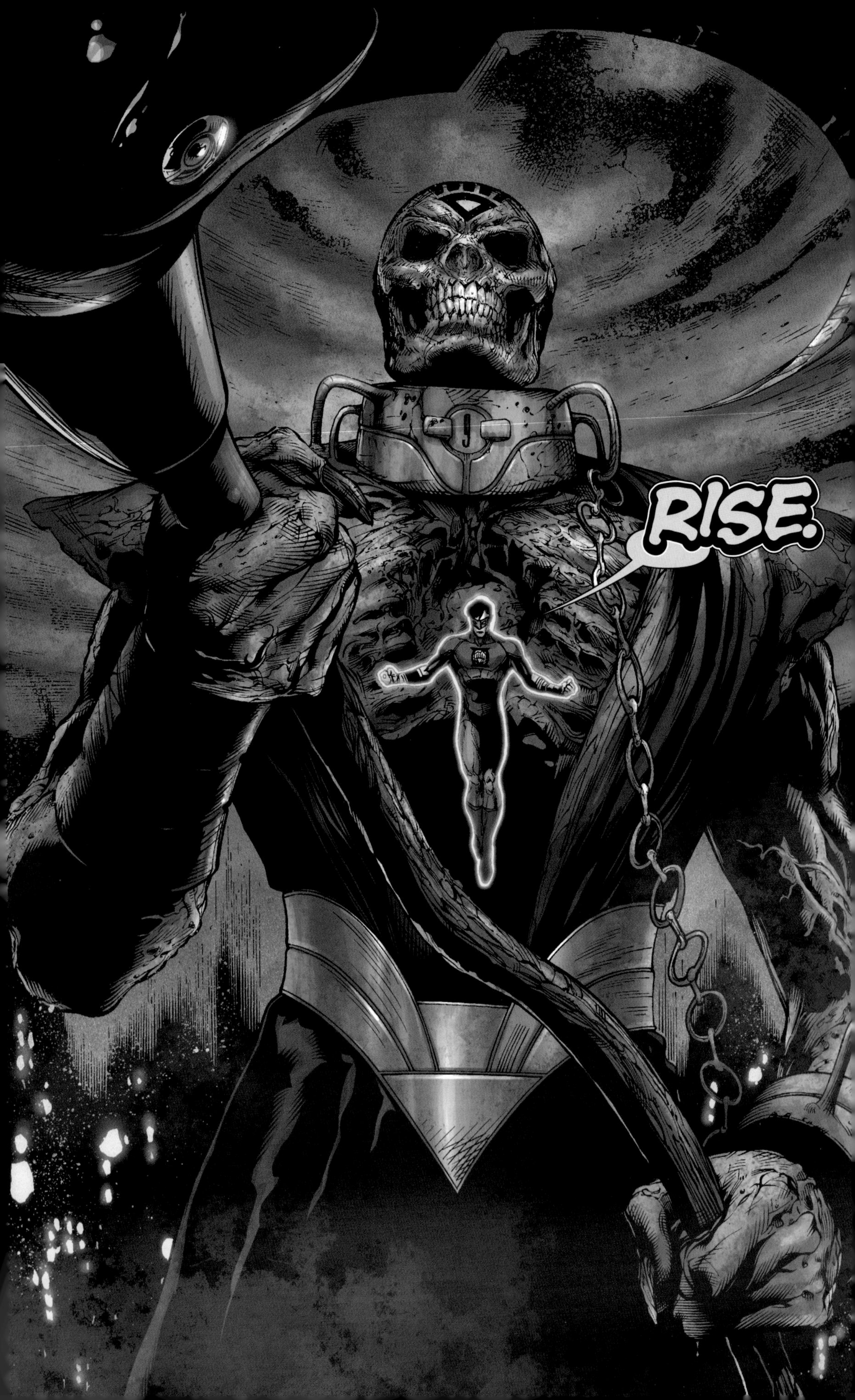
RISE.

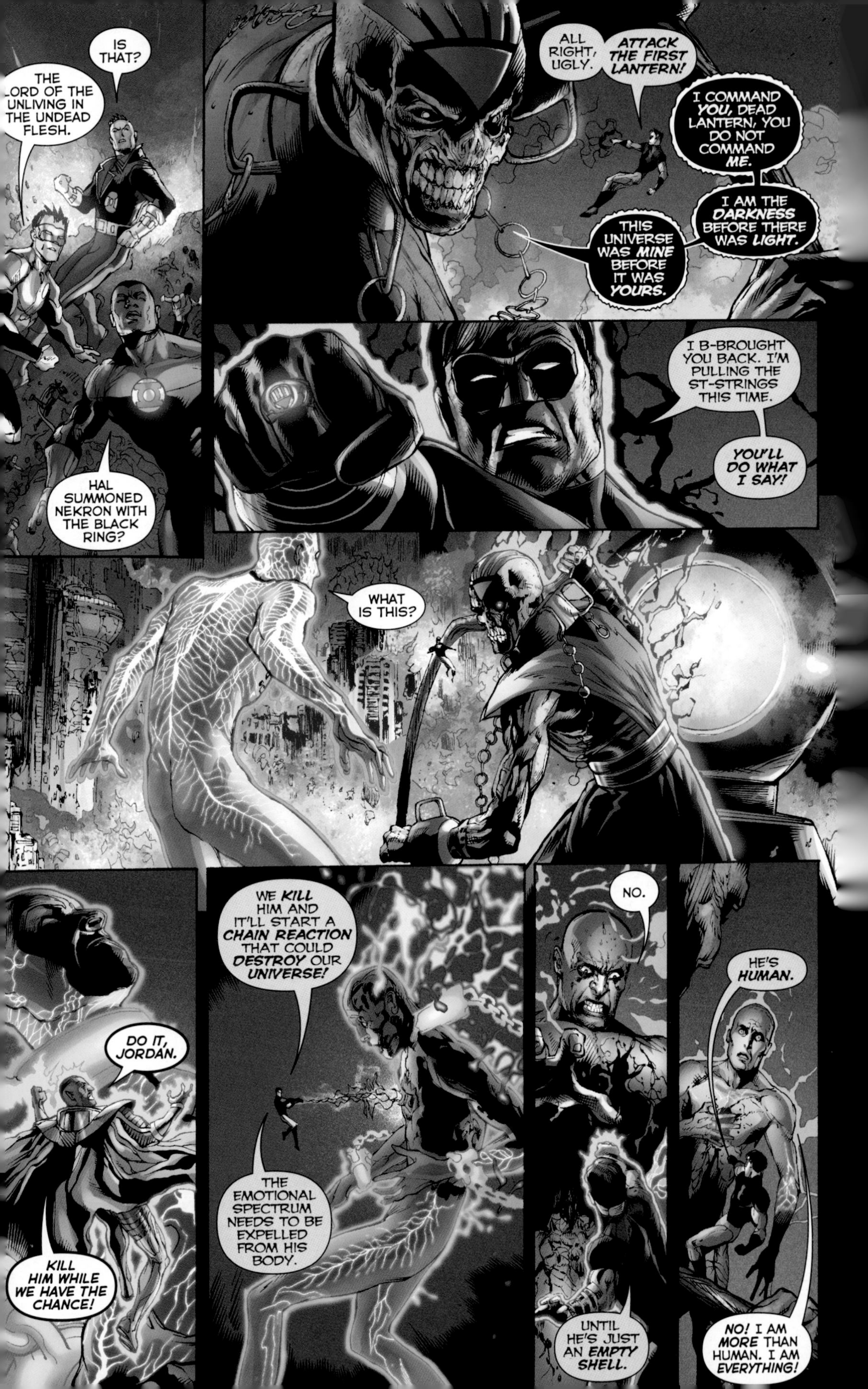
IS THAT?
THE LORD OF THE UNLIVING IN THE UNDEAD FLESH.
HAL SUMMONED NEKRON WITH THE BLACK RING?
ALL RIGHT, UGLY.
ATTACK THE FIRST LANTERN!
I COMMAND YOU, DEAD LANTERN, YOU DO NOT COMMAND ME.
I AM THE DARKNESS BEFORE THERE WAS LIGHT.
THIS UNIVERSE WAS MINE BEFORE IT WAS YOURS.
I B-BROUGHT YOU BACK. I'M PULLING THE ST-STRINGS THIS TIME.
YOU'LL DO WHAT I SAY!
WHAT IS THIS?
DO IT, JORDAN.
KILL HIM WHILE WE HAVE THE CHANCE!
WE KILL HIM AND IT'LL START A CHAIN REACTION THAT COULD DESTROY OUR UNIVERSE!
THE EMOTIONAL SPECTRUM NEEDS TO BE EXPELLED FROM HIS BODY.
NO.
UNTIL HE'S JUST AN EMPTY SHELL.
HE'S HUMAN.
NO! I AM MORE THAN HUMAN. I AM EVERYTHING!

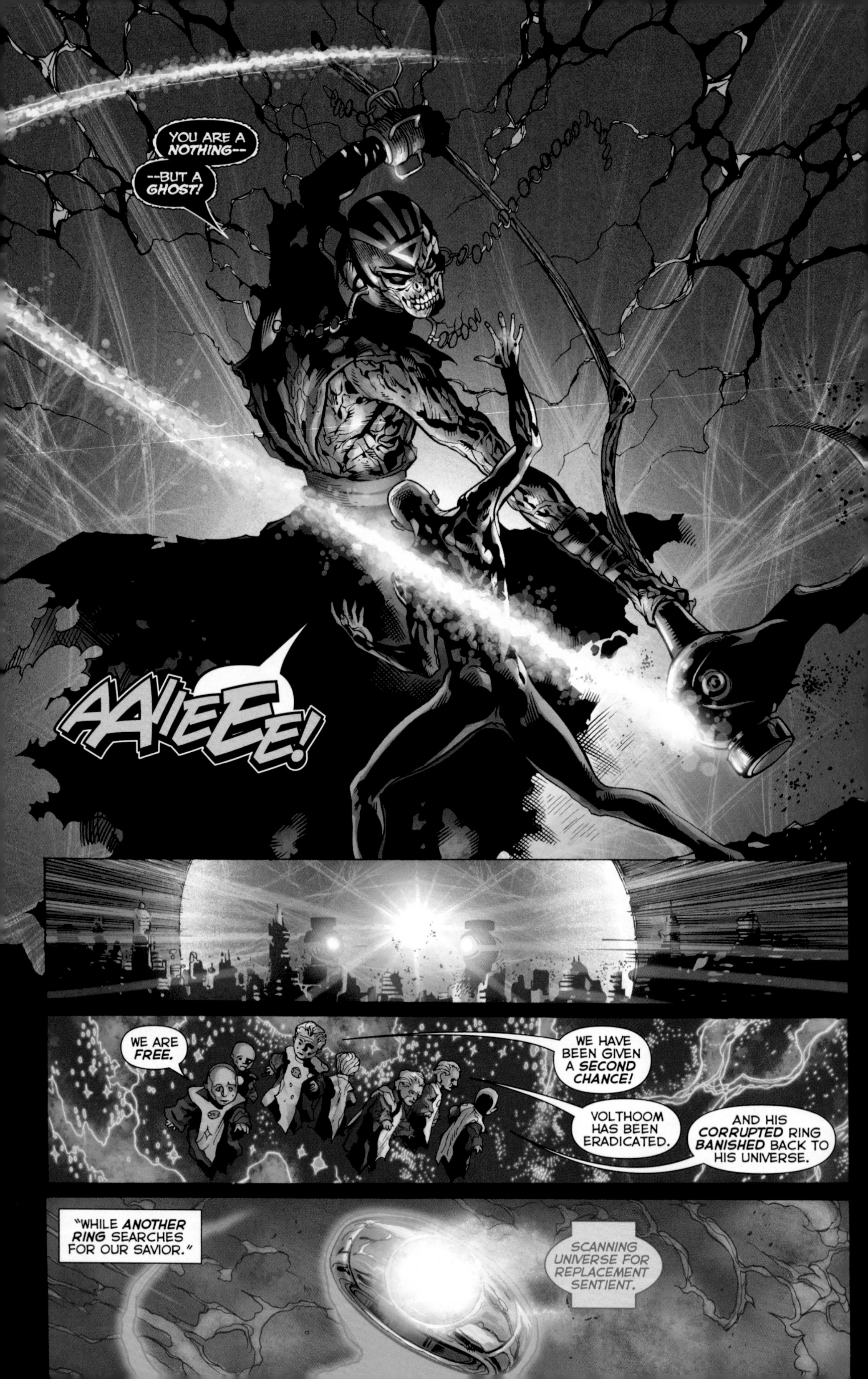
YOU ARE A NOTHING--
--BUT A GHOST!
AAIIEEEE!
WE ARE FREE.
WE HAVE BEEN GIVEN A SECOND CHANCE!
VOLTHOOM HAS BEEN ERADICATED.
AND HIS CORRUPTED RING BANISHED BACK TO HIS UNIVERSE.
"WHILE ANOTHER RING SEARCHES FOR OUR SAVIOR."
SCANNING UNIVERSE FOR REPLACEMENT SENTIENT.

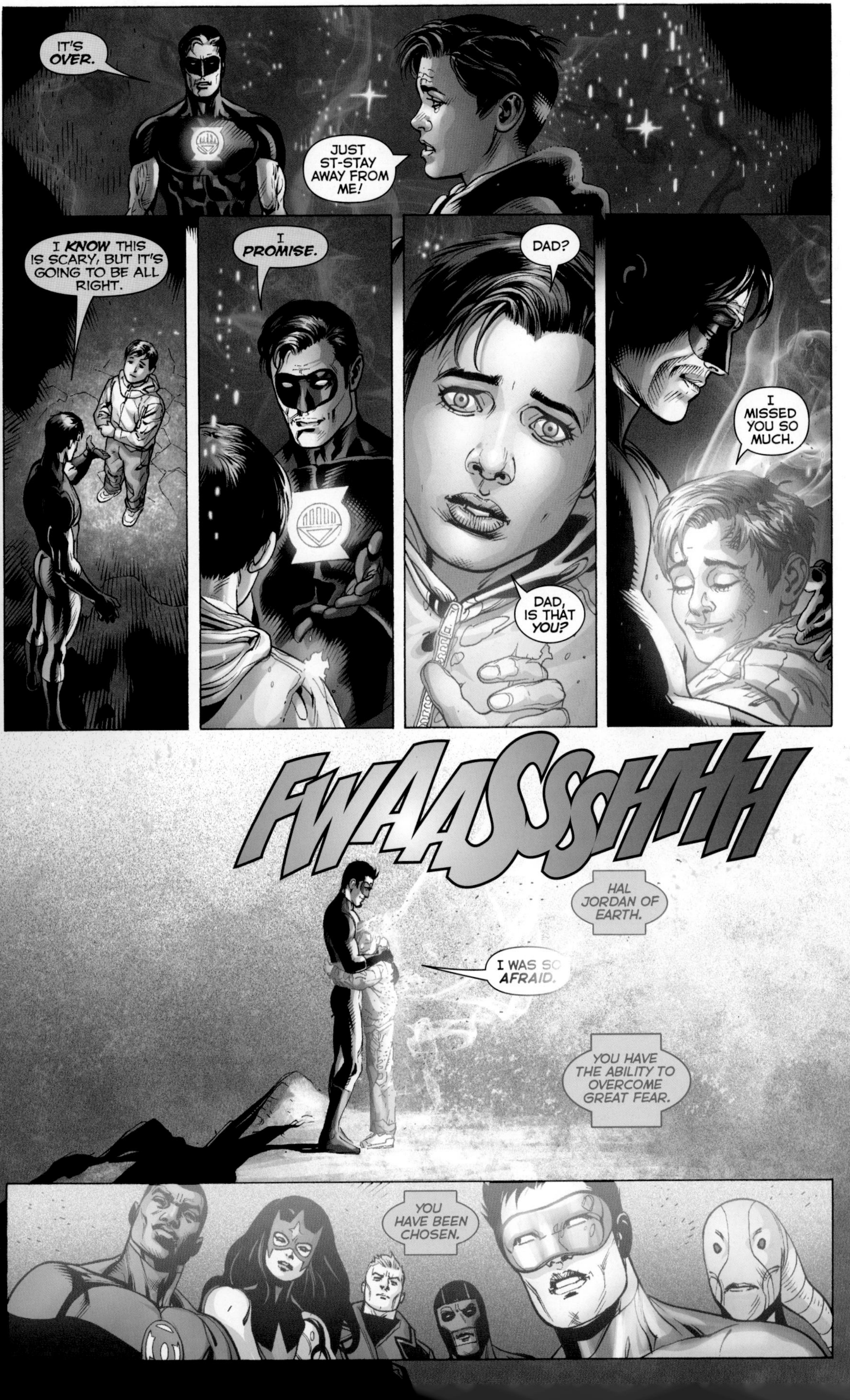
IT'S OVER.
JUST ST-STAY AWAY FROM ME!
I KNOW THIS IS SCARY, BUT IT'S GOING TO BE ALL RIGHT.
I PROMISE.
DAD?
DAD, IS THAT YOU?
I MISSED YOU SO MUCH.
FWAASSHHH
HAL JORDAN OF EARTH.
I WAS SO AFRAID.
YOU HAVE THE ABILITY TO OVERCOME GREAT FEAR.
YOU HAVE BEEN CHOSEN.

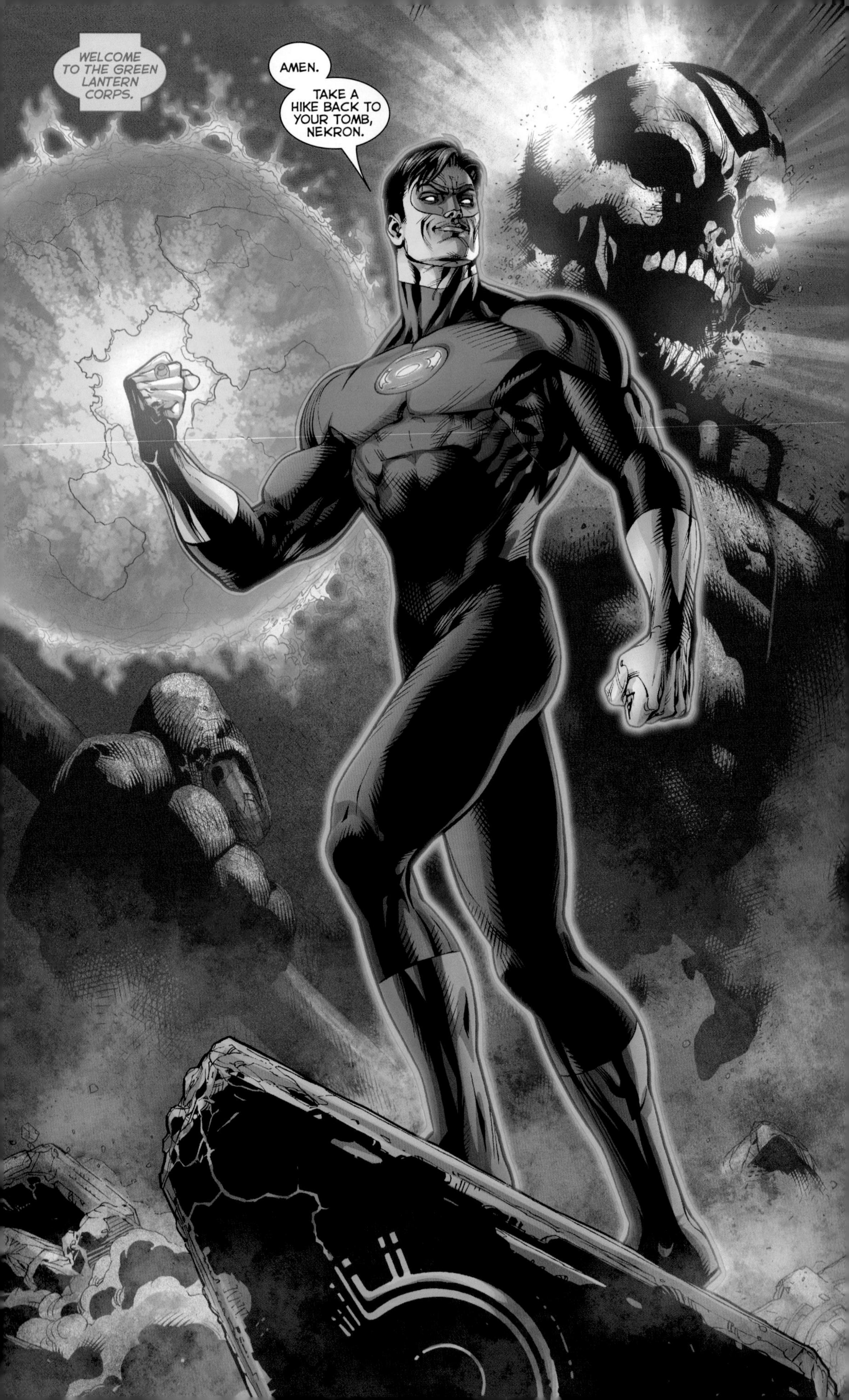
WELCOME TO THE GREEN LANTERN CORPS.
AMEN.
TAKE A HIKE BACK TO YOUR TOMB, NEKRON.

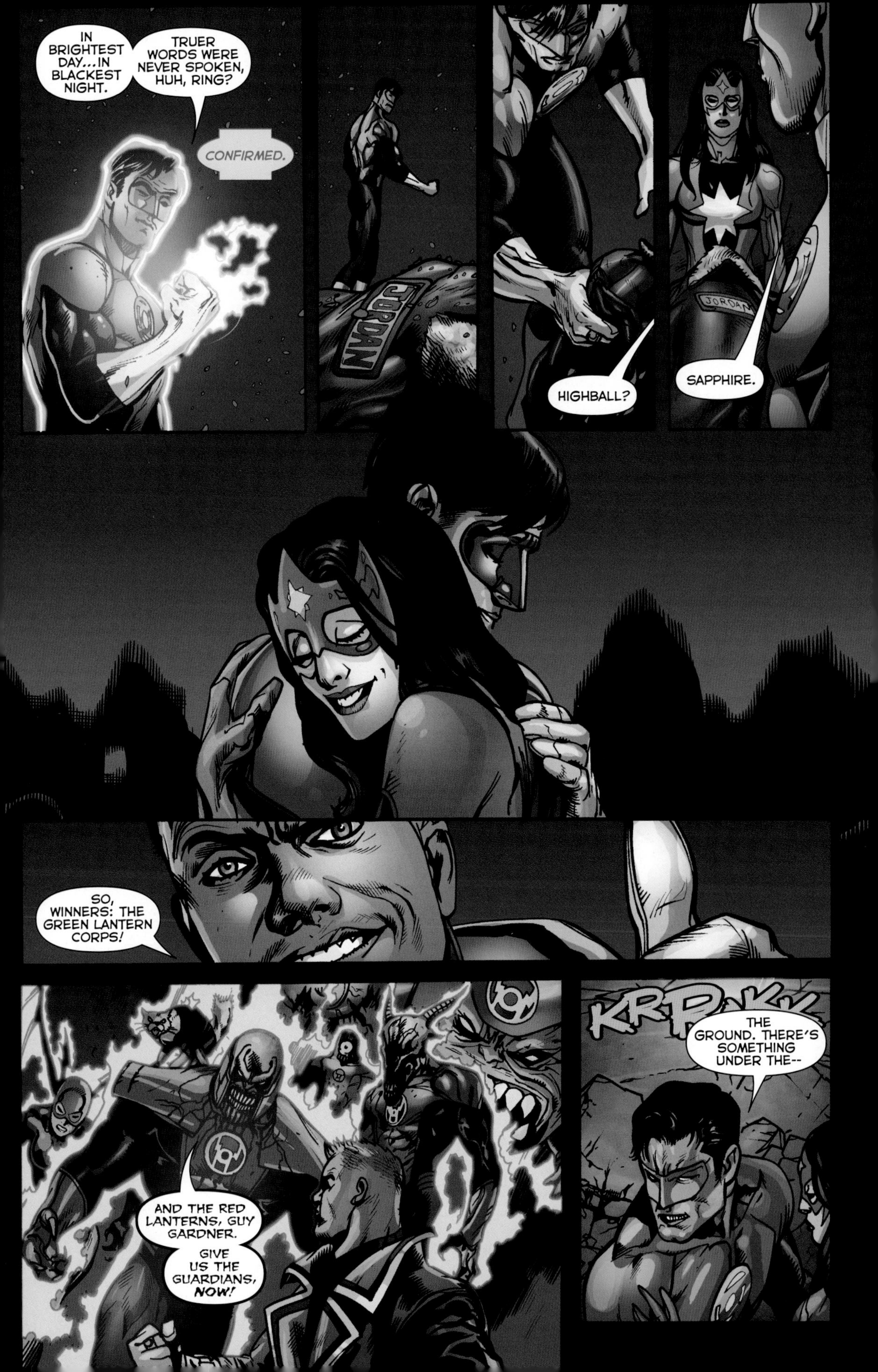
IN BRIGHTEST DAY...IN BLACKEST NIGHT.
TRUER WORDS WERE NEVER SPOKEN, HUH, RING?
CONFIRMED.
JORDAN
HIGHBALL?
JORDAN
SAPPHIRE.
SO, WINNERS: THE GREEN LANTERN CORPS!
AND THE RED LANTERNS, GUY GARDNER.
GIVE US THE GUARDIANS, *NOW!*
KRRKK
THE GROUND. THERE'S SOMETHING UNDER THE--

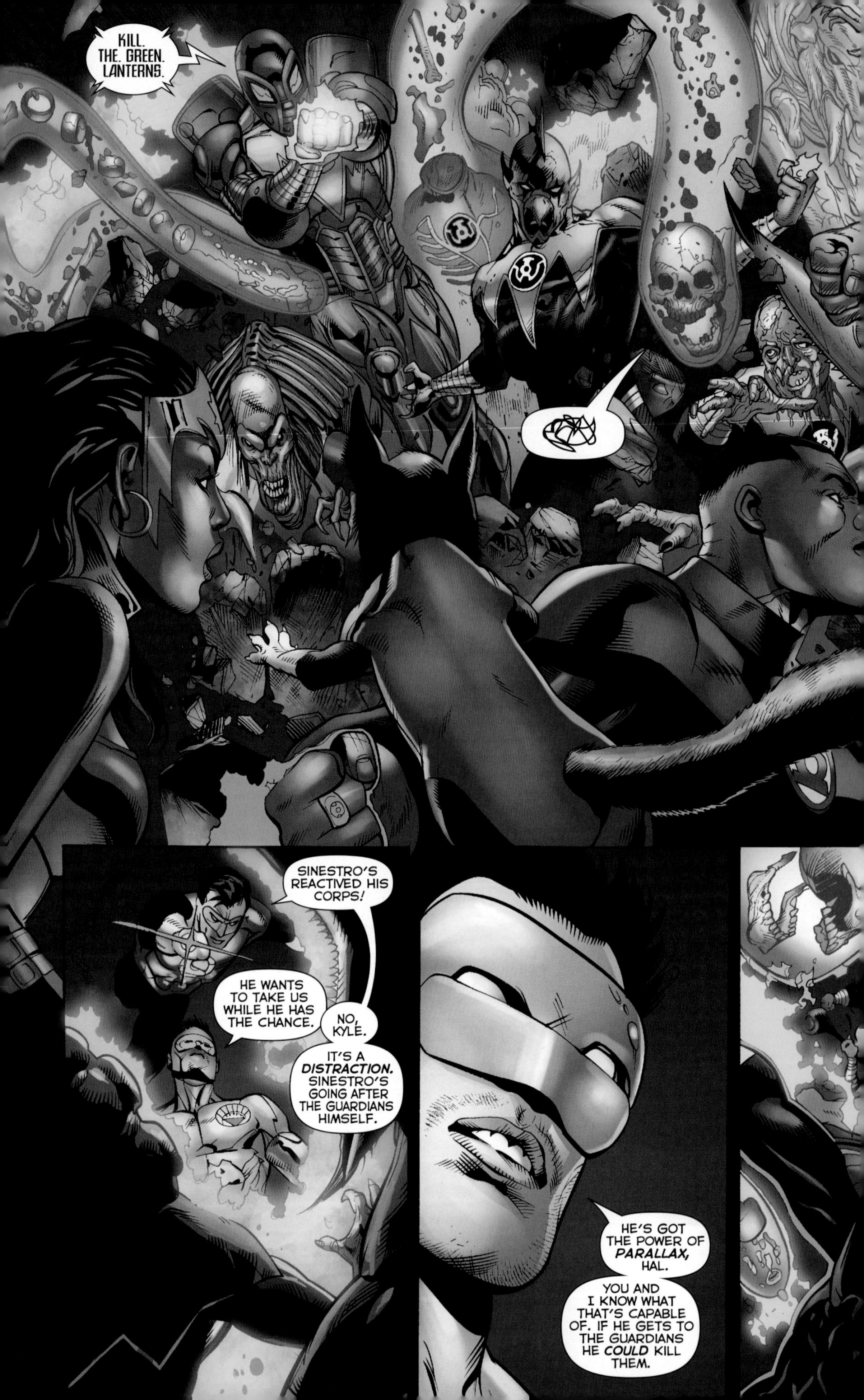
KILL. THE. GREEN. LANTERNS.
SINESTRO'S REACTIVED HIS CORPS!
HE WANTS TO TAKE US WHILE HE HAS THE CHANCE.
NO, KYLE.
IT'S A DISTRACTION. SINESTRO'S GOING AFTER THE GUARDIANS HIMSELF.
HE'S GOT THE POWER OF PARALLAX, HAL.
YOU AND I KNOW WHAT THAT'S CAPABLE OF. IF HE GETS TO THE GUARDIANS HE COULD KILL THEM.

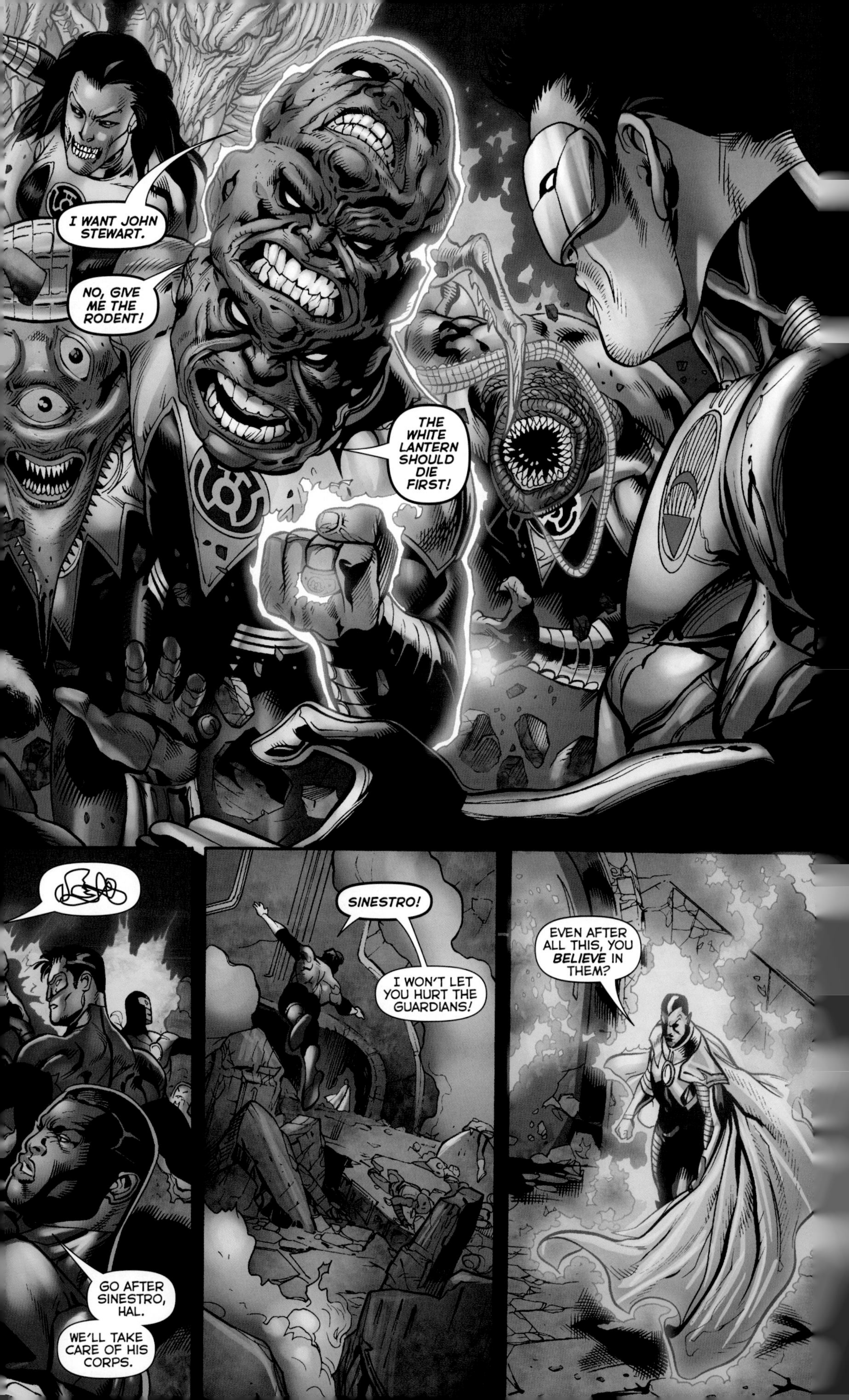
I WANT JOHN STEWART.
NO, GIVE ME THE RODENT!
THE WHITE LANTERN SHOULD DIE FIRST!
SINESTRO!
I WON'T LET YOU HURT THE GUARDIANS!
EVEN AFTER ALL THIS, YOU *BELIEVE* IN THEM?
GO AFTER SINESTRO, HAL.
WE'LL TAKE CARE OF HIS CORPS.

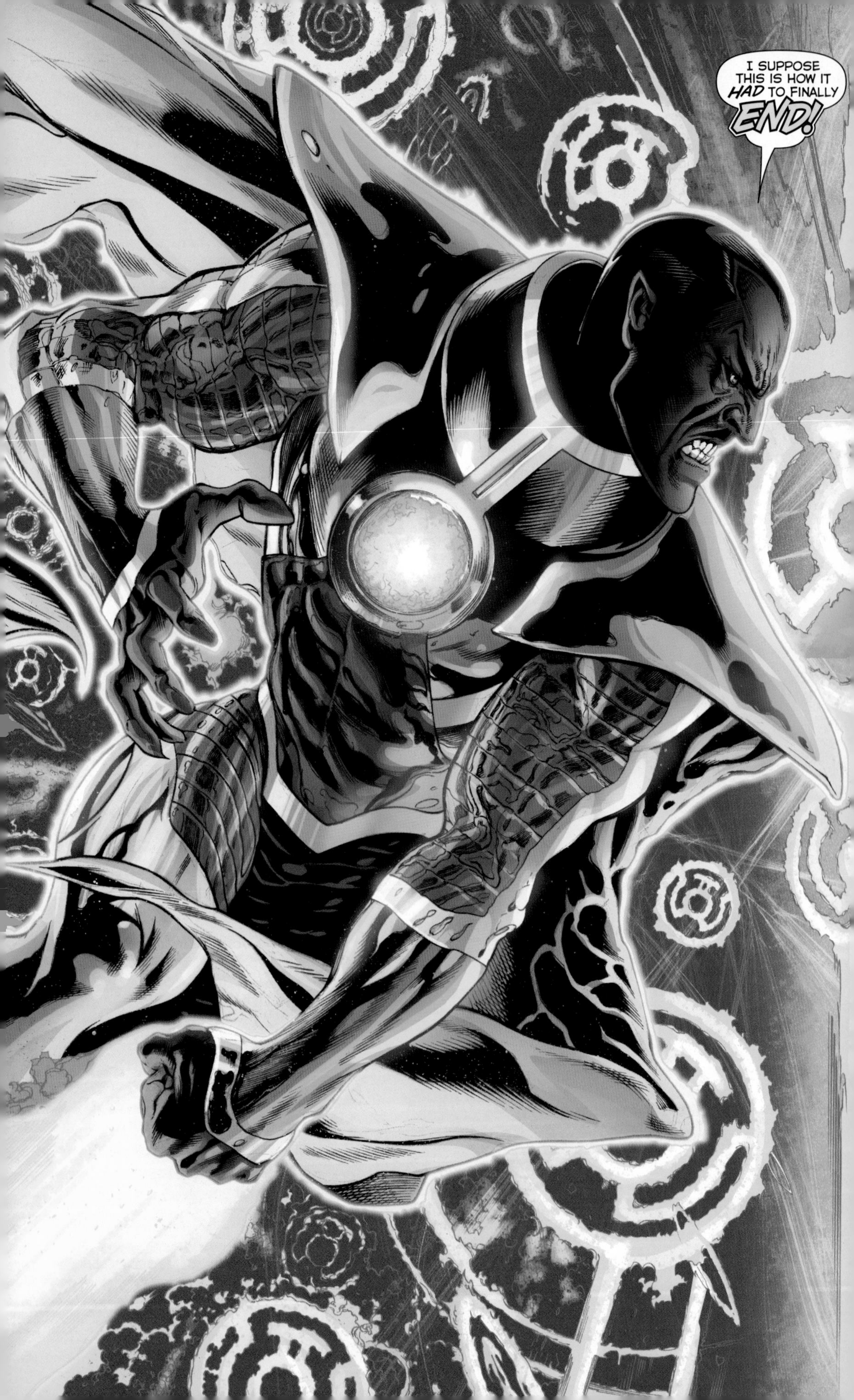
I SUPPOSE THIS IS HOW IT HAD TO FINALLY END!

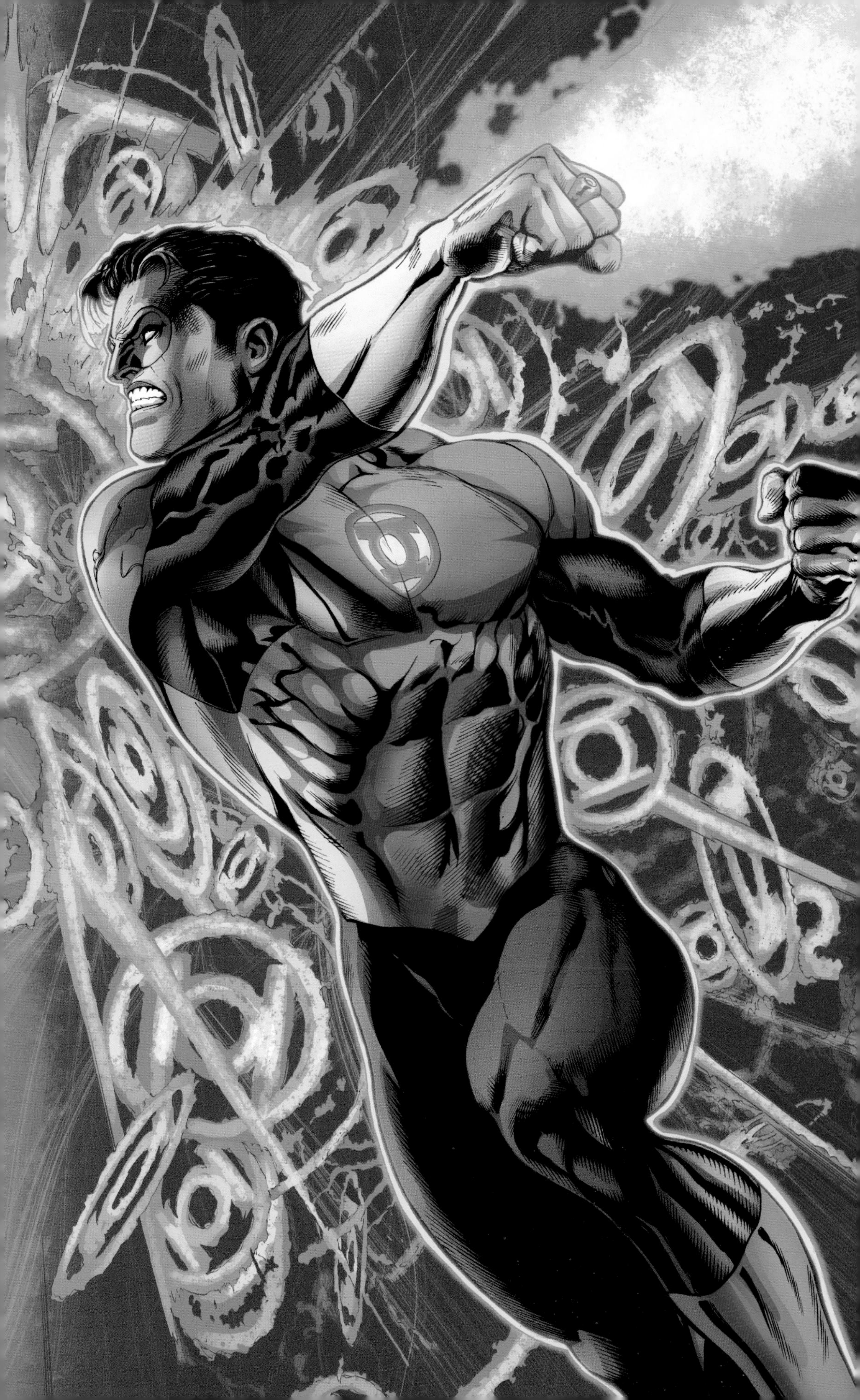

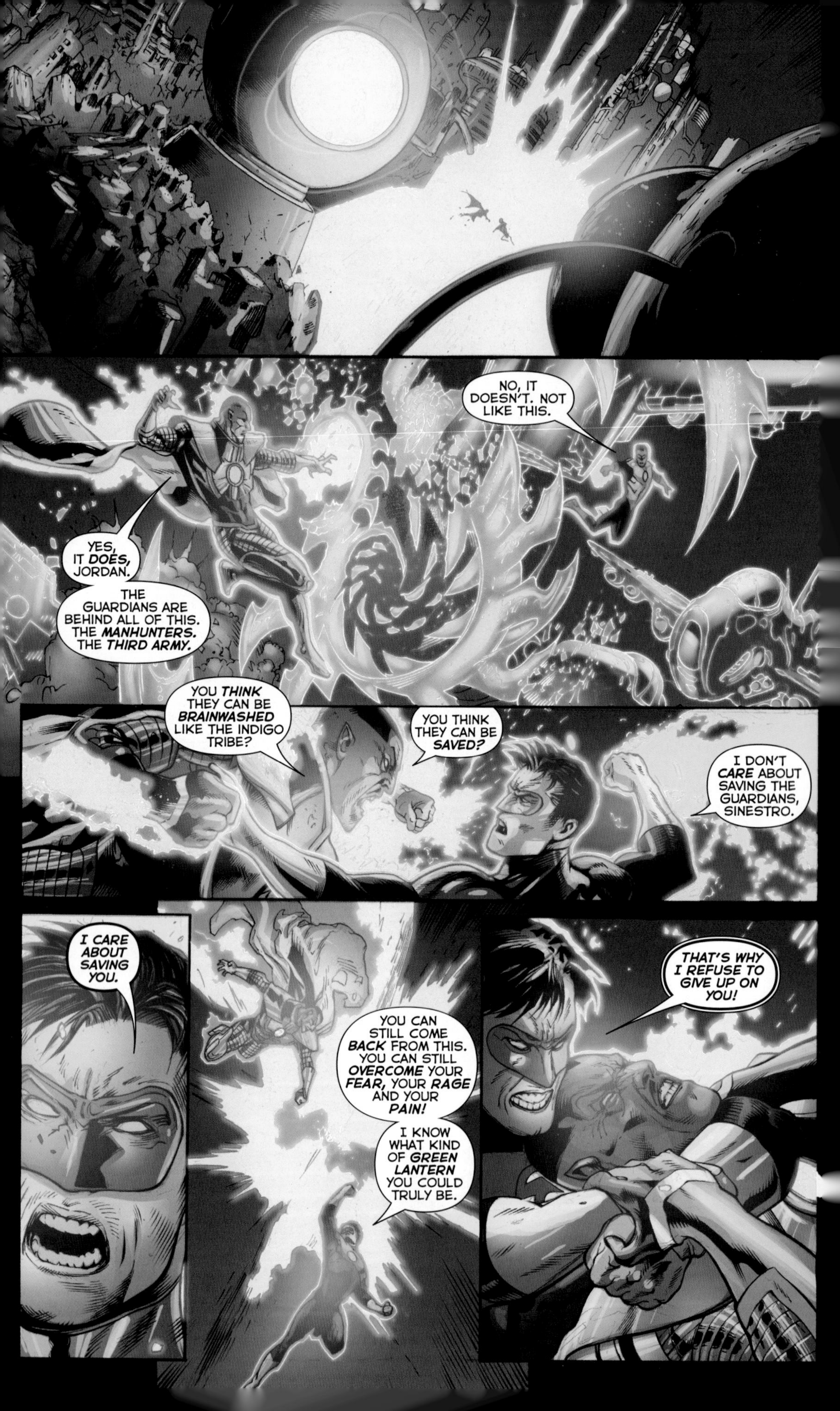

NO, IT DOESN'T. NOT LIKE THIS.
YES, IT DOES, JORDAN.
THE GUARDIANS ARE BEHIND ALL OF THIS. THE MANHUNTERS. THE THIRD ARMY.
YOU THINK THEY CAN BE BRAINWASHED LIKE THE INDIGO TRIBE?
YOU THINK THEY CAN BE SAVED?
I DON'T CARE ABOUT SAVING THE GUARDIANS, SINESTRO.
I CARE ABOUT SAVING YOU.
YOU CAN STILL COME BACK FROM THIS. YOU CAN STILL OVERCOME YOUR FEAR, YOUR RAGE AND YOUR PAIN!
I KNOW WHAT KIND OF GREEN LANTERN YOU COULD TRULY BE.
THAT'S WHY I REFUSE TO GIVE UP ON YOU!

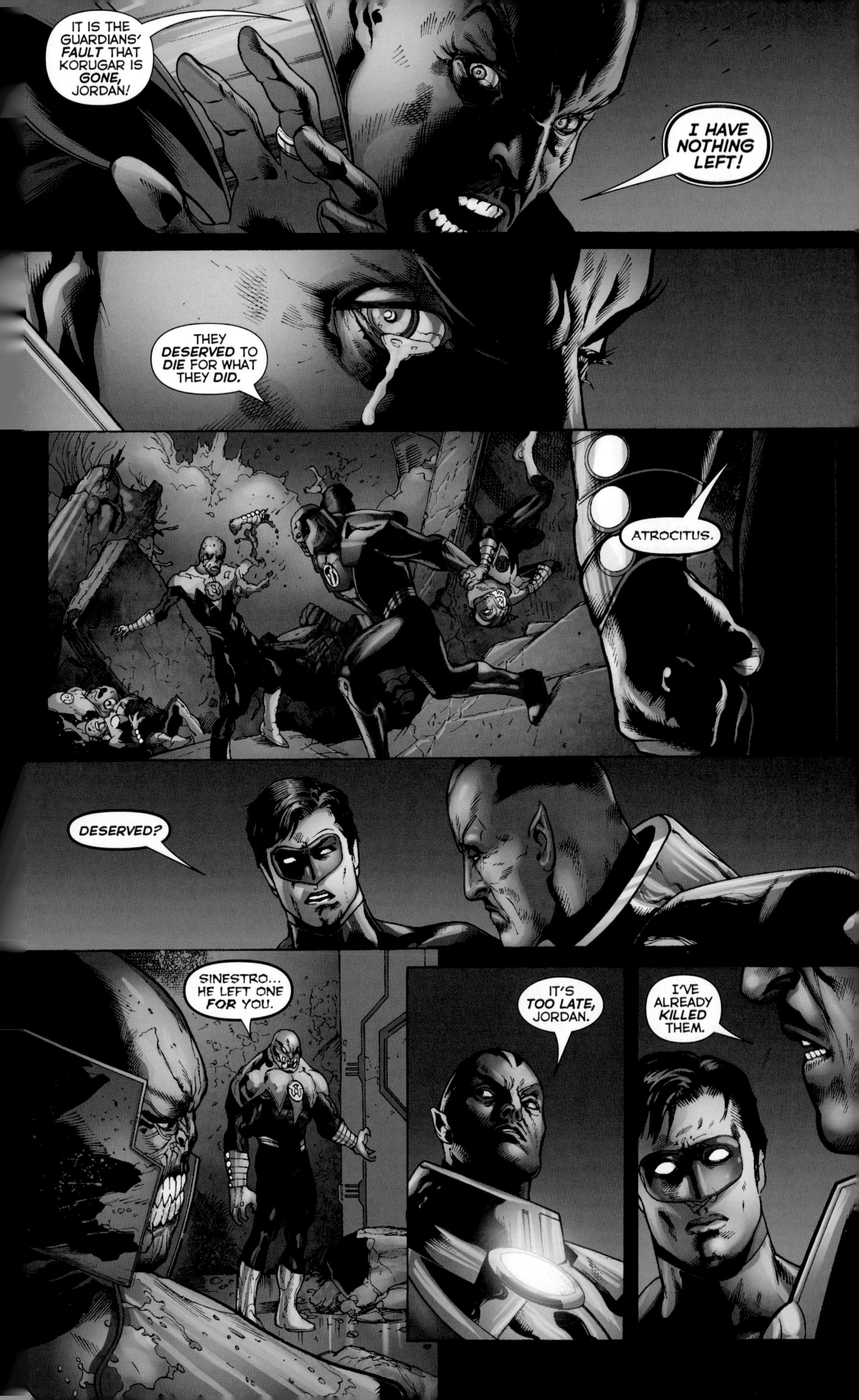
IT IS THE GUARDIANS' FAULT THAT KORUGAR IS GONE, JORDAN!
I HAVE NOTHING LEFT!
THEY DESERVED TO DIE FOR WHAT THEY DID.
ATROCITUS.
DESERVED?
SINESTRO... HE LEFT ONE FOR YOU.
IT'S TOO LATE, JORDAN.
I'VE ALREADY KILLED THEM.

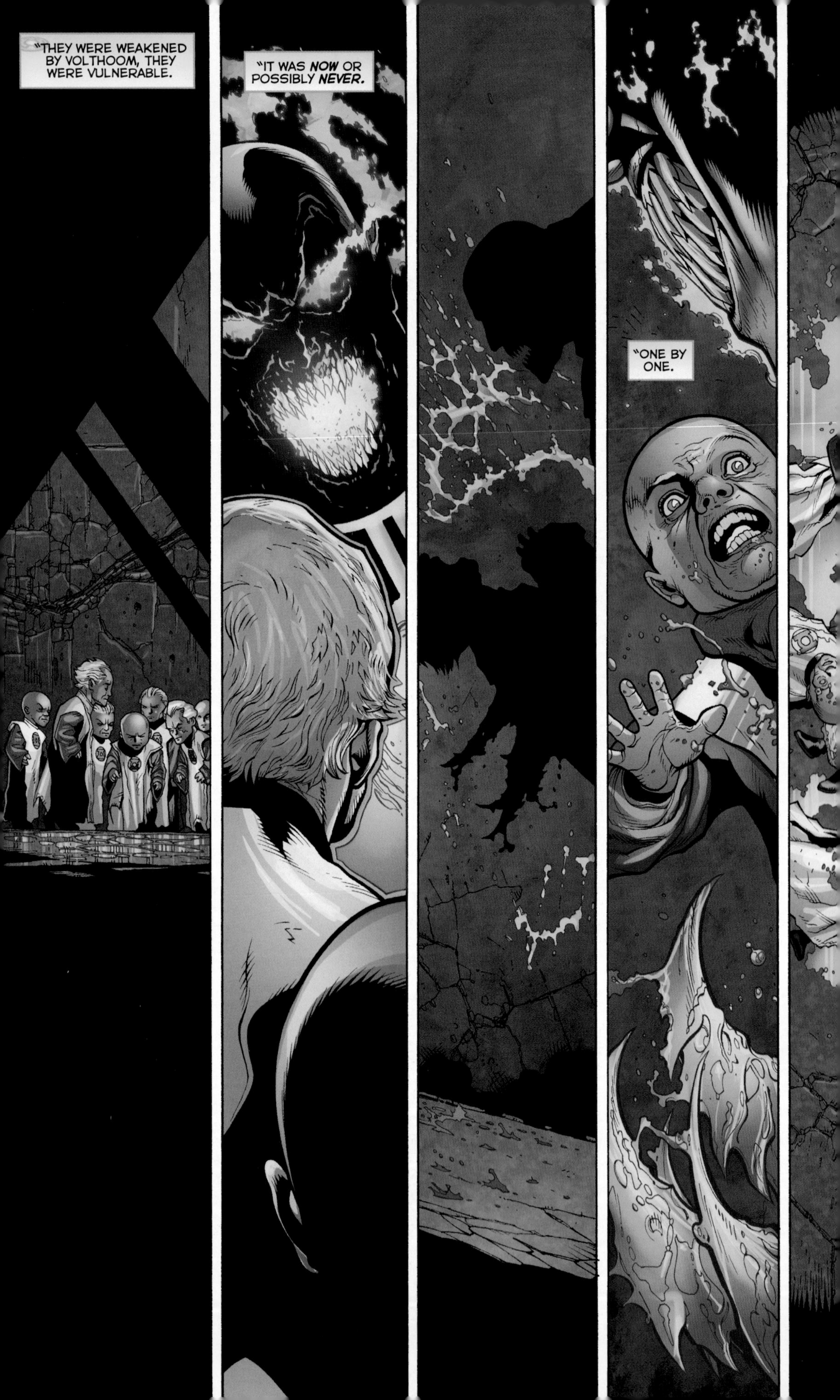
"THEY WERE WEAKENED BY VOLTHOOM, THEY WERE VULNERABLE.
"IT WAS NOW OR POSSIBLY NEVER.
"ONE BY ONE.

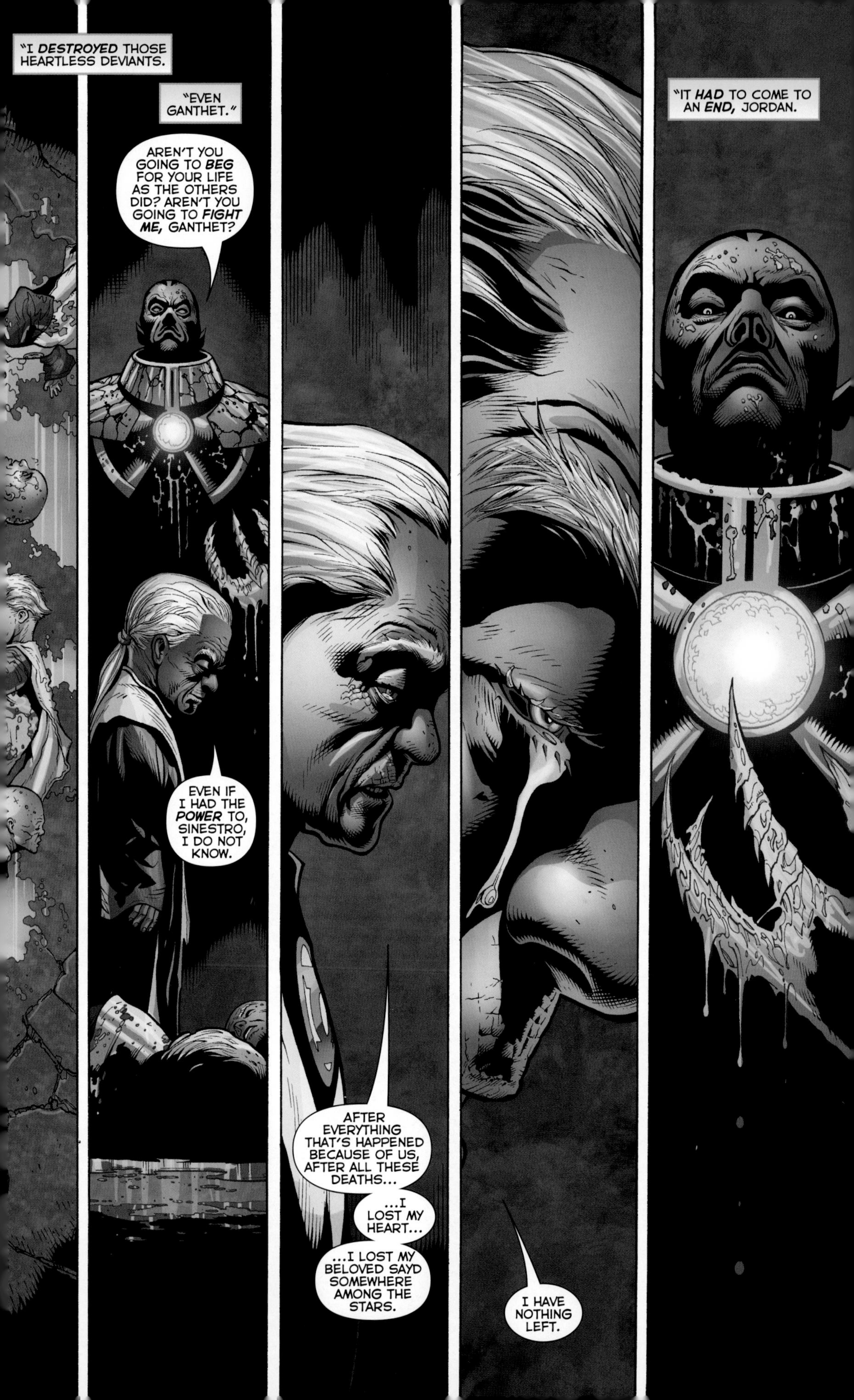
"I DESTROYED THOSE HEARTLESS DEVIANTS.
"EVEN GANTHET."
AREN'T YOU GOING TO BEG FOR YOUR LIFE AS THE OTHERS DID? AREN'T YOU GOING TO FIGHT ME, GANTHET?
EVEN IF I HAD THE POWER TO, SINESTRO, I DO NOT KNOW.
AFTER EVERYTHING THAT'S HAPPENED BECAUSE OF US, AFTER ALL THESE DEATHS...
...I LOST MY HEART...
...I LOST MY BELOVED SAYD SOMEWHERE AMONG THE STARS.
I HAVE NOTHING LEFT.
"IT HAD TO COME TO AN END, JORDAN.

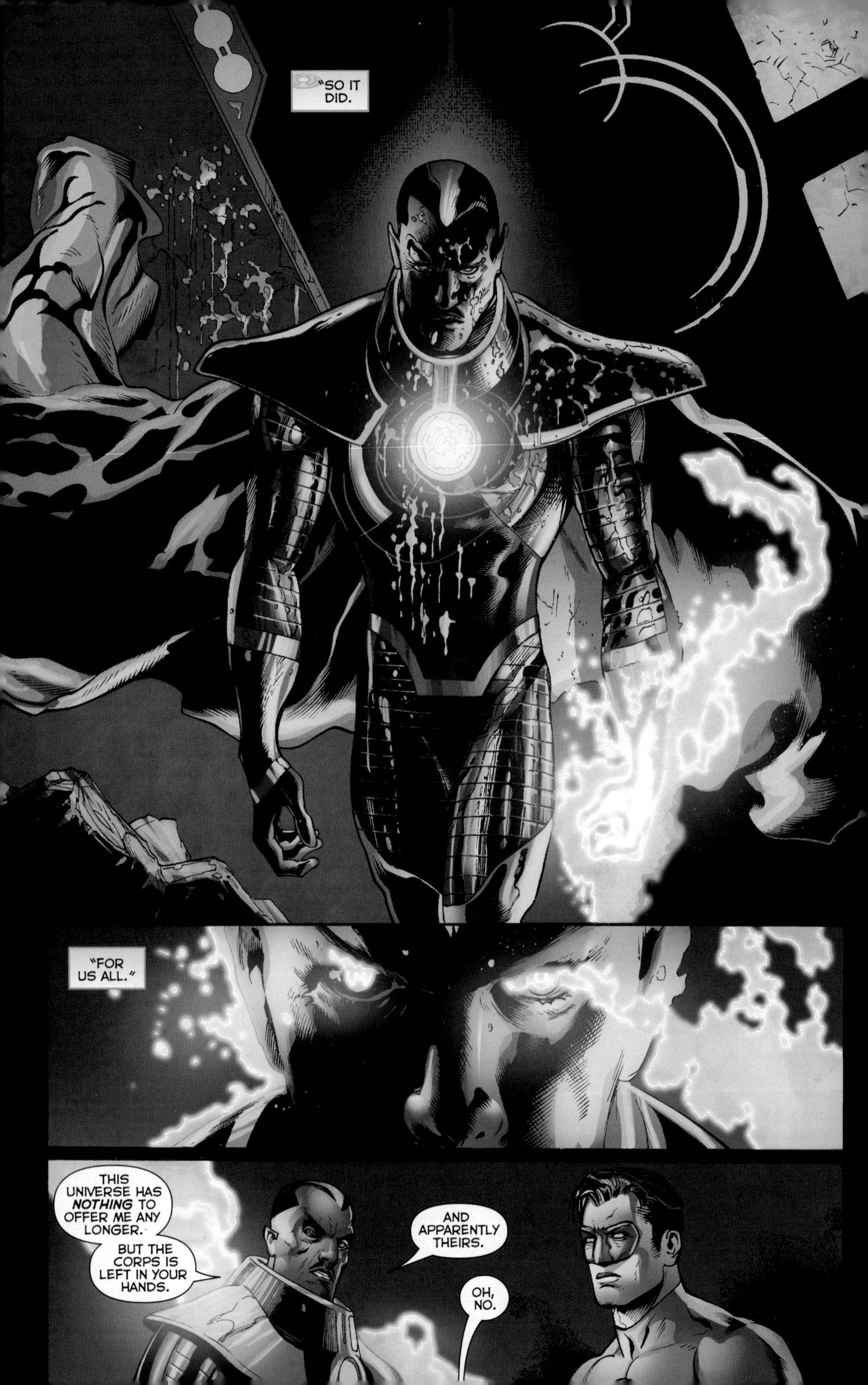
"SO IT DID.
"FOR US ALL."
THIS UNIVERSE HAS *NOTHING* TO OFFER ME ANY LONGER.
BUT THE CORPS IS LEFT IN YOUR HANDS.
AND APPARENTLY THEIRS.
OH, NO.

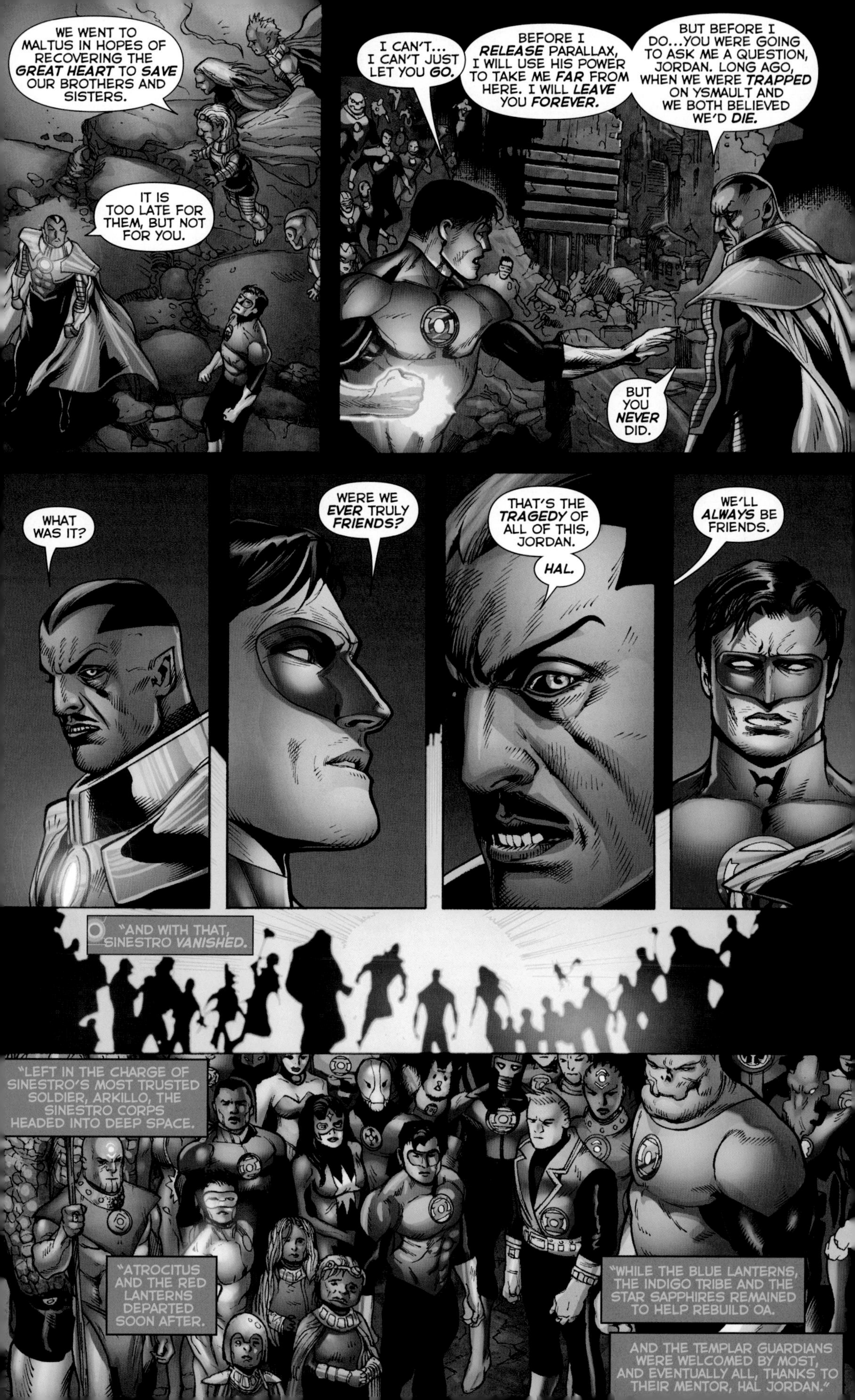
WE WENT TO MALTUS IN HOPES OF RECOVERING THE GREAT HEART TO SAVE OUR BROTHERS AND SISTERS.
IT IS TOO LATE FOR THEM, BUT NOT FOR YOU.
I CAN'T... I CAN'T JUST LET YOU GO.
BEFORE I RELEASE PARALLAX, I WILL USE HIS POWER TO TAKE ME FAR FROM HERE. I WILL LEAVE YOU FOREVER.
BUT BEFORE I DO...YOU WERE GOING TO ASK ME A QUESTION, JORDAN. LONG AGO, WHEN WE WERE TRAPPED ON YSMAULT AND WE BOTH BELIEVED WE'D DIE.
BUT YOU NEVER DID.
WHAT WAS IT?
WERE WE EVER TRULY FRIENDS?
THAT'S THE TRAGEDY OF ALL OF THIS, JORDAN.
HAL.
WE'LL ALWAYS BE FRIENDS.
"AND WITH THAT, SINESTRO VANISHED.
"LEFT IN THE CHARGE OF SINESTRO'S MOST TRUSTED SOLDIER, ARKILLO, THE SINESTRO CORPS HEADED INTO DEEP SPACE.
"ATROCITUS AND THE RED LANTERNS DEPARTED SOON AFTER.
"WHILE THE BLUE LANTERNS, THE INDIGO TRIBE AND THE STAR SAPPHIRES REMAINED TO HELP REBUILD OA.
AND THE TEMPLAR GUARDIANS WERE WELCOMED BY MOST, AND EVENTUALLY ALL, THANKS TO THEIR MENTOR, HAL JORDAN."

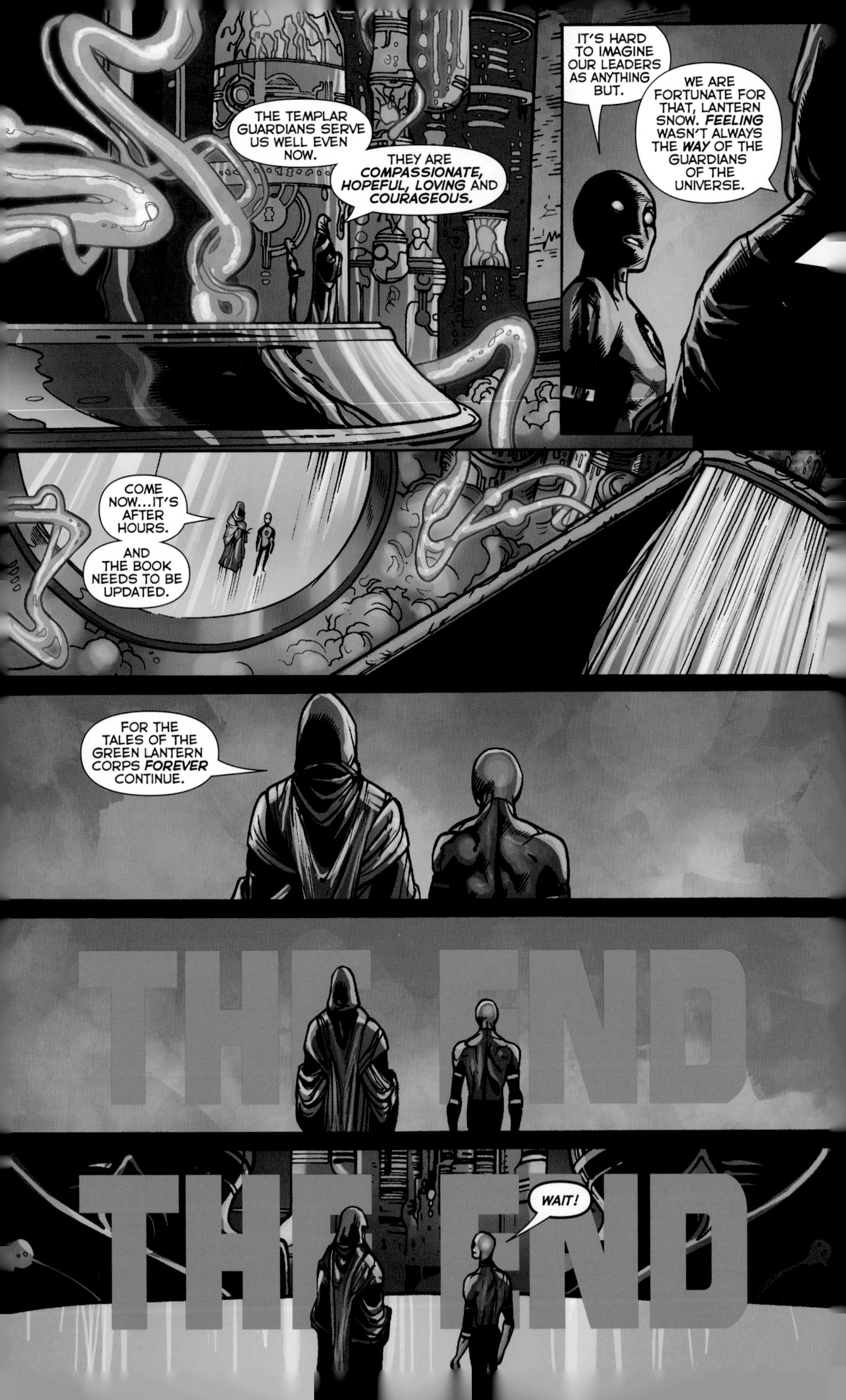
THE TEMPLAR GUARDIANS SERVE US WELL EVEN NOW.
THEY ARE COMPASSIONATE, HOPEFUL, LOVING AND COURAGEOUS.
IT'S HARD TO IMAGINE OUR LEADERS AS ANYTHING BUT.
WE ARE FORTUNATE FOR THAT, LANTERN SNOW. FEELING WASN'T ALWAYS THE WAY OF THE GUARDIANS OF THE UNIVERSE.
COME NOW...IT'S AFTER HOURS.
AND THE BOOK NEEDS TO BE UPDATED.
FOR THE TALES OF THE GREEN LANTERN CORPS FOREVER CONTINUE.
THE END
WAIT!
THE END

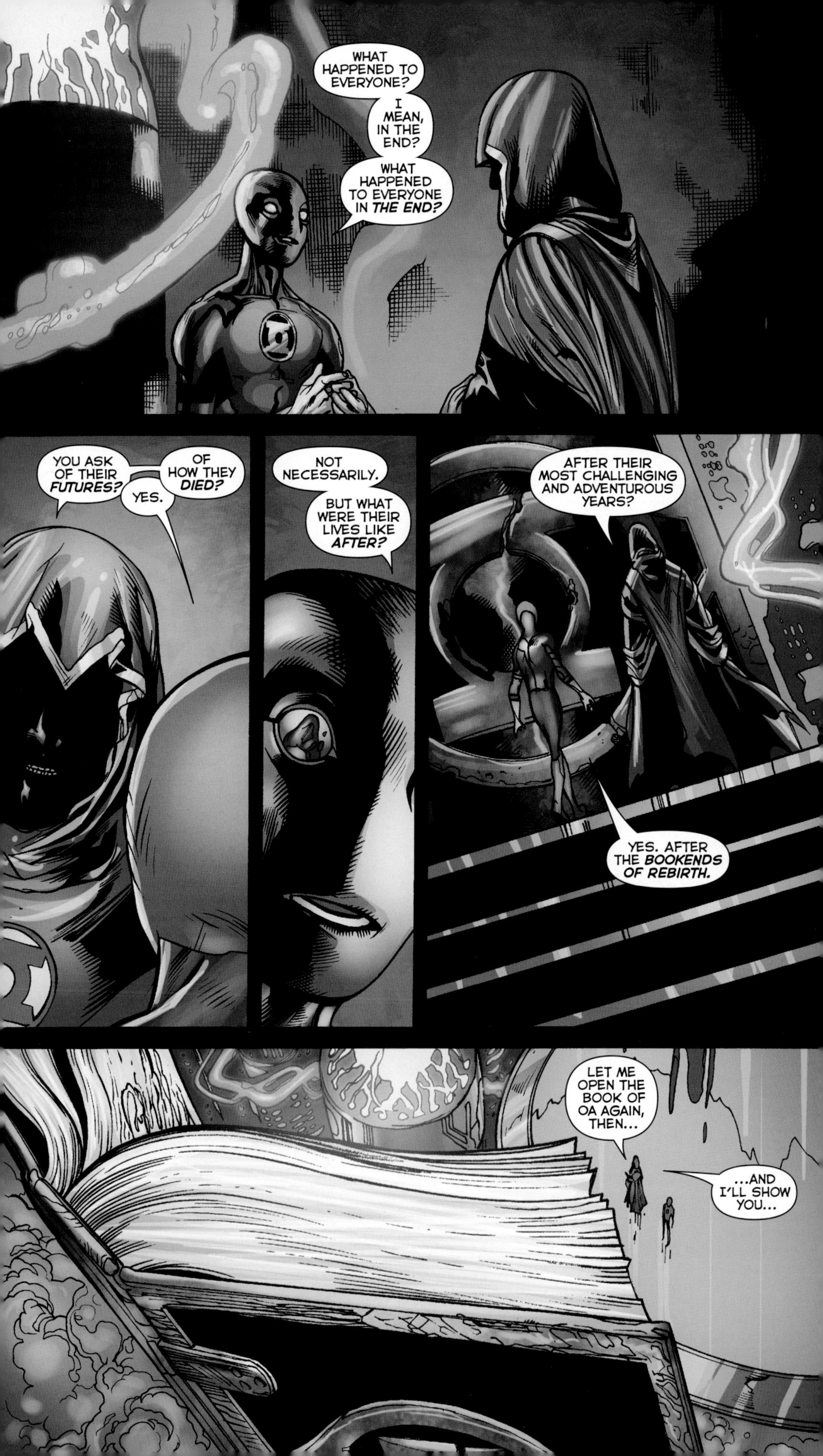
WHAT HAPPENED TO EVERYONE?
I MEAN, IN THE END?
WHAT HAPPENED TO EVERYONE IN *THE END?*
YOU ASK OF THEIR *FUTURES?*
OF HOW THEY *DIED?*
YES.
NOT NECESSARILY.
BUT WHAT WERE THEIR LIVES LIKE *AFTER?*
AFTER THEIR MOST CHALLENGING AND ADVENTUROUS YEARS?
YES. AFTER THE *BOOKENDS OF REBIRTH.*
LET ME OPEN THE BOOK OF OA AGAIN, THEN...
...AND I'LL SHOW YOU...

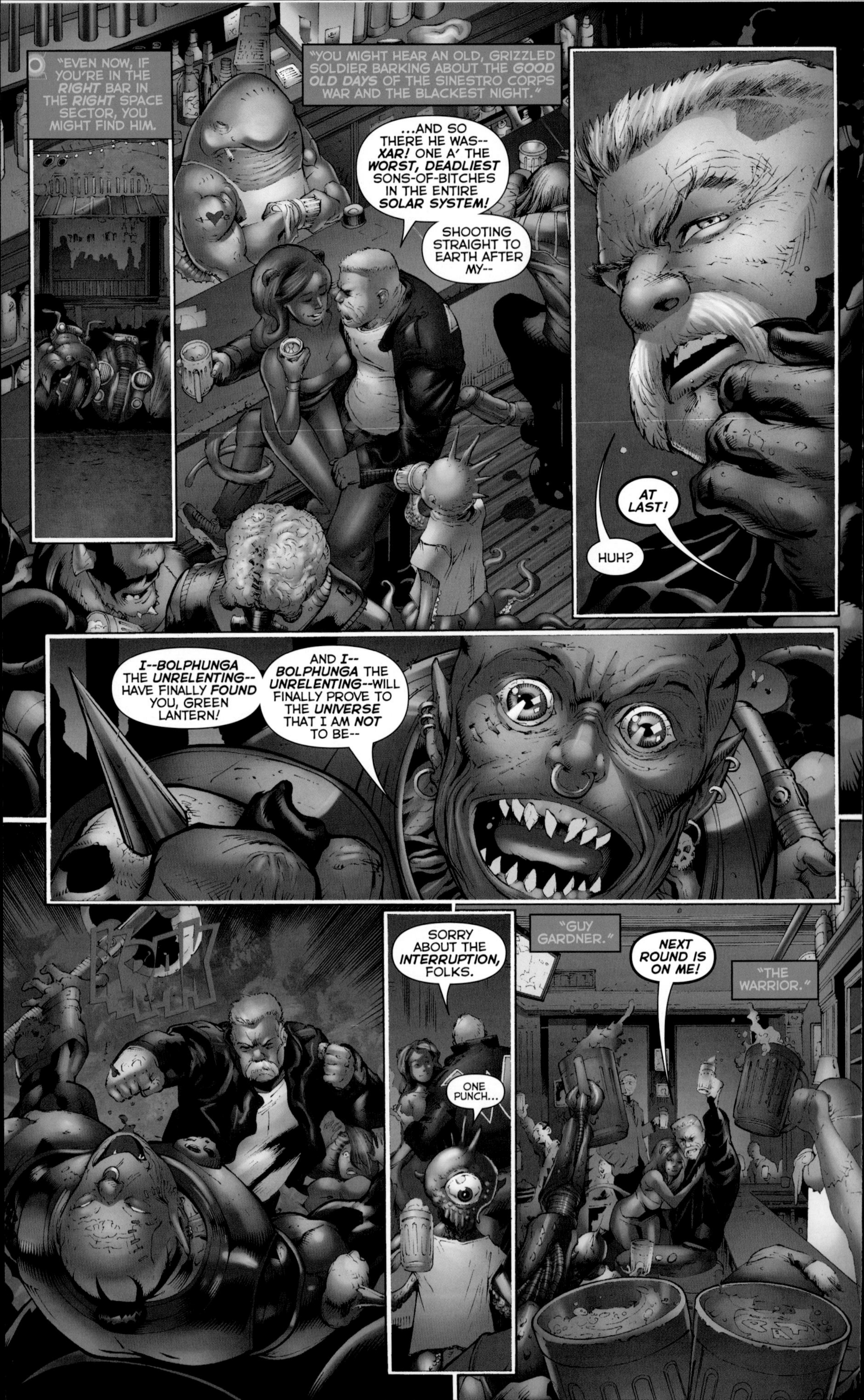
"EVEN NOW, IF YOU'RE IN THE RIGHT BAR IN THE RIGHT SPACE SECTOR, YOU MIGHT FIND HIM.
"YOU MIGHT HEAR AN OLD, GRIZZLED SOLDIER BARKING ABOUT THE GOOD OLD DAYS OF THE SINESTRO CORPS WAR AND THE BLACKEST NIGHT."
...AND SO THERE HE WAS--XAR! ONE A' THE WORST, DEADLIEST SONS-OF-BITCHES IN THE ENTIRE SOLAR SYSTEM!
SHOOTING STRAIGHT TO EARTH AFTER MY--
AT LAST!
HUH?
I--BOLPHUNGA THE UNRELENTING--HAVE FINALLY FOUND YOU, GREEN LANTERN!
AND I--BOLPHUNGA THE UNRELENTING--WILL FINALLY PROVE TO THE UNIVERSE THAT I AM NOT TO BE--
SORRY ABOUT THE INTERRUPTION, FOLKS.
ONE PUNCH...
"GUY GARDNER."
NEXT ROUND IS ON ME!
"THE WARRIOR."

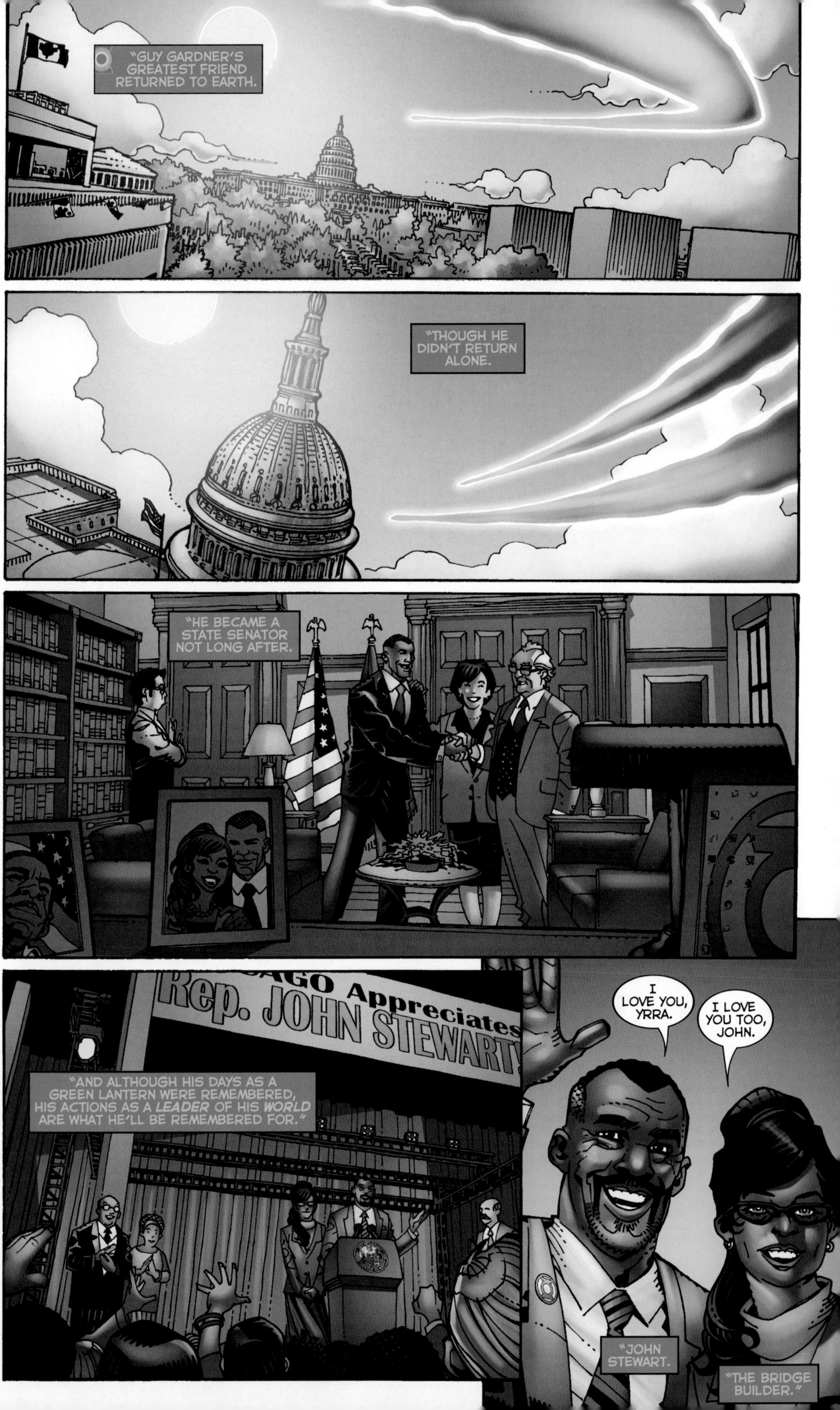
"GUY GARDNER'S GREATEST FRIEND RETURNED TO EARTH.
"THOUGH HE DIDN'T RETURN ALONE.
"HE BECAME A STATE SENATOR NOT LONG AFTER.
Rep. JOHN STEWART!
Appreciates
"AND ALTHOUGH HIS DAYS AS A GREEN LANTERN WERE REMEMBERED, HIS ACTIONS AS A *LEADER* OF HIS *WORLD* ARE WHAT HE'LL BE REMEMBERED FOR."
I LOVE YOU, YRRA.
I LOVE YOU TOO, JOHN.
"JOHN STEWART.
"THE BRIDGE BUILDER."

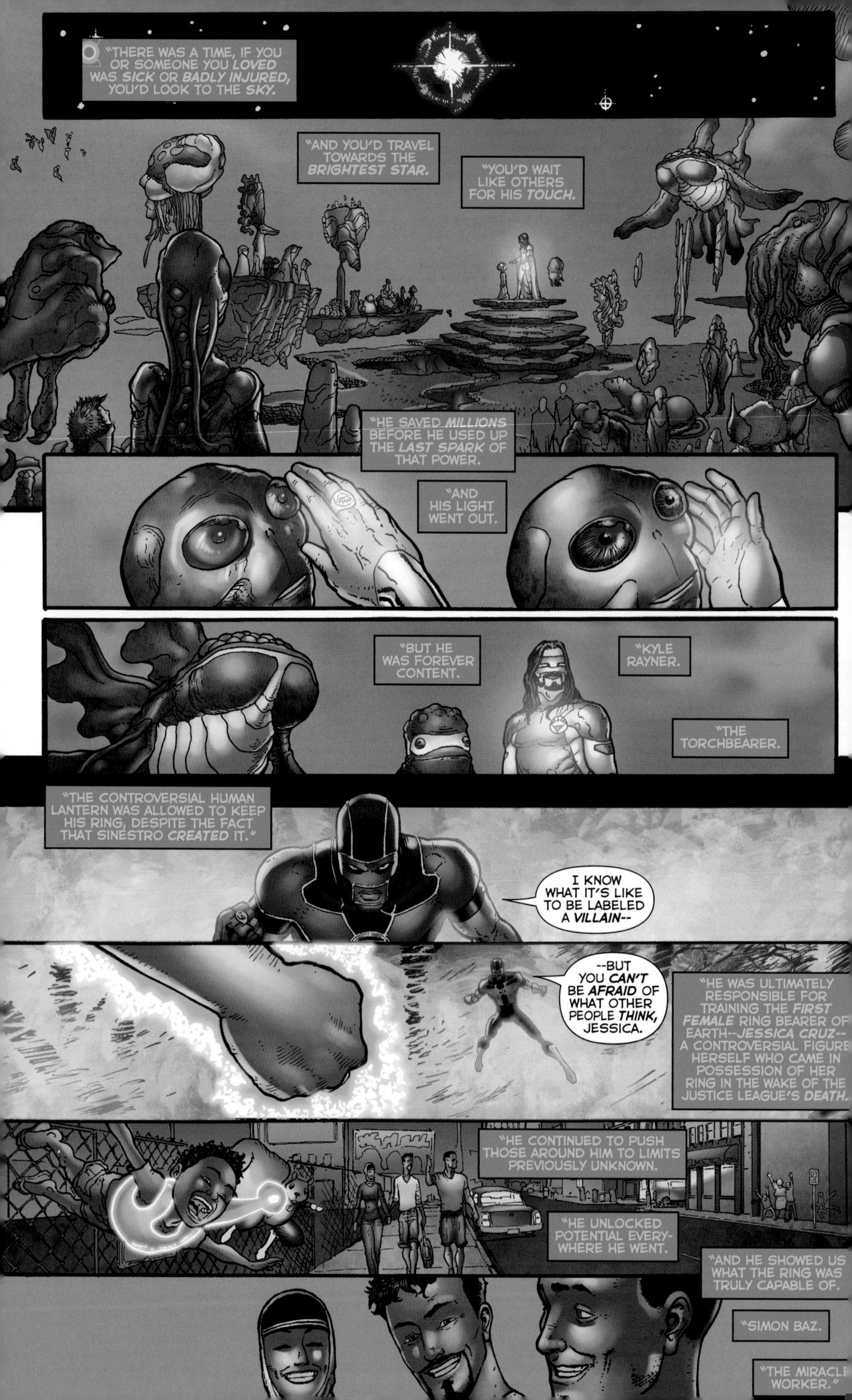
"THERE WAS A TIME, IF YOU OR SOMEONE YOU LOVED WAS SICK OR BADLY INJURED, YOU'D LOOK TO THE SKY.
"AND YOU'D TRAVEL TOWARDS THE BRIGHTEST STAR.
"YOU'D WAIT LIKE OTHERS FOR HIS TOUCH.
"HE SAVED MILLIONS BEFORE HE USED UP THE LAST SPARK OF THAT POWER.
"AND HIS LIGHT WENT OUT.
"BUT HE WAS FOREVER CONTENT.
"KYLE RAYNER.
"THE TORCHBEARER.
"THE CONTROVERSIAL HUMAN LANTERN WAS ALLOWED TO KEEP HIS RING, DESPITE THE FACT THAT SINESTRO CREATED IT."
I KNOW WHAT IT'S LIKE TO BE LABELED A VILLAIN--
--BUT YOU CAN'T BE AFRAID OF WHAT OTHER PEOPLE THINK, JESSICA.
"HE WAS ULTIMATELY RESPONSIBLE FOR TRAINING THE FIRST FEMALE RING BEARER OF EARTH--JESSICA CRUZ--A CONTROVERSIAL FIGURE HERSELF WHO CAME IN POSSESSION OF HER RING IN THE WAKE OF THE JUSTICE LEAGUE'S DEATH.
"HE CONTINUED TO PUSH THOSE AROUND HIM TO LIMITS PREVIOUSLY UNKNOWN.
"HE UNLOCKED POTENTIAL EVERYWHERE HE WENT.
"AND HE SHOWED US WHAT THE RING WAS TRULY CAPABLE OF.
"SIMON BAZ.
"THE MIRACLE WORKER."

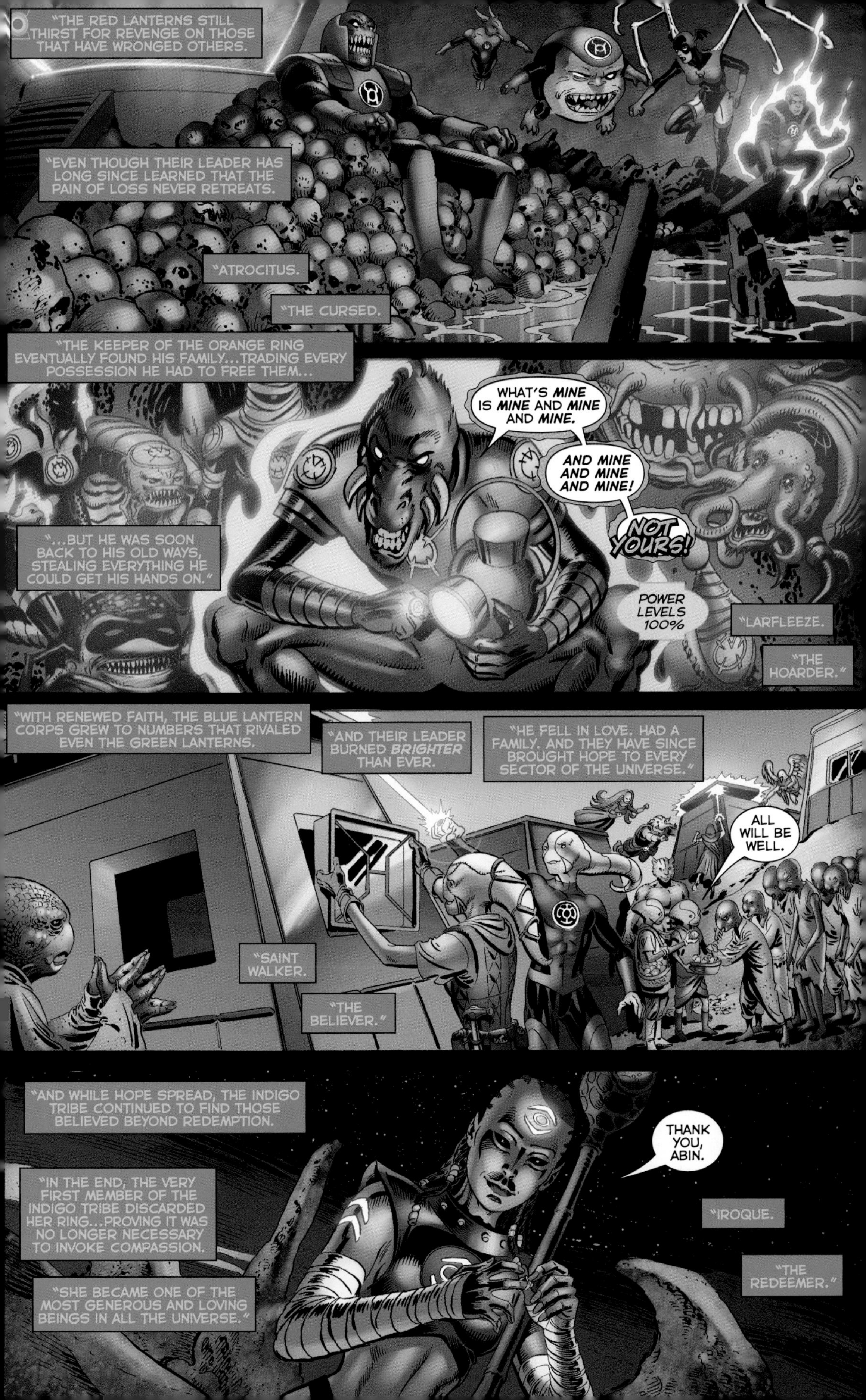
"THE RED LANTERNS STILL THIRST FOR REVENGE ON THOSE THAT HAVE WRONGED OTHERS.
"EVEN THOUGH THEIR LEADER HAS LONG SINCE LEARNED THAT THE PAIN OF LOSS NEVER RETREATS.
"ATROCITUS.
"THE CURSED.
"THE KEEPER OF THE ORANGE RING EVENTUALLY FOUND HIS FAMILY...TRADING EVERY POSSESSION HE HAD TO FREE THEM...
"...BUT HE WAS SOON BACK TO HIS OLD WAYS, STEALING EVERYTHING HE COULD GET HIS HANDS ON."
WHAT'S *MINE* IS *MINE* AND *MINE* AND *MINE*.
AND MINE AND MINE AND MINE!
NOT YOURS!
POWER LEVELS 100%
"LARFLEEZE.
"THE HOARDER."
"WITH RENEWED FAITH, THE BLUE LANTERN CORPS GREW TO NUMBERS THAT RIVALED EVEN THE GREEN LANTERNS.
"AND THEIR LEADER BURNED *BRIGHTER* THAN EVER.
"HE FELL IN LOVE. HAD A FAMILY. AND THEY HAVE SINCE BROUGHT HOPE TO EVERY SECTOR OF THE UNIVERSE."
ALL WILL BE WELL.
"SAINT WALKER.
"THE BELIEVER."
"AND WHILE HOPE SPREAD, THE INDIGO TRIBE CONTINUED TO FIND THOSE BELIEVED BEYOND REDEMPTION.
"IN THE END, THE VERY FIRST MEMBER OF THE INDIGO TRIBE DISCARDED HER RING...PROVING IT WAS NO LONGER NECESSARY TO INVOKE COMPASSION.
"SHE BECAME ONE OF THE MOST GENEROUS AND LOVING BEINGS IN ALL THE UNIVERSE."
THANK YOU, ABIN.
"IROQUE.
"THE REDEEMER."

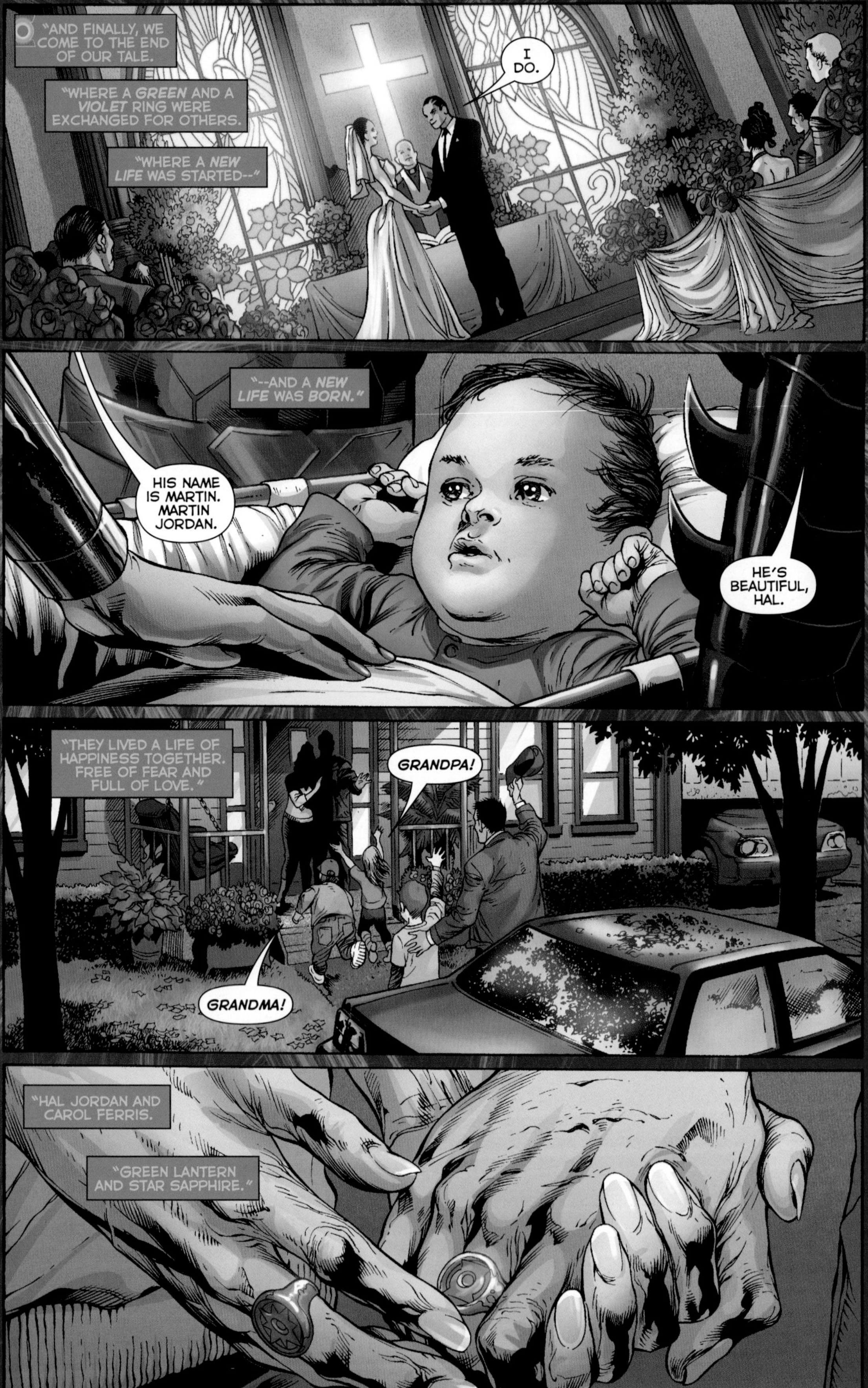
"AND FINALLY, WE COME TO THE END OF OUR TALE.
"WHERE A GREEN AND A VIOLET RING WERE EXCHANGED FOR OTHERS.
"WHERE A NEW LIFE WAS STARTED--"
I DO.
"--AND A NEW LIFE WAS BORN."
HIS NAME IS MARTIN. MARTIN JORDAN.
HE'S BEAUTIFUL, HAL.
"THEY LIVED A LIFE OF HAPPINESS TOGETHER. FREE OF FEAR AND FULL OF LOVE."
GRANDPA!
GRANDMA!
"HAL JORDAN AND CAROL FERRIS.
"GREEN LANTERN AND STAR SAPPHIRE."

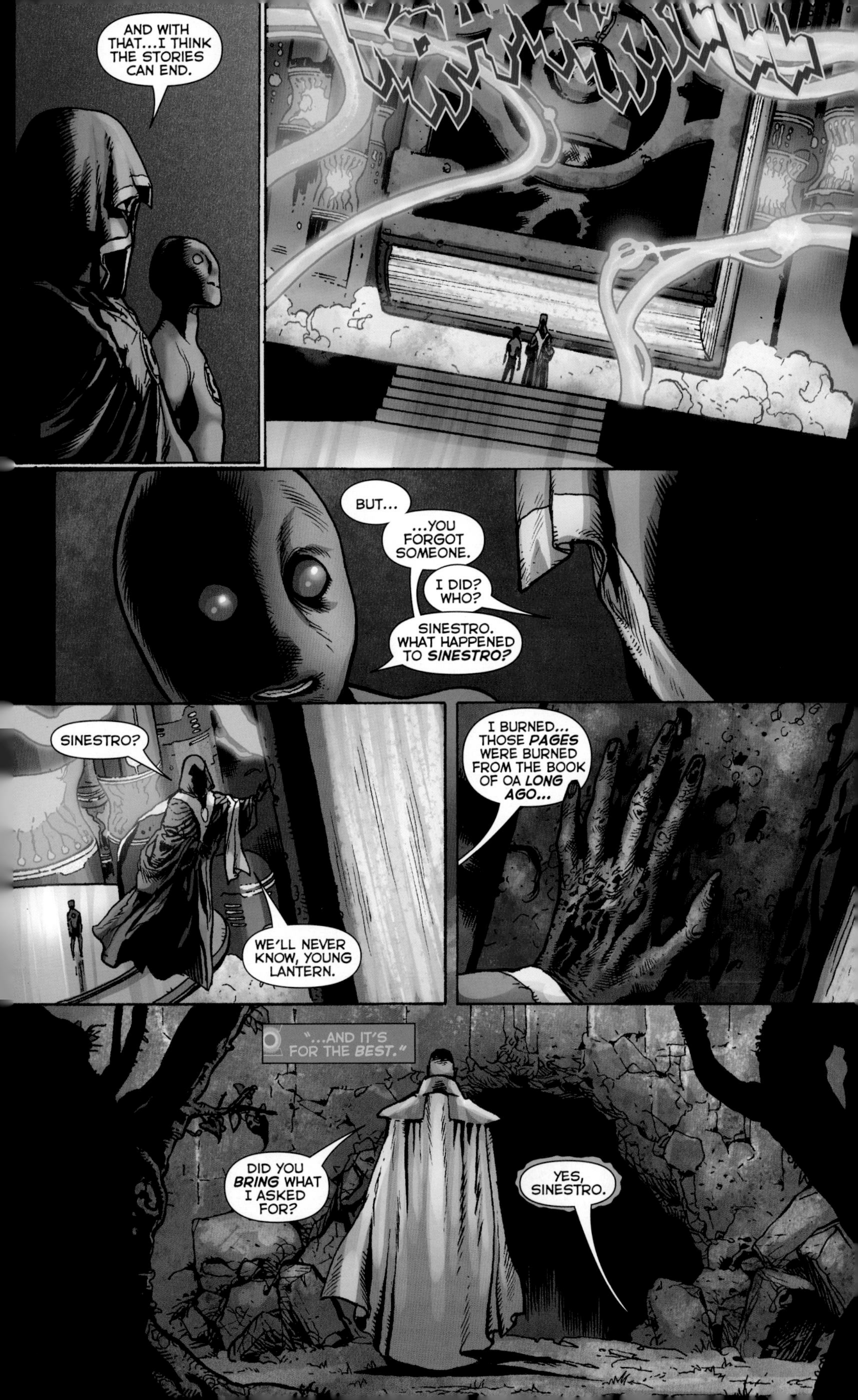
AND WITH THAT...I THINK THE STORIES CAN END.
BUT...
...YOU FORGOT SOMEONE.
I DID? WHO?
SINESTRO. WHAT HAPPENED TO *SINESTRO?*
SINESTRO?
WE'LL NEVER KNOW, YOUNG LANTERN.
I BURNED... THOSE *PAGES* WERE BURNED FROM THE BOOK OF OA *LONG AGO...*
"...AND IT'S FOR THE *BEST.*"
DID YOU *BRING* WHAT I ASKED FOR?
YES, SINESTRO.

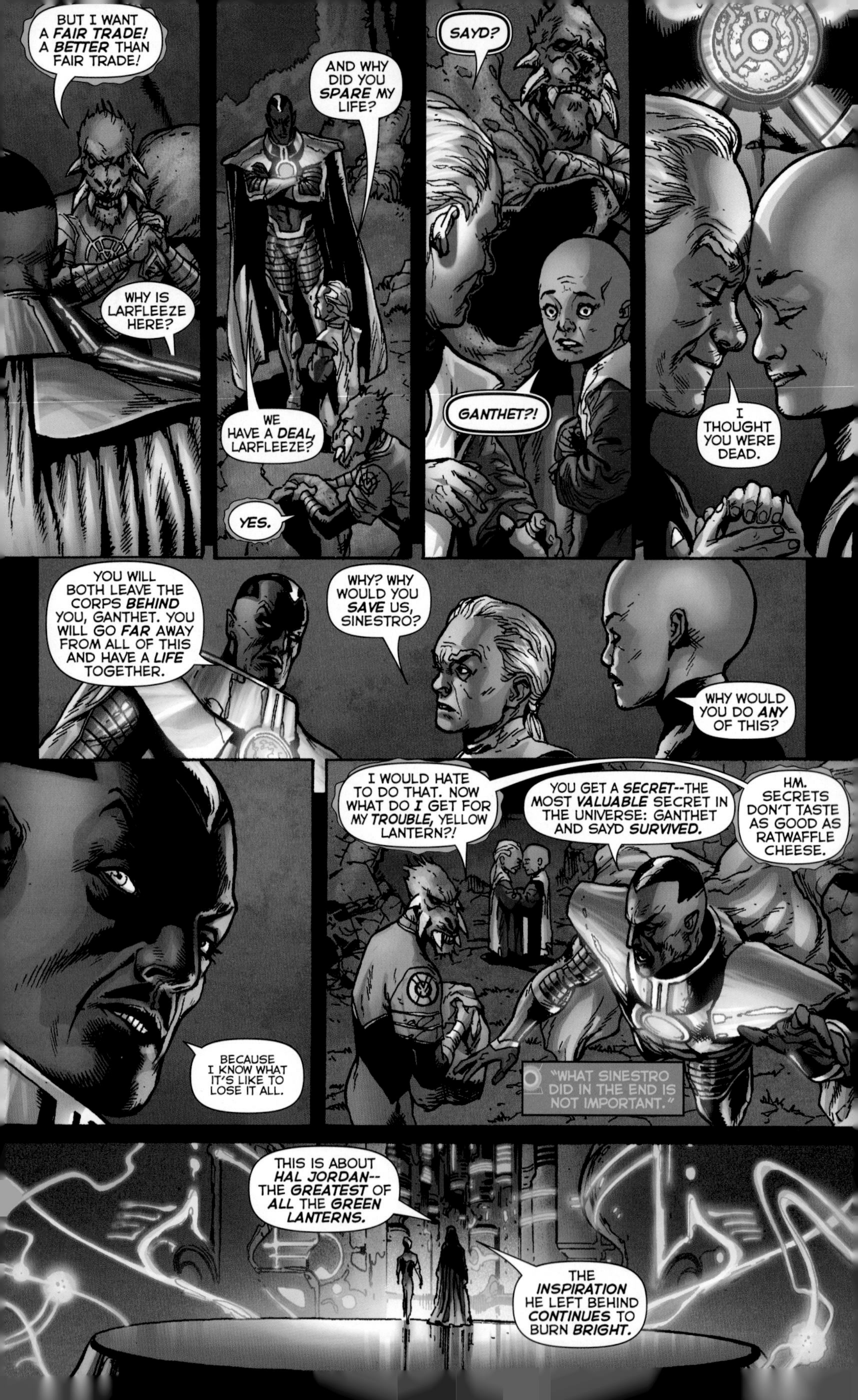
BUT I WANT A FAIR TRADE! A BETTER THAN FAIR TRADE!
WHY IS LARFLEEZE HERE?
AND WHY DID YOU SPARE MY LIFE?
WE HAVE A DEAL, LARFLEEZE?
YES.
SAYD?
GANTHET?!
I THOUGHT YOU WERE DEAD.
YOU WILL BOTH LEAVE THE CORPS BEHIND YOU, GANTHET. YOU WILL GO FAR AWAY FROM ALL OF THIS AND HAVE A LIFE TOGETHER.
WHY? WHY WOULD YOU SAVE US, SINESTRO?
WHY WOULD YOU DO ANY OF THIS?
BECAUSE I KNOW WHAT IT'S LIKE TO LOSE IT ALL.
I WOULD HATE TO DO THAT. NOW WHAT DO I GET FOR MY TROUBLE, YELLOW LANTERN?!
YOU GET A SECRET--THE MOST VALUABLE SECRET IN THE UNIVERSE: GANTHET AND SAYD SURVIVED.
HM. SECRETS DON'T TASTE AS GOOD AS RATWAFFLE CHEESE.
"WHAT SINESTRO DID IN THE END IS NOT IMPORTANT."
THIS IS ABOUT HAL JORDAN-- THE GREATEST OF ALL THE GREEN LANTERNS.
THE INSPIRATION HE LEFT BEHIND CONTINUES TO BURN BRIGHT.

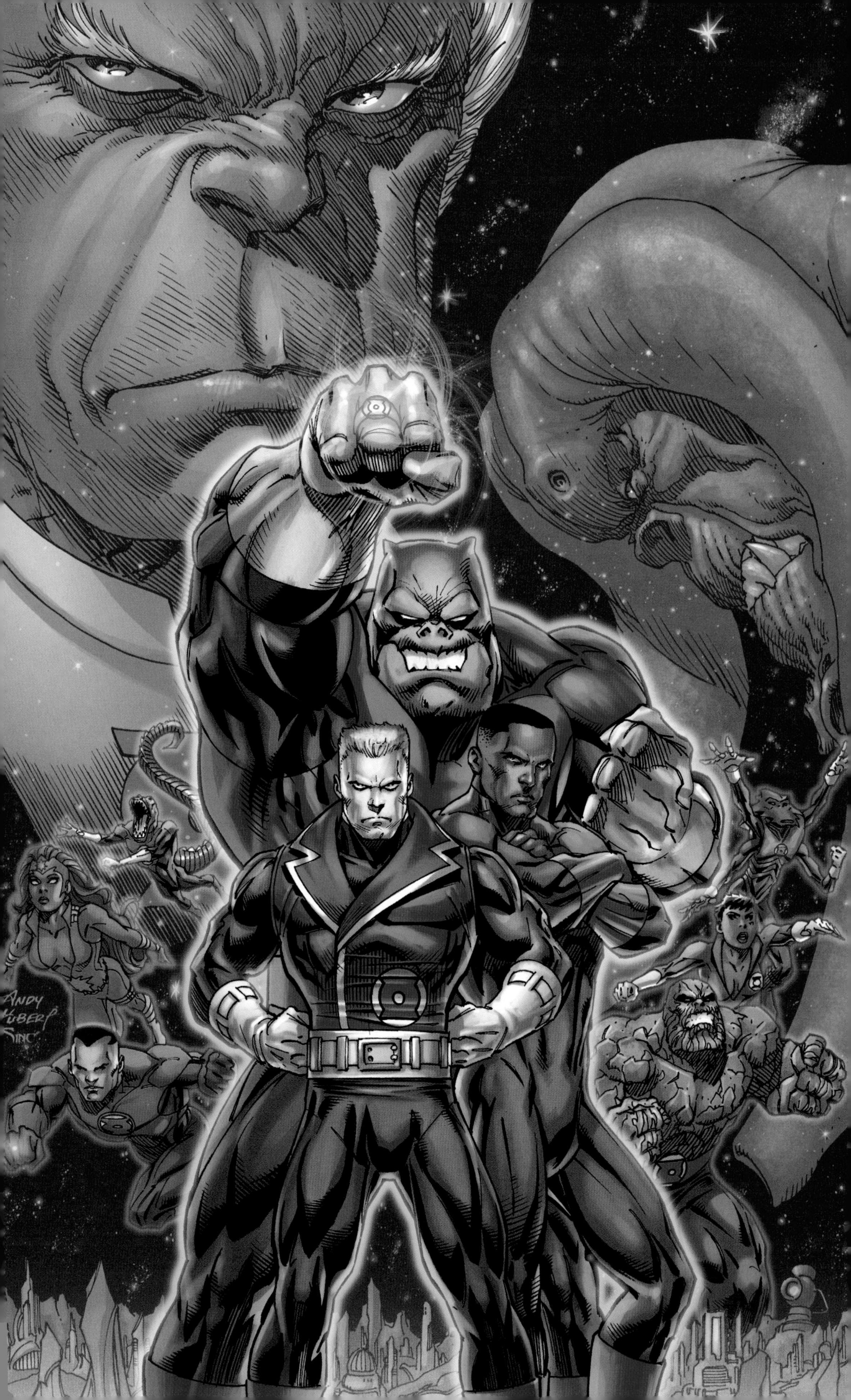

CODA

PETER J. TOMASI writer **FERNANDO PASARIN** penciller **SCOTT HANNA** inker cover art by **ANDY KUBERT & ALEX SINCLAIR**

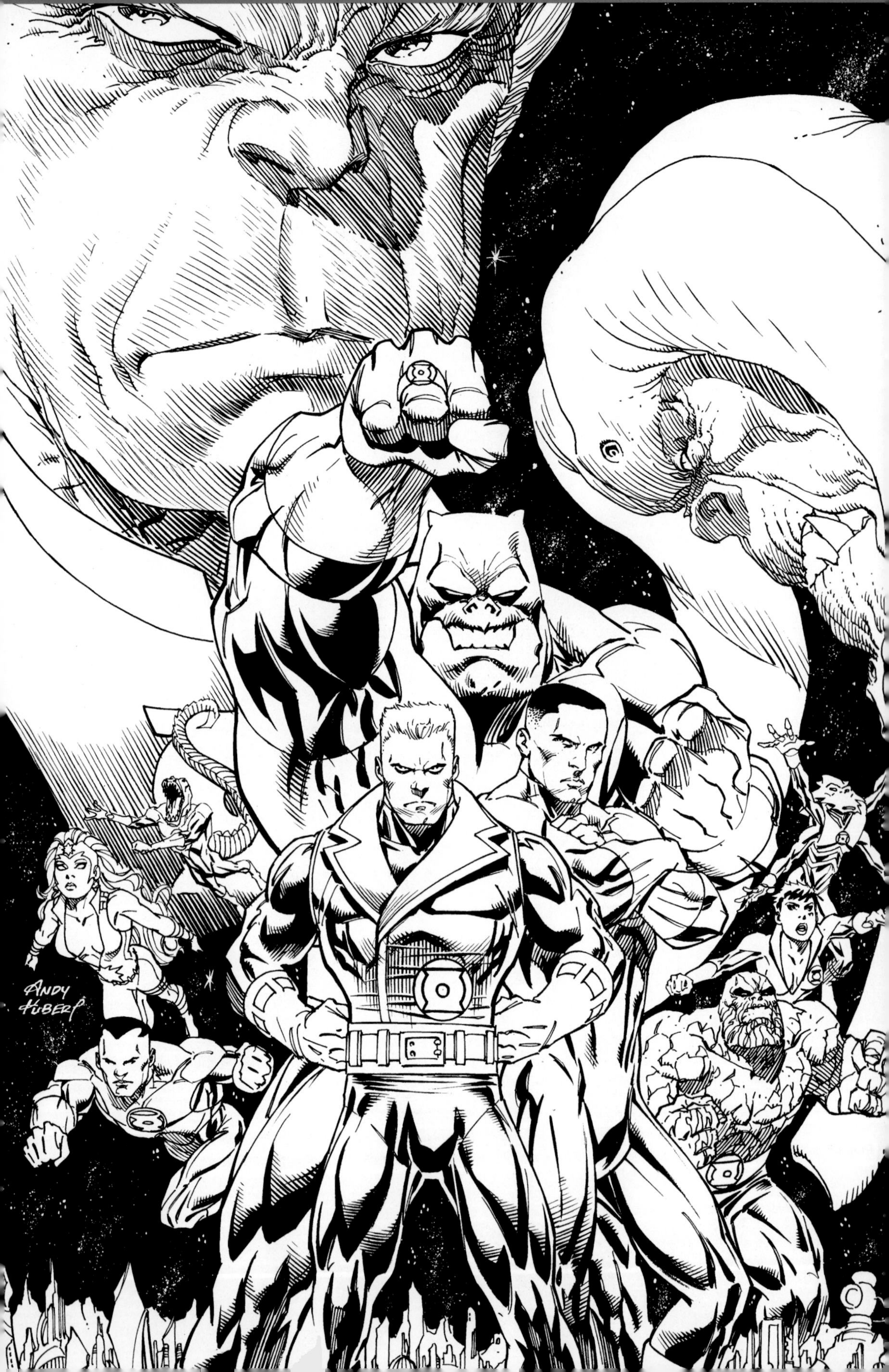
ANDY KUBERT

OA. THE GUARDIANS' PLANETARY CITADEL.
YOU SURE HE'S HERE?
NO I'M NOT SURE, BUT WE'VE CHECKED EVERY-WHERE ELSE.
KKKRRRKKKK
HEY, POOZER, YOU MISS US?

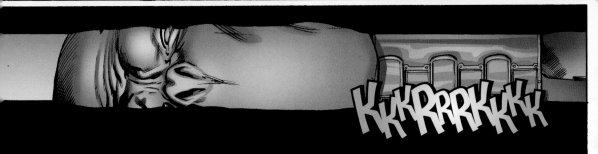

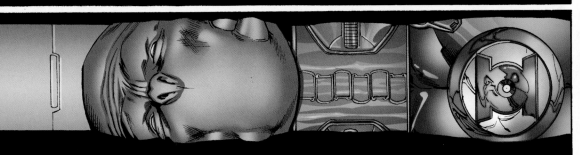

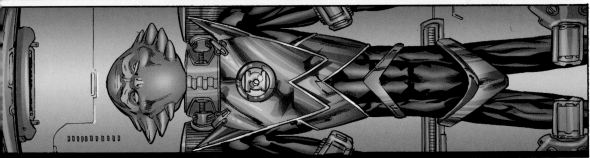

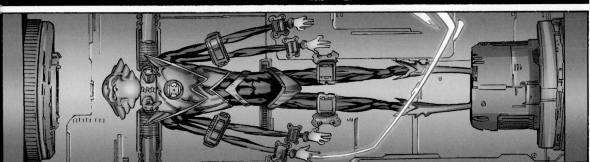

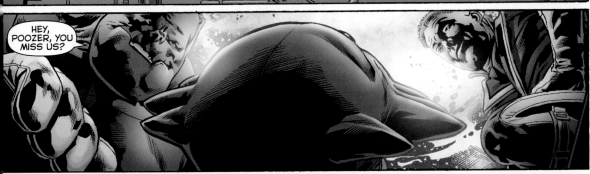

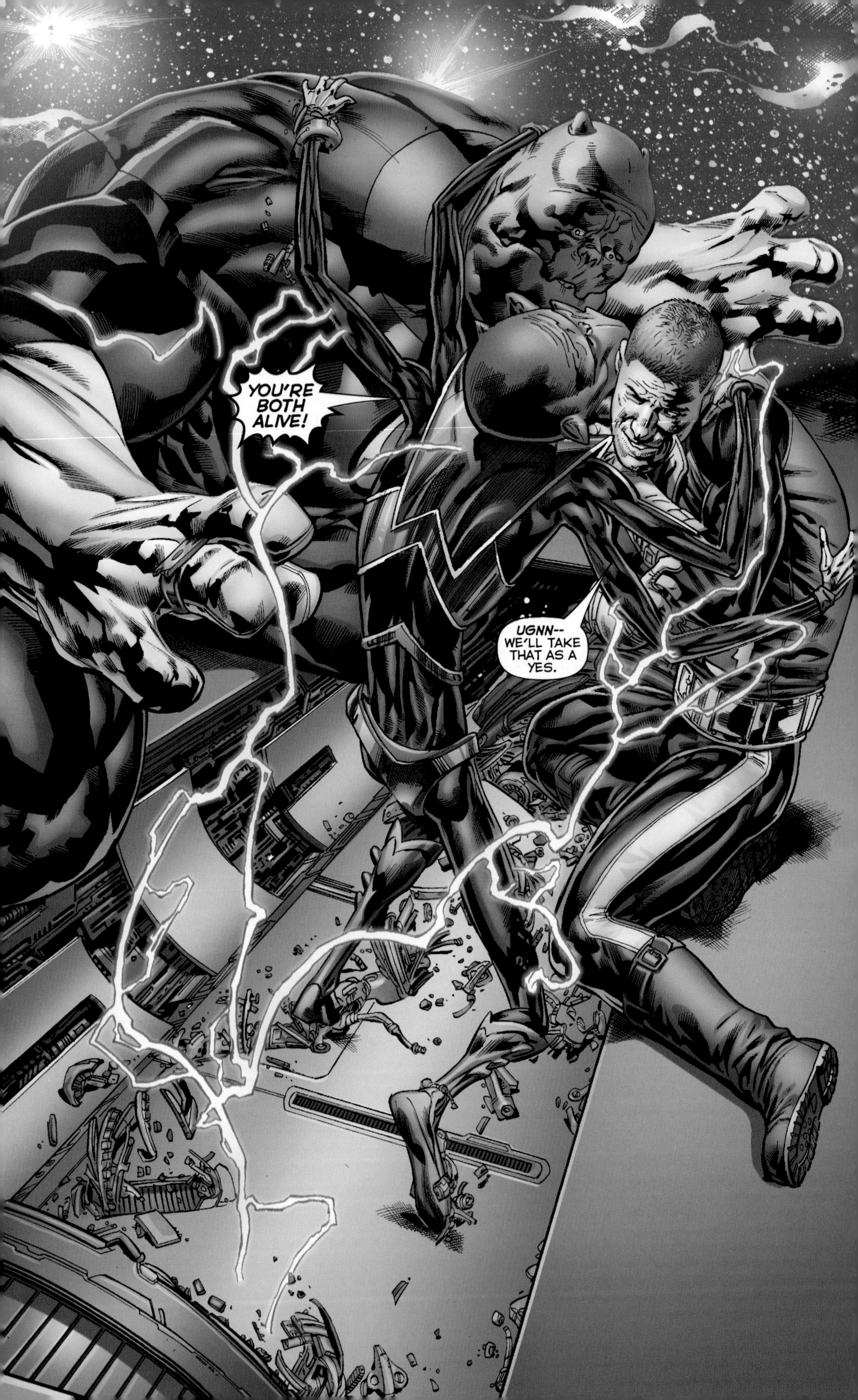
YOU'RE BOTH ALIVE!
UGNN-- WE'LL TAKE THAT AS A YES.

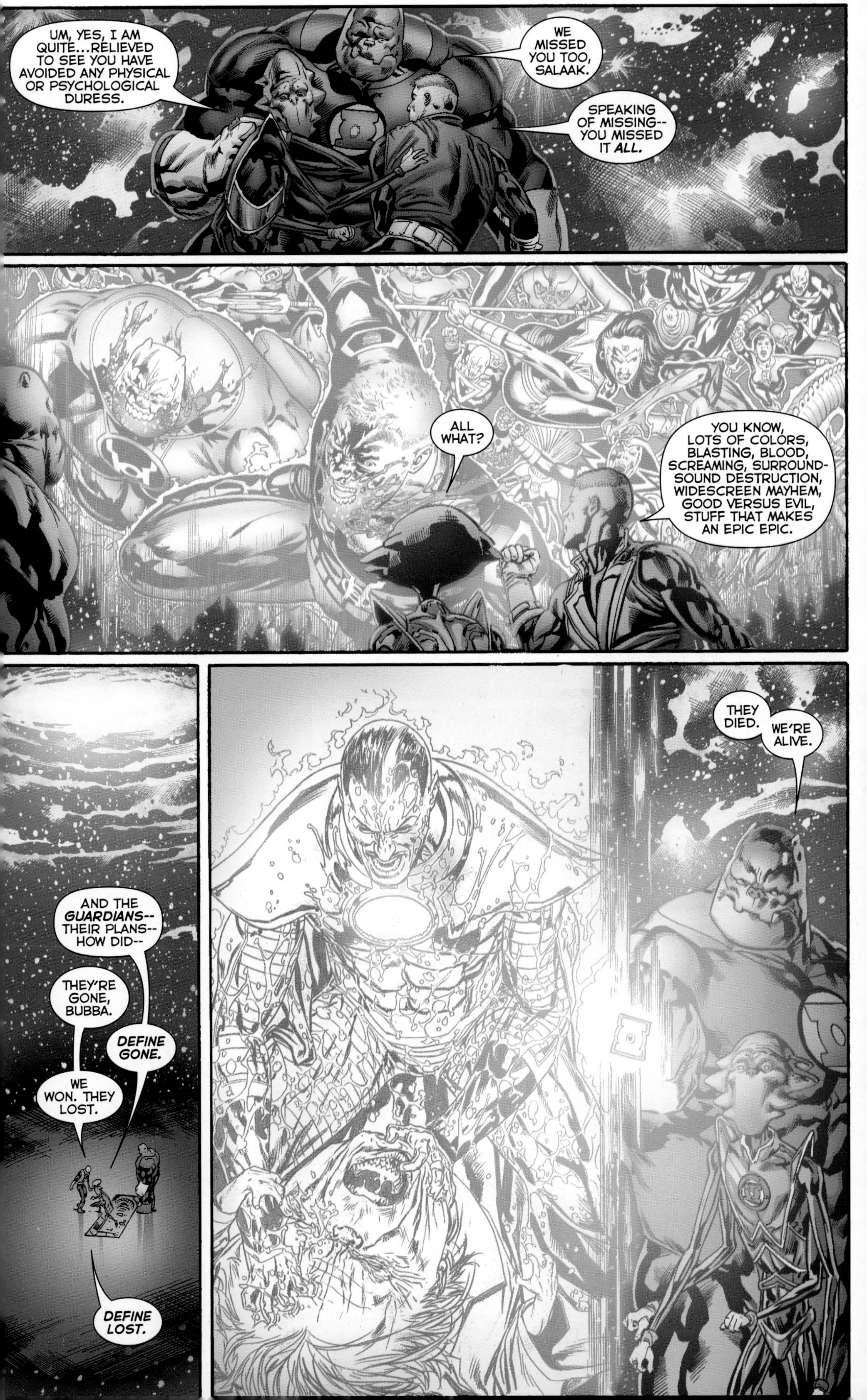
UM, YES, I AM QUITE...RELIEVED TO SEE YOU HAVE AVOIDED ANY PHYSICAL OR PSYCHOLOGICAL DURESS.
WE MISSED YOU TOO, SALAAK.
SPEAKING OF MISSING-- YOU MISSED IT *ALL.*
ALL WHAT?
YOU KNOW, LOTS OF COLORS, BLASTING, BLOOD, SCREAMING, SURROUND-SOUND DESTRUCTION, WIDESCREEN MAYHEM, GOOD VERSUS EVIL, STUFF THAT MAKES AN EPIC EPIC.
AND THE *GUARDIANS*-- THEIR PLANS-- HOW DID--
THEY'RE GONE, BUBBA.
DEFINE GONE.
WE WON. THEY LOST.
DEFINE LOST.
THEY DIED.
WE'RE ALIVE.

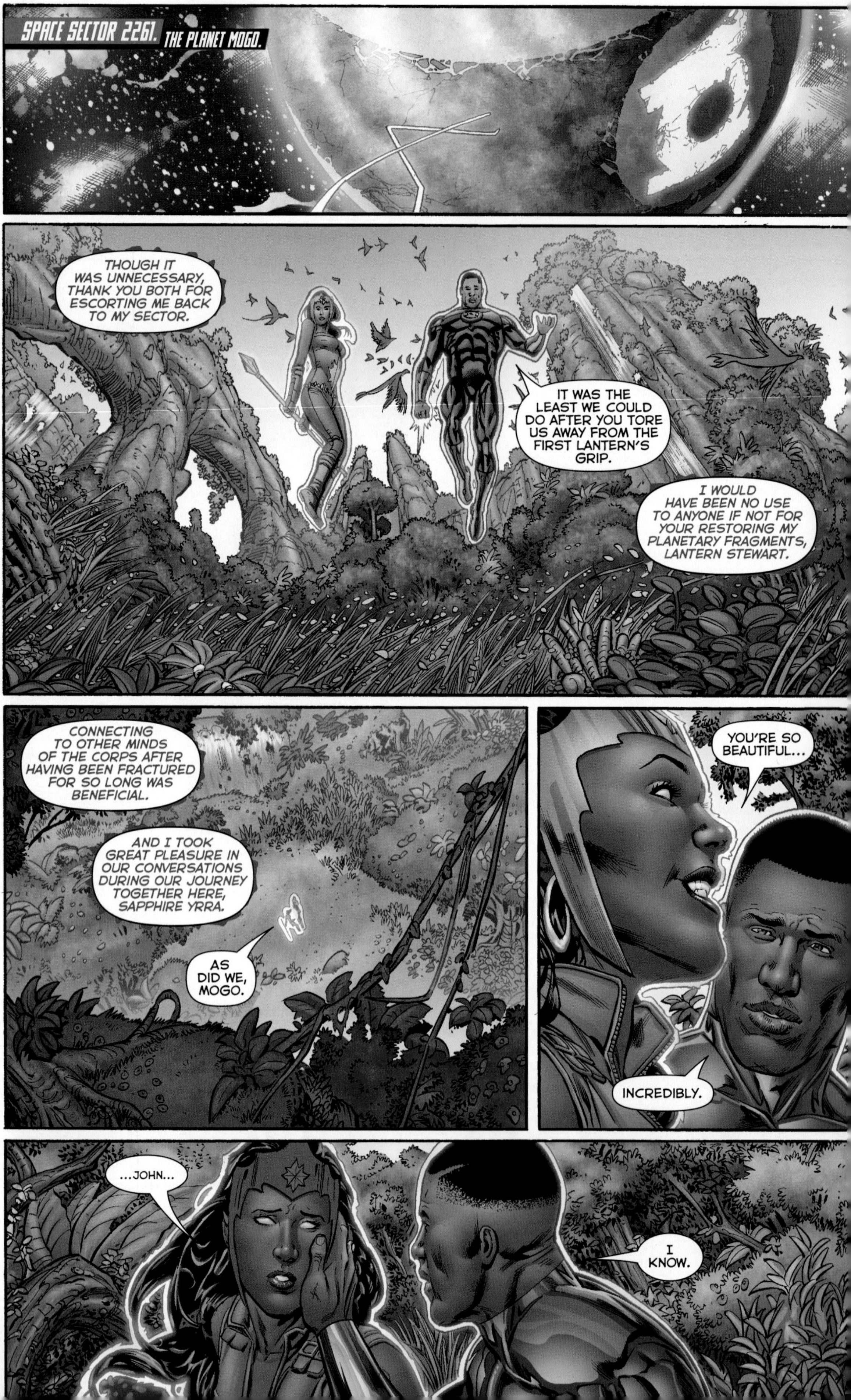
SPACE SECTOR 2261. THE PLANET MOGO.
THOUGH IT WAS UNNECESSARY, THANK YOU BOTH FOR ESCORTING ME BACK TO MY SECTOR.
IT WAS THE LEAST WE COULD DO AFTER YOU TORE US AWAY FROM THE FIRST LANTERN'S GRIP.
I WOULD HAVE BEEN NO USE TO ANYONE IF NOT FOR YOUR RESTORING MY PLANETARY FRAGMENTS, LANTERN STEWART.
CONNECTING TO OTHER MINDS OF THE CORPS AFTER HAVING BEEN FRACTURED FOR SO LONG WAS BENEFICIAL.
AND I TOOK GREAT PLEASURE IN OUR CONVERSATIONS DURING OUR JOURNEY TOGETHER HERE, SAPPHIRE YRRA.
AS DID WE, MOGO.
YOU'RE SO BEAUTIFUL...
INCREDIBLY.
...JOHN...
I KNOW.

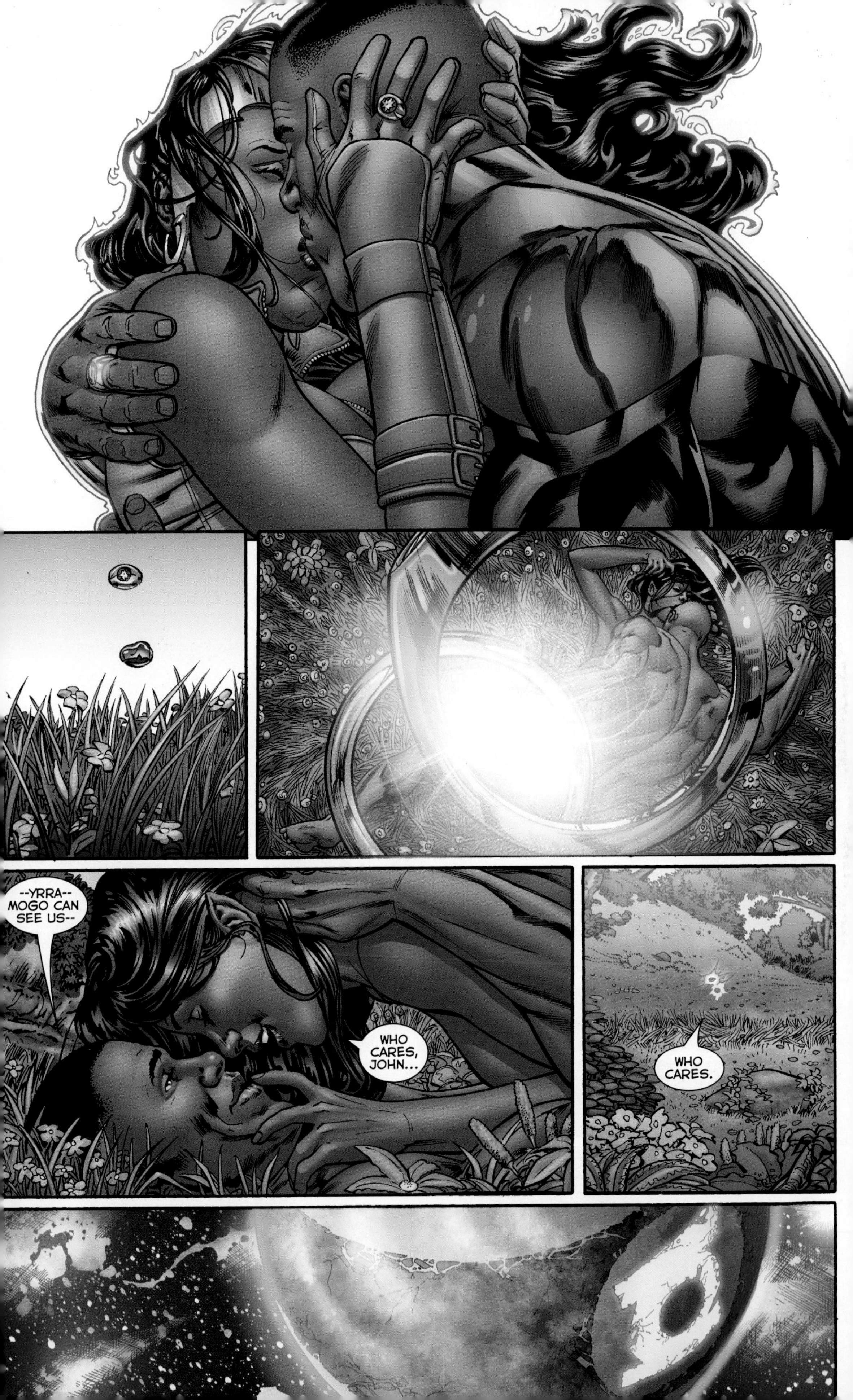
--YRRA--
MOGO CAN
SEE US--
WHO
CARES,
JOHN...
WHO
CARES.

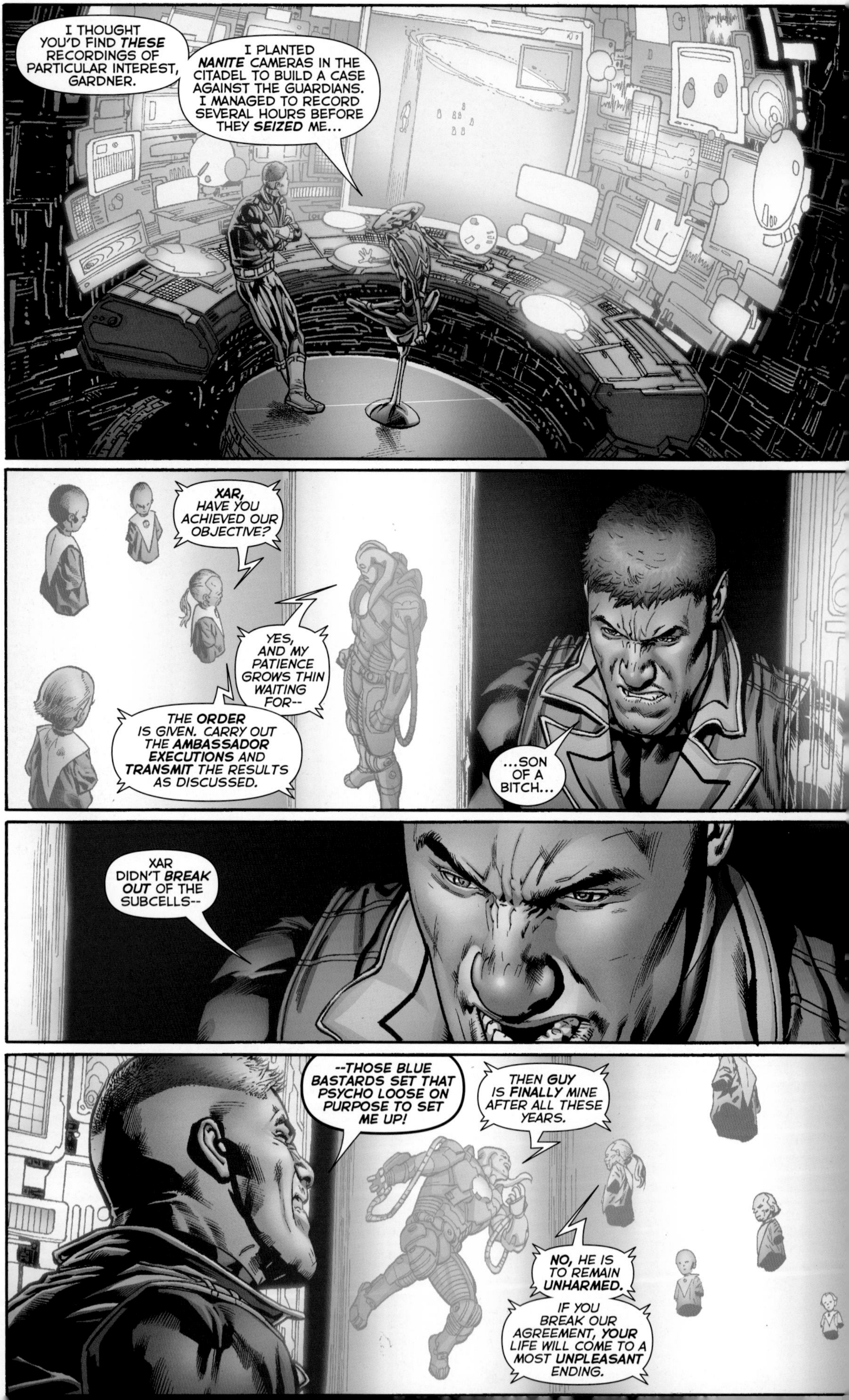
I THOUGHT YOU'D FIND THESE RECORDINGS OF PARTICULAR INTEREST, GARDNER.
I PLANTED NANITE CAMERAS IN THE CITADEL TO BUILD A CASE AGAINST THE GUARDIANS. I MANAGED TO RECORD SEVERAL HOURS BEFORE THEY SEIZED ME...
XAR, HAVE YOU ACHIEVED OUR OBJECTIVE?
YES, AND MY PATIENCE GROWS THIN WAITING FOR--
THE ORDER IS GIVEN. CARRY OUT THE AMBASSADOR EXECUTIONS AND TRANSMIT THE RESULTS AS DISCUSSED.
...SON OF A BITCH...
XAR DIDN'T BREAK OUT OF THE SUBCELLS--
--THOSE BLUE BASTARDS SET THAT PSYCHO LOOSE ON PURPOSE TO SET ME UP!
THEN GUY IS FINALLY MINE AFTER ALL THESE YEARS.
NO, HE IS TO REMAIN UNHARMED.
IF YOU BREAK OUR AGREEMENT, YOUR LIFE WILL COME TO A MOST UNPLEASANT ENDING.

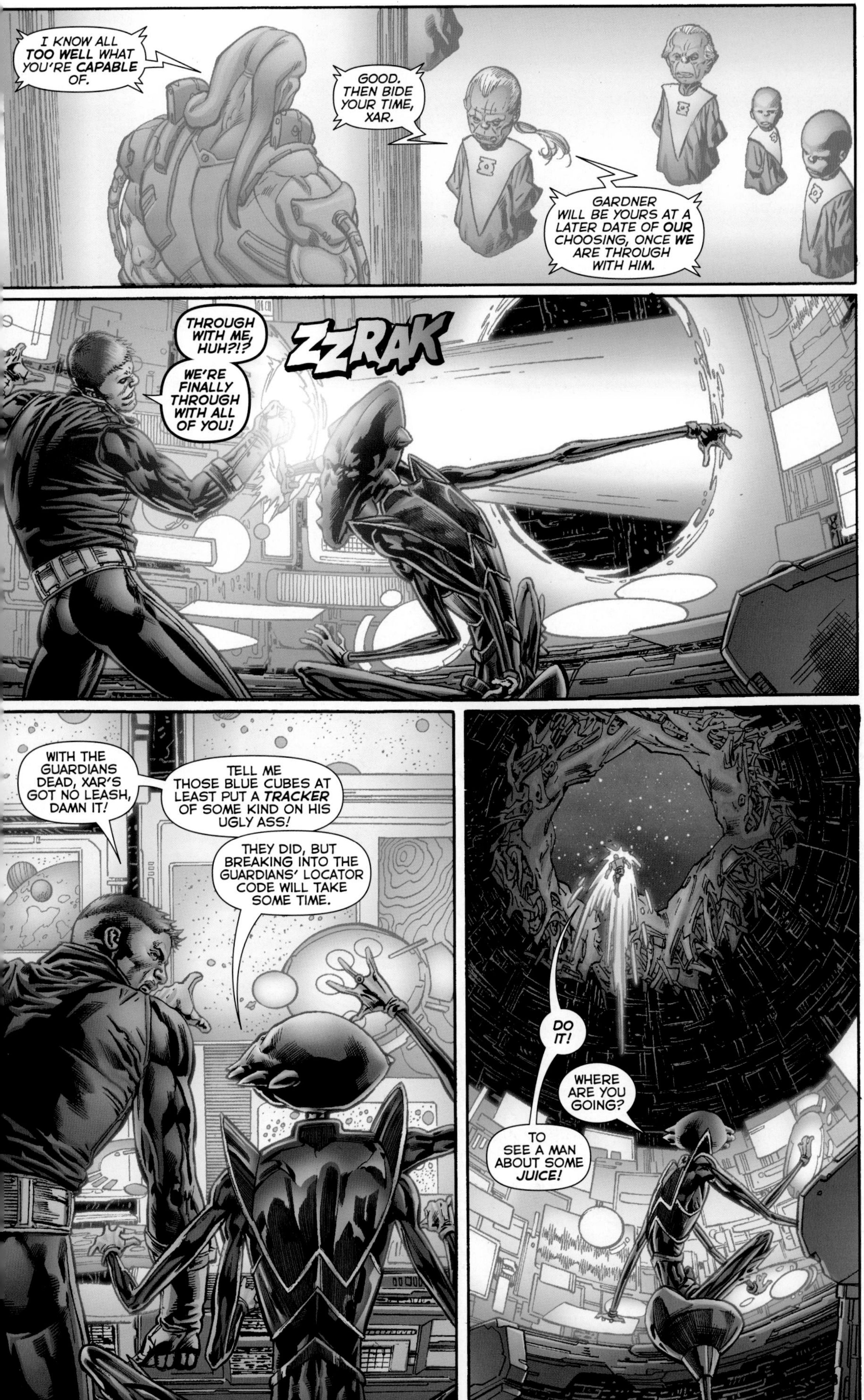
I KNOW ALL TOO WELL WHAT YOU'RE CAPABLE OF.
GOOD. THEN BIDE YOUR TIME, XAR.
GARDNER WILL BE YOURS AT A LATER DATE OF OUR CHOOSING, ONCE WE ARE THROUGH WITH HIM.
THROUGH WITH ME, HUH?!?
WE'RE FINALLY THROUGH WITH ALL OF YOU!
ZZRAK
WITH THE GUARDIANS DEAD, XAR'S GOT NO LEASH, DAMN IT!
TELL ME THOSE BLUE CUBES AT LEAST PUT A TRACKER OF SOME KIND ON HIS UGLY ASS!
THEY DID, BUT BREAKING INTO THE GUARDIANS' LOCATOR CODE WILL TAKE SOME TIME.
DO IT!
WHERE ARE YOU GOING?
TO SEE A MAN ABOUT SOME JUICE!

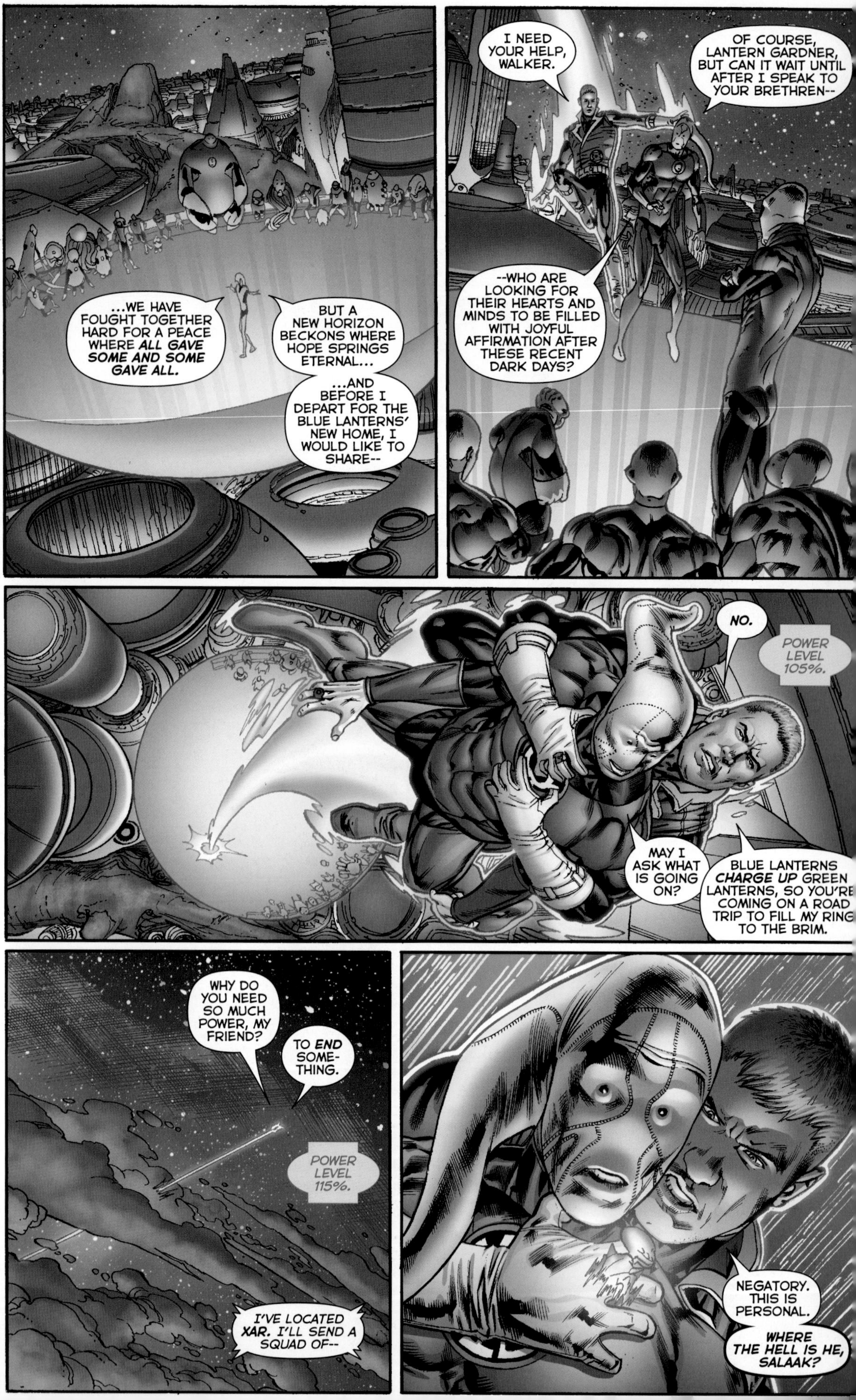
...WE HAVE FOUGHT TOGETHER HARD FOR A PEACE WHERE ALL GAVE SOME AND SOME GAVE ALL.
BUT A NEW HORIZON BECKONS WHERE HOPE SPRINGS ETERNAL...
...AND BEFORE I DEPART FOR THE BLUE LANTERNS' NEW HOME, I WOULD LIKE TO SHARE--
I NEED YOUR HELP, WALKER.
OF COURSE, LANTERN GARDNER, BUT CAN IT WAIT UNTIL AFTER I SPEAK TO YOUR BRETHREN--
--WHO ARE LOOKING FOR THEIR HEARTS AND MINDS TO BE FILLED WITH JOYFUL AFFIRMATION AFTER THESE RECENT DARK DAYS?
NO.
POWER LEVEL 105%.
MAY I ASK WHAT IS GOING ON?
BLUE LANTERNS CHARGE UP GREEN LANTERNS, SO YOU'RE COMING ON A ROAD TRIP TO FILL MY RING TO THE BRIM.
WHY DO YOU NEED SO MUCH POWER, MY FRIEND?
TO END SOME-THING.
POWER LEVEL 115%.
I'VE LOCATED XAR. I'LL SEND A SQUAD OF--
NEGATORY. THIS IS PERSONAL.
WHERE THE HELL IS HE, SALAAK?

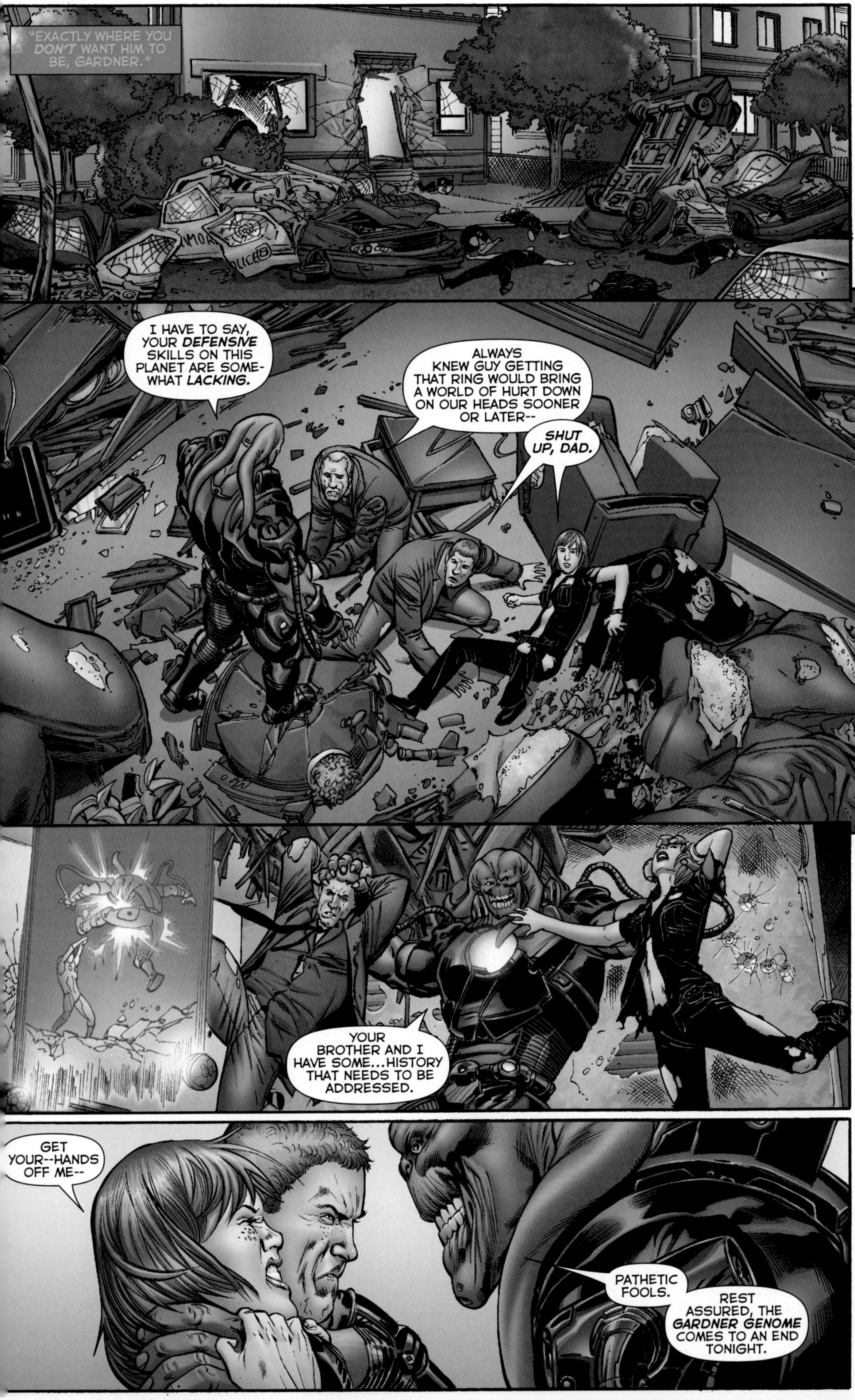
"EXACTLY WHERE YOU DON'T WANT HIM TO BE, GARDNER."
I HAVE TO SAY, YOUR *DEFENSIVE* SKILLS ON THIS PLANET ARE SOME-WHAT *LACKING.*
ALWAYS KNEW GUY GETTING THAT RING WOULD BRING A WORLD OF HURT DOWN ON OUR HEADS SOONER OR LATER--
SHUT UP, DAD.
YOUR BROTHER AND I HAVE SOME...HISTORY THAT NEEDS TO BE ADDRESSED.
GET YOUR--HANDS OFF ME--
PATHETIC FOOLS.
REST ASSURED, THE *GARDNER GENOME* COMES TO AN END TONIGHT.

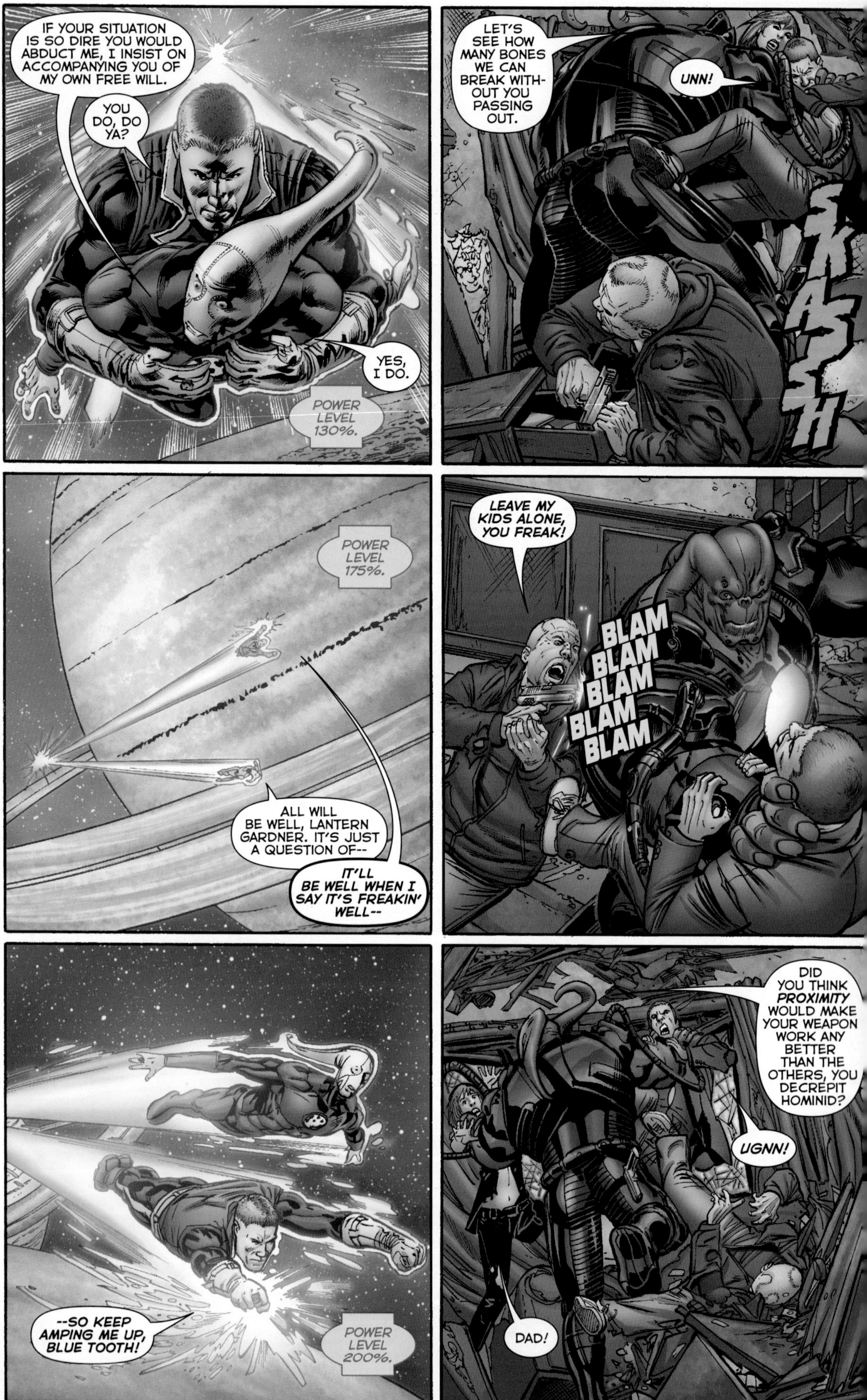
IF YOUR SITUATION IS SO DIRE YOU WOULD ABDUCT ME, I INSIST ON ACCOMPANYING YOU OF MY OWN FREE WILL.
YOU DO, DO YA?
YES, I DO.
POWER LEVEL 130%.
LET'S SEE HOW MANY BONES WE CAN BREAK WITH-OUT YOU PASSING OUT.
UNN!
SKASH
POWER LEVEL 175%.
ALL WILL BE WELL, LANTERN GARDNER. IT'S JUST A QUESTION OF--
IT'LL BE WELL WHEN I SAY IT'S FREAKIN' WELL--
LEAVE MY KIDS ALONE, YOU FREAK!
BLAM BLAM BLAM BLAM BLAM
--SO KEEP AMPING ME UP, BLUE TOOTH!
POWER LEVEL 200%.
DID YOU THINK PROXIMITY WOULD MAKE YOUR WEAPON WORK ANY BETTER THAN THE OTHERS, YOU DECREPIT HOMINID?
UGNN!
DAD!

POWER LEVEL 300%

I'M NOT SURE WHAT THE CAPACITY OF YOUR RING IS, BUT YOU NEED TO DISCHARGE THE IMMENSE POWER YOU'VE BUILT UP SOON.

YEAH. *THAT'S THE PLAN.*

IT'S TIME TO DIE.

IT WILL BE INCREDIBLY SLOW AND PAINFUL.

SMASH

YOUR LAST MOMENTS WILL BE RECORDED SO GUY GARDNER CAN WATCH HOW HE FAILED HIS OWN BLOOD-COVERED FAMILY.

THANKS FOR THE *COMPANY,* WALKER.

GOTTA DO THIS *ALONE.*

POWER LEVEL 325%

SO...

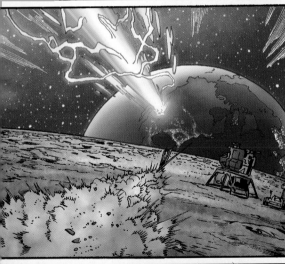

...WHO WANTS TO *SCREAM* FOR THE CAMERA FIRST?

I HAVE A FEELING IT'S GOING TO BE *YOU.*

HMM?

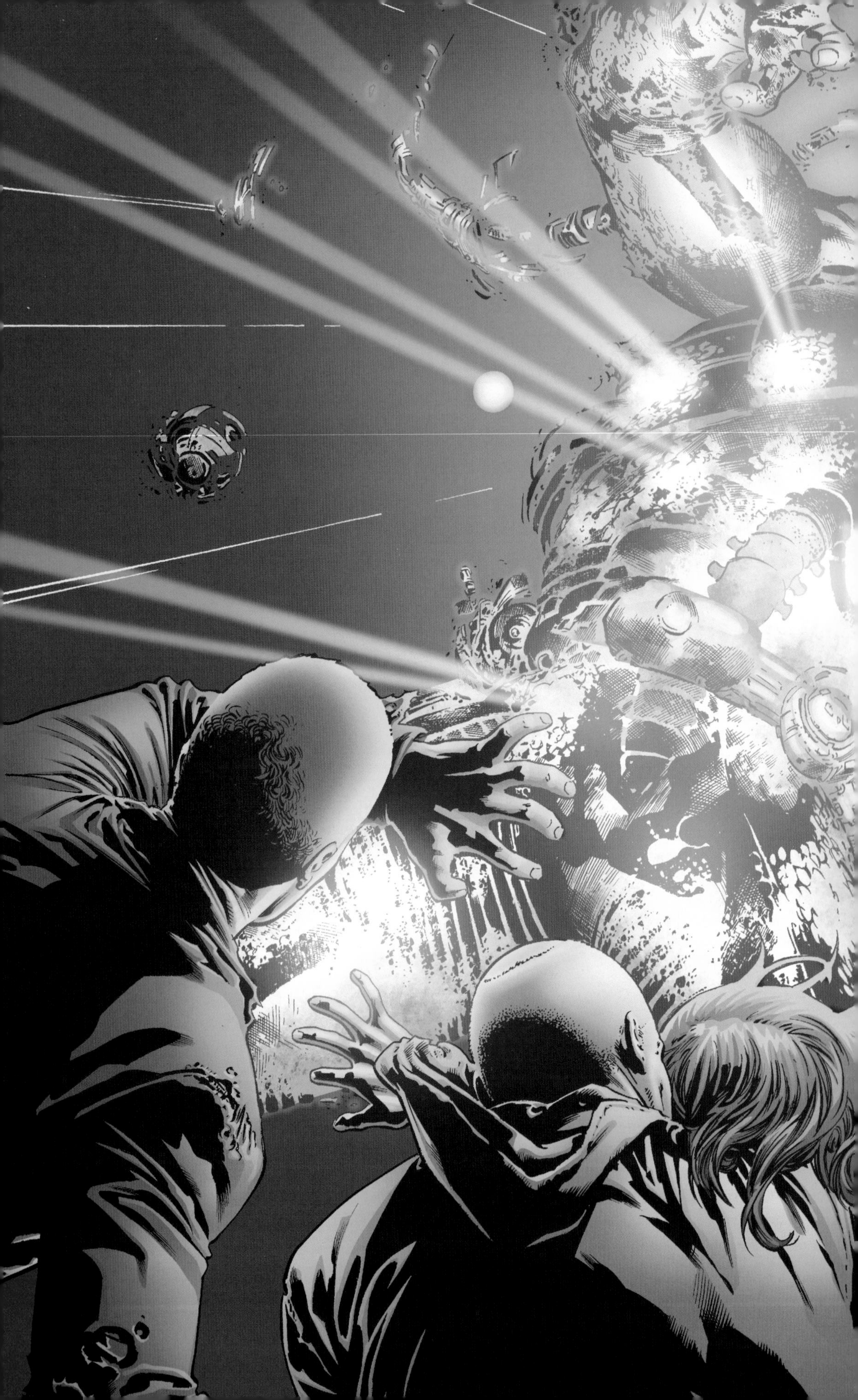

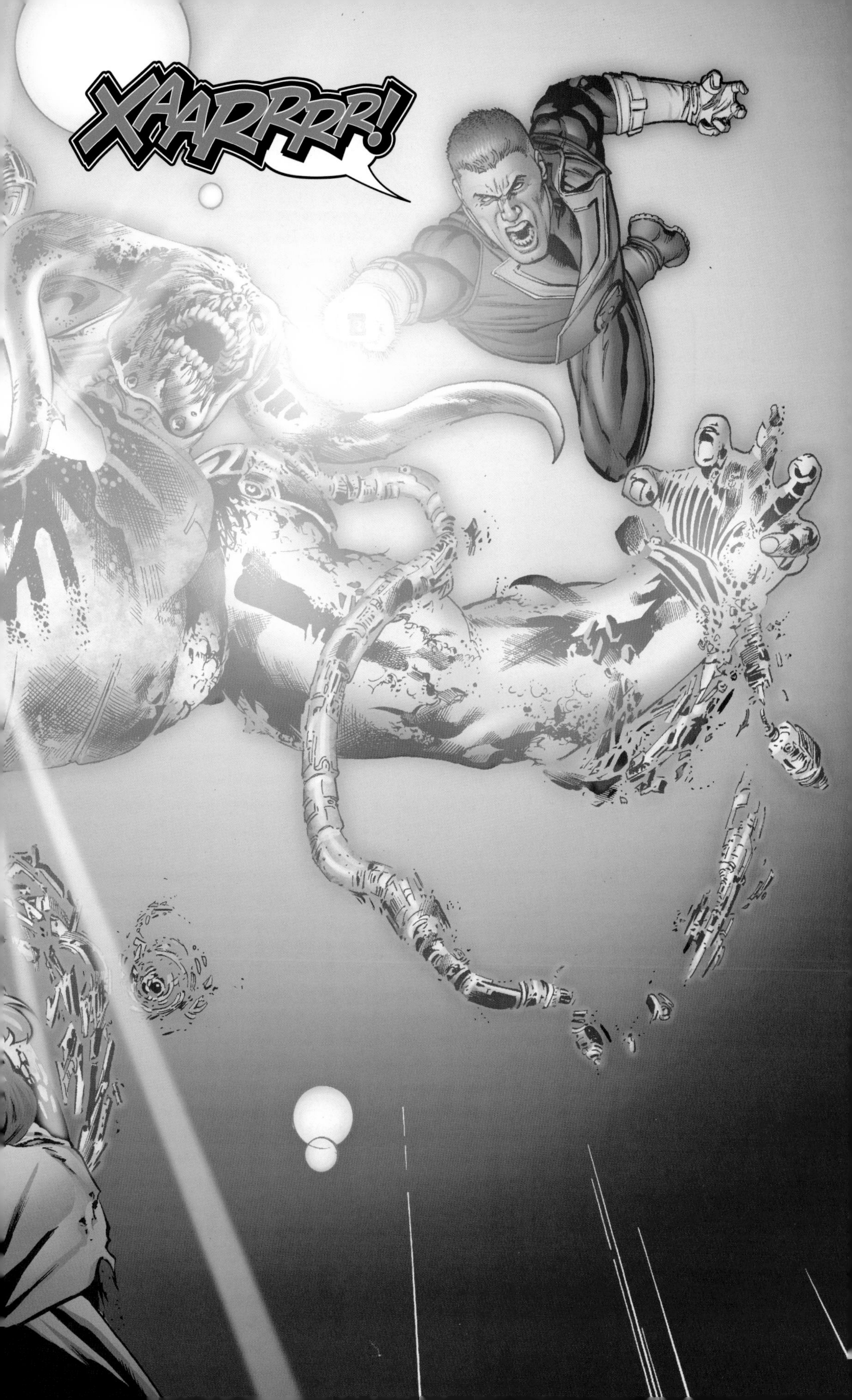
XAARRRR!

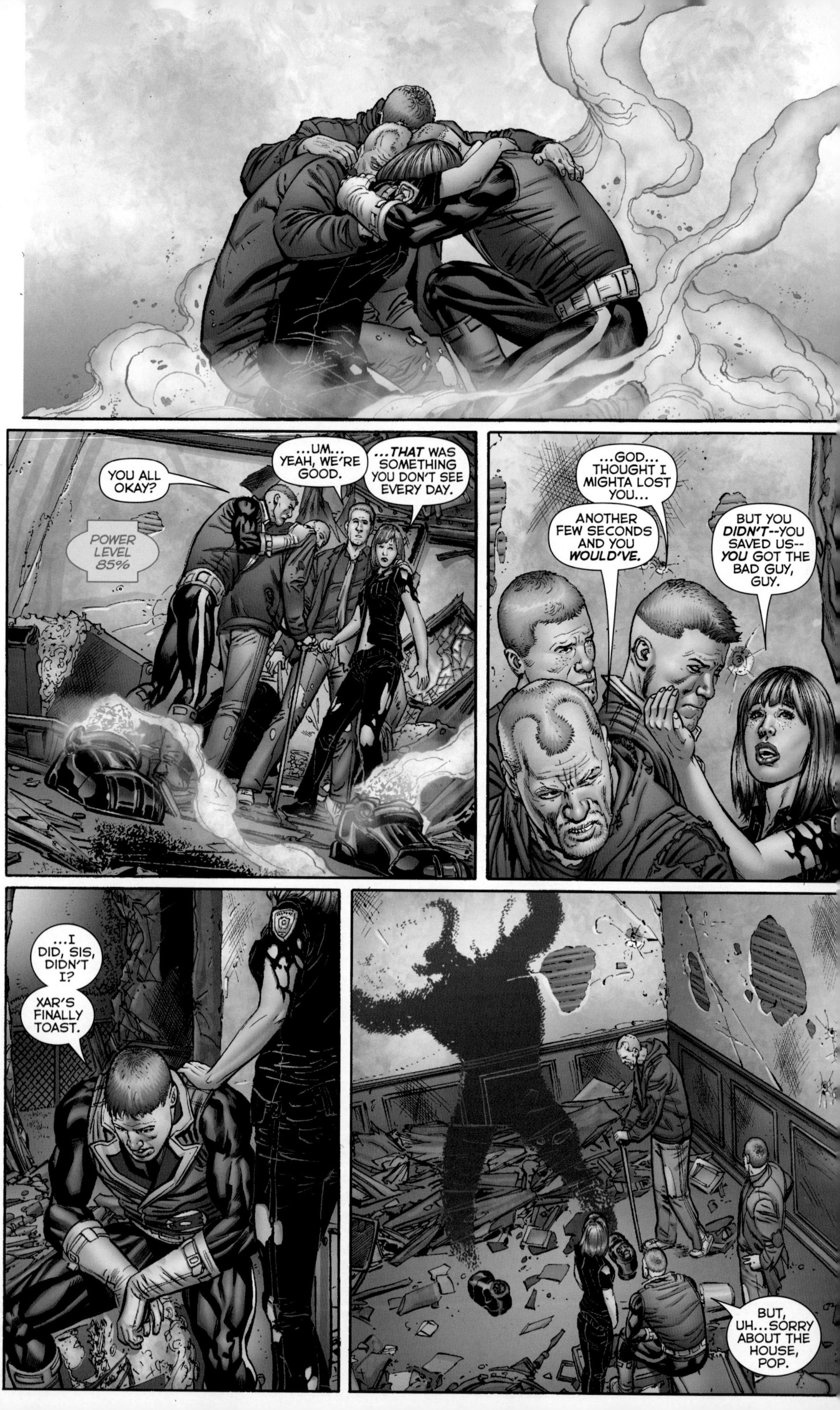
YOU ALL OKAY?
POWER LEVEL 85%
...UM... YEAH, WE'RE GOOD.
...*THAT* WAS SOMETHING YOU DON'T SEE EVERY DAY.
...GOD... THOUGHT I MIGHTA LOST YOU...
ANOTHER FEW SECONDS AND YOU *WOULD'VE.*
BUT YOU *DIDN'T*--YOU SAVED US--*YOU* GOT THE BAD GUY, GUY.
...I DID, SIS, DIDN'T I?
XAR'S FINALLY TOAST.
BUT, UH...SORRY ABOUT THE HOUSE, POP.

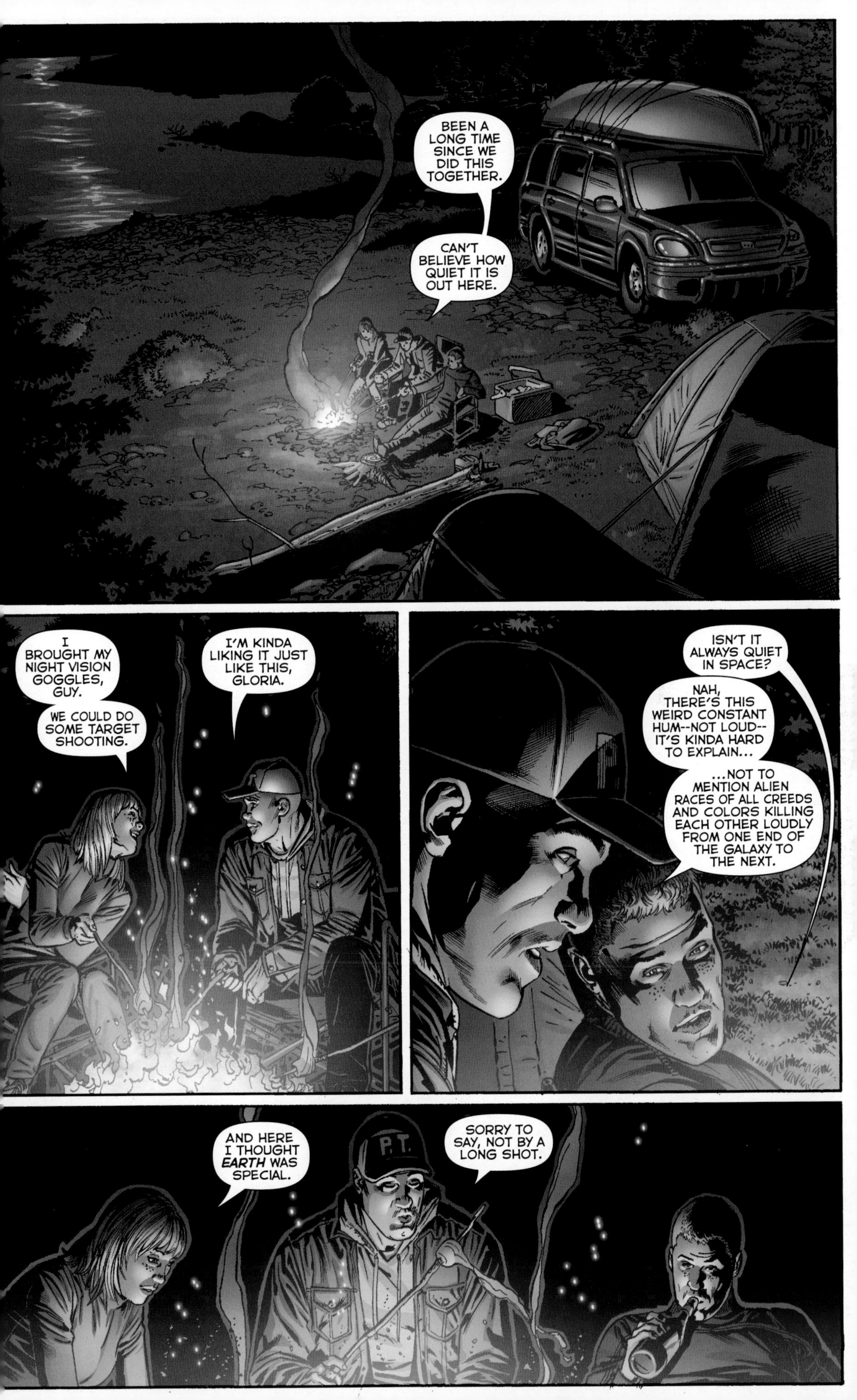
BEEN A LONG TIME SINCE WE DID THIS TOGETHER.
CAN'T BELIEVE HOW QUIET IT IS OUT HERE.
I BROUGHT MY NIGHT VISION GOGGLES, GUY.
WE COULD DO SOME TARGET SHOOTING.
I'M KINDA LIKING IT JUST LIKE THIS, GLORIA.
ISN'T IT ALWAYS QUIET IN SPACE?
NAH, THERE'S THIS WEIRD CONSTANT HUM--NOT LOUD--IT'S KINDA HARD TO EXPLAIN...
...NOT TO MENTION ALIEN RACES OF ALL CREEDS AND COLORS KILLING EACH OTHER LOUDLY FROM ONE END OF THE GALAXY TO THE NEXT.
AND HERE I THOUGHT *EARTH* WAS SPECIAL.
SORRY TO SAY, NOT BY A LONG SHOT.
P.T.

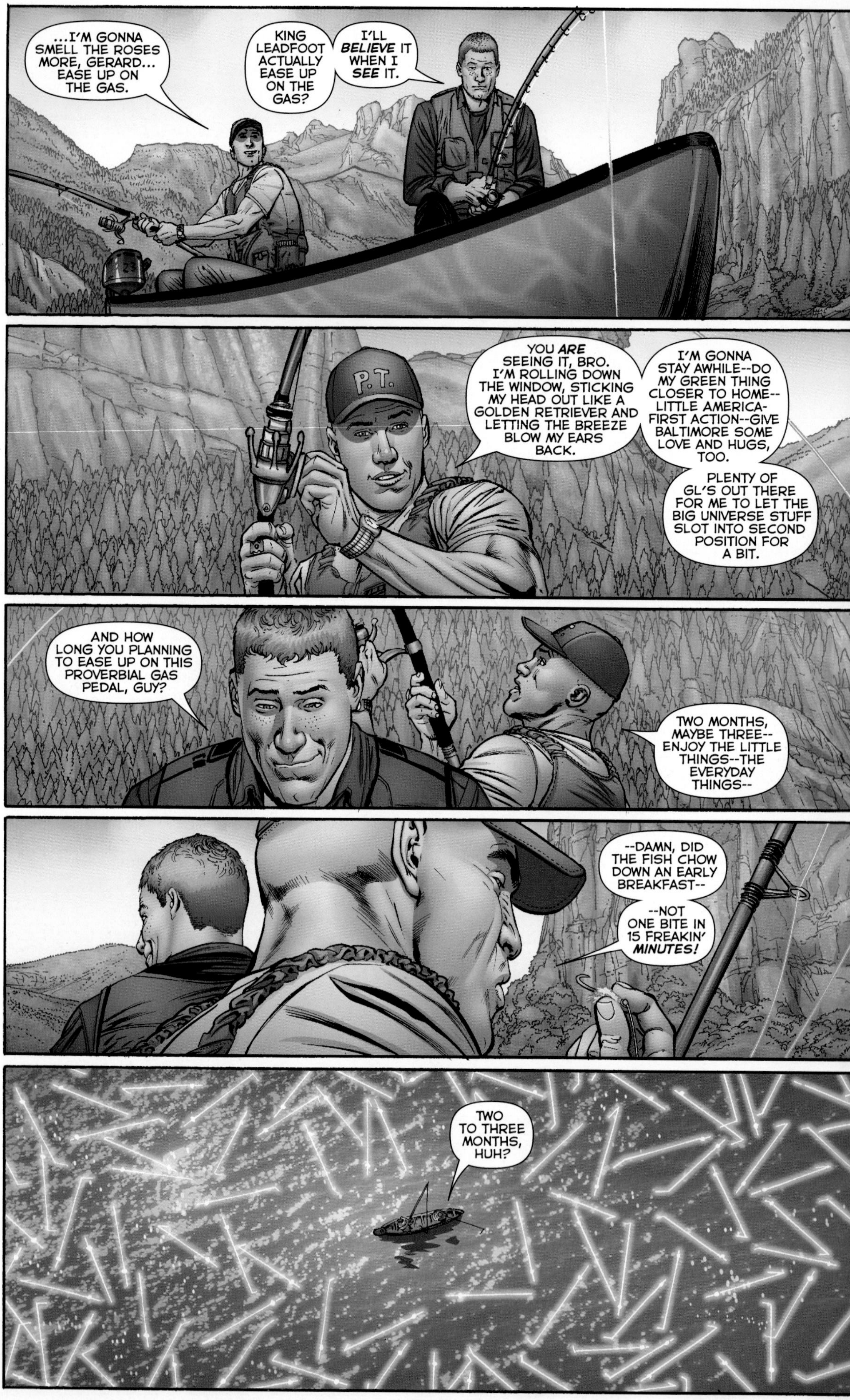
...I'M GONNA SMELL THE ROSES MORE, GERARD... EASE UP ON THE GAS.
KING LEADFOOT ACTUALLY EASE UP ON THE GAS?
I'LL BELIEVE IT WHEN I SEE IT.
YOU ARE SEEING IT, BRO. I'M ROLLING DOWN THE WINDOW, STICKING MY HEAD OUT LIKE A GOLDEN RETRIEVER AND LETTING THE BREEZE BLOW MY EARS BACK.
I'M GONNA STAY AWHILE--DO MY GREEN THING CLOSER TO HOME--LITTLE AMERICA-FIRST ACTION--GIVE BALTIMORE SOME LOVE AND HUGS, TOO.
PLENTY OF GL'S OUT THERE FOR ME TO LET THE BIG UNIVERSE STUFF SLOT INTO SECOND POSITION FOR A BIT.
AND HOW LONG YOU PLANNING TO EASE UP ON THIS PROVERBIAL GAS PEDAL, GUY?
TWO MONTHS, MAYBE THREE--ENJOY THE LITTLE THINGS--THE EVERYDAY THINGS--
--DAMN, DID THE FISH CHOW DOWN AN EARLY BREAKFAST--
--NOT ONE BITE IN 15 FREAKIN' MINUTES!
TWO TO THREE MONTHS, HUH?

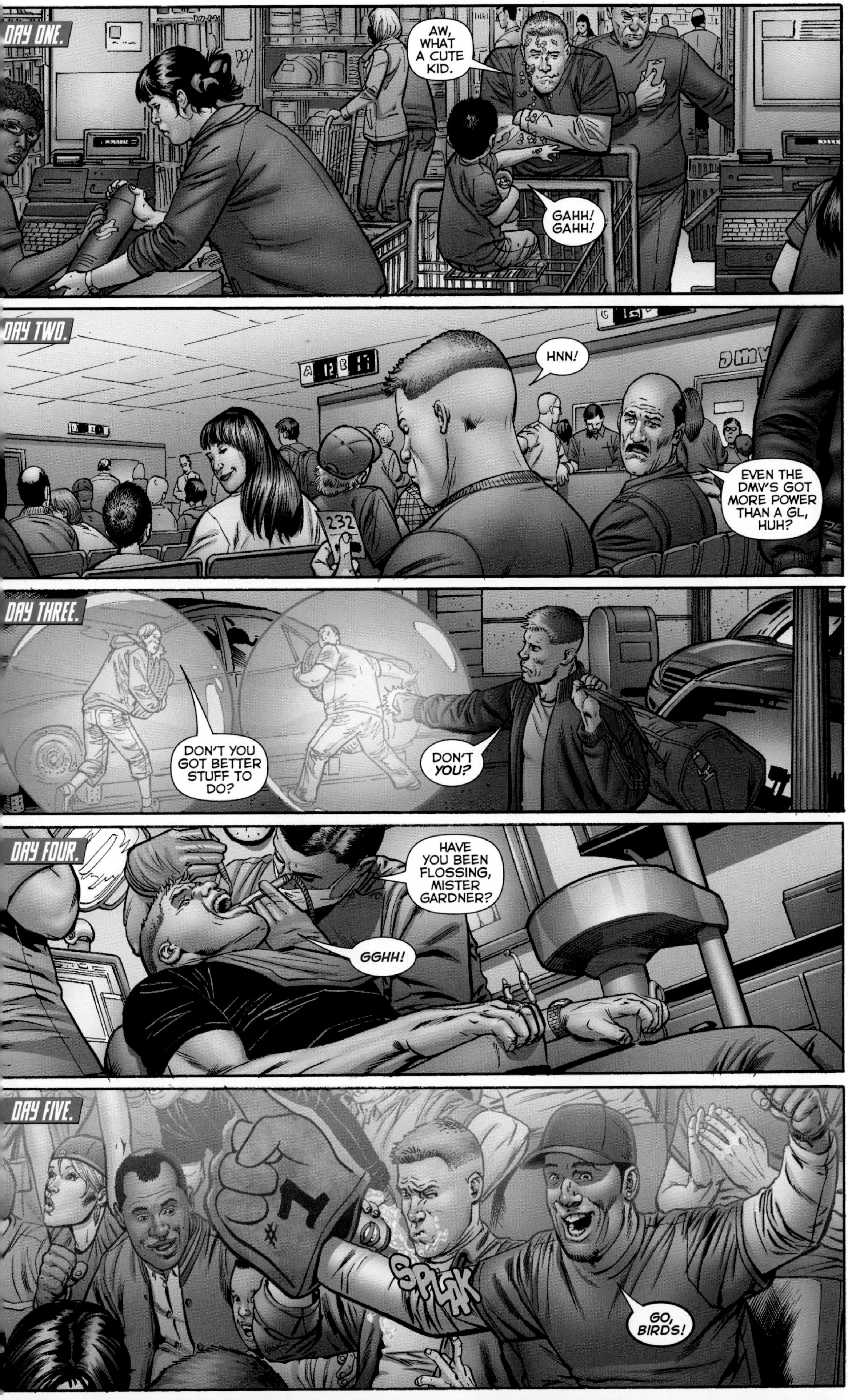
DAY ONE.
AW, WHAT A CUTE KID.
GAHH! GAHH!
DAY TWO.
HNN!
EVEN THE DMV'S GOT MORE POWER THAN A GL, HUH?
DAY THREE.
DON'T YOU GOT BETTER STUFF TO DO?
DON'T *YOU?*
DAY FOUR.
HAVE YOU BEEN FLOSSING, MISTER GARDNER?
GGHH!
DAY FIVE.
SPLAK
GO, BIRDS!

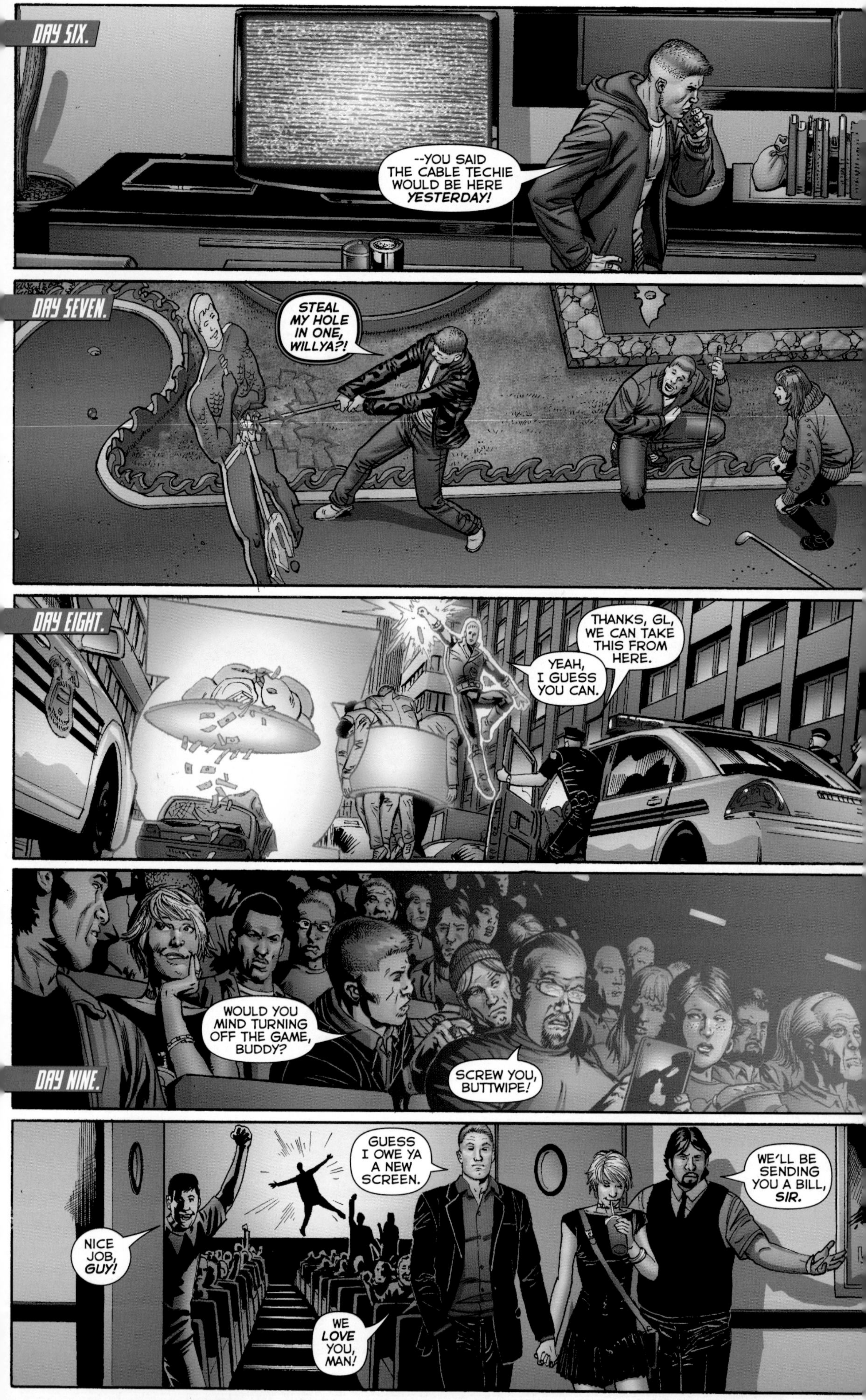
DAY SIX.
--YOU SAID THE CABLE TECHIE WOULD BE HERE YESTERDAY!
DAY SEVEN.
STEAL MY HOLE IN ONE, WILLYA?!
DAY EIGHT.
THANKS, GL, WE CAN TAKE THIS FROM HERE.
YEAH, I GUESS YOU CAN.
DAY NINE.
WOULD YOU MIND TURNING OFF THE GAME, BUDDY?
SCREW YOU, BUTTWIPE!
GUESS I OWE YA A NEW SCREEN.
WE'LL BE SENDING YOU A BILL, SIR.
NICE JOB, GUY!
WE LOVE YOU, MAN!

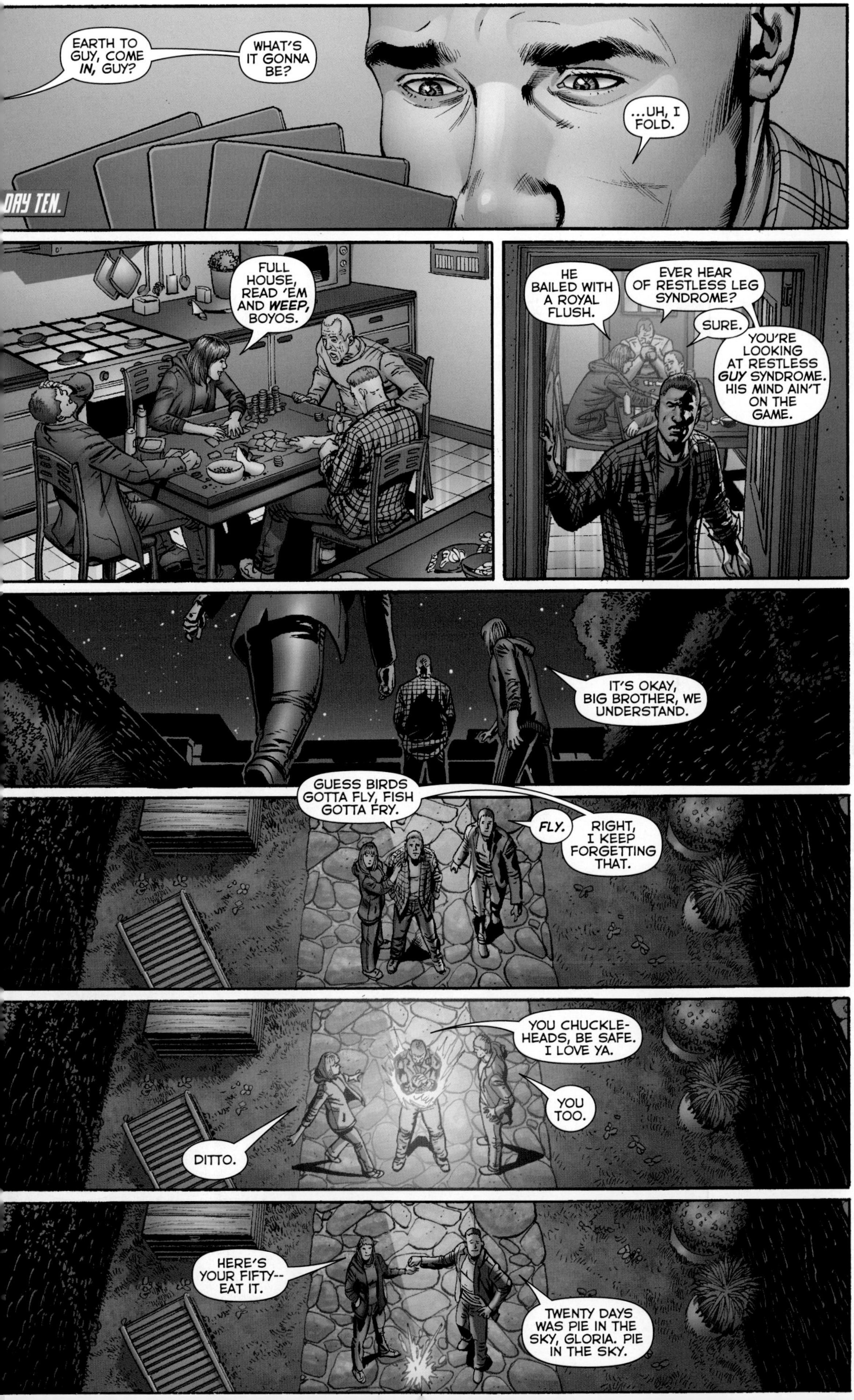
EARTH TO GUY, COME IN, GUY?
WHAT'S IT GONNA BE?
...UH, I FOLD.
DAY TEN.
FULL HOUSE, READ 'EM AND WEEP, BOYOS.
HE BAILED WITH A ROYAL FLUSH.
EVER HEAR OF RESTLESS LEG SYNDROME?
SURE.
YOU'RE LOOKING AT RESTLESS GUY SYNDROME. HIS MIND AIN'T ON THE GAME.
IT'S OKAY, BIG BROTHER, WE UNDERSTAND.
GUESS BIRDS GOTTA FLY, FISH GOTTA FRY.
FLY.
RIGHT, I KEEP FORGETTING THAT.
YOU CHUCKLE-HEADS, BE SAFE. I LOVE YA.
YOU TOO.
DITTO.
HERE'S YOUR FIFTY-- EAT IT.
TWENTY DAYS WAS PIE IN THE SKY, GLORIA. PIE IN THE SKY.

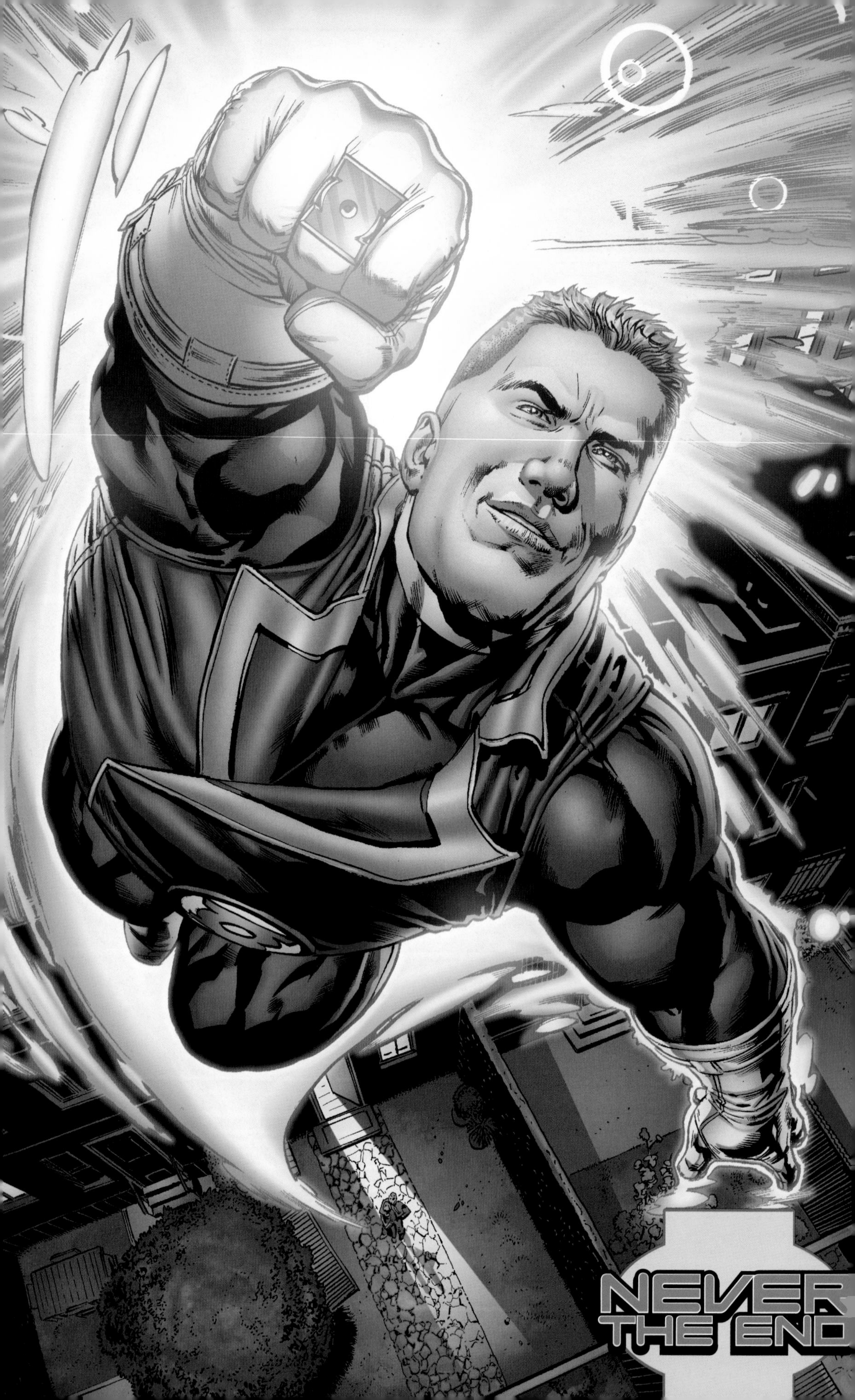
NEVER
THE END

PAGES 12 and 13

Double page spread, Fernando.

panel 1
Close only on Xar's face as he turns, the green energy of Guy is reflected in his unsuspecting eyes.

XAR: Hmm?

panel 2
This image takes up rest of the page.

Wicked cool shot as Guy, like a super-sonic green bullet, zips in cleanly, SCREAMING AS HE FIRES HIS RING AT XAR WHO HAS TURNED TO FACE HIM BUT IS BEING BLASTED APART. I'm seeing Xar looking like the moment when Doctor Manhattan is hit by the tachyons -- all tattered and stretched out blackness as he dies in extreme agony.

Guy hits him hard and fast. No fuss no muss. A quick and clean killshot to take out the creature who's murdered hundreds and was about to brutalize his family.

It all happens so fast and so cleanly that all Gloria, Gerard and Gavin can do is look on in shock as they are still on the floor.

Have the 2 digi-cams also being incinerated.

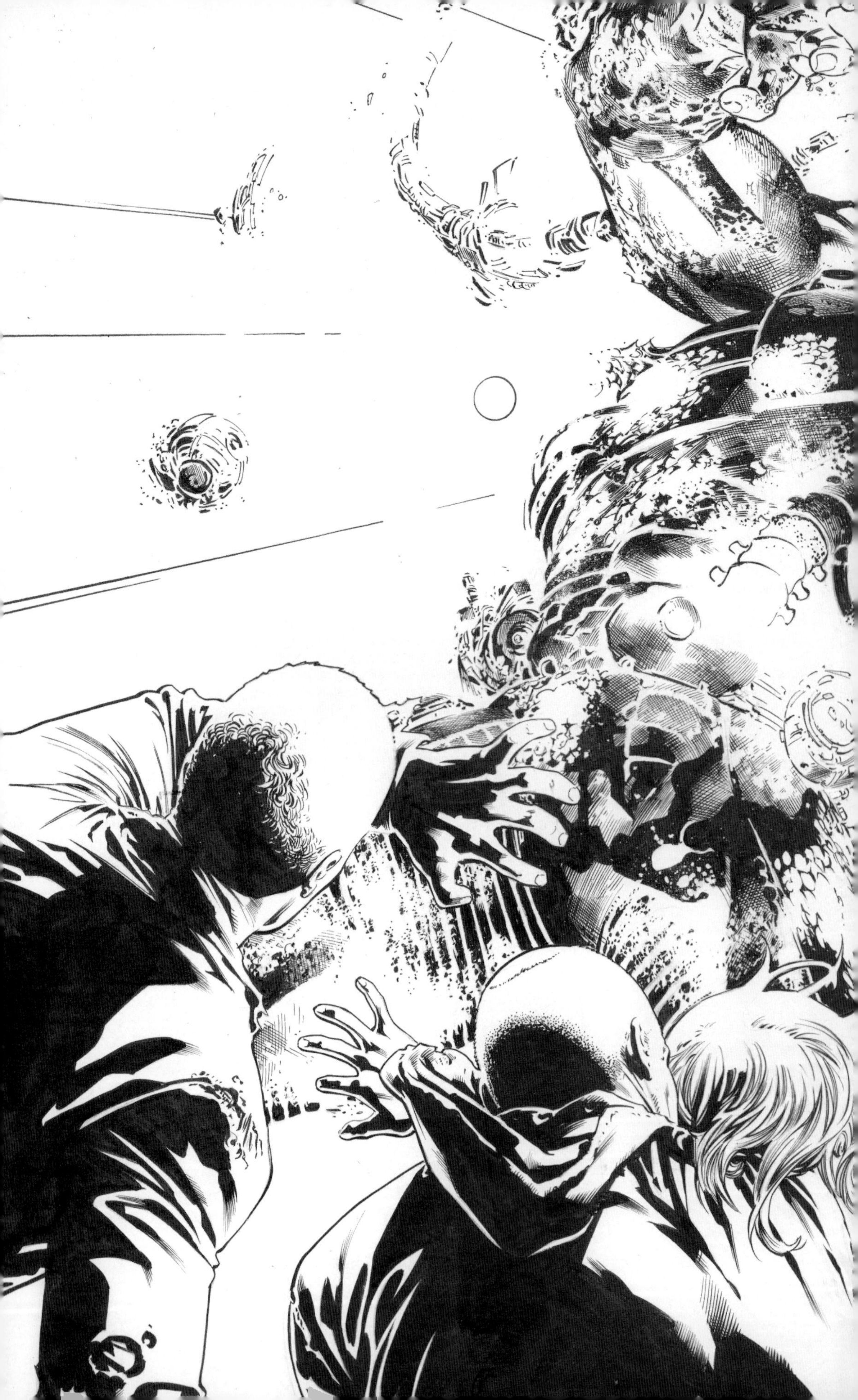

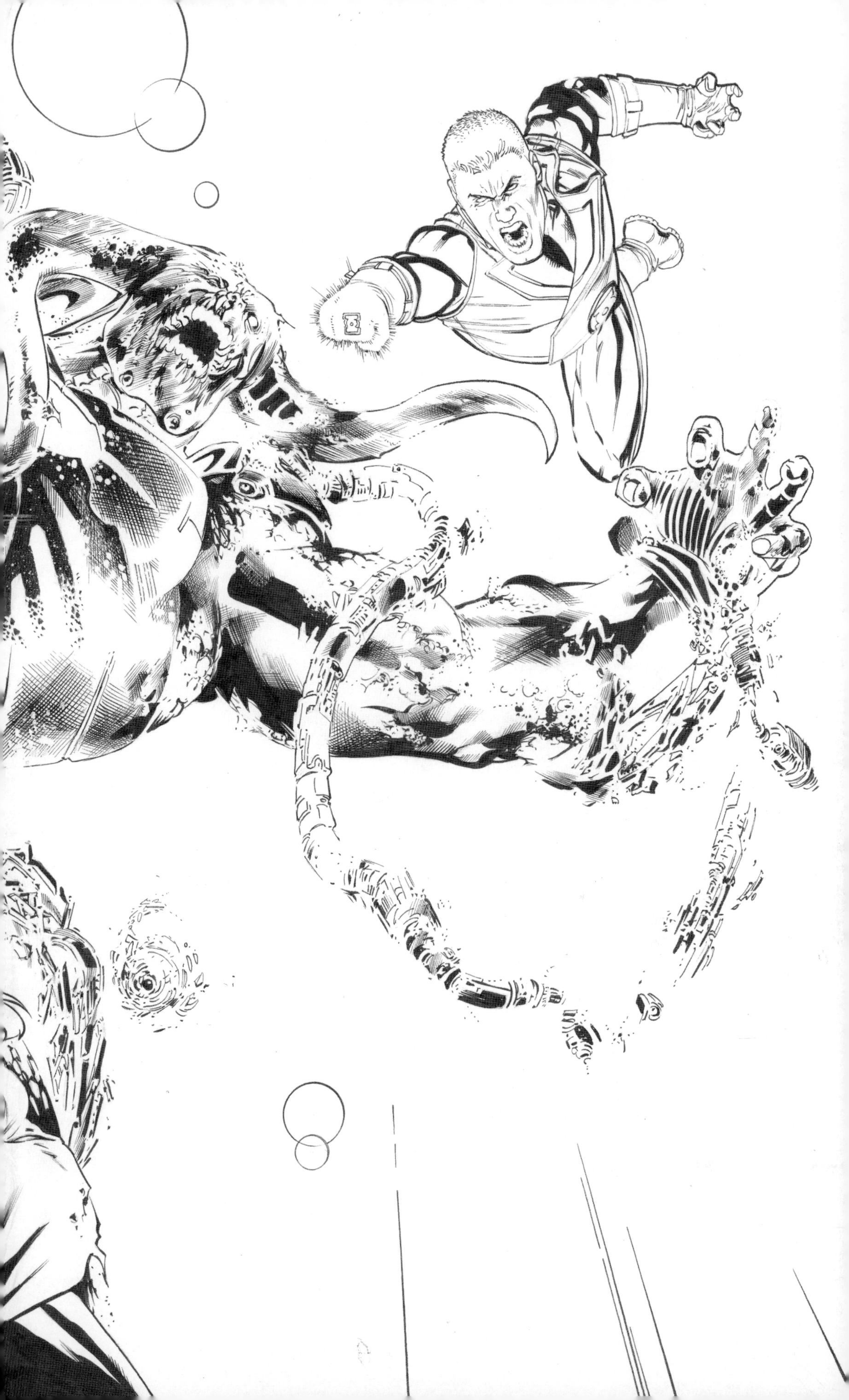

panel 1
Angle on Guy as he gathers all of his family into a big hug with energy construct arms, even his father, pulling them up from the floor; keep the mood serious for this page.

GUY:　　　　　SILENT

panel 2
Guy stands in the living room, exhausted, arms at his sides as the energy construct arms dissipate as his attention stays focused on his family who stand shaken and in awe at what they've just seen. Xar's feet up to his ankles are still standing in the spot where he was blasted; it's the only thing left of him. The ankles should appear smooth, as if sheared from the rest of his body, not bloody. Thin green tendrils of smoke waft off the remains.

GUY:　　　　　You all okay?

GERARD:　　　...um...yeah, we're good.

GLORIA:　　　...<u>that</u> was something you don't see every day.

RING:　　　　Power level 85%.

panel 3
Another angle on Guy and his family, still shaken from all this. Gavin of course is still mad at Guy, blames him for everything, always finds a negative way to look at his son.

GUY:　　　　　...god...thought I mighta lost you...

GAVIN:　　　　Another few seconds and you <u>would've</u>.

GLORIA:　　　But you <u>didn't</u> -- you saved us -- <u>you</u> got the bad guy, Guy.

panel 4
Only on Guy as he sits down on a half destroyed couch or chair, like a soldier who's adrenaline rush is over; he holds Gloria's hand who stands beside him.

GUY:　　　　　...I did, sis, didn't I?

GUY:　　　　　Xar is finally toast.

panel 5
Guy and the family as they look down at Xar's remains, his shadow left etched on the floor like the way Hiroshima victims close to the blast left theirs on walls and such.

GUY:　　　　　Um, sorry about the rug there, pop.

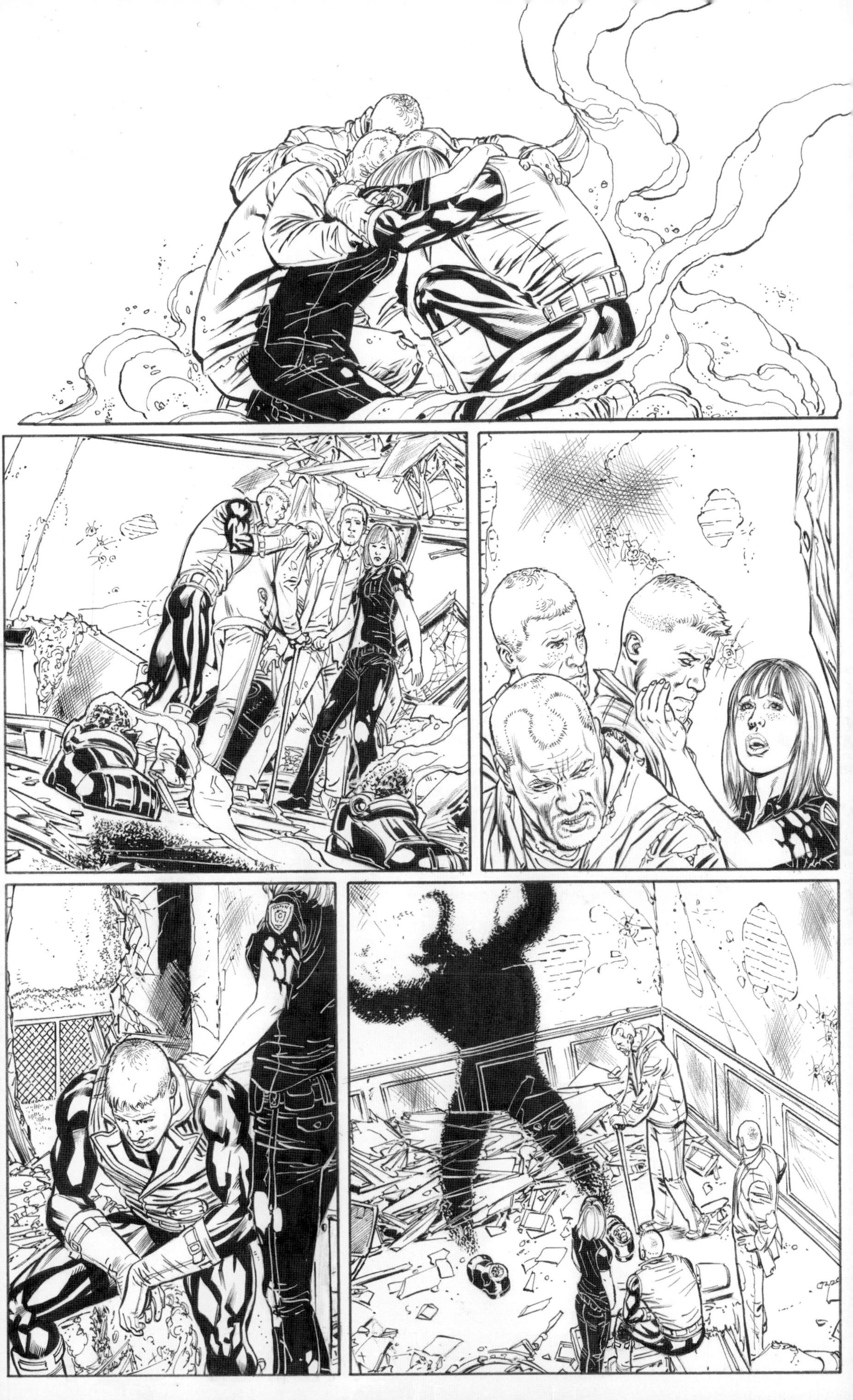

panel 1
Dusk. Angle on Guy, Gerard and Gloria sitting on some director's chairs beside a lake. Three mini tents, a campfire, they're roasting marshmallows with long tree sticks. Establish a canoe on top of their Honda Pilot in the background. Give them distinctive clothing to stand apart. Give Guy a baseball cap which he'll wear through sequence.

GUY: Been a long time since we did this together.

GUY: Can't believe how quiet it is out here.

panel 2
Angle close on Gloria and Guy roasting marshmallows.

GLORIA: I brought my night vision goggles.

GLORIA: We could do some target shooting.

GUY: No, no, I'm liking it just like this, Gloria.

panel 3
Angle on Gerard and Guy roasting marshmallows.

GERARD: Isn't it always quiet in space?

GUY: Nah, there's this weird constant hum -- not loud -- it's kinda hard to explain...

GUY: ...not to mention alien races of all creeds and colors killing each other loudly from one end of the galaxy to the next.

panel 4
Another angle on them. Have Guy blowing out his burning marshmallow.

GLORIA: And here I thought Earth was special.

GUY: Sorry to say, not by a long-shot.

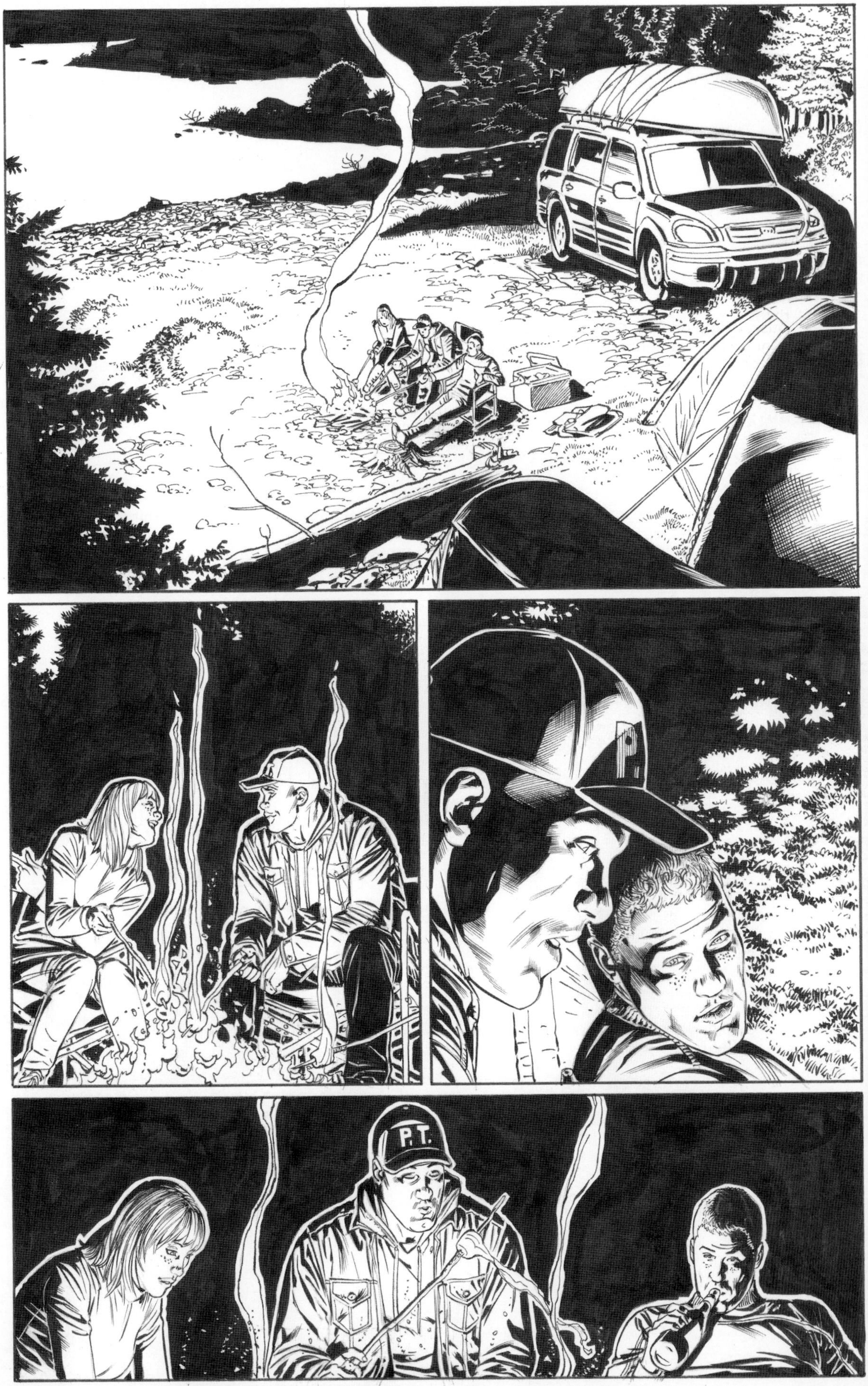
P.T.

panel 1
Morning. Guy and Gerard in canoe, fishing on the lake. Guy's got his baseball cap on (helps indicate speaker). Stay close, Fernando, save reveal for the last panel on the page.

GUY: ...I'm gonna smell the roses, Gerard. Ease up on the gas.

GERARD: King Leadfoot actually ease up on the gas?

GERARD: I'll <u>believe</u> it when I <u>see</u> it.

panel 2
Another close angle only on Guy as he gives his pole a tug to see if he's got anything.

GUY: You <u>are</u> seeing it, bro. I'm rolling down the window, sticking my head out like a Golden Retriever and letting the breeze blow my ears off.

GUY: I'm gonna stay awhile -- do my Green thing closer to home -- little America First action — give Baltimore some love and hugs too.

GUY: Plenty of GL's out there for me to let the big Universe stuff slot into second position for a bit.

panel 3
Gerard's got that look on his face; he knows Guy all too well. Guy is getting irritated that he hasn't caught a fish, starts reeling in.

GERARD: And how long you planning to ease up on this proverbial gas pedal?

GUY: Two months, maybe three -- enjoy the little things -- the every day things--

panel 4
Angle on Guy and Gerard as Guy looks at his hook with the bait/worm still on it.

GUY: — damn, did the fish chow down an early breakfast -- not one bite in 15 minutes!

panel 5
Horizontal across bottom of page. Now we pull back and get a nice establishing shot of Guy and Gerard fishing from the canoe on the lake along with a HUNDRED GREEN CONSTRUCT FISHING POLES HOVERING OVER THE WATER AND SPREAD OUT ALL ACROSS THE LAKE thanks to Guy's ring indicating his lack of patience. Establishing Gerard without the baseball cap earlier makes it clear who's speaking.

GERARD: Three months, hmm?

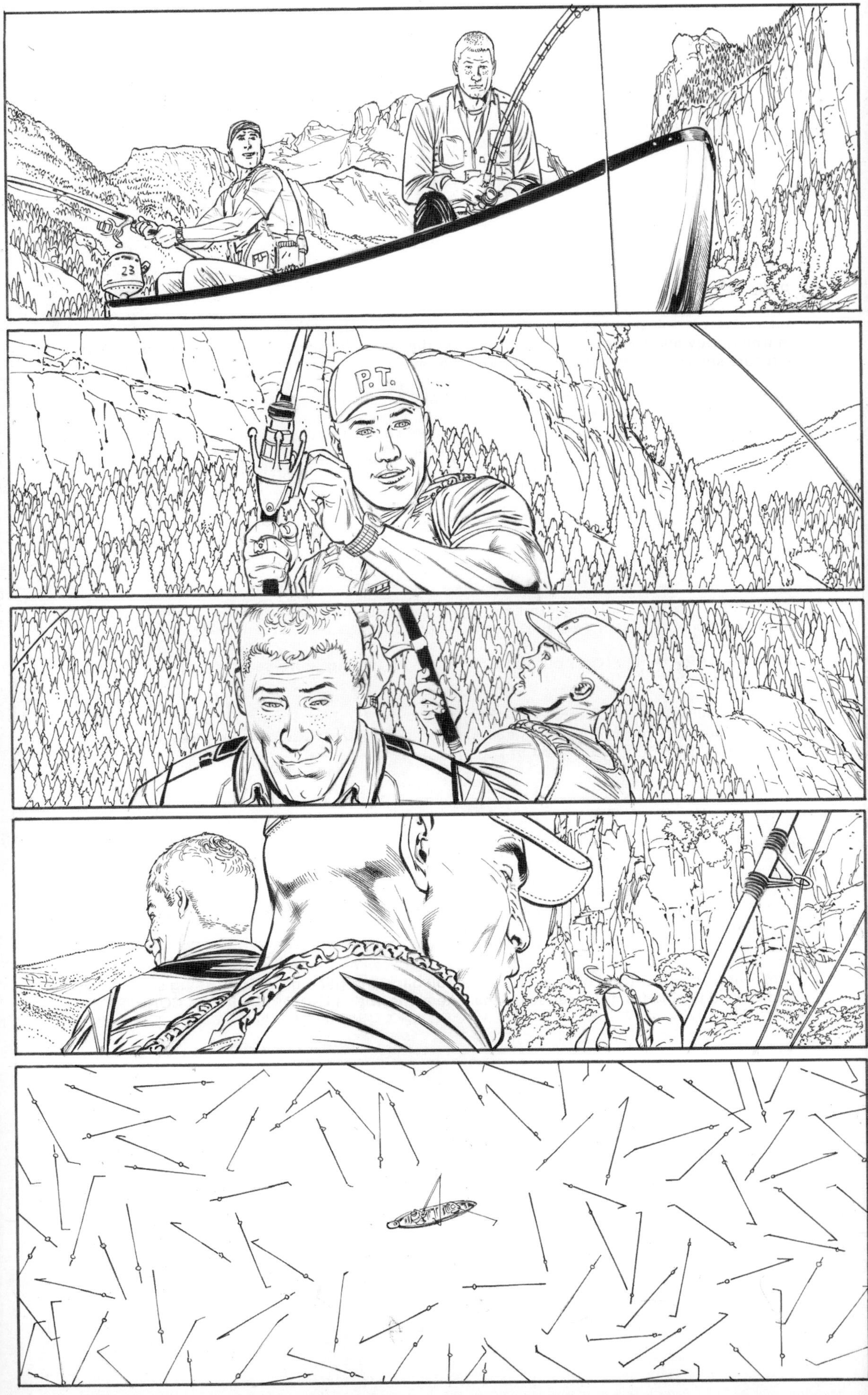
23
P.T.

What follows, Fernando, is Guy's attempt to just be a regular guy, doing the mundane things in life, enjoying the simple pleasures of every-day stuff. I'm seeing horizontal panels across for this sequence.

panel 1
Angle on Guy on line at the grocery store, a shopping cart filled with food, beer, snacks, etc. while in front of him is a young 2-YEAR OLD BOY sitting in the cart a mom is busy unpacking her groceries from and placing on the cash register belt. The Boy has a large bag of candy open and is flinging it at Guy, who is keeping one of those fake smiles plastered to his face as the candy bounces off his face and chest.

BANNER CAP: Day 1

GUY: Aw, what a cute kid.

panel 2
Angle on Guy at the Department of Motor Vehicles, he's on line with loads of other people holding a ticket that says 232 while a sign we can see says now serving 18.

BANNER CAP: Day 2

panel 3
Angle on Guy as a Green Lantern using his ring to put bubbles around TWO GUYS who were in the middle of stealing the tires off an expensive car. Guy should look bored like he can't believe this is what he's reduced to.

BANNER CAP: Day 3

panel 4
Angle on Guy sitting in a Dentist's chair and having a cavity drilled. He's clutching the armrests tight as the Dentist drills away.

BANNER CAP: Day 4

panel 5
Angle on Guy at a Baltimore Orioles game as a CHEERING FAN'S outstretched hand accidentally knocks Guy's cup of beer all over his face and chest.

BANNER CAP: Day 5

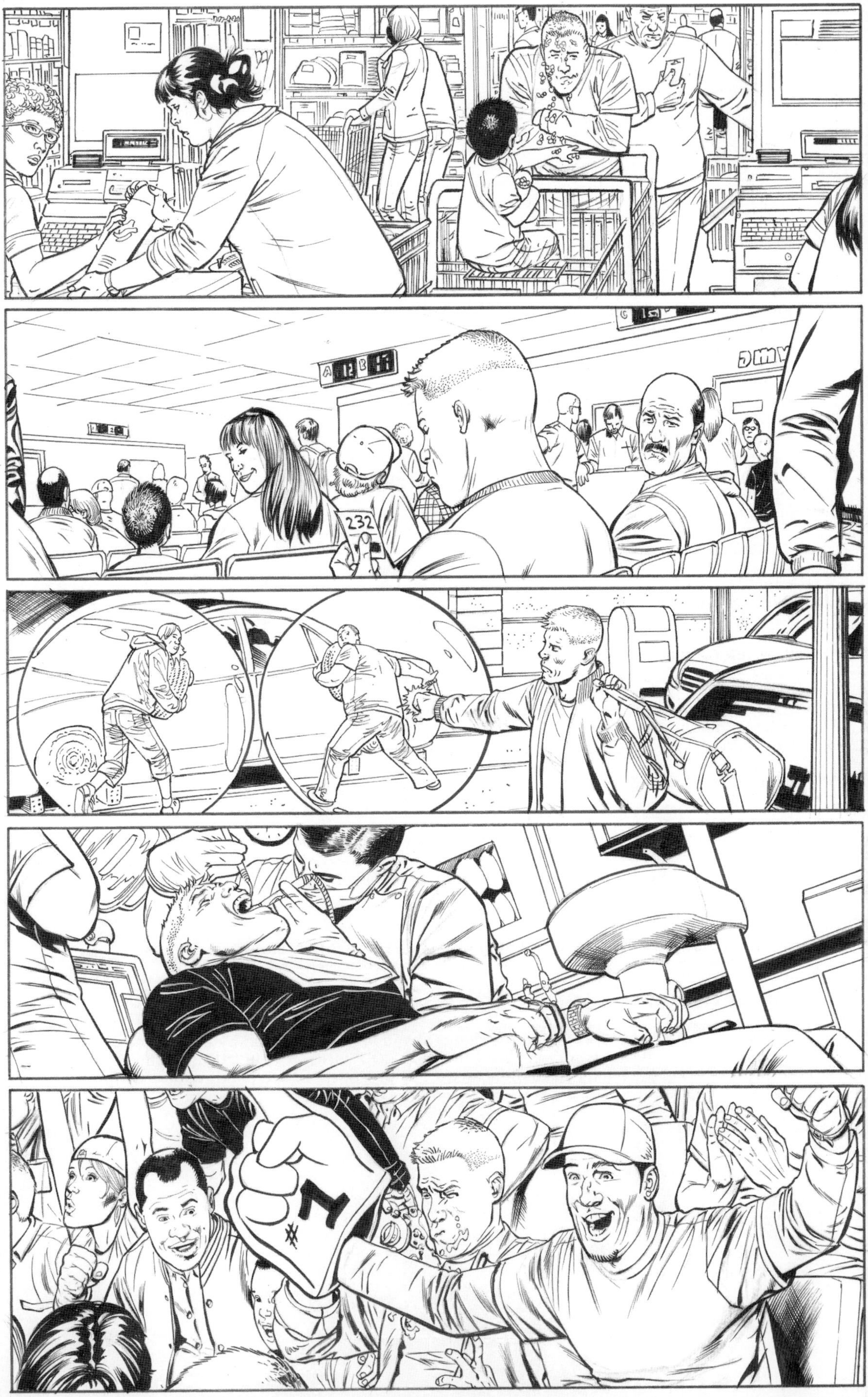
232
#1

PAGE 18

panel 1
Angle on Guy standing in front of his big screen TV, the picture is filled with static.

BANNER CAP: Day 6

GUY: — you said the techie would be here yesterday!

panel 2
Gerard and Gloria at DC hero-themed miniature golf course, as Guy (in HAPPY GILMORE mode) swings his golf club into the makeshift likeness of a LARGE AQUAMAN HOLE OBSTRUCTION, his Trident over the hole to prevent Guy's ball from going in. Gloria and Gerard are laughing as pieces of Aquaman fly all around.

BANNER CAP: Day 7

panel 3
Angle on Guy hovering in the air with 4 KNOCKED-OUT ARMED BANK ROBBERS wrapped tight in a green bow that he's lowering towards a group of POLICE OFFICERS, bags of money they stole held high in an energy tendril, some dollar bills drifting in the air and the car they were driving all smashed in the front thanks to a big giant construct GL symbol. Guy kinda looks matter of fact. Not much of an adrenaline rush.

BANNER CAP: Day 8

POLICE 1:   Thanks GL, we can take this from here.

GUY: Yeah, I guess you can.

panel 4
Guy sitting in a movie theater with a DATE, as he politely taps on the shoulder of a big-ass dude who's playing a game on his I-Pad Mini while the movie's on, the light from the pad really intrusive. The dude is turning his head slightly and telling Guy to fuck off.

BANNER CAP: Day 9

GUY: Would you mind turning off the game, buddy?

DUDE: Screw you, asswipe!

panel 4
Angle on Guy and his date leaving the theater hand in hand escorted by a manager, as the audience claps and cheers for him. We can see the OUTLINE OF THE DUDE on the movie screen like in a Bugs Bunny cartoon meaning Guy obviously threw him through it at some point.

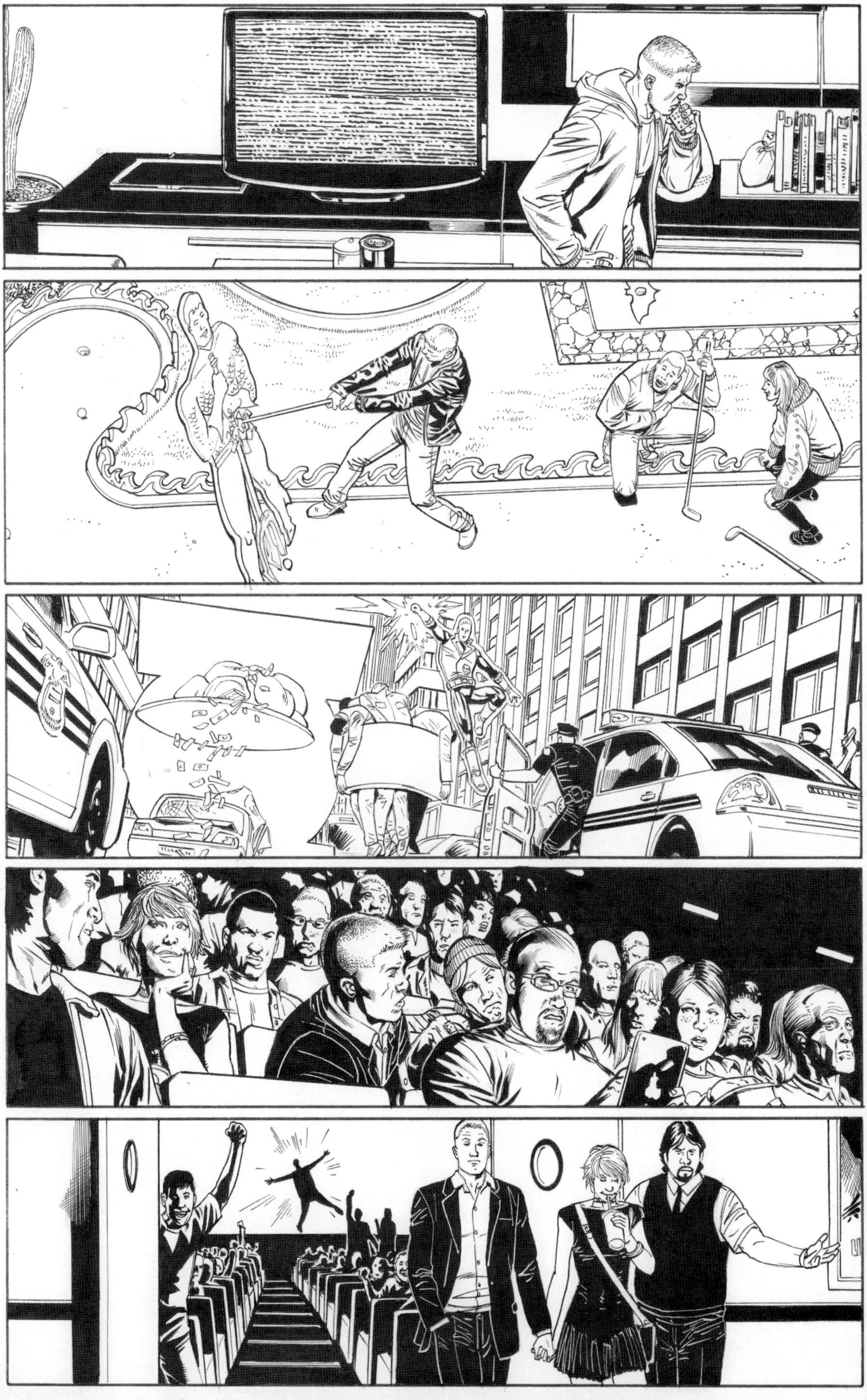

ISSUE # 19 wraparound cover by ANDY KUBERT, SANDRA HOPE and BRAD ANDERSON

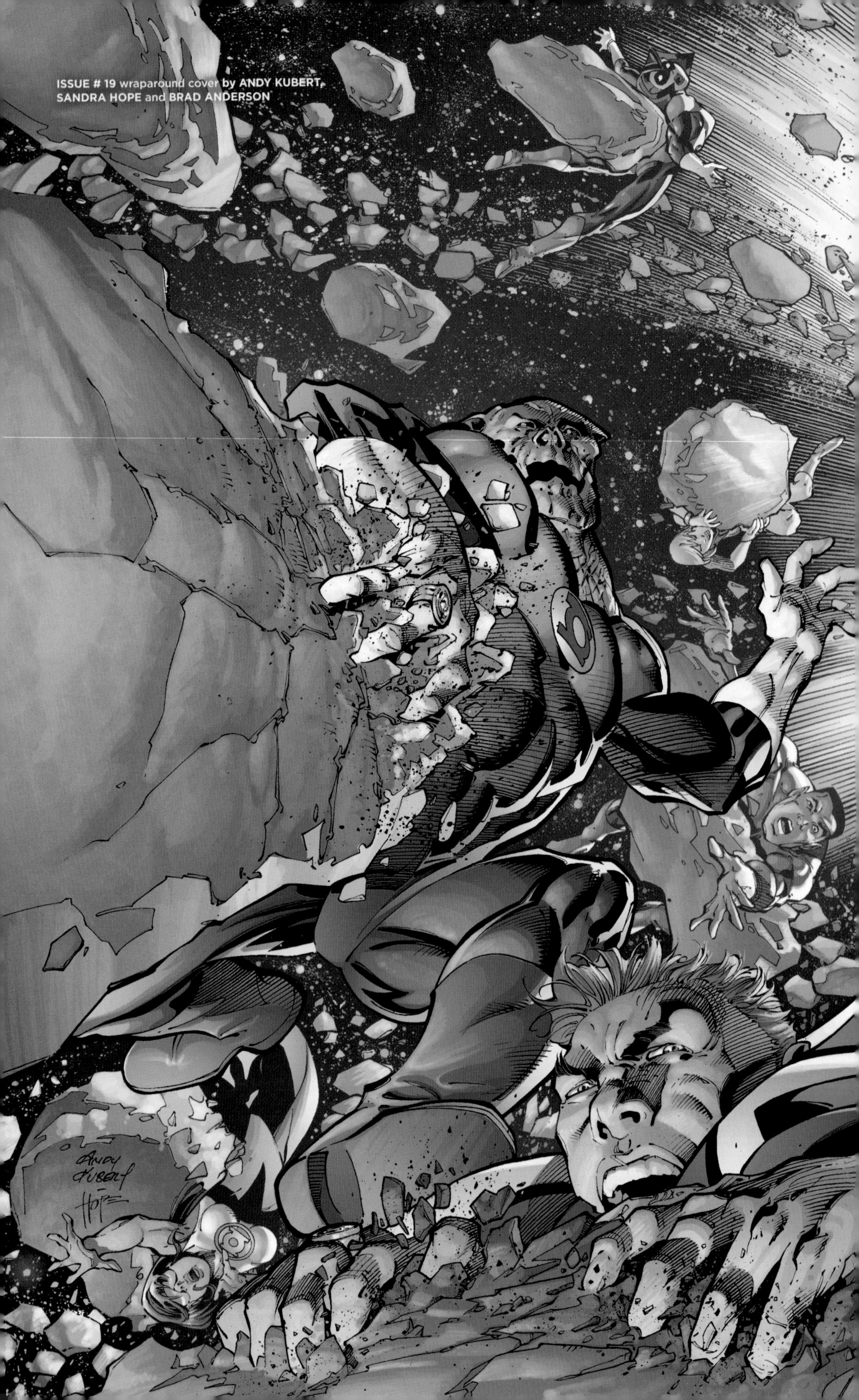
ANDY KUBERT
HOPE

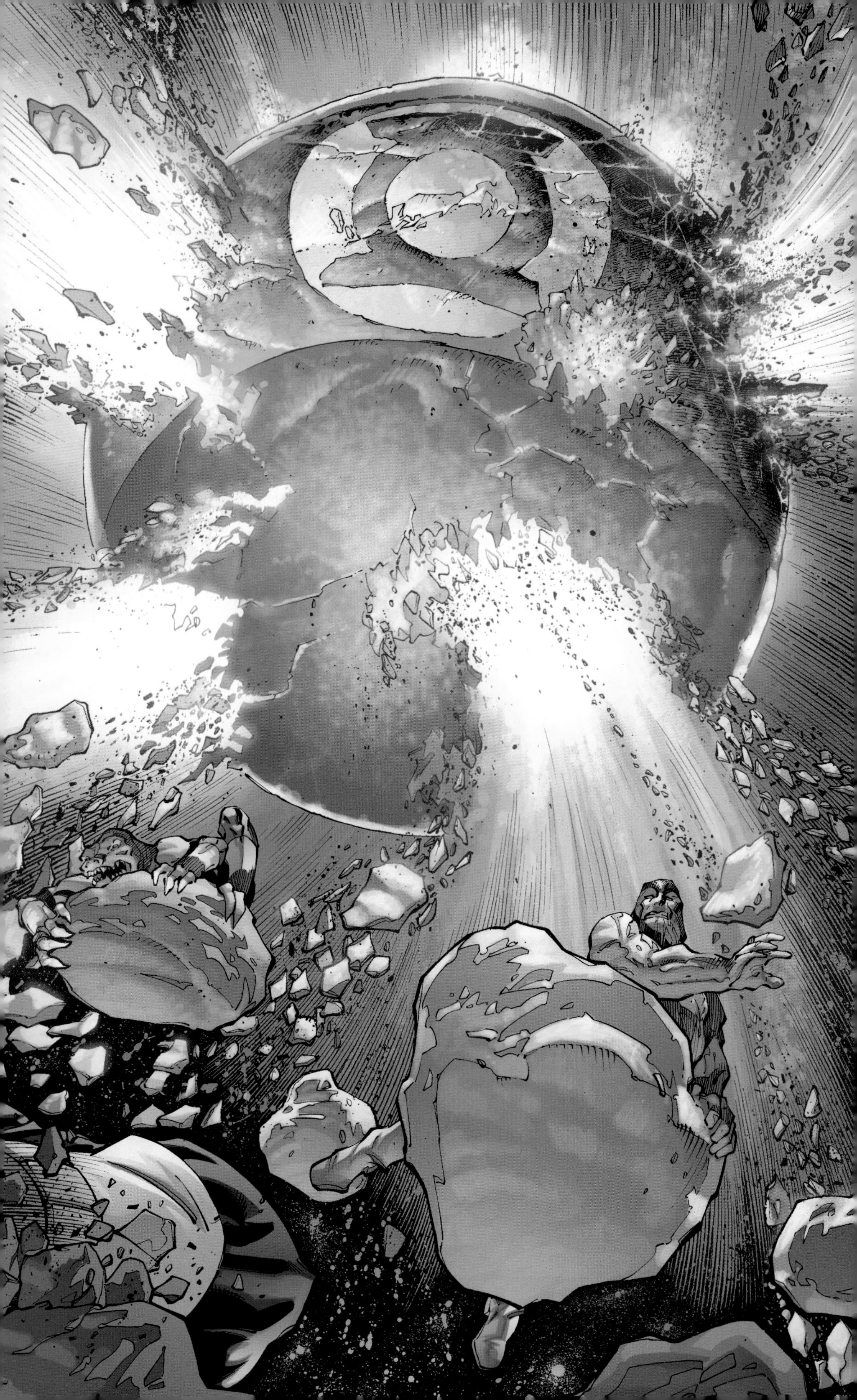

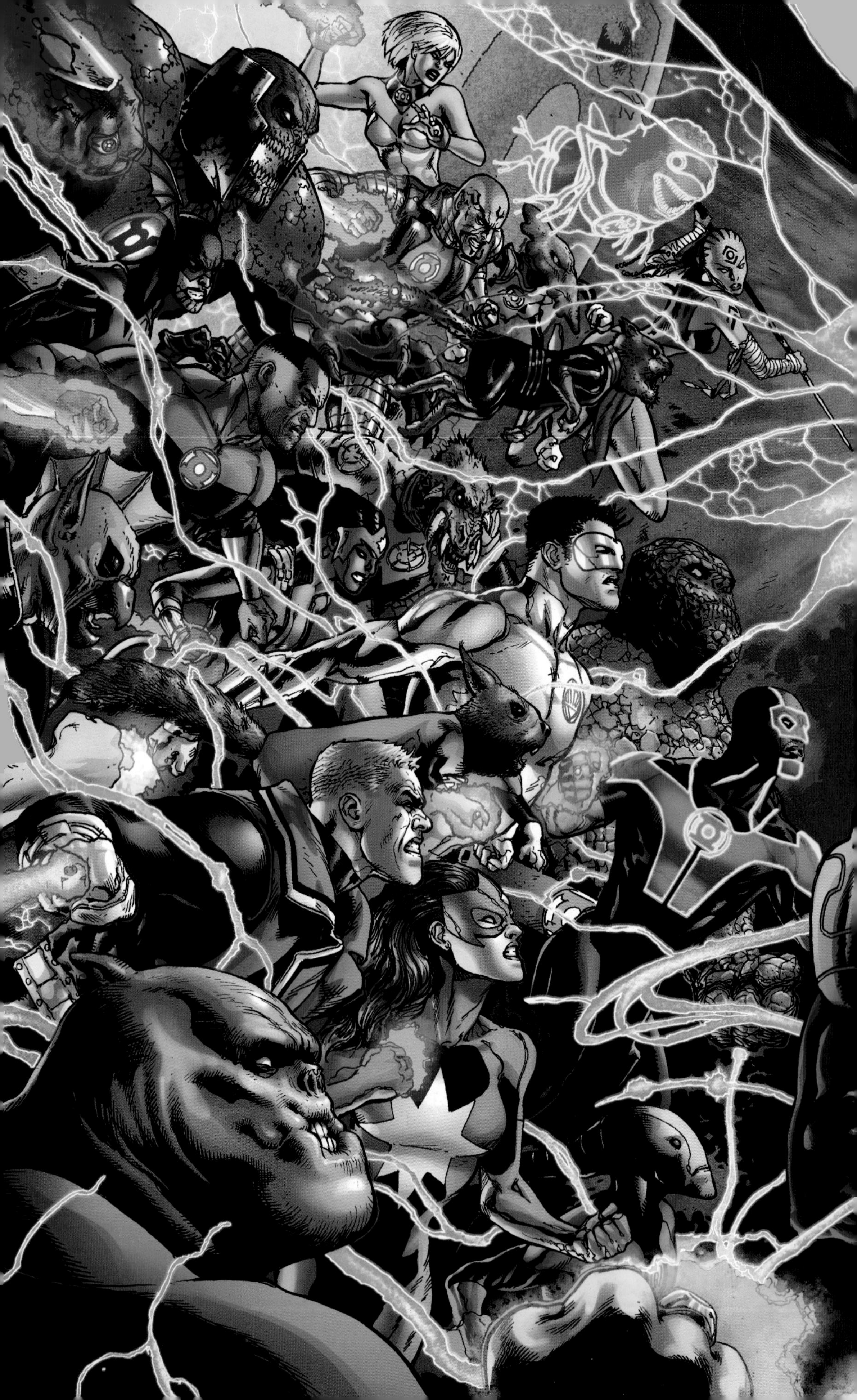

GREEN LANTERN ISSUE # 20 wraparound cover by
DOUG MAHNKE and **ALEX SINCLAIR**

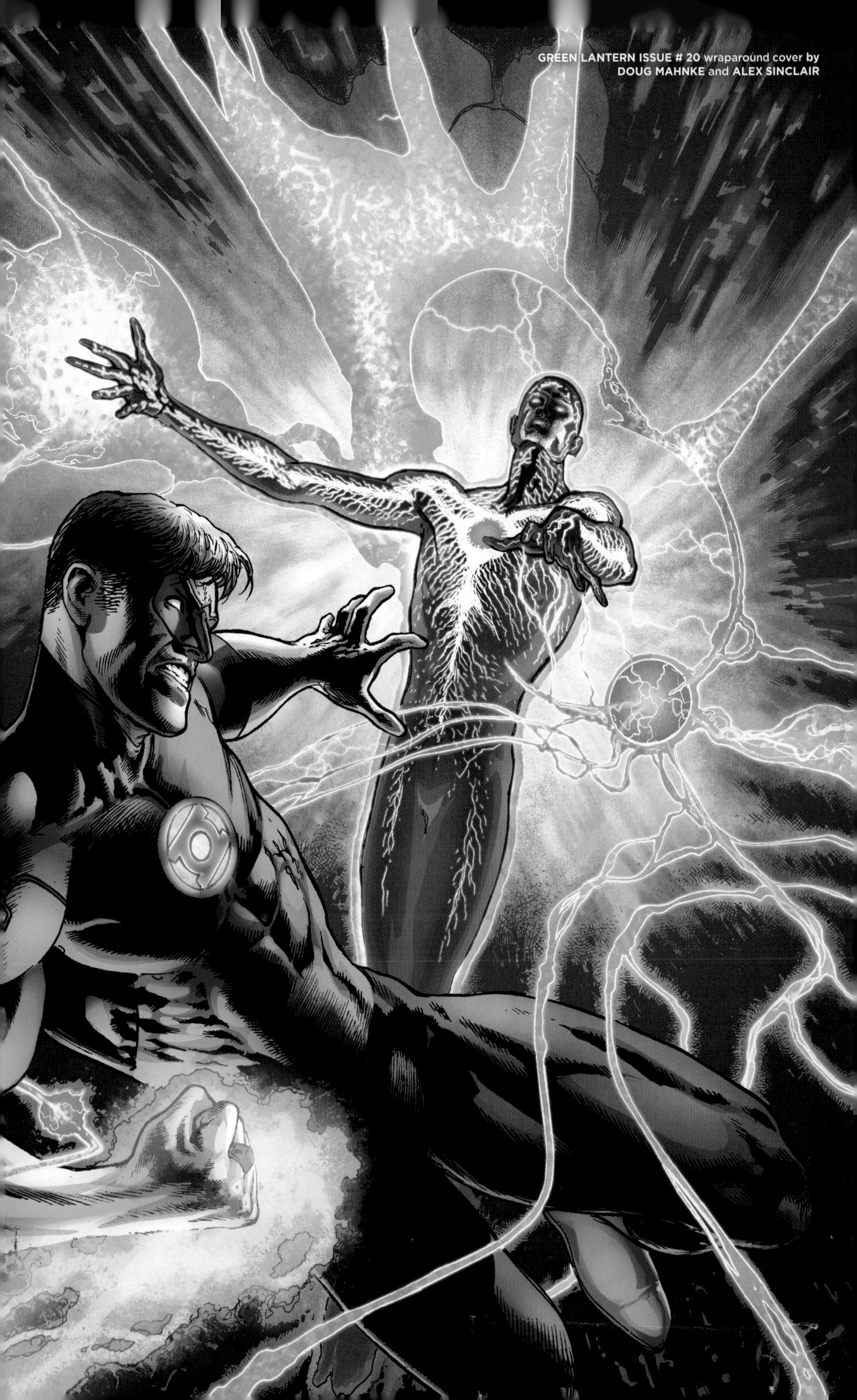

GREEN LANTERN CORPS

COVER SKETCHES BY ANDY KUBERT

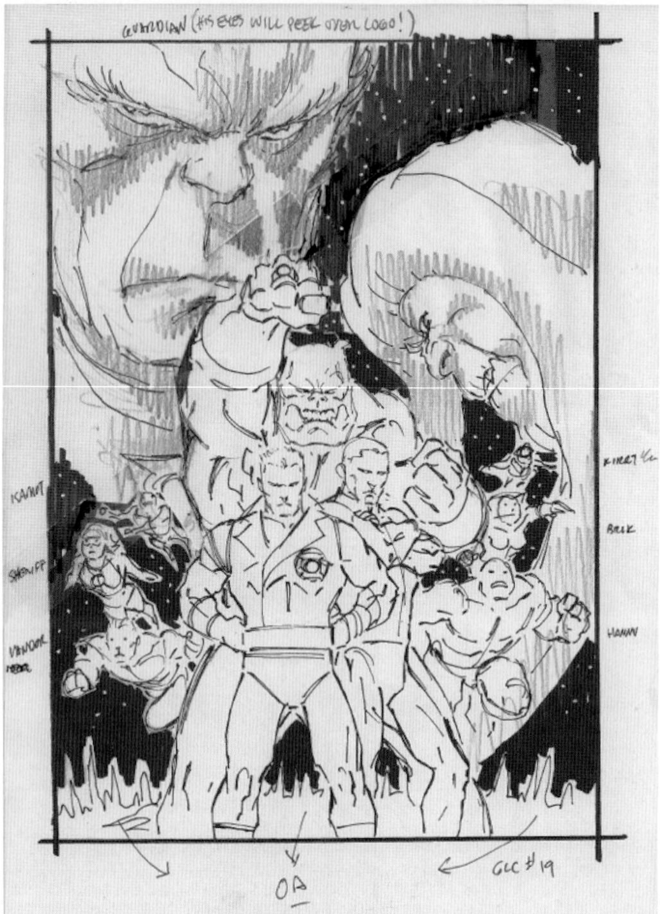
GUARDIAN (HIS EYES WILL PEEK OVER LOGO!)
OA
GLC #19

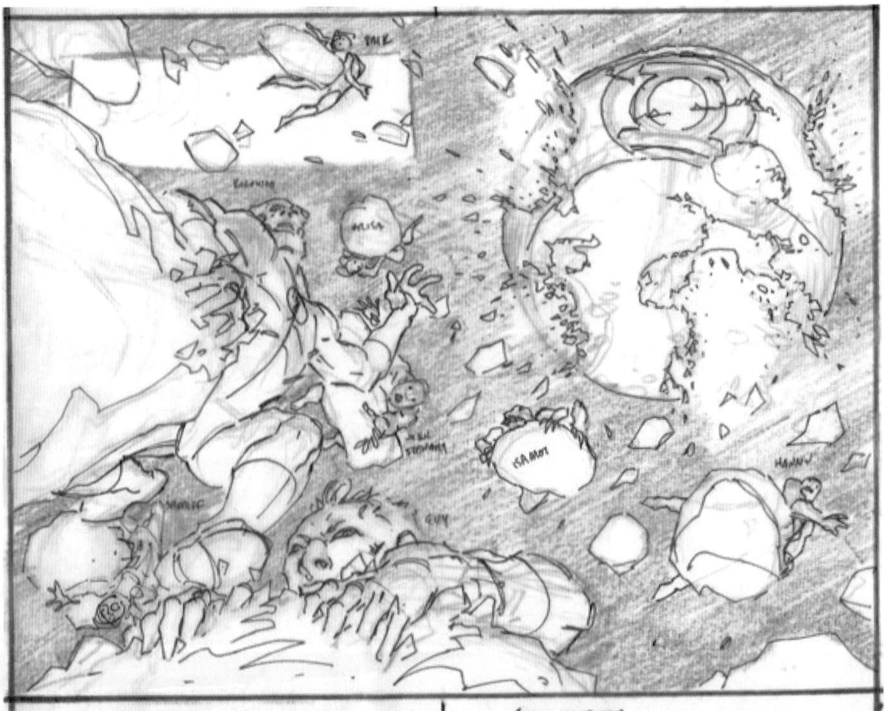
G.L. CORPS 19
ANDY KUBERT